Advertising in Canada

A MANAGERIAL APPROACH

RENÉ Y. DARMON
Ecole Supérieure des Sciences
Economiques et Commerciales (ESSEC)
Cergy-Pontoise, France

MICHEL LAROCHE
Concordia University

McGRAW-HILL RYERSON LIMITED

Toronto Montreal New York Auckland Bogotá
Caracas Lisbon London Madrid Mexico Milan New Delhi Paris
San Juan Singapore Sydney Tokyo

ADVERTISING IN CANADA: A Managerial Approach

ISBN: 0-07-549929-0

1234567890 JD 0987654321

This book has been manufactured on acid-free paper.
Printed and bound in Canada by John Deyell Company

Care has been taken to trace ownership of copyright material contained in this text. The publishers will gladly take any information that will enable them to rectify any reference or credit in subsequent editions.

Canadian Cataloguing in Publication Data

Darmon, René Y.
  Advertising in Canada

ISBN 0-07-549929-0

1. Advertising — Canada. 2. Advertising — Canada — Management. I. Laroche, Michel. II. Title.

HF5813.C3D37 1991   659.1′0971   C90-095030-7

SPONSORING EDITOR: KELLY SMYTH
PRODUCTION AND COPY EDITOR: KATHLEEN PRICE
PERMISSIONS EDITOR: NORMA CHRISTENSEN
COVER AND TEXT DESIGN: SHARON MATTHEWS
TECHNICAL ARTIST: PATRICIA CODE
COVER PHOTO: JEAN YVES BRUEL, MONTREAL

To
Nicole
and
Anne

CONTENTS

CASES

PREFACE

Advertising has always played a major role in the Canadian way of life. This country, in turn, has contributed substantially to the growth of modern advertising in North America. As early as 1878, concepts of advertising were being developed and refined in Canada. In 1904, a former member of the Royal Canadian Mounted Police, John E. Kennedy, formulated the definition of advertising as "salesmanship in print," which has been widely credited for the birth of modern advertising in North America. Not long after that, in 1920, the first radio station in the world started operations in Montreal. These are only some of the examples of the contributions of Canadians to the development of an exciting and dynamic industry.

This revised edition of the first original textbook on advertising in Canada published in 1984 provides a fresh new look into the advertising industry. It still looks at the functions of advertising mostly from management's point of view, but with more emphasis on the principles of advertising.

Canadian advertisers, advertising agencies, and media face unique problems because of the special nature of Canada's market environment. Thus, *Advertising in Canada: A Managerial Approach* provides the underlying knowledge (i.e., principles and frameworks) and develops the practical skills required to make advertising decisions within this environment. Since the advertising function within a firm requires many different kinds of decision making, methods relevant to each kind are described, discussed, and assessed.

Based on the useful input from all major Canadian sources, this text has been thoroughly revised to continue meeting the needs of several groups of people:
- Business majors and other students of courses of advertising principles given at Canadian universities and community colleges.
- Users of mass communication, including marketing and advertising managers in firms, government agencies and other institutions, advertising agencies, and media personnel.
- Public relations managers in profit and non-profit organizations.

- Anyone in this country or abroad who needs to have a good grasp of what makes advertising different in Canada.

This text has been reorganized into five major parts (chapter numbers in parentheses):
1. The role and functions of advertising within the marketing plan. This part places particular emphasis on the place of advertising within the marketing mix (**1**), and elaborates on the interactions and co-ordination with the other marketing mix variables (**2**). It assumes a minimal knowledge of marketing.
2. The structure and role of advertising organizations in Canada. Examining each major type of organization from a manager's point of view, these five chapters answer questions about how to select an advertising agency (**3**), the role of advertising for a retailer, an industrial firm, or a services organization (**4**), and how to evaluate print media (**5, 6**), broadcast media (**7**), or a sales promotion program (**8**).
3. Behavioural foundations of advertising. There is extensive knowledge in the behavioural sciences and in communication studies about processes that are directly related to the development of advertising campaigns (**9, 10**). These two chapters highlight the major findings of utmost interest to advertisers.
4. Management of advertising programs. This part describes the main decision areas and stages in the development of advertising campaigns, including:
    - the development of sound advertising objectives, and
    - the process of developing an advertising budget (**11**)
    - the development of a creative plan (**12**)
    - the creation of effective messages (**13**)
    - the development of an effective media plan (**14**)
    - the sources and methods of advertising research (**15**)
5. Advertising and the Canadian economy. This last part deals with two major contemporary topics: international advertising (**16**) and the economic and social effects of advertising on the Canadian society (**17**).

v

Another important new feature of this text is a complete set of 20 cases covering all major areas in advertising, and written by several fine Canadian authors. These cases should allow fruitful discussions, and they will help the student in understanding the material covered in the chapters, integrate various concepts, and apply this knowledge to developing his/her own campaign. In addition, with this text the instructor will receive a computer software program called TELPAK, especially developed by Marshall Rice (*York University*). This software provides some standard measures of a television schedule, and it can be used with any PC equipped with BASIC. It is very simple to use, and it allows the student to play with different schedules and to compare their effectiveness. It illustrates concretely many of the methods introduced in Chapter 14.

At the end of all chapters, there are summaries, questions for study, and small problems (some almost like mini cases) to solve. Appendices on broadcasting regulations and advertising production appear at the back of the book, along with a comprehensive glossary of advertising terms, including equivalent French terminology.

The development of this revised edition has, as for the first edition, generated an unusual amount of enthusiasm on the part of many individuals and organizations, and we are most fortunate to have benefited from their constant co-operation and encouragement. First, we would like to express our gratitude to Victoria Digby (*Sheridan College*), Sandra Mudd (*British Columbia Institute of Technology*), W.A. Inglis (*Capilano College*), Marie Louise Huebner (*Seneca College*), Douglas West (*University of Calgary*), Harold Simpkins (*Concordia University*), James Thurston (*Mohawk College*), Eunice Baxter (*College of New Caledonia*), Ross Richardson (*Humber College*), Colin Young (*Ryerson Polytechnical Institute*) for their thorough and thoughtful reviews of an early draft of this manuscript, and to Marshall Rice (*York*) for writing the TELPAK program to be used with this text. Robert E. Oliver (Past President, Advertising Advisory Board) provided us with several useful insights from his extensive experience in Canadian advertising.

We would also like to thank all the authors who have contributed their cases: Marvin Ryder (McMaster), Peter McGrady (Lakehead), Jacques Boisvert, Helen Lafrenière and Leo-Paul Dana (H.E.C.), Jane G. Funk, Thomas F. Funk and Peter Evans (Guelph), Gordon H.G. McDougall (Wilfrid Laurier), Douglas Snetsinger (Toronto), Robert M. MacGregor (Bishop), Harold J. Simpkins (Concordia) and David S. Litvack (Ottawa).

We are most grateful to all the firms and organizations which gave us permission to reproduce some of their material in the text. Their contribution is acknowledged throughout the book. We are particularly grateful to David M. Tattle (Nielsen Marketing Research), Lucy M. Wood (RBC), Michel Valois (Mediacom), Evelyne Tessier (Newspaper Marketing Bureau), Ross Wahl and Lyse Brunelle (Trans Ad), Alfred Stavro (Kitching Advertising) and Suzanne Keeler (Canadian Advertising Foundation).

In developing this text, we were fully supported by the able professionals at McGraw-Hill Ryerson, particularly Kelly Smyth, Kathleen Price, Laurie Graham, Michele MacDonald, and Norma Christensen. Our secretaries, Pina Vicario, Linda Meyer, Maureen McDonough, and Mary Genova deserve our gratitude for their patience, attention to detail and competent typing of the manuscript.

Finally, we are thankful to our families for their support and understanding during the process of developing the second edition of the first original textbook on advertising in Canada.

We sincerely hope that most participants in this exciting industry will recognize their trade in the various pages of this text, and that you, as an observer (or future participant) of this industry, will develop a sound understanding and appreciation of its role, importance and functions in the Canadian economy. We hope that you will enjoy reading this text as much as we have enjoyed researching and writing it!

René Y. Darmon

Michel Laroche

PART I

The Role and Functions of Advertising

Advertising is one of the most visible phenomena of modern times. No one can avoid being exposed to and, to some extent, influenced by advertising messages and commercials. At the same time, advertising is one of the least understood modern institutions, not only by the general public but also by many experts.

This text undertakes a systematic analysis of advertising in the Canadian context. Although the managerial perspective is favoured, advertising is also considered from the institutional, behavioural, economic, and social points of view. First, the role and functions of advertising in general and in Canadian society are examined. Then, the role and functions of advertising in a firm's marketing mix and in the promotional mix are discussed.

CHAPTER

1 *Advertising: Its Nature and Functions*

Wherever they live, Canadians are exposed to advertising material. As they walk or drive through the streets, listen to the radio at home or in the car, watch television, read newspapers or magazines, attend a sports event, go shopping, read mail, Canadians are exposed to advertisements for products, services, and ideas. All these advertisements are vying for the generally limited number of dollars they can spend, for their political votes, or for their involvement in or commitment to engage in some desirable social action. Advertising messages may be in the form of flashy, luminous posters or billboards, broadcast advertisements on local or national radio and television networks, full-page colour advertisements in national magazines, or small black and white advertisements in the local newspapers, advertising at the point-of-purchase at their usual retailer, or leaflets mailed to their homes—and this list is by no means exhaustive. It has been estimated that an American consumer is exposed to a daily average of 1500 commercials, and this figure might be only slightly lower for Canadians.

Because of advertising's continuous presence in daily life, everyone has some knowledge, beliefs, and often strongly held attitudes about it. Advertising is the most visible fact of marketing to many consumers; thus, not surprisingly, it has been attacked on social as well as on economic grounds. For some, advertising is a mischievous tool that marketers use to create needs, make consumers buy unwanted goods, and in general direct society toward the "false" values of mass consumption.

From another point of view, advertising is a necessary mechanism that has enabled Canadian society to achieve its present high standard of living. In either case, the controversy over advertising does not leave anyone indifferent, and unfortunately emotions are often involved in the debate.

Therefore, unless the nature and functions of advertising are studied objectively, its mechanisms, possibilities, and limitations cannot be understood and assessed properly. One objective of this book is to provide a framework in which to evaluate the institution of advertising. Thus a detailed study will be made of advertising's influence on human behaviour and of the role and functions of advertising management.

Before this task is undertaken, the text discusses the nature of advertising and proposes a definition of the advertising function. Then an outline of the historical background of Canadian advertising helps to explain the role that advertising presently plays in the Canadian economy and in business.

THE NATURE OF ADVERTISING

The Raison d'Etre of Advertising

camera
a time
travelling machine

Why is so much money spent on advertising? Is advertising necessary? The answer is that no purchase can take place without some form of communication between the seller and a potential buyer. The exchange of money for some product or service takes place when all the participants in such a trading activity have been informed of and have accepted the terms and conditions of the exchange. That is, a consumer or industrial purchase takes place when each participant in the transaction finds or expects to find satisfaction, or the fulfillment of some need. In a free market society, consumers buy goods and services because they hope to obtain satisfaction through their usage and consumption. In the same way, people give financial support to charitable organizations because they obtain some reward (if only psychologically) by doing so.

Traditionally, sellers have attempted to show prospective customers the advantages and satisfaction that the advertised goods are likely to bring. Even past forms of buying and selling, such as bartering, involved persuasive discussions between merchants and prospective customers. At one time, craftsmen showed the merits of their products and services to prospective clients. Today's salespersons, trained to perceive which arguments are likely to be most effective in selling goods to different categories of customers, are the craftsmen of marketing communications.

At the end of the nineteenth century, with the advent of the Industrial Revolution, marketing communications took on a new character. Entrepreneurs introduced mass production of goods, and the problem shifted from selling a custom-made product, manufactured according to the requirements of a specific client, to selling items produced on a large scale to a mass market. As a logical consequence of this trend, personal communications began to be replaced by mass communications. Rather than talking to one buyer at a time, the manufacturers' problem was how to communicate effectively with large and sometimes remote markets. Thus, mass production led to mass marketing.

In order to build a communication link between mass production and mass markets, a mass communication tool was needed, and the device was advertising. Of course, the characteristics and functions of advertising have evolved since the Industrial Revolution, but the roots and raison d'être of modern advertising can be traced to that period.

Advertising Defined

Most definitions of advertising stress three basic elements—that advertising is *communication* aimed at a *mass audience* and that it has a *socio-economic function*. For instance, the definition given by the American Marketing Association is as follows:

Advertising is any paid form of non-personal presentation and promotion of ideas, goods or services by an identified sponsor.[2]

The first element in the definition is that advertising is a set of *communications* originating from a sponsor. The flow of information is unidirectional and is directed at the advertiser's *customers* and *prospects*. The advertiser may be a business organization, a person, a firm, or a group of firms. It may be a manufacturing or a marketing organization, a producer, a middleman, or a retailer. The advertiser may also be a social organization, such as the Red Cross, or a religious organization, a political party, a government agency, or any organized group. The customers may be the final consumers of the product, other industrial firms, middlemen, or retailers. Consequently, advertising involves many kinds of communications, of which consumer advertising is only one type.

The second element is that advertising is *mass communication*, because it is directed at an entire market. It is different from such business communications as internal communication within a single firm or from marketing communications that a firm has with clients involving personal contact, such as personal selling through a sales force.

Third, advertising has a *socio-economic function*, resulting from its long-run objective of convincing customers and potential buyers to buy a firm's advertised products and services or to adopt the advertised idea or behaviour. Thus advertising plays an important role in *pursuasion*, and in supplying consumers with *information*. The economic nature of advertising is connected with advertising's high cost, since it is expensive to communicate with mass markets.

Table 1–1 shows how advertising differs from three other types of communications: *personal selling*, *publicity*, and *propaganda*. Although all fulfill a communication function, their differences lie in the scope and/or purpose of the communication. *Personal selling* differs in scope from advertising in that it is a personal rather than a mass communication. A salesperson directly addresses potential customers in this type of communication. *Publicity* departs from advertising in that it is not paid for by the beneficiary of the communication; it has more of a social than an economic purpose. Publicity often takes the form of editorial articles about a firm's performance or products and services and is published without charge by the media to inform consumers. *Propaganda* is significantly different from advertising. Although it is a type of mass communication, its source is not identified and it generally has a political rather than an economic purpose.

TABLE 1–1 **COMPARISON OF FOUR CURRENT TYPES OF COMMUNICATIONS**

	Advertising	Personal Selling	Publicity	Propaganda
Scope	Mass	Personal	Mass	Mass
Function	Communication	Communication	Communication	Communication
Purpose	Socio-economic	Economic	Socio-economic	Political

HISTORY OF ADVERTISING IN CANADA

The history of advertising in Canada is one of a fledgling industry that, in the space of forty years, grew to become a major force in the Canadian economy. Although it closely parallels the evolution of advertising in the United States (where modern advertising originated), its development in Canada differs in many respects. Canadian advertising operates in a specific cultural and geographic environment, and the imprint left by a few individuals lends it a distinct national flavour.

Beyond purely economic considerations, advertising has been instrumental in bringing about a revolution in Canadian lifestyles, outlook, and institutions. With its greatly increased sophistication and with advanced tools at its disposal, advertising now fulfills an essential role in the Canadian economy.

Early Advertising: 1752–1890

One could almost say that advertising is as old as Canada, since its presence in this country can be traced as far back as March 23, 1752. On this date the first issue of the *Halifax Gazette* was published, containing three advertisements.[3] Advertising was present, although in an embryonic form, in Canadian life throughout the 1800s. In the latter half of that century, economic trends paved the way for a growth of advertising as Canada started to industrialize.

After Confederation in 1867, newspapers multiplied and flourished, but their use of advertising was unsystematic and somewhat inefficient:

Advertising became an increasing source of revenue and the newspaper began to encourage and foster it. But even at the end of the eighties, advertising in Canada remained a more or less underdeveloped tool. Canadian advertising was still formless and haphazard, and what came to Canadian papers from "across the line" had scarcely more style or consistence.[4]

The 1890s, however, marked a radical departure from the concepts that had until then guided advertising. This last decade of the nineteenth century also marked the birth of modern Canadian advertising.

Evolution of Advertising Tools and Techniques: After 1890

The coming of age of advertising was closely related to the development of modern communications and mass production techniques. Without these, advertising would not have found a favourable environment in which to flourish.

Evolution of the Media

The first important factor that gave rise to modern advertising was the development of the modern mass media. After the first publication of the *Halifax Gazette*, Canadian newspapers steadily increased in numbers and circulation, but the 1890s was a period of great expansion. By 1891, Canada had a total of 1033 periodical publications—double the amount nine years earlier. Advertising was still infrequent, however, and printing techniques left much to be desired in the way of attractive illustration and copy presentation. At best, advertisements displayed simple line drawings or a few hand-lettered decorative headings.

But the giant technological leaps made by the printing industry, with such innovations as electrotyping, stereotyping, the rotary press, and the typesetting machine, made possible the expansion of printed media and the development of sophisticated advertising.

During the early twentieth century, newspaper distribution increased steadily, although the number of dailies fluctuated. As the newspaper industry became increasingly complex and required large investments, a more competitive economic environment made it difficult for marginal publications to survive. In the first half of the twentieth century, the number of newspapers declined at the same time as ownership became more concentrated. This concentration resulted in increased coverage but made it difficult for advertisers to reach specific market segments, since newspapers became more standardized. This trend was compensated, however, by a steady gain in the number, variety, and circulation of more specialized periodicals that catered to limited but well-defined social and professional groups. These magazines and periodicals were a powerful outlet for advertising. This early use of print media may account for its popularity as a source for advertising, even though print has had to compete with the more recent media of radio and television. The growth of audiovisual media irrevocably changed the nature of advertising. It gave advertisers a new and promising terrain in which to operate. The Canadian Broadcasting Corporation (CBC) rapidly extended its dominion beyond radio to television.

Economic Factors

The prominent place of advertising in Canada's economy is due in no minor fashion to the nature of the country's economic evolution. Such developments as standardization and mass production resulted in a more widely felt need for effective advertising. The generalization of branding and packaging during the 1890s, the development of manufacturing, the birth of the consumer society, and the expansion of the third sector were all instrumental in making advertising into what it is today. As we have seen, advertising is essentially a product of the Industrial Revolution, and it has accelerated and been a key factor in the advent of the modern consumer society. With the orientation of the Canadian economy toward greater reliance on services and on the third sector, which has been more apparent during the past decade, it appears that advertising will play an even more important and constructive role in the future.

The Evolution of Advertising Concepts and Institutions

Once a favourable environment for advertising was created, its potential still remained to be tapped. The evolution of concepts encouraging and fostering a more sophisticated and scientific approach to advertising also played an essential role. At the beginning of the 1890s, advertising was still a crude affair. Most printed ads merely exhibited a brand name, and possibly a price. The real efficiency of such advertising was far from established and elicited much scepticism in the business community. Furthermore, there was a widespread notion that it was somehow undignified for manufacturers to flaunt their merchandise. The sole function of advertising was therefore to maintain public awareness of a brand name.

FIGURE 1–1
Bissell's Carpet Sweepers

Source: H.E. Stephenson and C. McNaught, The Story of Advertising in Canada (Toronto: Ryerson Press, 1940).

Moreover, the persons who created advertisements tended to have little or no formal training in advertising techniques and were not trained to communicate effectively with mass markets. Advertisers did not try to translate their own experience into the language of the average consumer. As a result, advertisements were, more often than not, clever and humorous, but their wit was lost on most people; consequently they lacked real selling power.

This was further aggravated by the low quality of advertising design. The notion that an advertisement would be more attractive and attention-grabbing if it combined a half dozen different typestyles in copy that was also hopelessly overcrowded seemed to prevail among early advertisers. See, for instance, the advertisement for Bissell's carpet sweepers in Figure 1–1.

The first advertising agency appeared in Canada in 1889, with the founding of the McKim agency. Its sole function, however, was to sell newspaper space to advertisers. Most early advertising agencies served mainly as brokers of media space and had little to do with the content of the ads. The adoption of a more systematic approach to advertising was largely the work of a few individuals, whose accomplishments therefore merit some recollection.

The Canadian who probably did the most to bring about the birth of modern advertising was John E. Kennedy.[5] A former Mountie, he had a successful career in the garment industry by advocating what was then a revolutionary idea. Dividing consumers into nine broad categories, he produced large quantities of ready-made suits that could fit any standard build and were much less expensive than custom-made suits. The success of his clothing was due in no small part to advertising. Indeed, Kennedy used advertising to great effect and had a gift for communicating persuasively with mass markets. His experience in the clothing industry convinced him that advertising could and should play a fundamental role in any selling strategy. He therefore decided to test some of his theories in the United States.

In 1904, he went to the offices of Lord & Thomas, a major advertising agency of the time. While waiting in the lobby, he sent a note to two of the agency's top executives, Ambrose Thomas and Albert Lasker. The note read: "I am downstairs in the saloon, and I can tell you what advertising is. I know that you don't know. It will mean much to me to have you know what it is and it will mean much to you. If you wish to know what advertising is, send the word 'yes' down by messenger." Intrigued by this unusual communication Lasker sent for Kennedy. What he told Lasker was disarmingly simple: "Advertising is salesmanship in print."

This seemingly obvious truth landed Kennedy a job with Lord & Thomas for the unprecedented salary of $28 000 a year. His concept revolutionized the nature of advertising, for he had discovered the true function and driving force behind advertising—persuasion.

From then on, the role of advertising became more than exhibiting a brand name and keeping it in the public eye; it was extended to that of a salesperson who uses persuasive powers and argumentation to bring about a purchase. Although advertising concepts and techniques have been modified over the years, the underlying rationale—persuasion—remains basically unchanged.

Building upon this firm theoretical ground, Kennedy devised a wholly novel approach toward advertising and was one of the first advocates of what is called "reason-why" copy. "Conviction is not produced by bare affirmation, but by proof, by inference, by argument—in short, by 'reason-why talk'."[6]

Summing up Kennedy's achievements, one writer on the history of American advertising said:

It was not until his [Kennedy's] time that any appreciable number of advertisers got away from the old publicity theory of advertising effect as the sole end and aim of the art. While he doesn't by any means deserve all the credit, he had more to do with it than anybody else.[7]

With the idea introduced by John E. Kennedy, traditional advertising agencies underwent profound change. The turn of the century saw the establishment of agencies specializing in ad creation. This type of organization was short-lived, however, and soon merged with the traditional advertising agency. The results of such mergers were the forerunners of modern advertising agencies.

In the 1910s, advertising agencies became more sophisticated. From a small personal enterprise in 1889, the McKim advertising agency mushroomed to a full-fledged corporation, providing a comprehensive range of advertising-related services, including ad creation, production, and media planning. Modern advertising agencies are an outgrowth of the phenomenal expansion of advertising in the 1900s. Without this growth, advertising would not be the dynamic and vital institution it is today.

Like any other institution, Canadian advertising has evolved over the years. In many ways, advertising reflects its time, as well as the values, beliefs, and lifestyles of the time at which it was created.[8] It also reflects the progress and evolution of the advertising techniques and philosophies. This is illustrated by the sample of Canadian posters and ads which appeared in the print media in the 1930s reproduced in Figure 1–2 to 1–6.[9]

FIGURE 1–2

(top) The Westminster Hotel might well have appealed to an important choice criterion for a luxury hotel: "A real hotel without a bar."
Courtesy Westminster Hotel Ltd. and Martin Dennis

FIGURE 1–3

(bottom) What ever happened to Rogers radios?
Courtesy Rogers Communications Inc.

FIGURE 1–4
(left) Would such an advertising copy (run during
the First World War)
be conceivable in 1991?
FIGURE 1–5
(top, right) Laura
Secord's logo and
advertising appeal
have changed—along
with the Company's
image—since the time
of this poster.
Courtesy Laura Secord Inc.
FIGURE 1–6
(bottom, right) Would
this type of humour
sell nowadays?
Courtesy Best Foods Canada Inc.

ADVERTISING IN THE CANADIAN ENVIRONMENT

Environmental factors were instrumental in giving advertising the role it plays in the Canadian economy. Indeed, certain aspects of the Canadian scene led to the development of unique features in advertising in this country. The most relevant environmental factors include Canada's unique demography, its biculturalism, strong economic and cultural ties with its southern neighbour, and a tradition of high advertising spending, as well as highly developed communication channels, a high degree of advertising sophistication, and extreme and distinctive legislation regulating advertising activities.

Canadian Demography

Canada has approximately 26 million people scattered over a territory substantially larger than the United States, and unequally distributed. For example, the southern fringe, the St.Lawrence valley, the Great Lakes area, and the West Coast are highly populated areas, while the northern part of the country is sparsely populated.From a socio-demographic point of view, Canada is comprised of several easily identified markets which can serve as a basis for market segmentation. They are the Maritime Provinces, the French Canadian market (essentially, but not exclusively the Province of Quebec), Ontario, the Prairies, and British Columbia. In spite of this population concentration into relatively homogeneous markets, as will be seen, the unequal population distribution makes it difficult to reach isolated market segments effectively through the mass media.

Canada's Biculturalism

Language differences have proven another obstacle to effective mass communication. Quebec has a majority of Francophones, and there are sizeable francophone minorities in other provinces, notably, Ontario, New Brunswick, and Manitoba. The problem for advertisers has been reaching the two major language groups of this country through the proper media and in their own language. Other sizeable ethnic groups, such as the Portuguese, Italians, and

Chinese, should not be overlooked by advertisers who want to address these market segments and must therefore account for these groups' language, culture, and media habits. As will be discussed in Chapter 4, addressing these ethnic groups is much more than a mere translation of the basic message into the proper language. Often subtle cultural differences must be taken into account.

Canada's Ties with the U.S. Market

A major environmental factor is Canada's strong economic ties with the United States, which has recently been reinforced with the 1989 Free Trade Agreement between the two countries. These ties have made Canada especially vulnerable to changes in the American economy. In recent years, the economic recession, inflationary pressures, and a general slowdown in real income growth have been shared by both countries.

From an advertising point of view, this strong link between the Canadian and the U.S. economies and cultures results in a substantial spillover of advertising from the United States into Canada. Canadians receive American television through cable or through American border stations, and they buy American magazines. As American advertising conveyed by these media reaches Canadians, the spillover is likely to play in favour of large American advertisers who also operate in Canada and sell similar products in both countries. Thus, this spillover of American advertising creates a unique problem for Canadian advertisers, who must compete with American firms and are at a disadvantage even in their own country. In spite of attempts by the Canadian government to take corrective action, it has not been possible to change this situation substantially.

Canada's Advertising Spendings

The strong ties between the American and the Canadian economies also have definite advantages. It can be argued, for instance, that Canada would probably not have reached its present high level of economic development were it not for the close ties with the Unites States. For the same reason, Canadian advertising might not have been able to achieve its present high level of spending and sophistication.

Tables 1–2 and 1–3 give some indications of the position advertising enjoys in Canada's economy. From Table 1–2 it can be seen that the amount spent on advertising in the past 25 years has increased steadily and is now more than eight billion dollars. This increase is the result of a number of factors, such as the generally increasing gross national product and inflated dollars. On a per capita basis, advertising expenditures have grown from $38.00 in 1965 to $325.00 in 1989.

Table 1–3 gives a breakdown of Canadian advertising expenditures for each type of media. Newspapers (29.7 percent), direct mail (21.9 percent), followed by periodicals (16.6 percent) and television (15.6 percent) account for about 83.8 percent of total advertising expenditures.

Table 1–4 lists the twelve top advertisers in Canada in 1989. The first major advertiser by far is the federal government, and the government of Ontario is among the first 12 major advertisers. Also on the list are seven Canadian subsidiaries of multinational corporations.

TABLE 1–2 **TOTAL ADVERTISING EXPENDITURES IN CANADA**

Year	Total Advertising Expenditures ($ millions)	% Increase Over Last 5 Year Period
1965	798	
1970	1 060	+32.8
1975	1 938	+82.8
1980	3 763	+94.2
1985	6 210	+65.0
1989	9 049	+55.7

Source: Statistics Canada. Business Services Preliminary Estimates 1988, Cat. No. 63-015, Sept. 1990.

TABLE 1–3 **NET ADVERTISING REVENUES BY MEDIA (IN MILLIONS OF DOLLARS)**

	1984	%	1989	%
Radio	545	9.4	748	8.3
Television	970	16.7	1416	15.6
Newspapers	1729	29.8	2684	29.7
Periodicals	879	15.1	1504	16.6
Other Print	1295	22.3	1979	21.9
Outdoor[1]	392	6.7	718	7.2
Total	5810	100.0	9049	100.0

Source: 1983–1986 Statistics Canada actuals. 1987–1988 estimated by Maclean Hunter Research Bureau and published in CARD, May 11, 1989, p. 002. Business Services Preliminary Estimates 1988, Cat. No. 63-105, Sept. 1990.

[1]Incl. factory shipments of advertising signs and displays (Stat. Can. Cat. 47-209) and firms in other outdoor advertising businesses (renting space, putting up billboards or other displays, placing advertising matter on streetcars, buses, other transit systems and advertising revenue of other sign producers, show card writers, sign painters, etc.).

TABLE 1–4 **THE TWELVE TOP ADVERTISERS IN CANADA IN 1989**

	($ 000)
1. Government of Canada	76 045
2. Procter and Gamble	61 377
3. General Motors of Canada	56 735
4. Unilever	46 977
5. John Labatt Limited	44 706
6. Kraft General Foods Group	44 186
7. Cineplex Odeon Corporation	43 372
8. Paramount Communications	42 505
9. McDonald's Restaurants of Canada	34 849
10. RJR	33 484
11. Ontario Government	30 993
12. Molson Breweries of Canada	28 615

Source: Marketing (March 28, 1990), p. 2.

To sum up, Canadian advertising is characterized by a high level of expenditure and sophistication and is much influenced by the demographic, cultural, and geographic environment in which it operates. Although Canada's long history of close relations with the United States has had a profound impact on advertising, a number of unique features give Canadian advertising a particular flavour and originality.

ADVERTISING AS COMMUNICATION

The definition of advertising given previously has several implications about the distinctiveness of advertising. First, because it is a type of communication, advertising plays a specific role in the complex communication network of an industrial or commercial firm. Second, as a communication device, advertising draws upon the theories and findings of communication theory and social psychology. Third, because of the wide audience addressed, advertisers must have a comprehensive knowledge of their markets in order to deliver an efficient message. This is why advertisers must use research and apply the principles of scientific method. Fourth, because it is a type of mass communication, advertising plays a role in a firm's program that is markedly different from personal selling, which is the other major marketing communication tool. Fifth, because of its socio-economic function, advertising is assigned very precise objectives. In a marketing program, advertising's role should be consistent with the other elements of the marketing mix.

Advertising and the Social Sciences

The Communication Process

Because advertising is a special type of communication, the general model of communication theory is applicable. This model (see Figure 1–7) is comprised of six elements: the communicator (or the source), the message, the channels, the audience, the intended effect, and the feedback.

The *communicator* or *source* is the individual or organization initiating the communication. In an advertising context, the communicator is the firm advertising its products or services. The *message* includes the set of words, sounds, and images used by the communicator to convey an idea to the audience. In advertising, the message is a printed or broadcast piece of information. The communication *channels* are the media used to convey the message to the audience. In advertising, these channels are the mass media. The *audience* of the communication is the individual or group of individuals for whom the message is intended. In advertising, the audience is the potential market for the firm's products or services.

Any message has a precise objective or *intended effect*. For example, its purpose may be to inform an audience. When the additional information triggers a response from the audience, the intended effect is persuasive.

An advertiser gives consumers information about products or services in order to influence their attitudes. The final objective is to obtain a behavioural response, that is, the purchase of a product or service, or the adoption of an idea.

In Figure 1–7 the arrows indicate the direction of the information flow. Advertisers translate information into a specific message, in effect, coding the information. Then the message is delivered through a communication channel to a target audience. Individuals in the audience decode the message by attributing a meaning to the message and interpreting the information it contains. Obviously, a communicator must make sure the message has been properly deciphered, understood, and interpreted, and has thus produced the intended response. This process constitutes the *feedback.*

In advertising, the feedback is the effect of the advertising message on the consumer. It can be observed as a change in a consumer's attitude toward an advertised product, service, or idea, or as a change in the consumer's behaviour pattern (for example, a sales volume increase).

FIGURE 1–7

Theoretical Process of Advertising Communication

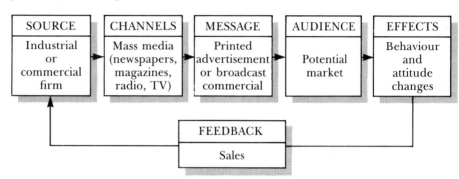

The Advertising Communications Process

The communications model suggests that for a communication to be effective, the same code must be used by the communicator and the receiver (Figure 1–8).[10]

In this diagram, the lines surrounding the communicator and the audience represent what is called their *field of experience* at the time of the communication.

FIGURE 1–8

Theoretical Process of a Communication

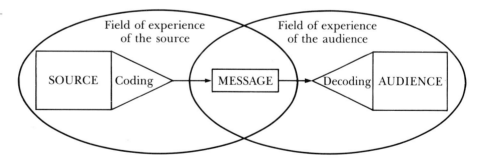

Communicators can only code a message in terms of their experience. For instance, a mathematical equation can be decoded (understood) by a scientist because mathematics is part of a scientist's field of experience. It could not be decoded by an individual who has not had some training or experience in mathematics. Consequently, a successful communication cannot take place without two conditions being fulfilled: first, the communicator and the audience must share at least part of their field of experience; they should at least be able to speak and understand a common language. Second, the message must be expressed in terms of their shared experience, that is, their common language.

Classifications of Advertising

This concept of the communication process can be used to describe different types of advertising. For example, advertising may be classified according to the communication element it emphasizes, as shown in Figure 1–9.

As illustrated, advertising may be classified according to the source of the communication, either business advertising or non-profit advertising. *Business advertising* can be further sub-divided into *manufacturer*, *wholesaler*, or *retailer* advertising. *Non-profit advertising* may be sponsored by *government*, by a *social organization*, or by a *political party*.

The type of message used can also be a classification. Advertising classified according to the content and/or format of the message links *product advertising*, which is intended to help sell a product, *service advertising*, which promotes a service, *idea advertising*, which attempts to "sell" an idea, and *institutional advertising*, which promotes a corporation rather than its products or services.

FIGURE 1–9
Current Classifications of Advertising

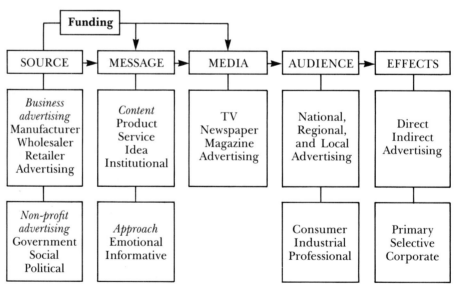

A classification according to the approach selected to deliver the message differentiates between *emotional advertising*, which appeals to consumers' conscious and abstract needs, and *informative advertising*, which emphasizes the physical characteristics of products. When advertising is classified based on the type of message, an advertiser either gives factual information about a product or appeals directly to consumers' desires, creating the advertising message so as to influence consumers. (This subject is discussed further in Chapter 9.)

Advertising may also be classified according to the media chosen, for instance, *television*, *newspapers*, or *direct mail* advertising, or according to the nature or geographical spread of a target audience. *Consumer advertising* is directed at final consumers, while *industrial advertising* is directed at industrial firms. *Professional advertising's* main objective is to reach professionals who are likely to influence the purchases of final consumers. An example of this would be doctors who prescribe certain drugs to their patients. *Middleman advertising* is intended for members of a distribution channel. In a classification according to the geographical dispersion of an audience, advertising is called *national advertising* when it is directed at the whole country, *regional advertising* if concentrated in a specific area, and *local advertising* if it is limited to a city or a smaller locality.

Advertising is also characterized by its intended immediate effects. Thus, it may be primary or selective, direct or indirect. *Primary advertising* promotes the consumption of a generic product category. An example is an advertising campaign aimed at convincing consumers to drink more milk. *Selective advertising* promotes the sales of a specific brand, for instance, a campaign for drinking Sealtest milk. *Direct advertising* tries to get an immediate response from the consumer (such as advertising for a specific offer). *Indirect advertising* tries to build a favourable image which, in the long run, would enhance a company's sales and profits.

Finally, advertising may be classified according to its source of funding. *Co-operative advertising* is partly paid for by a manufacturer and partly by a member of the distribution channel, for example, a retailer. Thus, a retailer who wants to advertise a certain brand might seek the support of the brand's manufacturer because such advertising is likely to benefit both of them.

Of course, these classifications of advertising are not mutually exclusive, since an advertising campaign might be initiated by a manufacturer, be informative, and be a national television campaign for industrial products.

*ADVERTISING
AS MASS
COMMUNICATION*

*Application
to the Mass
Communication
Process*

The Production and Consumption Worlds

As we have seen, many concepts from communication theory can be applied to advertising.[11] The experience gained by a firm and the experience acquired by a potential consumer of an advertised product are generally quite different. For example, a manufacturing firm evolves in a technological world. It has technical and scientific knowledge of its products and can code different information about its products in technical language. A firm also evolves in a professional world: to manufacture and market a product is the day-to-day task of the firm's officers and employees. In contrast, the product or service is part of consumers' private world. Consumers buy the product or service in order to experience some personal, familial, or social satisfaction. Therefore, their field of experience in relation to this product has more to do with product usage than with technical knowledge.

Because of these differences, a common language between a firm and its consumers does not develop either naturally or spontaneously. It must be worked out by the firm. This is why a firm must enlarge its experience in order to include in it consumers' experience of the product.

A Firm's Advertising Philosophy

The evolution of the prevailing advertising philosophies can be best explained in terms of these concepts. When craftspeople started to use mass production and began communicating with clients on a large scale, they lost personal contact with their clients. The gap between the experience of producers and consumers widened. Firms no longer knew their consumers and lacked the desire to know them. Figure 1–10a illustrates this phenomenon.

At one time, consumers needed the products and bought the goods available on the market without paying much attention to quality. Hence, advertising played only a minor role in a firm's marketing plans.

FIGURE 1–10

The Advertising Process before and after the Advent of the Modern Marketing Concept

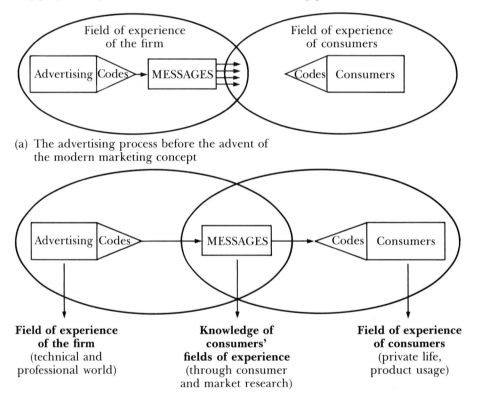

(a) The advertising process before the advent of the modern marketing concept

Field of experience of the firm
(technical and professional world)

Knowledge of consumers' fields of experience
(through consumer and market research)

Field of experience of consumers
(private life, product usage)

(b) The advertising process after the advent of the modern marketing concept

As mass production enabled basic consumer demands for goods to be met, consumers became increasingly difficult to satisfy and firms found it necessary to improve communications with their markets. Unfortunately, most firms knew very little about the reasons why consumers bought their products. Moreover, firms communicated with their clients in a language that the consumers hardly understood. Advertisers often coded a message that was not expressed in terms of the consumer's experience, thus the large amounts of money spent on advertising were for the most part wasted. This may explain the origin of the public's negative image of advertising as "persuasion at all costs."

With the advent of the modern marketing concept, manufacturers rediscovered consumers. They inquired about consumers' tastes, needs, and wants. So companies' communications with their markets came to be based on consumers' deepest motivations for buying a product and on sometimes hidden satisfactions consumers seek. Consequently, through consumer motivation and marketing research, advertisers must discover what motivates consumers.

The modern marketing concept holds that the language of advertising must be adapted to its target. Manufacturers and marketers must be able to predict clients' probable reactions. Advertising uses much the same selling techniques as last century's merchants, who presented their arguments in the manner most likely to be best appreciated by their customers. In the past, craftspeople relied on intuition to understand clients' psychology. Today this is accomplished by market surveys and motivation research, which help advertisers provide their mass communication with the content and format that best suit their market. This is shown in Figure 1–10b; the message is located in the middle where both fields of experience overlap.[12]

Advertising in the Canadian Bicultural Environment

Advertising campaigns must be adapted when they are used for a market segment other than the one they have been originally designed for. If a domestic firm uses commercials created for a national market in its international operations, the cost of advertising is reduced significantly. However, consumers' field of experience is deeply influenced by the culture to which they belong, and the same message can be interpreted very differently depending on consumers' culture or sub-culture.

In Canada a classic example of this is the Quebec market and how advertising evolved there.[13] Ever since advertising appeared in Quebec, advertising campaigns were mere French translations of English advertising campaigns originated by New York or Toronto advertising agencies.[14] The danger of such an approach, however, was that what was suitable for English Canada was often, for cultural and linguistic reasons, unsuitable for Quebec.

In the 1960s, advertising messages for the Quebec market were more or less successful adaptations of English commercials.[15] More recently, advertisements aimed at Quebec's francophone population have changed greatly.[16] In order to account for special characteristics of the Quebec market, advertising campaigns are generally conceived and designed by Montreal advertising agencies. Although this trend makes advertising creation more costly, it has the merit of recognizing that French and English Canadians have different cultural fields of experience.[17]

Advertising Research: A Consequence of Mass Communication

Advertising communications, like the other elements of the marketing mix, are elaborated from a precise knowledge of consumer needs, motivations, attitudes and opinions, behaviour, and purchasing habits. However, because of the high costs involved, advertising communications must be efficient. Thus, the various elements of an advertising communication program are the subject of formal research by advertisers and advertising agencies. (See Chapter 15 for a description of the research techniques used in advertising.[18])

What is important to keep in mind here is that the scientific method and systematic approach play a major role in an area that traditionally relied upon art and intuition. This does not mean that creativity and art have no part to play in advertising. An architect can design a masterpiece and still meet the functional constraints of the building. In the same way, advertisers must reconcile art and marketing communications. Their responsibility is to translate raw selling arguments into the words and images that are likely to induce consumers to buy what the economy has produced for them.

Personal vs. Mass Communications

Personal communications through sales representatives and advertising communications have a common objective: both are directed at potential customers to increase a firm's sales and profits. However, the two types of communication differ in their nature and effectiveness because of two essentially different characteristics they possess: the type of medium they use and their cost structure.

The Medium of Personal Communications

Advertising communications are transmitted through the mass media—newspapers, magazines, television, and radio. In contrast, sales force communications take place between a salesperson and a customer, a prospect, or at most a small group of potential customers.

FIGURE 1–11

Difference between Advertising and Personal Selling Communications

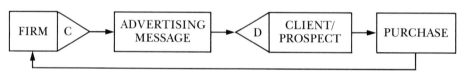

(a) Advertising Communication

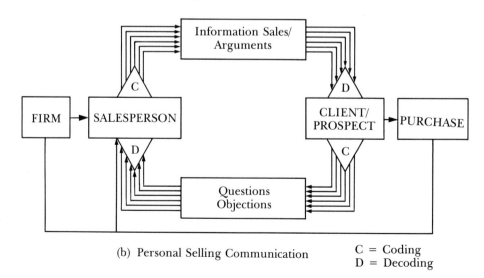

(b) Personal Selling Communication

C = Coding
D = Decoding

Figure 1–11 shows the difference between personal selling communications and advertising communications. A firm communicates with its sales force through training or retraining programs, which are formal communications systems. Sales meetings and directives that a sales manager periodically sends to sales personnel are examples of the more usual and recurrent formal communications. During sales calls a sales representative communicates information to customers and prospects. Unlike advertising, however, these communications occur more than once and are multidirectional: the information flows back and forth between the sales representatives and customers and prospects. For instance, a sales representative inquires about a customer's needs. To do so, the representative gives information about the products and services for sale and answers the questions and objections of prospective buyers.

This information goes back and forth between the sales representative and the customer in a continuous and two-directional communication flow. This continues until the customer ends the process by signing an order or by changing attitude.

These attitudinal or behavioural changes constitute the feedback on the effect of personal selling communications. Another important difference between personal communications and advertising is that during a sales call a sales representative can observe the effect of the sales pitch on potential customers. Consequently, the representative can adjust or reorient the message depending on the feedback received from the client. The sales manager can directly assess the quality and effectiveness of a sales communication by observing the customer's behavioural responses, that is, whether a customer places an order or is satisfied with the product or service.

Consequences of the Types of Communication Used

The use of personal or mass communications has several implications for the quality and efficiency of marketing communications. A comparison of the advantages and drawbacks of personal communication and advertising is shown in Table 1–5.

Differences Affecting the Communicator. The communicator of advertising messages generally has only a global knowledge of a market, that is, an "average profile" of a "typical" consumer in a target segment. Advertising messages are directed toward this average individual, who may resemble to a greater or lesser degree any of the actual individuals in the target market. A sales representative, however, communicates personally with customers and prospects and thus can learn a lot about them. Through intuition and observation (two important assets of a successful sales person) the motives and interests of customers can be detected and the communication adjusted accordingly. In marketing communications, sales representatives are to advertisers what craftspeople are to mass producers.

Differences Affecting the Message. Once an advertising communication has taken place, a sales manager must wait for the effects, if any, to become evident. In contrast, personal selling messages are adaptive: depending upon the feed-

TABLE 1-5 **COMPARISON OF THE ADVANTAGES AND DRAWBACKS OF ADVERTISING AND PERSONAL SELLING AS COMMUNICATION TOOLS**

		Personal Selling	Advertising
Source	Communicator's knowledge of the audience	+	−
	Flexibility and adaptability of messages	+	−
Message	Number of arguments that can be effectively used	+	−
	Control by the firm of the content and format of the message	−	+
	Personal contact	+	−
Medium	Possibility of communicating with many consumers in a short period of time	−	+
	Effects of coding errors	+	−
Audience	Ability to attract and hold consumers' attention	+	−
	Time at which communication takes place	+	−
Effects	Time lag between communication and purchase	+	−

back received during a sales presentation, a salesperson can adjust the message or leave it unchanged. Arguments that seem to satisfy potential customers' concerns can be emphasized or sales points that seem irrelevant to the customers' decision-making processes can be played down.

In the media, an advertiser can emphasize at most one or two reasons for buying a product. This is not the case for salespeople, who can stress many persuasive selling points during a single sales call.

An advertiser can, however, have some control over the sales message's content and presentation. Advertisers carefully select—often after formal research—the theme, copy, and layout of their advertisements. They make sure that the message can be properly understood by prospective buyers and can influence their target audience.

Sales managers can also test sales arguments and train the sales force to make effective presentations. However, a firm has no direct control over the exact content and wording of the message each salesperson actually delivers; a sales manager can do little to prevent salespeople from delivering poor presentations or being rude to customers.

Differences Affecting the Media. Personal and advertising communications have both advantages and drawbacks with regard to the effectiveness of the media through which a message is delivered. A sales representative has the advantage of establishing personal and often lively communication with a customer or prospect, while advertising, and especially print advertising, can be perceived by consumers as an impersonal way to communicate. However, advertising has an important advantage over personal selling: through the mass media, it can reach a large number of people in a short period of time, whereas a sales representative can make only a limited number of calls in a day.

Differences Affecting the Audience. This latter advantage of advertising over personal selling has a negative counterpart in its effects on the audience of the communication. Any blunder that a sales representative makes during a sales call affects only that customer or prospect. At worst, an inadequate salesperson affects sales negatively during the time he or she is part of the sales force and only in a limited territory. But an advertisement in poor taste has more damaging effects because it reaches an entire market simultaneously.

A salesperson also gets some attention from a client once the sales pitch has started. In contrast, the attention given to the mass media and to the advertising messages they convey cannot be controlled. Commercials often reach consumers during their leisure time, when they are watching television or reading newspapers or magazines. In contrast, a salesperson usually calls on customers during working hours; meeting sales representatives is often a part of the duties of the individuals on whom a sales representative calls. Thus, the audience is more favourably disposed toward listening to a sales pitch.

Differences Affecting the Effects. As far as communication effects are concerned, personal selling has a distinct advantage over advertising because it produces immediate responses. After a salesperson has succeeded in proving to a customer that the offer is superior to that of competitors, the selling process can be completed by persuading the customer to sign an order. In contrast, even when a commercial has been convincing enough to trigger the act of purchasing, this behavioural response cannot be immediate. There is always a time lag between the moment a commercial is seen or heard by a consumer and the moment the purchase is completed. This lag is the time necessary for the consumer to drive to a neighbourhood store or, more realistically, to wait for the next purchase occasion. Of course, during this time, the consumer may be subjected to other commercials from competitive products or may decide not to buy the product.

A Cost-Benefit Comparison of Both Types of Communications

From the comparison of the various aspects of advertising and personal selling, it can be seen that personal selling is a more effective and powerful communication tool than advertising. This does not mean that only personal selling should be used as a marketing tool and that advertising should have only a marginal role in a firm's marketing program. Contacting an individual through a sales representative costs about a hundred times more than an advertisement. Consequently, unless the personal element of a selling communication is essential to a firm, marketing managers will find that advertising is more time and cost efficient.

ADVERTISING AS A SOCIO-ECONOMIC COMMUNICATION

The Economics of Advertising Communications

The various socio-economic aspects of advertising are discussed more thoroughly in subsequent chapters. Here it is important to emphasize that commercial advertising has a precise economic objective. This objective is, in the long run, to contribute to the firm's sales and profits. To meet this objective, advertising is assigned short-run objectives that contribute to a firm's wider objectives.

To be justified from an economic point of view, advertising, along with the other elements of the marketing program, must help generate a firm's gross profits (long-run, and discounted at their present value, but excluding the direct costs of advertising). A marketer's task is to ensure that a firm's gross profits are greater than the costs of advertising, which include the costs of media, the costs of creating and producing the advertisement, and the research costs, so that the firm retains a flow of net profits.

The Social Objectives of Advertising

Increasingly, advertising is being used by non-profit organizations. For instance, an advertising campaign to raise funds for a cancer research institute, the Red Cross, or some other charitable organization, does not result in sales and profits. An advertisement campaign to induce Canadians to adopt better health habits, or to use safety belts in their cars, or advertising messages sponsored by a political party to gain citizens' votes for the next election do not result in dollar-measurable effects. Whenever advertising is used, however, certain social benefits are anticipated by the sponsors. Whether the social gains warrant the advertising expenditures is a far more difficult question to answer because the effects are not quantifiable as for business advertising. Nevertheless, no advertising campaign is likely to be run unless the sponsors feel that the social and/or economic gains warrant the advertising expenditures.

A PROSPECTIVE VIEW OF CANADIAN ADVERTISING

The direction advertising is likely to take in Canada over the next few decades may be determined by analyzing the influence of present trends on the various elements involved in advertising.[19] Because it is a mass communication tool, advertising will be affected by research in communications and in the behavioural sciences. Thus, advertising probably will become more efficient in the presentation of messages and in its diffusion processes, thanks to such technical innovations as communication by satellites, visual presentations by telephone, and other improvements in telecommunications. The use of scientific tools and techniques in advertising is likely to increase.

As a marketing tool, advertising will be linked to the evolution of the modern marketing concept. If marketing philosophy is applied to many other kinds of institutions, such as government agencies, educational institutions, and political parties, advertising will increase in scope to include what has so far been the domain of public relations.[20] On the other hand, as a result of increased market demand, a large number of products are likely to cater to smaller, more specific market segments. Consequently, advertising appeals will have to become more specific and will have to find new media vehicles for communicating with smaller market segments.

As for the future role of advertising research, new research techniques will undoubtedly be developed and at an accelerated pace. Because advertisers always need to reduce the uncertainty of their decisions, they will rely more on advertising research. Advertising research will then take a larger share of the advertising dollar. The economic and social effects of advertising will likely lead consumers to exert tighter control over marketing activities and especially over advertising, which is the communications link between manufacturers and consumers.

Two major trends can be predicted: the further evolution of the modern marketing concept will decrease the amount of misleading advertising and limit the use of exaggerated advertising claims. This trend should lead to a general acceptance of the ethical standards (discussed in Chapter 17) to which the largest advertisers have subscribed.

The other trend is toward more legislation to control advertising activities. Under the increasing pressure of consumer-related movements, legislators will have to exert more control over and restrict some activities of advertisers.

All these changes will affect the day-to-day decision-making tasks of advertisers. They will probably obtain increasing help from operational decision tools and, with the use of computers, will concentrate on more delicate problems. Advertisers will also be subject to new constraints from consumers, consumer groups, and legislators. At the same time, their potential for action will increase as new research methods and decision tools become available and as knowledge from the social sciences increases. Far from having their freedom to act curtailed, Canadian advertisers will face new challenges and tasks in the future.

SUMMARY

Advertising plays an important role in the Canadian economy. It can be defined as a mass communication tool with an economic purpose. There are several implications of this definition, and any study of advertising should include an analysis of communication theory and the role of advertising in a firm's communication system. Advertisers also need to understand the importance of advertising research as well as the role advertising and personal selling play in the marketing program.

From these analyses can be drawn some important conclusions. First, because advertising is a mass communication, it tends to lose contact with its audience and is efficient only if it is based on research initiated by the advertiser. Second, advertising is not an isolated phenomenon in a firm's activities. It is but one part of a firm's communication network and must be a consistent and integrated part of that network. Third, advertising is only one tool at the disposal of a marketer and therefore is subject to a firm's overall objectives. Therefore, it must be integrated with the other marketing elements into a coherent marketing program.

1. Canadian advertising expenditures reached a peak in 1988. The yearly increase of advertising expenditures is the result of several factors. Identify some of these factors, and show how each one contributes to the increase of advertising expenditure volume.

2. Explain how the modern marketing concept changed the nature of and approach to advertising.

3. After having been banned for some time, advertising was reintroduced in the USSR in the 1970s. What reasons do you think made this reintroduction necessary? Is there any economic system that could do without advertising? Explain.

4. Describe the differences in advertising for consumer products, industrial products, services, and charitable organizations.

5. Taking the buyer's point of view, contrast the quality and effectiveness of the information received from a sales representative and from an advertisement. Explain in what ways the concept of "salesmanship in print" was an innovation at the time it was first proposed by John E. Kennedy.

6. What are the main differences between an advertising campaign run by a retailer (such as Canadian Tire) and an advertising campaign for a consumer product (such as one run by Nabisco)? What are the main factors responsible for these differences?

7. Go through some magazine and newspaper ads. Find examples of:
   - manufacturer advertisements
   - retailer advertisements
   - product advertising
   - institutional advertising
   - emotional advertising
   - informative advertising
   - primary advertising
   - selective advertising
   - direct advertising
   - indirect advertising

8. Why would an advertiser want to use primary advertising? Give examples. Why would an advertiser want to combine primary and selective advertising campaigns? What important differences are likely to be found in both types of campaign? (Use Figure 1–2 to answer this question.)

9. Define advertising. Show how your definition applies to the different kinds of advertising listed in Question 7.

10. Describe the economic function of commercial advertising for a product or a service. Contrast these economic aspects with those of advertising by a non-profit organization.

PROBLEMS

1. Assume that you head the advertising department of a large electronic equipment manufacturer. In past years, the firm's main line of products has been computers, and until recently the firm's only clients have been important medium-sized organizations and businesses. In 1988, following trends in the data processing equipment industry, the firm introduced a new line of personal computers especially designed for consumer markets.
   a. What kind of adjustments to your advertising approach, advertising programs, and strategies do you think you would have to make in order to advertise this new line of products effectively?
   b. How could the concept of fields of experience described in Figure 1–9 help you make the necessary adjustments?

2. As a successful advertiser for a major detergent manufacturer in Canada, you have been approached recently by one of the major federal political parties to design their advertising strategy and campaign for a forthcoming election.
   a. Draw up a list of the relevant factors that you would like to account for before you would specify such a strategy.
   b. Are these factors different from those that you would consider if you were advertising a consumer product?
   c. In what ways (if any) could the concept of the field of experience help you to carry out your assignment?

NOTES

1. Raymond A. Bauer and Stephen A. Greyser, *Advertising in America: The Consumer View* (Boston: Division of Research, Graduate School of Business Administration, Harvard University, 1969).
2. Ralph S. Alexander and the Committee on Definitions, *Marketing Definitions* (Chicago, Ill.: American Marketing Association, 1963), p. 9.
3. H.E. Stephenson and Carlton McNaught, *The Story of Advertising in Canada* (Toronto: The Ryerson Press, 1940), p. 1.
4. Ibid., p. 8.
5. See John O'Toole, *The Trouble with Advertising* (New York: Chelsea House Publishers, 1981).
6. Stephenson and McNaught, p. 101.
7. Ibid., pp. 101–2.
8. Richard W. Pollay, "The Subsiding Sizzle: A Descriptive History of Print Advertising 1900–1980," *Journal of Marketing*, 49, (November 1985), pp. 24–37.
9. See the September 26, 1983 Issue of *Marketing*, from which the ads of Figure 1–2 to 2–7 have been reproduced.
10. Wilbur Schramm, "How Communications Works," *The Process and Effects of Mass Communication*, ed. Wilbur Schramm (Urbana, Ill.: University of Illinois Press, 1965).
11. Henri Joannis, *De l'Étude de Motivation à la Création Publicitaire et à la Promotion des Ventes* (Paris: Dunod, 1967) pp. 8–9.
12. Barbara B. Stern, "Medieval Allegory: Roots of Advertising Strategy for the Mass Market," *Journal of Marketing*, 52, (July 1988), pp. 84–94.
13. For example, see Serge Proulx, "Pour une Pratique de la Publicité au Québec", *Communications*, No. 14, (CECMAS, 1971).
14. For example, see Claude Cossette, *Communication de Masse, Consommation de Masse* (Sillery, Qué.: Boréal Express, 1975), p. 261.
15. Jacques Bouchard, "The French Evolution," *Marketing*, September 26, 1983, p. 60.
16. Robert MacGregor, "The Utilization of Originally Conceived French Language Advertisements in Parallel Canadian Magazines," *Marketing*, ed. Robert G. Wyckham (Montreal: Administrative Sciences Association of Canada, 1981), pp. 186–95.

17. Michel J. Bergier and Jerry Rosenblatt, "A Critical View of the Past and Current Methodologies for Classifying English and French Canadians," *Marketing*, ed. Michel Laroche (Montreal: Administrative Sciences Association of Canada, 1982), pp. 11–20. See also Roger J. Calantone and Jacques Picard, "Bilingual Advertising Revisited," *Marketing*, ed. Michel Laroche (Montreal: Administrative Sciences Association of Canada, 1982), pp. 31–38.

18. M. Lucas Darell and Steward H. Britt, *Measuring Advertising Effectiveness* (New York: McGraw-Hill, 1963); see also Paul Green and Donald S. Tull, *Research for Marketing Decisions*, 3rd ed. (Englewood Cliffs, N.J.: Prentice-Hall, 1975).

19. J.R.G. Jenkins, "The Canadian Advertising Industry in the 1980's." *ASAC Proceedings* (1975), pp. 4–125.

20. Philip Kotler and Sidney J. Levy, "Broadening the Concept of Marketing", *Journal of Marketing*, 33 (January 1969), 10–15.

CHAPTER

2 *Advertising in the Marketing Mix*

A properly developed advertising strategy is conceived and designed within the framework of the general marketing strategy. This is why an advertising campaign must be fully integrated into an overall marketing program. In the same way, an advertising plan should always be viewed as a part of the broader marketing plan. Thus, to design an effective advertising campaign, advertisers must understand the role and functions of advertising in the overall marketing program and advertising's contribution to the global marketing strategy.

This chapter analyzes how an advertising strategy can be derived from a marketing strategy and be made consistent with all the other elements of the marketing program. Then it is shown how advertising can be co-ordinated with the other dimensions of the promotional mix—personal selling and sales promotion.

FROM MARKETING TO ADVERTISING STRATEGY

Development of a Marketing Strategy

Generally, a single firm cannot supply all the consumers who have a broad generic need. For instance, no one firm is able to satisfy all the transportation needs in Canada. Therefore, a firm must select which part(s) of a market it wants to and/or can supply. To make such a decision, a firm must identify one or several consumer groups whose needs and behaviour patterns are sufficiently alike to enable them to receive satisfaction from the product or service being offered. Such a group of consumers is called a *market segment*. The program that is set up to fulfill some needs of a selected market segment is generally called the *marketing program*.

A marketing strategy is developed by selecting one or several market segments and designing marketing programs that result in effective market supply and consumer satisfaction. The strategy can be defined once a firm can identify a group of consumers (or market segments) and can develop a marketing program that is likely to satisfy the needs and wants of the consumer group. The firm's objectives and constraints must be met at the same time.

The marketing plan describes in detail the marketing program that a firm intends to follow. A short-term marketing plan usually covers a six-month to one-year period. Medium-term plans run from one to three years. A marketing plan covering a three- to ten-year period is called a long-term plan.

We have said that the marketing program must also account for various constraints, for example, the need to reach a sufficient profit level. Since profits are essential to a firm's survival, the search for market opportunities must aim toward increasing profits. Advertisers must also ensure that the marketing program benefits both the firm and its customers; the firm should be able to make a satisfactory level of profit to increase its resources and at the same time consumers should be able to satisfy some of their needs and wants.

In order to develop effective marketing and, consequently, advertising strategies, it is essential to have an understanding of the key concepts advertisers use: marketing environment, market segmentation, product positioning, marketing mix, and the product life-cycle.

The Marketing Environment Concept

The marketing process starts with an analysis of consumer needs and market behaviour so that the goods and services produced are wanted by consumers and likely to be accepted. This marketing philosophy has implications for the definition of a marketing strategy and for the tools marketers use to achieve their goals. A marketer's role can be compared to that of a marine officer. The officer's responsibility is to bring a ship safely back to harbour. The harbour that marketing managers must reach represents the marketing objectives.

The marine officer must allow for various forces that cannot be controlled, for example, storms, winds, currents, and the routes of other ships. In the same way, marketing managers are also affected by and must adjust to external constraints over which they have no control. Although they cannot control these elements, marketers must identify and, insofar as possible, predict them in the same way as marine officers cannot control the winds or the currents but can inquire about meteorological forecasts and consult ocean maps.

Thus, marketing actions are affected by the market environment at two different levels. On one level are the uncontrollable forces influencing a market: the socio-economic, competitive, institutional, technological, and legal environments. This is called the marketing macro-environment. At the second level are environmental forces over which marketers have no direct control but which can be influenced through promotional activities. This is called the marketing micro-environment. Such forces are, for instance, the consumers in the various target market segments. Marketers want to be able to affect the attitude and the behaviour of these consumers and have some tools at their disposal to do so.

The Marketing Macro-Environment. A market can be characterized by descriptive factors: size, population concentration, demographic trends, the average annual income of consumers or households, growth areas, and immigration or emigration trends. These basic factors are used to assess the importance of a particular market. For example, analysis of consumers' age group disribution in a given market indicates the important changes that will likely occur in consumer patterns for different product and service categories. Such other factors as ethnic origin, religious beliefs, education, income levels and sources, occupation, and language are also relevant market characteristics.

Competitive Market Structures. The competitive environment in which a firm operates is one of the most constraining factors when selecting a marketing strategy. A market of perfect competition is characterized by a very large number of small-size firms competing in an industry. No one firm can dominate the market and no marketer can profitably make the marketing program different from that of competitors. The product is essentially the same for all the firms in the market. The product's price is determined by the forces of supply and demand and not by any one firm. Promotion and advertising are useless tools because consumers are supposed to have complete and free information in a homogeneous market in which the same product is sold.

At the other extreme is a monopoly market, in which only one firm supplies a certain kind of service or product. In this situation a firm can set any price for a product and can decide on the level of all the other variables in the marketing mix. Marketing efforts and advertising can be profitably increased as long as the total demand for the product is sufficient to warrant the increase.

When a market has an oligopolistic structure, it is dominated by a small number of firms (the petroleum industry is one example). In this case, the marketing strategy of each firm is likely to affect competitors' market share significantly. Thus when one firm takes an aggressive marketing action, competitors usually react immediately to protect their market positions. The harshest competition typically takes place in markets with an oligopolistic structure. Since in this market structure a price decrease is likely to be immediately matched by competitors, price is not a very effective marketing weapon. Marketing efforts are more likely to hinge on advertising and sales promotion.

Finally, a market characterized by an imperfect competition structure has a certain number of firms manufacturing products that differ only slightly from one another. This is a common market structure, especially for such products as television sets and automobiles. In this type of market, each firm tries to cater to a specific market segment with a product and marketing program designed to meet that segment's needs, while trying to avoid any possible confusion between its products and those of competitors. In some ways, each firm has a quasi-monopoly in a very limited market segment.

Institutional Market Structure. In addition to its competitive structure, a market is also characterized by its institutional structure. Various organizations, for instance, wholesalers, brokers, retailers, selling organizations, and advertising agencies, specialize in distributing and promoting products. Moreover, certain relationships among these organizations have become a tradition in most markets. These relationships have evolved into their present form as the result of market forces and power structures within marketing channels. Thus the institutional structure of a market usually cannot be modified by a single firm.

The Technological Environment. Each industry is characterized by various degrees of technological evolution. Certain industries, such as electronics and aeronautics, have experienced dramatic change in the past few decades. Technological change compels the firms in these industries to keep abreast of and promote technological development.

In order to benefit from technological breakthroughs, a firm must constantly look for new market opportunities and for innovations that are desired by various market segments.

The Legal Environment.   Marketing managers and advertisers need to be aware of the laws designed to keep competition active or to protect consumers against unfair practices and abuse. In Canada, as will be discussed further in Chapter 17, the Competition Act is intended to discourage practices that might lessen competition. These practices include collusion among competitors, mergers, monopolies, discriminating practices, price fixing, illegal discounts, and false or misleading advertising.

The Marketing Micro-Environment.   The second category of environmental variables includes the factors that induce consumers to buy certain kinds of products (a given brand, at a specific point of purchase, at a certain time); in other words, how and why consumers behave in a certain way. To apply the modern marketing concept is to examine consumers' lives, to understand their needs, motivations, perceptions, attitudes, purchasing habits, and to be aware of the changes they want or are ready to accept.

The Concept of Market Segmentation

Definition.   Market segmentation[1] can be viewed as the process of dividing a given market into either distinct or homogeneous submarkets, according to consumers' reactions to the marketer's offer. This definition is borrowed from economic theory, and its application to marketing was originally proposed by Wendell Smith.[2] The concept of market segmentation was put forth to explain how a firm that sells a homogeneous product in markets with heterogeneous demand schedules could charge different prices to maximize profits. Wendell Smith defines market segmentation as the strategy that takes account of varying intensities of demand within a particular market. Consequently, a market segmentation strategy consists of adjusting the product and the marketing program to satisfy the demand and increase a firm's profits.[3]

Before the marketing concept was widely accepted, many firms followed a strategy of *product differentiation*. This is a strategy by which a firm sells its products to as many customers as possible through a single marketing program. The basic idea is to control, to some extent, the demand for the product through the emphasis of its differences from competitive products. For example, Coca-Cola used to sell its standard product in one bottle size, with a unique selling price, and a single advertising appeal as a selling proposition. With this approach, a firm could build its marketing program on the similarities of its potential customers, not on their differences. This strategy is not as popular as it once was, because "it is seldom possible for a product or brand to be everything for everybody at the same time."[4]

The concept of market segmentation is a corollary of the modern marketing concept. Because any marketing process starts from an analysis of consumer needs and preferences, one of the first findings of marketers was that needs and preferences differ from one customer to another. However, recognizing the heterogeneity of consumer needs and preferences would not have helped much if technological change had not allowed marketers to account for this fact. One of the reasons market segmentation is now a profitable strategy is that the minimum size of production series in most industries has decreased considerably. Thus, for a manufacturer, the additional profit to be earned through market segmentation should be higher than the foregone benefits of economy of scale in production runs. Thus, a strategy of market segmentation should be followed as long as certain consumer groups react differently to a firm's marketing program. Taking into account the costs of supplying each market segment, a firm can always transfer some resources from the least profitable segments to the most profitable until the profit margins generated in each market segment are equal.[5]

Market Segmentation Strategies. A firm may select various segmentation strategies, depending upon its objectives and its financial, technological, and/or managerial resources. Three commonly followed segmentation strategies are outlined below.

Concentrated Marketing. This strategy is represented in Figure 2–1a. It consists of cultivating only one market segment (out of several possible segments), because:

- the firm has limited financial or technical resources and cannot adequately serve several market segments. This may be the case when other firms are strongly entrenched in these segments.
- the firm has special know-how to serve this segment and prefers to concentrate on this market and build a strong position. In this case, the segment is viewed by the firm as its *niche*.

This strategy has the advantage of providing high rates of returns and ensures the firm a quasi-monopoly in the selected market segment. Some of the disadvantages are that a firm would be putting all its eggs in the same basket, and would be running the risk of demand in this segment shrinking, or a large competitor entering the segment. An example of this is the case of Apple serving the personal computer market segment until a large and powerful competitor, IBM, decided to enter this market.

Multi-Segment Marketing. In this case (see Figure 2–1b), a firm decides to serve several, or even all the defined market segments. A firm may prefer such a strategy when:

- a firm can capitalize on its name and build a synergy that will help penetration of several segments. Many firms in the automobile industry follow such a strategy by offering various models of different sizes and prices to many market segments. When consumers trade up, (i.e., change segments) they may remain loyal to their favourite car make.
- a company wants to build a strong position in a market and discourage new entrants because of its leading position.

The advantage of a multi-segment strategy is that it gives a company a more secure position in a market, making it less vulnerable to declining demand in one segment. The major disadvantage is the relative higher costs of building several marketing programs and of pursuing the less profitable segments.

FIGURE 2–1
**Market Segmentation
Strategies**

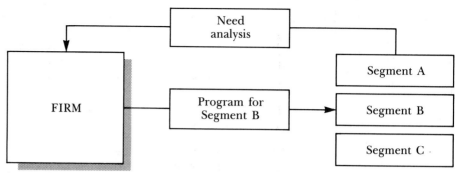

(a) Market Segmentation Strategy (concentrated marketing)

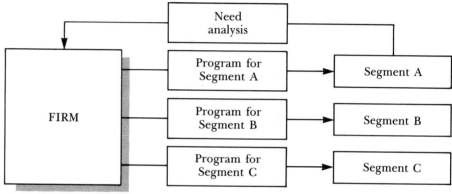

(b) Market Segmentation Strategy (multi-segment)

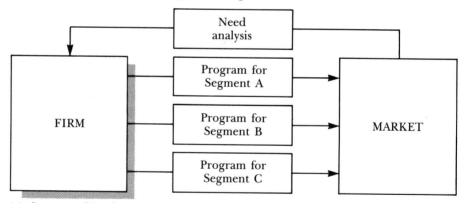

(c) Strategy of Product Variety

Product Variety Strategy. When it is difficult to identify and reach various market segments, a firm can use a product variety strategy (see Figure 2–1c).[6] Instead of marketing different products designed to cater to specific market segments, a firm can put a variety of products on the market. Among the reasons for such a strategy are:

• customers are not always different;

- competition among products of the same company is sometimes a good marketing practice;
- directing a series of specific marketing propositions to various market segments may be a better strategy than directing several propositions to an entire market (the costs, however, of reaching consumers in an entire market are generally much higher);
- it is often difficult to classify consumers into preference groups for products and brands;
- what seems to be market segmentation is often the result of random purchases made by many consumers buying a variety of products.

Implementing a Segmentation Strategy. The market segmentation concept may be simple, but its practical implementation is fraught with difficulties. The major problem is that segmentation is a two-way process; it goes from the market to the company (for the design of the marketing program) and then from the company to the segment (for actual implementation of the marketing program). Therefore, several steps are required to implement a market segmentation strategy effectively. The first step is to define the global market toward which the firm's activities shall be directed.

The second step is to identify sufficiently homogeneous and well-differentiated consumer groups. At this point a *conceptual segmentation criterion* must be determined, that is, the various groups must be defined on the basis of consumers' needs and desires. This means that the segments thus defined must be significant and that the demand elasticities in the various segments, with regard to changes in some elements of the marketing program, must be different for each segment.

Then, once the segments have been identified, the advertiser must evaluate their profit potential. To do so, the environmental forces affecting each segment should be evaluated and the marketing and advertising methods chosen. For a segmentation strategy to be worthwhile for a firm, the defined segments must be large enough to generate sufficient revenue and profits. Unfortunately, segments defined on the basis of consumer needs or likely behavioural responses to elements of the marketing program are usually not directly measurable; this is one of the major difficulties of a segmentation strategy. One must therefore define consumers in each segment by more practical criteria, for instance, demographic characteristics. It is easier to estimate the number of Vancouver residents between the ages of 18 and 65 than the number of people who buy toothpaste mainly to prevent cavities. It is necessary to define one or several criteria that can directly or indirectly evaluate the size of a market segment.

Next, a marketing mix that can respond to the specific needs of each target market segment must be determined. Once this is done, sales and revenue forecasts as well as cost estimates can be established. These combined estimates must give an acceptable profit level for the company. The economic analysis of each segment indicates whether a segment constitutes a market opportunity for the company.

Finally, the marketing program must be able to reach the target market segments. To establish clear communication and distribution channels that can reach consumers in each segment, an advertiser must identify the consumers in terms of geographic or socio-demographic variables. (As will be shown later, advertising media usually describe their audiences' profiles along such characteristics.)

The Choice of Segmentation Criteria. Market segments should ideally be identified by two sets of criteria: specific needs and behaviour of consumers, and socio-demographic variables (Table 2–1). Unfortunately, segments defined in terms of needs and/or behaviour generally do not coincide with socio-economic classifications. That is why the choice of a segmentation criterion is so important. When marketers use a definition based on consumer needs and behaviour, they can make better decisions about the product or service mix that best suits the segment's needs. On the other hand, it becomes more difficult to evaluate the size of the segment and to develop the other elements of the marketing program, especially the distribution and media plans. Conversely, if marketers use socio-economic variables as segmentation criteria, they may define segments that are easier to reach but less homogeneous in needs and behaviour. Keeping this dilemma in mind, advertisers must often rely on judgement and on formal market research in order to select the best possible segmentation criterion.

TABLE 2–1 **CHOICE OF SEGMENTATION CRITERION**

	Desirable Features for Each Segment		
	Significant Segments	**Measurable Segments**	**Segments That Can Be Reached**
Market Segmentation Objectives	Determination of product/service mix and prices	Determination of sales potential and profitability	Determination of the promotion and distribution programs
"Ideal" Segmentation Variables	Needs/desires behaviour psychographic variables	Socio-economic variables	Socio-economic variables

Traditionally, various segmentation criteria have been used in marketing. The most widely used criteria are listed in Table 2–2. They are:

Consumer Characteristics. This set of criteria includes socio-economic and demographic variables.[7] They also include psychological and social variables that characterize specific consumers and consumer groups.[8] Many studies have shown, however, that these variables tend to be weak in explaining and predicting consumer behaviour.[9]

Purchase/Consumption Situations. Analysis of the various situations or instances

TABLE 2–2 **CLASSIFICATION OF THE MAIN SEGMENTATION CRITERIA**

1. **Consumer Characteristics**
   A. Demographic Criteria
       Geography
           Provinces
           Regions
           Urban/Rural/Suburban
           City sizes
       Individual Characteristics
           Size
           Age
           Education
           Occupation
           Religion
       Families
           Composition
           Sizes
           Stage in life-cycle

   B. Economic Criteria
       Income
           Level
           Distribution
           – geographic
           – individual
           – families
       Spendings
           Use of credit
           Savings
           Level of asset formation

   C. Psychological Criteria
       General attitudes and beliefs
       Personality traits

   D. Sociological Criteria
       Families
           Types
           Role distribution
       Reference groups
           Opinion leadership
       Social Classes
           Cultural/subcultural
               groups

2. **Purchase/Consumption Situations**
   For example:
       At home
       In a restaurant
       For receiving guests

3. **Product Characteristics**
   Benefits

4. **Consumer Behaviour**
   Usage Level
       Non-users/light/heavy users
       Brand loyalty
       Price-sensitivity
       Promotional deal sensitivity

5. **Psychography**
   Interests
   Attitudes
   Opinions

in which a product is purchased or consumed can lead to meaningful segmentation. For instance, consumers may be looking for different brand characteristics for a beer depending upon the drinking occasion (such as, at night with friends in a bar, or to serve at home, or during the day, etc.).

Since there is no standard classification for situation segmentation, a marketing manager must develop a classification which is relevant to the specific product to be marketed.

Product Characteristics. Consumers differentiate between different brands on the market according to their perceptions of a brand's attributes, either real or imaginary, and choose the brand whose attributes they prefer. The advantage of these types of segmentation criteria is that it makes a market segmentation strategy consistent with the marketing concept, allowing a firm to design products perceived and desired by pre-specified market segments. Benefit segmentation can be considered as a special case of product segmentation: consumers are classified according to the perceived benefits of consuming a product. One example of benefit segmentation for the toothpaste market was provided by Haley, the proponent of this approach to segmentation (see Table 2–3). Four segments could be identified: the sensory, the sociable, the worrying, and the independent consumer, depending upon the blend of benefits they are looking for in toothpaste usage: good flavour or product appearance, brightness of teeth, decay prevention, and price.[10]

TABLE 2–3 **BENEFIT SEGMENTATION OF THE TOOTHPASTE MARKET**

	The Sensory Segment	The Sociables	The Worriers	The Independent Segment
Principal benefit sought	Flavour, product appearance	Brightness of teeth	Decay prevention	Price
Demographic strengths	Children	Teens, young people	Large families	Men
Special behaviour characteristics	Users of spearmint flavoured toothpaste	Smokers	Heavy users	Heavy users
Brands disproportionately flavoured	Colgate, Stripe	Macleans, Plus White, Ultra Brite	Crest	Brands on sale
Personality characteristics	High self-involvement	High sociability	High hypochondriasis	High autonomy
Life-style characteristics	Hedonistic	Active	Conservative	Value-oriented

Source: Russell I. Haley, "Benefit Segmentation: A Decision-oriented Research Tool," *Journal of Marketing* 32 (July 1968): 33: Published by the American Marketing Association.

Consumer Behaviour. Different market behaviour during the purchase or shopping stages, as well as different consumer reactions to various elements of the marketing program can serve as a meaningful basis for market segmentation. Thus, users versus non-users of a product, heavy versus light users, loyal versus non-loyal consumers often reflect basic different consumer needs and perceptions about the product. In the same way, various consumer sensitivities toward changes in prices, and in reactions to promotional deals have proved to be useful market segmentation criteria.

Psychography. Psychographic segmentation combines all the preceding forms of segmentation. It is based on consumers' lifestyle inventories, which include various activities (work, hobbies, travel, sports), interests (job, recreation, media habits), and opinions (about politics, consumption, culture). In addition, the psychographic variables include demographic and economic variables as well as variables related to product usage.[11]

The Concept of Product Positioning

A product can be defined according to a reference point (target market), physical, psychological, and sociological dimensions, and the time elapsed since the product was introduced. At a given moment, advertisers define their product strategy by deciding what the level of a product's attributes should be. The attributes may be weighed according to the perceived importance of each choice criterion. Thus, advertisers are said to decide the position of a product in the space defined by the attributes important to the firm's target market.[12]

Let us illustrate this concept with a hypothetical example representing a given market's perception of various competing brands of beer. We will assume that consumers use two important dimensions to evaluate these various brands, a physical dimension related to strength (alcohol content, sweetness, mild flavour), and a social dimension related to group influence (quality and price, or selectiveness). In this example, the perceptual map shown in Figure 2–2 has brands in all four zones. Of the four brands that are perceived as most selective, Beer 1 is perceived as the lightest and Beer 4 as the heaviest. Similarly, all the brands are positioned in the map according to how consumers perceive them in terms of their combination of the two important attributes.

When analyzing a market through a perceptual map, marketers should study the empty zones that no brand is presently occupying. These zones may

FIGURE 2–2

Perceptual Map of a Hypothetical Beer Market

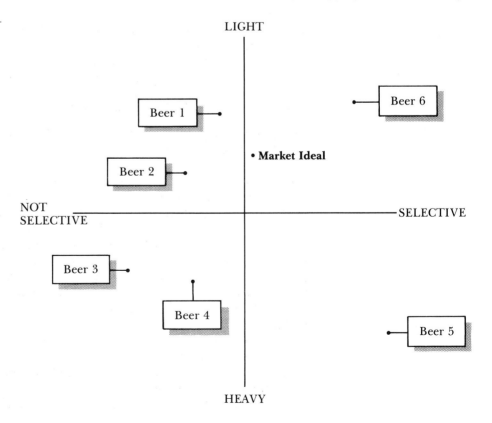

represent market opportunities. If a zone includes enough ideal points (or brands) to form a viable segment, this segment may be targeted either for a new product, or for a new promotional campaign.

The objective of product positioning is to identify the means of reducing the distance between the company's brand and the target market's ideal. There are three general types of strategies for positioning a product.

One strategy is to try to shift the position of a brand toward the ideal point. This can be achieved by improving the product and communicating this improvement to the target market. Another possibility is to improve consumers' perceptions of the company's brand. Pepsi-Cola pursued this strategy with the campaign, "More than half of Coke drinkers prefer Pepsi to Coke," by proposing a test in which blindfolded consumers chose the drink they preferred after tasting each one.

A second product positioning strategy is for advertisers to shift the ideal point of the target market toward their brand. This can be achieved by inducing consumers to use new choice criteria or by conducting an information campaign on the product or the product class in order to change consumers' perceptions of the importance of some criteria. This strategy may be successful only if the product is in one of the first stages of its life-cycle. As soon as consumers know the characteristics of a product class, it may be difficult to change their ideal point.

A third strategy is to shift the brand and the ideal point simultaneously toward a new intermediate position. This solution, which is a compromise between the first two strategies, may be easier and less costly to implement.

To conclude, the concept of product positioning is pertinent only at a given moment in a product's life-cycle. Most markets change constantly, with brand images shifting and new brands being introduced. As a result, advertisers must adjust the marketing mix according to changes in market situations.

Product Positioning as a Segmentation Tool. It is possible to position not only the competing brands and the ideal in the consumers' perceptual space, but also the ideal brand for every *individual* consumer.[13] If the ideal brands of a representative sample of consumers of a market are plotted on the perceptual map, the distribution of these ideal points will approximate that of the total market. These hypothetical points are indicated in Figure 2–3 by small dots. Marketing managers can then analyze the concentration of these points in order to identify groups with similar preferences. In this example, four segments could be easily identified. They are the circled areas A, B, C, and D. In practical applications, a market segment's shape and size are determined by the marketing analyst. The concentration of points may not be as obvious as in this example, but statistical techniques are available to assist when this task is difficult.

Segment A seeks a stronger and rather selective beer; it is natural for its members to choose Brand 5, even though it is more selective than required. Under these conditions, some consumers of this segment would rather purchase Brand 4. Segment B is less homogeneous and larger than Segment A. Brands 4, 3, and 2 all cater to this segment, and no brand has a clear competitive

FIGURE 2–3
Hypothetical
Distribution of
Individual Ideal
Points

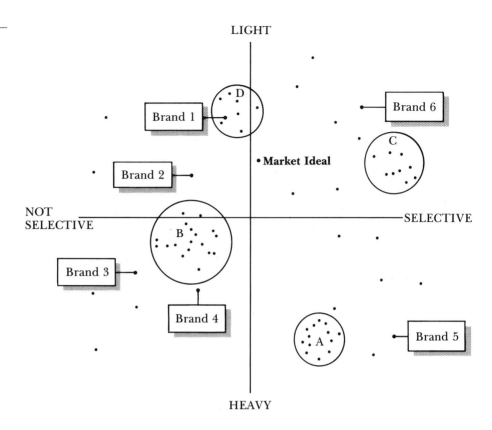

advantage in this larger, or probably more attractive segment. Segment C is probably dominated by Brand 6 because these consumers prefer a light and selective beer as Brand 6 is being perceived. Segment D is the segment which is the best attended to, because Brand 1 is very close to what this segment prefers. The marketing manager of Brand 1 has succeeded in serving a small, but profitable segment, as it is the only brand to supply these consumers.

The Marketing Mix Concept

Let us return to the comparison between a marketer's and a marine officer's tasks. Taking environmental constraints into account, the officer plans a route to take advantage of the wind and the current in order to reach a destination quickly and safely. Similarly, a marketing manager takes account of controllable marketing variables, and plans a marketing program. When the marketing manager makes a decision about all the controllable variables, he or she defines what is usually called the marketing mix. These controllable variables of the marketing program can be classified into the 4 Ps,[14] which are **P**roduct, **P**lace (distribution), **P**romotion (advertising and personal selling), and **P**rice (Table 2–4).

Product. An advertiser must make decisions that directly or indirectly affect a firm's products. These decisions include the quality level of the product or service to be marketed and the number and variety of product versions, styles, and sizes. Physical products are typically wrapped in a package with a label. Directions for use and other relevant information are generally written on the labels. More important, a name or brand name is prominently displayed on the label or on the package. This name may be the same name for all products sold by the firm, or it may be specific to a given product within the product line. The services included with the purchase of a product, such as the warranty, product maintenance, or service allowances, are considered part of the product offer. Advertisers must also establish policies for introducing, researching, and developing new products.

Place. Advertisers must determine the distribution channels through which products should flow from the producer to the final consumers. The decision about distribution channels are complex. For instance, products may be sold directly to the final consumers (through mail or catalogue sales), or through retailers or wholesalers. Whatever the method, marketers must ensure co-operation from the middlemen in the distribution channel selected and that

TABLE 2–4 **THE 4 Ps AND THEIR RELATED DECISION AREAS**

The 4 Ps	DECISION AREA
Product	Product line decisions (quality, type, sizes)
	Packaging and labelling decisions
	Brand name decisions (individual or family brand names)
	Product-related service decisions (trade-ins, maintenance and repair facilities)
	New product introduction decisions
	New product research and development decisions
Place	Selection of the distribution channels toward the final consumers
	Selection of the appropriate means to ensure channel members' co-operation
	Decisions about the distribution channel task allocation (transportation, handling, storage)
Promotion	Advertising decisions (advertising budget, advertising copy)
	Advertising directed at: • consumers • middlemen • the community
	Personal selling decisions
	Sales promotion decisions (couponing, cents-off)
Price	Pricing decisions (price level, specific prices—odd vs. even price)
	Price change policies
	Credit terms, payment procedures

the process of distributing goods from the factory to the final consumers runs smoothly. This process includes the transporting, handling, storing, and financing of the goods.

Promotion. Advertisers must establish communication channels with their markets. Mass communication, especially advertising, is typically directed toward the final consumer or sometimes to the middlemen in the firm's distribution channels or even to the entire community. Several types of marketing decisions are involved: what amount should be spent on advertising to do an effective communication job? Which ideas should be communicated to the target audience? Which media are most efficient for reaching the right people, at the right time and at the least possible cost? Communications through sales representatives are very often a vital part of a firm's marketing communication program. Sales promotion activities, which are the marketing actions designed to move products to distribution channels to the final consumers or middlemen, also require communication decisions. The promotional mix is the selected blend of advertising, personal selling, and sales promotions efforts.

Price. The fourth area of marketing decisions includes all the aspects of the marketing program dealing with the price of the transaction. Once the general price level of a product is determined, an advertiser must decide which specific figure(s) will be used as a price; for instance, should an even or an odd price be used; should a product be priced at 99¢ or $1? In competitive markets, pricing policies must be flexible so that a firm can act quickly to counteract competitive actions. The credit terms and payment procedures for final consumers or middlemen should also be carefully designed.

Marketers first set objectives and then define an appropriate marketing program to meet the objectives. To do this, allowances must be made in predictions of the future marketing environment. Even if these predictions are reasonably accurate, they will differ at least slightly from what actually happens. Thus actual marketing performance in terms of sales, profits, or market penetration will depart from the targeted objectives. If there is not too wide a gap between the objectives and the actual performance, one or more elements of the marketing mix may be adjusted slightly, e.g., by making practical adjustments. If the gap is too wide, the objective may be modified, or major changes made in the marketing program, or both.

The Concept of Product Life-Cycle

The concept of product life-cycle is the recognition of market dynamics. The conditions that cause a product to be adopted by a market at various stages change according to a firm's actions and that of its competitors.

This concept is useful in planning an advertising program because different market conditions may prevail at each phase of a product's life-cycle, and the survival of a product in a given market may be constantly threatened by those market conditions. All decisions required by the marketing program must fall between two important levels of product management: the long-term planning of product strategy, and the adjustments or tactics dictated by a particular situation.

Stages of the Product Life-Cycle. There are four stages in a product's life-cycle: introduction, growth, maturity, and decline (Figure 2–4). The stage in which a product may be at a given time can be determined by the evolution of the market's total sales for this product.

Introduction. During the introduction stage of a new product, sales rise at a slow pace. At first, the company can only activate this process with a small number of consumers. These may be consumers who have been in contact with one of the levels within the distribution channel or who have been exposed to a promotional message. Since the product is new, the objective of promotional efforts is to make potential consumers aware of and understand the new product. Therefore the advertising message must primarily be informative and secondarily mention the product's brand. It is not necessary to allocate larger sums to support the brand, since it is usually the only one on the market, but it is important to promote acceptance of this product. In addition to being aimed at potential consumers, product promotion must also be directed toward the various members of the distribution channel to convince them of the product's profitability and induce them to stock and distribute it.

Growth. During the growth stage, sales increase at an accelerated pace if the product is successful. If not, the product is taken off the market and the company suffers considerable losses. During the growth, the success of the product is largely due to a large number of consumers having made extensive information searches in order to decide whether to buy or at least try the product. In turn these new users act as information sources and convince other consumers to adopt or try the product. This process then goes on at an accelerated pace.

FIGURE 2–4
The Stages in a Product Life-Cycle

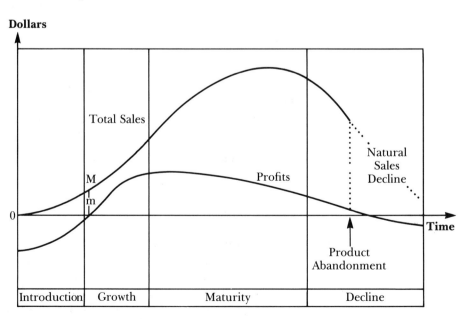

During the growth in sales, the firm's revenue increases rapidly and profits begin to appear. These profits may encourage other companies to offer products that are more or less improved imitations of the original product. Competition then forces the innovative company to promote its brand aggressively and to try to keep its leadership in product quality. At this stage the company may realize important reductions in manufacturing costs, since the process has been streamlined and "debugged," and in promotion costs, since spending is spread over a larger volume of sales.

As more firms penetrate the market, the original company's profits may reach a peak and begin to decline. Perceptible improvements may then be made to the product. At this point, conflicts usually emerge among institutions competing in a channel. This part of the growth stage, which also marks the beginning of the maturity phase, has been defined as the *turbulence* stage.[15] Promotional expenses are usually high and the product advertising emphasizes the superiority of the brand and its attributes. The methods of product positioning discussed previously may be used to develop marketing strategies.

The growth stage has a great influence on market share and profits, since during this phase it is relatively cheaper to build a strong market share and brand loyalty is developed. For these reasons companies with specific market share objectives must maintain an intensive promotion effort and steady sales growth.

Maturity.   The maturity stage corresponds to the natural sales ceiling of the target market, taking into account all the needs that the product satisfies. During this stage competing brands tend to have the same attributes. This convergence toward the same product quality is due to competing advertisers' increased knowledge of the market ideal.

Pressure on prices is generally strong during the maturity stage, and market profits gradually decline. The erosion of profits is also due to promotional efforts required to maintain market share by firms whose efforts are aimed at both the consumer and at the various distribution channels. During the maturity stage, each firm in an industry may have a promotional budget that is a fixed percentage of total sales, especially when sales are stable. Even so, some firms may spend more on advertising in order to maintain their market share. Others may spend a larger part of their budget on special offers in order to reduce inventories, stimulate consumer trials, strengthen consumer loyalty through repeat purchases, or attempt to get greater shelf space for their brand at the retail level.

Early in the maturity stage and toward the end of the turbulence stage, the number of competing brands on the market is probably at a maximum. At this point, inefficient firms may withdraw from the market. When all potential buyers have tried a product and sales become only replacement sales, the *saturation* phase has been reached,[16] and only the efficient firms remain. The competitive situation is then extremely stable, and each company is content to maintain its market share. An aggressive advertising campaign at this stage would probably not be profitable.

Decline. The decline stage starts when regular consumers of a product stop using it because the needs it satisfies have become less important or because the needs are better satisfied by a new product.

Competing firms have a choice between withdrawing the product from the market or supporting it because profits are still good. Generally, fewer are competing in this market, and those that remain try to lower their production, promotion, and distribution costs. In particular, there may be a shortening of product lines, and advertising campaigns may aim simply at reminding consumers that the product is still available.

Strategic Options For Advertising During a Product's Life-Cycle. The strategy of *market penetration* for a brand consists of attempting to increase the use of the brand and to reach new customers for the brand. Traditionally, this strategy is used by a company during the growth and maturity stages of its product. The total demand for a product generally follows the life-cycle evolution, and a company may increase its market share by taking sales from the natural growth of demand and/or from competitors.

The strategy of *product development* represents, with the next two strategies, a modification of the product's life-cycle. This strategy consists of developing a product with new characteristics aimed at the present target market. For example, the introduction of sweetened cereal and those with high nutritive value have raised the ceiling on total sales for cereals by about 40 percent. By the same token, milk has been at the maturity phase for a long time; most people stop drinking it after a certain age. The introduction of a new milk-based drink that would be appreciated by people of all age groups could raise the present sales ceiling considerably. Another example is the introduction of colour television, which repesented an improved product for families already owning a black and white television set. To families already owning a colour television set, new black and white portable sets may be offered for use in the bedroom, the basement, or the summer cottage.

The strategy of *market development* consists of adapting a product to other consumers or to other markets. For example, the adaptation to the feminine market of such male products as attaché cases, pants, and suits has lengthened the life-cycle of these products. It also works the other way: more men use cologne, skin cosmetics, and wear clothes made out of "feminine" fabrics.

Development of an Advertising Strategy

The strategy for the advertising component of the marketing mix is generally developed at the same time as the marketing strategy and is based on the communication objectives defined in the marketing plan.

An *advertising strategy* is developed by taking the market segment defined in the marketing strategy statement and designing an advertising program for achieving the communication objectives within a specified budget and time period. The *advertising plan* describes the advertising program that is to be followed over a specific period. The program may describe one advertising campaign or a series of consistent campaigns.

In order to design an advertising campaign, an advertiser must make decisions in five key areas:

- setting the advertising campaign objectives (see Chapter 11);
- setting the advertising budget (see Chapter 11);
- designing the advertising messages (see Chapters 12 and 13);
- determining the media to be used in conveying the message, as well as the advertising media schedule (see Chapter 14);
- and setting the mechanisms to control the effectiveness of the advertising campaign (see Chapter 15).

The decisions made in these areas are interrelated, as shown in Figure 2–5.

As has been pointed out, an advertising campaign should be designed to achieve precise marketing objectives. The means to achieve these objectives are the advertising message content and format and the media selected to convey the message to the relevant market segments. Decisions about the structure and format of the message depend on the types of media selected. These advertising tools involve costs that indicate what size budget is necessary in order to meet the marketing objectives.

This approach to determining an advertising budget is called the objective and task method. For an advertising campaign to be effective and profitable, an advertiser must select objectives in such a way that the costs involved still warrant their pursuit. It is always necessary to reassess the objectives in the light of costs whenever the difference between expected returns and costs are too great. Procedures for measuring an advertising campaign's effectiveness are designed to control the advertising process; advertising objectives can be reassessed for the following period because market penetration, the level of consumer awareness, or consumer attitudes achieved at the end of the campaign can be measured. These measurements affect the marketing objectives and consequently the advertising goals.

ADVERTISING AS PART OF THE PROMOTIONAL MIX

Advertising campaigns are not independent of a firm's other marketing activities, since all the elements of the marketing mix should fit into a homogeneous plan that can achieve the marketing objectives. In the same way, advertising must be co-ordinated with the other elements of the promotional mix: personal selling, publicity, and sales promotion.

Co-ordination with the Sales Force

Selecting the best possible mix between the two major communication tools—personal communication through sales representatives and mass communication through advertising—has strategic importance.

Figure 2–6 shows a common distribution channel that makes use of two different strategies: a manufacturer sells to wholesalers who in turn sell to retailers; the retailers then sell to the final consumers. This distribution channel is used to distribute small ticket items in the consumer market.

How does communication flow through this distribution channel? The communication system first takes into account a basic constraint, which is the cost of a communication. Studies have shown that the average cost of a sales call in 1988 was $250.[17] In contrast, the cost of reaching a potential customer through the mass media was a fraction of a cent.[18] Personal contact is, however,

FIGURE 2–5

**Relationships Among
the Various Decision
Areas in Advertising**

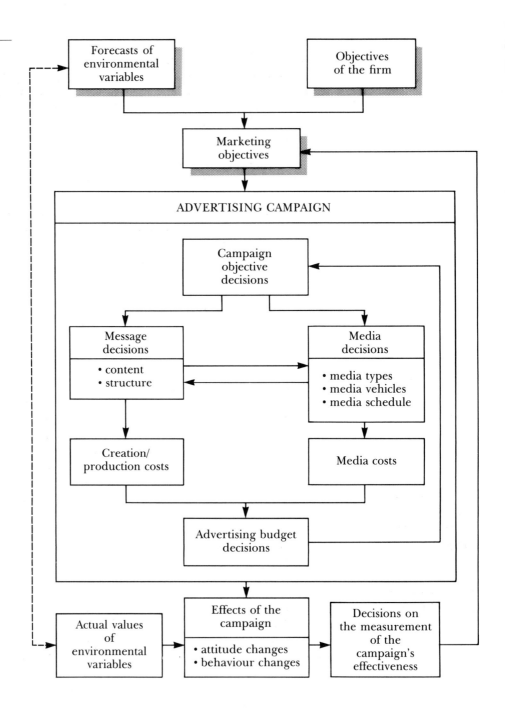

sometimes more effective despite the greater cost. For example, it may be important to have immediate knowledge of customers' reactions, or to interact between buyers and sellers, or to maintain personal ties with middlemen. If

FIGURE 2-6

Equilibrium between
Pull and Push
Strategies

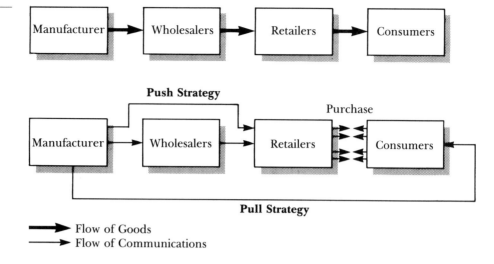

Push Strategy

Pull Strategy

→ Flow of Goods
→ Flow of Communications

personal contact is not essential, a marketing manager may reduce expenses by using advertising.

Pull and Push Strategies

With communication through advertising, a marketing manager attempts to stimulate market demand for a product. The objective is to create positive attitudes among consumers toward a brand, to give information about the positive attributes of a product or service, and eventually to induce consumers to buy the product. Through stimulation of market demand, goods flow through the distribution channel, and the final consumers play the role of a pump in keeping goods moving in the distribution channel. This strategy is known as the *pull strategy*.

With communication through personal selling, a marketing manager tries to make a product flow through the channel by persuading middlemen to keep inventories of the product and by making sure that the product gets enough shelf space. A strategy that pushes products into a distribution channel is the *push strategy*.

Figure 2–5 shows that the purchase of a certain brand takes place only when a consumer is ready to buy the product (knows of it, wants it, or insists on it) and can find it at a retail store.

If a consumer is ready to buy a certain product brand following some advertising pressure exerted within the framework of a pull strategy, and if the retailers do not carry this brand, the consumer will likely purchase a competitive brand. Conversely, if the brand has reached retailers' shelves but the consumer is not ready to buy it or try it due to a lack of information about the brand's attributes, the purchase will probably not take place. The two strategies should therefore complement each other so that an informed consumer can buy the brand from a retailer who can supply it.

Although a marketing manager may emphasize one strategy over the other, the two strategies should be mixed to reach a harmonious equilibrium. To do so, the communication task should be properly allocated to the two communication channels. For instance, Procter & Gamble launches most of its new products by using a pull strategy. The advertising campaign directed at the final consumers only starts once the product has achieved a high level of distribution among retailers. This objective can be met because Procter & Gamble sales personnel are able to convince retailers that the product will be backed by major advertising efforts and that they should be well stocked in order to meet the expected demand. With Procter & Gamble brand names, retailers are likely to co-operate. A firm less well known would probably have more difficulty achieving a high level of distribution before starting its pull effort; many retailers would want to make sure that the manufacturer's pull strategy was creating sufficient demand for the product to warrant keeping it in stock.

Other Factors Affecting the Advertising–Personal Selling Mix

Other factors likely to influence the advertising–personal selling mix are the type of product and the type of market. For instance, Cash and Crissy have noted that the mix between advertising and personal selling is affected by the phase a market is in.[19] According to these authors, a market goes through three phases: pretransactional, transactional, and post-transactional. Advertising plays a major part in the pretransactional phase (for cultivating the market) and in the post-transactional phase (for providing a rationalization to the buyer). Only in rare instances can advertising accomplish the transaction by itself; this role is best fulfilled by personal selling. In a sense, advertising can be considered as readying a market for a salesperson's personal effort.

Co-ordination Techniques

The sales force should be fully briefed and informed about the advertising campaign in order to reassure distributors and retailers about the promotional effort in support of the brand. The following are some of the techniques that may be used in co-operation with the sales force:

- The agency may prepare a film describing the product features, as well as the advertising campaign designed to support the brand. This film may be shown by the sales force to intermediaries.
- The agency may organize a sales meeting at which the new campaign is presented. This meeting may take place at a desirable location (e.g., a resort hotel), and use entertainers for impact. The objective of such meetings is to get the sales force enthusiastic about the product and the campaign.
- The sales force may be given copies of the print advertisement or the television commercial to show or distribute to intermediaries. The television com-

FIGURE 2–7

Storyboards such as the ones presented here show the television commercial on a single sheet of photographic paper.

Courtesy Colour Scripts Ltd.

Courtesy Broadcast Monitoring Services Ltd.

mercials are often presented in the form of colour storyboards with six to ten frames reproduced on photographic paper (Figure 2–7).

Co-ordination with Publicity

Activities related to *publicity* aim at realizing a firm's marketing objectives by obtaining free media space or time for articles, editorials, press releases, and photographs that provide information free of charge about products, services, or the firm itself. In general, the firm prepares the text of the message, which is given to the media by the public relations department. Since the message appears as editorial matter, it is more credible to an audience and thus is a more efficient communication form than a commercial message of similar size and repetition. This is because the medium is viewed by the public as objective and independent of the firm.[20] Publicity is also a relatively inexpensive form of promotion since the only costs involved are those related to preparing the message and finding the media that are willing to use it. The time or space the media allocates to such items is limited and is often given to a medium's best clients. The content of the message must be consistent with the advertising strategy in order to reinforce the campaign's effectiveness. Ideally, the message should be prepared by or in co-operation with the advertising agency.

Editorial matter that reports on problems with a product, a service, or a company is called *negative publicity*.[21] Examples of negative publicity are product recalls that are announced in the media. If sustained over a long period, such publicity may be damaging. As with other forms of promotion, however, negative publicity may be forgotten over time if it is not reinforced by the media. The rate of forgetting depends on the seriousness of the problem, consumers' experience with the problem, and the amount of negative publicity.

Co-ordination with Sales Promotion

Sales promotion activities are the activities other than publicity, advertising, and personal selling that promote the products and/or services of a firm or intermediary. These activities support, assist, or reinforce the other elements of the promotional mix. These aspects will be discussed in Chapter 8.

SUMMARY

Advertising plays a role both in the marketing mix in general and the promotion mix in particular. Marketing and advertising strategies are developed by taking into account various factors, in particular the market's environmental forces. The important concepts an advertiser uses to derive an advertising strategy from the overall marketing strategy are market segmentation, product positioning, and the product life-cycle. Advertising is but one part of a marketing program and should be integrated with the other elements of the marketing mix into a consistent and logical program.

Advertising is integrated into the overall marketing plan by planning and co-ordinating advertising actions with the other elements of the promotional mix, especially the sales force communication program, publicity, and sales promotion activities.

QUESTIONS FOR STUDY

1. Marketing and advertising strategies should follow from an analysis of consumer needs and wants. Why then is it necessary to segment a market?

How is the definition of a market segment likely to affect the definition of an advertising strategy?

2. How does a firm's decision to pursue a strategy of market aggregation, concentrated marketing, multi-segment marketing, or product variety affect the corresponding advertising strategy? Give specific examples.

3. Select a company with which you are fairly familiar. Describe its marketing strategy as best you can, including all the elements of its marketing mix. What is its advertising strategy? Is it consistent with the other elements of the marketing mix? Why?

4. Describe and contrast the use of advertising during the four phases of a product's life-cycle for: a) package goods, b) hard goods, and c) a service.

5. Discuss the concept of product positioning and its importance in the development of an advertising strategy.

6. Select three different products, one from a grocery store, one from a department store, and one from a specialty store. Describe the marketing strategy for each and recommend an advertising strategy.

7. Assume that you are a product manager reviewing the details of your advertising plan before starting an important campaign. How would you try to get the most out of your advertising effort even before the campaign reaches final consumers?

8. Discuss the promotional mix (advertising vs. personal selling) typically followed by firms selling

   • life insurance
   • beauty care products
   • household detergents
   • electronic equipment

   As much as possible, refer to actual examples.

9. Why, in your opinion, do industrial marketers tend to use advertising to a lesser extent than marketers of consumer goods?

10. Show how an analysis of market competition can influence the definition of an advertising strategy. Can the concept of product positioning be useful to carry out such an analysis? Give examples.

PROBLEMS

1. A manufacturer of electronic watches has developed a new concept for a digital watch that can be manufactured at a relatively low cost and that has unusual lasting characteristics in comparison with most similar products on the market. The firm's marketing manager is considering two possible product positioning and marketing strategies for this new product:

- Market the product to the price-conscious market segment.
- Market the product to the high-income market segment, which wants expensive and lasting watches.

    a. As an advertiser, show how these two marketing strategies are likely to affect your advertising program.

    b. For both alternatives, outline an advertising strategy and the major elements of the campaign (the objectives, budget, message, media plan).

    c. In both cases, show how the decisions on the other elements of the marketing mix and of the promotional mix are likely to affect your advertising decisions.

2. A brand manager for a leading biscuit manufacturer is in charge of the launching of a new brand of biscuits on the Canadian market. The brand manager must make consumers aware of the brand and induce them to try it. At the same time, trade acceptance and co-operation for launching and distributing the new brand must be ensured. Design the promotional mix for the launching of the new brand. Emphasize the co-ordination of the launch advertising campaigns, the sales promotion program, and the sales force communication effort.

NOTES

1. For a thorough analysis of the segmentation concept, see Ronald E. Frank, William E. Massey, and Yoram Wind, *Market Segmentation* (Englewood Cliffs, N.J.: Prentice-Hall, 1971); see also Yoram Wind, "Issues and Advances in Segmentation Research," *Journal of Marketing Research*, 15 (August 1974), 317–37.
2. Wendell R. Smith, "Product Differentiation and Market Segmentation as Alternative Marketing Strategies," *Journal of Marketing*, 21 (July 1956), 3–8.
3. Ronald E. Frank, "Market Segmentation Research: Findings and Implications," *Applications of the Sciences in Marketing Management*, ed. F. Bass et al. (New York: John Wiley and Sons, 1968).
4. Steven C. Brandt, "Dissecting the Segmentation Syndrome," *Journal of Marketing*, 30 (October 1966), 22–27; Burleigh Gardner and Sidney Levy, "The Product and the Brand," Harvard Business Review (March-April 1955), p. 37.
5. Henry J. Claycamp and William F. Massy, "A Theory of Market Segmentation." *Journal of Marketing Research*, 5 (November 1968), 388–94.
6. William M. Reynolds, "More Sense about Market Segmentation," *Harvard Business Review* (September-October 1965), pp. 107–14.
7. D.W. Greeno and W.F. Bennett, "Social Class and Income as Complementary Segmentation Bases: A Canadian Perspective," *Marketing*, ed. James D. Forbes (Montreal: ASAC), 1983, pp. 113–22.
8. David A. Boag, "Person-Situation Interaction in Product Choice: An Empirical Test of the Theory," in Proc. ASAC, Vol. 5, ed. Sherla Brown (1984), 51–61.
9. Norman L. Barnett, "Beyond Market Segmentation," *Harvard Business Review*, 47 (January-February 1989), 152–66.
10. Russell I. Haley, "Benefit Segmentation: A Decision-Oriented Research Tool," *Journal of Marketing*, 3 (July 1968), 30–35.
11. William D. Wells, "Backward Segmentation," *Insights Into Consumer Behavior*, pp. 85–100.
12. See, for example, Y. Allaire, "The Measurement of Heterogeneous Semantic, Perceptual and Preference Structures" (Ph.D. diss;, M.I.T., August 1972); R.M. Johnson, "Market Segmentation: A Strategic

Management Tool," *Journal of Marketing Research*, 9 (February 1971), 13–18; R.Y. Darmon, Multiple Joint Space Analysis for Improved Advertising Strategy," *The Canadian Marketer*, 10, no. 1 (1979), 10–14.

13. Johnson, "Market Segmentation," 13–18.
14. Jerome E. McCarthy and Stanley S Shapiro, *Basic Marketing* (Georgetown, Ont.: Irwin-Dorsey, Ltd., 1975), pp. 75–80.
15. Thomas A Staudt and Donald A. Taylor, *A Managerial Introduction to Marketing* (Englewood Cliffs, N.J.: Prentice-Hall, 1970), chapter 10.
16. *Management of New Products*, 4th ed. (New York: Booz, Allan & Hamilton, 1965), p. 4.
17. "Industrial Sales Call Tops $137, But New 'Cost to Close' Hits $589," *Marketing News*, 14, no. 22 (May 1981), 1.
18. Kenneth A. Longman, *Advertising* (New York: Harcourt Brace Jovanovich, 1971), p. 18.
19. Harold C. Cash and W.J.E. Crissy, "Comparison of Advertising and Selling," *The Salesman's Role in Marketing: The Psychology of Selling*, 12 (1965), 56–75.
20. Emmanuel J. Cheron and Jean Perrien, "An Experimental Study of the Effects of Commercial TV Advertising and Pro-Consumer Product Test-Results on TV," *Advances in Consumer Research*, vol. 8, ed. Kent B. Monroe (Association for Consumer Research, 1981), 423–27.
21. Carol A. Scott and Alice M. Tybout, "Theoretical Perspective on the Impact of Negative Information," *Advances in Consumer Research*, 8, ed. Kent B. Monroe (1981), pp. 408–10.

PART II

Advertising Organizations in Canada

The development of an advertising program requires the co-operation of many individuals and organizations. Chapter 3 explains and demystifies the advertising agency business in Canada. The different types of Canadian advertisers (including business-to-business, services, and retail institutions) and their approaches to the advertising function are described in Chapter 4. The large variety of media available in Canada are thoroughly covered in Chapter 5 for newspapers and periodicals, in Chapter 6 for out-of-home media and direct advertising, and Chapter 7 for radio and television. Finally, Chapter 8 describes the various sales promotion techniques available in Canada.

Advertisers, advertising agencies, and the media rely on countless outside suppliers that perform highly specialized tasks at all phases in the planning, execution, and control of the advertising campaign. These suppliers include freelance artists, art studios, production companies, and research firms. The role of these suppliers is mentioned throughout the text.

ANSON McKIM

Courtesy McKim
Advertising

CHAPTER

3 *Advertising Agencies in Canada*

Nearly everyone has heard or read something about advertising agencies, but what they actually do and how they operate is unclear to many business people, who often wonder whether or not to hire an agency or replace or fire their present agency. This chapter will discuss the advertising agency business in Canada, a business which has undergone many important changes in this century and will probably evolve even more quickly in the future.

EVOLUTION OF THE ROLE OF THE ADVERTISING AGENCY IN CANADA

The evolution of the modern advertising agency was the result of the merging of two functions: the older function of placing advertisements for the advertiser in various media, and that of assisting the advertiser in preparing the advertising copy.

Space Brokers for Newspapers

Until 1889, advertising agents working on a commission basis acted as intermediaries between advertisers and newspapers, selling space to advertisers for a commission. These agents helped advertisers deal with several newspapers and provided information on circulation and negotiated rates for the space.

In 1878 Anson McKim, a space broker who represented a Toronto newspaper, the *Mail*, was sent to Montreal to open an office and solicit business. McKim soon found that Montreal businessmen wanted information about and placement services for other Ontario newspapers. Since this information would help sell space in the *Mail*, the rates and circulation figures were collected in Toronto and sent to McKim's Montreal office. This office came to be called The Mail Advertising Agency.[1]

The agency was primarily doing business for the *Mail*, but McKim realized that he could be more effective if he were independent of any newspaper and could eliminate any conflict of interest with advertisers and other newspapers. In January 1889, he created the first Canadian advertising agency, A. McKim & Company, Newspaper Advertising Agency. The agency was established to obtain the most accurate information on newspaper circulation, to negotiate fair rates for advertisers, and to handle the negotiations between the two groups, including specifications for placing an advertisement, verifying the execution, and billing. This information was published in 1892 in the *Canadian Newspaper Directory*, which rapidly became the standard reference book on Canadian publications (Figure 3–1).[2]

FIGURE 3–1

**Title Page of the first
McKim Canadian
Newspaper Directory
(1892)**

Source: H. E. Stephenson
and C. McNaught, *The
Story of Advertising in Canada* (Toronto: Ryerson
Press, 1940), p. 31.

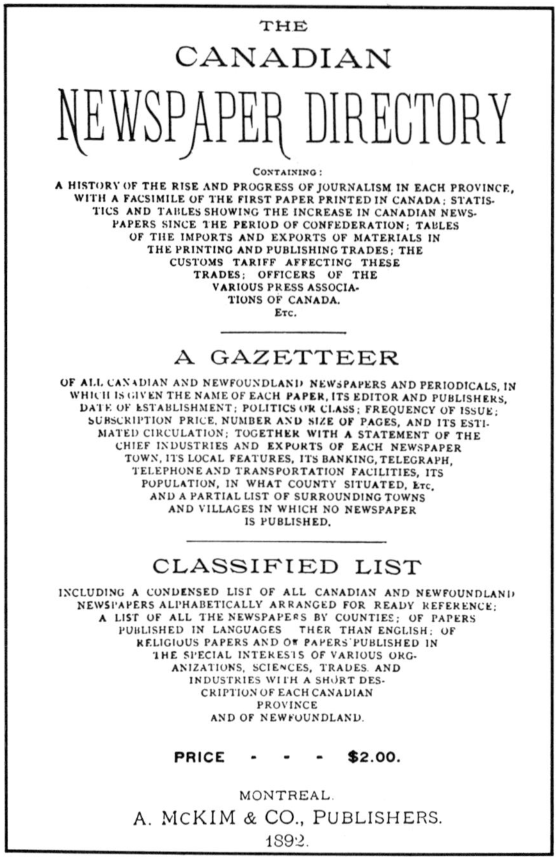

THE
CANADIAN
NEWSPAPER DIRECTORY

CONTAINING:

A HISTORY OF THE RISE AND PROGRESS OF JOURNALISM IN EACH PROVINCE,
WITH A FACSIMILE OF THE FIRST PAPER PRINTED IN CANADA; STATIS-
TICS AND TABLES SHOWING THE INCREASE IN CANADIAN NEWS-
PAPERS SINCE THE PERIOD OF CONFEDERATION; TABLES
OF THE IMPORTS AND EXPORTS OF MATERIALS IN
THE PRINTING AND PUBLISHING TRADES; THE
CUSTOMS TARIFF AFFECTING THESE
TRADES; OFFICERS OF THE
VARIOUS PRESS ASSOCIA-
TIONS OF CANADA.
ETC.

A GAZETTEER

OF ALL CANADIAN AND NEWFOUNDLAND NEWSPAPERS AND PERIODICALS, IN
WHICH IS GIVEN THE NAME OF EACH PAPER, ITS EDITOR AND PUBLISHERS;
DATE OF ESTABLISHMENT; POLITICS OR CLASS; FREQUENCY OF ISSUE;
SUBSCRIPTION PRICE, NUMBER AND SIZE OF PAGES, AND ITS ESTI-
MATED CIRCULATION; TOGETHER WITH A STATEMENT OF THE
CHIEF INDUSTRIES AND EXPORTS OF EACH NEWSPAPER
TOWN, ITS LOCAL FEATURES, ITS BANKING, TELEGRAPH,
TELEPHONE AND TRANSPORTATION FACILITIES, ITS
POPULATION, IN WHAT COUNTY SITUATED, ETC,
AND A PARTIAL LIST OF SURROUNDING TOWNS
AND VILLAGES IN WHICH NO NEWSPAPER
IS PUBLISHED.

CLASSIFIED LIST

INCLUDING A CONDENSED LIST OF ALL CANADIAN AND NEWFOUNDLAND
NEWSPAPERS ALPHABETICALLY ARRANGED FOR READY REFERENCE;
A LIST OF ALL THE NEWSPAPERS BY COUNTIES; OF PAPERS
PUBLISHED IN LANGUAGES THER THAN ENGLISH; OF
RELIGIOUS PAPERS AND OF PAPERS PUBLISHED IN
THE SPECIAL INTERESTS OF VARIOUS ORG-
ANIZATIONS, SCIENCES, TRADES, AND
INDUSTRIES WITH A SHORT DES-
CRIPTION OF EACH CANADIAN
PROVINCE
AND OF NEWFOUNDLAND.

PRICE - - - $2.00.

MONTREAL.
A. McKIM & CO., PUBLISHERS.
1892.

**Birth of the
Modern
Advertising
Agency**

Initially, most advertisers wrote their own advertisements. They would then give the manuscript with or without illustrations to the newspaper to have it set in type. Gradually, a new kind of specialist emerged who helped advertisers write copy. These people were often called "ad-smiths," since many were freelance writers offering their services to advertisers and agencies. One of the first of these freelance copywriters was Peter Rutherford, who worked in Toronto and promoted his services in advertisements (Figure 3–2).[3]

It was not until about 1910 that the two types of services—advertisement placement and copywriting—merged to form the modern advertising agency, and by this date most Canadian advertising agencies had permanent copy staffs.

The work of the copywriter originally included producing simple line illustrations. The layout and design of an advertisement eventually came to involve more than simple illustration and was integrated more closely with the advertising message. The need for more sophisticated art work gave rise to a new kind of expertise, that of the creative department. The copywriter evolved from a person clever with words to a specialist who could communicate effec-

FIGURE 3–2

Advertisement for Peter Rutherford, one of the first freelance copy writers in Canada, offering to write "four advertisements for a dollar."

Source: H. E. Stephenson and C. McNaught, *The Story of Advertising in Canada* (Toronto: Ryerson Press, 1940), p. 102.

tively with the market by using the market's language in talking about a product. This evolution marked the birth of the modern advertising agency, which grew by expanding its range of services and clients. After the First World War, emphasis was put on research and merchandising, and most large agencies gradually became full-service agencies.

THE NATURE AND ROLE OF A FULL-SERVICE AGENCY

The full-service advertising agency developed in response to advertisers' increasing needs, not only in terms of media placement and creative services but also in terms of marketing services. A full-service agency provides a complete range of marketing services, except for personal selling. Some agencies also organize sales conventions for the launching of a new product or service.

Types of Services

Full-service advertising agencies offer advertisers three broad types of services: account, creative, and media services. These services are covered by the commissions the agency receives.

Account Services

The account service group of the advertising agency is responsible for managing the relationship between the client and the agency staff assigned to this client. In co-operation with the client, the account service group manages the whole advertising process, from marketing strategy to advertising execution (Figure 3–3).

The account service group works closely with the advertiser to ensure that the flow of information between them is as efficient as possible. It obtains from

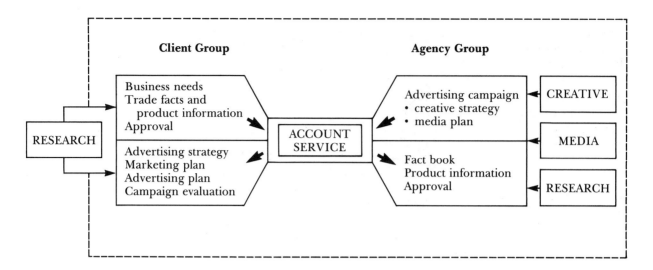

| Client Group | | Agency Group | |

FIGURE 3–3

Role of the Account Service Group in Managing the Relationship between the Client Group and the Agency Staff Assigned to the Client

the client all relevant trade facts and product information as well as a thorough understanding of the client's business needs. In addition to day-to-day consultation with the client, the account service group must obtain the client's approval for the work done by various agency departments.

The account service group also keeps the client informed by providing the marketing plan, the advertising plan, the creative strategy, and the campaign evaluation report.

Account service may also act as a marketing consultant to the client, particularly in the following areas:

- new product introduction (concept testing, branding);
- product strategies (packaging, repositioning);
- pricing (price deals, coupons);
- distribution (in-store displays, demonstrations).

In its relationship with various agency departments the account service group must ensure the client's needs and requirements are fully understood. Thus it provides agency personnel with a compilation of the relevant information on the client's product, called the *fact book*, as well as any other information requested by agency personnel.

With the creative media departments, the account service group co-ordinates media advertising, corporate graphics, point of sales material, packaging, and the planning and buying of media space or time.

Once the advertising campaign has been presented to and approved by the client, the account service group sees to the execution of the campaign and develops procedures to evaluate the campaign's effectiveness.

Creative Services

The creative services group provides the advertiser with the creative ideas and concepts for executing the campaign. This function is crucial, since agencies are often evaluated and compared on the basis of their creative talent, and this is the most visible part of the agency's work. The creative services group performs three main functions: copywriting, art direction, and print and broadcast production.

Copywriters transform the creative strategy into effective verbal or written communications that integrate illustrations, radio sound effects, and television. The copywriter works closely with the art director in developing the main idea for the campaign and then writes the headlines, subheads, and body copy for the print advertisement or the broadcast commercial.

Art directors translate the creative strategy into an effective visual communication that is integrated with the copy. They design the basic visual elements of the communication and work closely with copywriters, graphics specialists, art studios, and photographers in producing the final print advertisement or broadcast commercial. Detailed illustrations and most finished artwork is usually subcontracted to freelance artists or commercial art studios for final rendering.

Print and broadcast production managers prepare the print advertisements or broadcast commercials for production. In print production, the functions of typesetters, printers, and other graphic art suppliers must be co-ordinated and completed in time for publication. In broadcast production, the script or storyboard is developed into a radio or television commercial. Typically, this involves actors, film directors, music directors, cameramen, and other specialists. A commercial may be shot several times before the creative or art director is satisfied that the commercial effectively executes the creative concept. It is the responsibility of the production manager to ensure that all technical aspects in producing the commercial are successfully completed well before air date.

In some large agencies, a *traffic manager* is responsible for verifying that the final print advertisement and broadcast commercial have reached the selected media.

Media Services

The media services group provides the advertiser with a media plan based on the marketing strategy and the creative strategy (Figure 3–4). First a media strategy is developed, including the decisions on the media selected and the size, length, and timing of the media placements. Then, based on the media strategy, this group buys the selected time and space at the best possible price. Media research is often used to evaluate different media according to costs and suitability for the target market.

Media services are extremely important to the advertiser for several reasons:

1. In spite of the fact that it does not have the glamour of creative services, media services represent the traditional strength of an advertising agency.
2. It is essential that media planning be efficient, since a very large percentage of the advertising budget, usually more than 80 percent, is spent on media placements. In 1989, net advertising revenues of the various media exceeded $9 billion.[4]

FIGURE 3–4

Media Services
Offered by
Advertising Agencies

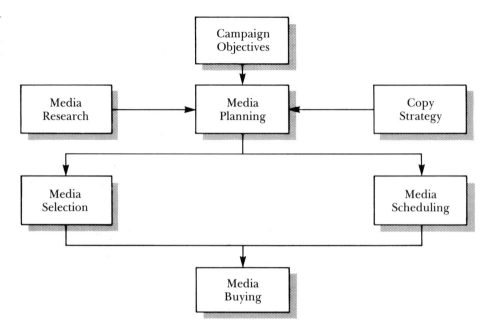

3. Media planning is a complicated task because a large volume of data is available on the various media and it is difficult to evaluate the effectiveness of each medium in relation to the others. Thus media planning requires well-trained specialists as well as computing services to carry out the large amount of analytical work involved.

Complementary
Services

As the need for more sophisticated marketing advice arose, some agencies set up specialized marketing services groups. Some of the most important are advertising and marketing research, sales promotion and merchandising, packaging and new product development, and publicity/public relations.

Advertising and marketing researchers provide the client and agency groups with planning information on all phases of a campaign, such as defining market segments, developing marketing plans, testing product concepts and creative executions, and measuring the effects of the campaign. Depending on the problem, they may use a variety of research instruments, from focus-group interviewing to large-scale mail surveys. They may draw heavily from outside research firms and organizations that supply such services as market research, copy testing, and media data, as well as computer software for evaluating broadcast media plans. Examples of such outside sources are A.C. Nielsen, the Print Measurement Bureau, the Bureau of Broadcast Measurement, and private research firms. The role of these outside suppliers is to provide agencies with the most accurate information on the market and its reaction to messages and media selections. This will be explained further in Chapter 15.

Sales promotion or merchandising specialists are most important to packaged goods accounts. They have specialized knowledge of the sales promotion industry and advise the other agency groups on developing marketing strategies and implementing such promotional activities as sampling, couponing, premiums, sweepstakes, and contests. Also, they provide counsel on co-operative advertising, point-of-purchase displays, and direct-mail advertising.

Packaging and new product development specialists help the client improve an existing package or design a new package for an existing product. Usually, they work in conjunction with the creative group. For new products, they may assist the client in many of the steps involved in new product development, from concept testing to the selection of a brand name, sales forecasting, pricing, and test marketing.

Publicity/public relations specialists respond to client needs and integrate public relations and advertising. To be effective, publicity about company products must be consistent with claims made in advertising and vice versa.

Organization of a Full-Service Advertising Agency

The organization of a full-service advertising agency may vary, but the basic structure is shaped by the functions described previously. Thus, most full-service agencies have an organizational chart something like Figure 3–5. Such titles as chairperson, chief executive officer, and vice-president establish comparable levels with those of the client group and designate department head status.

An organizational chart is merely an administrative tool to establish an agency's broad functional areas and services. Often, in small and medium-sized agencies, the same person may perform several functions and work on several accounts. As an agency becomes larger, there is a greater degree of specialization, with personnel assigned to one or two accounts. The various functional tasks may be organized by department or by group, depending on the size of the agency and the size of the account.

In a *departmental organization*, which is a functional type of structure, each account executive initiates work to be done with the various departments. Each department works on all accounts and is responsible for allocating the tasks among its specialists and for meeting deadlines prescribed by the account executive. This type of organization is often found in small agencies or for small accounts in large agencies.

In a *group organization*, which is a modular type of structure, a complete team including service, creative, and media personnel is responsible for a specific account or a line of products. Each group is responsible for developing a complete campaign for the client, and its tasks may include formulating a marketing plan, developing an advertising strategy, creating and testing several advertisements, and executing and controlling the campaign as approved by the client. This type of structure is most often used for large clients, whose complex businesses are more effectively handled by the personal attention offered by the group system. Group members are completely responsible for all advertising activity on that account.

To ensure that an agency's output is of sufficient and consistent quality, a *plans board* may be set up. This board, usually composed of senior executives representing the various agency disciplines, is responsible for approving the advertising strategy developed before it is shown to the client. The board acts

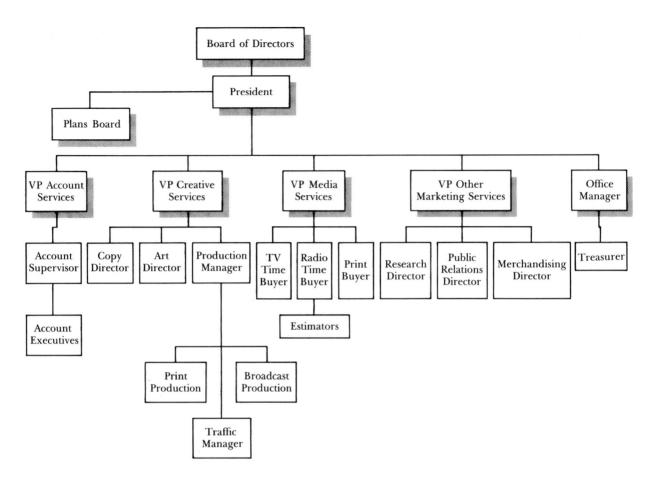

FIGURE 3–5

*A Typical
Advertising Agency
Organization Chart
Organized along the
Major Advertising
Functions*

as a quality control mechanism, and in this role it can help improve the quality of the agency's presentation to the client.

Finally, agencies have the personnel common to most businesses: an office manager, a treasurer, secretaries, and switchboard operators. In addition, because of the numerous laws and regulations in force in Canada and its provinces, a lawyer may be retained by the agency. Since the agency is legally responsible for the advertising it creates, it could be convicted, if found guilty, for false or misleading advertising.[5] Thus the role of the lawyer is to make sure that copy claims prepared by the agency are fully supported by facts.

OTHER TYPES OF AGENCIES

Alternatives to the complete package offered by full-service advertising agencies arose from advertisers' desire to improve the value received for their commissions or fees. Advertisers' concern that full-service agencies did not give them the best possible counsel in all areas of advertising encouraged the creation of *à-la-carte agencies*, *creative boutiques*, *media buying services*, and *in-house agencies*.

**A-la-carte
Agencies**

A-la-carte agencies provide the services of a full-service agency, but they allow the clients to choose, for a specified or negotiated fee, the services to be performed. This unbundling of services allows advertisers to organize an ad hoc group by selecting the best talents in various à-la-carte agencies.

**Creative
Boutiques**

A creative boutique is a special type of à-la-carte agency that became popular in the late 1960s and the 1970s. Intense competition in several markets led advertisers to depend on the creativity of their advertising to give them an advantage over competitors. Competition for the best creative talent led many art directors and copywriters to leave full-service agencies and set up their own creative shops, which became known as creative boutiques. The term "boutique" was initially used by full-service agency people as a derogatory term conveying the idea of narrowness. However, its other connotation—that of personal attention and unique creative styles—led to its adoption to describe the new shops. The popularity of creative boutiques waned as advertisers realized they needed a whole range of services not provided by the boutiques. Some boutiques added other types of services and became full-service agencies or à-la-carte agencies. In general, creative boutiques provide only creative services to advertisers, for a negotiated fee.

**Media Buying
Services**

Media buying services sprang from the dramatic increase in media costs, particularly in spot television, and the willingness of certain media to negotiate prices on the basis of dollar volume. The independent media buying service looks for special buys priced at lower than regular advertising rates. In turn, they sell broadcast time or print space to clients and agencies at a rate lower than the one that could be obtained by the agency. The difference between these two rates represents the service's gross profit. They have forced advertising agencies to improve their media buying procedures, thus encouraging the industry to provide advertisers better value for their media dollars.

**In-House
Agencies**

Some advertisers own and operate an advertising agency under their supervision. This in-house agency is entitled to all media commissions and usually works on the company's products or product lines. If solicited, they may handle outside accounts. They provide the same services performed by the traditional full-service advertising agency but at a total cost that is usually lower than the commissions from media buying. This is the economic rationale for establishing such an agency.[6] For campaigns with a straightforward creative approach or that are lifted from the U.S., this arrangement may work reasonably well, particularly with heavy television advertisers. However, critics point out that by working on the same product line, the creative group of in-house agencies becomes stale and cannot attract top talent. In addition, the advertiser loses the point of view and experience of outside agencies. Despite these drawbacks, this form of arrangement appears to be most popular with large U.S.-based consumer packaged-goods companies.

lecture

Agency-of-Record (AOR)

An agency-of-record is not a new type of agency. It is an agreement between a large advertiser and any agency selected by the advertiser. That agency (of any type) is appointed by the advertiser as its agency-of-record, responsible for the media buying for all the products advertised by the client. The advertising plan for each one of these products may be developed by a different agency, but all the media buying is centralized in the AOR. This is to allow the client to take advantage of the various media discounts and other benefits of large volume buying. For its services, the AOR is paid a fee and all the savings are returned to the client.

STRUCTURE OF THE CANADIAN AGENCY BUSINESS

Size Distribution of Canadian Advertising Agencies

The precise number of advertising agencies in Canada is difficult to determine since there is no complete list of Canadian agencies. In 1977, there were approximately 300 agencies in Canada; today the actual number is between 400 and 500. A partial list of agencies, their addresses, and the names of their personnel can be found in the monthly publication *Canadian Advertising Rates and Data* (CARD).[7]

There is a wide disparity in size among Canadian agencies. Most of the largest ones belong to the Institute of Canadian Advertising, which has about 70 members accounting for about 85 percent of national advertising. Thus, one finds the traditional 80–20 rule in action, i.e., 20 percent of advertising agencies account for about 80 percent of total billings.

Table 3–1 presents a list of the top 20 Canadian advertising agencies in 1989, compiled on the basis of the amount of advertising business handled by each advertising agency, including all branch offices but excluding subsidiary companies or satellite agencies. Based on this definition of total billings, the largest advertising agency in Canada in 1989 was MacLaren:Lintas, with $220 million in billings. The second one was Cossette Communication-Marketing with $215 million, and the third one was FCB/Ronalds-Reynolds with $202 million.[8] There are 17 agencies with billings over $100 million, only 27 with more than $50 million, and 87 with more than $15 million. These statistics reveal that this is a highly concentrated industry.

Distribution of Billings

In order to understand the agency business, it is useful to understand how the money received from the client is spent. The 80–20 rule mentioned above is also a good benchmark: about 80 percent of total billings is spent on media placements, and 20 percent is mostly for production charges, with the rest used for market surveys, research, and other services.

In addition, very small agencies tend to favour the print media, because of the size of their advertising budgets, while large agencies tend to spend a large share of their budgets on television. In between, medium-sized agencies tend to use all media. These differences reflect a number of factors, including the size of their clients' advertising budgets, the availability of good creative talent (especially for television), and agencies' attempts to develop specific areas of expertise.

TABLE 3-1 **THE TOP 20 CANADIAN ADVERTISING AGENCIES IN 1989 (IN BILLINGS)**

Rank	Agency	$Million
1	MacLaren:Lintas	220
2	Cossette Communication-Marketing	215
3	FCB/Ronalds-Reynolds	202
4	J. Walter Thompson Company	195
5	Young & Rubicam	194
6	McCann-Erickson Advertising of Canada	191
7	McKim Advertising	185
8	Ogilvy & Mather (Canada)	183
9	Saffer Advertising	180
10	Vickers & Benson Advertising	169
11	Baker Lovick	159
12	Grey Canada	145
13	Saatchi & Saatchi Compton Hayhurst	128
14	Backer Spielvogel Bates Canada	122
15	Leo Burnett Company	110
16	Scali McCabe Sloves (Canada)	107
17	BCP Strategy-Creativity	101
18	D'Arcy Masius Benton & Bowles Canada	99
19	The Collier & Park Group	95
20	Palmer Jarvis Advertising	85

Source: "Canada's Top 100," *Marketing* (11 December 1989), pp. 23–25.

Salaries of Agency Personnel

Salaries of agency personnel are a result of the supply and demand for qualified individuals. However, they tend to fall within ranges. The salary ranges for 12 agency positions are indicated in Table 3–2. These figures were compiled for large agency personnel, but they also apply to other types of agencies. Entry-level positions in account services, creative, and media tend to receive similar salaries, somewhere between $10 000 and $25 000. Personnel in the creative group have, in the last 20 years, received some of the highest salaries, reflecting a strong demand for creative talent. Recently, competition between full-service agencies and media buying services has increased demand for experienced media personnel, and their salaries have increased faster than the other groups. Future changes in agency salaries will depend on the supply of and demand for qualified personnel.[9]

Geographic Distribution of Agencies

Most large agencies are located in Toronto and Montreal, near the head offices of major corporations. Other major cities have local or regional agencies, as well as branches of major national agencies. Montreal has the additional characteristic that most agencies there have personnel specializing in French creative and thus often handle the French component of a national advertising

TABLE 3–2 **AGENCY SALARY RANGES FOR FOUR TYPES OF POSITIONS**

Agency Salaries

The following chart was compiled after talks with more than a dozen senior ad agency executives. The figures represent the lower and upper level annual salary ranges found in the creative, account management, and media departments of agencies with $25 million in billings and up. Also, the figures reflect total remuneration packages, but they do not include money earned from equity participation.

Creative	Account Management	Media
The creative director and vice-president $45,000 to $100,000+*	Director of client services and vice-president $35,000 to $85,000	Media director $30,000 to $100,000+**
Assistant creative director or senior writer/art director $35,000 to $80,000	Account group supervisor $30,000 to $60,000	Associate media director $25,000 to $55,000
Intermediate writer or art director $20,000 to $35,000	Senior account executive $25,000 to $55,000	Media supervisor $20,000 to $35,000
Junior writer or art director $12,500 to $20,000	Junior account executive $11,000 to $25,000	Media estimator, traineee $10,000 to $25,000

* There are probably between five and ten big-name creative directors earning more than $100,000.
** Traditionally the lowest salaries have been in the media department. But recently overall salaries have increased throughout agency media departments and several of the most prominent media directors are now in the $100,000+ category.

Sources: Mark Smyka, "JWT Takes the Lead in Training Recruits," *Marketing* (13 December 1982), p. 39; Martin Mehr, "Low salaries and long hours result in a shortage of good media people," *Marketing* (11 December 1989), p. 59.

campaign that may have been developed in Toronto or Vancouver. As the need for original French creative arose,[10] several advertising agencies with strong creative talent in French grew in size and volume. This in turn forced some of them to open branches in Toronto in order to become truly national agencies.[11] Table 3–3 presents the top ten agencies in Quebec with the total billings for their Quebec office only. The top Quebec agency is Cossette Communication-Marketing with $138 million in billings (it is also the second largest in Canada), followed by the BCP Group, with $101 million. These two agencies have been among the fastest growing agencies in Canada in the last ten years.

TABLE 3–3 **THE TOP TEN QUEBEC ADVERTISING AGENCIES BASED ON THEIR BUSINESS IN QUEBEC ONLY (IN BILLINGS)**

Rank	Agency	Billings $million	Number of Employees
1	Cossette Communication-Marketing	138	325
2	The BCP Group	101	129
3	Marketel/Foster/McCann-Erickson	79	114
4	Publicité Martin	55	80
5	Groupe Morrow	52	70
6	Groupe Everest	38	78
7	J. Walter Thompson	37	50
8	PNMD Communications	35	55
9	Léveillé Vickers et Benson	35	55
10	Provost/Ronalds-Reynolds	32	55

Source: "Quebec's top 50 agencies," *Marketing* (19 March, 1990), p. 28.

HOW ADVERTISING AGENCIES ARE COMPENSATED

The method of compensation for most agencies is still based on the commission system of the nineteenth century newspaper space brokers. The 15 percent commission rate was first used by Albert Lasker in the early 1900s, and institutionalized in 1918 by the AAAA (American Association of Advertising Agencies). This system has been criticized over the years, but it remains the preferred method of compensation, as about 45 percent of Canadian companies use this method.[12]

As agencies added services, the charges billed to the client were determined in a manner consistent with the standard 15 percent commission. Other revenues come from fees for use of agency personnel. The three main sources of revenue for agencies are commissions, charges, and fees.

Commissions

A bona fide agency receives a commission from the medium in recognition of its traditional role as an agent. Advertisers do not bear any cost in media placement and thus are not entitled to a commission.

For example, suppose an agency places a contract with one television station for $100 000 (Figure 3–6). If the rate is $1000 for each 30 second prime time slot, the client receives 100 prime time slots. The station allows the agency to deduct from the total buy a 15 percent commission. This means the agency revenue would be $15 000 in order to cover salaries, overhead, and make a profit. If the bill is paid within ten days, the agency may also deduct 2 percent of the net amount ($85 000) to be paid to the station. The agency may in turn pass this cash discount on to its client for prompt payment.

Technically, the commission of $15 000 is paid by the television station to the agency. In turn, the agency plans and executes the advertiser's campaign and assumes full responsibility for contractual dealings with the media. It is estimated that more than 80 percent of all advertising agency revenues are derived from the 15 percent commission from the media. Two recent studies

FIGURE 3–6

*The Commission
System of
Compensation*

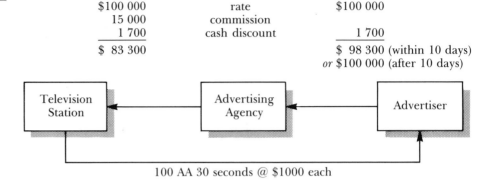

$100 000   rate $100 000
15 000   commission
1 700   cash discount   1 700
$ 83 300 $ 98 300 (within 10 days)
or $100 000 (after 10 days)

Television Station ← Advertising Agency ← Advertiser

100 AA 30 seconds @ $1000 each

on Canadian advertisers reveal that about 45 percent of companies are using the commission system.[13]

Charges

Additional costs the agency incurs in developing the advertising campaign are charged to the client. For example, the costs of using outside services to produce an advertisement are charged to the client, and this amount is usually marked up by 17.65 percent. This percentage on costs leads to the same amount as the 15 percent on the amount billed to the client. For example, suppose in producing a television commercial an agency uses an outside television studio, for the amount of $8500. In billing the client, the agency would add $1500, for a total of $10 000. The mark-up of $1500 represents either 17.65 percent of $8500 or 15 percent of $10 000. Thus the charge system is consistent with the commission system.

Fees

Fees are negotiated between the agency and the client whenever the commission or charge systems provide inadequate compensation. The agency may feel it is receiving too little compensation, or the advertiser may feel that the agency is not providing enough value for its commission.

Under the fee system, the advertiser and the agency negotiate a total fee for services rendered. Often, this is done on a project basis. The agency usually agrees to rebate all commissions to the client and to absorb all charges. The agreed-upon total fee may be higher or lower than the sum of the commissions and the charges, but the essential point is that both sides agree that the compensation is fair for the services rendered. In developing the agreed-upon fee, the agency often uses a multiple of the hourly rate of its personnel. This multiple may vary between 2.5 and 3, with 2.75 often selected. It is used to cover overhead costs and a reasonable profit in addition to the time agency personnel spend on the account. According to agency personnel, less than 10 percent of advertising agency revenues are derived from fees. Two recent studies on Canadian advertisers reveal that between 25 and 30 percent are using the fixed fee method.[14]

Guaranteed Revenue System

A variant of the fee system, the guaranteed revenue system calls for the client to guarantee a minimum profit target for the agency. For example, the costs incurred by the agency in developing a campaign for a client may generate insufficient profit or a loss after all media commissions have been collected. Under this system, the client agrees to reimburse the agency the difference between the costs plus the profit target and the revenues. The advantage of this system is that the agency can make a satisfactory profit, while the client obtains the best services the agency can offer. The client has no guarantee, however, that the agency will be cost efficient. To date, very few Canadian companies (2.4 percent) are using the guaranteed revenue system.[15]

Advantages and Disadvantages of the Commission and Fee Systems

There has been much debate over the advantages and disadvantages of both the commission system and the fee system.

The commission system has been criticized on the grounds that agencies are tempted to suggest excessive advertising budgets, relatively expensive media, or media that minimize the agency input and costs. In addition, the system leads to heavy competition for large accounts, often to the detriment of smaller or medium-sized accounts. Proponents of the commission system argue that it is very simple to administer and has been working reasonably well for more than a century. As we have seen, agency profit margins tend to be low, which indicates that agencies provide some value for their revenues. Even though it is still the most widely used method, the percentage of Canadian companies using it has declined from 76 percent in 1970 to 45 percent in 1986.[16]

The fee system has been criticized on the grounds that agencies may try to compete on the basis of price, rather than on quality of services. Also, the client may try to cut costs by eliminating such services as research; conversely, the agency may be tempted to add services in order to increase its fee. Proponents of the fee system claim that the bias toward commissionable media is removed and that the agency is more likely to provide non-commissionable services. Also, an agency receives a more stable income; it is not affected greatly by budget changes. The agency makes a fair profit on all accounts. An advertiser is more likely to receive good value for the agreed-upon services to be performed. The percentage of Canadian companies using the fee system has grown from 10 percent in 1970 to 25–30 percent in 1986.[17]

Each system has advantages and disadvantages. The real problem lies in the exchange relationship between the agency and the advertiser and the concept of "value" provided by the agency to the advertiser in exchange for a certain sum. Ultimately, the key to this relationship lies in the objectives the advertiser assigns to the advertising function and the cost of reaching these objectives. Thus, proper determination of the advertising objectives and budget is critical, and some form of *objective* or *incentive system* may be more appropriate. With an objective system both the advertiser and the agency agree on some precise goal and result for the advertising campaign (see Chapter 11). The incentive system bases compensation on the results achieved by the campaign.[18]

AGENCY RECOGNITION

Because newspapers paid agencies a commission for their services, newspapers needed assurance that an agency was solvent. A credit system instituted and managed by the Canadian Daily Newspaper Publishers Association (CDNPA) was founded in 1859 and incorporated under federal law in 1913.[19] The credit system of the CDNPA is revised periodically to allow for inflation and growth of the overall economy. In April 1982, the credit ratings of the CDNPA were adjusted to the following:[20]

- *AA rating:* for agencies showing a current surplus of liquid assets over liabilities of at least $100 000. A portion of that excess may be a letter of credit from a Canadian chartered bank.
- *A rating:* for agencies showing a current surplus of liquid assets over liabilities of at least $50 000.
- *B rating:* for agencies showing a current surplus of liquid assets over liabilities on a two-to-one ratio of at least $15 000, or a letter of credit in the amount of $15 000.
- *C rating:* for agencies without one of the above ratings providing a cheque with the insertion order.

When an agency satisfies one of these requirements it is said to be "enfranchised" or "recognized" and thus entitled to the 15 percent commission. Recognition from the CDNPA only indicates an agency's credit worthiness; it does not confer any recognition or implication in terms of creative or marketing ability.

Four other associations grant recognition to agencies: the Periodical Press Association, the Canadian Community Newspapers Association, the Canadian Association of Broadcasters, and the Outdoor Advertising Association of Canada.

GROWTH IN AGENCY BUSINESS

In the highly competitive advertising business, agencies must make sure that their revenues grow from year to year. Agencies may ensure continued growth in profits by keeping present clients satisfied, acquiring other agencies, and obtaining new business.

Keeping Present Clients Satisfied

This is probably the most important objective, since it is harder to obtain new clients than to retain existing ones. The average length of a client-agency relationship is probably between three and five years, and every year a large amount of billings change agencies. The main reasons for these changes are:

Lack of Proper Communication

Communication between the advertiser and the agency may be poor because of neglect, the advertiser's failure to understand clients' needs and expectations, or clients' unreasonable expectations. It is the responsibility of the account service personnel to ensure a complete understanding of client needs and to communicate to the client what the agency can and cannot do.

Lack of Chemistry or Trust

A client may feel uneasy about the agency, its personnel, or the advertising campaign's effects on the target market. The role of the agency's president is to make sure that clients are properly matched with agency personnel.

New Management

A change of management on the client side may lead to a change of agencies, since a new manager many want to renew previous ties with other agencies or change the company's creative approach.

Changes in Market Performance

Positive or negative changes in client's sales growth may cause an agency to lose an account. This may be because the company has grown larger and management feels that they need a bigger or different agency or the advertising agency may be made the scapegoat for the company's financial setbacks.

Account Conflict

In principle, an agency cannot handle two competing accounts in the same market. But what about non-competing products from competing companies? Should the agency handle both accounts? To minimize potential problems, some agencies will set up or acquire separate advertising agencies to handle one of these two accounts and to ensure that both clients are satisfied.

Acquiring other Agencies

By acquiring other agencies, an agency can obtain new accounts that may or may not conflict with its present accounts. Acquisitions of or mergers with other agencies are quite frequent, and may be the result of account changes or losses of qualified personnel.

The mid-1980s saw the beginning of a wave of big mergers in various industries. As the wave continued, advertising agencies worldwide started going "global," creating mega-agencies billing over $5 billion. This trend has had its effect on Canadian agencies; the list of top agencies in 1989 is very different from the list from previous years. These mergers have intensified account conflicts, increased personnel turnover rates, and resulted in some rethinking in clients' strategies. For example, large clients with worldwide operations are tempted to use global agencies to develop more consistent advertising in different countries (the "standardization approach" to international advertising). Other clients wishing to take advantage of the free trade agreement (FTA) with the United States may choose a U.S.-owned agency with a wide network in the U.S. Finally, clients which are only interested in the Canadian market and want personal attention may prefer a small- to medium-size agency.[21]

Obtaining Additional Business from Present Clients

Good performance on the client's business and soliciting business on new product launching or proposing a change of positioning for an existing product can be a means of obtaining business from present clients. The idea is to be knowledgeable in the client's business and to assume marketing leadership and partnership with the client. New product ideas, market segments, uses of existing products, and channels of distribution may be proposed to the client by the account service or creative personnel.

Obtaining New Business

It is challenging but essential for a growth-oriented agency to obtain new business. Most "good" accounts already have an agency and must be won over aggressively. Three methods are often used, singly or in combination:

Advertising the Agency

The reputation and high profile of the name of the agency is often important in deciding which agencies the client should contact. These agencies often advertise in order to keep their name in the public eye. The approach varies from listing services, describing their personnel, giving examples of successful campaigns, or mentioning important changes in personnel. An example of an agency advertisement is shown in Figure 3–7.

Calling on Selected Companies

This may be done by suggesting to the appropriate advertising manager that the agency make a presentation on the agency's strengths and demonstrate how these may benefit the company. If the manager is dissatisfied with the company's present agency, the presentation may lead to a switch of agencies.

Contacting Companies Openly Dissatisfied with Their Agencies

Contrary to the preceding method, this is a highly competitive method, since the information on these companies appears in advertising trade magazines like *Marketing* or in newsletters like *Adnews*; thus many other agencies are probably soliciting the dissatisfied company. Often the company may ask four or five agencies to do a "speculative presentation," that is, a campaign proposal on their product. The company then reimburses the agency for some of the costs of preparing the proposal. Some agencies refuse to participate in speculative presentations on the grounds that it is an excuse for a company to obtain free advice. Other agencies consider such presentations as part of the cost of doing business. For the client, this method is a means of selecting the best agency for its product when it is difficult to choose an agency on the basis of its past record or its standard promotional presentation.

FIGURE 3–7

Advertisement for an Advertising Agency

With permission of McBride Advertising

SUMMARY

Advertising agencies were born of newspaper publishers' need to sell space and collect bills. They evolved into independent businesses filling the needs of both media owners and advertisers for marketing and advertising counsel.

A full-service advertising agency offers clients three basic types of services: account management, creative services, and media planning. Complementary services include research, publicity, and sales promotion.

Advertisers who want to cut costs may use à-la-carte agencies, creative boutiques, or media buying services. Large advertisers may also set up in-house agencies, and use an agency-of-record.

The Canadian agency business is influenced strongly by the size of the agency. A few large agencies representing about 20 percent of all agencies are responsible for about 80 percent of the billings. They use television heavily and tend to attract the best talent. Small agencies use proportionally more print than large ones because their clients' budgets are smaller.

Advertising agencies derive their income from a combination of the 15 percent media commission, charges, and fees. They may also negotiate a guaranteed profit target with clients. Over the years, there has been much criticism of the commission system, but it is still the preferred method of compensation. In order to receive the 15 percent commission from the media, an advertising agency must be recognized by the various media associations. This recognition merely indicates an agency's credit worthiness.

In order to survive, agencies must maintain or increase their billings. The first rule is to keep present clients satisfied. Growth in billings may come from acquiring or merging with another agency, obtaining additional business from existing clients, or attracting new clients.

With an understanding of the nature, role, structure, and functioning of advertising agencies in Canada, their contribution to the growth of an industry, firm, or organization can be evaluated.

QUESTIONS FOR STUDY

1. Explain under what conditions creative boutiques can be viable in the long run.

2. Explain under what conditions media buying services can be viable in the long run.

3. Discuss the advantages and disadvantages of using a full-service agency versus à-la-carte agencies, creative boutiques, and media buying services.

4. Under what conditions does it make sense for an advertiser to set up an in-house agency?

5. Read the last five issues of *Marketing*. Make a list of account changes and suggest some reasons why these changes took place.

6. Discuss the pros and cons of speculative presentations. Under what conditions should an advertising agency agree to do such a presentation? When does it make sense for an advertiser to request four or five agencies to develop speculative presentations?

7. Should an advertising agency handle competing accounts? Explain your answer.

8. Why is the 15 percent commission system still the preferred method of compensation? Does it favour the large advertiser to the detriment of the small one?

9. Do you think that conflict may arise between agency personnel in two different functional groups?

10. It has been said that an agency's inventory or assets go down the elevator every night at five o'clock. What does this mean, and what are the implications for an agency's upper management?

1. Assume that you are the owner of OEM Ltd., a very small advertising agency billing about $2 million a year with about ten clients of similar sizes. You have one creative and one media person, and one secretary.

   a. Analyze your overall situation and identify the main problem(s) that you will be facing in the next five years. Be sure to define clearly your business objective (mission).

   b. Evaluate the different options that are open to you.

   c. Develop a plan of action for OEM Ltd.

2. Select an advertising agency in your town and develop a complete picture of that agency in terms of its services, types of clients, organization, and method of compensation. If possible, interview key people in the agency, e.g., one or two account executives, the media director, and the creative director.

   If an agency is not available, write to one agency in a large metropolitan area and ask for their promotional package. Work from there.

NOTES

1. H.E. Stephenson and C. McNaught, *The Story of Advertising in Canada* (Toronto: The Ryerson Press, 1940), pp. 20–24.

2. Ibid., pp. 28–32.

3. Ibid., pp. 99–109.

4. "The best of the big time spenders," *Marketing* (10 April 1989), pp. 1, 3.

5. "The Canadian Media Directors' Council Media Digest, 1989/90," *Marketing*, p. 10.

6. Robert G. Wyckham and Frank Anfield, "In-house Advertising Agencies—A Trend?," *The Canadian Marketer* (Fall 1974), pp. 25–27.

7. *Canadian Advertising Rates and Data* (monthly publication), section called "Advertising Agency Personnel."

8. "Canada's Top 100 Advertising Agencies," *Marketing* (11 December 1989), pp. 23–29.

9. Mark Smyka, "JWT Takes the Lead in Training Recruits," *Marketing* (13 December 1982), p. 39; Martin Mehr, "Low salaries and long hours result in a shortage of good media people," *Marketing* (11 December 1989), p. 59.

10. Madeleine Saint-Jacques and Bruce Mallen, "The French Market under the Microscope," *Marketing* (11 May 1981), p. 14.

11. Rob Wilson, "The Anglo Connection: Taking a Nibble from the 'Big Apple'," *Marketing* (13 December 1982), pp. 42–44.

12. John Oldland, "Twilight years of commission system," *Marketing* (26 January 1987), p. 29.

13. Michel Laroche and Louis Desjardins, "The Agency Compensation Decision in Canada: the Current View from Both Sides," Working paper, Concordia University (1990); "Agency Compensation," Association of Canadian Advertisers (February 1986), p. 5.

14. Ibid.

15. Ibid.

16. Ibid.

17. Ibid.

18. Roger G. Calantone and Donald H. Drury, "Advertising Agency Compensation: A Model for Incentive and Control," *Management Science* (July 1979), pp. 632–42.

19. Stephenson and McNaught, p. 264.

20. "CDNPA Adds 'AA' Agency Rating," *Marketing* (31 May 1982), p. 2.

21. Randy Scotland, "As global agencies get bigger by gobbling up each other, it could mean a big future for the little guy," *Marketing* (12 December 1988), pp. 12, 16, 36–38; Gail Chiasson, "Free trade and Quebec agencies: today Canada, tomorrow the world," *ibid*, pp. 12, 52–54.

CHAPTER

4 *Canadian Advertisers*

The first large-scale advertisers in Canada were patent medicine men who used direct mail to advertise their products. The patent medicine almanac contained jokes, stories, and general interest articles, and may be considered the forerunner of today's magazines.

These modest beginnings contrast sharply with the $9 billion that was spent on advertising in Canada in 1989. The variety of media available to advertisers includes 110 daily newspapers, over 530 consumer magazines, about 690 radio stations, and 120 commercial television stations.[1]

In contrast to the previous chapter which looked at the role and functions of advertising from the agency's perspective, this chapter will look at the advertiser's perspective. The role of advertising and the amount spent on advertising vary according to the nature of the industry and the organizations within one industry or one sector of economic activity.

WHO ARE THE MAIN CANADIAN ADVERTISERS?

Type of Product

Advertisers may be classified according to the type of product, the type of marketing organization, and the size and nature of the firm.

The nature of the advertising effort varies according to the type of product being advertised. The most important distinctions in product classifications are between business-to-business and consumer products and between durable and non-durable goods.

Business-to-Business vs. Consumer Advertising

This is a very important distinction since business-to-business advertising is becoming more sophisticated and better understood. In addition, since the costs of personal sales calls are becoming extremely expensive and out of reach for many small- to medium-size businesses, advertising has received more attention and resources.

Business-to-Business Advertising. This form of advertising is directed toward a professional who is responsible for evaluating competitive products for use by a firm. The copy in such advertisements is usually lengthy, and the approach tends to be rational and informative. The aim of business-to-business advertising is to create awareness of a company's name, to improve its image, and to open the door to sales representatives. Figure 4–1 shows an example of business-to-business advertising.

FIGURE 4–1

**An Example of
Industrial
Advertising**

In this advertisement
the judicious use of a
headline and an illus-
tration related to a
common industrial
problem leads into the
long copy explaining
the advertiser's
"early involvement"
approach.

Courtesy AMP of Canada
Ltd.

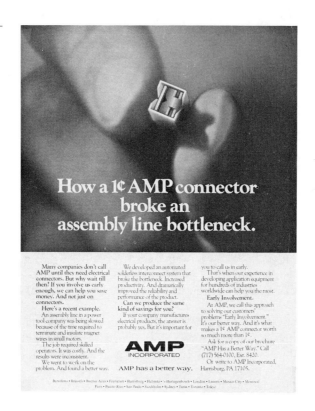

How a 1¢ AMP connector
broke an
assembly line bottleneck.

Major Types of Business-to-Business Advertising. Depending on the intended
audience there are three major types of business-to-business advertising:

1. *Industrial advertising* is directed toward a manufacturer who uses the firm's
   product in its operations. This could be raw materials, semi-finished products, finished products, services, or supplies. Advertising may be placed in
   industrial journals, use direct mail, or even mass media such as television
   or consumer magazines (e.g., copiers, courier services).
2. *Trade advertising* is directed toward the members of the firm's distribution
   channels (e.g., wholesalers, retailers, or agents). The objectives may be to
   inform them of special promotions, maintain loyalty, or create a positive
   image. Advertising may use direct mail or trade magazines such as the
   Canadian Jeweller or *Sales & Marketing Management in Canada.*
3. *Professional advertising* is directed toward decision makers or influencers in
   various professions, such as doctors (e.g., ethical drugs, or medical equipment), lawyers (e.g., computerized research tools), or teachers (e.g., new
   textbooks). Advertising may use direct mail or trade journals such as the
   Canadian Banker, the *Canadian Pharmaceutical Journal*, or the *Canadian Journal of Administrative Sciences.*

Objectives of Business-to-Business Advertising. Business-to-business advertising may be used with several possible objectives in mind:

First, business-to-business advertising helps a firm increase the awareness of its name among potential customers. Since the selection process for a complex product (for example, a new machine tool, or a new fleet of cars) may be involved, business-to-business advertising increases the chances of the advertiser being considered as a supplier.

Second, business-to-business advertising is often used to supply specific information about an advertiser's products or services to some of the key individuals involved in a firm's purchasing decision. The copy usually conveys technical information about the product. Thus, such advertising prepares a potential customer for a visit from the advertiser's sales representative. This is important, considering that in 1987, the average cost of *one* industrial sales call was estimated at $229.[2]

Third, business-to-business advertising is used to create a highly favourable image of a firm among its present customers, reinforcing their loyalty to the firm's products.

Finally, business-to-business advertising is used to complement the sales effort in other ways, such as to generate new leads, or to reach smaller accounts. The advertising budget is a relatively small portion of the total promotional budget in business-to-business marketing, but it is expected to grow in the 1990s.

Business-to-Business Media. Business-to-business customers are often concentrated and highly specialized. Thus, business-to-business advertisers have found using print media such as trade publications or direct mail the most efficient. Some newer forms of direct response advertising, such as telemarketing and electronic mail (e.g., using fax machines), have found useful applications in the business-to-business area.

Nevertheless, the media decision may be complicated by the customer's purchase decision process, as well as by the number of people involved in the customer's organization. Also, some firms have used some mass media successfully, such as consumer magazines or television (e.g., Canon copiers, Federal Express, or Bell Canada).

Consumer Advertising. In contrast to the previous form of advertising, consumer advertising is directed toward groups of individuals during their leisure time. Thus it must be more intrusive, entertaining, and rather short. The role of consumer advertising is to create awareness of a brand name, increase consumers' interest, and create desire for the product. Most large advertisers are in this category since advertising is their main promotional tool. Unlike business-to-business advertising, consumer advertising has to fully convince its audience that the firm's products or services are the best available. The reason for this is retail salespersons may not provide sales support for a particular item or there may be no salesperson, as in self-service operations.[3] However, consumer advertising may also be used by an advertiser's sales force to persuade the distributors to carry the firm's products.

FIGURE 4–2

An Example of Hard Goods Advertising

This advertisement for the new Kodak Carousel projectors makes good use of different types of lettering and composition to communicate how the new models can solve real consumer problems with other types of slide projectors.

Reprinted Courtesy Eastman Kodak Company

Durable Goods vs. Non-Durable Goods vs. Services

Another important distinction in product classifications is made among durable (or hard) goods, non-durable (packaged and soft) goods, and services.

Durable (or Hard) Goods. These are products that are rather expensive and require a long search process by the consumer. Examples are automobiles, appliances, stereo systems, and sophisticated cameras. Since consumers rely rather heavily on advertisements when considering whether to purchase durable goods, ads must be attractive, informative, and properly targeted. Figure 4–2 is a good example of this type of advertising.

The advertising campaign must also be co-ordinated with the personal selling effort, since the retail salesperson plays an important role in the customer's decision process. For example, in 1989, some of the top national advertisers were automobile manufacturers, who spent more than $194 million on national advertising alone. In addition, dealer associations spent another $44 million, and individual dealers had their own campaigns.[4] One objective of these campaigns was to draw traffic into the showrooms and induce customers to trade up. To accomplish this objective, the package offered by the advertiser had to

FIGURE 4–3

An Example of Packaged Goods Advertising

In this advertisement no copy is used. The message is communicated by a handsome picture of the package and the product.

Courtesy Parfumerie Versailles Limitée

be attractive to the target market and the salespeople had to be sensitive to consumers' needs.[5]

Non-durable goods. These are of two types, packaged goods and soft goods.

Packaged Goods. These are convenience items, frequently purchased, low-priced, and distributed widely. Packaged goods advertisers tend to be among the largest users of advertising, as evidenced by their presence among the top 50 national advertisers (Table 4–1). Since for packaged goods, a brand is promoted to the consumer solely through advertising, packaging, and sales promotion, advertising is critical to a brand's success. Figure 4–3 gives an example of packaged goods advertising.

Soft Goods. These are shopping good items, moderately priced, and distributed selectively. Thus, the retailer is important to the success of a brand, since consumers often need help when purchasing a product. Examples of soft goods are clothing, carpeting, and linens; such retailers as Sears, Eaton's and Canadian Tire are among the 1989 top 100 national advertisers.[6] In addition to using co-operative advertising, manufacturers advertise directly to consumers to reinforce an image of quality, as with designer clothes. Figure 4–4 illustrates soft goods advertising.

FIGURE 4–4

An Example of Soft Goods Advertising

This example of soft goods advertising uses a clever device to call readers' attention to the product and the signature.

Courtesy Pegabo Shoes Inc. Advertising Campaign of Pegabo Shoes, 1982

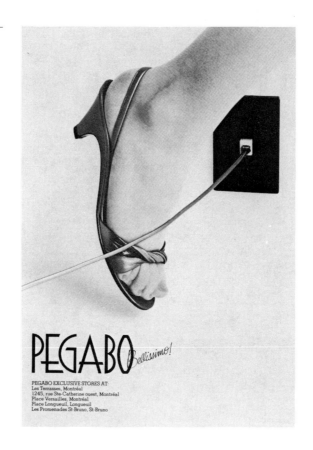

PEGABO *Bellissimo!*

PEGABO EXCLUSIVE STORES AT:
Les Terrasses, Montréal
1245, rue Ste-Catherine ouest, Montréal
Place Versailles, Montréal
Place Longueuil, Longueuil
Les Promenades St-Bruno, St-Bruno

TABLE 4–1 **TOP 50 NATIONAL ADVERTISERS, 1989**

Advertiser	Expenditures[1] ($000s)	Rank by Revenues[2]	Net Income[3] ($000s)	A/S Ratio (%)
1. Government of Canada	76 045	—	—	—
2. Procter & Gamble	61 377	P38	1 369 742	4.5
3. General Motors of Canada	56 735	P1	19 650 614	0.3
4. Unilever	46 977	P54	1 002 944	4.7
5. John Labatt Limited	44 706	26	4 856 800	0.9
6. Kraft General Foods Group	44 186	N/A	1 485 000	3.0
7. Cineplex Odeon Corporation	43 372	122	668 680	6.5
8. Paramount Communications	42 505	121*	870 000*	4.9
9. McDonald's Restaurants of Canada	34 849	89*	1 256 000*	2.8
10. RJR	33 484	P177	291 584	11.5
11. Ontario Government	30 993	—	—	—
12. Molson Breweries of Canada	28 615	N/A	N/A	N/A
13. Chrysler Canada	28 338	P2	8 237 600	0.3

TABLE 4–1 **TOP 50 NATIONAL ADVERTISERS, 1989** (continued)

Advertiser	Expenditures[1] ($000s)	Rank by Revenues[2]	Net Income[3] ($000s)	A/S Ratio (%)
14. BCE	27 104	1	17 084 000	0.2
15. The Molson Companies	26 790	69	2 603 841	1.0
16. The Thomson Group	26 454	8	5 240 000	0.5
17. Imperial Oil	26 362	10	10 086 000	0.3
18. Kellogg Canada	25 411	P194	288 429	8.8
19. PepsiCo	25 174	N/A	N/A	N/A
20. Coca-Cola	24 843	P188	303 926	8.2
21. PWA Corporation	24 732	50	2 736 472	0.9
22. Sears Canada	22 001	30	4 562 300	0.5
23. Ford Motor of Canada	21 589	2	15 394 500	0.1
24. Quebec Government	21 342	—	—	—
25. Imasco Holdings Canada	20 224	31	4 387 800	0.5
26. Warner-Lambert Canada	20 123	N/A	N/A	N/A
27. Kodak Canada	18 542	N/A	N/A	N/A
28. Toyota Canada	18 515	P33	1 498 035	1.2
29. Canadian Tire Corporation	18 147	46	2 977 424	0.6
30. American Home Products	18 147	N/A	N/A	N/A
31. Nissan Automobiles of Canada	18 116	P85	634 685	2.9
32. Nestlé Enterprises	17 312	P56	960 000	1.8
33. General Motors Dealers Association	16 570	N/A	N/A	N/A
34. George Weston	16 570	9	10 459 000	0.2
35. Honda Canada	16 009	P23	2 164 844	0.7
36. Shell Canada	15 397	25	4 917 000	0.3
37. Johnson & Johnson	15 103	P269	190 633	7.9
38. Dairy Bureau of Canada	13 087	—	—	—
39. General Mills Canada	12 988	P170	330 536	3.9
40. Nutri/System	12 960	N/A	N/A	N/A
41. Quaker Oats of Canada	12 515	P166	342 371	3.7
42. Government of British Columbia	12 451	—	—	—
43. Effem Foods	12 166	N/A	N/A	N/A
44. Ford Mercury Dealers Association	12 016	N/A	N/A	N/A
45. Provigo	11 803	14	7 389 800	0.2
46. Hyundai Auto Canada	11 318	P246	210 403	5.4
47. Trilon Financial Corporation	11 262	22	5 060 000	0.2
48. Groupe Desjardins	11 110	194	388 627	2.9
49. Gillette Canada	10 986	N/A	N/A	N/A
50. Brick Warehouse	10 723	N/A	437 900 *	2.4

* These figures are for 1988 only.

[1] These expenditures are for space and time only in daily newspapers, print supplements, magazines, billboards, television, and radio. They do not include production expenditures.

[2] Rankings with a P are for private companies. Those without are for companies listed on Canadian stock exchanges.

[3] Sales or revenue figures include services and rental revenues, but exclude investment income. Net income for banks is before extraordinary items.

Sources: "Ad cutback not what it seems," *Marketing* (March 26, 1990), p. 2; *The Financial Post* (Summer 1989); "The top 1000 companies," *The Globe and Mail Report on Business Magazine* (June 1990), pp. 73–200.

FIGURE 4–5

*An Example of
Service Advertising*

This advertisement for
Iberia uses several
devices to reinforce an
image of quality. The
"I" shape of the layout,
the use of white space,
the integration of the
headline and illustra-
tion, and the composi-
tion of the signature
make the advertise-
ment visually
interesting.

Courtesy Iberia Airlines of
Spain

Services. Services are more difficult to advertise than products, since they are intangible, and thus cannot be shown.[7] However, there is much opportunity for creativity in promotional activities, for example, painting airplanes, or decorating banks or hotel lobbies. Hotels often provide "extras," such as free drinks or a complimentary towel. Figure 4–5 is an example of service advertising.

Objectives of Service Advertising. Advertising may be used by the service provider for the following objectives:

- To provide information on the service's benefits, availability, location, and price. Since the service is intangible, only the derived benefits may be stressed in the message. Testimonials may be used to add credibility to the message and to personalize the service.
- To introduce new services, or to launch special consumer promotions, for example a free glass for every gasoline purchase of more than 20 litres.
- To improve or maintain the reputation of the service provider, which has important implications for the perceived quality of the service. This can

be accomplished by using well-known personalities (e.g., Peter Ustinov for American Express), or impressive tangible cues (e.g., a famous building, rock, or bull).

- To lower the perceived risk of purchasing the service, which may be high since the service cannot be shown (e.g., a surgery).
- To motivate employees, and to influence them in improving their performance of the service. This is a critical part of any service since the employee is often the one who produces and delivers the service, and that performance will affect the perception of the quality of the service. This is a critical factor in the tourism industry, for example, where an employee's lack of courtesy may generate negative word of mouth.

In addition to advertising, publicity and sales promotion are also used to promote services. Techniques of sales promotion may be used to smooth out demand to off-peak time, or to introduce a new service. For example, coupons may be distributed by a restaurant to increase demand during the early evening (5:00 PM to 6:30 PM), or late evening (11:30 PM to 1:30 AM), during weekdays, or to encourage customers to try a new restaurant. A tanning salon may use sampling techniques and offer a free half-hour of tanning to new potential clients; a hotel may offer a free towel as a premium to encourage patronage. The airlines' frequent-flyer-programmes or Zellers' Club Z are modern versions of the old trading stamp technique. Finally, contests and sweepstakes have been used successfully to launch a new branch of a bank or a trust company, or to attract new clients.

Major Service Advertisers.   Services are also well represented in the 1989 top 100 national advertisers, particularly governments, entertainment companies, and banks. Since they have adopted the marketing concept, banks have been advertising heavily to inform their target markets about their new or improved services.[8] Advertising is also used to promote hotels, car rental companies, and airlines.

Types of Marketing Organizations

Advertisers may be either *producers* of products or services or they may be *intermediaries* between producers and customers. The nature and extent of the advertising effort depends largely on the location of the target market.

Producers

Most major manufacturers of goods and services advertise on a national or regional basis, using mass media to reach a large number of people with one campaign. Some campaigns may have very large budgets, and it may be critical for an advertiser to efficiently spend that budget. Thus they must hire an advertising agency with a proven track record.

Producers may also advertise to impress the members of the distribution channels, and gain their co-operation in properly distributing and promoting their products.

Retailers

Intermediaries and in particular retailers tend to advertise on a local basis and to run a series of small campaigns.[9]

Objectives of Retail Advertising. A retailer's objective is to offer selected merchandise for sale based on the target market's needs. Over the long run, the retailer's advertising should be designed to strengthen the retailer's image as a reliable buying agent for the consumer. More specifically, retail advertising may pursue the following objectives:

- Clearly define or improve the image of the retailer or some particular aspect of the retailer or its stores.
- Obtain customer acceptance of a specific line or group of lines within a merchandise category.
- Develop or increase customers' store loyalty.
- Increase the frequency of patronage by the current retail customers.
- Attract new customers in order to increase store traffic.
- Announce special events to take place in the store within a specific time period (for example, holiday specials such as Halloween, Easter, or Mother's Day).
- Announce specific sales or clearances to take place in the store within a specific time period. These allow the retailer to increase inventory turnover and sell off old inventory, for example during the low season, as in February.

Planning the Retail Campaign. Since retailers are not entitled to commissions from the media and have very tight schedules, the planning of the campaign tends to be done by the firm's advertising department with the assistance of manufacturers, other retailers, and the media.

Role of Manufacturers. Manufacturers provide retailers with *matrices* and *co-operative advertising* funds. Matrices are papier maché moulds of the manufacturer's product or package designs, and they are used by newspapers in making stereotypes to be included in the retailer's advertisement. In *co-operative advertising*, the manufacturer provides the retailer with an advertising allowance that usually covers half of the costs of advertising the brand in the retailer's advertising program. Since local advertising is cheaper than national advertising, both parties benefit from this type of arrangement.

Co-operative Efforts by Retailers. Retailers in the same product category, such as hardware stores or realtors, may join forces in some form of co-operative advertising. This allows a bigger budget, the use of professional services, access to mass media, and extension of the retailer's audiences.

Role of Media. Most media have in-house personnel to assist retailers in developing their creative approach and their media schedules. These copy service departments may also call on outside freelance artists, stock shops that sell photographs to be used in the layout of the retailer's advertisement, or advertising service companies that sell prepackaged advertisements, called "idea service." The media provide these services free of charge to the retailer to make it easier for small retailers to advertise in their media.

Role of Advertising Agencies. In planning their advertising activities, some retailers may use the services of an advertising agency. The main role of the agency is to develop an *image campaign* for the retailer. In turn, the retailer would use the agency's work to design in-house campaigns based on *event advertising*, which involves special sales and promotions that may be timed to coincide with holidays and seasons.

In addition, retail advertising is affected strongly by seasonal factors or broad market trends and is designed to respond quickly to change. The retailer is mostly interested in building traffic and thus in maximizing the number of people reached by the advertisement. Consequently, repetition is not important. The advertisement has a short-term effect (in terms of the event advertised), and in-store promotions should be co-ordinated with the advertising campaign to maximize its effect.

The Size and Nature of the Advertiser

The size of a company's sales as well as the industry in which it operates may influence the amount of advertising it does. A distinction can be made between large and small businesses in order to explain the influence of company size on the advertising effort.[10]

Large Advertisers

Large advertisers are generally national advertisers. National advertisers use mass media to advertise their products or services throughout Canada. Overall, total advertising spending reached the $9 billion mark for the first time in 1989, which is almost double the total for 1982. Table 4–1 shows that the largest national advertiser in 1989 was the Government of Canada, with expenditures of $76 million. The largest private advertiser was Procter & Gamble, which spent $61 million. Among the 100 largest advertisers are the following categories:

- Governments: Canada, Ontario, Quebec, British Columbia, Alberta
- breweries and distillers: Labatt, Molson, Seagram
- cigarette manufacturers: RJR, Rothmans/Benson & Hedges
- car manufacturers: GM, Ford, Chrysler, Toyota, Nissan
- banks and other financial institutions: Trilon, Groupe Desjardins, Royal Bank, American Express
- retailers: McDonald's, Sears, Canadian Tire, Eaton's, Brick Warehouse
- packaged-goods manufacturers: Procter & Gamble, Kraft General Foods Group, Johnson & Johnson, General Mills, Pepsico, Coca-Cola
- oil companies: Imperial Oil, Shell Canada
- conglomerates: Gulf & Western, Unilever, Imasco
- entertainment companies: Cineplex Odeon, Paramount, Walt Disney

In addition, there are wide variations in advertising efforts compared to a company's sales. The advertising to sales ratio (A/S) in Table 4–1 has been calculated by using the 1989 advertiser's sales or net income. A comparison of these ratios across the categories of advertisers indicates that the nature of the industry influences advertising efforts. For example, car manufacturers, large department stores, financial institutions, and oil companies spend a fraction of one percent on advertising, while cigarette manufacturers and packaged goods companies spend a much higher proportion of their sales, such as 3 percent for Kraft General Foods Group and 8.8 percent for Kellogg. In the latter group, advertising is more important for promoting products or services than for the first group, where personal selling has a dominant role or where distribution is more important than promotion.

Small Advertisers

By contrast with large advertisers who may use a variety of mass media to reach a national audience with a high level of repetition, small advertisers may use only one medium and concentrate on exposure rather than on repetition. Small advertisers fall into several categories or industries. Retailers and business-to-business firms have been discussed; this section concentrates on other types of small advertisers.

Because their budgets are more limited, small advertisers must be resourceful. They must look for low-cost special space units or time periods. Since they are not able to use large advertisements or long commercials, the creative approach must attract attention, especially if position in the medium cannot be controlled. In addition, small advertisers often cannot afford to advertise nationally, so they must carefully select the regions in which to concentrate their advertising effort. In this case, advertising may be a part of a phased penetration on a region-by-region basis.

Many small advertisers cannot afford to hire an advertising agency, because agencies are often reluctant to take these advertisers' accounts on a commission basis and they request additional fees or a guaranteed revenue to cover costs. Their limited budgets also prevent small advertisers from receiving from agency personnel the attention given to large advertisers. Sometimes an advertising agency will take on a promising client in the hope that today's small account may be tomorrow's large account. Otherwise, it is better for small advertisers to have a consistent planning approach with well-defined basic marketing objectives and strategies, and then to use the services of outside suppliers. Small advertisers who cannot afford an advertising manager may use the services of an outside consultant who acts as a part-time advertising manager.

FACTORS INFLUENCING THE ORGANIZATION OF THE ADVERTISING FUNCTION

Since advertising must be co-ordinated with other marketing functions and because it receives public attention, it is conducted through a variety of organizational structures at three levels: the position of the advertising function in the overall organization, the responsibilities of the advertising manager, and the structure of the advertising department. The actual structure may depend on many other factors, such as the size of the company, the nature of the industry, and top management philosophy. The principle behind these structures is described below.

Position of the Advertising Function in a Firm's Overall Structure

As mentioned previously, it is desirable to have the advertising manager report directly to the marketing manager, since the latter is responsible for the marketing plan and is trained to evaluate the quality of the advertising effort. This reporting arrangement is particularly important in the case of packaged goods manufacturers, for whom the advertising effort is the most important promotional ingredient.[11]

Product or Brand Manager

In many large packaged goods companies with numerous brands, the advertising function is the responsibility of *product* or *brand managers*. A product or brand manager is responsible for planning, executing, and controlling the advertising campaign for one or several brands and for co-ordinating the advertising effort with the outside agency and the firm's in-house marketing specialist.

Advertising Department

In some companies, a separate advertising department is added to the brand management structure in order to assist and advise the product managers. The advertising department also may co-ordinate the brand managers' and their agencies' media buying in order to obtain the greatest media discount. This function may be the responsibility of one selected advertising agency, called the *agency of record* (see Chapter 3).

Under the Sales Manager

Some companies place the advertising function under the responsibility of the sales or marketing services manager, because the main promotional tool is personal selling, and advertising is used to complement this effort by creating awareness of the company name, generating inquiries, or opening doors for the sales force.

Under the President or CEO

Corporate advertising may be used to enhance a company's image among selected target groups, e.g., businesspersons, politicians, employees, investors, or the public. With corporate advertising, the advertising manager reports directly to the company's president or chief executive officer. An example of corporate advertising is presented in Figure 4–6.

Level of Centralization

With a centralized advertising function, scale economies may be realized, particularly in media buying. The centralized department usually reports to the president and may be staffed with specialists in research, public relations, and merchandising. It can often control the total advertising effort better. Centralizing the co-ordination of advertising campaigns for dissimilar products may, however, create major planning problems.

FIGURE 4–6

An Example of Corporate Advertising

In this advertisement, the company attempts to convey how the use of aluminum is enhancing the well-being of countless individuals, thus its aim is to improve the public's attitude toward the company.

Courtesy Alcan Aluminum Limited

AFRICAN SAFARI.   ALCAN ALUMINUM.

Alcan is a Canadian company, yet when photographers go to Africa to shoot big game, most use Nikon, Canon, Minolta and Konica cameras made with precision tooled aluminum from our Japanese partners.

Aluminum is being used increasingly in the precise engineering and manufacture of camera bodies, lenses, meters and tripods. Indeed, it is replacing heavier metals in practically every component of advanced professional photo equipment.

Alcan aluminum has been at home in the wilds of Africa and around the world for decades in many types of 4WD vehicles as well, including the venerable Land Rover and its swank sister, the Range Rover.

In fact, aluminum gear has become the new norm on all kinds of expeditions, from mountaineering, to undersea, to NASA space exploration.

In photography, exploration, automotive, aerospace, marine, research, recycling and corporate citizenship, Alcan is aluminum to the world.

ALCAN IS ALUMINUM

With a decentralized advertising function, each operating division has its own advertising department. Advantages of this structure are that the department can focus on its specific needs and is better able to make its objectives consistent with other marketing decisions for a product. Disadvantages are the loss of scale economies in media buying and a possible lack of support from specialists.

To obtain the advantages of both types of structure, some companies adopt a mixed structure. A large firm with decentralized advertising departments may also set up a centralized advertising department in order to take advantage of scale economies in media buying and to co-ordinate advertising planning and execution.

Responsibilities of the Advertising Manager

The advertising manager's major responsibilities are analyzing, planning, executing, and controlling the advertising campaign. These functions involve co-ordination with the advertising agency, marketing specialists, and top management.

Analysis

The advertising manager must have all pertinent information on the product and the trade. The manager must also communicate to the advertising agency the company's business needs and corporate objectives.

Planning

Together with the agency's account service group, the advertising manager develops the advertising plan, which is based on the marketing plan's objectives and strategy. This process includes preliminary approval of the creative and media recommendations and the advertising budget, before these matters are presented to top management for final approval.

Execution

The advertising manager monitors the execution of the approved advertising plan and co-ordinates the execution with the department's other functions and with the activities of the firm's marketing specialists.

Control

The advertising manager also evaluates the campaign's effectiveness in terms of its stated objectives. In doing so, the manager constantly evaluates the agency's performance and reports the findings to top management. If the agency's performance is considered unsatisfactory, it is the manager's responsibility to take appropriate action with the account service group. Firing the agency should be a decision made when everything else has failed, since the search and breaking-in period for a new agency can take up to twelve months, during which time the company can lose momentum and continuity in its advertising.

Structure of the Advertising Department

Companies with a large marketing department may have one of the following five basic structures for the advertising department:

1. *According to advertising functions.* With this type of structure, individual employees are responsible for the various advertising functions. This structure is justified if the advertising department actually handles some of these functions or has to co-ordinate them among several agencies. An in-house advertising agency is a department with this type of structure.
2. *According to media types.* A firm may have different specialists whose job is to co-ordinate the various media budgets in order to take advantage of volume discounts.
3. *According to product lines or brands.* Each product or brand manager is in effect an advertising manager. Co-ordination may be carried out by an advertising director with or without additional staff members.
4. *According to customer types.* The advertising effort may be given to different specialists. For example, one manager may be responsible for business-to-business advertising, while another may handle consumer advertising.

5. *According to geographical or international markets.* The advertising effort may be decentralized, with responsibilities divided among divisional advertising managers. This structure is particularly important for international markets, where cultural and market-related factors usually require a different form of advertising. In some cases, control and/or co-ordination may be carried out by a centralized advertising department servicing all divisional departments.

SELECTING AN ADVERTISING AGENCY

A thorough analysis of advertising's role within a firm's marketing effort can help the marketing manager decide whether an advertising agency is necessary, and if one is, what kind of services are needed and what kind of agency best suits the firm's needs.

Is An Advertising Agency Necessary?

In evaluating whether an advertising agency is necessary, the advertiser must have a thorough understanding of the role, functions, and compensation methods of advertising agencies.

Advantages of Using an Advertising Agency

The advantages of using an advertising agency are:

- Standard services are generally provided to the advertiser without charge, since agencies are compensated by the commission they receive from the media.
- Agencies often have some of the best resources and professionals, and they spread their costs over several accounts.
- Agencies can provide marketing assistance to small- or medium-sized firms, which often do not have a marketing department. They also provide advertisers with an objective point of view and experience in specific industries.
- Agencies have considerable experience in all phases of campaign planning.

Thus, whether an advertiser is small or large, the services of an advertising agency are recommended unless the advertiser is able to handle all phases of campaign planning at a lower cost. For the advertiser who does not qualify for retail rates and who has a medium-size advertising budget, it is often more expensive to handle the advertising internally than through an advertising agency.

Disadvantages of Using an Advertising Agency

The disadvantages of using an advertising agency are:

- Local advertising is non-commissionable, thus agency services have to be compensated by the advertiser, and these tend to be expensive for small- or medium-size local businesses.
- Agencies are generally not organized to provide services on very short notice. For example, retail campaigns are often planned to respond to competitive

moves or to take advantage of special environmental conditions, so it may be more efficient to handle the advertising internally.

- The main strength of advertising agencies is in advertising requiring broadcast media or special colour printing. Many small- or medium-size advertisers make heavy use of newspaper advertising, which is relatively simple to undertake in-house.

Thus, the services of an advertising agency are generally not recommended when timing is important, the advertiser qualifies for retail rates, and the types of services needed can be easily obtained from outside suppliers or from the media. For some retailers or advertisers with small budgets, it may be more economical to handle the advertising function internally than through an advertising agency.

Choosing the Services Needed from an Advertising Agency

The advertising manager should state clearly and in writing the kind of services the firm needs most and should evaluate how the agency can meet the firm's needs.

Agency Business Philosophy

The advertising manager must ensure that the agency's business philosophy and attitudes toward advertising and marketing are compatible with those of the firm. This factor is important because it permeates all exchanges between the two groups and affects the quality of their relationship.

Types of Services Needed

The advertising manager must also make decisions in the following areas:

Account Services. The following questions are important to raise.

- How much marketing input is needed?
- What type of marketing counsel is required?

Creative Services. Similarly, one must ask:

- What are the creative styles of the agency's personnel?
- What is their past experience with similar products?
- What is their success record? Can it be documented?

Media Services. In terms of media selection, it is important to find out:

- What is the ability, background, and level of experience of the media personnel?
- Do they have any clout with the media?

Other Marketing Services. In situations where these are needed, one must ask:

- Does the agency provide merchandising, sales promotion, research, and publicity/public relations services?

Other Selection Criteria

Additional criteria used to select an advertising agency are as follows:

Size of the Agency in Relation to the Size of the Account

This criterion relates to the attention the agency can be expected to give to the account. A medium-size advertiser may get more attention from a small agency than from a large one, where it would be competing with other large accounts.

Method of Compensation

The advertiser evaluates the compensation system required by the agency in relation to the services to be provided.

Location of the Agency

This is an important criterion for firms operating in several markets and particularly in international markets, where they may choose among agencies with foreign branches. Within Canada, most large agencies have offices in Toronto and Montreal as well as other major metropolitan areas.

Conclusion on Agency Selection

In conclusion, selecting an advertising agency is an important task for the advertising manager and a critical decision for the firm. Some firms and organizations consider the selection of an advertising agency so important that they use the services of a consultant, who acts as an intermediary between the two groups.[12]

Advertisers may find it helpful to consult an Institute of Canadian Advertising publication entitled *How to Select an Advertising Agency*, which provides a set of guidelines and recommendations as well as a sample questionnaire (Figure 4–7).

ADVERTISING NEEDS AND PROBLEMS IN OTHER AREAS

Most principles developed in this book are general in nature. However, different areas may have specific problems and require more specialized advertising objectives and strategies. Three such areas are institutional, non-profit, and multicultural advertising. International advertising will be covered in detail in Chapter 16.

Institutional Advertising

Institutional advertising is undertaken by either a profit or a non-profit organization. Its purpose is to change an organization's image. There are three main types of institutional advertising:

The Organization as a Good Corporate Citizen

This kind of advertising aims to enhance an organization's reputation or image and is handled in various ways. For example, the campaign may convey the impression that the organization is concerned about the well-being of consumers or the public (see Figure 4–6). Another example of this type of advertising is sponsorship of a cultural event or a sports event.

HOW TO SELECT
AN ADVERTISING AGENCY

Introduction.

Selecting a new advertising agency is a major decision for any company. The choice of the right agency can have a significant effect on the company's long term sales and profit performance. The new agency will not only be responsible for making significant purchases on behalf of the company but also, and more importantly, for the care and maintenance of the company's most important asset: — its reputation with the consumer.

Selecting a new agency is also a bewildering decision. Very few marketing executives, even senior ones, have had much experience in selecting agencies. Despite the industry's reputation, account shifts are not common. Probably fewer than 10% of all Canadian accounts shift in a year. Thus many advertisers simply do not know how to go about an agency search, because it has been so many years since their company has done one.

There is no universally accepted approach to the best way to select an agency. How do I even know if I need a new agency? How do I screen the vast array of alternatives? What is the value of a screening questionnaire? What are the best questions to ask? How many agencies should I look at? How do I evaluate them? And many more.

Since the Institute of Canadian Advertising is the national association of advertising agencies, we thought it appropriate to produce a guide to help answer these questions. A committee of senior agency people, all of whom have been involved in new business efforts, went through a great deal of material that has been published on the subject. They sifted out what they thought was most relevant, added some of their own ideas, and this outline is the result.

We hope that this booklet will take some of the mystery out of selecting an agency. How to do it effectively and efficiently. And most importantly, to conduct your search in a professional way that will bring credit to you and your company from all the agencies you contact during the search process, even the ones that are unsuccessful candidates.

Defining your needs.

Selection of an advertising agency is perhaps best approached in the same manner in which a new staff member is employed. Indeed, when an advertising agency is hired, the advertiser has in reality employed a group of individuals to work with him.

Just as a precise job description is a sound basis for a successful employee acquisition, the same ground work is essential to the advertising agency selection process.

A specific definition of needs (i.e. job description) is essential to enable the advertisers to more easily sort through the wide variety of services offered by agencies. It helps each of the agencies under consideration to respond more precisely to the advertiser's requirements.

Most advertising agencies have a variety of talent available. The more clearly an agency can understand the advertiser's expectations, the better able it is to select the most appropriate people from its staff to work with him.

The consulting firm of Booz, Allen & Hamilton, in its report entitled "Management and Advertising Problems" classified advertisers into five broad categories which illustrate the range of services that might be required from an advertising agency.

1. Companies where advertising is of limited importance. These companies are reasonably self-sufficient in other key marketing areas, such as marketing research, new product planning and sales promotion. Examples might be industrial companies or insurance companies. Because of the specialized technical nature of these companies, agencies can make only a limited contribution. All that companies in this first category want from their agencies, therefore, is *advertising help* — copy and media.

2. Companies where advertising is of limited importance, but which are not self-sufficient in some other key marketing areas. Examples might be an industrial company that needs agency help in developing trade exhibits and promotional material, or some consumer packaged goods companies that have decided to do part of their marketing work internally. Companies in this second category, therefore, want *advertising help plus certain selected services* (such as market research and sales promotion).

3. Companies where advertising is important and which have fully developed capabilities in all key marketing areas. Examples might be a large manufacturer of consumer durable goods or a large industrial company that wants to advertise past its customers to the ultimate consumer. Companies in this third category want not only advertising help, but objective and sound *marketing counsel* of the broadest sort.

4. Companies where advertising is of critical importance and which have fully developed capabilities in key marketing areas. Large, multi-agency consumer packaged goods companies frequently fall into this category. These companies want agencies that can offer in-depth, specialized talents and can share responsibility with the company for total marketing results — a *full marketing partnership*, in other words.

FIGURE 4–7
Continued

5. Companies where advertising is critically important, but which do not have fully developed capabilities in other key marketing areas. Many smaller consumer goods fall into this category. Companies in this fifth category look to their agencies for *marketing leadership*.

This review clearly indicates that the kinds of service needed by an advertiser can vary widely. It also explains why an advertiser must define these needs very clearly before the agency selection process is begun.

A comprehensive written check list of requirements which takes into account both present and possible future needs is essential to the selection process. It will help the advertiser sort through any broad claims by advertising agencies that they "do everything". Just as important, it helps prevent vulnerability to an emotional appeal on a personality basis. Having matched services from competing agencies against the list of requirements in an unemotional way, the advertiser can then weigh in the "chemistry" aspect, i.e. "would I enjoy working with these people?"

Here's a list of needs you might consider:

Development of	Creative Work on
— Marketing Plans	— Media Advertising
— Product Strategies	— Brochures, Catalogues
— New Products	— Point of Sale
— Advertising Strategies	— Packaging
Marketing Counsel on	Distribution Analysis
— Product Mix	Marketing Research
— Pricing	Media
— Sales Targets	— Planning
	— Buying
	Public Relations

If you already have an agency.

If you already have an agency, before you search for another you should be very sure that a change is what you really want. You have invested a great deal of time and money in your agency, and in turn, they have learned a great deal about your business, about your people, and about the way you like to work. Before dissolving the relationship then, you should sit down with your agency to see if they can modify their operation to suit you. Perhaps a change of personnel on your account is indicated, or there may be other steps that will result in the very improvement you hope to find in a new agency (but always risk failing to find). Thus the list of needs you have prepared to help define your agency search should be analyzed in order to set down where your current agency is not performing. Then discuss the list with your agency. Ask your agency if it is a fair list. Does it match their understanding? Why have the shortfalls occurred?

You are urged to proceed very carefully through these steps. Changing an agency is a difficult, time consuming and expensive process. The expense is not just involved in the time demands and costs your management team will incur, but in the disruption of your advertising and other parts of your marketing mix, both during the search period and while your new agency is "getting up to speed" in your business.

If you have satisfied yourself that you have been fair with your agency, given them ample time to correct their shortcomings, and that there is no way to make a new beginning with your current relationship, then you should proceed with a search for a new agency. Only you and your executives can determine whether your present agency will stay on the "short list". If you feel that they have already been given every chance, perhaps it would be fairest to be frank, and have a mutually-agreed termination.

If you are choosing an agency for the first time.

If this is your first agency search, you should still go through the analysis of services you are searching for. This will help define the kind of agency you need, how involved in your business it will be, and therefore, in the end, how much you should be prepared to pay for its services.

Involvement of key executives in the entire process.

Your firm must be prepared to devote a substantial amount of time of key executives to the entire process. The selection of an advertising agency should be like selecting a new partner in your business. In order to make the partnership a real success, each executive must feel comfortable with the selection, not only in order to have confidence in the advice the agency will give, but also to feel comfortable in sharing the confidential information the agency must have to do its complete job.

Getting a "feel" of the market.

Ultimately, you will probably want to send a questionnaire to a list of 10 to 15 agencies that seem to fit roughly into the requirements you have determined. This will help you prepare your "short list" of 3 to 5 from whom you will elicit presentations.

If you have no "feel" for the market, you should go through several steps to develop ideas to help you develop this first list. Here are some suggestions:

Ask ICA for a list of its members, who together account for about 85% of the advertising agency business done in Canada. Membership in ICA is a sign that an agency has joined with its colleagues in supporting the building of a more professional, and more effective industry. ICA will also be able to supply some details of size and type of operation for those of its members who submit such data to it.

Examine the agency listings in Canadian Advertising Rates and Data, a Maclean-Hunter publication most likely in your library. It lists most of the senior personnel of each agency. Since agencies usually employ between 3 and 5 persons per million dollars of billing, this is a good way to get an idea of relative sizes.

Read the National List, an annual publication of Maclean-Hunter that sets forth the accounts that each agency has. Here you will be able to exclude agencies on the basis that they already have accounts that conflict with yours.

Talk to people in other companies to get their help in preparing a list. You will most often find that people whom you scarcely know are very glad to be of help.

Visit a few agencies of different sizes. You will be welcomed and this may help you more than any other way of getting a feel of the market.

The questionnaire.

A recommended questionnaire is provided at the end of this booklet. It elicits all of the information you should need in order to narrow the replies down to a short list. Agencies don't

FIGURE 4–7
Continued

mind answering questions that require factual answers. Some advertisers seem to like to add questions that require philosophical dissertations. Try to avoid this, because most replies will be so general (because the respondent won't know what you are looking for, and tries to give a bland answer to avoid being washed out at this point) they will not be helpful to you. The time to search for answers to your deeper questions is during the presentation stage.

Set a reasonable time, at least 3 to 4 weeks for receipt of replies.

If you stick to the questions recommended in the questionnaire, agencies can respond quickly and factually and allow you to get on with the really important part of the work, listening to the presentations of the agencies who have made it to the short list.

Your agency briefing document.

Your questionnaire will be most helpful to you if you send out a detailed briefing document with it. It will help the respondent agencies better determine whether they can serve you, and also give them common information on which to base their replies.

Your briefing document should describe your company, product lines and involvement with other agencies, as well as provide as much history on the product or service category in question as you can release. It is at this point that your own work, or evaluating what type of agency services you require, will be most valuable.

Evaluating the replies.

Some of your questionnaires will come back with more material than you asked for. You may even find content that leads you to expand your "needs" list.

Remember that some agencies may have more insight into your product or service because of past associations, but that does not mean that they can serve you better. You should therefore, consider amending your briefing document in order to give all the "first wave" agencies a chance to reply before proceeding with the next step.

When all the replies are in, you are ready to proceed to the next step — preparing your short list. Review the replies against the "needs" that you set forth for yourself at the beginning of the process, and aim to get down to a list of not more than 3 or 4 agencies.

We recommend that you judge any contacts you get from agencies who were not on your list against these same criteria. As word gets out that you're looking, you will be contacted, and these contacts can lead to an enormous time investment on your part if they are not carefully controlled.

Some thoughts on agency presentations.

Your final agency selection will likely be based on presentations made by each of the contenders on your short list.

This means that you will be depending on about a two hour presentation from each agency to guide you to the right choice. It is, therefore, extremely important that the presentations be meaningful to your business, and that they permit an honest comparison among the agencies.

To achieve these objectives, we recommend that you supply an identical presentation outline to each of the prospects. The outline should include the criteria that you feel

are essential. For example, if research is an important subject to you, then you want to be sure that each agency fully discusses their research capabilities.

The standard outline is not intended to restrict individual presentations. Beyond the areas you want covered, there should be ample scope for the agency to discuss its particular strengths, and other factors they feel will be of interest to you.

There are normally 3 types or levels of agency new business presentations:

1. Capabilities — limited to the agency's experience, service facilities, and people.

2. Strategic — thoughts on your company's marketing situation and strategy alternatives.

3. Creative Project — development of actual advertising creative, in response to objectives supplied by you; may also include media planning recommendations.

Usually, Levels 1 and 2 will provide sufficient information on which to base an agency selection decision. Level 3 requires extensive briefing of the agencies, and considerable time and effort. You should also be prepared to pay a reasonable amount of money for this degree of presentation. Keep in mind that a reliable assessment of an agency's strategic thinking and creative ability can be made on the strength of the work they have done for other clients.

Perhaps the single most important aspect of the presentation is your opportunity to meet the people who will work on your account. You should insist on having in the presentation the key account service, creative and media people who will form your team. They should each take an active part, so that you can judge their ability and compatibility to your business and people. Remember that personal chemistry is a very valid criterion for selection.

Finally, ask to have the presentations at the agencies' offices. This will ensure that you are not interrupted and it will give you a good opportunity to size up each agency in its own environment. In fact, you may want to visit the office, and/or have lunch with some of the people in each agency before making up your mind.

It is also at this point that you "get into people's heads" before making up your mind. As well you can resolve any unclear issues such as staffing, compensation, new personnel and so on.

Making the decision.

Make the decision and let everyone know right away. This is a business decision and prolonged speculation will only affect the attitude with which the new agency enters the partnership.

Welcome your new agency as a partner in your business. Agency people respond to contact. A note of optimism and high expectations can prove to be excellent motivation.

An agency agreement.

ICA recommends that you make a formal agreement with your new agency. It is at this point that many future misunderstandings can be avoided if each party sets down those business details that either have been or should be decided. Matters such as method of compensation, how commissions and trade discounts are to be handled, details of billing and payment should be covered. If compensation is by a commission arrangement, a detailed list of services to be expected as part of the arrangement should be outlined.

FIGURE 4–7

Continued

Details of how new product assignments or other projects which may come up from time to time can simply be covered under a "fee to be negotiated" category.

Remember that the best time to work out all of the details of the business arrangement is at the beginning of the relationship. ICA can supply an agreement format, if you're interested.

Letting the trade press know.

The trade press loves to know when an advertiser is beginning to look around. Often an advertiser, wanting not to disrupt the relationship with his current agency, will try to quietly look around to see if a new relationship should be investigated. In spite of the best efforts to keep the secret, the trade press often finds out, and the current agency finds out it's in trouble by reading the story.

The result of these leaks most often is an agreement to part when usually the advertiser had not formed that intention.

The best solution, then, if you've decided that you are unhappy enough to begin to look around, is to level with your agency. Discuss the reasons for your dissatisfaction as set forth in the section "If you already have an agency". It is at this time that you may decide that there is no point in continuing your relationship. If so, give the agency a chance to resign gracefully. Whether you decide to part company or keep your current agency in the running, work out a mutually satisfactory statement for the press.

After you've completed your search, there are again some ideas you should follow if you are to be seen as a thoughtful and gentlemanly advertiser.

• Obviously you'll want to build up the winner with praise and good wishes for the future. You can do much at this point to creating the healthy harmony and respect that is the basis for good work from any agency.

• Don't name the losers, for it cannot possibly help them to do so. Remember that they've put in a lot of work to try to get your account, so reward them all by making some graceful general statements about the quality of the competition.

• A thoughtful letter to each of the losing agencies can both thank them for their efforts, and may give them some help in assessing why they lost.

At both the beginning of the search and at its end, you will find many opportunities to do some excellent public relations for both yourself and your company by careful planning and management of the publicity which will surround your search, whether you want it or not.

Reviewing operations with your new agency.

You should document your decision and the criteria you used to make it, both for the successful agency and those who were not successful.

You should review the expectations you had with the management of your new agency within 3 to 6 months and periodically after that. This will help you to keep the relationship at its most productive level.

You will have invested a lot of time in choosing an agency, and a lot more time and money in bringing them to the full understanding of your business and how you operate it. By

working on the relationship to keep it happy and productive no one will want to conduct another search for a long time.

ICA has written a booklet that discusses regular agency reviews in detail and you should ask your agency (if it is a member of ICA) to go over the details of such a review with you.

Parting with your agency fairly and equitably.

Any agency will arrange to hand over all production elements and documentation. Make sure this happens as quickly as possible.

All outstanding billing and projects should be resolved at this time.

You might note at this time also that it could have been helpful to have an agreement with your agency that was, in effect, a divorce agreement. This may convince you to add such a section to the agreement with your new agency.

Although there is no "standard" practice for a termination notice for an agency, 90 days is considered to be a fair period during which the new agency will be selected and be ready to take over.

You should treat your agency fairly, making sure that their compensation, whether by fee or commission, continues for the notice period, for it is likely that it has not been fully compensated for its work when you give notice, for a variety of reasons:

• When the agency took on your account, there was a period when they invested a good deal of time learning your business, and about your company, and you were not billed for much of that time.

• The agency may have just gone through an intensive period of work developing a new campaign just prior to receiving notice, and it should receive some benefit for that work.

• If you are a seasonal or sporadic advertiser, the agency would be very unfairly treated if it was terminated during a period when there was no advertising activity. In that case, the 90 day notice period should be translated into "compensation for ¼ of the year's expected advertising."

Why this booklet was written.

This book was produced by The Institute of Canadian Advertising (ICA), the national association of advertising agencies in Canada. It has been created to help you with what can be two difficult tasks.

First, not all advertising agency listings contain just full-service advertising agencies. Your Yellow Pages directory will list dozens, sometimes hundreds, of advertising agencies, but many are printers, photographers or others whose main business is not of a full-service advertising agency. There is no source that lists all of the advertising agencies in Canada, but there are believed to be somewhere between 300 and 450.

Your second task will be to determine which of the bona fide agencies you should select. ICA has almost 70 members who account for approximately 85% of all of the advertising agency produced advertising in Canada. Among its members can be found an agency that can look after the needs of almost any client, regardless of size of budget or type of business.

FIGURE 4–7
Continued

What Membership in ICA Signifies?

Like most industries, not every company in the industry belongs to its national trade association, which, for the full service advertising agency industry in Canada is the ICA.

Those that do belong make several important statements about themselves, including:

1. They have demonstrated prudent financial management. To become a member of ICA, an agency must submit financial statements to an independent Trustee, who evaluates whether the agency has sufficient working capital to properly carry on its business, and to have a sufficient capital cushion to survive the loss of some of its business.

2. That they have pledged to abide by a Code of Ethics that is administered by the President and Board of Directors of ICA.

3. That they support both the self-regulation and advocacy of advertising, by providing that a portion of their membership fees in ICA be given annually to the Canadian Advertising Foundation.

Agency selection questionnaire.

SECTION I—BASIC FACTS

1. AGENCY NAME

2. ADDRESSES   TOTAL NUMBER OF EMPLOYEES

Head Office:

Branches:

3a. OWNERSHIP

☐ Public Company   ☐ Limited Partnership   ☐ Private Company   ☐ Chartered Federally   ☐ Provincially

3b. NAMES AND TITLES OF PRINCIPAL SHAREHOLDERS/PARTNERS

4a. PRINCIPAL CLIENT LIST	YEAR ACQUIRED	SENIOR CLIENT PERSON DEALT WITH	MAY WE CONTACT? YES NO
1.			☐ ☐
2.			☐ ☐
3.			☐ ☐
4.			☐ ☐
5.			☐ ☐
6.			☐ ☐
7.			☐ ☐
8.			☐ ☐
9.			☐ ☐
10.			☐ ☐

4b. SPECIFIC NUMBER OF CLIENTS IN EACH SIZE CATEGORY

UNDER $100,000 _____ $100,000 to $500,000 _____ $500,000 to $1 Million _____

$1 Million to $3 Million _____ Over $3 Million _____

5a. LIST CLIENTS GAINED OVER PAST 24 MONTHS

5b. LIST CLIENTS LOST OVER PAST 24 MONTHS	YEAR ACCOUNT ACQUIRED	REASON FOR LOSS (Attach longer explanation if desired)

6a. APPROXIMATE AGENCY BILLINGS

This year (estimated) $_____ Last year $_____ Year before $_____

6b. WHAT PERCENTAGE OF YOUR BILLINGS ARE:		6c. HOW DO YOUR BILLINGS BREAK DOWN BY THE VARIOUS MEDIA?	
Consumer packaged goods	_____ %	Newspapers	_____ %
Consumer durables	_____ %	Consumer Magazines	_____ %
Industrial products	_____ %	TV	_____ %
Office and commercial products	_____ %	Radio	_____ %
Retail advertising	_____ %	Outdoor	_____ %
Service organizations	_____ %	Business & Financial Press	_____ %
Agency of Record	_____ %	Sales promotion/Collateral Materials	_____ %
Other	_____ %	PR/Publicity	_____ %
		Other (specify)	_____ %

6d. WHAT PERCENTAGE OF YOUR BILLINGS ARE FOR:

English language advertising _____ %

French language advertising _____ %

FIGURE 4-7

Continued

4. That they will fight for both the freedom of advertising from needless government regulation, and for its fair treatment by the taxation system. Their pledge is made both in the form of financial support for ICA with membership fees, but also the volunteering of staff to ICA committees and projects.

5. That they support the development of better advertising people, by both sending employees to educational classes and seminars organized by ICA, and by lending staff as instructors.

6. That they are anxious to be kept up to date by ICA's many bulletins and advisory services, on every nuance of change in the practice of professional advertising in Canada.

7. That they want to work through ICA with the other associations that represent other parts of the advertising industry, such as the Association of Canadian Adver-

tisers, the various media associations, and such organizations as the Bureau of Broadcast Measurement, the Print Measurement Bureau, and Canadian Outdoor Advertising Measurement Bureau and many others.

More help available.

For a number of years, advertisers who read this booklet would later ask for a list of ICA members to start their search. Since a list of names was of small help, the Institute offered its members space in a book titled "Who's Who in Canadian Advertising". In the two pages each is offered, an agency can tell prospective advertisers, in as creative a way that it can, why it believes it should be considered for appointment as your agency.

That booklet may be purchased from ICA.

SECTION II—FACILITIES, EXPERIENCE AND OPERATING METHODS

7. NUMBER OF PEOPLE BY DEPARTMENT

	Head Office	Branch	Branch	Branch	Branch	Branch
Account Management						
Creative — Copy						
— Art						
Media — Planning						
— Buying						
Production						
Research and Planning						
Billing and Checking						

8a. WHICH TYPE OF COMPENSATION ARRANGEMENT DO YOU PREFER?

☐ Commission   ☐ Fee   ☐ Combination

8b. IF "COMBINATION", PLEASE COMMENT ON WHICH SERVICES YOU FEEL MERIT SPECIAL FEES:

9a. DO YOU HAVE A FORMAL COST ACCOUNTING SYSTEM, WHEREBY YOU KNOW THE PROFIT PICTURE ON EACH ACCOUNT?

☐ Yes   ☐ No

9b. IF "YES", DO YOU REVIEW ACCOUNT PROFITABILITY WITH YOUR CLIENTS?

☐ Yes   ☐ No

Comment

10. PLEASE COMMENT ON THOSE ACCOUNTS ON WHICH YOU FEEL YOU HAVE MADE A SIGNIFICANT CONTRIBUTION TO THE CLIENT'S SUCCESS.

11. PLEASE COMMENT ON BOTH THE OPERATING AND THE CREATIVE PHILOSOPHY OF YOUR COMPANY.

12. COMMENT ON THE PROCEDURES THAT YOUR AGENCY FOLLOWS TO EVALUATE QUALITY OF WORK SPECIFICALLY WITH REGARD TO:

Development of Advertising Strategy:

Development of The Creative Product:

DATE THIS QUESTIONNAIRE COMPLETED:

BY:

Name   Title

The Organization as a Good Employer

This kind of advertising tries to create positive feelings among employees about the organization in order to improve loyalty, morale, or productivity over the long term. The organization's employees may be called upon to execute the campaign.

Advocacy Advertising

Through this type of advertising an organization advocates a particular position or course of action on a controversial issue, such as the effects of acid rain or the construction of nuclear power plants. Since the organization would benefit from the advocated course of action, the problem here is to make the advertiser seem credible. The organization can better assert its credibility to the target audience by designing its communication in accordance with the basic principles of persuasion.

Non-Profit Advertising

Through non-profit advertising an organization seeks to encourage behaviour that benefits society in general or a particular community. The organization may be a government, a non-profit organization such as the Red Cross, or a political candidate. For some non-profit organizations, some agencies may offer their services free of charge, as a public service.

With this kind of advertising it is difficult to design effective messages, since the "product"[13] may be an *organization*, such as a university that advertises courses and programs to increase or maintain enrolment.[14] The product may also be a *place*, such as a city that advertises its attractions to increase tourism. Or it may be a *person*, such as an incumbent running for re-election or a political candidate conducting an election campaign.[15] Finally, the advertised product may be an *idea*, such as the need to wear seat belts, help cancer research, fight crime, or recycle.[16]

Organization Advertising

A large number of non-profit organizations use advertising to increase enrollment, patronage, or attendance. Some examples are:

- University advertising to increase enrollment to regular or advanced programs, or to special courses or seminars.
- Museum advertising, mostly to announce special events, such as selected works by famous Canadian or French painters, or cultural exhibitions from other countries (Inca or Chinese "treasures").
- Performing arts advertising to increase attendance, as well as the purchase of season tickets.
- Churches advertising to announce regular services during the week, with the title of the upcoming sermon.

Place Advertising

Advertising may be used to promote a place, such as a city, a region, or even a country.

- One of the biggest Canadian advertising campaigns took place almost a century ago when Canada was advertised to European audiences as an attractive place in which to settle, and was very successful in attracting large numbers of immigrants.
- As tourism becomes more popular, a number of places are advertising to attract more tourists: cities such as Montreal, Toronto, or Vancouver; regions such as the Niagara peninsula, the Canadian Rockies (very popular with Japanese honeymooners), or the Maritimes; countries such as Canada, Greece, or Mexico.
- Advertising of places is also used to attract investors to a region, and it is mostly run by city, provincial, or federal governments.

Person Advertising

Advertising may also be used to promote a person, such as an applicant for a job, or a political candidate. Political advertising has been developed to an art form over the years, and has become quite sophisticated.[17] In fact, traditional methods of campaigning have been replaced by a blend of publicity (e.g., the media event, or the prime time clip), and advertising developed by well-known agencies. The candidate's image is paramount, and great efforts are expended to project the right image, including market and advertising research.

In terms of advertising strategies, new candidates seeking office are like new brands being launched in test markets, while established politicians seeking re-election are like mature brands that must retain the loyalty of traditional voters.

Idea Advertising

Also called *social advertising*, non-profit organizations use advertising to promote social causes, such as "stop smoking," "don't drink and drive," "practise safe sex," "give blood." In the case of idea advertising it is difficult to show the product in the message, since it is an intangible. Plus, there is the problem of creating motivation to encourage or discourage a practice, or to generate donations.

Multicultural Advertising

Most Canadian advertisers operate in multicultural markets, both within and outside the country. In this section, only the Canadian markets are covered: the French Canadian markets, the ethnic markets, and the regional markets. The cultural situation in Canada has been described as a "salad bowl," or mosaic, in which all cultural groups are explicitly encouraged to maintain their identity while mixing with each other.[18] This situation creates serious challenges for most Canadian advertisers.

The French Canadian Market

The French Canadian market can be defined as including the province of Quebec, eight adjacent counties in Ontario, and seven counties in New Brunswick.[19] The French Canadians represent about 29 percent of the Canadian population, with their largest concentration in Quebec (81%). Quebec alone represents 26 percent of the Canadian population and 25 percent of its retail sales.[20] Thus, it is a substantial market for Canadian firms, and many opportunities are available in this market. Because of its French population, the Quebec market also presents to the advertiser major cultural and linguistic problems.[21] For instance, should a campaign designed for an English Canadian market be translated with minor adaptations for the French Canadian market? For a little humour, the reader may refer to Table 4–2 which illustrates the problems that occur when literal translations from one language to another do not take into account culturally based language intricacies and subtleties, which are often the stock and trade of advertising creators.

TABLE 4–2 **EXAMPLES OF MISUSE OF THE TWO LANGUAGES IN ADVERTISING**

Literal translation from English to French

1. Car wash: Lavement d'auto. (Car enema.)
2. Fresh milk used: Lait frais usagé. (Used fresh milk.)
3. They are terrific: Elles sont terrifiantes. (They are terrifying.)
4. Big John: Gros Jos. (Large breast.)
5. Chicken to take out: Poulet pour sortir. (Chicken to go out with.)

Literal translation from French to English

1. He there knows that: Lui y connait ça. (He really knows what he's talking about.)
2. There is in it: Y en dedans. (There's a lot to it.)
3. That—that walks: Ça, ça marche. (That really works.)
4. One chance out of thirteen. Une chance sur treize. (Thirteen to one.)
5. That's all a number: C'est tout un numéro. (He's a hell of a guy.)

Source: Adapted from Madeleine Saint-Jacques and Bruce Mallen, "The French Market Under the Microscope," *Marketing*, May 11, 1981, p. 14.

In order to understand the French Canadian markets, advertisers have developed several frameworks of cultural traits to explain some observed behaviours. The most important ones are described next.

Cultural Differences Between English and French Canadians. One of the first attempts to understand the French Canadian market, Table 4–3 provides a comparison between the two groups. Francophones are said to represent a different group because of language, religion, and family ties. They are described as more introspective, humanistic, and emotional, and less pragmatic than English Canadians.[22] Religion is not as important as it used to be, but some related values may still hold. Similarly, although the Quebec families are getting smaller, the kinship system is still very strong, and leisure is still a function of the extended family. Finally, their attitude toward the environment is still largely individualistic, in the sense of being more concerned about individual welfare.[23]

TABLE 4–3 **CULTURAL DIFFERENCES BETWEEN ENGLISH AND FRENCH CANADIANS**

Cultural Characteristics	English-Speaking	French-Speaking
Ethnic Origin	Anglo-Saxon	Latin
Religion	Protestant	Catholic
Language Spoken	English	French
Intellectual Attitude	Pragmatic	Theoretical
Family	Matriarchy	Patriarchy
Leisure Time	In function of the professional class	In function of the family circle
Individual vis-à-vis the Environment	More social	More individualistic
Business Management	Administrator	Innovator
Political Tendencies	Conservative	Liberal
Consumption Attitudes	Propensity to save; conformist; financier more than financed	Propensity to spend; innovator; financed more than a financier

Source: Georges Hénault, "Les conséquences du biculturalisme sur la consommation," *Commerce* 73, no. 9 (September 1971): 78–80.

Typologies of Cultural Traits of French Canadians.

There are three major such typologies which have mostly been developed by advertising agency people.

Sensate, Conservative, and Non-Price Cognitive. The *sensate* trait relates to touch, smell, taste, sight, hearing, and social hedonism. The *conservative* trait relates to low risk-taking behaviour, and explains a high degree of brand loyalty. The *non-price cognitive* trait is an outcome of the two previous ones; if a product is liked, price (within bounds) will not be an obstacle to purchase. This helps explain the failure of generics among French Canadians in 1978, and the finding that they react more to the *source* of the communication than to the *message* itself, while the opposite is true for English Canadians.[24]

The Thirty-Six Responsive Chords. According to advertising executive Jacques Bouchard, Francophones have six common historical and cultural roots, and each root produces six responsive chords, for a total of thirty-six, which are most useful to advertisers.[25] Figure 4–8 illustrates this typology.

- *Rural:* The transformation of the society from a rural to an urban one is fairly recent, and many have relatives in rural areas.
- *Minority:* Because of their numbers in North America, there is a sense of insecurity, a complex of inferiority which may be triggered by political and economic events.

- *North American:* It reflects the materialism, the super consumption typical of the continent, for instance, the desire for the newest and latest models of automobiles.
- *Catholic:* As explained in the previous section, some of these values might still be present, and such chords as conservatism explain low risk-taking and brand loyalty.

FIGURE 4–8

The Thirty-Six Responsive Chords of the French Canadians

Source: Jacques Bouchard, *Differences*, translated from *Les 36 cordes sensibles des Québécois*. Courtesy of Jacques Bouchard. (Montreal: Editions Héritage Inc., 1980), p. 19.

Courtesy Les Editions Héritage Inc.

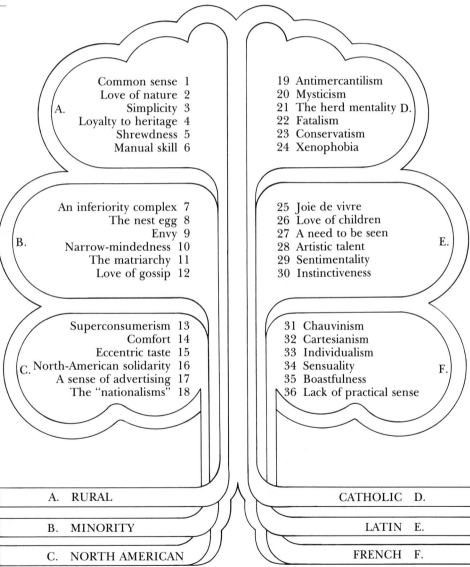

A.
Common sense 1
Love of nature 2
Simplicity 3
Loyalty to heritage 4
Shrewdness 5
Manual skill 6

B.
An inferiority complex 7
The nest egg 8
Envy 9
Narrow-mindedness 10
The matriarchy 11
Love of gossip 12

C.
Superconsumerism 13
Comfort 14
Eccentric taste 15
North-American solidarity 16
A sense of advertising 17
The "nationalisms" 18

19 Antimercantilism
20 Mysticism
21 The herd mentality D.
22 Fatalism
23 Conservatism
24 Xenophobia

25 Joie de vivre
26 Love of children
27 A need to be seen
28 Artistic talent
29 Sentimentality
30 Instinctiveness E.

31 Chauvinism
32 Cartesianism
33 Individualism
34 Sensuality
35 Boastfulness
36 Lack of practical sense F.

A. RURAL

B. MINORITY

C. NORTH AMERICAN

CATHOLIC D.

LATIN E.

FRENCH F.

- *Latin:* Many of these chords explain the effectiveness of emotional approaches over rational ones, of the source over the message, as well as the fashion consciousness of Quebec women.
- *French:* Beyond language, it reflects a sharing of a common heritage, and an understanding of that heritage is essential in designing advertising communications; for example, an ad using a local celebrity, such as a comedian or hockey player, would be more effective than one using a non-Francophone celebrity.

This brief description clearly indicates the value of such an understanding for advertisers. For example, French Canadians tend to select products that bring instant gratification, satisfy some aesthetic sense, and are somewhat affordable. They are also more demanding of service providers.[26]

Openness to Change. According to advertising creator Claude Cossette, French Canadians can be distinguished on the basis of their openness to change and their ability to react to innovation.[27] Underlying this theory are five major traditional values: faith, family, country, opposite sex, and whatever is the most important value for the individual. From these, Cossette defines four major groups which are described in Table 4–4, for their attitudes and values, and Table 4–5, for their characteristic behaviours.

- *Inerts* (35%): For these Francophones, faith, family, work, and morality are permanent values. They get their information from television, and they have consumption habits similar to those of their parents.
- *Detached* (40%): If forced by their environment, these Francophones would change in the hope of improving their economic situation, or to move up the social scale. They have few sources of information, prefer eating at home, and like bowling.
- *Mobiles* (15%): These Francophones are more open-minded, believe in scientific progress, like to develop "useful" acquaintances outside the family circle, like to read, to eat out, to take vacations, especially in the winter ("Canadian snowbirds"), to buy a big car or a nice house.
- *Versatiles* (10%): These Francophones are the most open-minded, tend to be reformists, like to make new friends, to access many information sources, to try new exotic foods, restaurants, or vacation destinations. They tend to be highly educated and critical of social institutions.

This framework is a useful way of looking at different segments within the French Canadian market, and of developing more refined and effective marketing and communication programs, depending on the segment(s) targeted by the advertiser.

The Ethnic Markets

A similar reasoning may be applied to the Canadian ethnic groups representing the Canadian "salad bowl," where these groups represent large, identifiable, and concentrated markets. However, they have not been studied to the same extent, and our understanding is more fragmentary. This section will examine the most numerically important ethnic markets in Canada.

- *The German Canadians:* Mostly concentrated west of Ontario, they are 1.2 million strong, and are maintaining their ethnicity through rituals and celebrations. Their biggest concentration is in Kitchener (20%), Regina (18%), Saskatoon (15%), and Winnipeg and Edmonton (9%). As for language, only 12 percent speak German at home.

TABLE 4–4 **COSSETTE'S TYPOLOGY: A. ATTITUDES AND VALUES**

	Inerts (35%)	Detached (40%)	Mobiles (15%)	Versatiles (10%)
Traditional Moral Values				
1. Faith	"Simple Faith"	Detached without crisis	Go to church without conviction	Rational detachment
2. Family	Extensive and important family ties	Ties with close relatives	Belief as a social institution	Bounds of friendship more important
3. Country	Trust Canadian leaders (refer to Quebec)	Feel inferior as Quebeckers	Somewhat xenophobic, Americans are role models	Friendship has no border, but with a Quebec flavour
4. Opposite Sex	"A man is a man, a woman is a woman"	"Men (or women) are not what they used to be!"	"My sailboat, my German Shepherd, and my woman"	"A man or a woman both are human beings"
5. Most important value	clannishness	work	order	authenticity
Interrelationships				
6. Social class	Same as their parents	Try to improve their lot	Often from lower classes	Climbed social ladder or from middle class
7. Social life	Little outside, intense with relatives	Some relatives and friends	Very active with "utilitarianism"	Rather good, involved with several groups
8. Political life	Unconcerned	Vote for traditional parties	Conformists	Reformists
9. Critical mind	Grumble without aim	Rising social conscience	Almost absent	Rather sharp
10. Index of mobility-versatility	Almost null	Mostly at social level	Mostly at professional, behavioural level	Mostly at the level of ideas and attitudes

Source: Adapted from Claude Cossette, "Typologie du Québécois en quatre portraits," *Cahiers de Communication Graphique*, No. 4, Université Laval (1976).

• *The Italian Canadians:* Mostly concentrated in Ontario and Quebec, they number more than 800 000, and they are maintaining their culture through limited contacts with other groups.[28] Their biggest concentration is in Toronto (10%), St. Catharines-Niagara (9%), Thunder Bay, Windsor (8%), and Montreal (6%). About 48 percent speak Italian at home, and in Toronto, for instance, some firms are advertising in Italian. The Italian Canadians have developed their own stores, cinemas, newspapers, radio stations, TV programs, and social events. Recent studies have also shown that consump-

TABLE 4–5   **COSSETTE'S TYPOLOGY: B. CHARACTERISTIC BEHAVIOURS**

	Inerts (35%)	Detached (40%)	Mobiles (15%)	Versatiles (10%)
Leisure				
1. Vacations	None; stay at home	One or two weeks; to relations' or to friends' cottage	Several times a year to "classical" destinations	Several weeks, tour Quebec, Americas, Europe
2. Journeys	From one part of town to another	From one town to another	In the Americas	From one continent to another
Development of Knowledge				
3. Information sources	Television	Reader's Digest	Time-Life books, encyclopedia	Movies, Express, Time, books
4. Continuing education	None	Sometimes	Yes, to establish social relationships	Often, as leisure
Education				
5. Studies	Primary	Secondary	Secondary or College	College or university
6. Employment	Unskilled workers	Skilled workers, white collars	Commerce, traditional professions	Professionals
Typical Consumption Behaviours				
7. Food	Bologna	"Canadian" meals	Steak	Exotic foods
8. Alcoholic beverages	Geneva gin	Beer, sometimes Geneva gin	Rye, Scotch	Wines, spirits
9. Car	Old model	Intermediate, American, a few years old	Large American	European
10. Sports	None	Bowling, snowmobile	Golf, snowmobile	Camping, cross-country skiing

Source: Adapted from Claude Cossette, "Typologie du Québécois en quatre portraits," *Cahiers de Communication Graphique*, No. 4, Université Laval (1976).

tion behaviour may be different from that of other groups, and may require a different approach in advertising.[29]

- *The Ukrainian Canadians:* Mostly concentrated west of Ontario, they number more than 500 000. Their biggest concentration is in Winnipeg, Saskatoon, and Edmonton (10%), and Thunder Bay (8%). There are distinct types of foods, crafts, clothing, home decoration techniques, and leisure activities among the members of this group.[30] Only 17 percent speak Ukrainian at home.

- *The Chinese Canadians:* Mostly concentrated in the metropolitan areas of Ontario, British Columbia, and Alberta, they number more than 300 000. Their biggest concentration is in Vancouver (7%), and Toronto and Calgary (3%). About 65 percent speak Chinese at home. A study showed that they are becoming a more independent and self-sufficient community, that a significant percentage do not use English at work, and are exposed to Chinese media only: television (70%), radio (14%), and newspapers (78%). They reported that firms advertising to them in Chinese would receive more business (70%).[31] A study of the Chinese in Montreal also indicated very specific consumption behaviour.[32]

- Finally, other significant groups which may be of interest to advertisers are the Dutch Canadians (400 000), the Jewish Canadians (265 000), the Polish Canadians (260 000), the Indo-Pakistani Canadians (200 000), the Portuguese Canadians (190 000) and the Greek Canadians (160 000).[33]

The Regional Markets

Some authors have also argued that there are regional differences in Canada which may call for differentiated marketing and communication strategies.[34] In fact, the Canadian "salad bowl" described in the previous sections, as well as the concentrated patterns of French Canadian markets, is only one facet of Canadian regionalism. The uneven distribution of the Canadian population, with 60 percent of the Canadian population living in the 25 CMAs, and one-third of economic activity found in the three largest urban centres, is also a major factor for the presence of regional and local markets.[35]

The Six "Nations" of Canada.[36]   It has been suggested that consumers should be regrouped according to life-styles, consumption behaviours, economic activities, and reactions to their environments. Such groups are called "nations," and six nations were identified to cover Canada and parts of the United States.

The New England Nation.   This nation includes the Atlantic provinces and the six New England states. This area has few raw materials, few industries, many farms, and high taxes, making it the poorest nation with a hopeful future. It is the oldest anglophone region, whose inhabitants are elitist, environmentally aware, tolerant, intelligent, political, and fair.

The Quebec Nation.   This group is strongly characterized by history, tradition, ethnic pride, a homogeneous culture, plentiful hydroelectric power, a diversified economy, and a high acceptance of new technologies.

The Foundry Nation.   Mostly centred in the industrial heartland of the United States, it includes southeastern Ontario. It is characterized by the availability of work, and by abundant water supplies. There has been a history (mostly in the U.S.) of obsolete technologies, decaying infrastructures, and declining population, jobs, and investments. Its future will depend on the growth prospects of some industrial sectors, as well as on the increasing value of water as a resource.

The Breadbasket Nation.   This nation encompasses the great plains of North America, and is mostly characterized by large scale agriculture. It includes southeastern Saskatchewan, southeastern Manitoba, and southwestern Ontario. Its inhabitants are conservative, hardworking, religious, and ratifiers of social change. Because it is so dependent on agriculture, its prosperity is at the mercy of the weather, and world prices for its products.

The Empty Quarter Nation.   The largest area in terms of land, this nation includes the Yukon, the Northwest Territories, eastern British Columbia, Alberta, northern Manitoba, north and southwestern Saskatchewan, and northern Ontario. It has few people, but lots of space, energy, and minerals. Its inhabitants still believe in the frontier ethic. Its bright future prospects will attract many immigrants from the other five nations.

The Ecotopia Nation.   This nation includes a long narrow strip along the coast of the Pacific, and in Canada it includes western British Columbia. It is characterized by an adequate supply of water and renewable resources. Its people prize their quality of life, want to be left alone, and favour energy conservation, recycling, and clean high-tech industries. Their outlook is west to the emerging Pacific Rim countries.

Implications for Advertisers.   This interesting and surprising view of Canada suggests that advertisers take into account the differences in life-styles, values, and needs among these different markets, such as:

- differences in preferences for product categories and brands, for example in the liquor market;[37]
- differences in advertising appeals which may build upon values and attitudes;[38]
- differences in reactions to new products, which may put into question the validity of test marketing across nations.

However, other authors have cautioned advertisers about putting too much faith into this theory, and more testing is expected before it can be fully validated.[39]

SUMMARY   Canadian advertisers are a heterogeneous group with different needs, problems, and resources.

Business-to-business advertising is directed toward the professional. Its goals are to increase awareness of a firm as a suitable supplier, to provide information to individuals involved in the decision process, and to help salespersons gain entry, improve the selling effort, and reduce selling costs.

The nature of the advertising message and the type of media used also depend on the type of products advertised. In advertising for durable goods, the goals are to provide information and to draw traffic into the stores. For packaged goods, the goal is to pre-sell the brand before the consumer reaches the self-service retail establishment. For soft goods, advertising attempts to create a favourable brand image and assist retail salespeople. The advertising of services requires a great deal of creativity to communicate the intangible benefits of the "product."

Retailers develop an advertising effort with two main goals. First, long-term development of the store image is the guiding principle of all retail advertising, and an advertising agency may be helpful. Second, retailers increase store traffic through in-house campaigns based on event advertising. Retailers receive free assistance from producers and media, and they use the services of outside suppliers.

In contrast to the large advertiser, the small advertiser is forced to use fewer media and to concentrate on increased exposure rather than frequent repetition of the message. Small advertisers may not be able to afford an advertising agency or have an advertising manager. Thus, the advertising campaign is often done in-house with the help of outside suppliers.

The main factors influencing the organization of the advertising function are the position of the advertising function within a firm's overall structure, the responsibilities of the advertising manager, and the structure of the advertising department.

The important questions in hiring an advertising agency are whether an agency is necessary, and if it is, what kind of services are needed.

There are three additional areas with special advertising needs and problems. Institutional advertising is directed to the general public or to the organization's employees, with the objective of improving its image or advocating a particular course of action. Advertising is used by non-profit organizations to promote an organization, a place, a person, or an idea. In advertising to different cultures, one of the main issues is whether a campaign designed for one group may be transferred to another. Canadian advertisers should look at the specificities of the French Canadian market, the ethnic markets, and the regional markets. In dealing with the French Canadian market, there are three typologies which advertisers can use in developing communication programs directed at that market. Among the emerging ethnic groups, attention is being directed toward the German, Italian, Ukrainian, and Chinese Canadians. Finally, the theory of the "six nations of Canada" sheds some light on the notion of regional markets.

QUESTIONS FOR STUDY

1. Describe the differences in the decision process between a "typical" consumer buying a home computer and the purchase of a computer for use by a small business. What does this imply for the advertising to these two groups?

2. Select an advertisement for one durable good, one packaged good, one soft good, and one service. Explain for each one how the nature of the product has influenced the advertising strategy, the creative execution, and the media selection.

3. Why are services difficult to advertise? Give three examples to illustrate your answer.

4. What are the main differences between an advertising campaign run by a retailer (e.g., Sears) and the advertising campaign of a consumer product (e.g. Coca-Cola)? What are the main factors responsible for these differences?

5. Describe the role of advertising for the largest department store in your town. Try to find out how the entire campaign is planned.

6. Select a small- or medium-size business and describe the process of choosing an advertising agency for the company.

7. Find three examples of institutional advertisements. Analyze them in detail, paying particular attention to the advertisements' objectives, their target audience(s), and the media selected.

8. Explain in detail how advertising may be designed to appeal to the two main cultural groups in Canada and to other Canadian cultural groups (Italian, German, etc.).

9. Select a recent advertising campaign used by a non-profit organization and analyze its objectives, the target audience(s), and the media selected.

10. Review the notion of regional markets in Canada and the theory of the "six nations of Canada." Explain the implications of such a view of Canadian markets, and give some examples of how regional differences may affect advertising strategies.

PROBLEMS

1. Assume that you are POCHI, a manufacturer of potato chips, and that your market is the province in which you live. You have determined that you can spend $100 000 for your advertising and you think that an advertising agency could help you with the marketing and advertising program.
   a. Analyze your needs to select the best agency available. Try to interview as many agencies as possible, using the questionnaire in Figure 4–7. If a personal interview is not possible, try to fill in the questionnaire basing your answers on the promotional brochures distributed by the agencies.
   b. Justify your final choice of an agency.

2. Assume that you are the same manufacturer as in Problem 1. You have decided that you do not need an advertising agency, and that you should handle the advertising campaign yourself with the help of the media and

outside suppliers. Based on the information in Chapters 1 to 4, develop an advertising campaign for your product, paying particular attention to the following elements: marketing strategy, advertising objective, advertising strategy, the message, and media selection.

NOTES

1. *Canadian Media Directors' Council Media Digest, 1990/91* (1989), pp. 16, 31, 40, 50.
2. McGraw-Hill Research, *LAP Report*, New York: McGraw-Hill, 1987; Jo Marney, "DM Plays Vital Role in the Total Media Mix," *Marketing* (12 July 1982), pp. 7–9.
3. John Oldland, "Brand Loyalty and the Change in the Marketing Mix for Packaged Consumer Goods," *Canadian Journal of Administrative Sciences*, Vol. 4:3 (September 1987), pp. 266–75; John Oldland, "Advertising and Brand Loyalty, 1973–1983," in *Marketing, Vol. 6*, ed. Jean Charles Chebat (Montreal: ASAC, 1985), pp. 264–74.
4. 'Ad cutback not what it seems," *Marketing* (March 26, 1990), p. 2.
5. "Auto Ad spending to stay on par with '81," *Marketing* (22 February 1982), p. A8; see also Ted Wood, "Ah Yes, Those Were The Days," *Marketing* (22 February 1982), p. A4.
6. "Ad cutback not what it seems," op. cit.
7. Gordon H. G. McDougall, "Determinants of Ease of Evaluations: Products and Services Compared," *Canadian Journal of Administrative Sciences*, Vol. 4:4 (1987), pp. 426–46; Lynn G. Shostock, "Breaking Free from Product Marketing," *Journal of Marketing*, Vol. 41 (1977), pp. 73–80.
8. Michel Laroche and Thomas Taylor, "An Empirical Study of Major Segmentation Issues in Retail Banking," *International Journal of Bank Marketing*, Vol. 6:1 (1988), pp. 31–48; Michel Laroche, Jerry Rosenblatt and Terrill Manning, "Services Used and Factors Considered Important in Selecting a Bank," *International Journal of Bank Marketing*, Vol. 4:1 (1986), pp. 35–55.
9. For more details, see J. Barry Mason, Morris L. Mayer, Hazel F. Ezell, Michel Laroche, and Gordon H.G. McDougall, *Canadian Retailing* (Homewood, IL: Irwin, 1990), Chapter 15.
10. John R. G. Jenkins, "The Canadian Advertising Industry in the 1980s," *Proceedings of the Third Annual Conference* (Administrative Sciences Association of Canada, 1975), Section 4, pp. 125–33.
11. John Oldland, "Departments are losing their control," *Marketing* (July 6, 1987), p. 16.
12. Randy Scotland, "Are Agency Searches Turning Inside Out," *Marketing* (13 December l982), pp. 48–50.
13. Philip Kotler, "A Generic Concept of Marketing," *Journal of Marketing* (April 1972), pp. 46–54; see also Philip Kotler and Gerald Zaltman, "Social Marketing: An Approach to Planned Social Changes," *Journal of Marketing* (July 1971), pp. 3–12.
14. G. H. Church and D. W. Gillingham, "The Description of Marketing Strategies and Their Influences in the University Context," *Marketing, Vol. 1*, ed. Vernon J. Jones (Administrative Sciences Association of Canada, 1980), pp. 107–16.
15. Gary A. Mauser, "Broadening Marketing: The Case of Political Marketing," *Marketing*, vol. 4, ed. James D. Forbes (Administrative Sciences Association of Canada, 1983), pp. 201–9.
16. Gordon H. G. McDougall, "Alternative Energy Conservation Appeals: Relative Effects," *Marketing in the 80s*, ed. Richard P. Bagozzi *et al.* (Chicago Marketing Association, 1980), pp. 432–35; C. Dennis Anderson and John D. Claxton, "Barriers to Consumer Choice of Energy Efficient Products," *Journal of Consumer Research* (September l982), pp. 163–70.
17. Gary Mauser, "Broadening Marketing . . .," op cit.
18. Gurprit S. Kindra, Michel Laroche and Thomas E. Muller, *Consumer Behaviour in Canada* (Toronto: Nelson Canada, 1989), Chapter 8.
19. Pierre C. Lefrançois and G. Chatel, "The French Canadian Consumer: Fact or Fancy?," *New Ideas for Successful Marketing*, ed. J.S. Wright and J.L. Goldstucker (Chicago: American Marketing Association, 1966), pp. 706–15.
20. *Canadian Media Directors' Council Media Digest*, op. cit., p. 7.
21. Bruce Mallen, *French Canadian Consumer Behaviour* (Montreal: Advertising and Sales Executives Club, 1977); M. Brisebois, "Industrial Advertising and Marketing in Quebec," *The Marketer*, 2, no. 1

(1966), p. 13; Robert M. MacGregor, "The Utilization of Originally Conceived French Language Advertisements in Parallel Canadian Magazines," *Marketing, Vol. 2*, ed. Robert G. Wyckham (Administrative Sciences Association of Canada, 1981), pp. 186–95.

22. Bruce Mallen, "How Different is the French-Canadian Market?," in *Marketing: Canada*, eds. B. Mallen and I.A. Litvack (Toronto: McGraw-Hill, 1968), p. 26.

23. S.A. Ahmed, R. de Camprieu, and Paul Hope, "A Comparison of English and French Canadian Attitudes Toward Energy and the Environment," in *Marketing, Vol. 2*, ed. R.G. Wyckham (Montreal: Administrative Sciences Association of Canada, 1981), pp. 1–10.

24. Robert Tamilia, "A Cross-Cultural Study of Source Effects in a Canadian Advertising Situation," in *Proceedings ASAC*, eds. J.M. Boisvert and R. Savitt (Montreal: ASAC, 1978), pp. 250–56.

25. Jacques Bouchard, *Differences* (Montreal: Éditions Héritage Inc., 1980), p. 19.

26. Steve B. Ash, Carole Duhaime, and John Quelch, "Consumer Satisfaction: A Comparison of English and French-Speaking Canadians," in *Marketing, Vol. 1*, ed Vernon J. Jones (Montreal: ASAC, 1980), pp. 11–20.

27. Claude Cossette, "Typologie du Québécois en quatre portraits," *Cahiers de Communication Graphique*, No. 4 (Quebec: Laval University, 1976).

28. C. Jansen, "The Italian Community in Toronto," in *Immigrant Groups*, ed. J.L. Elliott (Toronto: Prentice–Hall, 1971).

29. "Montreal Ethnics Focus of New Study," *Marketing* (March 5, 1984), pp. 12–13.

30. A. Anderson, "Ukrainian Ethnicity," in *Two Nations, Many Cultures*, ed. J.L. Elliott (Toronto: Prentice–Hall, 1979).

31. Stan Sutter, "Advertisers missing out," *Marketing* (October 20, 1986), pp. 22–23.

32. "Montreal Ethnics."

33. Carl Lawrence, Stanley J. Shapiro, and Shaheen Lalji, "Ethnic Markets—A Canadian Perspective," *Journal of the Academy of Marketing Science* (Summer 1986), pp. 7–16.

34. Harrie Vredenburg and Peter Thirkel, "Canadian Regionalism: A Marketplace Reality?," in *Marketing, Vol. 4*, ed. James D. Forbes (Montreal: Administrative Sciences Association of Canada, 1983), pp. 360–70.

35. Leonard Kubas, "Medium is siphoning national budgets," *Marketing* (June 8, 1987), pp. 26–27; René Y. Darmon, Michel Laroche and John V. Petrof, *Marketing in Canada* (Toronto: McGraw-Hill Ryerson, 1989), Chapter 3.

36. Joel Garreau, *The Nine Nations of North America* (New York: Avon, 1981).

37. E. Clifford, "Tippers Reflect Diverse Tastes of National Mosaic," *The Globe and Mail* (June 30, 1979).

38. Bernie Whalen, "Ad Agency Cross-Tabs VALS with 'Nine Nations'," *Marketing News* (January 21, 1983), p. 20.

39. Lynn R. Kahle, "The Nine Nations of North America and the Value Basis of Geographic Segmentation," *Journal of Marketing* Vol. 50 (April 1986), pp. 37–47; John Oldland, "Beware the hype of regionalism," *Marketing* (July 13, 1987), p. 10.

CHAPTER

5 *Canadian Newspapers, Consumer Magazines, and Other Periodicals*

Most media plans include advertising in print media. In 1989 Canadian advertising revenues for all print media accounted for about 76 percent of advertising revenues for all media (Table 5–1). A variety of print media are available for carrying advertising messages. The four general categories of print media in Canada are newspapers, periodicals, outdoor, and other print media.

Newspapers include dailies, weeklies, and semi-weeklies. Newspapers receive the largest share of advertising revenues of all media. In 1989, this share was about 30 percent (Table 5–1). As a category, newspapers still have the largest share of advertising revenues.

Periodicals include consumer magazines, business publications, and farm publications. In 1989 their share of revenues was about 17 percent.

Outdoor media, including transit, has seen its share of advertising revenues reach almost 8 percent in 1989.

Other print media are catalogues and direct mail. Those media increased their share of advertising revenues to about 22 percent in 1989.

This chapter will cover newspapers and periodicals, while the next chapter will deal with outdoor and other print media.

Before looking at each type of media, it is important to understand three basic media terms. *Reach* (R) is the percentage of a target audience exposed at least once to one medium. *Frequency* (F) is the average number of times one member of the target audience is exposed to one medium. *Gross Rating Points* (GRPs) measure the number of times members of the target audience are exposed to one medium as a percentage of the target audience. Unlike reach, GRP includes multiple exposure to the same person. The relationship among these concepts is reach multiplied by frequency equals gross rating points (R x F = GRP). A more complete treatment of these concepts, as well as their use in media planning, is presented in Chapter 14.

NEWSPAPERS

Evolution of Newspapers as an Advertising Medium

A Boston printer, Bartholomew Green, established the first Canadian newspaper, the *Halifax Gazette*, which appeared on March 23, 1752. His father printed the first American newspaper, the *Boston News Letter*, in 1704. This paper was one single sheet printed on both sides. A Philadelphia printer, William Brown, founded *La Gazette de Québec*, in 1764. It was Canada's second newspaper and was printed in both French and English.

TABLE 5–1 **COMPONENTS OF NET ADVERTISING REVENUES BY PRINT MEDIA (IN THOUSANDS OF DOLLARS)**

Type of print medium	1984		1989		Annual rate of growth (%)
	amount	%	amount	%	
NEWSPAPERS—*Total*	*1 729 172*	*29.8*	*2 684 600*	*29.7*	*9.2*
Dailies—*total*	*1 353 280*	*23.3*	*2 032 000*	*22.5*	*8.5*
national	276 734	4.8	424 000	4.7	8.9
local	766 377	13.2	1 019 000	11.3	5.9
classified	310 169	5.3	589 000	6.5	13.7
Weekend Supplements—*Total*	*36 115*	*0.6*	*24 400*	*0.3*	*−7.5*
national	6 200	0.1	4 000	0.0	−8.4
local	29 915	0.5	20 400	0.2	−7.4
Weeklies, semi, tri, etc. (includes controlled distribution)—*Total*	*339 777*	*5.8*	*628 200*	*6.9*	*13.1*
national	26 042	0.4	41 800	0.5	9.9
local	313 735	5.4	586 400	6.5	13.3
PERIODICALS—*Total*	*879 333*	*15.1*	*1 504 100*	*16.6*	*11.3*
Magazines, general	255 860	4.4	283 500	3.1	2.1
Business publications	164 894	2.8	183 600	2.0	2.2
Farm publications	23 112	0.4	22 000	0.2	−1.0
Directories, phone, city	415 200	7.1	931 400	10.3	17.5
Religious, school & other	20 267	0.3	83 600	0.9	32.8
OTHER PRINT—*Total*	*1 294 919*	*22.3*	*1 978 900*	*21.9*	*8.9*
Catalogues	187 690	3.2	258 000*	2.9	8.7
Other printed advertising	706 124	12.2	1 148 000*	12.7	10.2
Imported advertising matter	61 105	1.1	73 900*	0.8	3.9
Postage cost	340 000	5.8	499 000*	5.5	8.0
OUTDOOR—*Total*	*391 500*	*6.7*	*718 100*	*7.9*	*12.9*
TOTAL PRINT MEDIA	*4 294 924*	*73.9*	*6 885 700*	*76.1*	*9.9*
TOTAL ALL MEDIA	5 809 951	100.0	9 049 000	100.0	9.3

Source: Based on *Canadian Advertising Rates and Data* (May 1989) p. 402; CMDC *Media Digest, 1990/91*, pp. 10-11; and estimates (*) using historical data.

A Frenchman, Fleury Mesplet, arrived in Quebec on May 6, 1776 to set up a printshop and publish a newspaper in order to assist Benjamin Franklin in wooing Quebec to become the fourteenth colony. When this plan failed, Mesplet was arrested. Because of an acute need for a printer, however, he was released three weeks later to set up a print shop. On June 3, 1778, he published the first issue of *La Gazette du Commerce et Littéraire*. This paper later became an English-language newspaper, the *Gazette* of Montreal.[1]

As the Canadian population and the volume of trade grew, so did the number of newspapers. By 1857 there were 243 publications. By 1987 this number had quintupled to over 1250 publications.[2] The real growth occurred in the circulation figures with the growth in population and trading activity. Between 1890 and 1990 Canada's population increased five times, while the average circulation per paper increased eleven times.

There are now 110 daily newspapers in Canada with a combined average circulation of 5.3 million copies a day.[3] Daily newspapers represent by far the largest medium in terms of net advertising revenues, which passed the $2 billion mark in 1989 for the first time (Table 5–1). They represent almost a quarter of net advertising revenues for all media. If one adds net advertising revenues for other types of newspapers (weekend supplements, weeklies, and others), the proportion is about 30 percent. Although the number of daily newspapers in Canada has not changed much in the past thirty years, the industry has undergone major changes in distribution and structure. The number of cities with two or more daily newspapers is declining, while most of the new newspapers were originally weekly newspapers. Almost half of all Canadian daily newspapers and of the average daily circulation of newspapers is controlled by two chains: Southam Inc. (15 papers) and Thomson Ltd. (40 papers).[4]

Competition from broadcast media and the declining household penetration of daily newspapers, from 1.06 copies daily per household in 1948 to 0.60 in 1988, has changed the nature of newspapers.[5] They have evolved from a medium for informing people about major news events to a medium with in-depth analysis of news events, investigative reporting, local news, special sections, and so on. However, the number of people who read at least one newspaper per week has increased during the same period.[6] Irregular readers account for this increase. Newspapers are trying to make them regular readers so that present levels of penetration can be maintained or increased.

Newspapers are also getting involved in the protection of the environment by introducing new organic, smudge-free, bio-degradable inks (made from canola or soybeans), and newsprint made from kenaf (a fast growing fibre plant).[7]

Differences among Newspapers

Newspapers have several formats and publication frequencies and provide different types of advertising services.

Formats

In Canada, two basic newspaper formats are used: the *broadsheet* and the *tabloid* (Figure 5–1, page 117). The broadsheet is a full-size newspaper approximately 330 mm wide and 560 mm deep (13 in. x 22 in.). Examples of broadsheets are the *Globe and Mail*, the Montreal *Gazette*, the *Vancouver Sun Province*, and the *Winnipeg Free Press*.

The tabloid is approximately 254 mm wide and 356 mm deep (10 in. x 14 in.). Examples of tabloids are the *Calgary Sun*, the *Toronto Sun*, and the

Halifax *Daily News*. Canada has 11 English and 5 French tabloid daily newspapers.

The units of measurement of newspaper space have traditionally been the agate line and the column width. A *line* (or agate line) is a unit of space measurement one column wide and 1.8 mm (1/14 in.) deep. The *column width* is specified by the newspaper, and it affects the number of columns for that newspaper, creating for the advertiser a major problem of comparing newspaper rates, and adjusting to different sizes. However, in October 1985, the newspaper industry introduced a standardized system of measurement, called the CNU format:

1. The *Modular Agate Line (MAL)* is a unit of space measurement one standard column wide and 1.8 mm ($^1/_{14}$ in.) deep.
2. The *Standard Column Width* is 52 mm (2 $^1/_{16}$ in.) for a broadsheet and 49 mm (1 $^{15}/_{16}$ in.) for a tabloid.
3. The *Canadian Newspaper Unit (CNU)* is one standard column wide and 30 MALs deep.
4. Broadsheet newspapers consist of six units wide and ten units (or 300 MALs) deep for a total of 60 CNUs (or 1800 MALs) per page. The size of a standard page is thus 330 mm by 544 mm (13 in. by 21 $^3/_7$ in.).
5. Tabloid newspapers consist of five units wide and six units (or 180 MALs) deep for a total of 30 units (or 900 MALs) per page. The size of a standard page is thus 260 mm by 327 mm (10 $^1/_4$ in. by 12 $^6/_7$ in.).

All broadsheet newspapers use the CNU format, while only a few tabloids are using it. However, it is expected that all newspapers will eventually adopt this system.

Publication Frequency

Newspapers are also classified by frequency of publication: daily and community newspapers.

Daily Newspapers. In 1989 Canada had 110 daily newspapers with an average daily circulation of 5.3 million copies and net advertising revenues of about $2 billion.[8] Daily newspapers are published as morning or afternoon newspapers, but the trend has been toward morning newspapers. This is due to a shrinking "window of time" in the evening and the strong competition from television. Thus, the afternoon newspaper is slowly disappearing.

Most daily newspapers reach a high percentage of households within a particular geographic area. On average, gross circulation is about 60 percent of households. This geographic characteristic of daily newspapers influences the type of news and other features carried, although more daily newspapers are including special sections like lifestyle or regional editions in large metropolitan areas in order to increase reader interest and daily circulation.

Some daily newspapers have developed into national daily newspapers. For example, the *Globe and Mail* is sold in all provinces and territories and about 42 percent of its circulation is outside its primary market area in Toronto.

FIGURE 5–1

Characteristics of Broadsheets and Tabloids under the CNU Format

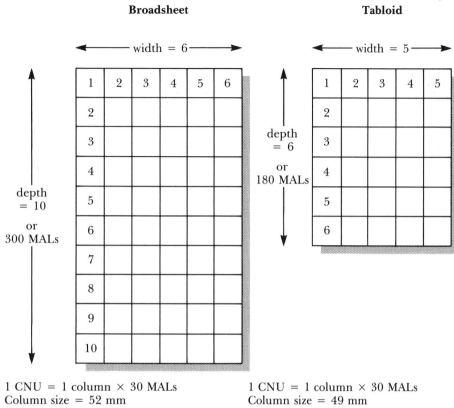

Broadsheet

Tabloid

1 CNU = 1 column × 30 MALs
Column size = 52 mm
CNUs per page = 6 × 10 = 60 CNUs
Total lineage per page = 60 × 30
= 1 800 MALs

1 CNU = 1 column × 30 MALs
Column size = 49 mm
CNUs per page = 5 × 6 = 30 CNUs
Total lineage per page = 30 × 30
= 900 MALs

Most newspapers are published Monday through Friday, plus Saturday or Sunday, with special features that attempt to keep readership high. Some days have a high proportion of advertisements for food, banking services, and so on. This policy is a shopping convenience for readers and for advertisers it ensures high reader interest.

Some daily newspapers publish seven consecutive days, with a Sunday edition similar in style to the Saturday edition of other daily newspapers. This edition contains a blend of news, news summaries and analysis, radio and television listings, comics, and special sections on sports, travel, and entertainment. In Canada the trend is to more Sunday editions of daily newspapers.

Community Newspapers. This is the second major group of newspapers. Most community newspapers are published once a week, but some are published two or three times a week, and a few once a month. The circulation varies between 400 and 190 000 copies, and in Table 5–1 they are included under the category 'Weeklies, semi, tri, etc.' Canada has approximately 1056 community newspapers. Many of these papers use the CNU format, and some are regularly reported in the Print Measurement Bureau studies.[9]

The Canadian Community Newspaper Association (CCNA) has about 690 members and centralizes buying from all member papers, using the one insertion order/one invoice method of making a complicated or multiple buy.

Some community newspapers are distributed freely while others have a paid circulation. The increased number of free community weekly newspapers has led to a phenomenal growth in household penetration, from 0.66 copies per household per week in 1948 to over 1.3 in 1988. Circulation, number of titles, and net advertising revenues have all grown. The number of Canadians reading a community newspaper each week has been estimated at 13 million.[10] This trend contrasts with the decline of household penetration by daily newspapers and indicates a shift in the reporting of purely local news from the daily newspapers to the weekly newspapers. Some large daily newspapers have separate community sections in the regular issues, particularly in the Sunday edition, to cover local news. These are distributed in large suburbs of major metropolitan areas in order to increase household penetration.

There are seven main types of community newspapers that have historically developed in reaction to the dailies and the magazines:[11]

• The grass roots weekly, generally independent, rural, and paid.
• The suburban weekly, generally corporately owned, and free.
• The saturation advertising vehicle, with very little editorial content (less than 25%), and low cost classified advertising. A successful example of this type are the "shoppers" or "pennysavers," which are listed under a separate category in CARD. Coverage tends to be uneven in Canada, with a majority found in Ontario.[12]
• The weekend newspaper, published only on Saturday or Sunday, and dealing with local or regional news.
• The local business publication, with local business editorial and advertising support.
• The ethnic or cultural publications, dealing with unique linguistic, cultural, or religious local issues.
• The special interest publications, covering entertainment or consumer products (e.g., cars), at the local or regional level.

Additional Services Offered by Newspapers

In order to improve flexibility and compete with other media, newspapers provide a number of special advertising and printing services.

Colour has long been one of the main problems of newspapers because the quality of the standard newsprint is low. To correct this situation, advertisements are preprinted on higher quality paper and then fed in roll form into the newspaper during a normal run. Two types of pre-printed colour inserts are available: hi-fi and spectacolour. *Hi-fi* appears in a continuous pattern that bleeds off the top and bottom of the page. It is offered by most newspapers. *Spectacolour* has the width and depth of a newspaper page. About seven Canadian dailies offer spectacolour to advertisers. In contrast to the preprinted advertisement, *ROP* (run of press) colour is printed on standard newsprint paper along with editorial material and other advertisements. Although the quality of ROP colour printing is still far from that of magazines, it is adequate for many creative requirements. Most daily newspapers offer ROP colour with minimum line requirements (400 to 660 MALs), and cost premiums depend on the number of colours.

Inserts are advertisements printed in advance by the advertiser and bound or inserted into a newspaper by hand or by machine. Most newspapers offer this service.

Flexform is any advertising shape that does not conform to the standard rectangular format. Most daily newspapers offer this service for a premium charge.

Newspapers as an Advertising Medium

Advantages

The main advantages for advertisers using newspapers may be grouped into five categories:

Market coverage. Daily newspapers reach an average of 67 percent of all adults (18 years and over) during the week and 75 percent of all adults during the weekend. In metropolitan areas of 100 000 to one million inhabitants, these figures are, respectively, 70 percent and 77 percent.[13] The average daily reach has been falling since 1962, when it stood at 71 percent.[14] Newspapers also provide advertisers with broad coverage of several demographic sub-groups, although here they reach only about half of teens aged 12 to 17 and half of adults with less than a high school education, and a household income less than $10 000.[15]

Flexibility. Newspapers allow very short lead times both for closing and cancelling advertisements. Advertisers may be allowed 24 hour's notice to take advantage of fast-changing market conditions, fads, or to respond to actions by competitors.

In planning the campaign, since most newspapers are a local medium, they can be selected according to the brand's regional market conditions. In addition, newspapers provide merchandising properties (e.g., dealer tie-ins, co-operative plans, colour inserts, and couponing).

Newspapers provide creative flexibility for a low production cost. A wide range of spaces, sizes, and shapes is available. Time flexibility allows for creative use of news items and special events.

Reader interest. Canadians spend about $350 million a year on newspapers. Four out of five readers go through daily papers page by page.[16] Readers differ, however, in the way they read the various sections of a newspaper.[17] As shown in Table 5–2, the most read section is Canadian News, and the least is Stock Market Listings. Differences are also found between men's and women's readership patterns. As shown in Table 5–2, there are major readership differences in the Sports, Fashion, Women's Pages, Food/Recipes and Automotive sections.

TABLE 5–2 **NEWSPAPER READERSHIP BY SECTION AND SEX**

Section	Men 18+	Women 18+
Canadian News	80.4%	74.4%
World News	77.8	69.3
Local News	77.7	71.7
Business/Finance	59.8	43.0
Editorial/Letters	56.5	53.2
Stock Market Listings	36.3	21.9
Classified Ads	63.1	56.6
Help Wanted	43.7	42.7
Careers	44.2	40.4
Colour Comics	55.9	50.9
Sports	72.9	46.3
Movies/Entertainment	72.5	69.4
Fashion	44.8	67.7
Horoscope	48.6	62.5
Family/Lifestyle	51.7	63.3
Women's Pages	26.9	65.5
Food/Recipes	43.7	65.8
Travel Pages	61.3	58.9
Homes/Real Estate	54.9	47.2
Home Decorating/Living	49.5	58.0
Automotive/Wheels/Car Market	61.4	28.0

Source: NADbank 1988.

Newspapers are an excellent medium for long copy and factual information. In addition, advertisers may benefit from the editorial environment in which their advertisement will appear.

Many consumers use newspapers as a shopping guide when looking for a specific item (e.g., car, stereo system, or sports equipment), or before a shopping trip to a food store, a hardware store, or a car dealer.

High Frequency Potential. Daily publication of newspapers provides the advertiser with high frequency potential against a large number of readers. On an average weekday, daily newspapers provide about 67 percent reach with a frequency of 1.2 for one insertion. Thus, on the average, readers are exposed to an advertisement 1.2 times.

Accessibility to Small Advertisers. Newspapers' high reach, timing, and creative flexibility make the medium accessible to advertisers with a small budget, particularly retail advertisers who are charged local rates and given free creative assistance.

Disadvantages

The main disadvantages of newspapers may be grouped into three categories:

Creative Negatives.   Although the quality of ROP colour is constantly improving, newspapers cannot compete effectively with magazines. This is a serious drawback for campaigns in which colour is an important ingredient in communicating some product benefit, for example, for food products or fashionable clothes. Another drawback is that newspapers lack audio capabilities and movement, thus it is impossible to demonstrate a product in use or to use special effects. There is also the problem of clutter: newspaper advertisements have to compete for attention with many other advertisements and with a large number of inserts. Newspapers have a short life per issue. As a result, the advertisement must attract the reader the first time it is seen. Finally, advertisers have little control over an advertisement's position on a particular page, although newspapers try to accommodate the advertiser's requested position. Many newspapers have some form of position charges, which vary from newspaper to newspaper.

Audience Selectivity.   Because their coverage is broad, newspapers are an expensive medium for reaching a specific target group. The advertiser may be paying for a large amount of wasted circulation. This is also aggravated by a low pass-along circulation and the lower reach in such demographic groups as teens aged 12 to 17 and those with less than a high school education.

Problems for National Advertisers.   Some newspapers may require national advertisers to provide separate insertion orders and material, because space sizes are not standardized. Thus newspapers can be a difficult medium in which to buy space. To alleviate this problem, the Newspaper Marketing Bureau (NMB) was formed in 1979. The NMB represents 50 of Canada's daily newspapers and 80 percent of daily newspaper circulation. It provides both centralized representation and centralized research with the Newspaper Audience Databank (NADbank).[18]

On a national basis, an advertising campaign run in daily newspapers can be expensive. For example, in 1990 a 600 MAL black and white newspaper advertisement in all markets of more than 100 000 people costs about $100 000. If the advertiser's audience is general, this may compare favourably with television, but if the audience is more selective, newspapers may be more expensive than television.

National advertisers pay a higher rate than local advertisers, who are the daily newspapers' best customers. National advertisers have often argued against the dual rate structure, and some publishers have either eliminated the rate differential or have narrowed it.[19] To justify the rate differential newspaper publishers point to the higher costs involved in servicing national advertisers, including the 15 percent commission paid to the advertising agency and the commission paid to media representatives.

Newspaper Advertising Rate Structure

Advertising rates depend on the nature of the advertising and the additional services requested of newspapers. There are three basic types of advertising rates for newspapers: general (or national) rates, retail (or local) rates, and

FIGURE 5–2

General Rate Card for a Newspaper

Courtesy The Gazette

The Gazette

250 St. Antoine W., Montreal, Quebec H2Y 3R7
Tel: (514) 282-2750   Fax No.: (514) 282-2322
National Advertising Manager: Doris Bradley

NATIONAL RATE CARD NO. 53
Effective
January 1, 1990
Contracts subject to written notice of increase.

Note Unless otherwise stated, all rates shown are for Sunday through Friday. **To determine Saturday rates, add 25%.** (Saturday circulation is approximately 35% higher than weekday circulation throughout the year.)

1. R.O.P. VOLUME RATES (12-month contract)

Modular Agate lines	Sun./Fri.	Sat.	Modular Agate lines	Sun./Fri.	Sat.
2,000	$4.70	$5.87	35,000	4.40	5.50
5,000	4.60	5.75	50,000	4.37	5.46
7,000	4.55	5.69	65,000	4.34	5.42
10,000	4.50	5.62	75,000	4.31	5.39
15,000	4.47	5.59	100,000	4.28	5.35
25,000	4.43	5.54			

2. R.O.P FREQUENCY RATES

(All dates reserved in advance for 8 week period or less - size and copy may vary)

	Per m.a.l. Sun./Fri.	Per m.a.l. Sat.
1 time	$5.50	$6.87
2 times	5.25	6.56
3 times	5.00	6.25
4 times	4.80	6.00
5 times	4.70	5.87
6 times	4.50	5.62
7 Plus	4.40	5.50

3. SPECIAL CLASSIFICATIONS

- APPOINTMENT/ANNOUNCEMENT NOTICES
  (With or without photo)
  Per modular agate line . . . . . Sun./Fri. $14.25 . . . . . Sat. $17.81
  (Glossy photos preferred. Top of advertising column guaranteed: 30%.)

- CAREERS

	Per m.a.l. Sun./Fri.	Per m.a.l. Sat.
1 insertion	$6.30	7.87
2 insertions	5.50	6.87
3 insertions	5.00	6.25

- NATIONAL/PROVINCIAL FUND-RAISING RATE
  Per modular agate line . . . . . . Sun./Fri. $2.55 . . . . . Sat. $3.19

- NATIONAL/PROVINCIAL CULTURAL RATE
  Per modular agate line . . . . . . Sun./Fri. $3.59 . . . . . Sat. $4.49

- BOOK PUBLISHERS
  Per modular agate line . . . . . . Sun./Fri. $4.00 . . . . . Sat. $5.00

- LEGALS, TENDERS,
  Per modular agate line . . . . . . Sun./Fri. $5.50 . . . . . Sat. $6.87

- ADVOCACY ADVERTISING
  Per modular agate line . . . . . . Sun./Fri. $5.50 . . . . . Sat. $6.87

4. POSITION PREMIUMS

- No advertising on pages 1, 3, or editorial page.
- Break page ads and banners; island advertising — availability and premiums on request.
- Page 2: 75% extra (160 modular agate lines × 4 columns maximum).
- Pages 4 to 7 of first section: 50% extra.
- First section guaranteed at 15% extra (no specific page).
- Stock-table pages: 50% extra for exclusivity — limited availability — minimum sizes on request.
- All other guarantees: 30% extra

5. COLOR ADVERTISING

	Sun./Fri.	Sat.
B/W + 1 color	$1,600	$2,000.00
B/W + 2 colors	1,850	2,312.50
B/W + 3 colors	2,225	2,781.25

Under 400 modular agate lines: advertisement may not be guaranteed page exclusivity for color.

STAND-BY COLOR

B/W 1 color . . . . Sun./Fri. $615 . . . . Sat . . $768.75

The "stand-by color" rate is applicable when an advertisement is located on a page where spot color becomes available at the last moment.

6. SATURDAY COLOR COMIC ADVERTISING

Available on request

7. MINIMUM & MAXIMUM PAGE REQUIREMENTS

- Minimum depth: 10 modular agate lines by 1 column, 20 modular agate lines by 2 columns, 30 modular agate lines by 3, 4, 5 or 6 columns. Any advertisement in excess of 270 modular agate lines will be billed at full depth of column (310).
- Tabloid ordered in excess of 150 modular agate lines will be billed at full depth (182 lines).
- Banner advertising within sections — minimum depth 30 modular agate lines.

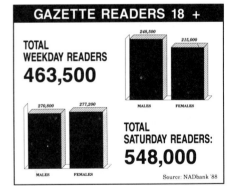

GAZETTE READERS 18 +

TOTAL WEEKDAY READERS
463,500

MALES   FEMALES
248,500   215,000

MALES   FEMALES
270,800   277,200

TOTAL SATURDAY READERS:
548,000

Source: NADbank '88

classified rates. Information on rates and data about each type of advertising is available from each newspaper in the form of a *rate card*. Rates and data of interest to national advertisers are also available in *Canadian Advertising Rates and Data (CARD)*.

General or *national* advertising is placed by an advertising agency and is subject to the traditional 15 percent commission as well as cash discounts. Newspapers may also use the services of media representatives, who sell adver-

FIGURE 5–2
Continued

8. COPY & RESERVATION DEADLINES

	Reservations & camera-ready material	Copy for proofs (minimum 120 m.a.l.)
• B/W		
Sun. insertion	Fri. noon	} Thurs., Noon
Mon. insertion	Fri. noon	
Tues. insertion	Fri. 3 p.m.	
Wed. insertion		5 p.m.,
Thurs. insertion	Noon	3 working
Fri. insertion	2 days	days prior
Sat. insertion	prior	
• Color advertising, Flexform, double truck	Noon, 3 working days prior	5 p.m. 4 working days prior
• Science (Sat.)	Noon Wed.	Noon Tues.
• Travel (Sat.)	Noon Wed.	Noon Tues.
• Living (Sat.)	Noon Wed.	Noon Tues.
• Special sections and features	Deadlines on request	Deadlines on request

9. MECHANICAL REQUIREMENTS

Mechanical and material requirements card available on request.
• CDNPA Group #6 newspaper.
• Half-tone screen: 65.
• Printing process: letterpress.
• Double truck: Minimum 1,000 modular agate lines. Use CDNPA Group No. 6 column measurements and include ½'' for gutter column. Gutter charged as one column. Negative required for double truck.

10. CREATIVE SERVICES

Layout and copy services available at no extra charge. Charges for special artwork.

11. CLASSIFIED ADVERTISING

• Rates on request
• Classified advertising format: 10 columns

12. TERMS OF PAYMENT

• All accounts are payable upon receipt of invoice. A commission of 15% will be granted for national advertising to recognized advertising agencies (as defined by the CDNPA).
  Recognized agencies are allowed an additional 2% cash discount if invoice is paid **within 20 days of billing date.**
• Terms: Interest on overdue accounts 1.5% per month (18% per annum).

13. MISCELLANEOUS

a. The publisher reserves the right to increase the rate stipulated herein at any time upon notice in writing to the advertiser or his agent. The advertiser reserves the right to cancel at any date upon which the higher rates are made effective by the publisher. Furthermore, should publication of this paper be restricted or curtailed in any way, the rate quoted herein and the amount of space contracted for, as well as the size, location and volume of the advertisements, shall be subject to revision or regulation by the publisher at any time without notice.

b. All advertising subject to publisher's approval. The publisher reserves the right to reject, discontinue or omit any advertisement, or to cancel any advertising contract for reasons satisfactory to the publisher without notice and without penalty to either party. The publisher reserves the option to insert the word "advertisement" above or below any copy. All advertising subject to Federal and Provincial Government regulations.

c. No contract made for a period exceeding 12 months.

d. Advertising instructions and/or information not in accordance with the current rate card will be regarded as a clerical error and any advertising will be billed at the rate in force.

e. All contracts are subject to the approval and written acceptance of the publisher or his appointed representative. The publisher shall not be bound by any stipulations or conditions other than those set out in contracts and evidenced by the signatures of the parties.

f. All telephone orders and cancellations must be confirmed in writing. Advertisements cancelled after reservation deadlines will be charged at full rate.

g. Failure to receive copies of The Gazette containing advertisements will not be considered reason to delay payment. Tearsheets for advertisements under 200 modular agate lines placed within the Census Metropolitan Area will not be mailed. Advertisers requiring tearsheets may pick them up at The Gazette Advertising Department, 250 St. Antoine St. W., Montreal.

h. Advertisements set and not used will be charged at $70. per hour (min. $70.).

i. The advertiser agrees that the publisher shall not be liable for any damages whatsoever arising from errors in advertisements beyond the actual amount paid for the space used by the part of the advertisement containing the error. Notice of such error is required before second insertion. The publisher shall not be liable for non-insertion of any advertisement.

j. All property rights, including copyright in the advertisement, shall be vested in and be the property of the newspaper. No such advertisement or any part thereof may be reproduced without the prior written consent of the newspaper.

k. Contest advertising shall include the publication of results.

l. Contingent orders not accepted.

m. Setting of key numbers not guaranteed.

n. Material sent collect or on which customs or excise taxes are charged, will be charged back to the client at our cost.

---

tising space to agencies for a commission. For these reasons, general advertising rates exceed retail rates by about 15 to 50 percent. About 20 percent of daily newspapers' net advertising revenues come from national advertising. (For community newspapers this rate is about 7 percent.) The general rate card for the *Gazette* is reproduced in Figure 5–2. The types of rates and data available in CARD for a newspaper are shown in Figure 5–3. In 1990 the rate for a full column (310 MALs) black and white advertisement in a weekday edition of the *Gazette* was $1705. A full-page advertisement cost $10 230. In addition, Figure 5–3 shows the special rates for special classifications of advertising: tender and legal notices, notices of redemption, career advertising, marine advertising, and reader advertisement. The latter classification uses the same type as for editorial matter and is marked "advertisement" at the top in order to identify it as such to the reader.

Retail (or local) advertising is placed directly by a retail store and is not commissionable. As mentioned before, the retail rates may be much lower than the general advertising rate. The retail rate card for the *Gazette* shown in Figure 5–4 can be compared with Figures 5–2 and 5–3. In 1990, a 2000 MAL advertisement cost a retailer $7340, while the same size ad would cost a national advertiser $9400, almost 30 percent more.

The Gazette

Since 1778

The Audit Bureau

Member CDNPA

The Southam Newspaper Group

Data confirmed for May/90 CARD

(Broadsheet) Est. 1778. Morn. Mon-Sun. Publishers: The Gazette Montreal/Montréal Limitée, 250 St. Antoine W., Montreal H2Y 3R7. Phone: 514-282-2750. WATS: Eastern Canada & U.S. 1-800-361-6172; Western Provinces 1-800-363-6765. Fax: 514-282-2322; Editorial 514-282-2141. ABC Coupon Verification Service.

CLOSING DATES: Regular page: b&w noon 2 days pre.; noon Fri. pre. for Sun., Mon. & Tues. If proof req'd, mat'l & space 3 working days pre. Travel pages (Sat.) preprint: Wed. noon for b&w; and for col.; Living-Sat. preprint inc. religion, education, art galleries-deadline: Wed. noon. Careers (Sat. only) preprint-deadline-Wed. noon. Restaurant pages (Fri.) 2 p.m. Wed.; double truck: 3 days pre. Color: Wed.-Sat. b/1c, b/2c, b/3c: 3 weekdays pre. Thurs. for Sun., Mon. & Tues editions. Special sections: 10 days pre. for space & mat'l.

COMMISSION & CASH DISCOUNT: 15%; 2% 20th fol. mo.

GENERAL ADVERTISING: Rate Card No. 53. Effective Jan. 1, 1990.

☞Uses CNU advertising units as indicated.

Sat.: 25% extra on all rates.

CNU modular agate line rate (MAL)	5.50
CNU modular unit rate	165.00
Full column depth rate	1705.00

MULTI-DEALER CO-OP RATE: Available on request.

R.O.P. volume rates (12 mo. contract):

2,000	4.70	35,000	4.40
5,000	4.60	50,000	4.37
7,000	4.55	65,000	4.34
10,000	4.50	75,000	4.31
15,000	4.47	100,000	4.28
25,000	4.43		

Sat. add 25%.

R.O.P. Frequency: (All dates reserved in advance for 8 week period or less—size & copy may vary).

1 ti.	5.50	5 ti.	4.70
2 ti.	5.25	6 ti.	4.50
3 ti.	5.00	7+ ti.	4.40
4 ti.	4.80		

Sat. add 25%.

COLOR	B/1c	B/2c	B/3c
Sun.-Fri.	$1600	$1850	$2225

Sat. add 25%.

Standby: b/1c $615. Sat. 25% extra. 400 MAL. advtr. guaranteed to be only color advt. on page. Dbl. truck: appropriate color charge for each page used. Min. 1000 MAL. Gutter charged as 1 col. Use CDNPA Group No. 6 col. measurements & incl. 1/2″ for gutter col. Gutter charged as 1 col. Negative req'd for dbl. truck.

TV/TIMES—See Class 405.

SAT. COLOR COMIC ADVERTISING: available on request.

CLASSIFICATIONS:

†Appt. notices	14.25
Guaranteed top of column, extra	30%

Careers:

1 ti.	6.30
2 ti.	5.50
3 ti.	5.00
Nat'l/Provincial fund raising rate	2.55
Nat'l/Provincial cultural rate	3.59
Book publishers	4.00
Legals, tenders	5.50
Advocacy Advtg.	5.50

†With or without photo. Glossy photos preferred. Sat. add 25%. Resort & travel area, pick-up & gatefold advtg.—rates on request. Reader ads (carried under dbl. cutoff rule & marked "advt."). Dbl. rates apply.

FLEXFORM ADVERTISING: Rates on request. Color add'l. Reservations 3 weekdays pre. Noncancellable. Subject to pubr.'s approval.

POSITION CHARGES: No advtg. on pages 1 or 3 & editorial page. Break page ads & banners; island advtg.—availability & premiums on request. Page 2; 75% (max. 160 MAL x 4 cols.); Pages 4 to 7 of 1st section 50%. 1st section guaranteed 15% (no specific page). Stock table pages; 50% for exclusivity—limited availability—min. sizes on request. All other positions 30%.

MINIMUM & MAXIMUM REQUIREMENTS: Min. depth: 10 MAL x 1 col., 20 MAL x 2 cols., 30 MAL x 3, 4, 5 or 6 cols. Any adv. in excess of 270 MAL billed at full depth of col. (310 lines). Banner advtg. within sections—min. depth 30 MAL.

CLASSIFIED:

Commissionable	Sun.-F.	Sat.
Per agate line	4.00	Extra 25%

Volume contracts & consecutive issues—rates on request. Noncommissionable. Box number $20. Deadlines: 4 p.m. pre. day; display noon 2 days pre., with proof 3 days pre.

MECHANICAL REQUIREMENTS

Printed size: 13 x 22-1/8.

Col. width: 12.4 picas. Depth: 310 MAL.

Halftone screen: 65. B&W, blk. & 1 color material: photocomp prints (Velox); repro proofs, negative film. Appointment notices: photocomp prints acceptable. Glossy photos preferred. Blk. & 2 colors, Blk. & 3 colors: negative on 20 x 24 film; to be same size as printed full page 13 x 22-1/8; partial page pre-positioned to lower right-hand corner of 20 x 24 film; register marks in bearer area; with right reading from emulsion side up. For unregistered blk. mat'l, photocomp. print (velox) to make-up col. width & depth. Full page direct cast mats not acceptable. Dbl. Truck: neg. req'd.

PERSONNEL

Pubr.: David Perks.
Dir. Mktg.: Bruce Stevenson.
Adv. Dir.: Jean Sanche.
Nat. Adv. Mgr.: Doris Bradley.

Class. Adv. Mgr.: James Thivierge.

BRANCH OFFICES/REPRESENTATIVES

The Southam Newspaper Marketing Div.:
Toronto M2P 2C2: Greg Varga, 20 York Mills Rd., Ste. 401. Phone: 416-222-8000. Fax: 416-222-3400.
Ottawa K1R 6K7: Ken Winchcombe, Ste. 707, 880 Wellington St. Phone: 613-234-1492. Fax: 613-234-2694.
Montreal H5A 1G5: Shannon McPeak, 35 Edison, Box 1173, Place Bonaventure. Phone: 514-878-9794. Fax: 514-878-3516.
North Burnaby V5C 6E7: Glen Sayers, Sales Mgr., P.O. Box 82230. Phone: 604-433-6125. Fax: 604-433-9549.
Mexico D. F.: 11500: Towmar Representaciones, Presa de la Angostura 8. Phone: 905-395-5888.

CIRCULATION

A.B.C. publisher's statement for 6 mos. ending Sept. 1989.

	M-F	Sat.	Sun.
Average:			
Paid	177,544	254,398	159,447
City zone	145,173	199,324	129,973
Retail trading zone	18,001	32,939	17,825
All other	14,370	22,135	11,649

WEST ISLAND EDITION: Issued every Thurs. Closing 3 p.m. pre. Mon.

COMMISSION & CASH DISCOUNT: Rates commissionable to recognized agencies.

GENERAL ADVERTISING: Rate Card No. 7. Effective Jan. 1, 1990.

Frequency discounts per MAL:

1 ti.	1.52
2 ti. (within 13 wks)	1.44
3 ti. (within 13 wks)	1.40
4 ti. (within 13 wks)	1.36
8 ti. (within 26 wks)	1.33
16 ti. (within 26 wks)	1.32
26 ti. (within 52 wks)	1.28
52 ti. (within 52 wks)	1.24

FREQUENCY DISCOUNT: Advtr. must make commitment to level of frequency when placing initial advtmt.—will not be applied retroactively.

PICK-UP RATES: Advtr. must have appeared once in The Gazette & be repeated in The West Island Zoned Edition with no copy changes. Regular West Island color rates apply.

COLOR	B/1c	B/2c	B/3c
Per page	$359	$388	$494
Last minute color			$100

Double truck: Appropriate color charge for each page used.

CIRCULATION

WEST ISLAND EDITION ONLY.

Sworn July 1989.

Average circulation per issue	51,581
Average net paid circulation per issue	49,673

Retailers provide daily newspapers with about 50 percent of net advertising revenues (excluding classified advertising). For community newspapers, this percentage goes up to 93 percent. Newspapers may be the best medium for retailers in terms of costs, timing, product presentation, and market coverage. Newspapers offer retailers assistance in designing their advertising creative, in selecting the size of the advertisement, the layout, and the illustrations, as well as providing retail research through NADbank.

Classified advertising may be placed by individuals or firms and is grouped according to various categories. Classified advertising rates are non-commis-

FIGURE 5–4

Retail Rate Card for a Newspaper

Courtesy The Gazette

The Gazette

250 St. Antoine W., Montreal, Quebec H2Y 3R7
Tel: (514) 282-2750   Fax No.: (514) 282-2342
Sales Manager, Retail Advertising: Joyce Hammock

**RETAIL
RATE CARD
NO. 52**
Effective
January 1, 1990

1. RETAIL DISPLAY ADVERTISING
(in modular agate lines)

Contract size	Sun./Fri. per line	Contract	Sun./Fri. per line
Transient	$ 5.50	50,000	3.26
1,000	4.45	65,000	3.23
2,000	3.67	75,000	3.20
5,000	3.47	100,000	3.18
7,000	3.42	200,000	3.15
10,000	3.39	400,000	3.12
15,000	3.35	500,000	3.09
25,000	3.32	700,000	3.06
35,000	3.29	1,000,000	3.00

SATURDAY:
Add 25% to Sun./Fri. line rates.

DISCOUNTS:
Discounts available for multiple pages in one edition from same advertiser.

2. SPECIAL CLASSIFICATIONS

- Religious services in Metropolitan Montreal churches and synagogues, appearing on religion page $2.17 per line
- Fund raising activities by Metropolitan Montreal charitable organizations   Sun./Fri. $2.17 per line   Sat. + 25%
- Community and cultural organizations that primarily serve Metropolitan Montreal   Sun./Fri. $3.05 per line   Sat. + 25%
- Art Galleries $3.57 per line
- Book pages (Sat.) $3.57 per line
- Restaurants $3.57 per line
- Educational institutions in Metropolitan Montreal   Sun./Fri. $3.57 per line   Sat. + 25%
- Hookers   Sun./Fri. $42.00   Sat. + 25%
- Political (and para-political) organizations
- Appointment notices   See National Advertising Rate Card.

3. FREQUENCY RATES
To obtain a frequency discount, the advertiser must make a commitment as to the level of frequency when placing the initial advertisement.

	Price per line Sun./Fri.
2 - 6 times within 13 weeks	$ 4.09
7 - 12 times within 26 weeks	3.80
13 - 19 times within 26 weeks	3.62
20 + times within 52 weeks	3.47

Saturday: Add 25% to Sun./Fri. modular agate line rates.

4. COLOUR ADVERTISING

	Sun./Fri.	Sat.
B/W + 1 colour	$ 1,300	$ 1,625
B/W + 2 colours	1,500	1,875
B/W + 3 colours	1,800	2,250

- 400 modular agate lines or more: advertiser is guaranteed to be the only colour advertiser on the page.
- Under 400 modular agate lines: the advertisement can be preempted, and there is no guarantee of exclusivity for colour.
- When advertisements are located on pages where it is predetermined that spot colour is available at the last moment, the same colour may be used by those advertisers at a cost of $500.
- One set of progressive proofs (preferred) or colour keys required for process colour advertising.
- Double truck: appropriate colour charge for each page used.

5. POSITION
- No advertising on pages 1, 3, or editorial page.
- Break page banners and ads available. Limited sizes. Monday to Saturday. 75% extra.
- First section guaranteed at 15% extra (no specific page).
- Page 2: 75% extra (40 modular agate lines x 2 columns minimum, 160 modular agate lines x 4 columns maximum).
- Pages 4 to 7 of first section: 50% extra (100 modular agate lines x 3 columns minimum).
- Other positions in first section 15% extra.
- Stock-table pages: 50% extra (50 modular agate lines x 6 columns only).
- Guarantees other than in the first section 30% extra.

sionable, except for general advertising placed by advertising agencies that is in regular or display classified style. Newspapers derive about 29 percent of their net advertising revenues from this source.

Future of Newspapers as an Advertising Medium

As we have seen, the nature of newspapers has changed considerably over the past century and will likely evolve further as market conditions change and new technologies are implemented.

Newspapers have benefited greatly from the development of such technologies as offset printing and its superior reproduction quality, particularly for

FIGURE 5-4
Continued

6. RESERVATIONS/MATERIAL DEADLINES
- Travel section (Sat. insertion): 5 p.m. Wed.
- Living section (Sat. insertion): Noon Wed.
- Science pages (Sat. insertion): Noon Wed.
- Weekly Review pages (Sat. insertion): 5 p.m. Fri., one week prior.

REGULAR NEWSPAPER
- B/W advertising: 12 noon 2 days before insertion for all material and copy; 3 working days before insertion if proofs are required. (Excessive copy changes or advertising copy set and not scheduled will be charged at $70 per hour, minimum $70.) No proofs on advertisements 120 modular lines or less.
- For Mon. issue: 12 noon Fri. preceeding
- For Tues. issue: 3 p.m. Fri. preceeding
- Camera-ready material: 11 a.m. day prior to publication.
- Flexform advertising: 3 days preceeding, non-cancellable
- Colour advertising: B/W + 1 colour - 3 working days before insertion for reservation and material (add 1 day if proof is required), non-cancellable. B/W + 2 colours and B/W + 3 colours - 3 working days before insertion for reservation and material (add 2 days if proof is requi-red), non cancellable.
- Double truck advertising: reservation and material 3 working days before insertion, non-cancellable.

7. FLEXFORM ADVERTISING
Rates available on request.

8. DOUBLE TRUCK
Gutter charged as one column. Minimum 1,000 lines overall.

9. SATURDAY COLOUR COMICS
Separate rate card available on request.
Deadline for reservations: 5 p.m. Fri., 4 weeks prior.

10. TV TIMES
Full-colour offset magazine appearing every Saturday. Flat rates for regular advertising units. Separate rate card available on request.

11. INSERTS
Separate rate card available on request.

12. ZONED EDITIONS
Separate rate cards available on request.

13. PICK-UP ADVERTISING
Separate rate card available on request.

14. MECHANICAL REQUIREMENTS
- Column width: 2 1/16''.
- Column depth: 310 lines.
- Full page type space: 13'' x 22 1/8''.
- 6 columns to a page.
- Minimum space, display: 10 modular agate lines by 1 column, 20 modular agate lines by 2 columns, 30 modular agate lines by 3, 4, 5 or 6 columns.
- Half-tone screen: 65.
- Double truck material: minimum 1,000 modular agate lines overall. Normal column widths apply to either page of a double truck. The gut-

ter space charged as one column, measures ½'' or 3 picas. Negative film required for half tones. Appropriate colour charge for each page used.

- Any advertisement in excess of 270 modular agate lines will be given full depth of column (310 lines) and charged accordingly.
- Advertising material not claimed or used within a period of 4 months will be destroyed at the option of the publisher.
- The mechanical requirements of The Gazette are subject to change without notice.

15. CORPORATE CONTRACT RATES

Available to companies owned 51% or more by parent company or offering proof of effective control by parent company. Volume used by each corporate division accrues to corporate contract.

16. TERMS OF PAYMENT

Invoices payable upon receipt. The publisher reserves the right to apply interest on overdue accounts at the rate of 1 1/2% per month (18% per annum).

17. MISCELLANEOUS

(a) The publisher reserves the right to increase the rates stipulated herein at any time. The advertiser reserves the right to cancel at any time upon which higher rates are made effective by the publisher. Furthermore, should publication of this paper be restricted or curtailed in any way, the rate quoted herein and the amount of space contracted for, as well as the size, location and volume of the advertisements, shall be subject to revision or regulation by the publisher at any time without notice.

(b) All advertising subject to publisher's approval. The publisher reserves the right to reject, discontinue or omit any advertisement, or to cancel any advertising contract for reasons satisfactory to the publisher without notice and without penalty to either party . The publisher reserves the option to insert the word "Advertisement" above or below any copy.

(c) All property rights, including copyright in the advertisement, shall be vested in and be the property of the newspaper. No such advertisement or any part thereof may be reproduced without the prior written consent of the newspaper.

(d) No contract made for a period exceeding 12 months.

(e) Contest advertising shall include the publication of results.

(f) Tearsheets for advertisements under 200 mudular agate lines placed within the Census Metropolitan Area will not be mailed. Advertisers requiring tearsheets may pick them up at The Gazette Advertising Department, 250 St. Antoine St. W., Montreal.

(g) The advertiser agrees that the publisher shall not be liable for any damages whatsoever arising from errors in advertisements beyond actual amount paid for space used by that part of the advertisement containing the error. Notice of such error is required before second insertion. The publisher shall not be liable for non-insertion of any advertisement.

(h) Contingent orders not accepted.

(i) Advertising instructions and/or information not in accordance with the current rate card will be regarded as a clerical error and any advertising will be billed at the rate in force.

colour reproduction. The communications industry is one of the biggest users of computers in Canada and is rapidly adopting word processors, desktop publishing, satellite transmission, fibre optics, and lasers.[20] Also, as mentioned earlier, newspapers are using environmentally friendly organic inks and newsprint made from a fibre plant. Thus, the quality of newspapers will continue to improve.

Newspapers are strengthening their *market orientation* by better tailoring their content to readers' local interests and specific needs. They are improving their research capabilities and establishing reliable data-bases on their audiences with the various NADbank studies. Up-to-date and comprehensive information is essential to media buyers and should encourage greater use of newspaper advertising in national campaigns.[21]

In their role as a communication medium, newspapers will provide more information retrieval services, such as Southam/Torstar's Infomart or the *Globe and Mail*'s InfoGlobe. Such home-delivery information systems as videotex are still a few years away from the high penetration rate necessary for affordable advertising. However, several forms of electronic publishing, especially the "electronic newspaper" are on the horizon. The impact of these developments on advertising revenues is difficult to estimate and depends on two factors:

- How people will allocate their time among the various media; in particular, how much time they will spend reading newspapers.
- How advertisers will allocate their advertising dollars among the growing number of media, particularly if the total media demand is not very elastic.[22]

CONSUMER MAGAZINES

Consumer magazines are issued periodically and are intended for the ultimate consumers of retail goods and services. As an advertising medium, consumer magazines have experienced growth and have been able to adapt to advertisers' changing needs and to competition from other media.

Growth of Consumer Magazines as an Advertising Medium

In Canada and in the United States consumer magazines started as literary publications aimed at highly educated readers. Because Canada's population is so small and scattered, publishers had enormous financial difficulties and came to rely on advertising as a major source of revenue. Between 1833 and 1893, more than 18 magazines appeared in Ontario; many of them survived only one to three years. The *Canadian Monthly* (1867) and the *New Dominion Monthly* (1867) lasted 10 and 11 years respectively. A French magazine, *Le Samedi*, founded in 1889, lasted more than 50 years.[23]

To survive, many literary magazines were forced to broaden their appeal or become more specialized. Even so, such magazines as *Canadian Magazine* (1893) was forced to cease publication.[24] Despite these difficulties, the number and circulation of magazines kept growing, and at a much faster rate since the early seventies. In 1989, there were over 530 consumer magazines listed in CARD, compared with 190 in 1971.[25]

In addition to the difficulties of dealing with a small and sparsely distributed population and bilingualism, Canadian consumer magazines have had to withstand competition from U.S. magazines, which have used the Canadian market to extend their circulation and thus their advertising revenues. Canadian magazines, however, could not hope to penetrate the U.S. market to add to their already small Canadian-based circulation. In 1989, there were about 59 U.S. consumer magazines with an issue circulation of more than 25 000 distributed in Canada.

The competition from U.S. magazines forced Canadian magazines to focus on Canadian concerns in terms of editorial policy. This strategy proved to benefit the industry greatly, as evidenced by the growth in numbers, circulation, and net advertising revenues. Table 5–1 shows that the advertising revenues of consumer magazines reached $283 million in 1989.

The evolution of consumer magazines also resulted from competition from the other information and entertainment media—film, radio, and television. Radio forced some magazines to adopt the weekly news format, with narrative and photographs. Television pushed magazines into more audience specialization, with specific interests appealing to both readers and advertisers. Thus, one finds magazines on soccer, photography, nature, stamp collecting, vintage vehicles, the military, and secretaries.[26] In effect, magazines have reacted to the threat of television by targeting markets, thereby offering advertisers a means of reaching very specific audiences and complementing the coverage provided by television.

Various associations have played an active role in promoting magazines as a medium: Magazines Canada (The Magazine Association of Canada), the Canadian Magazine Publishers' Association (CMPA), and the Periodical Publishers Exchange (PPE).

Differences among Consumer Magazines

Like newspapers, magazines have various formats, frequencies of publication, editorial policies, and circulation bases, and offer different types of special services to advertisers.

Format

Canadian magazines are published in formats ranging from the pocket size (14 cm x 19 cm) of the *Readers' Digest*, to the standard size (21 cm x 28 cm) of *Time* or *Chatelaine*, to larger sizes such as for *Decormag* (23 cm x 30 cm). Advertisements that are to appear in several magazines should be adapted to these sizes.

Frequency of Publication

Magazines vary greatly in frequency of publication, ranging from weekly magazines to quarterly magazines. About 28 percent of consumer magazines are published monthly, 15 percent weekly, and 11 percent are published 10 to 11 times a year.[27] Frequency is an important consideration for advertisers concerned about message repetition, or for advertisers who are planning a new product introduction or promoting products whose sales are influenced by seasonal factors.

Editorial Policy

As was seen, magazines have developed editorial appeal *vertically*, by targeting a more or less narrowly defined audience. There were 52 categories of consumer magazines listed in CARD in 1989. The most important group of magazines is "general interest," with 61 titles. In this category one finds such diverse publications as *Canadian Geographic*, *Western Living*, and *Readers' Digest*. Other important categories are sports and recreation (34 titles), television and radio (47 titles), and women's magazines (30 titles). In the last group, one finds *Homemaker's Magazine*, *Chatelaine*, and *Canadian Living*.

Their range of editorial content and specific target market combined with high reader interest make magazines an attractive advertising medium.

Circulation Base

Magazines may be classified into three categories according to their type of circulation: traditional, controlled circulation, and special interest.

Traditional Magazines. These magazines are the broad circulation magazines bought by subscription or on a newsstand, for example, *Chatelaine* or *Canadian Geographic*. Most of these magazines' circulation is from subscription. It has been estimated that Canadians annually spend about $500 million buying magazines and periodicals, about $125 per household per year.[28]

Traditional magazines are generally well established, with high prestige for advertisers. They have maintained their circulation and volume of advertising revenues. Most of them are audited by the Audit Bureau of Circulations (ABC) and the Canadian Circulations Audit Board (CCAB).

Controlled Circulation Magazines. These magazines are distributed without charge to a specific group of readers selected according to socio-demographic and economic variables, e.g., young apartment dwellers in downtown Montreal or Calgary. The first such magazines were the weekend newspaper magazine supplements (also called roto publications or rotogravures), which were introduced in 1951. *Homemaker's Magazine* and *Madame au Foyer* were controlled circulation magazines introduced in 1966 to selected groups of women. These magazines used research to prove to advertisers that they could not only provide efficient target group reach but also high readership levels.

Controlled circulation magazines is the fastest-growing category of magazines and of total circulation. This growth is largely responsible for the increase of household consumption of magazines.

Special Interest Magazines. These magazines form the third category, and they also represent a fast-growing segment. Their average circulation is between 20 000 and 25 000 copies. There are more than 100 special interest magazines, among them *Canadian Yachting*, *Hockey News*, *Destinations*, and *The Atlantic Salmon Journal*. Of the three groups of magazines, they have the most selective audience and the most specific editorial environment, along with high reader interest.

Additional Services Offered by Consumer Magazines

Colour. In addition to excellent colour reproduction, some magazines offer five or more colours, instead of the traditional four, and metallic inks, which create striking effects. As printing technology improves, magazines will likely be the first to use the new processes.

Bleed Pages. Bleed pages are printed to the edge of the paper; there is no margin whatsoever. They give advertisements a contemporary look and allow for special effects.

Free Form. This service, also called *flex-form*, allows creative directors to use an abstract form to contain the advertisement, subject to the magazines's mechanical requirements. The magazine runs editorial matter around the free-form advertisement. *Checkerboards* are a simple example of free-form: advertisements are made up of squares set up in the form of a checkerboard with alternating advertising and editorial material.

Gatefolds.   Gatefolds are pages that fold out from a two-page spread advertisement. They are especially useful when an advertiser has lengthy copy or wants to make an impact by being the dominant advertiser in a magazine. Because they are physically different from the others, gatefolds are usually noticed by readers. Gatefolds are often used as an extension of the front or back covers of magazines.

Special Positions.   Most magazines offer two types of special positions: covers and guaranteed positions. (Magazines usually try to accommodate, without additional charges, the wishes of advertisers who want special positions.) These are often called *preferred* positions.

Covers.   Of the four covers of a magazine, three are available for advertisements. The most expensive one is usually the back cover. The second and third covers may be charged the same rate but at a premium to the four-colour page rate. For example, in 1989 the rate for the second and third covers (four colours) of Maclean's was $23 845. For the fourth cover it was $26 010, while the rate for one page, four colours, was $16 475.[29]

Guaranteed Positions.   These may be offered at a premium and are useful whenever the effectiveness of the advertisement may be enhanced by the proper editorial environment; for example, an advertisement for an album by a rock group next to a story on that group.

Inserts.   These may be supplied either by the advertiser or by the magazine. Inserts command more attention, because they may be printed on thicker paper, or appeal to the senses (e.g., smell, touch), or offer samples, or have a tear-off or cut-off postal card.

Split Runs.   Some consumer magazines reproduce different advertisements in alternate copies of the magazine. This service allows the advertiser to test two creative approaches for their effectiveness on two matched samples.

Regional Editions.   Consumer magazines may also offer some regional editions, thus offering more flexibility to advertisers. *Maclean's* with 16 editions and *Readers' Digest* with 15 editions offer the best market flexibility. Others include *Chatelaine, Canadian Living, Financial Post* and *TV Guide.*[30]

Magazines as an Advertising Medium

Advantages

The main advantages of magazines can be grouped into four categories:

High Selectivity.   By carefully selecting the appropriate magazines, advertisers can reach a target with minimal waste circulation, especially if the target is narrowly defined. Since magazines are mostly a national medium, the coverage of the target group is obtained on a national basis. Regional editions of magazines allow advertisers the flexibility to adjust for regional differences in product distribution and market penetration.

The wealth of information on magazine readers, their consumption patterns, and life-styles is extremely useful to advertisers. Magazines understood very early the value of research as a tool for competing with other media.

Starch Readership Studies and Print Measurement Bureau (PMB) studies have been largely sponsored by magazines and have helped magazines grow by convincing advertisers of magazine advertising's effectiveness (Figure 5–5). These studies are described in detail in Chapter 15.

A High-Quality Medium. Magazines are a high-quality medium. The quality of colour reproduction of magazines is unsurpassed by newspapers or television. This allows advertisers to create a certain mood, present food and beverages in an appealing manner, build a prestigious image, or attract attention and interest by a dramatic use of colour. When combined with appropriate editorial content, colour advertisements are well read, since magazines' believability, authority, and prestige are often extended to advertisements. In addition, the editorial content stimulates the reader's information gathering, and advertisements are one readily available source of information. Finally, advertising in prestigious magazines enhances the advertiser's image in the eyes of both customers and distributors.

A Durable Medium. Magazines have a long life and may be read several times by one reader. Thus one advertisement may be noticed several times. A study based on 39 consumer magazines shows that on the average, adult readers pick up a magazine on 3.2 separate reading occasions and spend about an hour reading one issue.[31]

Magazines also have a high secondary or pass along readership. What is important to advertisers is not a magazine's circulation, but its total audience, i.e., the number of people who read a particular issue. The total audience is

FIGURE 5–5

Advertisement for a Consumer Magazine Using Research Results to Promote the Magazine to Potential Advertisers

Produced by Prime Time Publishing Inc., created by Ruth Kelly and Julie Wons

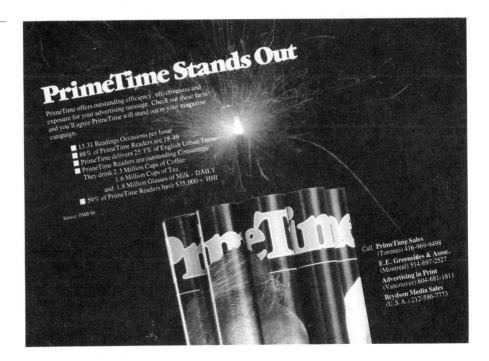

made up of a primary and a secondary audience. The *primary audience* or *readership* is composed of individuals belonging to the subscribing or purchasing household. The *secondary* or *passalong audience* is composed of individuals who do not belong to the subscribing household but who receive the publication second hand. Magazines measured in the PMB'88 study attracted an average of 2.7 readers per copy.[32]

The relationship among total audience, circulation, and readers per copy is: *total audience = circulation × readers per copy*.

For example, the PMB'88 found that there were on the average 2.7 readers per copy. If the paid circulation of a magazine in 1988 was 100 000, the total audience of that magazine was: *100 000 × 2.7 = 270 000 readers*.

Additional Services. Additional services magazines provide are split-run and advertisement reprints, which are given to sales representatives who in turn distribute the advertisements to the trade.

Disadvantages

There are four main disadvantages to using magazines as an advertising medium:

Lack of Flexibility. Magazines lack flexibility for two main reasons. First, they require long lead times for including an advertisement in a specific issue. The closing date varies according to the type of magazine and is usually between four to twelve weeks before the issue (or cover) date. The on-sale date of a particular issue is often several days or weeks prior to the issue date. This long lead time does not allow advertisers to take account of rapid changes in market conditions. Second, magazines' circulation patterns do not always match a product's distribution pattern, and many magazines do not have regional editions. Even magazines with regional editions find it difficult to vary the intensity of advertising geographically. Finally, Canada does not have a real general interest magazine, so it is impossible to reach men and women as a group with one publication or type of publication.

Low Frequency and Penetration. Magazines cannot offer high frequency of exposure and thus are inappropriate when high frequency is required. Because of its selectivity, the coverage offered by an individual magazine may be lower than for other media. Moreover, because a magazine is around for a long time, people do not read it right away. Although reach is not immediate as it is with TV or newspapers, people do look at a magazine several times. Thus the actual reach of a magazine may not be attained at the publication date. This is a corollary of the long life of a magazine.

Creative Drawbacks. For the creative director, magazines present some problems. There is no limit on the number of advertising pages in a magazine, so the problem of clutter is very acute. This creates a difficult competitive environment for creative directors, who must find ways to improve an advertisement's chances of being noticed and read. A variety of techniques is used, often at a higher cost: special inks, preferred positions, covers, use of a celebrity endorsement, pop-ups, and large-size insertions. As with other print media,

SDA Division

An Ottawa Magazine Inc. Pubn.

Data confirmed for June/90 CARD

Est. 1979. Published by Ottawa Magazine Inc. 192 Bank St., Ottawa, ON K2P 1W8. Phone: 613-234-7751. Fax: 613-234-9226. Issued 10 times a year, Dec./Jan., Feb., March, April, May, June/July, Aug., Sept., Oct., Nov. Closing dates: space 5 wks pre.; camera-ready mat'l 4 wks. pre. Cancellations 5 wks pre. Per year $18.
COMMISSION & CASH DISCOUNT: 15%; 2% 10 days.
GENERAL ADVERTISING: ♧ "Publisher warrants deduction of advertising costs is not restricted by Section 19 of Income Tax Act. Advertisers who file Canadian tax returns can claim advertising costs of this publication as business expense."
Rates effective Jan. 1, 1990.

B&W:	1 ti.	4 ti.	8 ti.	10 ti.
1 p.	$3065	$2940	$2820	$2760
2/3 p.	2515	2415	2315	2265
1/2 p.	2085	2000	1915	1875
1/3 p.	1600	1540	1475	1445

COVERS:

2nd or 3rd	$4025	$3865	$3705	$3625
4th	4600	4415	4240	4140

COLOR: Incl. spot color.

1 p.	$3835	$3680	$3530	$3450
2/3 p.	3145	3020	2895	2830
1/2 p.	2610	2505	2400	2350
1/3 p.	2005	1925	1845	1805

Match ink rates on request. Fashion & Homes supplements, extra 5% of b/w & color rates.
POSITION CHARGES: 10% extra.
BLEED: No extra charge. Full page only + 1/4" all around.
INSERTS: Rates on request.
MECHANICAL REQUIREMENTS
Type page: 7 x 9-7/8.
Trim size: 8-1/8 x 10-7/8.
Bleed page: 8-7/16 x 11-1/8.
D.p.s. trim: 16-1/4 x 10-7/8.
D.p.s. bleed: 16-7/8 x 11-1/8.

Unit	Wide	Deep	Unit	Wide	Deep
2/3 p.	4-5/8	9-7/8	1/3 s.	4-5/8	4-7/8
1/2 h.	7	4-7/8	1/6 v.	2-1/4	4-7/8
1/2 v.	4-5/8	7-3/8	1/6 h.	4-5/8	2-3/8
1/3 v.	2-1/4	9-7/8			

Printing process: web offset lithography. Binding method: saddle-stitched. Halftone screen: 120 process magenta, cyan, black; 133 process yellow. 4-color: supply 1 set of screened final negatives, right reading, emulsion down with proofs. Under color removal should be total density in darkest areas will not exceed 260%. D.p.s. advtmts. supply on 1 sheet.
PERSONNEL
Adv. Sales Dir. & Gen. Mgr.: Peter Ginsberg.
Editor: Louis Valenzuela.

BRANCH OFFICES/REPRESENTATIVES
Scarborough, ON M1S 2M4: E.T. Pearce & Assocs., 9 Overdon Sq., Phone: Ed Pearce, 416-299-1469, Fax: 416-299-5344; Marion Bogert 416-622-6412.
CIRCULATION
C.C.A.B., S.D.A. Div. publisher's statement for 6 mos. ending Sept. 1989.

Average circulation per issue	45,867
Selected distribution Aug. 1989 issue	45,624

†Distribution:

Selected households in Ottawa area	31,287
Selected apts., condominiums	8,303
Delivered in bulk to Welcome Wagon for redistribution	600
Delivered in bulk to airlines for redistribution	50

Single copy distribution (4,734):

Mbrs. of Parliament & Senate	575
Foreign embassies	49
Other single copies mailed to professional offices in Ottawa area	3,604
Subscriptions	506
Net news stand sales	650

†Geographical Breakdown:

Nfld.	1	Man.	6
P.E.I.	2	Sask.	3
N.S.	8	Alta. & N.W.T.	10
N.B.	1	B.C. & Yukon	37
Que.	1,502	U.S.	20
Ont.	44,028	Foreign	3

†Based on Aug. 1989 issue.

In addition to above & audited as to quantity only: Advtrs., agencies 1,530; other 2,000.

FIGURE 5–6

CARD Listing for a Consumer Magazine

Courtesy *Ottawa Magazine*

magazines do not have audio capabilities nor can they use movement to demonstrate a product.

High Production Costs. Magazine production costs are higher than for newspapers, particularly for four-colour advertisements or special devices like metallic inks and microfragrances (e.g., for sampling a perfume).

Magazine Rate Structures

Magazine rates are determined according to circulation, audience, and editorial content. Circulation figures may be audited by the Audit Bureau of Circulations (ABC) or the Canadian Circulations Audit Board (CCAB). Magazines with audited circulation represent about 55 percent of consumer magazines that report circulation. Other magazines provide either sworn statements or guarantees, and about 30 percent of consumer magazines do not report circulation.[33]

This information, as well as all other relevant data, is provided by an individual magazine rate card, which is similar to the newspaper general rate card. A standardized version of the magazine rate card is available in CARD. Figure 5–6 shows the CARD listing for the *Ottawa Magazine.*

The rate structure for magazines may be based on regular rates, a variety of discounts, and additional services advertisers require.

Regular Rate

The regular rate may vary according to an advertisement's size. Most magazines quote their rates according to a full page or a portion of a page. For example, for the *Ottawa Magazine* one finds the following symbols in Figure 5–6 with the corresponding four-colour rate, and one insertion (1 ti.):

1 p.	(one page)	$3835
$2/_3$ p.	(two-thirds of a page)	$3145
$1/_2$ p.	(one-half of a page)	$2610
$1/_3$ p.	(one-third of a page)	$2005

Advertising space covering two pages facing each other is called a *double-page spread* and may be sold at a discount. Part of a spread may also be bought, for example, a half-page spread. A *gatefold* allows an advertisement to run three pages or more and is subject to a special rate, usually at a discount from a multiple of the page rate.

Discounts

Some magazines offer discounts. Magazines that do not offer discounts have what is called a flat rate policy. There are several types of discounts, which may be combined according to the publication:

Frequency discounts are based on the number of issues in which the advertisement appears during a twelve-month period.

Volume discounts are based on the number of full (or equivalent) pages bought within a twelve-month period.

Continuity discounts are combined with volume discounts when an advertiser contracts for a space equivalent to one full page or more in each issue for twelve, twenty-four, or thirty-six consecutive months.

Consecutive-page discounts apply when several consecutive pages are bought in any one issue.

Run-of-book (ROB) discounts allow publishers flexibility in placing an advertisement.

Cash discounts of 2 percent of net amount may be offered when the bill is paid within a specified period of time.

The *short rate* prevails if the advertiser does not use all the space contracted for. The adjustment is based on the discounts applicable to the amount of space used, and it results in amounts to be paid in excess of those already paid. If the amount of space used is higher than the one contracted for, the advertiser receives a *rebate* at the end of the year.

The Future of Magazines as an Advertising Medium

The evolution of magazines in response to competition from other media and U.S. magazines will likely take new directions with the introduction of new technologies.

New printing processes will improve the quality of magazines while new computerized colour graphic systems and other processes will allow a shortening of closing dates. Another technological innovation is called "selective binding" and it may allow development of personalized magazines and advertising. This process uses a computer to read the information from the subscription database to produce a magazine with the contents suited to the subscriber (e.g., medical ads or editorial matter for a doctor), and even insert the name of the subscriber into the ad itself.[34]

The *verticalization* of magazines is likely to continue, with the introduction of more special interest magazines that have smaller audiences but offer advertisers better advertising exposure. More national magazines will develop regional or city editions. City-oriented magazines (e.g., *Calgary Magazine*) or even more restricted demographic areas like business districts or high- income, well-educated residential areas (e.g., Vancouver's *V Magazine*) will offer advertisers better quality audiences.[35]

The proliferation of media and the increased verticalization of magazines will increase the importance of the media director as well as the use of media research. To illustrate this point, the Print Measurement Bureau is increasing the frequency and scope of its research studies.[36]

The introduction of home information delivery systems may eventually lead to the electronic magazine, allowing magazines to increase their coverage of a particular group and generate new revenues to cover increasing costs.

OTHER CANADIAN PERIODICALS

In addition to consumer magazines, periodicals include business publications, farm publications, and directories as well as religious and school publications. Most of what has been said about consumer magazines applies to these periodicals, but there are some important differences.

Business Publications

Business publications developed in Canada with the growth of various trades or professions and were often started by a target group member as a business sideline. They preceded consumer magazines and some eventually became consumer magazines, such as the *Canadian Sportsman*, founded in 1870. Like consumer magazines, the mortality rate of these periodicals was high. The first business publications were aimed at trades or professions. The *Canadian Pharmaceutical Journal* was founded in 1868. The *Canadian Mining Journal* and the *Canada Lumberman* were founded in 1879 and 1880, respectively.[37]

In 1940, there were about 215 Canadian business papers under about 75 classifications, with a total circulation of about a half a million.[38] By 1989, the number of Canadian business publications was over 700, under more than 200 classifications, with a total circulation of more than 100 million.[39] In 1989, net advertising revenues of business publications were $184 million, and growing at an average annual rate of 2.2 percent (Table 5–1).

Differences from Consumer Magazines

Business publications are specialized and are used to advertise products or services to industrial users, distributors, and other professional groups. Business publications differ from consumer magazines in several ways:

- They are directed to professionals who are experts in their fields and for whom the advertising must be informative, and often precedes a sales call.
- They are one of the few sources of new information for professionals.
- They provide advertisers with less readership information than do consumer magazines or daily newspapers (since 1987, a few business publications are included in the PMB annual survey).
- They are represented by several different organizations: the Canadian Business Press (CBP), which is the largest; the Periodical Publishers Exchange (PPE); and the Canadian Magazine Publishers' Association (CMPA).

- Most business publications have low circulation figures (usually below 20 000 copies) compared to consumer magazines. A few like the *Financial Post* have very large circulations (about 200 000).

Rates and Rate Cards

The rate structure of business publications is similar to that of consumer magazines. Like consumer magazines, business publications are audited by the CCAB or ABC or give sworn statements. Since many business publications have controlled distribution, the accuracy of circulation figures is an important factor for advertisers to consider when buying space.

Business publications are expected to show growth in the future, with this growth coming from new publications and improvement in the "total product"—better information on circulation, audiences, and readership.

Farm Publications

Farm journals were one of the earliest types of periodicals in Canada, often associated with daily newspapers. The oldest survivor is the *Free Press Report on Farming*, founded in 1872. Two of the oldest farm journals not associated with daily newspapers are the *Country Guide*, founded in 1882, and the *Grower*, an Ontario journal founded in 1879.[40]

As with other periodicals, farm journals evolved from a general publication to more specialized editorial content, often focusing on the managerial aspects of farming. This trend paralleled the transformation of farming from the small family farm to the large agri-business. A high level of verticalization can be attributed to the heterogeneous farm audience in terms of climatic conditions and types of farm products and competition from other media. Thus, several farm magazines have regional editions. For example, the *Country Guide* offers national, regional, and provincial editions, plus demographic breakdowns by census division for producers with specific needs. This explains why most farm magazine advertising is placed in regional magazines or regional editions of national magazines.

Approximately 99 farm publications are listed in CARD. In 1988 net advertising revenues reached $22 million (Table 5–1). Most are monthly publications, and some are weeklies.

Farm publications are expected to develop along the same lines as consumer magazines, with more specialization, particularly for the large publications.

Directories, Annuals, and Yellow Pages

These publications appear annually and usually contain an alphabetical or classified list of names, addresses, and other information. Advertisers may be charged to have their name listed, to have it appear in special type, or to include an advertisement near their listing.

Approximately 120 directories and annuals are listed in CARD, 80 percent of which are classified as business publications, 13 percent as consumer magazines, and the rest as farm, university, and school publications. Examples are the *Crops Guide* and the *Canadian Directory of Professional Photography*.

Yellow page advertising is often the only form of advertising used by local merchants, since it is an effective and inexpensive medium. Canada has more than 337 yellow page directories with a total circulation of more than 22 million.[41] The large circulation explains why some national advertisers use the yellow pages for promoting a local branch or distributor or for providing information and other services to consumers.

Net advertising revenues for directories reached $931 million in 1989, or 10.3 percent of all media advertising revenues, and these revenues are expected to grow. The medium will likely evolve along the same lines as other periodicals. For example, telephone directories may become widely available through such electronic systems as Alex (Bell Canada).

Religious, University, School, and Scholarly Publications

One early group of Canadian periodicals was the religious publication. Among the oldest surviving ones are the *Atlantic Baptist*, founded in 1827, and the *United Church Observer*, founded in 1829.[42] Twenty-four religious publications are listed in CARD, with circulation ranging from about 1600 to 280 000 and a total circulation of over one million.

About 212 university, community college, alumni, and scholarly publications with a total circulation of over 320 000 are listed in CARD. Some of the oldest publications are *The Brunswickan*, established in 1865, and the *Queen's Journal*, established in 1873.[43] These publications may belong to one of five networks that centralize the selling of space: Access Media with 52 members and about 400 000 circulation, Alumni Plus with 15 members and a circulation of 720 000, the Campus Network with 27 members and a total circulation of over 257 000, Campus Plus, with 49 members and a total circulation of over 300 000, and Publi-PEQ with 46 members and 180 000 circulation.

Foreign-Language Publications

One manifestation of Canadian society's multicultural character is the growth in foreign-language publications (also called the *ethnic press*). This growth is consistent with the overall trend in magazines toward special interest groups.

TABLE 5–3 **NUMBER OF FOREIGN-LANGUAGE PUBLICATIONS IN CANADA**

Language	Number	Language	Number
Italian	18	Hungarian	5
Ukrainian	12	Punjabi	5
Chinese	8	Urdu	5
Greek	8	Korean	4
Arabic	7	Polish	4
Spanish	6	Multicultural	3
German	6	Portuguese	3
Croat, Macedonian,		Slovak & Czech	3
and Slovenian	5	Other*	31
Dutch	5	*Total*	*138*

*Armenian, Byelorussian, Danish, East Indian, Estonian, Inuit, Filipino, Finnish, Gujarati, Hindi, Icelandic, Japanese, Jewish, Latvian, Lithuanian, Malayalam, Native Peoples, Pakistani, Russian, Scandinavian, Scottish, Swedish, and Tamil.

With foreign-language publications language and culture are the main segmenting characteristics. CARD lists approximately 138 publications belonging to 40 language or ethnic groups. The most important ones are Italian, Ukrainian, Chinese, and Greek (Table 5–3).

Most of these publications are recent, but some are quite old, such as the German semi-weekly publication *Mennonitische Rundschau*, established in 1877, and the Icelandic weekly publication *Logberg-Heimskringla*, established in 1886.

TABLE 5–4 **MAIN STRENGTHS AND WEAKNESSES OF NEWSPAPERS, CONSUMER MAGAZINES AND OTHER PERIODICALS**

MEDIUM	Strengths	Weaknesses
Daily newspapers	• high reach • broad coverage • flexible (geographic, lead time, creative) • high reader interest • high frequency potential • affordable to small business • well-researched (NADbank)	• poor colour reproduction • low audience selectivity • low pass along rate • national coverage is difficult/expensive
Community newspapers	• high local reach • broad local coverage • flexible (geographic, lead time, creative) • high reader interest • very affordable to small business	• poor colour reproduction • low audience selectivity • low pass along rate • national coverage very difficult/expensive • low frequency
Consumer magazines	• highly selective • high pass along rate • high-quality reproduction • long life • high prestige and credibility • well-researched (PMB)	• little flexibility (lead time, geographic) • low penetration • high cost of production • low frequency • clutter
Other periodicals	• extremely selective • high-quality reproduction • long life • high reader interest • high prestige and credibility	• little flexibility • low penetration • high production costs • low frequency

SUMMARY

There are various print media available in Canada for carrying advertising messages. Each medium has evolved to meet the needs of the advertiser and compete for a share of the advertising budget. They will continue to do so as needs change and new technologies transform the nature of the media. Table 5–4 highlights the main strengths and weaknesses of each medium.

Newspapers provide high reach and coverage of most demographic subgroups. It is a flexible medium offering short lead times, regional flexibility, and good creative opportunities at low cost. Reader interest tends to be very high for both daily and community newspapers. For daily newspapers, high frequency can be achieved, but not for community newspapers.

Thus, newspapers are a worthwhile medium for regional marketers or small local business. Colour reproduction is sometimes a problem, and national coverage may be relatively expensive and cumbersome to buy. Audience selectivity may be expensive for advertisers with specific audiences.

Periodicals, including consumer magazines, business, farm publications, directories, and others are aimed at a highly selected audience with a high pass along readership. High quality reproduction and long life of messages in a prestigious medium are the major advantages of periodicals. However, periodicals tend to have long lead times and a low penetration of some subgroups. High frequency is difficult to achieve, and the cost of production is often higher than for radio and newspapers.

QUESTIONS FOR STUDY

1. Select the listing of one of your local newspapers in the latest CARD catalogue and try to describe its contents. What would a 300 MAL black and white advertisement in the business section cost a national advertiser?

2. What are the pros and cons of the two-rate structure of national and local advertising? Present the two viewpoints and indicate the kind of policy you would follow as a newspaper publisher or a national advertiser.

3. Compare the use of your local daily newspaper and community newspaper as an advertising medium for a) a local retailer, and b) a national advertiser.

4. Compare newspapers and consumer magazines as advertising media for a) cereals, b) power tools, and c) cheese advertisements.

5. Find three different magazine or newspaper advertisements using flex-form or free-form. Comment on the appropriateness of each. Under what conditions do you think a free-form advertisement would perform better than the traditional rectangular one?

6. Describe the similarities and dissimilarities of promotion through a sales force and through a) newspapers, b) consumer magazines, and c) business publications.

7. Find three different examples of the use of colour in newspaper advertising, and analyze for that product why newspaper was selected as the

advertising medium as well as the role of colour in the advertisement. Answer the same question with consumer magazines.

8. What does verticalization of consumer magazines mean? Explain why this trend occurred. Do you believe it will continue? Justify your answer.

9. Discuss the advantages and disadvantages of your school publication as an advertising medium.

10. Discuss when it is advisable to use consumer magazines or business publications to attract professional readers for a) a manufacturer, b) a financial institution, and c) a pharmaceutical company.

PROBLEMS

1. Assume that you are a retailer of women's fashion shoes in the downtown area of a large metropolitan centre near your home. Your objective is to stimulate traffic in your showroom, and someone suggested that you advertise in one of the local print media. You have budgeted $5 000 for advertising, and you are deciding which print medium to use. In order to understand each medium, you have decided to look at each one separately and evaluate how much exposure your store would be getting by using that medium. Which medium seems to be the best one for your store?

2. Select one particular group of retailers who tend to advertise heavily in local media (for example, auto dealers, electronic retailers, department stores, or supermarkets). Prepare a detailed portfolio of ads, and analyze the choice of media in relation to the probable marketing and advertising strategy. Evaluate the strategy of each retailer in your portfolio, and come up with recommendations regarding media selection.

NOTES

1. H.E. Stephenson and C. McNaught, *The Story of Advertising in Canada* (Toronto: The Ryerson Press, 1940), pp. 1–4.
2. Ibid., pp. 262–68; *Canadian Advertising Rates and Data* (May 1989). Henceforth cited as *CARD*.
3. *The Canadian Media Directors' Council Media Digest, 1990/91*, p. 40. Henceforth cited as *CMDC*.
4. "Canadian daily newspaper chains and independents," *Marketing* (November 14, 1988), p. 45.
5. *CMDC*, pp. 7, 40.
6. T.R. Bird, "Analysis of the Impact of Electronic Systems on Advertising Revenues in Canada," (Working paper, Montreal: Institute for Research on Public Policy, 1982), p. 14.
7. Margaret Bream, "Soybeans and hibiscus plants make reading the paper cleaner, clearer," *Marketing* (November 14, 1988), p. 43.
8. *CMDC*, p. 40; Margaret Bream, "Some habits never die, a paper every day," *Marketing* (November 14, 1988), p. 15.
9. "Weeklies use PMB to show their might," *Marketing* (September 9, 1985), pp. 10–11.
10. Margaret Bream, "Small newspapers make hay while the sun shines," *Marketing* (July 25, 1988), pp. 11–12; Bird, *op. cit.*, p. 19.
11. *CMDC*, p. 45; Leonard Kubas, "For innovative marketers boom times lie in wait," *Marketing* (September 9, 1985), pp. 15–16.

12. *CARD*, pp. 64–65.
13. *NADbank*, 1988.
14. Bird, p. 14.
15. *NADbank*, 1988.
16. Newspaper Marketing Bureau, *Canadian Daily Newspapers: The Facts*, March 15, 1981, p. 30; *NADbank* 1988.
17. Fred H. Siller and Vernon J. Jones, "Newspaper Campaign Audience Segments," *Journal of Advertising Research* (June 1973), pp. 27–31.
18. "NMB Leads in Market Research," *Marketing* (November 2, 1981), pp. 43–45; John Finneran, "Black and white and read with zeal...still," *Marketing* (November 14, 1988), p. 32.
19. "What's hot in the 'hot medium'," *Marketing* (November 9, 1987), pp. 14–22.
20. Finneran, p. 32; David Cadogan, "Mom and Pop move over for the 'real' trends," *Marketing* (July 25, 1988), p. 11; Leonard Kubas, "Newspapers making their own news," *Marketing* (November 9, 1987), p. 31.
21. Finneran, p. 32; Kubas, p. 31.
22. Joe Mullie, "The Videotex Threat? Fear and Loathing in the Newsroom," *Marketing* (November 8, 1982), pp. 11–12.
23. Stephenson and McNaught, pp. 273–76.
24. Ibid., pp. 277–79.
25. *CMDC*, p. 50; Jo Marney, "Demographic Changes Favour Future Growth," *Marketing* (April 12, 1982), pp. M6–7.
26. CARD, p. 74.
27. Jo Marney, "In the beginning was the Word...," *Marketing* (June 22, 1981), pp. 36–37.
28. Len Kubas, "Upper-income households are the top magazine buyers," *Marketing* (April 4, 1988), pp. 40–42.
29. *CARD*, p. 136.
30. *CMDC*, p. 53.
31. Karen Dean, "Magazines Canada Industry Round-up," *Marketing* (April 12, 1982), pp. M14–16.
32. "Readership and circulation on even keel, survey shows," *Marketing* (July 11, 1988), p. 10.
33. Bird. p. 25.
34. Rob Wilson, "Magazines just for you," *Marketing* (April 17, 1989), p. 28.
35. Leonard Kubas, "Is publishing greener on the other side?," *Marketing* (April 17, 1989), pp. 30, 40; "Magazine sets its sight on city core," *Marketing* (June 22, 1981), p. 60.
36. Hugh Dow, "PMB moves to annual reporting with the release of 1983 study," *Marketing* (April 12, 1982), pp. M12–13.
37. Stephenson and McNaught, pp. 271–72.
38. Ibid., p. 272.
39. Estimated from *CARD*, p. 197, and *CMDC*, 1986/87, p. 43.
40. Stephenson and McNaught, p. 270.
41. *CMDC*, p. 77.
42. *CARD*, pp. 171–73.
43. *CARD*, pp. 174–180.

CHAPTER

6 Canadian Out-of-Home and Direct Response Media

A variety of other print media are available to advertisers, the two major categories being out-of-home and direct advertising.

Out-of-home advertising is growing rapidly and reached $718 million in net advertising revenues in 1989, which is about double the 1984 figure (see Table 5–1). The two major forms of out-of-home advertising are *outdoor advertising* and *transit advertising*.

Direct response advertising, particularly *direct mail advertising* and *telephone advertising*, is also growing rapidly, is becoming more sophisticated, and will likely benefit from new technologies.

The total net advertising revenues of direct response almost reached the $2 billion mark in 1989, which represents about a 22 percent share of all media. With outdoor media at 7.9 percent, these other Canadian print media represent almost 30 percent of all revenues.

OUTDOOR ADVERTISING

Evolution of Outdoor as an Advertising Medium

Outdoor advertising is a very old medium and may be traced back to Babylonian bas reliefs. Early Canadian tradesmen and merchants used rocks, fences, barns, and chimneys to advertise their trade. Then came the printed poster, which was initially used by circuses, theatrical companies, and the patent medicine industry. In 1891, bill posting companies formed the Associated Billposters and Distributors of the United States and Canada. This helped standardize poster sizes and rates. Sign painting companies merged with the bill posting companies in 1925 to form the forerunner of the Outdoor Advertising Association of Canada.[1] The most important factor in the growth of the medium was the growth of the automobile industry early in the twentieth century. Outdoor displays grew in size and in geographical coverage and the copy became simpler, thus effectively attracting attention. After standardization of sizes and rates, the most pressing need for advertisers was for research that would verify audience data. In 1933, the Traffic Audit Bureau was created for this purpose. Today this task is performed by the Canadian Outdoor Measurement Bureau (COMB).

Types of Outdoor Formats

Space for outdoor advertising is usually offered as predetermined sets of packages in each city. For any market, the packages are designed according to daily circulation figures expressed as a set percentage of the total population: 25, 50, 75, and 100 GRPs. The number of panels needed for each level varies from market to market.

There is a great variety of outdoor formats, and it is likely that new ones will be created where there is both a shortage of traditional space, and high traffic. The following will review the main formats available in Canada.

Posters

Poster panels are large structures that can accommodate three different sizes of posters: the 24-sheet, the 30-sheet, and bleed posters (Figure 6–1, page 144). Another common format is 305 cm × 610 cm (10 ft × 20 ft). Posters are available in more than 400 Canadian markets and in 14 extended market areas, reaching more than 70 percent of the Canadian population. They are the most common format of outdoor advertising.

Tri-laterals are a form of poster panel, in which a series of triangular posts rotate at regular intervals to reveal one of three ads. This allows an element of novelty and movement, and maximizes the use of locations where space is scarce or severely restricted. However, these structures are difficult to set up and to maintain.

Junior Panels

Junior panels (also called eight-sheets) have a non-illuminated single pole structure of 366 cm x 183 cm (12 ft x 6 ft) placed in six census metropolitan areas (CMAs). The actual copy area is 335 cm x 152 cm (11 ft x 5 ft), and they are usually positioned at a lower level than regular posters. They can be used for local advertising or to supplement at a lower cost a poster campaign.

Superboards

Superboards (also called painted bulletins) are hand painted or printed designs on structures larger than posters and are positioned at heavy traffic locations in major markets. The designs are rotated to different locations every two months to offer a more balanced coverage. Extensions made of wood or plastic affixed to the unit may extend the face of the bulletin for more dramatic effects.

A modern variation of superboards are the superflex posters made of flexible vinyl stretched over wood or metal, with either painted or printed designs. They are available in two sizes:

- the Series 14, which are 427 cm x 1463 cm (14 ft x 48 ft), available in six major markets;
- the Series 10, which are 305 cm x 1340 cm (10 ft x 44 ft), available in 18 major markets.

Backlit Outdoor

There are three kinds of backlit posters available in Canada.

Backlights are units of 305 cm x 610 cm (10 ft x 20 ft) located in high traffic areas, printed on reinforced translucent plastic, and illuminated from behind. They allow better colour reproduction, particularly at night. They are located

FIGURE 6–1

***Characteristics of the
Three Main Types of
Standardized Posters***

*Source: The Instructor's
Manual: An Inside Look
at Outdoor Advertising*
(New York: Gannett
Foundation, 1981).

The common poster panel is usually 747 cm long and 366 cm high (24′6″ × 12′) and can accommodate three different sizes of posters: the 24-sheet, the 30-sheet, and the bleed. All sizes involve a proportion of $2\frac{1}{4}$ to 1.

24-Sheet Poster

Many years ago, when printing presses were smaller, a poster panel required 24 sheets of paper. Today, with larger presses, fewer sheets are needed but the original term remains. This is a typical pattern for a 24-sheet poster which measures 594 cm by 264 cm. The area between the design and the frame is covered with white blanking paper.

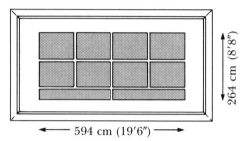

30-Sheet Poster

The 30-sheet poster, measuring 658 cm by 292 cm, provides about 25% more space for the design than does the 24-sheet poster. The additional space is taken from the blanking area. This is a typical pattern for the 30-sheet poster. Through careful planning of the pattern, 4-colour printing can be limited to a minimum number of sheets for lower production costs.

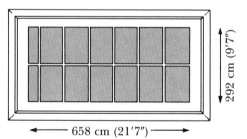

Bleed Poster

In the bleed poster—40% larger than the 24-sheet—the design is carried all the way to the frame. This is done by printing the minor variations in the overall size of poster panels; essential elements of the design—such as copy or logo—should be positioned at least 15 cm from the edges. This will ensure their appearance on the smallest panels.

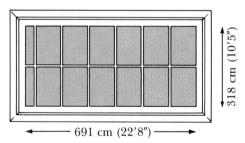

at high traffic points in 27 urban markets. They are rotated every eight weeks to different locations.

Airport backlights are units of 305 cm x 915 cm (10 ft x 30 ft), made of similar material and located near airports in 15 urban markets. They are rotated every 60 days, and are generally purchased for a longer term than regular backlights.

Urban-lites are units of 305 cm x 700 cm (10 ft x 23 ft), printed on translucent plastic and internally illuminated. They are located in high traffic points in 25 urban markets, and are rotated every 60 days.

Spectaculars

Spectaculars are custom designed and come in varying shapes and sizes. They use electrical or mechanical devices or inflatable vinyl-coated nylon to create a three-dimensional display. Other devices can be used, such as steam in a coffee advertisement, or reflective disks to create an impression of movement.

Transit Shelters

Transit shelter advertising is available in 21 major markets along the high traffic areas. The ads are 122 cm x 168 cm (4 ft x 5 ft 6 in.), and each shelter can carry two backlit ads.

Mall Posters

As the name indicates, mall posters are located in about 420 malls and shopping centres in 25 major markets. The size of the display is 107 cm x 152 cm (3 ft 6 in. x 5 ft). They are reverse printed and illuminated from behind the glass, and they are rotated every 30 days to provide a complete market coverage of the message.

Pillar-Ads

Pillar-Ad is going West to Calgary, Edmonton and Vancouver

These pillar units are placed at eye-level with two or four faces and located on private or public property adjacent to the sidewalk in the downtown areas of major markets across Canada, and seven smaller markets in Ontario (Figure 6–2). The size of the backlit display is the same as transit shelters, 117 cm x 171 cm (46 in x 67 in.). In addition, new units called *Pillar-Box* are available in Toronto at the entrances to subway stations, and they incorporate newspaper vending machines with two regular displays and two smaller ones (2 ft 5 in. x 5 ft 6 in. or 74 cm x 168 cm).

FIGURE 6–2
An Example of Pillar Ads

Courtesy Pillar Ads

Electronic Boards

These new types of outdoor advertising are electronic message and animation centres. Called *Pixelboards*, they display electronic messages for ten seconds, twenty-four hours a day.[2] They are currently available in ten markets.

Outdoor as an Advertising Medium

Advantages

The advantages of outdoor can be grouped into four categories.

High Reach and Frequency. Outdoor is a mass medium with high reach; it covers all demographic groups. In addition, outdoor provides high frequency very quickly because it has broad strategic location throughout a market.

Flexibility. Outdoor can be purchased market-by-market, thus providing advertisers with geographic flexibility. Also, advertisers may vary the time period for showing the advertisement.

High Message Impact. Outdoor has a long life, and because of its size and artistic quality, it is an effective medium for many products that need reminder advertising or for new product introductions, which need quick brand awareness. Research has shown that 73 percent of those who see a poster, and 80 percent of those who see a junior poster, can recall the brand.[3]

Efficient. Outdoor is a relatively inexpensive medium on a relative cost per thousand impressions basis. Advertising messages can be placed close to the actual point-of-purchase, which is important during seasonal shopping rushes.

Disadvantages

The disadvantages of outdoor advertising can also be grouped into four categories.

Creative Negatives. Outdoor can only be used for very short product stories. The advertisement must use few words and illustrations for the message to be communicated effectively. In addition, the environment in which the advertisement is placed can be highly distracting, and there is no editorial or program content to enhance it. Also, outdoor is not considered a prestigious medium and it may create some negative feelings among consumers who object to its environmental impact.

Audience Selectivity. The medium's broad reach means that it is difficult, if not impossible, to focus on a specific target group. Thus some circulation may be wasted. Outdoor is not consistently available in all major markets. It is banned in some cities (e.g., Victoria, B.C.) or severely restricted (in Quebec only French copy is allowed). Finally, statistics used to measure audiences reflect only the level of traffic flows by the boards and thus do not necessarily compare with those of other media.

Long Lead Times. Outdoor requires long lead times because of the long production time of outdoor messages. Often a two-month lead time is necessary.

High Total Costs. The absolute costs for national coverage are high. In addition, the production costs are fairly high compared to radio, magazines, and newspapers.

Outdoor Advertising Rate Structure

Information on rates and data about each type of outdoor advertising is available from the corresponding outdoor company, as well as from the latest issue of CARD. An example of a CARD listing for outdoor is presented in Figure 6–3.

Mediacom Airport Advertising

Data confirmed for June/90 CARD

COMMISSION & CASH DISCOUNT: 15% to accredited advtg. agencies.
CANCELLATION: Contracts are noncancellable.

INTERIORS
GENERAL INFORMATION: Airport advertising displays are located in 20 Canadian airport terminals in 19 major markets. Displays include Air Posters, Spectaculars, Display Cases, Travellers' Service Centres & free standing display space. Western Sales Office: Vancouver, BC V6G 1J3: Ronald G. Smith, Sales Mgr., Mediacom Inc., 1905-2020 Haro St. Phone: 604-250-5553. Fax: 604-926-1417.
AIR POSTERS: 40" h. x 50" w., rear-illuminated advtg. displays. Std. posters not protected for guaranteed location. Permanent posters purchased on permanent basis with guaranteed location.
TRAVELLER SERVICE CENTRE: A backlit display of photographs depicting an advertisers place of business. A phone line provides direct communication between traveller and advertiser.
SPECTACULARS: Large rear illuminated displays ranging in size up to 8' x 12'.
DISPLAY CASES/DISPLAY SPACE: Floor &/or wall mounted cases or aisle space to display products or service.
EXTERIOR AIRPORT: Displays provide outdoor coverage of the airport in selected Internationals.
CONTRACT PROCEDURE: One contract books media space across Canada. If contract cannot be fulfilled as requested, advtr. may approve or reject alternative coverage or dates.
SHORT TERM RATES: Rates quoted are for 52 wk. campaigns; shorter term rates avail. upon request.
LOCATION LISTS/MAPS: Location lists/maps will be supplied by your sales rep. on request.

SERVICE CHARGES: Apply for copy/design changes on Air Posters. See rep. for details.
CLOSING DATES: Production of all copy mat'l is responsibility of advtr. & must be provided to appropriate market 10 days pre. installation date.
ADVERTISING COPY: All artwork must have bilingual Eng./Fr. copy of equal prominence except in Quebec where all "non-service" copy must be in universal "non copy" format. English to appear 1st in all provinces except Que. where French to appear 1st. All artwork must be approved by Transport Canada via Mediacom before production.
SHIPPING: Advtr. will be supplied with list of shipping addresses & is responsible for shipping mat'l to each market.
ART SPECIFICATIONS: For 40" x 50" faces, mat'l should be in proportion & may be supplied as: transparencies or negs., min. 4" x 5", to max. 8" x 10" (good quality 35mm, usage possible); or reflective artwork min. 8" x 10" to size as. A 10% prodn. overrun is recommended in case of loss or damage in shipment. Sales rep. can suggest production sources.
AIRPORT ADVERTISING RATES: 52 week min. purchase. Rates are 52 week rate per unit.
INTERIOR:

Market	Air Poster 40x50	Spectacular 8x16
Western Region		
*Vancouver	$17,820	$44,340
*Calgary	14,616	36,540
*Edmonton	10,176	—
*Winnipeg	9,996	—
Thunder Bay	3,204	—
Regina	3,204	—
Saskatoon	3,204	—
Ontario/Quebec Regions		
*Toronto Terminal I	$19,248	$48,132
*Toronto II	24,408	61,056
*Dorval	20,076	50,160
*Mirabel	7,092	—
Quebec City	3,396	8,496
*Ottawa	10,704	—
Atlantic Region		
*Halifax	$ 8,940	$18,600
Saint John, N.B.	3,396	—
Moncton	3,396	—
Fredericton	3,396	—
Charlottetown	3,396	—
Sydney	3,396	—
St. John's, Nfld.	3,396	—

*International Airports

EXTERIOR
GENERAL INFORMATION: Displays provide outdoor coverage of the airport in selected internationals.
SHORT TERM RATES: Rates quoted are for 52 wk. campaigns. Shorter term rates: 0-26 wks., 50% extra; 27-51 wks., 20% extra.
CLOSING DATES: Finished art must be rec'd 10 working days pre. to scheduled start date. Artwork rec'd within 10-days may be subjected to production & posting premiums.
ADVERTISING RATES: Information received Nov. 24, 1989.

	Airport	*Location	52 wk.
10 x 30 backlights	*Dorval	A	†
10 x 30 backlights	Dorval	B	†
10 x 30 backlights	Dorval	C	†
10 x 30 backlights	*Mirabel	—	†
10 x 30 backlights	Que. City	1	$18,900
10 x 20 posters	Que. City	2	9,120
10 x 20 posters	Que. City	3	9,120
10 x 20 posters	Que. City	4	9,120
10 x 20 posters	Que. City	5	9,120
10 x 20 posters	Sudbury	—	5,980
10 x 20 posters	Timmins	—	5,980
10 x 20 posters	North Bay	—	5,980

*International Airports.
†Consult Poster Network rep.

FIGURE 6–3

An Example of CARD Listing for Outdoor Advertising

Courtesy Mediacom Inc.

Rates for outdoor advertising are based on three main factors. The first is the level of daily GRPs, i.e. the average daily circulation as a percentage of the total population. The circulation figure is the number of persons walking or driving by the outdoor display each day. The most commonly used levels are 25, 50, 75, and 100 GRPs. Junior and mall posters use different levels. These rates are usually quoted for a four-week period, although short-term contracts are available at a premium.

Outdoor panels are not generally bought individually, and the number of panels that deliver a given level of GRPs varies from market to market. For example, in 1990 the rate for posters in all 62 urban markets and 50 daily GRPs was about $560 000 for 997 panels. For 100 daily GRPs, the cost was about $1 million for 1826 panels.[4]

Production charges must be added to the other costs, particularly for superboards, spectaculars, and backlights. Continuity discounts based on the number of consecutive weeks purchased are available in some markets.

Future of Outdoor Advertising

Because its main strengths are high reach and frequency, outdoor is likely to grow as an advertising medium. The supply of outdoor space will have to increase without creating a negative public reaction, which would restrict its growth or even ban it from certain high traffic areas. Thus outdoor structures may have to become more adapted to their environment. Some ways of accomplishing this may involve making innovative use of available space, using the new electronic and laser technologies,[5] and providing public services, such as time of day and news.

TRANSIT ADVERTISING

Evolution of Transit as an Advertising Medium

Streetcar advertising was first handled directly by the companies themselves. By 1902, street railways carried 135 million passengers in Canada, and by 1937 the number had grown to 827 million.[6] Advertising companies contracted with the various street railways for space to sell to advertisers. The industry grew with the number of passengers and number of public transportation systems. Today, most streetcars have been replaced by subways and buses, and transit advertising has changed accordingly.

Types of Transit Advertising

There are several types of transit advertising, the most important ones being interior transit cards and the exterior bus boards.

Interior Transit Cards

Interior transit cards (also called car cards) are displayed inside the vehicles. Because the travelling public is a captive audience, it is an effective communication medium. Car cards are available in more than 73 markets and are offered in standards sizes of 28 cm x 59 cm or 118 cm, depending on the market (11 in. x 23$\frac{1}{4}$ in. or 46$\frac{1}{2}$ in.). Back-lit car cards are available in several markets.

Car cards are sold on the basis of level of service. Full service means that every vehicle has one or two cards. Service may also be offered in multiples or fractions. For example, half service means that half of the full service boards will be distributed among the vehicles, i.e., among every other vehicle or one card per vehicle instead of two. Car cards may also be sold on the same basis as for outdoor—by level of GRPs.

Exterior Bus Boards

Exterior bus boards may be purchased for the front, sides, and back of vehicles. They are, in effect, travelling outdoor displays; their audience extends beyond the travelling public to pedestrians and motorists.

Exterior bus boards are available in more than 65 markets across Canada. The standard sizes are:

- king size, 76 cm x 353 cm (30 in. x 139 in.);
- queen size, 53 cm x 223 cm (21 in. x 88 in.);
- taillight, 53 cm x 178 cm (21 in. x 70 in.).

They may be sold according to the number of boards (showings) per month, or according to set levels of weekly GRPs.

Total Painted Buses

This is a relatively new medium, in which the complete outside of the bus is hand painted with one single message (see Figure 6–4). The result is very striking and the message is surely noticed.[7] In addition, the advertiser buys the entire interior space of the vehicle. Total painted buses are available in 22 markets across Canada, and are contracted for a minimum of one year.

Other Transit Formats

Other forms of transit advertising are subway posters, which may be platform posters on the walls of the platform, or interior sidedoor cards located on each side of the car door. Other options include back-lit displays placed in high traffic areas of subway stations, digital clock advertising within subway stations, and bus top spectaculars, custom-designed as for outdoor spectaculars.

Transit as an Advertising Medium

Advantages

As for outdoor advertising, transit is a mass medium with a high degree of market flexibility.

It also commands attention and has high visual impact. Another strength is that advertising copy can be longer than for outdoor displays.

It is a relatively inexpensive medium for reaching urban markets and operates close to the point-of-sale. It also allows advertisers to provide riders with coupons or response cards.

Disadvantages

Transit is inefficient for non-urban and narrow audiences. In addition, there is a lack of extensive audience research on transit that would provide informa-

FIGURE 6–4

An Example of a Total Painted Bus

Courtesy Trans Ad

FIGURE 6–5

*An Example of CARD
Listing for Transit*

Media Marketing Associates Ltd.
(St. John's, Nfld.)

Data confirmed for May/90 CARD

P.O. Box 5634, St. John's, NF A1C 5W8. Phone: 709-726-4100. Fax: 709-739-7724.
COMMISSION & CASH DISCOUNT: 15% to recognized agencies.
GENERAL ADVERTISING: Information received Dec. 22, 1988.
CORNER BROOK TRANSIT SYSTEM
No. of buses: 9.
Exterior Bus Boards

	Per month/ Per Panel
Tail-light sections (70″ x 21″)	$110
(60″x13″)	89
Side Sections (70″ x 21″)	84

Interior

		Mo. per panel
Car cards (11″ x 23-1/4″)		$13
Dbl. car cards (46-1/4″ x 4″)		17
Transfers	Distribution	Rate 300./
2″ x 2″ copy area	10,000/mo.	10,000

Conditions: Rates for space only, advtrs. to supply cards.
Continuity Discount: 6 mos.—5%; 12 mos.—10%.
PERSONNEL
Sales: Paul Dunne, Robert Meaney.

tion on audience characteristics and reach/frequency figures.

The advertisements tend to be expensive and time-consuming to produce and thus have long lead times. Also, as a medium it lacks prestige among consumers and the trade.

Transit Advertising Rate Structure

Information on rates and data about each type of transit advertising is available from the corresponding company, as well as from the latest issue of CARD. An example of a CARD listing for transit is presented in Figure 6–5.

The rate structure for transit is similar to that of outdoor advertising, although the actual rates may be different. For example, full service on a national basis for the smallest interior card size in 1990 cost about $80 000 per month, based on a three-month purchase.[8]

Future of Transit Advertising

The use of transit advertising will likely grow with the development of transit systems and with the increase in the proportion of the urban population using it instead of the automobile. Also, transit may benefit from the potential shortage of outdoor space. Better research may show that costs per thousand impressions are low, making transit a good buy for many small- or medium-sized advertisers.[9] Increased demand for transit space may bring about innovative ways of using the available space while maintaining reach and frequency levels.

OTHER OUT-OF-HOME MEDIA

As explained earlier, tradesmen and merchants have historically used a variety of out-of-home supports to advertise their trade, including rocks and barns. This tendency has taken many modern forms, the most important ones being new outdoor structures, as well as new forms of transit advertising. This section will briefly review other forms of out-of-home media. The reader may readily think of other ones that have not been introduced yet.[10] Information on rates and data, as well as on the various companies offering this service, is available from the latest issue of CARD.

Aerial Advertising

This is advertising in the sky at special events or in the downtown areas when there are many people outside. This form of advertising includes sky writing, banner towing, advertising on blimps and hot air balloons,[11] and lighted messages for night viewing. An example of aerial advertising is reproduced in Figure 6–6.

FIGURE 6–6

An Example of Aerial Advertising

Courtesy Darryl Dahmer, Topcam Inc. and Goodyear Canada Public Relations

Bench Advertising

This includes advertising on benches situated in high traffic areas, with either pedestrian and/or motor vehicles.[12] Most of the sites are currently in Ontario. An example of bench advertising is presented in Figure 6–7.

Elevator Advertising

In some high-rise buildings, many people tend to circulate and have to travel by elevator. Some companies have been selling small display areas to advertisers (13 cm x 17 cm, or 5 in. x 7 in.). These tend to be local advertisers, mainly retailers.[13]

Shopping Centre Advertising

This is different from the mall advertising described in the section on outdoor. Shopping centre advertising includes showcases that travel from centre to centre, kiosks, distributing brochures, or other forms of information displays.

Sports Advertising

This includes all forms of advertising in locations where there are usually a large number of participants and spectators, such as at stadiums, ski lifts,[14] golf courses, and health and fitness clubs.

Taxicab Advertising

Taxicab rooftop displays, mostly illuminated, are available in Vancouver and Toronto. Like buses, these taxis are constantly moving and their "travelling displays" can be seen by many people in urban areas.

FIGURE 6–7

An Example of Bench Advertising

Courtesy Creative Outdoor Advertising

Truck Advertising

These work on the same principle of mobile outdoor displays and are available in Toronto and Montreal. Because of their size, trucks can accommodate large posters, which make a strong impact (Figure 6–8). Also, with their mobility they can expose the message to a large number of people.[15]

Theatre and Video Screen Advertising

Advertising is shown in theatres during each performance,[16] or in shopping malls during public service information clips.

DIRECT RESPONSE ADVERTISING

Direct response advertising is defined as any form of advertising message that is sent directly to a pre-selected audience through the mail, by telephone, or through any of the traditional advertising media. This form of advertising has seen tremendous growth both in terms of revenues, as well as in the means used to convey the message. In this medium, the advertiser has a message that contains an offer, and the objective of this message is to sell a product, a service, or an idea. Companies offering these kinds of services are represented by the Canadian Direct Marketing Association (CDMA).

There are several forms of direct response advertising, with the most important one being mail and telephone advertising (also called *telemarketing*, although the latter is also used in conjunction with personal selling).

- *Direct mail* advertising is the largest form of direct response advertising. Due to its importance, it will be studied in detail in the next section.
- *Telephone* advertising (telemarketing, with the above distinction) is growing very rapidly in Canada. Telemarketing has in recent years grown spectacu-

larly and accounts for a large share of direct marketing revenues.[17] The main reasons for its popularity are, first, that it is a fast method of reaching prospects, with a high degree of control. Second, it can be used effectively with other promotional activities, such as direct mail and sales force efforts. Third, the costs of a telephone call may vary between $3 and $10, compared to the cost of sales call, which may reach $230.[18] Today, everyone has a telephone, and some have more than one (including one in the car). Advertising messages to promote the sale of a product or service can be made quite inexpensively from a centralized location. Advertisers have the choice of using trained operators (out-bound service),[19] or using toll-free "800" numbers contained in messages sent through other media like newspapers or television (in-bound service). Some companies have been experimenting with computer calls using an automatic dialing-announcing device (ADAD). However, the lack of personal interaction makes ADAD somewhat ineffective. Telemarketing is expected to be the fastest growth area of direct response advertising in the 1990s.

- *Direct print* advertising includes preprinted inserts in newspapers, magazines, and other periodicals, as well as advertisements which contain some form of direct response. These were covered in Chapter 5, as part of the services offered by the print media to advertisers. Outdoor may also be used for a direct response, such as providing directions to a retail outlet, or an address or phone number.

- *Direct television* advertising is often well suited for many products that are rather inexpensive and can be shown or demonstrated to the viewers. The commercials for these products then provide either a toll-free "800" number

FIGURE 6–8
An Example of
Truck Advertising

Courtesy Flashmedia

or an address to order the product. An extension of this principle is the introduction of various home shopping programs or networks where more expensive merchandise can be promoted. Distribution of advertising messages through cable television will probably experience very rapid growth in the 1990s with the spread of new communication technologies.[20]

• *Direct radio* advertising can be used for products which do not need to be seen, for example tapes or compact disks of popular singers or composers.

DIRECT MAIL ADVERTISING

Evolution of Direct Mail as an Advertising Medium

Direct mail advertising was one of the first media used in Canada by merchants and has its roots in handbills and pamphlets as well as the advertising card. The growth of direct mail advertising was spurred by developments in printing technology, the growth in postal delivery methods and postal rate structures, as well as by efforts to organize the industry. In 1917, the Direct Mail Association of America was formed with the active participation of Canadian representatives.[21]

Direct mail has been growing rapidly in Canada—an average of 8.9 percent per year between 1984 and 1989. Net advertising revenues of direct mail were almost $2 billion in 1989, representing about 22 percent of all advertising revenues. Thus in terms of advertising revenues, direct mail is the second largest medium after daily newspapers. This growth is likely to continue. Americans receive three times the amount of direct mail material that Canadians do, but because Canadians are more collectively oriented than Americans, response rates in Canada are about 40 percent higher than in the U.S. Response rates are also higher in Quebec than in English Canada.[22]

Characteristics of Direct Mail Advertising

Direct mail is characterized by format and mailing lists, as well as production and distribution.

Formats

Direct mail comes in a variety of formats, with letters being the most common.

Letters. Most people like to read interesting letters, so considerable work has been done to improve the effectiveness of the creative approaches in designing letters. New technologies are being incorporated in the production of direct mail material to make them more involving, interesting, and personalized. The wide use of computers in the last two decades brought about the *computerized letter*, which is becoming more and more sophisticated and attractive. For example, the use of laser processes for addressing allows the display of copy in half-inch type, adding strong visual impact to the message and increasing attention and response rates.

Other formats of direct mail may be used in conjunction with or instead of a letter.

Broadsides. Also called *bedsheets*, these are large sheets with full colour illustrations and folded for distribution. Layout and copy are very important in keeping the reader's interest.

Booklets.   Booklets are used when the message is too long for a broadside or a folder, or when several offerings are described.

Folders.   These direct mail pieces are commonly used to present short, simple printed messages and may be used with or without an accompanying letter.

Circulars.   Also called *leaflets*, *throwaways*, or *fliers*, circulars are one of the least expensive forms of direct mail advertising and are used for a quick impact, for example, to announce a special sale.

Brochures.   These are a more elaborate, higher quality type of booklet.

Postcards.   Postcards are used for short messages that need to be sent inexpensively. They may include a reply feature.

Catalogues.   Catalogues are books describing several or all of the products available from either a manufacturer or a distributor. Because Canada's population has strong rural roots and is sparsely distributed, catalogues and particularly department store catalogues have always been popular[23] and will likely see rapid growth in the future.

Some upscale advertisers have recently introduced a catalogue resembling a magazine, with articles on a subject somewhat related to the merchandise. These are called *magalogs*, and they tend to be expensive to produce and distribute. An example of a magalog is Birks' "The Spirit of Adventure" (Figure 6–9), which contains articles on the theme of an African safari.[24]

FIGURE 6–9
An Example of "Magalog"

Courtesy Henry Birks & Sons Ltd.

Mailing Lists

A good, up-to-date mailing list is an essential requirement in direct-mail advertising. A message is lost if the address is incorrect or if the recipient is not in the target market. Since direct mail is an expensive medium, it is particularly important to minimize wasted circulation. With a proper mailing list the advertiser can truly practise relationship marketing, by paying particular attention to respondents' likes, dislikes, and past behaviour/purchases.[25]

Mailing lists come from several sources.[26]

Internal (or House) Lists.   Internal lists are available to many advertisers from their own records of clients, distributors, stockholders, inquiries, complaints, and so on. Further breakdowns may be done based on the information available on these individuals or companies.

Solicitation (or Response) Lists.   These are lists of individuals who responded to various forms of direct mail solicitation, to other forms of direct response, or to promotion incentives. They are generally considered to be the best lists available. They are available from specialized companies, most of them with several demographic breakdowns.

Directories.   Directories are another source of potentially useful mailing lists. They may be broad like the telephone directory, or very narrow like the list of members of the Administrative Sciences Association of Canada.

Compiled Lists.   These lists are developed by one organization according to a common criterion and then made available to advertisers. They are compiled from a variety of sources, such as directories, public records, or trade show registration. For example, these could include a list of new house buyers or graduating students.

Production and Distribution

Production of direct mail pieces may be done by an advertiser or its agency or by a direct mail agency. These agencies handle all the details from the initial layout and the development of the mailing list to the final distribution program.

Since a direct mail campaign can be extremely complex and expensive, advertisers may also use the services of several specialists:

- freelance designers and/or writers for the creative side;
- a mailing list company or a list broker for the rental, purchase, or creation of a mailing list;
- list managers for the actual housing and on-going maintenance of the list (addition, deletion, and correction), as well as analysis of the responses achieved with the list;
- letter shops (or fulfillment houses), which handle the actual printing of direct mail material and stuff, seal, address, and sort (according to postal codes) the envelopes.

Direct Mail as an Advertising Medium

Advantages

The advantages of direct mail can be grouped into four categories.

Selectivity. Direct mail is a highly selective medium; it allows advertisers to reach a narrowly defined target audience with a well-targeted message. Mailing lists often allow the advertiser to reach the best prospects for a product with a minimum amount of wasted circulation. In particular, the F.S.A. (Forward Sortation Area) codes, which are the first three digits of the postal codes, provide very precise indications of the demographic characteristics of the addressee. This is because census information is available according to F.S.A. codes. In addition, direct mail allows complete flexibility in the degree of coverage to be reached by the campaign.

Creative Flexibility and Effectiveness. From the creative director's viewpoint, direct mail is a highly versatile medium. It is very flexible in the type of creative approaches, format, length of copy, and type of layouts it allows. In particular, the ability to use long copy is a strong point in favour of direct mail compared to other media. Communication with the market may be highly personal, quick, and has the possibility of feedback that can be measured. In addition, direct mail commands a high level of attention, free from the distraction of other media or competitive messages. Finally, a direct mail message may have a long life, with many prospects keeping it for future action, as a reminder, to show a spouse, a friend, or to pass along.

High Degree of Control. From an overall communications viewpoint, direct mail provides a high degree of control. The advertiser has some certainty that the message has reached the intended audience. In addition, the advertiser may measure the performance of the campaign quite accurately, both for the total target or for some demographic or psychographic breakdowns.

Complements Sales Promotion. Direct mail can also be used for a variety of sales promotion activities: to distribute coupons, refund offers, contest announcements, and small product samples.[27]

Disadvantages

The disadvantages of direct mail can be grouped into three categories.

High Relative Costs. The major disadvantage of direct mail is its high relative cost. The cost per thousand impressions may run as much as 100 times the cost per thousand viewers for television. This high cost makes it imperative for the communication to be effective.

Creative Negatives. Direct mail has some creative negatives. The message must stand on its own, without editorial support. The reader may have little interest in the material or have a negative reaction to this form of advertising. Studies show that a high percentage of people open their "junk mail," but the response rate of direct mail is often extremely low. Although the response rate depends on several factors, such as the value of the item advertised or the type of market reached, it is not unusual for response rates to be less than 1 percent.

Operational Problems. The effectiveness of a direct mail advertising campaign depends heavily on the speed of postal delivery. Also, the accuracy of the information contained in the mailing list, including demographic and psychographic information, affects the success of the campaign.

Cost Structure of Direct Mail

The costs of a direct mail campaign are related to production, mailing lists, and distribution.

Production costs vary with the type, length, and quality of the message. A one-page black and white flyer costs much less than a four-colour broadsheet. The costs of the creative work for preparing the direct mail material must also be added.

Mailing lists may be rented, purchased, or compiled specifically for an advertiser. Costs vary with the type, length, and quality of the list.

A final cost factor is the *distribution* of the mailing, which involves folding, collating, stuffing, addressing, stamping, and bundling envelopes. The cost is based on the number of steps involved and the number of names in the list. One important item in the distribution is the cost of postal delivery, which varies according to the weight and the postal class used. For example, first class is the most expensive but also the fastest type of mail delivery, and it should be used when timing is important.

Future of Direct Mail Advertising

The future of direct mail will be influenced by innovations that will improve the attractiveness of a mailed advertisement and reduce its costs. The industry will continue to improve its use of computer technology, laser technology, fax technology, and new printing processes. This will help make advertisements more personal, more relevant, and lower the cost per unit. Better research will help advertisers to target their audiences more selectively and increase the response rates.

Direct mail advertising may be affected by changes in public attitudes toward the medium and by deterioration (or improvement?) in postal delivery and costs. The industry will have to invest in home-delivery information systems (videotex and two-way cable) since these are expected to become very important in the 1990s.

SPECIALTY ADVERTISING

This is also a very old medium which can be traced back to the industrial revolution. *Specialty* (or remembrance) advertising includes a wide range of products that contain some form of advertising and are given away free or sold to a selected group. These are widely used by many businesses from a calendar imprinted with the name or logo of the business, all the way to a gold pen or desk clock (Figure 6–10). *Marketing* publishes in several issues during the year a list of various *premiums* and *incentives*, as well as the names and addresses of companies specializing in these products.

There are three types of companies dealing with specialty advertising: *suppliers* are companies which produce the product used in specialty advertising; *specialty distributors* are agents representing various suppliers; *direct selling houses* are agencies dealing with all aspects of specialty advertising.

Because these products are practical and have a degree of permanence, they expose the recipient and users to the message every time the product is used. It may be used in conjunction with other forms of advertising, by reproducing the slogan, logo, or character used in the other message. Its main benefits are in terms of name awareness and reminder advertising. However its cost is very high, and it is best used for a narrow specialized target. It is expected to grow and evolve as new types of specialty products are created using new technologies such as microchips and miniaturization.

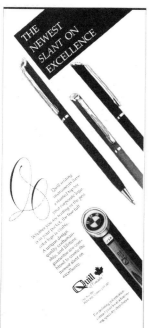

FIGURE 6–10

An Example of Specialty Advertising

Courtesy Quill of Canada

TABLE 6–1 **MAIN STRENGTHS AND WEAKNESSES OF OUTDOOR, TRANSIT, DIRECT RESPONSE, AND SPECIALTY ADVERTISING**

MEDIUM	Strengths	Weaknesses
Outdoor	• high reach & frequency • geographic flexibility • long life of message • high message impact	• short message • no selectivity • long lead time • high production costs
Transit	• high reach & frequency • high readership • low cost per thousand	• no selectivity • long closing dates • high production costs
Direct Response	• highest selectivity • flexible (creative, coverage) • high degree of control	• high relative cost • no editorial support • low response rate
Specialty	• high selectivity • long life • high interest	• high cost • short message

SUMMARY

This chapter has described in detail the "other" print media available in Canada, in addition to newspapers and periodicals. They are the out-of-home media (outdoor, transit, and others), the direct response media (direct mail, telemarketing, and others), and the specialty media. These should not be overlooked by advertisers as they may be more efficient than traditional media. Table 6–1 highlights the main strengths and weaknesses of each medium.

Outdoor advertising is a mass medium with geographic flexibility. Its size and permanence provide impact and command attention. But messages must be short and universal (no selectivity). Production of outdoor messages leads to high costs and long closing dates.

Transit advertising is a mass medium in urban areas and it has some geographic flexibility. Size, permanence, and location provide for high readership, and relative costs per thousand impressions are low. As with outdoor advertising, production costs are high and closing dates can be long. Transit offers very little audience selectivity and only reaches consumers who use public transportation.

Direct response advertising can be very selective and provides advertisers with a high degree of control and feedback. The main types of direct response advertising are direct mail and telemarketing. In particular, direct mail is very flexible both in terms of creative content and market coverage. Without editorial support, however, the advertising message may lack credibility or be ignored. Also, the relative costs are very high.

Specialty advertising may be used for maintaining brand awareness and image. It is very selective, and has a long life, but the cost is high and the message must be very short.

QUESTIONS FOR STUDY

1. From your community, find some examples of campaigns using outdoor or transit advertising. Evaluate this choice of medium for the particular products advertised.

2. What are the major unique characteristics of outdoor advertising, and what conclusions can you draw from them?

3. Describe the similarities and dissimilarities of promotion through a sales force and through
   a. out-of-home media
   b. direct response media

4. Discuss the advantages and disadvantages of using complete painted buses with one single message.

5. Review the various forms of out-of-home media described in this chapter. Explain the rationale behind the ones that are currently available in Canada. Can you think of other ones? Explain.

6. Discuss the advantages and disadvantages of outdoor versus transit as an advertising medium for a new brand of yogurt.

7. "Direct mail is inefficient as an advertising medium, since most people think of it as 'junk' mail." Comment.

8. Explain how you would plan a direct mail advertising campaign. Develop a numerical example with a one-page black and white flyer addressed to homeowners in your community.

9. "Mailing lists are the Achilles' heel of any direct mail campaign." Do you agree? Justify your answer.

10. Explain the rationale behind the use of specialty advertising. Give some good examples and others that you think are not appropriate.

PROBLEMS

1. Jeremy McInnis has just thought of a new business opportunity. Jeremy is well aware that good out-of-home locations are at a premium, particularly in the downtown core of major metropolitan areas. Furthermore, he has noticed that there are thousands of parking meters across most such areas. These structures could very well support small display ads that could be seen by pedestrians as well as passengers in cars driving by or looking for a parking space. Local merchants could be interested in advertising their store to draw in more traffic. Evaluate this idea, assuming that permission may be obtained from the city government to place such structures on the posts. What kind of formats, rates, minimum requirements, rotations, etc. would you suggest to Jeremy? How can the space be sold to merchants?

2. You have invented a revolutionary burglar-proof lock that works without a key. The lock operates with a small device attached to the wrist that emits a special coded sound. An electronics firm located in a nearby metropolitan area has agreed to produce the locks at $5.00 per unit provided that you order at least 5000 units. You have $20 000 of your own money, and a local bank has agreed to give you a loan of up to $50 000. You have decided that $15 is a good price for the new lock and that the best medium to use is direct mail. You are thinking of naming your invention Surelock, and your firm the Surelock Homes Company. Prepare a complete direct mail campaign in order to sell your lock to Canadian home owners. Make sure that all assumptions are clearly stated, and that all the costs are accurate.

NOTES

1. H.E. Stephenson and C. McNaught, *The Story of Advertising in Canada* (Toronto: The Ryerson Press, 1940), pp. 280–84.
2. "Pixelboard sees its name up in lights," *Marketing* (September 5, 1988), p. 29.
3. Jo Marney, "Posters turn all their heads," *Marketing* (September 6, 1986), pp. 16, 31.
4. Mediacom, *Rate Card, 1990*, p. 11.
5. Margaret Bream, "Laser billboards: A bright new idea," *Marketing* (September 7, 1987), p. 21.
6. Ibid., p. 284.
7. Laura Medcalf, "Toronto Transit's rolling milk carton," *Marketing* (September 5, 1988), p. 19; "Newfoundland wants to be remembered in a national buy," Ibid., p. 27.
8. The *Canadian Media Directors' Council Media Digest*, 1990/91, p. 68.
9. "New research is in transit," *Marketing* (September 6, 1986), p. 22.
10. Gail Chiasson, "Outdoor media not left in the cold," *Marketing* (September 7, 1987), pp. 13, 28, 30.
11. Ian Timberlake, "Ads that are full of hot air," *Marketing* (September 7, 1987), p. 23.
12. "Go sit on it," *Marketing* (September 5, 1988), p. 32.
13. Ken Riddell, "The ups and downs of elevator ads," *Marketing* (September 5, 1988), p. 23.
14. "Mediaski: The medium's definitely not on the skids," *Marketing* (September 5, 1988), p. 28.
15. "Good buddy, these ads are truckin'," *Marketing* (September 6, 1986), p. 17; "Going where no ad has gone before...," *Marketing* (September 7, 1987), p. 19.
16. Jim McElgunn, "The least popular of out of home media," *Marketing* (September 5, 1988), pp. 30–31.
17. Terry Belgue, "Telemarketing the latest trend," *Marketing* (July 18, 1988), p. 19; Phil Brown, "A direct hit is one in a hundred," *Marketing* (12 July 1982), p. 12.

18. McGraw-Hill Research, *LAP Report* (New York: McGraw-Hill, 1987).
19. Ken Riddell, "Fighting the tainted image of . . . telemarketing sweatshops," *Marketing* (July 10, 1989), pp. 20–21.
20. "Videotex leads the way in DM revolution," *Marketing* (12 July 1982), p. 8.
21. Stephenson and McNaught, p. 284.
22. Stephen J. Arnold and James G. Barnes, "Canadians and Americans: Implications for Marketing," *Current Topics in Canadian Marketing*, eds. J.G. Barnes and M.S. Sommers (Toronto: McGraw-Hill Ryerson, 1978), pp. 84–100. These figures were given by Frank Ferguson, President, Canadian Direct Marketing Association.
23. Jo Marney, "DM plays vital role in the total media mix," *Marketing* (12 July 1982), pp. 7–9.
24. Ken Riddell, "Birks gets into Spring with a new 'magalog'," *Marketing* (March 14, 1988), p. 1; Margaret Bream, "Hybrids on hold," *Marketing* (February 27, 1989), p. 12; Richard Siklos, "'Magalogs' reach out to upscale consumers," *Financial Times* (December 7, 1987), p. 4.
25. Stephen Shaw, "A new era dawning for direct mail," *Marketing* (July 10, 1989), p. 24; Margaret Bream, "Goodbye to the 'bucket shop' system," Ibid., p. 36.
26. R.S. Hodgson, *Direct Mail and Mail Order Handbook* (Chicago: Darnell, 1965), p. 323.
27. Marney, "DM plays vital role," p. 12.

7 *Canadian Broadcast Media*

Canada has been among the foremost nations in introducing new technologies in the area of broadcast media. When they were first introduced, radio and television radically transformed the entertainment and advertising industries, and forced the print media to change their strategies.

In net advertising revenues, radio has been growing at a slower rate than television, and both shares of total advertising revenues have declined during the last five years. Table 7–1 shows the components of net advertising revenues of radio and television. In 1989, net advertising revenues of radio reached $748 million, and its share of total revenues dropped to 8.3 per cent from 9.4 percent in 1984. Similarly, television's net advertising revenues reached $1.42 billion, and its share of total revenues dropped to 15.6 percent from 16.7 percent in 1984. Overall, the share of the broadcast media declined to 24 percent in 1989 from 26 percent in 1984, although total revenues will continue to grow. What explains this decline: is it increased cost, or the availability of more effective print media? To help answer this question, this chapter examines the role of radio and television as potential media for the advertiser.

RADIO

The Changing Role of Radio as an Advertising Medium

In December 1920, the Canadian Marconi Company, located in Montreal, began broadcasting regularly on a wavelength of 1200 metres. From that first radio station in the world (which later became CFCF), the new medium grew rapidly. By 1923, 52 broadcasting licences had been granted.[1] The first receiving sets were battery-powered. The growth of radio penetration was based on improvements in technology and lower prices for receiving sets.

Because of the uneven distribution of the Canadian population, only large centres had operating radio stations and families with a set in other areas were listening to more powerful U.S. stations. The solution to the problem of providing radio programs to all Canadians was to set up a national broadcasting system, first as the Canadian Radio Broadcasting Commission, and in 1936 as the Canadian Radio Broadcasting Corporation (CBC), modelled after the British Broadcasting Corporation. Radio penetration grew rapidly, from 49 percent in 1936 to 85 percent in 1939, when 85 stations were in operation, nine of which were owned by the CBC. Initially, the CBC operated on licence fees levied on receiving sets as well as government loans and advertising revenues. In 1974, the CBC decided to stop selling advertising time for broadcast in all of its stations.

TABLE 7–1 **COMPONENTS OF NET ADVERTISING REVENUES BY BROADCAST MEDIA (IN THOUSANDS OF DOLLARS)**

Type of broadcast medium	1983		1988		Annual rate of growth (%)
	amount	%	amount	%	
RADIO—Total	*544 729*	*9.4*	*747 600*	*8.3*	*6.5*
national	145 850	2.5	176 000	1.9	3.8
local	398 879	6.9	571 600	6.3	7.5
TELEVISION—Total	*970 298*	*16.7*	*1 415 700*	*15.6*	*7.8*
national	762 545	13.1	1 062 400	11.7	6.9
local	207 753	3.6	353 300	3.9	11.2
TOTAL BROADCAST MEDIA	*1 515 027*	*26.1*	*2 163 300*	*23.9*	*7.4*
TOTAL ALL MEDIA	**5 809 951**	**100.0**	**9 049 000**	**100.0**	**8.4**

Source: based on Canadian Advertising Rates and Data (May 1989) p. 402; CMDC *Media Digest, 1990/91*, pp. 10–11.

Battery-operated receiving sets received a strong impetus with the invention of the transistor in 1948. This allowed a reduction in size and an increase in mobility. The invention of the transistor allowed more cars to be equipped with radio. The growth and vitality of the medium was also spurred by other inventions and new technologies that led to FM (frequency modulation) and stereophonic broadcasting, more stable reception, and less interference.

In 1952 a new technology, that of television, pre-empted radio and soon became the favoured entertainment medium. In response to this competition, radio became more specialized and developed programming directed at specific audiences. Radio changed from an involving entertainment medium to a background medium. Thus, radio came to be positioned as a complement of rather than a direct competitor to television.

By 1987, there were 580 independent stations, and 118 CBC owned and operated stations. About 60 percent are AM stations and 40 percent are FM stations. A breakdown by region is shown in Table 7–2. On the average, about 94 percent of Canadians aged seven and older listen to AM radio in a given week (61 percent for FM radio), and 95 percent of all households own at least one FM set.[2]

Characteristics of Radio

Radio stations are characterized by their mode of broadcasting, type of ownership, and programming.

Mode of Broadcasting

AM (amplitude modulation) stations transmit radio waves that may cover a very large area. AM stations are the most important in terms of numbers and amount of advertising carried. As seen in Table 7–2, there were 385 AM stations in Canada in 1989, 56 percent of all radio stations.

TABLE 7–2 **NUMBER OF RADIO STATIONS (AS OF MARCH 1989)**

Region	CBC O&O			Private Independent			Total Stations		
	AM	FM	Total	AM	FM	Total	AM	FM	Total
Atlantic	12	11	23	52	31	83	64	42	106
Quebec	10	8	18	62	76	138	72	84	156
Ontario	10	8	18	89	85	174	99	93	192
Prairies	8	5	13	74	34	108	82	39	121
West	11	8	19	57	37	94	68	45	113
Canada	*51*	*40*	*91*	*334*	*263*	*597*	*385*	*303*	*688*

Source: CRTC, 1988–1989, p. 53. Annual Report.

FM (frequency modulation) stations cover a limited area, but their signal has the major advantage of clear reception. FM stations have seen rapid growth in their advertising revenues and audience share in recent years. FM audience share has grown dramatically, particularly among teenagers.

Types of Ownership

Radio stations may be classified into three groups according to the type of ownership: independent stations, network affiliates, and owned-and-operated stations.

Independent stations are individually responsible for programming and advertising. The majority of radio stations are in this category and the overwhelming majority of advertising expenditures are placed with independent stations.

Network affiliates stations must carry some of the programs of the network, as well as the advertising sold by the network for some time periods. Otherwise, affiliates have complete responsibility for their programming. Examples of such networks are the Farm Market News and the Canadian Radio Networks.

Owned and operated (O&O) stations belong to one network, and individual stations have great flexibility for local programming. Examples of such networks are the CBC Network (no commercial advertising allowed), and the World Radio Network.

Types of Programming

Radio stations define, attract, and hold their audience by the kind of programs they select. Programming decisions are based on demographic composition and tastes of the population covered by the station, changes in audience flow during the day, and competition from other stations.

Music formats. In Canada, there are basically six types of music formats used in radio programming:

Adult-contemporary stations play adult or easy listening music, show tunes, and popular music. These stations are sometimes called middle of the road

(MOR) stations. Their audience is typically in their late 20s and up. Examples are CJOB in Winnipeg, CFRB in Toronto, and CJAD in Montreal.

Rock-oriented or top 40 stations play recent rock music and appeal mainly to teenagers and young adults. Most of them are AM stations. A recent variation of this format is called a *gold station*, which plays solid gold hits and appeals mainly to the baby boomers (i.e., those born between 1946 and 1966). One example is CHUM-AM in Toronto.

Album-oriented rock (AOR) stations play rock albums on a continuing basis. They appeal mainly to teenagers and young adults. Most of them are FM stations. One example if CJAY-FM in Calgary.

Country music stations play a variety of country music, which is most popular in the western provinces. One example is CKWX in Vancouver. The audience tends to be downscale on the key demographic dimensions of occupation and income.

Classical music is played on many Canadian stations but only during certain times of the day. In addition to the CBC network, there is only one pure classical music station in Canada, CFMX-FM in Coburg (Ontario). For most radio stations playing some classical music, the proportion of classical programming varies from 1 percent to 25 percent. The audience tends to be older, with higher education and income than for other music formats.

All-news stations do not play any music but provide local, regional, and national news and other related information on a 24-hour basis. These types of stations are relatively new in Canada and are experiencing difficulties in attracting audiences.[3]

Syndicated Radio. A recent development is the creation of syndication companies who are producing special radio programs available on a sponsorship basis. These programs range in contents from sporting events to rock concerts and they are offered for syndication to a pre-determined list of radio stations. They are represented by the Canadian Association of Radio Syndicators.[4]

Population Composition and Tastes. Population characteristics of the area covered by a radio station can influence the type of programming. Age, sex, occupation, level of education, geographic location, and employment status affect the number of hours per day (or week) tuned to radio, AM or FM. Radio programming in a small town may be different from that in a large metropolitan or rural area. Examples of such differences are provided in Table 7–3 for age, sex, and geographic location.

Changes in Audience Flow. The listening habits of various demographic groups are also quite important in deciding on programming formats, since there are major changes in audience composition during the average day. Between 8 A.M. and 4 P.M. there are more women listeners than men, while the reverse is true before 8 A.M. and after 4 P.M. Proportionally, more teenagers listen to radio than adults or children after 6 P.M.

Based on these characteristics, radio uses one of two programming strategies: a station selects a demographic group and caters to its tastes, developing

TABLE 7-3 **CHARACTERISTICS OF RADIO AUDIENCES**

Region	Women 18+	Men 18+	Teens 12–17	Children 7–11
	(Average weekly hours tuned)			
Maritimes	21.1	18.3	12.5	7.0
Quebec	24.3	21.9	11.6	6.6
English Quebec	*24.7*	*21.6*	*12.3*	*5.7*
Ontario	22.5	20.7	13.5	7.2
Prairies	21.1	21.1	13.2	7.1
British Columbia	21.1	18.9	11.7	7.4
	(Weekly reach of) (%)			
AM Radio	74	72	65	58
FM Radio	64	66	62	44

Source: CMDC Media Digest 1990/91, p. 32.

a strong image as, say, a rock station or an adult-contemporary station; or a station varies its programming in order to follow the audience flow pattern.

Competitive Situation.   In a given market, the amount of competition for the same audience may lead a station to change its music format or to expand its revenue base by targeting several groups at different times.

Radio as an Advertising Medium

Advantages of Radio

The main advantages of radio can be grouped into five categories:

High Frequency.   Radio is the best medium for advertisers who require high message frequency at a relatively low cost. Specific audiences may be reached several times a day, for several days or weeks. High frequency using one vehicle may allow the advertiser to qualify for a volume discount.

High Potential Reach.   Because almost everybody listens to radio and most households own several sets, including car radios and portable radios, the medium has the potential for high reach by combining several stations. In addition, radio listenership is strong all year round. Radio's weekly reach by region is presented in Table 7–4. Reach figures are very high, especially for teenagers and adults.

Low Cost.   The costs of using radio are relatively low for four reasons. First, production costs of radio commercials are usually very low. Second, radio requires short deadlines and rapid copy changes can be made in order to take advantage of changes in market conditions. Third, unit costs of radio (the cost per thousand listeners) are among the lowest of all media, thus allowing advertisers to supplement the reach of other media or to generate high message frequency. Fourth, because of its relatively low production and time costs, advertising in radio is affordable to many retailers, with or without co-operative advertising dollars.

TABLE 7-4 **WEEKLY RADIO REACH BY REGION (%)**

Region	Women 18+	Men 18+	Teens 12–17	Children 7–11
Maritimes	96.4	94.3	88.3	75.5
Quebec	96.6	94.9	90.4	72.9
English Quebec	*96.7*	*97.3*	*94.5*	*71.7*
Ontario	96.8	96.0	91.5	81.5
Prairies	97.4	96.2	90.6	83.5
British Columbia	94.5	94.8	87.9	77.9
Canada	*96.6*	*95.1*	*90.3*	*78.7*

Source: CMDC Media Digest 1990/91, p. 31.

High Selectivity.   Radio stations have attracted very specific audiences through careful programming. Some stations appeal to narrowly defined demographic subgroups, thus allowing the advertiser to match the target market with the audience of one or several stations with a minimum of waste. Radio is considered the best medium to reach teenagers. Specific ethnic groups may be reached through ethnic radio stations or programs. Some stations, particularly in small communities, change programming during the day according to the changes in audience composition.

Great Flexibility.   Radio is a highly flexible medium. It allows short lead times in most markets for both production and scheduling, generally two to four weeks. In the top five or six markets, lead times of two to three months are often necessary, because of the nearly sold-out positions of the stations. Radio allows flexibility in market coverage, i.e., precise targeting both in terms of demographic characteristics and geographical coverage, which allows advertisers to vary the intensity of advertising according to market potential. Radio also allows a great deal of creative flexibility through a variety of sound effects, music, and voice types, and by relying on listeners' imagination. Radio has often been termed "the theatre of the mind." Thus the message may be highly adaptable to a more heterogeneous audience. The low cost of producing radio commercials allows more experimenting with various approaches, until the right one is found.

Disadvantages of Radio

The main disadvantages of radio may be grouped into three categories:

A Low Reach Medium.   Although it has the potential for high reach, radio can present many problems in terms of reach. First, the total audience for radio is often highly fragmented, depending on the number of stations available in a particular market and the changes in audience composition during the day. Second, the audience is segmented further due to differences in program quality, individual listening habits, and personal taste. Thus, radio is mostly a high frequency/low reach medium.

Creative Negatives.   For the creative director, radio presents several problems. Since radio is mostly a background medium, it has low listener attention levels.

Message registration often requires repetition, attention-getting devices, and learning aids, such as catchy jingles and closure. A radio commercial has a very short life and has to accomplish its objectives in 30 or 60 seconds. In addition, particularly in AM radio, advertising messages have to compete for attention. Thus, clutter severely restricts the effectiveness of a particular message. Radio messages lack visual registration, particularly in providing package identification for products sold in self-service retail establishments. In writing radio commercials, it is inadvisable to use long copy because of low listener attention levels.

Media Planning Problems. Radio also presents several problems to the media planner. Most radio contracts contain a two-week cancellation clause, thus preventing the advertiser from responding within days to changes in the marketplace. It is often difficult to buy radio time in major markets because demand is high and availability limited. Stations are limited by law in the amount of commercial time they are allowed to sell. In a week, AM stations are allowed 1500 minutes; FM stations affiliated with AM stations are allowed 840 minutes; and independent FM stations are allowed 1050 minutes. Other constraints applying to FM stations limit the amount of commercial time per day or per hour. (See Appendix 1 for a listing of radio advertising regulations.) There is a need for more and better research data about radio in order to assist the media director in choosing vehicles and schedules. The use of research is increasing, and radio is just beginning to offer the extent and quality of data that consumer magazines provide. BBM started to offer Radio Product Measurement (RPM) data in 1986, and the second generation RPMII was released in 1989.[5]

Finally, from the agency viewpoint, radio is an expensive medium for administrative costs because of the high number of independent stations.

Radio Advertising Rate Structure

The cost of advertising on Canadian radio depends on the nature of the advertiser, the scheduled time (daypart), the length of the commercial, package plans, and discounts or special features.

Nature of the Advertiser

There are two basic types of rates for radio: general and retail.

General (or National) Rates. General advertising is placed by agencies and is commissionable. General rates are published monthly in CARD. Unless noted in the general rate card, these rates are usually higher than local rates. On the average, national net advertising revenues represent 24 percent of total revenues (Table 7–1).

Retail (or Local) Rates. Retail rates are non-commissionable, and commercials are placed by a local businessperson, with or without production assistance from the station. Retail rates are generally lower than national rates, and these revenues provide an average of 76 percent of total revenues (Table 7–1).

Time Classification (dayparts)

Radio time is usually divided into dayparts, and each such time segment has a different rate assigned to it. Unfortunately, dayparts are not standardized and the media buyer must look at each station's rate card. For example, two CARD listings are reproduced in Figure 7–1. The Swift Current station has three dayparts, against five for the Toronto station. For the Toronto station, the class AAA (Breakfast) rates are from 5:30 to 10 A.M., Monday through Saturday, while for the Swift Current station the AAA rates are from 6 A.M. to 1 P.M., Monday through Sunday.

The audience composition by time period for four demographic groups are shown in Figure 7–2 and the audience composition by commonly used time blocks (dayparts) is shown in Table 7–5. The pattern for adult men and women are fairly similar with more women listening in the morning. The pattern for teenagers is similar in shape to that of children, but a greater percentage of teenagers listen to radio.

TABLE 7–5 **AUDIENCE COMPOSITION BY TIME BLOCK**

Time Block		Women 18+	Men 18+	Teens 12–17	Children 7–11
Breakfast	M–F or M–Sat, 6–10 A.M.	50	42	5	3
Midday	M–F, 10 A.M.–4 P.M.	55	42	2	1
Drive	M–F, 4–7 P.M.	46	45	6	3
Evening	M–F, 7 P.M.–Midnight	41	44	12	3
Weekend	Sat–S, 7 A.M.–7 P.M.	51	40	6	3

Source: BBM, Fall 1989.

Length of Commercial

All radio stations sell radio time by blocks of 30 or 60 seconds, the former being the most popular. Rates for 30 seconds are usually more than half the rate for 60 seconds.

Package Plans

Since one of the drawbacks of radio is low reach, stations have designed plans to maximize their reach. These plans are called reach plans or total audience plans (TAP). The rationale is that since audience composition varies with dayparts, the number of different people listening to the commercial may be increased if the commercial is rotated among various dayparts. In Figure 7–1, CHUM-FM offers a choice of five reach plans, while CIMG-FM offers three plans. The unit rate for these plans is offered at a discount from the regular rates.

In addition, more specific rotations may be offered to increase reach. A *horizontal rotation* places a spot in the same daypart on different days, while a *vertical rotation* places a spot in different dayparts on the same day.

FIGURE 7–1
CARD Listing for Two Radio Stations

Source: Canadian Advertising Rates and Data (1990), pp. 451, 465.

Courtesy CHUM-FM and 94FM

Toronto—CHUM-FM

Member CAB

Data confirmed for May/90 CARD

Est. 1963. Owned & operated by CHUM Ltd. Studio: 1331 Yonge St., Toronto, ON M4T 1Y1. Phone: 416-925-6666. Fax: 416-926-4026. Tlx.: 06-22063. *Format:* Adult contemporary.
FREQUENCY-POWER-TIME
Frequency: 104.5 MHz.
Power: 40,000 w. ERP. Transmitter: CN Tower, Toronto. Stereo.
Time: Eastern.
OPERATING SCHEDULE: 24 hours daily.
TIME CLASSIFICATIONS
Class AAA: 5:30-10 a.m. Mon.-Sat.
Class AA: 3-8 p.m. Mon.-Sat.
Class A: 10 a.m.-3 p.m. Mon.-Sat.
Class B: 8 p.m.-1 a.m. Mon.-Sun.
Class C: 6 a.m.-8 p.m. Sun.
COMMISSION & CASH DISCOUNT: 15% on station rates to all recognized advtg. agencies. No commission on talent. No cash discounts. Invoices rendered monthly. Bills due & payable when rendered.
GENERAL ADVERTISING: Rate Card No. 24. Effective Dec. 8, 1988.
ANNOUNCEMENTS
CLASS AAA

Grid:	1	2	3	4	5
60 sec.	$420	$460	$480	$510	$540
30 sec.	380	400	420	450	480

CLASS AA

	1	2	3	4	5
60 sec.	$305	$325	$340	$355	$370
30 sec.	280	300	315	330	345

CLASS A

	1	2	3	4	5
60 sec.	$305	$325	$340	$355	$370
30 sec.	280	300	315	330	345

CLASS B

	1	2	3	4	5
60 sec.	$165	$175	$185	$195	$205
30 sec.	135	145	155	165	175

CLASS C

	1	2	3	4	5
60 sec.	$185	$195	$205	$215	$225
30 sec.	160	170	180	190	200

Split 60 sec. anncs. available at double the 30 sec. rate. Grid protection on avail presentations limited to 5 working days.
REACH PLANS: To be used within 1 b'cast week.
12 UNITS: 3AAA, 3AA, 3A, 3B.

	1	2	3	4	5
60 sec.	$3000	$3360	$3600	$3780	$3900
30 sec.	2700	2880	3060	3240	3420

15 UNITS: 3AAA, 6AA, 3A, 3B.

	1	2	3	4	5
60 sec.	$3750	$4200	$4500	$4725	$4875
30 sec.	3375	3600	3825	4050	4275

18 UNITS: 3AAA, 6AA, 6A, 3B.

	1	2	3	4	5
60 sec.	$4500	$5040	$5400	$5670	$5850
30 sec.	4050	4320	4590	4860	5130

21 UNITS: 3AAA, 6AA, 6A, 3B, 3C.

	1	2	3	4	5
60 sec.	$5040	$5670	$6090	$6405	$6615
30 sec.	4515	4830	5145	5460	5775

24 UNITS: 6AAA, 6AA, 6A, 6B

	1	2	3	4	5
60 sec.	$5760	$6480	$6960	$7320	$7560
30 sec.	5160	5520	5880	6240	6600

ALL NIGHT SHOW: Mon.-Sun. 1-5:30 a.m.—rates on request.

COMMERCIALS/PRODUCTION REQUIREMENTS
Preferred deadline: 48 hours.
PERSONNEL
Pres.: Allan Waters.
V.P./Gen. Mgr.: Jim Waters.
Retail Sales Mgr.: Jack Addis.
Traffic Dept.: Cathy McNeil (416-926-4013).
REPRESENTATIVES: Can.: Major Market Broadcasters Ltd., Toronto, Montreal, Vancouver, Halifax, Winnipeg.
U.S.: Hooper Jones Associates, Inc., New York, Chicago.

Swift Current—CIMG-FM

Data confirmed for June/90 CARD

Owned & operated by Grasslands Broadcasting Ltd. Studio: 28-4th Ave. N.W., Box 1590, Swift Current, SK S9H 4G5. Phone: 306-773-1505. Fax: 306-778-3737. *Format:* Adult contemporary & contemporary hit radio.
FREQUENCY-POWER-TIME
Frequency: 94.1 MHz.
Power: 100,000 w. Tower height: 450 ft.
Time: Central.
TIME CLASSIFICATIONS
Class AAA: 6 a.m.-1 p.m. Mon.-Sun.
Class AA: 1-7 p.m. Mon.-Sun.
Class A: 7 p.m.-mid. Mon.-Sun.
OPERATING SCHEDULE: 24 hours daily.
COMMISSION & CASH DISCOUNT: 15% on station rates to recognized agencies. No commission on talent. Invoices rendered monthly. No cash discounts.
GENERAL ADVERTISING: Rate Card No. 3. Effective Feb. 1, 1989.

CLASS AAA	1 ti.	200 ti.	300 ti.
60 sec.	$29	$26	$21
30 sec.	25	21	19
CLASS AA			
60 sec.	$23	$21	$18
30 sec.	20	18	15
CLASS A			
60 sec.	$16	$14	$12
30 sec.	14	12	11

REACH PLANS: Plan No. 1: Mon.-Sun. 1/2 6 a.m.-1 p.m.; 1/2 1-7 p.m. Min. 28 occ.
60 sec. .... $25   30 sec. $21
Plan No. 2: Mon.-Sun. 1/3 6 a.m.-1 p.m.; 1/3 1-7 p.m.; 1/3 7 p.m.-mid. Min. 28 occ.
60 sec. .... $21   30 sec. $18
Major Information Packages: Major news, weather, sports & agri business/farm reports, 1 rate $30.
PERSONNEL
Pres./Gen. Mgr.: Jim Warren.
Sales Mgr.: Kim Sather.
Traffic Mgr.: Jan Broccolo.
REPRESENTATIVES: Can.: Target Broadcast Media REPS, Winnipeg, Toronto, Montreal, Vancouver.

Other Discounts

Four types of discounts are available:

Volume Discounts. The unit rate is lower if a certain number of spots are purchased. For example, Swift Current's CIMG-FM offers the first discount at 200 spots (ti.) and the second at 300 spots (Figure 7–1).

Frequency Discounts. The unit rate is lower if a certain number of spots are bought for a number of consecutive weeks.

Run of Station (ROS) or Best Time Available (BTA). The radio station schedules the commercial at its discretion. ROS or BTA rates are often combined with a minimum volume.

Combination Rates. Discounts are offered when several stations (either AM, FM, or both) are owned by the same company and spots in two or more stations are bought.

FIGURE 7–2

Audience Composition (Flow) by Time Periods and for Four Demographic Groups

Source: Fall 1989 TV Sweep Survey

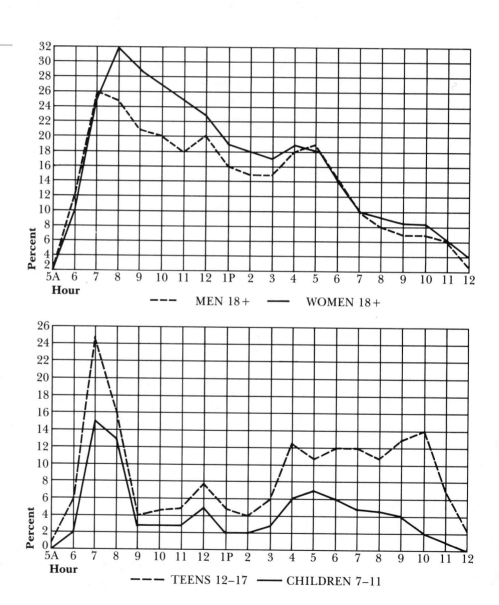

Special Features

Special features offered to advertisers include sponsorship of a specific program, feature inserts, and tie-ins with retail outlets.

The Future of Radio as an Advertising Medium

The trend in favour of FM stations and an increasing use of radio by advertisers, particularly local advertisers, will likely continue because of cost considerations. The latter may be stimulated by industry efforts to improve their marketing orientation through standardization of rate cards. There is also a trend toward increased use of research beyond the mere demographic variables by using psychographic, media, and product usage variables (improved RPM studies). The industry, through more and better radio syndication may attempt to produce effective programs and spread the costs over larger audiences. Networking using satellite technology will become more important.

Radio will be affected by demographic and socio-economic trends in the Canadian population: aging, working women, rising education levels, and changing leisure patterns. In particular, radio will be profoundly affected by the aging baby boomers and the emerging over-50 market. New music formats will be created to cater to these groups. Finally, the changing ethnic composition of the Canadian society will create new opportunities for radio stations and formats.[6]

Radio may be affected by new technological developments, but not as much as other media. These developments will include increased penetration of cable, dish antennas, home information delivery systems, and other innovations related to the transmission of sound. The increasing use of AM stereo by stations will be facilitated by standardization of the technology used in Canada.

The evolution of radio will also be influenced by government regulations by the CRTC, in particular content regulations, as well as by the free trade agreement with the United States (for instance, stations may be forced to pay royalties for playing records).

TELEVISION

Growth of Television as an Advertising Medium

Three years after it was introduced in the United States, television became the newest Canadian medium in 1952 with one station, CBFT, operating in Montreal and another, CBLT, in Toronto. Both stations were owned and operated by the Canadian Broadcasting Corporation.

As the CBC expanded its network and privately owned stations were licensed, by 1955 seven CBC and 19 privately owned stations were reaching ten million Canadians. Based on the two main languages in Canada, the CBC expanded into a French and an English network.

In 1961 the third Canadian network, the CTV television network, was licensed to operate in eight major urban areas. The fourth Canadian network, the TVA television network, was established in 1971 to cover the province of Quebec. One year later the fifth Canadian network, the Global Television Network, was licensed to serve the province of Ontario. Today, there are three national networks, eight regional networks, and ten specialty networks.

In 1966, barely 14 years after the introduction of television, another momentous development occurred: the introduction of colour. In 1970, about 12 percent of Canadian households were equipped with a colour television set. By 1989, this figure had risen to 95 percent.

As this brief overview indicates, the medium of television is becoming extremely diverse and complicated, particularly as new technological innovations are introduced.

Technological Developments Affecting Television as an Advertising Medium

The following technological developments are affecting the nature of the industry:

CATV. Cable (or community antenna) television was first developed to reach areas with poor reception and came to be used to provide distant channels to the public in high density areas. Cable penetration of households rose from 25 percent in 1970 to 73 percent in 1989,[7] making Canada one of the most "wired" nations in the world.

Converters. Converters allow the public to pick up more channels with a standard television set connected to a cable. About 55 per cent of all households owned a cable converter in 1989. The acquisition of a cable converter was found to increase total viewing and satisfaction with viewing.[8] However, the extent of switching among channels after acquisition of cable converters is probably related to the use of remote controls.

Pay TV. Pay TV allows the public to receive selected programs for a fee through sets connected to a cable and with the use of a decoder to unscramble the signal. Pay TV penetration has been growing slowly, and the weekly reach in 1989, of the combined pay TV and specialty stations (basic cable) was 34 percent. Canadians spent about four hours per week tuned to pay-TV, and depending on the region, they have currently up to three English, four French, and three ethnic channels available.[9]

Satellites and Dish Antennas. Satellites and dish antennas may improve the speed and efficiency of communication, particularly for business.

VCRs. Home video players/recorders allow the public to tape programs and delete commercials for viewing at a later date and to use their television sets to view commercial-free movies. In 1989, penetration of VCRs was 62 percent of Canadian households, and they spent about four hours per week watching their VCR. The average weekly reach of households is 20 percent.[10]

Videotex. Videotex systems/home computers allow the viewer to control the information received through the television set in the form of words or symbols. The Canadian videotex system, Telidon, is used in the NAPLPS (North American Presentation Level Protocol Syntax), and in the Alex system introduced by Bell Canada in 1989. Other systems using videotex are the French Minitel service, the Videoway system (Videotron), and Grassroots (targeted to farmers).

Two-Way Cable. Two-way cable allows viewers and the cable company to control information other than text received through the television set. Two-way cable systems may be used to develop interactive programs such as electronic shopping (e.g., Videoway), or electronic market surveys. This type of system is in its infancy but it is expected to grow very rapidly in the 1990s.

Thus, the medium of television, just 40 years after its birth, is undergoing major changes that will shape its future.

Basic Facts About Television

Today 99 percent of Canadian households are equipped with at least one television set and more than 95 percent own at least one colour set. More than 56 percent own more than one set, and 73 percent are equipped with cable.[11] Table 7–6 provides a breakdown by major markets. The highest penetration rate of cable (92%) and converters (72%) is in Vancouver/Victoria. Calgary has the highest percentage of households with a VCR (70%).

TABLE 7–6 **PENETRATION OF MULTIPLE TELEVISION SETS, CABLE, CONVERTERS, PAY TV AND VCRs**

Market	2 + TV Sets	Cable	Converter	Pay TV specialty*	VCR
St. John's	63	77	46	41	60
Halifax	57	73	56	36	61
Saint John/Moncton	55	69	49	33	60
Montreal	61	69	55	33	57
Quebec	59	68	53	30	59
Sherbrooke	48	63	50	33	56
Kitchener	53	79	64	37	61
London	51	77	59	34	59
Ottawa/Hull	60	73	60	39	63
Sudbury/Timmins/North Bay	60	74	55	43	62
Toronto/Hamilton	56	86	71	37	68
Windsor	66	41	34	24	65
Winnipeg	63	69	41	28	60
Regina/Moose Jaw	60	74	49	37	59
Saskatoon	62	65	40	34	56
Calgary	59	79	58	37	70
Edmonton	61	73	45	34	62
Okanagan/Kamloops	46	74	49	44	61
Vancouver/Victoria	45	92	72	38	65
Canada	*56*	*73*	*55*	*34*	*62*

* Reach of combined pay TV and specialty stations (at no charge on basic cable service).
Source: CMDC Media Digest, 1990/91, pp. 22–23.

There are currently 138 commercial television stations in Canada, reaching an average of 37 percent of all adults on any quarter hour during prime time. On the average, 78 percent of Canadians watch television at least once a day.[12]

FIGURE 7–3

Average Weekly Hours Tuned per Capita

Source: Fall'89 BBM

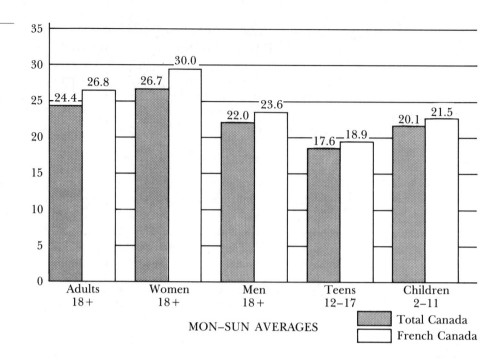

Figure 7–3 shows the average number of hours per week of television viewing for different groups. Women watch four and a half hours more of television than men, and all adults watch more television than teenagers or children.

Net advertising revenues for television reached $1.4 billion in 1989, about one and a half times the 1984 figure. Television's share of advertising revenues for all media dropped from 16.7 per cent in 1984 to 15.6 percent in 1989.

Television is mostly a national medium, with more than three-fourths of its revenues coming from national advertisers. It tends to be an expensive medium, well beyond the reach of small- and medium-sized advertisers and thus is generally a medium for mass marketers, for example, packaged-goods companies.

Characteristics of Television

Television has various vehicles for carrying an advertising message: the type of station, the scheduled time period, and the type of program selected by the advertiser and its agency.

Type of Station

Television stations are classified according to the frequency of transmission and the networks to which they are affiliated.

Frequency. Since signals are transmitted by radio waves, television stations are assigned special frequencies by the CRTC. The first stations were assigned *very high frequencies (VHF)*, which are channels two to 13. In 1989 there were 90 VHF stations in Canada. In 1972, when the VHF range could not accommodate more stations, *ultra high frequencies (UHF)* were assigned to new stations. These are channels 14 to 83.

Network or Individual Stations.   Television stations may be either independent or affiliated with one or several networks.

Independents.   Independent stations, like CKND-TV (Winnipeg), are not affiliated with any network. They sell their time directly or through media representatives.

National Networks.   English CBC network stations are affiliated with the CBC English Network. There were 41 English stations in 1990, 14 owned and operated stations and 26 affiliates. The CBC Metronet network was comprised of the major stations affiliated with the CBC and included CBC stations in 15 markets. The coverage of the full network was about 98 percent of households, while that of the Metronet was about 80 percent.[13]

French CBC network stations are affiliated with the CBC French network called Radio-Canada. There were 20 French CBC station affiliates in 1990, with a coverage of 99 percent of Quebec households.

There were 16 English stations affiliated with the CTV network in 1990. They have a 97 percent English household coverage. All CTV stations are independently owned and operated.

Regional Networks.   There were eight regional or provincial networks in Canada in 1990:[14]

The *Atlantic Satellite Network* serves the Maritimes, Newfoundland and the Eastern Arctic, and is offered in conjunction with the *ATV Network*, which serves New Brunswick, Nova Scotia, and Prince Edward Island.

The *Maritime Independent Television* serves Nova Scotia and New Brunswick.

The *Global Television Network* has one studio in Toronto and another in Ottawa and serves southern Ontario (96 percent coverage).

The *Saskatchewan Television Network* has a 94 percent coverage with four stations.

TVA/the Network Plan is a French network with ten affiliates in 1990 with a household coverage of about 99 percent of the francophone population of Quebec.

The *Quatre Saisons Network* has nine stations in the province of Quebec with a 94 percent coverage.

Radio Quebec was established by the Quebec government and has 17 stations.

Educational Stations.   Non-commercial educational stations in Canada are TVOntario, Access Alberta, and Knowledge B.C., and they may allow some program underwriting with credits.

Specialty Networks.   Specialty networks are being developed to meet some needs and are provided either as part of basic cable service or as a pay TV service. Some may sell commercial time. There are currently 11 such channels:[15]

- MuchMusic: shows music videos around the clock
- The Sports Network (TSN)
- Vision TV: shows family programs
- Weathernow, Meteomedia: weather information
- The Youth Channel (YTV): children (no commercial), teens and family programs
- MusiquePlus: French music video
- Le Réseau des Sports (RDS)
- TV5: French programming from francophone countries
- Chinavision (Cantonese and Mandarin)
- Telelatino: in Italian and Spanish
- CBC News World (part of CBC Network)

U.S. Border Stations.   Another type of station that has a profound effect on Canadian television are U.S. border stations, which are powerful enough to broadcast to large populated areas in Canada. They further fragment the audience and put pressure on the operating costs of Canadian stations by pulling away advertising revenues from Canadian advertisers. Since 1976, however, these expenditures are not allowed as a deductible business expense (Bill C-58).[16] Nevertheless this competition makes it economically difficult for Canadian networks and stations to develop the high quality programming needed to attract the large audiences advertisers seek. Since U.S. programs were developed for the large U.S. market, the high production costs are spread among many stations; the exposure of the Canadian market to these programs is merely an added benefit. The same is true for the cable distribution of these U.S. stations and will continue as the penetration of cable television increases.

To combat U.S. competition, Canadian stations have resorted to scheduling the same episode of a popular program at the same time as in the U.S. This practice is called simulcasting, and the station may demand that cable companies replace the U.S.-originated signal, including commercials, with that of the Canadian station showing the same episode. With simulcasting, the Canadian station can cater to the public taste for American programs and still receive additional revenues by offering Canadian advertisers a much larger Canadian audience. However, this may change in the future depending on the course taken with the implementation of the free trade agreement with the United States.[17]

Types of Advertising Time

For network affiliates, there are three types of advertising time: network, spot, and local. Independent stations have spot and local advertising.

Network Advertising.   Network affiliates are linked by microwave relay stations or satellite transmission. Affiliates agree to carry a set of specific programs at a specific time, with the commercials sold by the network. These programs are mostly run during the evening prime time, with a few shown during the day. Commercials broadcast during these programs are called *network* advertising (or *network time*). For advertisers, the advantage of buying network time is in terms of the number of people reached during popular programs over a wide geographical area. This translates into high reach and low cost per thousand viewers. Another factor is the glamour or halo effect of advertising during popular programs, potentially giving additional status to the brand advertised and impressing the trade.

Spot or Local Advertising. Once a station agrees to carry the network programs and commercials, it is fully responsible for the balance of the schedule. The station may select its own programs and sell commercial time within the programs.

Commercial (non-network) time may be sold to a national advertiser, in which case it is called spot advertising. The advantage of *spot* advertising is that it allows advertisers to adjust the advertising pressure to local market conditions and to supplement basic network coverage.

Commercial time may also be sold to local advertisers, such as retailers. This is called *local* advertising and is non-commissionable. About 25 percent of net television advertising revenues come from local advertisers (Table 7–1).

Types of Programming

The most important vehicle for carrying the advertising message is the program in which it is positioned. Since each type of program, and even each program, has its own individual audience composition, it is important to select the right one.[18]

General drama and films attract a balanced distribution of both French and English viewers, with a bias toward more women than men and more French Canadian women than English Canadian women.

Suspense and adventure programs attract a balanced distribution of English and French Canadians.

Situation comedies are viewed more by French Canadian women than their English Canadian counterparts.

Variety shows are viewed more by women than men and least by teenagers in both French and English Canada.

Documentaries are viewed mostly by adults.

Talk shows and educational programs are also viewed mostly by adults, with a higher proportion of English Canadian men and French Canadian women.

Sports programs are dominated by men.

News programs are mostly viewed by adults. The share of French Canadian males watching the early evening news is surprisingly low compared to the other groups, and conversely for females.

Research conducted for the CBC shows that Canadians allocate their television viewing time as follows: 49 percent for drama, 19 percent for variety shows, 12 percent for news, 10 percent for sports, and 7 percent for public affairs.

In addition to selecting the program, the advertiser has the option of *sponsoring* or *co-sponsoring* a particular program: one (or more) advertiser(s) agree(s) to buy all commercial time within that program. The advantage is for the advertiser to be associated with a popular program and to gain goodwill with a selected audience, for example, male adults watching a sports program. At the same time, the advertiser prevents other competitors from becoming associated with the program.

Television as an Advertising Medium

Advantages of Television

The main advantages of television can be grouped into four categories:

High Message Effectiveness. Television is the preferred medium of most creative personnel, and the best creative directors work more with television than with any other medium. Television allows an infinite variety of creative approaches by combining sight, sound, and motion to create a strong, effective impact. Television allows effective demonstration of the product in use, particularly for new product introductions; thus it is often the best medium for new product launches. Also, television is an intrusive medium; it encourages relatively high levels of attention thereby increasing the effectiveness of the communication. Finally, the advertiser selects the programs in which to broadcast a commercial, thus assuring compatible editorial content. Alternatively, the creative approach can be adapted to the type of program selected.

High Reach and Frequency. Because it is a mass medium with the potential to reach 99 percent of Canadian households, television can deliver high reach for the advertiser. On the average, 78 percent of Canadians turn on the television set at least once a day, of which 37 percent do so during prime time. These figures mean that although television is expensive in absolute terms, it can be cost effective in terms of costs per thousand impressions (CPMs). Television can reach all demographic groups, thus providing unmatched high reach for mass marketers, such as Procter and Gamble and General Foods, which are among the heaviest users of television.[19] Again, this may lead to relatively low CPMs compared to other media.

For advertisers with large budgets, television provides a high level of message repetition, thus increasing reach and frequency. Messages may be repeated with any frequency within the hour, the day, or the week. Repetition is an important learning device and is critical to a product's success during the introduction and growth stages. High frequency may also be attained by placing an advertisement within the same program over a period of time. There is viewer loyalty to certain programs or program types, and if the audience of the program matches the target market profile, frequency can be built.

A Prestigious Medium. There is a certain glamour associated with television advertising both from a consumer and trade perspective. Television allows advertisers to pre-sell products that are distributed in self-service retail establishments (i.e, a pull strategy). In particular, it promotes package identification, which is an important factor in that retail environment. Wholesalers and retailers are impressed with television advertising's ability to "pull" customers and increase their turnover rates.

Advertisers may sponsor (or co-sponsor) a popular program and provide worthwhile entertainment to the viewing public. This creates goodwill toward the advertiser and it is hoped the goodwill will carry over to the advertiser's products.

Some Flexibility. Advertisers can complement the networks' broad coverage through spot buying to adjust the advertising emphasis to local market conditions. Advertisers may also adjust the schedule to seasonal variations in demand for their products.

Disadvantages of Television

The main disadvantages of television may be grouped into five categories:

High Costs. Television is an expensive medium. The CPM may be relatively low, but the absolute cost of advertising on television can be very high. A 30-second commercial on one of the major national networks may cost up to $25 000 in air time alone during the regular season. Thus, television is often out of reach for the small- or medium-sized advertiser.

Production costs for a commercial are also very high because of the technology involved, the cost of equipment, actors' fees, on-site filming, and special effects. More than one commercial is often produced and tested for effectiveness before it is aired, thus adding to the total cost. It is not unusual for the production of one 30-second commercial to cost more than $75 000. High production costs are becoming a serious problem for advertisers who are trying to find various ways of reducing this component of their advertising budgets.[20]

The taxes levied on advertising must also be added to the high budgets typical of television advertising. In Quebec, all broadcast advertising is subject to a 2 percent tax on net dollars, while in Newfoundland all advertising (print and broadcast) is subject to a 4 percent tax on net dollars (Bill 46).

Lack of Flexibility. Television is a rather inflexible medium for media buyers. It has long lead times both for booking and for production. Most networks are booked in June for the 52-week period that starts the following September. Usually these contracts can not be cancelled. Other networks have minimum requirements for the length of a campaign. Selective spots may be purchased at any time but with two- to four-months' notice. Spots may be cancelled with a notice of one month, but at least four weeks of the booking must be run and paid for.

Good time periods for advertising on television are limited and competition for them is stiff. Thus booking has to be done well in advance for the desired time slots.

Creative Negatives. Television messages are very short; more than 80 percent of all commercials aired are for 30 seconds. The rest are for 60 seconds and 15 seconds. Thus, the commercial has to reach all of its objectives during this period. As a result, it is highly perishable.

Television is an entertainment medium and viewers often regard commercials as an annoyance, often switching off, changing channels, or engaging in other activities while the commercials are being aired.

It is difficult to use long copy in television; the story must be short and simple.[21] One major selling point is usually the best strategy to follow.

There is the problem of clutter, which is the practice of clustering messages together during a station break. Here the position of the message is important, with the first and the last receiving greater attention than the middle ones.

Commercials tend to wear out; they become stale and lose their effect over time. It is important to know when to pull a worn-out commercial and to replace it—at additional cost.

Reach Problems. A problem of *audience fragmentation* results from the number of channels available to viewers. The audience is divided up and this leads to reduced reach and higher costs. The problem is aggravated in many markets by the powerful U.S. stations and by the penetration of cable, pay TV, and cable converters. It may also be influenced by videotex systems, two-way cables, dish antennas, and video recorders. Television viewing tends to drop dramatically during the summer, further reducing reach. Summer drop-off is not uniform across the country, as illustrated in Table 7–7 for adults in 12 major markets. The highest drop-off level in 1989 is found in Quebec City and the lowest in Edmonton. Finally, network reach and frequency are uneven across Canada. This may create problems in using television networks in such highly fragmented markets as Toronto and Vancouver.

TABLE 7–7 **TELEVISION SUMMER DROP-OFF**

Markets	Central Area Ratings* (% Difference)
Halifax	−21
Quebec City	−41
Montreal	−30
Ottawa/Hull	−23
Toronto	−23
Kitchener	−18
London	−23
Windsor	−22
Winnipeg	−30
Calgary	−26
Edmonton	−16
Vancouver	−21

*Basis: all stations, adults 18+, Monday-Sunday 7–11 P.M.
Source: BBM Fall '88 vs. Summer '89.

Heavy Regulation. Because of its wide exposure and impact on the public, television is subject to a series of rules and regulations that can severely restrict advertising copy claims. The most important ones are:[22]

- The CRTC must approve all scripts for nationally aired commercials for food, drug, and cosmetic products.
- The Advertising Standards Council must approve all commercials directed at children 12 years old and under. "Directed" usually means either a commercial message designed for them, or run during children's programs.
- In Quebec, it is illegal to advertise to children 12 years old and under. The Committee for the Application of Articles 248 and 249 of the Quebec Consumer Protection Act gives written opinions on whether or not a commercial is directed to children under 13. This law was upheld by the Supreme Court in 1989 (Irwin Toy case).
- The CBC Commercial Acceptance Committee must approve all commercials to be aired on CBC on the basis of good taste, factual (and documented) presentation, and competitive claims.
- The Telecaster Committee (CTV affiliates and one independent) must also approve all commercials to be aired on its stations.
- The federal Department of Consumer and Corporate Affairs must approve all national commercials for food products.
- There are a number of content rules that affect the programming of television stations, and are meant to encourage more Canadian content.[23]

Television Advertising Rate Structure

Although television rates are often highly negotiable and based on demand and supply, rates also depend on the nature of the advertiser, the length of the commercial, the types of programs/dayparts, and the available discounts.

Nature of the Advertiser

There are three basic types of published rates for television advertising: network, spot, and local. Information and data for each type of advertising rate is available from the networks and/or stations in the form of a *rate card*. Rates and data of interest to national advertisers are available in CARD. An example of such a listing is provided in Figure 7–4.

Network advertising is placed by advertising agencies and is subject to the traditional 15 percent commission. The rates are published in the network rate cards and in CARD under the name of the appropriate network. Most of the network time is booked well in advance, usually in late spring. Actual schedules must be negotiated with the networks, and the heavier advertisers tend to obtain the most desirable programs.

Selective spot advertising is also placed by advertising agencies and is subject to commission. The rates are published in the individual station rate cards and in CARD under the name of the station (Figure 7–4). Rates vary according to the daypart, and the time and the nature of the program.

Local advertising is sold directly to local businesses, mostly retailers, and is non-commissionable. Local rates are usually much lower than national rates. About 25 percent of net advertising revenues come from this source. Stations are trying to encourage local businesses to advertise on television, particularly

Edmonton—CFRN-TV

8 Red Deer; 3 Peace River; 13 Grande Prairie; 12 Whitecourt; 12 Ashmont; 2 Lac la Biche; 12 Rocky Mountain House; 9 Crimson Lake; 7 Lougheed; 4 Slave Lake; 18 High Prairie.

| Member CAB | Member TVB | |

A CTV Network Station

Data confirmed for June/90 CARD

Est. 1954. Owned & operated by Sunwapta Broadcasting Ltd., Box 5030, Stn. E., Edmonton, AB T5P 4C2. Studio: 18520 Stony Plain Rd., Edmonton, AB. Phone: 403-483-3311. Fax: 403-486-5121. Tlx.: 03-72257. Member Telecaster Committee of Canada.
NETWORK AFFILIATION—CTV.
FREQUENCY-POWER-TIME
Frequency: Channel 3.

Power: Video 250 kW. Audio 50 kW. Antenna ht. 720′ EHAAT. Mono.
Time: Mountain.
COMMISSION & CASH DISCOUNT: 15% to all CAB certified adv. agencies. No cash discounts. Accounts rendered monthly. Bills due & payable when rendered.
GENERAL ADVERTISING: Rate card effective Sept. 1, 1988.
30 SEC. ANNOUNCEMENTS
Prime Time:

6-11 p.m.	$823-$2823

Daypart:

6:30-9 a.m.	60-175
10 a.m.-4 p.m.	124-353
4-6 p.m.	235-600
11 p.m.-mid.	324-470
Mid-2:30 a.m.	94-235
2:30-6:30 a.m.	18-59

60 sec.: double 30 sec. rate. 15 sec.: 75% of 30 sec. rate. 2 15's must run in same program. Split 30 sec./1 reel—125% of 30 sec. rate.
MANDATORY ROTATIONS:
10 a.m.- 4 p.m. Mon.-Fri.
4-6 p.m. Mon.-Fri.
6-8 p.m. Mon.-Sun.
Mid.-2:30 a.m. Mon.-Sun.
2:30-6:30 a.m. Mon.-Sun.

CHILDREN'S PACKAGES	†	††
Noon-12:30 p.m. Mon.-Fri. Flintstones	$425	$500
9:30-11 a.m. Sat. Slimer/Ghost	425	500
6 a.m.-2 p.m. Sat. rotation	88	88
6-8 a.m. Sun. rotation	59	59

†Jan. 1-Sept. 14. ††Sept. 15-Dec. 31.
COMMERCIALS/PRODUCTION REQUIREMENTS
1-inch tape. 1 dub. Preferred deadline 72 hours.
COMMERCIAL POLICY: Comm'ls. & instr. must arrive at station 96 hours pre. scheduled broadcast. Station will bill for spots contracted but missed due to non-arrival of comm'ls. Anncts. which run in same programming pattern as booked, but delayed up to max. of 15 min. due to conditions beyond station's control, will be charged as booked.
PERSONNEL
Pres.: B. Cowie.
Televison Station Mgr.: J. F. Little.
Gen. Sales Mgr.: Alan R. Mabee.
Sr. Traffic Operator: Gloria Letourneau.
REPRESENTATIVES: Can.: Paul Mulvihill Ltd., Toronto, Montreal, Vancouver; Messner Media, Winnipeg.
U.S.: Minn. & East, incl. Dallas & Houston: Brydson Media Sales Int'l, New York; Hugh Wallace Inc., Los Angeles & Western U.S.

FIGURE 7–4

CARD Listing for a Television Station

Source: *Canadian Advertising Rates and Data (1990)*, pp. 484–485.

by offering them creative counsel and technical assistance in producing commercials.

Length of the Commercial

About 80 percent of all commercials sold in Canada are 30 seconds long, a few are 60 seconds or more, but the recent trend has been the introduction of commercials 15 seconds long, either as stand alone 15s or as split 30s (i.e., two 15s following each other). Pricing of 15-second commercials may vary from 50 to 75 percent of the 30-second rate, subject to a number of conditions, depending on the station. Similarly, pricing of split 30s may vary from 100 to 130 percent the corresponding 30-second rate, again with a number of conditions, depending on the station.[24]

Types of Program/Daypart

Rates vary according to the type of program selected for the commercial and the time the program is aired. The rates take into account the audience available at a particular time segment as shown in Figure 7–5, as well as the individual ratings of a program. The three main types of times and programs are prime time, fringe time, and daytime.

Prime time usually runs from 7 to 11 P.M. and it is the most expensive time. Networks and independents schedule their most widely appealing programs during prime time and compete for a share of the viewing audience (Figure 7–5).

Fringe time precedes or follows prime time, from 5 to 7 P.M. and 11 P.M. to 1 A.M. Early fringe time appeals primarily to individual adults or children returning from school. Stations often schedule situation comedy reruns, talk shows, and local news during this period. Late fringe appeals primarily to young adults, and stations usually schedule talk shows or movies in this period.

FIGURE 7–5

Patterns of TV Viewing by Daypart

Source: Fall'89 BBM

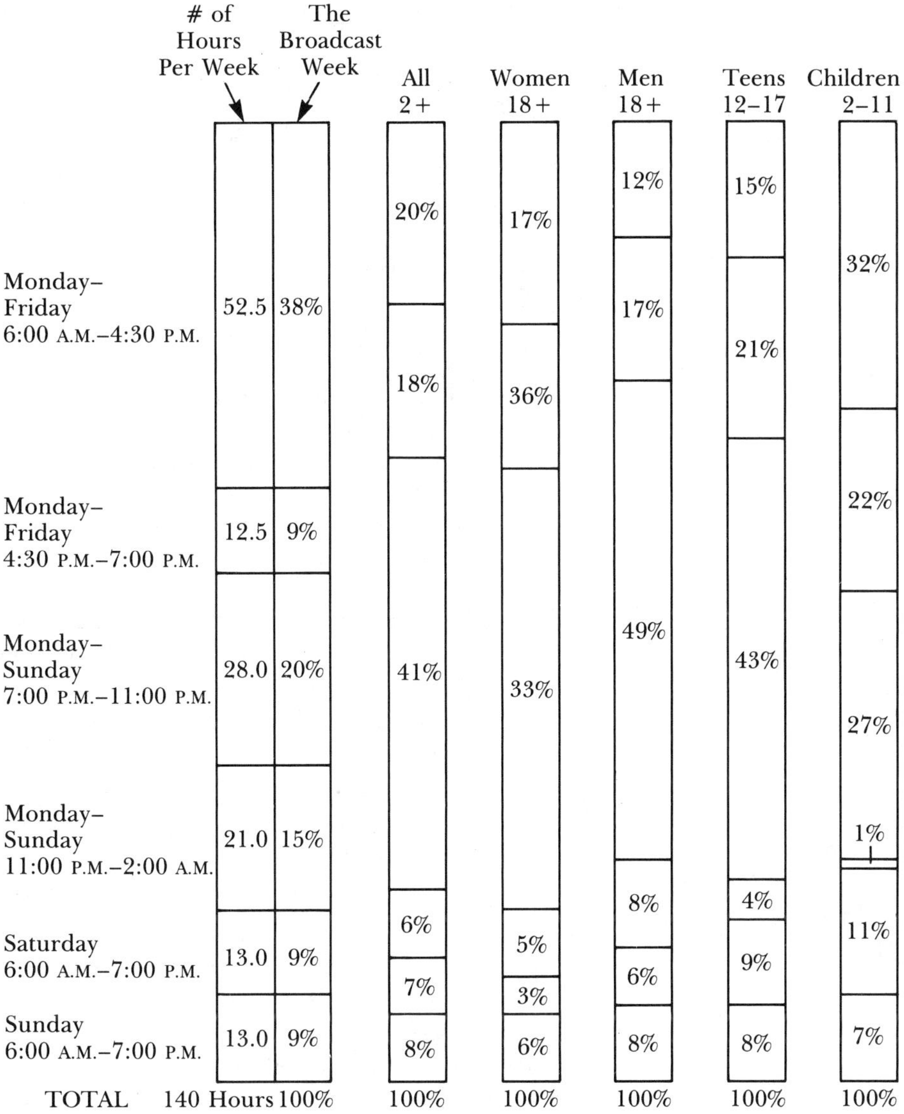

Daypart	# of Hours Per Week	The Broadcast Week	All 2+	Women 18+	Men 18+	Teens 12–17	Children 2–11
Monday–Friday 6:00 A.M.–4:30 P.M.	52.5	38%	20% / 18%	17% / 36%	12% / 17%	15% / 21%	32%
Monday–Friday 4:30 P.M.–7:00 P.M.	12.5	9%					22%
Monday–Sunday 7:00 P.M.–11:00 P.M.	28.0	20%	41%	33%	49%	43%	27%
Monday–Sunday 11:00 P.M.–2:00 A.M.	21.0	15%					1%
Saturday 6:00 A.M.–7:00 P.M.	13.0	9%	6% / 7%	5% / 3%	8% / 6%	4% / 9%	11%
Sunday 6:00 A.M.–7:00 P.M.	13.0	9%	8%	6%	8%	8%	7%
TOTAL	140 Hours	100%	100%	100%	100%	100%	100%

Daytime runs from the morning to 5 P.M. and appeals primarily to women through local news programs, game shows, and soap operas. Some daytime programming is done by the networks.

Discounts

In addition to the published rates, various discounts are available.

Frequency discounts are earned when a minimum number of spots are purchased within a defined period, usually 13, 25, or 52 weeks.

Volume discounts are based on the amount of dollars spent within a period of time, usually 13, 25, or 52 weeks.

Continuity discounts are earned when a contract involves buying at least one spot every week over a given number of weeks.

Special package plans are offered by television stations to sell off fringe time or daytime at a discount or in combination with prime time. Often the purchase of a package is mandatory for advertisers who want to buy prime time. Other packages include sports, movies, and entertainment specials.

Network discounts are available for buyers of full or partial network time slots or packages.

Special Rates

These include ROS or BTA, rotation, and pre-emption rates.

Run-of-schedule (ROS) or *best time available* (BTA) is a discount the station offers advertisers if the station is allowed to schedule the commercial at its discretion.

Rotation is a discount the station offers for scheduling a commercial at will during specific programs or time periods. (See Figure 7–4 for an example of rotation.)

Pre-emption rates are lower rates given to the advertiser in exchange for the right to pre-empt a commercial with or without some notice with the commercial of another advertiser who is paying a higher rate, or by an unexpected event, e.g., a major news story or a sports program. A pre-empted commercial is "made good," that is, the station will run it free later in an equally priced time segment.

The Future of Television as an Advertising Medium

Fragmentation of television audiences may continue as viewers are given more opportunity to use their sets with:

- increased penetration of cable television and of pay TV;
- home-delivery information systems, such as Telidon or Alex, with all its potential applications for entertainment, working at home, and electronic data transmission (e.g., directories and newspapers);
- television video games and home computers connected to television sets;
- dish antennas that pick up signals from satellites and bring programs from all over the world;
- video recorders that delete commercials, re-schedule viewing, or allow for viewing of special tapes (movies and educational material) at home.

The important questions for advertisers concern audience viewing patterns and commercial exposure:

- Is total viewership going to increase with the penetration of new technologies?
- What is the composition of the new, smaller audiences, i.e., narrowcasting instead of broadcasting?
- What is the role of advertising in these new technologies?

- Would Canadians be willing to continue paying for all these services (being tested in Regina, Saskatoon, and Yorkton by Allancom Pay Television Limited), including the planned *pay-per-view* system?[25]

The answers to these and other questions will determine the direction that advertising takes in the television medium. But it is very likely that the task of the media director will become much more complex in dealing with television.

Television may become an even more sophisticated communication medium by appealing to other senses like smell, using the new high definition technology (HDTV), using larger screens with three-dimensional capabilities, incorporating stereophonic sound, or becoming more portable. Thus, the creative director may have different ways of employing its creative possibilities.

The costs of advertising on television will likely continue to increase, not only as a result of inflation but also as the medium itself becomes more complex. Stations will have to find ways of incorporating the new technologies, and of improving their programming to maintain audience share. They will also have to strengthen their marketing orientation to compete with other stations and media for advertising revenues.

Research data on television viewing patterns, particularly viewing of commercials, will become more important to advertisers as audiences become more fragmented and stations try to attract more narrowly defined audiences. Research tools will become more sophisticated and may benefit from such new technologies as people meters (discussed in Chapter 15), two-way cable, and other interactive systems.[26]

SUMMARY

The two broadcast media available in Canada for carrying advertising messages are radio and television. Since the birth of broadcast media in 1920, with the first radio station in the world, Canada has been at the forefront of its technological and commercial development. Canada is one of the most "wired" nations in the world and is among the leading nations in developing videotext systems (Telidon), pay TV, and two-way cable systems.

Table 7–8 highlights the strengths and weaknesses of each broadcast medium.

Radio is mainly a frequency medium, with high flexibility in terms of lead times and market coverage. The cost of radio time is relatively low. However, radio messages have a short life, the medium is not intrusive, and stations must compete for attention. Radio time in major markets is not always available when advertisers need it.

Television is the ultimate communication medium, providing mass coverage and geographic flexibility. It is the only medium that permits sound, colour, and motion, but television advertising is expensive both for time and for production. Television requires long lead times for both booking and for production. As is the case with radio, the television messages have a short life and must reach their objectives in spite of fragmentation, clutter, and negative viewer reactions.

TABLE 7–8   **MAIN STRENGTHS AND WEAKNESSES OF RADIO AND TELEVISION**

MEDIUM	Strengths	Weaknesses
Radio	• high frequency • high selectivity • flexible (coverage and time) • affordable to small business	• fragmentation (low reach) • clutter • short life of message • limited availability in major markets • background medium
Television	• complete communication • high reach and frequency • flexible (geographic and creative) • high prestige and credibility	• high absolute costs (time and production) • fragmentation • short life of message • long lead time • heavy regulation

QUESTIONS FOR STUDY

1. Compare television and radio as advertising media for a) a moving company; b) a restaurant; and c) a political candidate.

2. Compare television and magazines as advertising media and give examples of products that should be mostly advertised in one of these media. Explain your choices.

3. Explain the problem of audience fragmentation and indicate how an advertiser may try to control it.

4. Explain the problem of commercial clutter and indicate how an advertiser may try to control it.

5. "Television is well suited to most advertising budgets." Do you agree? If not, explain under what conditions television should be used by a media planner.

6. It has been said that "radio is the theatre of the mind." Explain what this means with three specific examples, and contrast the creative approaches and effectiveness of television and radio.

7. a. Discuss the role of cable television in changing people's viewing patterns. What effect would increased penetration have on the advertising industry?
   b. Answer the same question for
      • converters and dish antennas;
      • pay television;
      • video recorders, home computers, and video games.

8. Radio has been described as a frequency medium and a background medium. Do you agree? Explain your answer and develop the implications for you as an advertiser.

9. Under what conditions should spot radio commercials be used heavily? Spot television commercials?

10. Contrast AM and FM radio as an advertising medium for a retailer whose target market is composed of a) teenagers, b) young female adults, c) young male adults.

PROBLEMS

1. You are the owner of Beefun, a small chain of fast food restaurants in your community that sells mostly hamburgers and french fries to young adults. You have decided to advertise regularly on radio, using a humorous approach and emphasizing that eating in your restaurant is a fun experience with a relaxed atmosphere. You have determined that you should spend $50 000 a year for your advertising.

   Develop the advertising strategy in detail and select the best radio station(s) and program(s) for carrying your radio commercial(s). Be sure to explain the reasons behind your choice and the rationale for rejecting the other stations.

2. You are the owner of the Surelock Homes Company (see Problem no. 2, Chapter 6). After looking at all the print media, you have decided to evaluate the use of broadcast media to advertise your lock.
   a. Construct a table summarizing the advantages and disadvantages of using each medium for your advertising.
   b. You think that you need to show your target market how the new lock works. Perhaps you may be forced to use television advertising. Since your advertising budget is limited, you are thinking of introducing your product in stages. The first market to enter is the largest metropolitan area in your province. Develop this strategy further, including your selection of television station(s) and program(s) as well as the rationale for rejecting the other stations.

NOTES

1. H.E. Stephenson and C.McNaught, *The Story of Advertising in Canada* (Toronto: The Ryerson Press, 1940), p. 192.
2. The *Canadian Media Directors' Council Media Digest, 1990–91*, p. 32. Henceforth cited as CMDC; Jo Marney, "Who's listening? Radio reaches everyone," *Marketing* (March 21, 1988), pp. 13–15.
3. "CKO Head into the Black at Last," *Marketing* (March 1, 1982), p. R2.
4. "Good shows key to success," *Marketing* (March 21, 1988); Jim Macdonald, "Syndication: For Some Clients It's a Great Way to Augment 'Spot' on Superior Programs," *Marketing* (February 23, 1982), pp. 36–37.
5. Martin Mehr, "Radio isn't static, but change is still slow," *Marketing* (March 13, 1989), pp. 11, 18; "An industry of winners and losers," *Marketing* (March 23, 1987), pp. 9, 12; "New BBM data takes mystery out of buying," *Marketing* (March 17, 1986), p. 12.
6. Leonard Kubas, "Back to the future of radio," *Marketing* (March 13, 1989), p. 26; Leonard Kubas, "Radio aims at baby boomers," *Marketing* (March 21, 1988), p. 26.
7. *CMDC*, p. 12.

8. Kenneth C. Hardy and Ian S. Spencer, "Television Viewers' Responses to Acquisition of a Cable Converter," *Marketing*, *1*, ed. Vernon J. Jones (Administrative Sciences Association of Canada, 1980), pp. 172–78.

9. *CMDC*, pp. 24–25.

10. Ibid., p. 27.

11. Ibid., p. 23.

12. Ibid., p. 12.

13. Ibid., p. 12.

14. Ibid., pp. 12–13.

15. Ibid., pp.14–15; "Special Report on Television," *Marketing* (October 24, 1988), pp. 13–36.

16. Vernon J. Jones and Sherry Monahan, "An Investigation into the Effects of Bill C-58 on Advertising Media Decisions," *Marketing 1977*, ed. Réjean Drolet and Gordon H.G. McDougall (Administrative Sciences Association of Canada, 1977), pp. 82–90.

17. Martin Mehr, "Confusion rules the tube," *Marketing* (October 24, 1988), p. 16.

18. Jo Marney, "Passive viewers are now media controllers," *Marketing* (October 26, 1987), p. 35.

19. *TV Basics*, p. 16.

20. Jim McElgunn, "Price of production: Is it right?," *Marketing* (October 24, 1988), pp. 13, 23–24; Laura Medcalf, "Keep your eye on the $," *Marketing* (July 4, 1988), p. 15.

21. Gordon H.G. McDougall, "Alternative Energy Conservation Appeals: Relative Effects," *Marketing in the 80's*, ed. Richard P. Bagozzi et al. (Chicago: American Marketing Association, 1980), pp. 432–35.

22. *CMDC*, pp. 26–27.

23. Mehr, "Confusion . . .," pp. 13, 16.

24. *CMDC*, p. 17; Anne Parkes, "15s: They're short, but are they sweet?," *Marketing* (February 1, 1988), pp. 23–24; Jo Marney, "15 seconds: The big squeeze countdown," *Marketing* (October 27, 1986), p. 42.

25. Mehr, "Confusion . . .," p. 16; CMDC, p. 25.

CHAPTER

8 *Sales Promotions*

As discussed in Chapter 2, advertising is part of the promotional mix, which represents the communication dimension of the marketing program. Advertising shares this marketing communication task with two other major communication tools: personal communications through a sales force, and sales promotions. Because sales promotion activities are generally closely associated with advertising, this chapter will be devoted to an analysis of sales promotion. Most of the time, the advertising campaign and the sales promotion campaign are conceived, planned, and executed at the same time because these activities are complementary. Without tight co-ordination, both campaigns might well be doomed to failure. In the following paragraphs, we will examine the role and purpose of sales promotions, the part sales promotions play in the Canadian economy and in Canadian firms' marketing plans, and the most recent trends in sales promotion techniques. The various sales promotion techniques will be described and discussed. Finally, this chapter will examine the major steps to be taken when planning a sales promotion campaign.

SALES PROMOTIONS IN CANADA

Sales Promotions Defined

Sales promotion has been defined as "media and non-media marketing pressure applied for a predetermined, limited period of time at the level of consumer, retailer, or wholesaler in order to stimulate trial, increase consumer demand, or improve product availability."[1] Consequently, sales promotion is the name given to a wide variety of tools and techniques that tend to complement the two other major marketing communication devices, advertising and personal selling. Depending on the objectives, sales promotion programs are set up to emphasize a pull and/or push strategy in the distribution channels.

Unlike advertising, a sales promotion's target audience can be the consumer, the trade, or a sales force. It also differs from advertising in its objective to trigger immediate action. In addition, sales promotion actions are always scheduled for a short period of time and at a more or less frequent pace.

Promotion Spending Trends

The exact amount of money spent on sales promotions in Canada is difficult to determine. It has been estimated at over $8 billion in 1988 (compared to $95 billion in the United States).[2] It is also known that currently more is being spent on promotion than on traditional advertising. For instance, the gas station chain Ultramar has reported spending about $3.5 million on promotion versus only $2 million on media advertising and $1 million on sponsorship. This trend is no exception.[3] Depending upon the company and industry,

50 to 70 percent of the promotion budget is devoted to sales promotion activities. This fast increase in promotion spendings, not only in absolute terms, but also in terms of its share of the promotion dollar suggests that sales promotion has recently gained the status of an essential and strategic marketing tool. Sales promotion expenditures are growing at a rate of 12 to 14 percent per year, while advertising is growing only at a 6 to 7 percent rate per year, showing that sales promotion is growing at a faster rate and is taking an ever increasing share of the promotion dollar in Canada.[4]

In terms of the split between trade and consumer promotion, it is clear that trade promotion still dominates. Consumer promotion spendings, however, take an increasing share of the sales promotion dollar. In 1984 it was estimated that 42 percent of all promotional dollars were spent on consumer promotion compared to 40 percent in 1983 and 36 percent in 1982.[5]

Major Factors Underlying the Trends

What are the main factors that may contribute to the sharp increase in sales promotional spendings over the last few years? A first explanation can be found in the evolution of consumption trends. For instance, it has been found that 81 percent of consumers' final buying decisions were made in the store (versus only 65 percent in 1977). In the same way, impulse purchases have jumped from 47 percent to 60.4 percent over the same period of time. In contrast, specifically planned purchases have declined during the same period from 35.2 percent to 19.3 percent.[6] These data suggest that consumers can be strongly influenced by in-store promotions and special deals at the expense of other more traditional communication devices. As a result, consumer promotion has often become the opportunity for marketing advantage.[7]

A second major reason for the increased use of sales promotion over advertising can be found in the increased fragmentation in the traditional broadcast sector. As a result of more viewing options being made available to households by cable TV, channel switching devices, and VCRs, advertisers are looking for new and more efficient ways to reach their target markets.[8]

Other reasons may include:

• Sales promotion has become more "fashionable" and there may be a bandwagon effect as more and more competitors become promotionally minded.
• Consumers are becoming increasingly inclined to use coupons and other sales promotion material.
• The number of brands on the market is still increasing. Consequently, product managers may have to rely more heavily on sales promotion to introduce their products effectively, and to vie more aggressively for the limited retailers' shelf spaces.
• As products become less differentiated, competition on brand characteristics tends to give way to competition through promotional deals.

These are of course only a few of the plausible reasons for the recent usage of sales promotion in the marketer's communication mix. In any case, there is one sure fact: sales promotion activities are likely to increase at an accelerated pace over the years to come.

THE MAIN SALES PROMOTION TECHNIQUES

In order to describe the different sales promotion techniques, it will be useful to consider when, where, and why those activities take place in the distribution channel. Figure 8–1 describes a typical distribution channel: a manufacturer sells goods to final consumers through a number of intermediaries (including retailers). In order to communicate with the final consumers, manufacturers and intermediaries develop promotional mixes which are their marketing communication programs. It has been shown in Chapter 2 how marketers use advertising and personal selling to emphasize a pull or a push strategy. Sales promotions can be viewed as activities that complement, reinforce, or emphasize advertising and personal selling to obtain a proper balance between the two strategies through the distribution channels. Consequently, sales promotion techniques can be classified into three major categories, depending upon the group of individuals targeted. As mentioned earlier, sales promotion tools may be used for directly influencing *consumers'* actions, or *intermediaries'* behaviour

FIGURE 8–1

Consumer Promotion Techniques

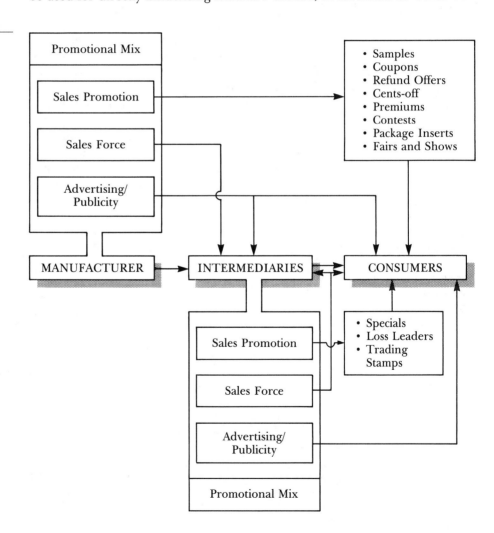

and programs, or *salespeople's* actions. These tools constitute what is called consumer promotions or trade promotions or sales promotions, respectively. Each category will be described in the following paragraphs.

**Consumer
Promotions**

Consumer promotions are essentially used for enhancing a pull strategy. They can take two major forms, depending on whether they are initiated by manufacturers or by intermediaries (especially retailers).

Consumer Promotions Initiated by Manufacturers

As shown on the upper right part of Figure 8–1, these promotional activities tend to encourage brand trial or brand loyalty through sampling, coupons, refund offers, cents-off, premiums, sweepstakes, contests, package inserts, or trade fairs and shows.

Samples. A sample promotion campaign involves the free distribution of a product in regular pack sizes, or more frequently, in special small size packs. The rationale is to provide potential customers with an opportunity to try the product without bearing the financial risk of a first purchase of the brand. It is an effective way to skip the awareness stage of the purchase decision process: providing a free sample is a sure way to have the brand known and tried out. Sampling is therefore effective for introducing a new or improved product, and for inceasing product trial of an existing product.

A sample promotion campaign generally involves substantial costs to a company. Consequently, it should be carefully planned in order to get the most out of it. For instance, the cost of a sampling campaign can be reduced by a proper identification of the target market, and by a careful selection of the distribution method. Samples can be sent directly to households separately or by co-operative direct mailing, which distributes the sample along with

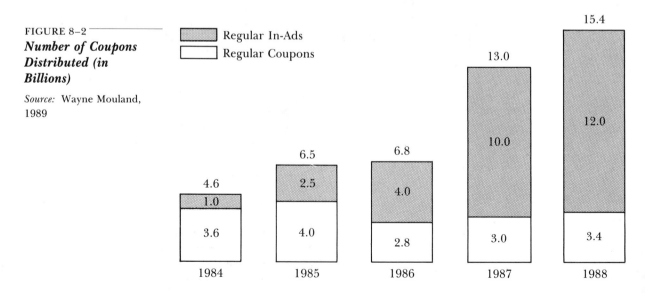

FIGURE 8–2

Number of Coupons Distributed (in Billions)

Source: Wayne Mouland, 1989

coupons or other direct mail pieces. Sampling may also be done in-store with product demonstration or by including the sample with other products.

Coupons.   Coupons have become the most popular form of consumer promotions over the last few years.

Definition and Trends.   Coupons are price-off offers to potential consumers. Couponing is the most widely used sales promotion technique in Canada. In 1988, 15.4 billion coupons were distributed and 250 million were redeemed by consumers (an average percentage of 11.6).[9] This accounts for about 70 percent of all consumer promotion activities.[10] As shown in Figure 8–2, coupon usage by marketers has been growing at an accelerated pace over the last few years. It is interesting to note, however, that this level of couponing activity is much lower than that occurring in the United States. The average Canadian consumer receives 15 percent as many coupons and redeems only 25 percent as many coupons as the average American consumer.[11]

Figure 8–3 shows that the number of coupons redeemed has kept increasing over the years.

The increase in coupon use has been enhanced by the SmartScan Bar Coding System. This system allows a large percentage of coupons to be processed directly by computers from scanner codes. Consequently, because of reduced costs of manual processing, the system allows for faster, more accurate, and better controlled couponing campaigns.

Couponing Objectives.   Coupons are most often used to generate brand trial of existing brands, or to introduce new products. Some advertisers use couponing to increase market share or to defend the brand against competitive actions. Coupons are in fact effective at inducing product trial and repeat buying from existing customers. It is important for advertisers to carefully define the

FIGURE 8–3
Number of Coupons Redeemed (in Millions)

Source: Wayne Mouland, 1989

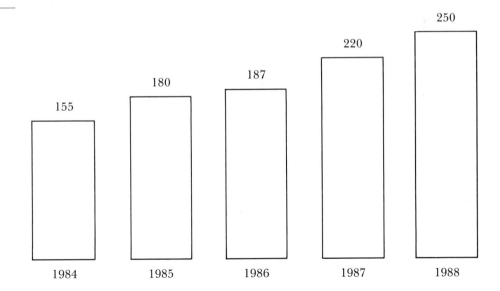

objectives of a specific couponing campaign. This definition will result in a clear identification of the target market for the campaign, as well as the most appropriate media and coupon distribution methods.

Coupon Distribution Methods. Depending on the objectives of the couponing campaign, as well as on the intended target market, an advertiser has a number of options to choose from for distributing the coupons. Among the most frequently used methods are:

1. *Free Standing Newspaper Inserts.* These are four-colour, tabloid size inserts that are distributed within a given newspaper issue (see Figure 8–4). These inserts often contain a large number of coupons for a wide variety of products. This method of coupon distribution is flexible because it permits national or regional distribution. It can be scheduled so as to reach a large number of households on the same day. Its main advantage, however, is its low distribution costs. Through Free Standing Inserts (FSI), some households can receive several inserts of the same offer, especially in areas where FSIs are delivered in both daily and weekly newspapers.[12] In Canada, most FSI insert distribution is limited to newspapers that are home delivered on Wednesdays.

2. *Co-operative Direct Mail.* With this method, coupons are distributed to households in non-addressed mail. A marketer can select certain postal walks for coupon distribution. This method of distribution is flexible because it can reach as many households or areas as desired. It permits the marketer to adapt to the desired geographical market (national, regional, provincial, or smaller areas), with flexible delivery timing. In addition, co-operative direct mail is characterized by reasonable unit distribution costs. Each household can be reached only once, if desired. Co-operative direct mail generates good redemption rates, and it is widely accepted by consumers and by retailers. In fact, the co-op envelope is typically used by a large number of advertisers, and it contains all types of offers for various product types. An example of coupons distributed through co-operative direct mail is provided in Figure 8–5.

3. *Selective Direct Mail.* When a marketer wants to target specific customers who have answered a questionnaire, he can send the coupons to the address of the identified customers.

4. *In/On Pack.* In this distribution method, the coupons are included in the package itself, or on the package, for immediate or future use by the consumer. In this case, the attention of the customer is often drawn to packaging containing such an offer. This method of distribution is economical and effective because the coupon may help attract new users to the brand and provide an incentive for buying it again. This method also stimulates retailers to stock the brand. However, since non-users of the product category are not reached, the direct delivery of coupons to potential users is the preferred method.

Coupons that are instantly redeemable can be especially effective at influencing brand purchase decisions by the consumers. This type of cou-

FIGURE 8–4

Free-Standing Inserts from One Single Wednesday Issue of a Canadian Newspaper

FIGURE 8–5

Examples of Co-operative Direct Mail Distributed Coupons

With the compliments of Steinberg Quebec

pon allows a marketer to directly influence a brand's price at the store level, where as already mentioned most purchase decisions are being made. The redemption rate for instantly redeemable coupons depends on:

- the ease with which coupons can be removed from the product;
- the prominence of the coupon in/on the package;
- the size of the coupon; and
- whether the coupons are attached at the store level by the manufacturer's sales force, or at the factory before retail distribution.[13]

5. *Newspaper Run of Press (ROP)*. With this method, coupons are part of a newspaper advertisement for the brand. This method lacks the flexibility of FSIs or co-operative direct mail. It is also limited in its use of colours. However, it can be effective from a cost-benefit point of view.
6. *In-Store Coupons*. In this case, coupons are distributed within a store through hand-outs or through coupon-information centres.
7. *Magazine coupons*. Such coupons are distributed through consumer magazines. They provide the same advantages and drawbacks as ROP except that they can use four colours and benefit from the editorial climate created by the magazine.

Table 8–1 gives the percentage of coupons being distributed through each method,[14] as well as the evolution of these percentages over the last few years. One can see that Free Standing Inserts are increasingly being used as a method of distribution. Of regular coupons, 49 percent (i.e., 1.65 billion coupons) have been distributed through this channel in 1988. This is a faster growing couponing distribution method, having doubled its market share in five years. This success of FSIs is a result of relatively lower distribution costs, a reasonable redemption rate, and the use of four-colour advertisements accompanying the coupons.

TABLE 8–1 **SHARE OF COUPONS DISTRIBUTED (1986–1988) (REGULAR MARKETER ISSUED COUPONS)**

Media	1986	1987	1988
	%	%	%
FSI	43	45	49
Co-op Direct Mail	18	15	10
Sel. Direct Mail		1	3
In/On Pack	11	12	12
Newspaper (ROP)	14	10	8
In-Store	7	7	7
In-Store Cpn Books	1	2	4
Magazine	5	5	4
Other/Unclassified	1	3	3
Regular Coupons Distributed (in Billions)	2.8	3.0	3.4

Source: Wayne Mouland, 1989

Direct mail offers, which tend to be less cost efficient than FSI offers, seem to lose some ground on a percentage of usage basis.

Coupon Redemption Rates. The redemption rate of a couponing campaign is an important dimension of the campaign success. One of the most important factors influencing redemption rate is the coupon distribution method. Table 8–2 gives the median redemption rates of the various distribution methods, as estimated by the Nielsen Promotion Company. As can be seen, the redemption rate for a couponing campaign can vary from a low 1.7 percent for newspapers run-of-press distributed coupons to 37.9 percent for instantly redeemable coupons.

TABLE 8–2 **COUPON REDEMPTION RATES BY METHOD OF DISTRIBUTION**

Method of Distribution	Median Redemption Rate (%)
Free-Standing Insert	4.8
Co-operative Direct Mail	9.8
Selective Direct Mail	20.3
In Pack	23.1
On Pack	14.4
Instantly Redeemable	37.9
Newspaper Run-of-Press	1.7
In-Store Handouts	30.3
In-Store Entrance	7.7
Magazines	2.7

Source: A.C. Nielsen Company

Other factors are also likely to influence the redemption rate of a specific couponing campaign. For instance, the frequency of product purchase by consumers, the use of an expiry date, the products's market share, the extent of a brand's consumer franchise, the coupon's face value, the percentage discount implied by the coupon, and the product's availability at the retail outlet.[15]

Evaluation of Couponing Campaigns. The effectiveness of a campaign is strongly affected by the choice of a specific distribution method. Effectiveness refers to how the coupon campaign will help achieve the brand's objectives. Efficiency, which refers to the cost per coupon redeemed, is another important consideration for evaluating the success of a coupon campaign. Several factors affect the cost of the campaign: the face value, the cost of redemption, the redemption rate, the expiration date, the method of redemption , and the nature of the advertising campaign. On the other hand, many advertisers are very concerned about the risk of misredemption by dishonest dealers.[16]

Table 8–3 shows how to compute the cost per coupon redeemed for an FSI coupon program.[17] The cost of coupon redeemed is the basis for comparing different programs and distribution methods. Two types of cost need to be taken into account: 1) the fixed, up-front costs (design, printing, distribution); and 2) the variable redemption costs which account for the redemption rate, the offer's face value, and the retailer's handling allowances.

TABLE 8-3 **CALCULATING COST/COUPON REDEEMED FOR AN FSI COUPON PROGRAM (BASED ON TYPICAL COSTING FACTORS & REDEMPTION RATES FOR FSI COUPONS)**

Unit Distribution Cost Factors	
Distribution	3.5 Million
Distribution Cost/M	$15.60
Printing	Included
Artwork/Plates	$4 000/program
Distribution Costs for FSI Program	
Distribution	$54 600
Printing	Included in Distribution
Artwork/Plates	$4 000
Subtotal	$58 600
Unit Redemption Cost Factors	
Face Value	40¢
Unit Handling Costs	14.4¢
Median Redemption Rate	4.2%
Coupons Redeemed	147 000
Redemption Costs	
Face Value Paid	$58 800
Coupon Handling Paid	21 200
Subtotal	$80 000
Total Program Costs	$138 600
Coupons Redeemed	147 000
Cost/Coupon Redeemed	94.3¢

Source: A.C. Nielsen Company

Refund Offers. Refund or rebate offers are prespecified amounts of money that a manufacturer promises to return to the final consumer. Generally, the consumer must send back to the manufacturer some proof that he/she has purchased the product. Recently, this technique has been extended to programs where the discount value varies with the amount purchased, or to refunds for multiple product purchases. In the latter case, the products are generally sold by the same manufacturer.

Rebate programs are often used by manufacturers of durables such as appliances or automobiles. In any case, the refund value must be high enough to influence the purchase decision. A study has shown that rebate offers brought several specific advantages to a producer:[18]

1. *Large Refunds and Negligible Accumulation Requirements.* Unlike trading stamps, which require the collection of books in which stamps are posted, or coupon offers which may require filing systems, most rebate offers omit accumulation needs. They typically call for immediate action (usually within one to four weeks) by the consumer. At the same time, while stamp and coupon values for typical purchases are measured in pennies, few refunds are currently less than fifty cents, and many amount to a substantial number of dollars.[19]

2. *Minimal Risk by Consumers.* Unlike sweepstakes and lotteries (discussed below) few consumers perceive that reputable companies will fail to honour their rebate promises.[20]

3. *Ease of Scheduling by the Manufacturer.* Rebate offers can be introduced with small set-up costs and minimal advance planning and then terminated by the announced expiration date.

4. *Little Opportunity for Fraud.* The manufacturer can be assured that the refund will be sent directly to the consumer since the retailer is not involved in the dealing of money to the shopper. Refunds are sent directly to anyone who submits the required proof of purchase.

5. *Slippage.* A proportion of consumers who are enticed to purchase as a result of the rebate offer fail to request refunds to which they are entitled. This lack of follow-through by consumers (i.e., slippage) results in increased consumer purchases without cost to the manufacturer. Thus, the producer's average refund cost per product unit is less than the face value advertised. Research has shown that the slippage rate often exceeds 30 percent.[21]

Cents-Off. Cents-off offers a temporary price reduction to encourage consumers to try or repurchase a brand. Consumers may stock up on the product, and if the product is satisfactory, the consumer may purchase it at the regular price. The promotion should not run too long or be repeated too often, because consumers then consider the reduced price as the maximum amount they should pay.

Premiums. Premiums give consumers a product "bonus." The premium may be unrelated to the product, like a beach towel for a detergent brand, or related to the product, like a razor with a package of razor blades. It may be free, like a small plastic toy in a cereal box, or sold at or below cost with proof of purchase. Some premiums may be included in the package, while with others the consumer must write the manufacturer and include proof of purchase and a payment for the premium. Premiums may be used to attract attention to a package or to enhance interest in advertisements for the brand. Since it is a rather complicated technique, premiums are not as popular as couponing or refund offers.

Sweepstakes. Sweepstakes ask consumers to fill out contest entry forms. At a fixed date, the winners are selected by random drawing from all entries. Because the prizes are often spectacular, sweepstakes generate high interest from consumers and from the trade. This interest in turn may translate into additional trade support and increased consumer awareness of the brand. Sweepstakes must be co-ordinated closely with the advertising campaign to generate excitement about the product and to ensure that the product's image is not compromised.

In Canada, the Criminal Code outlaws the use of a sweepstake that forces a consumer to buy the product. Consequently, marketers have developed contest rules that are designed to permit the entry into the contest while encouraging, but not forcing brand purchases. For instance, entrants may have to provide a facsimile of the proof of purchase instead of an actual proof of the purchase. Unfortunately, this has recently led some consumers to become "professional contest entrants." They enter such sweepstakes on a large scale by submitting large numbers of submissions.[22]

Contests.   This is a technique similar to sweepstakes, except that consumers must demonstrate some skill. As with sweepstakes, "instant-win" contests help generate excitement about a brand, encourage multiple product purchases, and increase brand loyalty. This type of contest is often used by soft drink companies and fast food chains.

Package Inserts.   A package insert is included in a package, and is a promotional piece about a product, a line of products, or a related product. They are a convenient way to reach the current purchasers of a brand, and to communicate to them information about complimentary products, or different versions of the same brand.

Fairs and Shows.   Fairs and shows for consumers help manufacturers promote their products to highly interested audiences. Examples of consumer fairs are book fairs, antique fairs, auto shows, and video shows. For industrial marketing, trade shows are an economical means of contacting customers.

Consumer Promotions Initiated by Intermediaries

As shown in the lower part of Figure 8–1, several promotion activities are designed for stimulating consumer demand and are typically initiated by intermediaries in the distribution channel, especially by retailers. These promotional activities include specials, loss leaders, and trading stamps. These activities stimulate traffic in the premises of the distributor or retailer.

Specials.   Specials are products a distributor sells at a discount for a limited time. The distributor temporarily lowers the profit margins on that item or passes on to the consumer the manufacturer's discounts. Specials are an effective tool for distributors to build traffic and increase store loyalty.

Loss Leaders.   Loss leaders are items sold at or below cost and are used to attract attention to the store and/or its advertisements. The products are used regularly and are often perishable, e.g., milk, eggs, bread, or meats.

Trading Stamps.   Trading stamps increase loyalty to the retail store by providing some merchandise according to the cumulative value of goods purchased. The consumer is given stamps in proportion to the amount purchased, and these may be exchanged for goods once a certain volume has been reached. This technique is not as popular now as it was twenty years ago. One version of the technique offers consumers a set of products in exchange for receipts totalling a given amount; for example, a set of glasses for receipts of $100 per glass.

Trade Promotions

Trade promotion techniques are devices that can enhance a manufacturer's push strategy. They are designed to directly influence demand among intermediaries in the distribution channel, or to contribute to the promotion programs that those intermediaries (and especially the retailers) have designed for stimulating final consumer demand. These trade promotion activities are shown in Figure 8–6.

Promotion Techniques for Stimulating Intermediary's Demand

As shown in Figure 8–6, the major promotion techniques that manufacturers use for stimulating demand from the various members of the distribution channel are trade deals, free goods, volume discounts, and trade shows. These techniques encourage intermediaries to stock a brand and promote it to other intermediaries or to the final consumers.

Trade Deals.   Trade deals reduce prices to the intermediary for a limited time and are an incentive to carry the brand being promoted. These deals may be offered as a percentage reduction, or as a predetermined dollar amount off the list price. They can take the form of an immediate reduction on the invoice. Alternatively, they can be computed on the total quantity purchased during the deal period and consequently computed at the end of this period.

Free Goods.   Free goods are an alternative to trade deals. A firm offers free goods for the purchase of a quantity of a brand, e.g., "Buy twelve cases, get one free."

Volume Discounts.   Volume discounts encourage an intermediary to carry large stocks of a brand in anticipation of heavy demand spurred by the advertising campaign. The discount rate may increase as the volume ordered increases.

Trade Shows.   Trade shows are an economical means of contacting distributors and getting their support for a brand. Examples of trade shows are fashion shows.

Promotion Techniques for Contributing to the Intermediary's Promotion Program

Assistance to the intermediary's promotion program may be offered by a firm at all levels in the promotional program. For instance, a manufacturer may support an intermediary's sale promotion program, sales force, or advertising campaign toward the final consumers.

Assistance to the Sales Promotion Program.   A manufacturer may provide its distributors with point-of-purchase (POP) display materials, posters, flyers, in-

FIGURE 8–6
*Trade Promotion
Techniques*

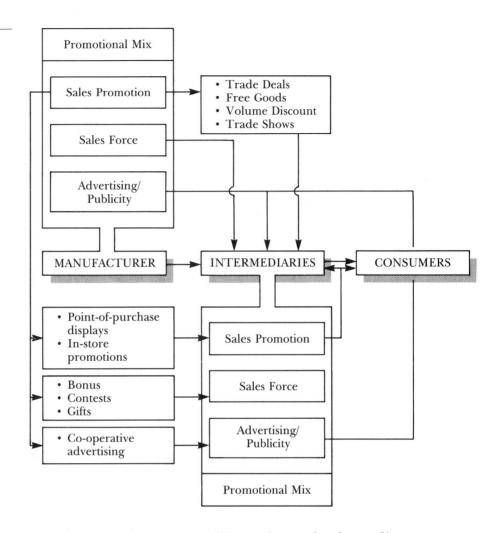

store demonstrations, merchandising racks, or other forms of in-store promotion. It is up to the retailer whether or not to use the promotion materials provided by the manufacturer. Frequently, the manufacturers' sales force must convince the retailers to provide the necessary space, and to set up the display. Obviously, many manufacturers vie for the retailers' co-operation in using their point-of-purchase materials. On the other hand, retailers tend to become increasingly selective in using them. Generally, retailers prefer those displays that exhibit an exciting promotion theme, adapt to store-wide promotions on a chain-wide basis, are in line with the store image and environment, sell several related products, install easily, and fit the store outlay. Sometimes, retailers rent those spaces to manufacturers.

Assistance to an Intermediary's Sales Force. A manufacturer may provide incentives to the distributor's sales force by giving them bonuses (often called push money or spiffs), gifts, or participation in a contest. These special incen-

FIGURE 8–7
*Sales Force
Promotions*

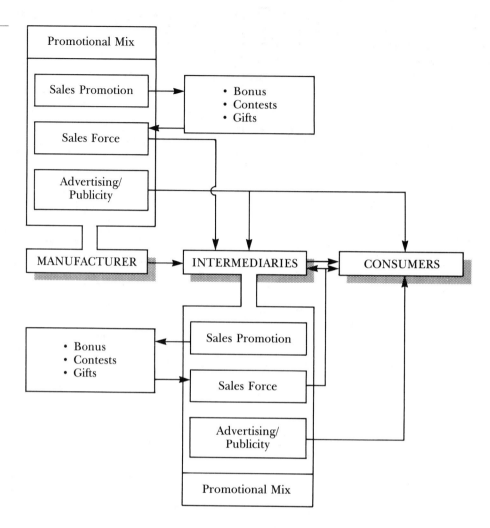

tives are designed to induce the intermediary's sales force to give an extra selling effort during the promotion campaign. In addition, a manufacturer often provides the intermediary's sales force with the necessary promotional material. This may include catalogues, brochures, pamphlets, price lists, or any other promotional aids that may be needed by the sales representatives to make more effective sales presentations.

Assistance to an Intermediary's Advertising. The firm may also finance some of the distributor's costs of advertising to consumers. This is called a co-operative advertising allowance, and the distributor is often required to use in the advertisement illustrations provided by the firm.

It is common practice for a manufacturer to build an integrated trade promotion plan which combines several kinds of allowances, in such a way as to balance the retailers's push/pull strategies, and to provide them with an incentive to increase volume and to achieve fast inventory turnover.

Sales Force Promotion

As shown in Figure 8–7, a manufacturer (or an intermediary) may provide some special incentive to its own sales force in order to ask some special effort during a promotion campaign. Such actions tie sales objectives to a short-term incentive program that uses cash bonuses, gifts, or contests. Gifts can take the form of trips, plaques, rings, jackets, or any object that sales people are likely to value and/or is likely to boost their reputation within their sales organization. These activities are non-recurring and separate from the normal remuneration the sales force receives. They are used to increase the momentum of the promotional plan and to ensure that the sales force pushes the brand when the advertising campaign is attempting to build a strong demand.

PLANNING THE SALES PROMOTION CAMPAIGN

In order to plan a successful sales promotion campaign, at least six steps need to be carried out. These steps are listed in Figure 8–8 and they will be discussed in the next few paragraphs.

Setting the Sales Promotion Campaign Objectives

A promotion campaign should satisfy general as well as specific marketing objectives. Among the first questions to answer when planning a sales promotion campaign are: What is the sales promotion program supposed to accomplish in the overall marketing plan? Is it strategic, or tactical, or both? Is it used as a defensive or an offensive weapon in order to gain market share? How is it supposed to contribute to the balance between pull and push strategies in the distribution channels? How must it fit with the other elements of the marketing communication mix, and especially, advertising? This is why very often the sales promotion and the advertising campaigns are planned together. Sometimes the sales promotion plan is developed by the advertising agency itself. More and more frequently, however, a sales promotion agency is also hired. In the latter case, strong co-ordination is an essential prerequisite to

FIGURE 8–8

The Sales Promotion Planning Process

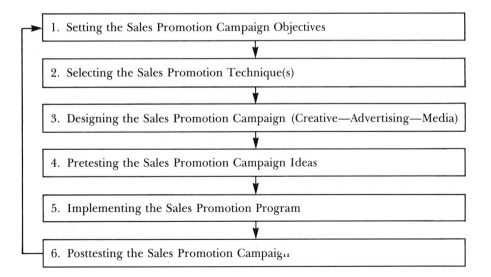

1. Setting the Sales Promotion Campaign Objectives

2. Selecting the Sales Promotion Technique(s)

3. Designing the Sales Promotion Campaign (Creative—Advertising—Media)

4. Pretesting the Sales Promotion Campaign Ideas

5. Implementing the Sales Promotion Program

6. Posttesting the Sales Promotion Campaign

successful sales promotion campaigns. As is also the case with advertising, clearly defined objectives will help control and measure the effectiveness of the sales promotion program. Examples of possible sales promotion general objectives are provided in Table 8–4.

TABLE 8–4 **EXAMPLES OF GENERAL SALES PROMOTION OBJECTIVES**

CONSUMER PROMOTION

- Build new product awareness
- Enhance trial purchase
- Build up brand loyalty
- Induce repeat purchase
- Induce stockpiling at the consumer's level

TRADE PROMOTION

- Increase brand distribution
- Build volume
- Increase sales support
- Induce retailers to stimulate consumer demand

SALES FORCE PROMOTION

- Induce salespeople to "sell" POP material to retailers
- Induce salespeople to install display racks at retailer level
- Induce salespeople to build inventories at retailer level

The specific objectives of a sales promotion campaign imply the definition of a precise target for the promotion action. It should be specified whether the sales promotion campaign should be addressed:

1. To the final consumers; in this case, what consumer groups or subgroups should be targeted? For instance, should the promotion be designed to reach consumers who have not tried the product yet, or those who are price sensitive, or any other particular segment?
2. To the trade; in this case, what type(s) of intermediaries will be involved? In what region(s)?
3. To a sales force; which sales force will be the target?

The second part of a definition of specific sales promotion objectives is to precisely define which actions are being sought from the people in the sales promotion target. For instance, should young consumers be induced to try the product? Should working women be induced to remain loyal to the brand? Should the promotional action induce retailers to hold a larger inventory for the brand? And so on.

Finally, if ever possible, the sales promotion objectives should be quantified and they should specify a time horizon over which this action should take place.

Selecting the Sales Promotion Technique

It is clear that the choice of specific sales promotion techniques should follow logically from a clear definition of the sales promotion objectives. For instance, if the objective is to increase brand awareness, contests and sweepstakes may be the most appropriate techniques. If the objective is to attract new customers, the advertiser may have the choice between single purchase cash refunds, mail couponing, single purchase premiums, or sampling. Finally, for increasing sales to present customers, there is a choice between bonus packs, multiple purchase cash refunds or premiums, in/on pack couponing, and price-offs.[23]

When selecting the proper sales promotion technique, special attention should also be given to the nature of the target audience, and which technique is likely to be effective with the target audience. For instance, research suggests that coupon usage is low among young, working women.[24] Consequently, a marketer whose objective would be to reach this market segment should use another sales promotion device.

Another important consideration in the choice of a sales promotion technique is the phase the promoted product has reached in its life-cycle. For instance, a brand in its introduction phase should be promoted through sales promotion techniques that generate awareness and trial purchases. At the decline stage, promotional actions that maintain distributors' or retailers' loyalty are generally more appropriate.[25]

Designing the Sales Promotion Campaign

The sales promotion program should be consistent with the advertising campaign. This is why it is especially important at this stage that the advertising and the promotion agencies work together and in perfect co-operation. Creativity is often considered a key factor to successful sales promotions. As one senior vice-president and creative director of a large promotion agency puts it, there are only three ways to make sales promotion work: through look, theme, or nuance."[26] By properly combining these three elements, one can generate a "creative envelope" that makes the difference between an outstanding campaign and the rest of the pack.

Because sales promotions are activities which supplement the communication mix, and are carried only over a short period of time, they should be consistent and in perfect harmony with the main advertising campaign. Under no circumstances should they disrupt it. More specifically, the sales promotion planners should carefully watch that the intended action is consistent with the brand and the product image. Note also that too frequent promotional actions may affect a brand's image. Consequently, careful consideration should be given to the length as well as to the frequency of sales promotion campaigns for a given brand.

Finally, given that promotional actions should be advertised, promotion advertisement is often part of the regular advertising during ther sales promotion campaign. At this stage, advertisers should decide which main selling theme or promotional theme should be the most prominent in the advertisements. Advertising copy and media should be selected to effectively reach the sales promotion target audience, with the proper (generally, higher than usual) frequency, through the proper media.

Pretesting the Sales Promotion Campaign

Pretesting of promotional programs is an essential part of promotion planning. It helps evaluate whether the most appropriate promotional technique has been selected, and whether it is being used in the most efficient manner. Unfortunately, pretesting of promotional programs is often overlooked because of time pressures. It has been estimated that only 30 percent of firms do some formal pretesting of their sales promotion programs.[27] In fact, after a rough executional development, several ideas should be pretested. At this stage focus groups, mall intercept surveys (techniques that will be briefly discussed in Chapter 15) can be effectively used.

Implementing the Sales Promotion Program

When implementing a sales promotion program, the sales force is considered as one of the key elements for its success. First, the media campaign must be run along with the promotional campaign. In the same way, the sales force has an important role to play at the implementation stage. It may be for putting up displays in retail outlets, for getting additional shelf space for the brand from retailers, or for inducing retailers to order additional quantities. Obviously, obtaining such co-operation from retailers requires a lot of convincing, and that can be facilitated by trade incentives. This requires extra work and effort from the sales force, without which the sales promotion campaign may fail. To induce the sales representatives to carry out this extra effort properly, the use of sales force promotion devices provide motivation, training, and incentive. This is why a short-term incentive program linked to the promotion results may be used to that effect.[28]

Post-testing of the Sales Promotion Campaign

Finally, after it has taken place, any sales promotion program should be carefully evaluated. This evaluation should be quantitative as well as qualitative. The objective is to assess the extent to which the campaign has fulfilled the objectives that had been set at the beginning of the planning process. This evaluation enables marketers to make recommendations for future programs and to learn the effectiveness of various sales promotion techniques in the firm's specific situations.

SUMMARY

Sales promotion has been defined as "media and non-media marketing pressure applied for a predetermined, limited period of time at the level of consumer, retailer, or wholesaler in order to stimulate trial, increase demand, or improve product availability." Sales promotion is an $8 billion industry in Canada. It is fast growing and it has been taking an increasing share of the advertising dollar over the last few years, at the expense of advertising. Several reasons explain why consumer promotions are increasing so fast: changing consumption brands, and increased fragmentation of the broadcast media are among the most important factors.

Consumer promotion techniques are essentially used for enhancing a pull strategy. Among the main promotion techniques generally initiated by manufacturers are sampling and couponing. Couponing is the most popular consumer sales promotion technique, and can use a wide variety of distribution methods. Other consumer sales promotion devices include refund offers, cents-off, premiums, sweepstakes, contests, package inserts, and fairs and shows. Specials, loss leaders, and trading stamps are consumer sales promotion techniques that are typically used by retailers.

Trade promotion techniques are used for enhancing a manufacturer's push strategy. Among the techniques that manufacturers use for stimulating intermediaries' demand are: trade deals, free goods, volume discounts, and trade shows. Other techniques are used to contribute to the sales promotion, advertising, or sales force aspects of intermediaries' promotion programs. Sales force promotion techniques provide short term incentives to the sales force to induce them to carry out additional tasks and extra effort.

Planning a sales promotion campaign involves the following steps: setting objectives, selecting a sales promotion technique, designing the campaign, pretesting the promotion ideas, implementing the promotion program, and evaluating the results. Through the sales promotion planning program, emphasis should be put on the importance of co-ordination of the sales promotion activities with the two other major marketing communication tools: advertising and personal selling.

QUESTIONS FOR STUDY

1. Define and explain the objectives of 1) consumer promotion; 2) trade promotion; 3) sales force promotion.

2. Compare the relative advantages and disadvantages of a couponing campaign over a sampling campaign.

3. List and describe each of the techniques typically used for consumer sales promotions.

4. List and describe each of the techniques typically used for trade sales promotions.

5. Show how the sales promotion program for a brand of breakfast cereal is likely to evolve over the life-cycle of the product.

6. Find examples of consumer sales promotions. From what you can observe, try to infer the manufacturer's/retailer's (plausible) objectives for these sales promotion programs.

7. What are the different methods typically used for distributing coupons to the consumers? Explain the advantages and disadvantages of each of them.

8. What are the main advantages and disadvantages of a product rebate campaign for a producer? Explain the concept of slippage.

9. What major steps should be followed for designing a sales promotion campaign? Describe each step in detail.

10. Why is it essential for the advertising and the sales promotion agencies to co-operate at the planning stages of both advertising and sales promotion campaigns? How should such a co-operation materialize in practice?

PROBLEMS

1. A large personal care product manufacturer intends to enter the Canadian toothpaste market six months from now. The product, which is being positioned as a product for teenagers, will use in its advertising a good breath theme. An intensive TV campaign has been scheduled for the first six months of introduction, followed by six months of sustained advertising.

   Outline a *consumer* sales promotion campaign that could take place during the introduction phase of the new brand. Clearly specify the objectives to be achieved, the sales promotion techniques and methods to be used, the design of the campaign (as precisely as you can), the schedule and timing for the campaign, as well as a plausible budget.

2. In the same context as problem 1, design a trade promotion for the first year of introduction. Make sure that both consumer and trade promotions are consistent and supplement each other. Specify what role the manufacturer's sales force should play at the implementation stage of these sales promotion campaigns.

NOTES

1. Don E. Schultz, *Dictionary of Marketing Terms*, American Marketing Association, 1988.
2. Miles Nadal and John Pudly, "No Longer the New Kid on the Block," *Marketing*, February 15, 1988, p. 22.
3. "Sales Promotion: Costs Higher in Canada," *Marketing*, February 15, 1988, p. 20.
4. Ibid, p. 20.
5. Nadal and Pudly, op. cit., p. 22.
6. Nielsen Promotion Services, "Survey and Study Show's," March 1989.
7. John Oldland, "On the Sales Promotion Bandwagon," *Marketing*, October 31, 1988, p. 19.
8. Nadal and Pudly, op. cit., p. 22.
9. Wayne Mouland, "More Exciting Times Ahead for the Consumer Promotions Industry," *Canadian Premiums and Incentives*, supplement to *Marketing*, February 20, 1989.
10. Nadal and Pudly, op. cit., p. 22.
11. W. Mouland, op. cit.
12. Wayne Mouland, "Evaluation,—A Key to Successful Couponing," *Marketing*.
13. Wayne Mouland, "A Marketers' Guide to Couponing—Instantly Redeemable Coupons Add Selling Power," Nielsen Promotion Services, March 1988.
14. W. Mouland, "More Exciting Times . . ." op. cit.
15. A.C. Nielsen Company of Canada.
16. Wayne Mouland, "Coupons Are the Most Important Consumer Promotion Method," *Canadian Premiums & Incentives* (August 1982), pp. 11–14.
17. Wayne Mouland, "Evaluation . . ." op. cit.
18. Marvin A. Jolson, J.C. Wiener, and R.B. Roseely (1987), "Correlates of Rebate Proneness," *Journal of Advertising Research*, 27 (February/March), 33–43.
19. A.C. Nielsen Company (1983), *Promoting with Consumer Refunds*. A special report from the Nielsen Clearing House. Chicago: A.C. Nielsen Company.
20. Patricia Bransford (1982), "An Analysis of the Cash Rebate as a Promotion Tool of the 1980's," unpublished study, University of Maryland.

21. Jolson et al., op. cit.
22. R.W. Peacock, Nielsen Promotion Services, "Controlling Facsimile Use in Sweepstakes," October 1989.
23. Nadal and Pudly, op. cit., p. 22.
24. "Coupon Use Low Among Young, Working Women," *Marketing News*, April 10, 1987, p. 24.
25. "Pretesting Phase of Promotions Is Often Overlooked," *Marketing News*, February 29, 1988, p. 10.
26. Jeff Davis, "Best Promotions Come Inside a 'Creative Envelope'," *Marketing News*, December 5, 1988, p. 20.
27. "Pretesting . . .," op. cit., p. 10.
28. Thomas McCann, "Sales Force Involvement Critical to Promotions," *Marketing News*, March 19, 1990, p. 9.

PART III

Behavioural Foundations of Advertising

To make sound decisions, advertisers should not only have a thorough knowledge of advertising institutions and the industry, but should also be able to recognize and analyze the opportunities available in an ever-changing environment. Most of these opportunities lie in consumer behaviour and in consumers' reactions to advertising messages. The third part of this text provides advertising students with a framework for understanding how advertising can influence consumers' behaviour.

To design effective advertisements, an advertiser must have a thorough knowledge of individual buyers' motives, attitudes, and purchasing habits. Chapter 9 describes how advertising affects individual buyer behaviour. Then, Chapter 10 specifies the role of advertising in influencing the consumer's purchase decision process.

CHAPTER

9 *Advertising Effects on Individual Behaviour*

Why do advertisers need to understand human and market behaviour? This chapter addresses this question and describes the basic market mechanisms that make advertising an efficient communication tool. To design an advertising campaign that has the intended effect, the advertising message must be compatible with the characteristics of the target audience, that is, the consumers or potential buyers of the advertised brand. As is true of the design of the entire marketing program, an advertiser needs extensive knowledge of potential consumers in order to perform this task. For instance, how can a marketer advertise a certain brand of instant coffee if it is not known what benefits buyers are seeking when they purchase the product?

Because advertising is a mass communication tool, an understanding of individual buyers is necessary but not sufficient. If all buyers were motivated by the same forces and possessed identical attitudes toward the advertised ideas, products, brands, or companies, a standardized advertising message could have approximately the same effect on all the individuals in a target market. Of course, people are extremely diverse. Some are economy oriented, others buy only luxury items. Some people like Mozart; others enjoy accordion music.

The wide heterogeneity of audiences forces advertisers to develop a global understanding of the marketplace. Since advertising is a mass communication tool, it is intended to influence an entire market at a time. Thus, advertisers should know and be aware of the various flows of consumers in a target market. The problem is still more complex, however, because markets are not static; they evolve constantly. Some consumers enter and others leave the marketplace in more or less continuous flows. This explains the saying often heard in advertising circles that a firm does not advertise to an audience but to a parade.

An advertiser who is responsible for setting up a campaign for a brand of instant coffee generally tries to find answers to such questions as: Why is a significant proportion of consumers loyal to Maxwell House? What is the proportion of potential customers who are aware of our brand? Why are the new buyers of instant coffee more likely to try a competing brand first? Here again, it is seen how different advertising message decisions are likely to result from the answers to these questions.

Advertisers need to have a micro view of the market, which is an understanding of individual potential buyers or of the different types of buyer for a product category, as well as a macro view of the market, which is market behaviour at an aggregate level (the whole mass market). The objectives of an advertising campaign are based on both a micro *and* macro understanding of the market. In contrast, decisions on the advertising message content and format, which must reach and influence each buyer individually, are based on a good understanding of buyer behaviour. Media buying decisions are based on the knowledge of where to reach consumers or what the media habits are in the market segments. These decisions imply that advertisers have a macro knowledge of the market.

ADVERTISING EFFECTS ON BUYER BEHAVIOUR

A simplified view of buyer behaviour is given in Figure 9–1.[1] When buyers are subjected to certain marketing stimuli coming from the environment (such as a product or an advertising message) there is some probability they will respond. The behavioural response may be, for instance, the purchase of the product. The study of consumer behaviour is the determination of the elements that influence the consumer response.[2]

Three conditions must be simultaneously met before potential buyers are willing to or even can buy a certain product or brand:

1. They must feel the need or have the desire to acquire a certain category of product or service. They should be motivated to fulfill a basic need or desire.
2. They must perceive the product and the brands as likely to fulfill this need. They should also have a sufficiently favourable attitude toward acquiring the product and the specific brand to consider purchasing it.
3. The product should be available for purchase (adequate distribution) and the consumer must be able to afford it (adequate pricing).

For instance, some individuals could have very favourable attitudes toward IBM and its products. However, they will not purchase an IBM personal

FIGURE 9–1

Simplified View of Marketing and Advertising Effects on Consumer Behaviour

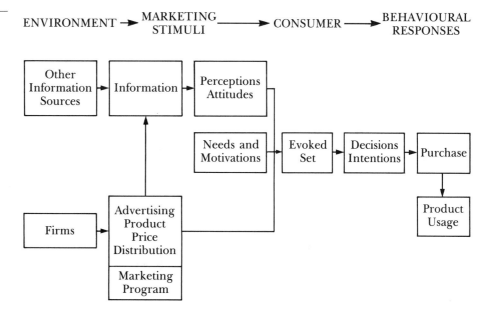

computer (PC) unless they experience the need or desire to acquire one. Let us assume that one day one such potential buyer starts a business, hires an office assistant, and decides to by a PC. The buyer may or may not decide to purchase an IBM PC, despite the buyer's decision to acquire such a piece of equipment and favourable attitude toward IBM. For instance, the PC may be too expensive, or there may be no local IBM dealer. It may also be that the PC is too heavy to be carried along on business trips if necessary.

It may be, however, that this business person has a favourable attitude toward several brands and models of personal computers and that several of these brands are in the same price range and are available at a nearby dealer. In this case, which brand is the entrepreneur likely to select?

When a specific brand of a product category simultaneously meets the three essential prerequisites listed above, this brand is considered to be in the buyer's *evoked set*. A buyer's evoked set is composed of all the brands a potential buyer considers as possible purchase alternatives to satisfy the same general need or desire. Now, a buyer must decide which brand in the evoked set is likely to best satisfy. The outcome of the evaluation process is a purchase decision, generally followed by the purchase itself (behaviour) and by product usage. However, the outcome may also be a non-purchase decision.

In the preceding example, let us assume that the buyer has three brands in the evoked set for PCs: IBM, Apple, and Digital. The buyer must decide which among these three brands is most likely to best satisfy his specific need. After a careful evaluation of the features of each PC in relation to his needs, he may select an Apple, purchase it, and use it. Under certain circumstances, however, he may decide that none of these three PCs really fits his requirements and may decide to withhold his purchase decision until he finds a satisfactory solution or completely give up the idea of purchasing a personal computer.

To what extent does advertising play a role in the purchasing process? Advertising is an important marketing stimulus that provides information to consumers. However, as can be seen in Figure 9–1, it is not the unique source of marketing information used by consumers. The other elements of the marketing mix also convey a lot of information. Not only can they determine whether or not a brand is part of a buyer's evoked set, but they can also carry information to potential buyers that can affect their attitudes toward the brand. Buyers also receive many pieces of marketing information from outside environmental groups (from family members, neighbours, or consumer associations).

ADVERTISING AND BUYERS' NEEDS AND MOTIVATIONS

The Role of Motivations in Purchase Behaviour

Motivation can be defined as the underlying force of any action. By inducing an individual to perform a certain act, this force tends to reduce the state of psychological tension generally aroused by an unsatisfied need or desire. Thus, motivations can be physiological (such as hunger, thirst, or sex) but, more often, they are psychological (for instance, security, esteem, or prestige).[3]

Psychologists distinguish between positive and negative motivations. Positive motivations favour certain acts. They are often called needs or desires. Negative motivations, on the other hand, prevent the performance of certain acts. They are also called fears, aversions, or inhibitions.

The products and services consumers buy reflect their needs. Consequently, a purchase cannot take place without a need being aroused, consciously or not. The same type of product may be bought by different consumers as the result of very different needs and motives. A car may fulfill a transportation need for some consumers and a social status need for others. The need for social status and recognition may have outlets other than buying a certain style of car, however.

These simple and somewhat intuitive facts have clear implications for advertisers. First, advertisers must identify properly the needs they want to satisfy through the advertised product. Second, they must identify actual competitors, i.e., the other consumption means typically used by consumers to fulfill the same need category. For instance, a car manufacturer may find that its main competitor is not General Motors but a large travel agent or a well-known brand of stereophonic equipment. Finally, because advertising is part of a buyer's environment, it has the capacity to arouse certain needs in consumers.

Lewin's Field Theory

Several theories of motivation have been proposed.[4] Among them, Field Theory may be the most useful in advertising. According to Kurt Lewin[5] an individual's behaviour is the result of a number of motives and forces in this individual's *life space*, or perceptions of the surrounding world (the environment). As a consequence, to understand buyer behaviour is to identify all the forces to which a potential buyer is subjected at the time he considers making a purchase and all the barriers that block efforts to reach these goals.

Certain forces induce buyers to purchase and are considered to have a *positive valence*. Forces that prevent them from buying have a *negative valence*. These forces can be represented by vectors, the direction of which would represent the valence of the motives. This set of vectors can be thought of as the configuration of the nature and the relative strength of the motivations involved in a certain purchase situation. The conflict between motivations with positive and negative valences generates a state of psychological tension, which is directly linked to the number and intensities of all the forces involved. Thus, the conflicting nature of any human action, and of purchasing behaviour in particular, is highlighted. While certain motives induce a consumer to purchase a product, other motives (especially those urging the satisfaction of other needs) tend to prevent the purchase.[6] Thus, it would be unusual for a given action not to go against the satisfaction of other needs. This is always true of a purchase: when consumers buy a product, they give up a certain part of their purchasing power.

For example, let us assume that a student whose financial resources are somewhat limited is subjected to conflicting motives for buying a used car (Figure 9–2, next page). Certain positive forces may induce the student to make such a purchase: the desire to get to school more conveniently and pleasantly every morning; the need to impress friends (love needs); and the need to feel important (self-actualization need).

However, purchasing a car may be inhibited by other negative forces. For instance, the student may fear that the car could break down (security needs).

FIGURE 9–2

Example of Motive Conflict in a Used Car Purchase Decision for a Given Consumer

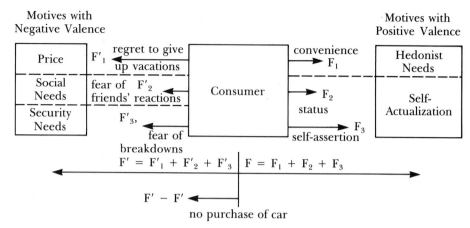

Purchasing a car may also prevent the student from making some other expensive purchase.

If the sum of the forces pushing the student toward a purchase decision is larger than the sum of the forces pulling him or her away from this decision, the student will buy the used car; otherwise, the student will probably decide to postpone the purchase.

How Advertising Can Influence Consumer Needs

Psychologists recognize that a latent desire can be stimulated by a subject's physiological change. For instance, hunger may result from the changes in an organism that are provoked by deprivation of food during a certain period of time. A latent desire can also be aroused by stimuli from the subject's environment. For instance, the subject may become thirsty at the mere sight of a bottle of Coca-Cola or the stimulus may be an advertising message that arouses a latent need or desire.

It must be stressed, however, that exciting a latent need is *not* "creating" a need. An advertisement can awaken, reinforce, or even strongly stimulate a latent need. However, it cannot stimulate a desire that does not exist already. The sight of even the most delicious meal cannot arouse the appetite of anyone who has just finished a hearty meal.

An advertiser can exert some action upon consumer needs only by remaining as present as possible in the consumer's environment in order to stimulate latent needs. This is especially true when the need is frequent and easily satisfied. Advertisements of drinks at points of purchase are an example of this. Note that in addition to being influenced by physiological changes, needs and motivations are also influenced by a consumer's personality and past experience.

ADVERTISING AND BUYER PERCEPTIONS

Buyers gain product and brand awareness and knowledge through the information flow they receive from various sources. They are exposed to at least four sources of marketing information.

1. *Direct sensorial information.* Buyers receive such information through physical contact with the product. For instance, when they look at a product in

a retail outlet or when they are exposed to the package, when they watch a commercial, when they see a model in a showroom, or in any other circumstances, they receive or infer a certain amount of information about the product and/or the brand. Consumers may also infer information about the product characteristics after product usage.

2. *Retailer or seller's information.* A buyer may receive product or brand information from retailers or from people in the distribution channels. Industrial buyers get valuable information from salespeople. This information may be factual, for instance, when it results from a demonstration of the product or from a description of the product's technical features and characteristics. It may also be "subjective" information, as when the retailer tries to use persuasive arguments to induce the customer to buy a specific brand or when the customer asks the retailer's personal and subjective advice on which brand to select.

3. *Advertising information.* This is the bulk of information about companies, products, services, and brands that potential buyers receive through the advertising media.

4. *Interpersonal information.* Consumers receive a large amount of marketing information as they interact with various reference groups, which are the social groups to which they belong or to which they aspire to belong.

With the information received through these different communication channels, consumers develop an image of a brand that more or less matches the real and "objective" physical product. In other words, one could think of consumers as matching a brand with a typical consumer with a certain profile. Consequently, buyers see products and brands as more than a set of technical and physical attributes. The set of attributes that consumers associate with a brand is what is generally called the *brand image*. In other words, a brand image can be defined as the personality traits consumers ascribe to a brand.

A brand image is favourable as long as a buyer perceives some congruence between needs (as perceived by the buyer) and the brand image. That is, the brand image is favourable if there is a small or no gap between buyers' perception of themselves (their self-concept) and the brand image. Conversely, the brand image may be unfavourable if there is too wide a gap between the two profiles. For instance, if a consumer perceives a certain brand of men's shoes as suitable for playboys, he will probably develop a positive attitude toward this brand if he perceives himself as a playboy. A conservative businessman, however, may develop a negative attitude toward the brand.

Buyer Perceptions of Brands

Buyer Perceptions of the Physical Attributes of a Brand

Buyers often have only a partial knowledge and understanding of the products they buy. Sometimes, the product is technically sophisticated (for example, a personal computer or video recorder). Therefore, unless consumers are electronics engineers or technicians, they are unlikely to understand or evaluate all the technical and complex features of the product. Even when the product is not technically sophisticated, manufacturers are often surprised to learn through a market study that consumers have a high level of technical ignorance about facts that have become obvious and natural to them. Advertisers should thus be aware of the level of technical knowledge buyers have reached on a product if they want an advertising communication to be properly decoded by potential buyers.

Buyers tend to perceive only the attributes that are important to them. These are the *salient attributes*. Knowledge of which attributes are salient for which buyers in which circumstances is essential, since buyers are likely to compare the performance of the various brands available on these salient attributes before they purchase a brand. Moreover, consumers interpret and infer all kinds of information from certain physical attributes of the product.[7] This inferred information may seem absurd to a well-informed specialist. For instance, from the light weight of an electrical appliance, some consumers may (unconsciously) infer that the appliance is not sturdy. Some may infer that a piece of furniture is of inferior quality because some of its ornaments are made of plastic (for many consumers, a good piece of furniture can only be made of wood).

Buyer Perception of a Product's Price

The price charged for a product has different meanings for buyers. One is that part of the consumer's purchasing power must be sacrificed to acquire the product. Buying product A often means giving up the prospects of buying products B, C, or D, which would satisfy other needs. This is why in *absolute terms* the price characteristic of a product can never be an inducement to purchase it.

Another meaning of price was not recognized, however, by classical economists, who assumed that consumers would have access to immediate, perfect, and free information. If this were the case, what would be the point of advertising? Price often gives consumers information about the quality of the product. In this case, the demand for a product increases as the price also increases, because consumers associate price with quality and the demand is higher for high quality products.[8]

Buyer Perceptions of a Brand's Intangible Attributes

It was shown how a product's physical characteristics and attributes, including its price, tend to generate in buyer's minds new attributes that may be real or sometimes irrelevant and false. As soon as a potential buyer comes into contact with a product, the brand image formation process starts. Advertisement of a brand, interpersonal communications about products, and in general everything that is related to a brand and falls into a buyer's visual field are also sources of information about a product. For instance, the general display at a bank head office, the thickness of the carpets at its branches, and the courtesy of its employees are but a few of the multitude of details that are visible to the public and that give a bank its personality (image).

Although advertising is not the only source of brand image formation, it is one of the few information sources that is often completely under a firm's control. Therefore, advertisers are generally interested in these kinds of questions: What is the present image of the brand as perceived by consumers? How is this image different from those of the competing brands? What is the "ideal" brand image toward which the brand should tend in a specific market segment? What should and could be done to bring the present brand image as close as possible to the ideal one? Consequently, brand image analysis is an important task of an advertiser.

Brand image analysis can be conducted according to a brand's proximity, content, and value.[9]

Image Proximity. Image proximity refers to how present a brand is in buyers' minds. Some brands are always present in practically every consumer's mind; others are not. To demonstrate this, one has only to ask people which brands of a product category they can mention without any aid. A brand with a high level of presence will always be among the first mentioned because it will probably come readily to consumers' minds as soon as they think of the relevant product category. For instance, when Canadian consumers are asked to give a few brand names of snowmobiles, Ski-doo is likely to be mentioned frequently, Eaton's for a department store, Kodak for a camera, Molson's for a beer, and so on.

In contrast, certain brand names are unknown to many consumers. Other brands are well known but not frequently mentioned because consumers do not readily think of such brands when they consider a product category. These brands have a low presence level in consumers' minds.

Image Clarity. A brand image is perceived with different levels of clarity. This is evidenced by the amount of consensus among consumers as to what the personality of a brand is. Thus, a brand of detergent may be perceived by practically all customers as being young, modern, and effective. This would be an example of a clear image. If, on the other hand, a brand is perceived as young, modern, and effective by certain customers, as old, traditional, and rather ineffective by others, and as a brand for poor or vulgar people by yet another group of consumers, this brand would not have a clear image in the market.

Image Content. The content of a brand image includes all the personality traits that characterize the brand. As shown in Figure 9–3 (next page) two brands (General Electric and private Brand X) could be perceived as having their profiles defined according to a set of bipolar adjectives such as young/old, reliable/unreliable. Average profiles across consumers in a market segment are typically estimated on such scales for analyzing brand image content. Thus, in Figure 9–3 the General Electric brand would be perceived as more powerful, reliable, and modern than Brand X.

Brand Image Value. The profile of a certain brand image has little significance in itself. It gets its full meaning only when compared with the traits that buyers

FIGURE 9–3

**Image Profiles of
Two Brands**

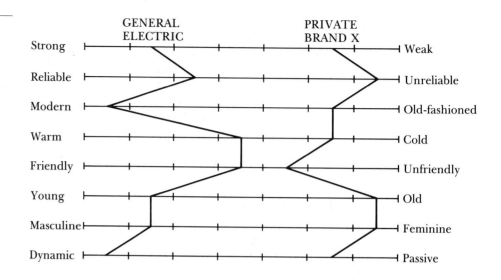

in a market segment would consider positive or negative for a brand in a particular product category. For instance, a brand can be perceived as feminine by consumers. This might be a positive characteristic for a beauty care product or for a brand of cigarettes directed at the women's market segment. However, it would certainly be an undesirable characteristic for an after-shave lotion.

Buyer Perceptual Maps

It was shown how buyers perceived a brand according to certain characteristics and attributes. These attributes can be objective (such as the package or product colours, or its shape), or abstract (such as masculine/feminine, or modern/old-fashioned). In practice, advertisers are interested not only in buyers' perceptions of their brand but also in how these perceptions compare with competing brands. A buyer perceptual map helps advertisers understand and visualize these perceptions of a buyer or of a whole market segment, if it can be assumed that buyers' perceptions of different brands are sufficiently similar to warrant their aggregation.

The use of a brand perceptual map for developing advertising strategies was mentioned in Chapter 2. In the perceptual map, actual brands of a same product class are represented as points in a geometrical space. Interpoint distances between brands represent overall similarities as perceived by buyers of a market segment. The underlying dimensions of this space are considered to be the attributes used by buyers to discriminate among brands.

For instance, assume that a brand manager for Minute Maid, a fruit-juice company, wants to find out how consumers' perceptions of Minute Maid compare with two competing brands, Sun Pac and Tropicana. Also assume that only two main attributes are used by consumers to differentiate among the different brands,[10] for instance, sugar content and colour. (In practice, an advertiser does not know which or even how many attributes are used by

FIGURE 9-4

Perceptions of Three Brands of Fruit Juice on Two Relevant Attributes by a "Typical" Buyer

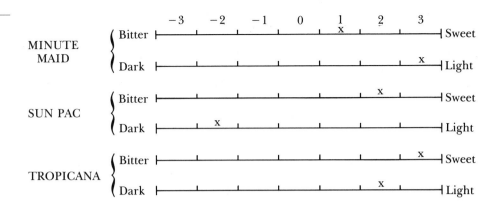

consumers.) Figure 9-4 shows how an average consumer in a market segment has rated Minute Maid, Sun Pac, and Tropicana on these two characteristics. It can be seen that Tropicana is perceived as being more similar to Minute Maid than Sun Pac.

These data could be presented directly on the same diagram, where the two axes represent the two attributes and the scores of each brand on these two dimensions can be used as the co-ordinates to position each brand as a point in this two-dimensional space (Figure 9-5).[11]

If more brands and more attributes were involved, direct comparisons of the brands' relative positions would be very difficult. This is where the perceptual map concept can help an advertiser. It can provide the spatial representation of the perceptions of the various brands in buyers' minds, the number of relevant dimensions used by buyers to perceive brands, and the nature of these dimensions.

FIGURE 9-5

Configuration of Three Brands of Fruit Juice in a Consumer's Perceptual Space

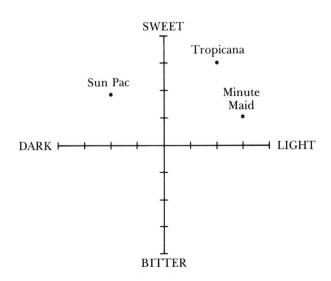

Buyer Perceptions of the Communication Elements

All the elements of an advertising campaign contribute to brand image formation. When properly designed, a message conveys to consumers what the advertiser has to say about a product; in addition, the individual who actually delivers the message (source), the media vehicles carrying the ads, and the featured consumption scenario in which the product is advertised also communicate.

This is an important area for advertisers because an integrated brand image strategy should include the elements that are compatible and are likely to convey the same information to the consumer or at least information that is not inconsistent with the target brand image.[12]

Source Credibility

Even before any communication takes place, a source is perceived by an audience as carrying a certain amount of information[13] and, hence, as more or less competent and credible. Source credibility is essential in advertising because communication effectiveness depends on it.[14] The source of a communication may be perceived as being either the firm advertising the brand or the individual(s) who deliver(s) the message, especially in the case of testimonial advertising. Source credibility depends on whether the source is perceived as being competent to make the statements contained in the message or whether the individual delivering the message is considered truthful. Credibility has two major components: a cognitive and an effective component.[15] The cognitive component refers to the source's competence as perceived by the communication's recipient. A doctor is generally more credible when he or she makes a statement about some medical matter than would be a janitor. The affective component refers to whether the source is perceived as objective and trustworthy. A politician who makes a speech on the national economy may be perceived as competent but biased because of her or his political allegiance. Thus, credibility is not an intrinsic characteristic of a source; it is granted to the communicator by an individual. A source may seem quite credible to one individual and absolutely untrustworthy to another.

Two factors enhance the perception of a source's competence. First, the source must be effectively recognized as an expert. Dentists (because of their officially recognized expertise) are more credible than a non-medical specialist when they make a statement concerning the effects of sugar consumption on cavity proneness. A second factor is the assurance with which the statement is made. The rationale is that experts are supposed to talk confidently about their field of expertise. This is why experts may lose some or all of their credibility[16] when they speak on topics outside their field.

The level of agreement between a communicator and an audience is a primary determinant of the affective component of source credibility. In other words, a source is more credible when it is perceived as holding opinions similar to those of the audience on other matters. One evidently tends to agree with people with whom one already shares a certain number of opinions. A second determinant is whether the source is perceived as having some interest in defending the stand taken in the message.

FIGURE 9–6
The Use of a Recognized Expert for Testimonial Advertising

Courtesy Procter & Gamble Inc.

FIGURE 9–7
The Use of a "Typical" Consumer for Testimonial Advertising

Courtesy Japan Airlines Co., Ltd., from a mid-1980s advertisement.

"Dryness is extremely important for healthy skin. And Pampers is a very dry diaper."

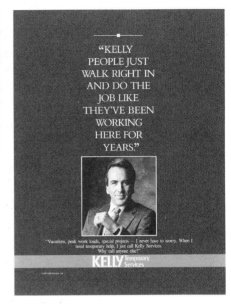

"KELLY PEOPLE JUST WALK RIGHT IN AND DO THE JOB LIKE THEY'VE BEEN WORKING HERE FOR YEARS."

These have important advertising implications. One is that an advertiser should be perceived as a credible source, and this cannot be achieved unless the company is perceived as *competent* and *objective*. Although a company can build a reputation of expertise and competence, it will practically never be able to show it has no vested interest in convincing its audience.[17] This reality may be somewhat overcome by a well-established reputation of competence.

A company that has not been able to establish such a reputation can use testimonial advertising. The objective of this approach is to dissociate the source of the message from the company. An advertiser can ask an outside person to "testify" for the product. Thus, the testimony of a recognized expert can be used to act upon the competence element[18] (Figure 9–6), while a "typical" consumer may be used to act upon the affective element by reporting on a positive experience with the product or service (Figure 9–7). The assertive tone of most broadcast commercials can also be explained by advertisers' desire to ensure that the source is perceived as competent and credible.

How Advertising Can Influence Buyer Perceptions

It was shown how advertising, like any buyer information source, must overcome buyers' perceptual defense mechanisms in order to increase their information level about an advertised product, brand, or service.[19] In order to break down the barriers of selective attention, an advertiser can try to bypass the obstacle of selective attention and use mechanical devices to attract the audience's attention.

Factors such as the size of a print advertisement, the length of a telecast message, the use of colour, repetition, high message intensity, or motion can decrease the effectiveness of consumers' selective attention. Consequently, in order to be more effective communicators (regardless of the costs involved), advertisers are likely to prefer for magazine and newspaper advertisements:

- a full page to a half or quarter page,
- four colours to black and white,
- an advertisement that contrasts with the rest of the information conveyed by the medium.

For a broadcast commercial, advertisers generally prefer:

- a one-minute commercial to a shorter one,
- a commercial whose intensity contrasts with the rest of the program it is broadcast on.

For a flashlight billboard, advertisers should prefer:

- the largest possible billboard,
- the use of several colours of lights,
- the use of a moving rather than a still advertisement.

Another effective mechanical device that applies to all kinds of media is the use of message repetition. Several studies have shown a direct relationship between message repetition and message recall and comprehension. One study showed that the percentage of a television audience that could recall a telecast advertisement increased from 33 percent to 65 percent, depending on the total number of minutes the advertisements of the specific brand were seen.[20] Other studies have shown similar results.[21]

ADVERTISING AND BUYERS' ATTITUDES

Attitude may be defined as a hypothetical construct that intervenes between buyers' perception formation process and their actual behaviour as they are exposed to stimuli and communications from the market environment. Broadly speaking, an individual's attitude toward an object is the inclination to act positively or negatively toward this object. It includes the individual's judgements about these objects and the affective reactions (e.g., liking or disliking) aroused by such information. Attitudes are modified in strength and nature as new information from all kinds of sources is received, perceived, and processed by a consumer.

Especially relevant to a study of buyer behaviour are buyers' attitudes toward products, product usage, firms, and the brands on the market. Other relevant attitudes are those toward various communication sources, different media vehicles, advertisements, and buyers' attitudes toward risk.

Attitude Structure

Three types of attitude components can be identified: the cognitive, the affective, and conative elements.

Cognitive attitude components include the knowledge (or cognitions) individuals have acquired, as well as their evaluation of the importance of this information. During the evaluation process of the perceived information, a piece of information can be rejected if, for instance, it is not believed to be true. This information is likely to be rejected if it cannot be harmoniously integrated into the coherent system of cognitions that the individual has developed over the years. For instance, a glue manufacturer advertised that a single drop of Krazy Glue is sufficient to support a man hanging from a steel bar. One can easily imagine that this information runs a high risk of not being believed by potential customers. This is absolutely independent of the (possible) technical truth of this assertion. The fact that a message content is technically accurate is irrelevant. A message that is not perceived as truthful is rejected and cannot add to the consumer's knowledge about the product (glue) or the brand (Krazy Glue).

Affective attitude components include the feelings and affective reactions provoked by the object toward which the attitude is being formed. These affective components are intimately linked to the evaluation of the information concerning the object. For instance, a piece of information is likely to be evaluated as important if it helps or hinders the satisfaction of some need(s). When it is perceived as hindering the satisfaction of some need or the aspirations of the individual, it is likely to generate negative affective reactions. Conversely, when it is perceived as helping to satisfy some needs and aspirations, it is likely to generate positive affective reactions.

Conative attitude components refer to an individual's tendency to act toward the attitude object. When positive affective elements dominate, these actions are likely to be in favour of the object. Otherwise, they are likely to be against the object. The conative elements of attitudes may be considered the logical consequence of the cognitive and affective attitude components.[22]

One important property of attitudes is that their elements tend to be consistent with one another. Thus, cognitive elements tend to be mutually compatible. In the same way, this is also true of the affective elements among themselves, as well as of the cognitive with the affective elements. Of course, attitude components are not organized into perfectly logical systems. People are often subjected to conflicting pieces of information or may simultaneously lean toward values that cannot be reconciled. Most individuals can cope with a certain amount of inconsistency among their attitudes or attitude components, but only to a certain extent. When an attitude includes elements that are inconsistent with one another, it becomes unstable, and it can be easily changed. Conversely, when the attitude elements are homogeneous and consistent among themselves, the attitude is stable and difficult to change. At the extreme, when individuals are exposed to information that contradicts pre-existent attitudes, they are likely to reject the information, as was the case in the preceding example. But because the different elements that are part of an attitude are consistent among themselves, individuals' attitudes toward various aspects of their environment also tend to be consistent among themselves.

The various components of attitudes can also be characterized by the *valence* (intensity) and by their level of *multiplexity* (the number of elements that they include). Thus, an attitude involving a large number of cognitive, affective, and conative elements can be characterized as a *central* attitude, because it involves important values to the individual. An attitude essentially involving one single affective dimension (product liking, for instance) would be simple, in contrast to an attitude that involves a large number of emotions such as fear, anxiety, and pleasure.

Attitude Models   ## *The Communication Models of Attitude Formation*

Some authors have postulated that potential customers who are exposed to persuasive communications are likely to go through a number of stages. These stages fall into the three attitude components described previously.[23] At least two models have been proposed to describe the stages through which buyers supposedly progress when they receive persuasive communications. These models, which are also called *hierarchy of effects* models, are shown in Figure 9–8.

1. *The AIDA Model.*[24] This model is one of the most popular in the advertising literature. According to this model, an effective advertisement should first attract a consumer's Attention (cognitive stage), arouse Interest and then Desire for the advertised product or brand (affective stage), and, finally, trigger an Action, i.e., a trial or a purchase (conative stage).
2. *The Hierarchy of Effects Model.*[25] Lavidge and Steiner have proposed a six-step hierarchy through which buyers progress when they are exposed to advertising messages. These steps are: product-brand awareness, product knowledge, brand liking, brand preference, brand conviction, and purchase of the product or brand.

These models of the communication effects rely on certain assumptions that are more or less relevant depending on the purchase situation to which they are applied. One of these assumptions is that consumers move sequentially from one stage of the hierarchy to the next, that consumers cannot reach a certain stage without having gone through all the preceding stages of the hierarchy.

A second assumption implied in all the communications effect models is that consumers' progression in the hierarchy is unidirectional (as shown by the direction of the arrows in Figure 9–8). Consequently, the purchase probability of consumers who are at each stage of the hierarchy increases as they get closer to the last stages.

In fact, the cognitive and affective components of attitudes are not necessarily sequential and do not always follow a hierarchy.[26] They are often simultaneous and interrelated. For instance, an advertiser may give some information about a product (cognitive elements) and, at the same time, try to push the

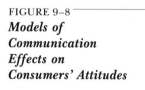

FIGURE 9–8
*Models of
Communication
Effects on
Consumers' Attitudes*

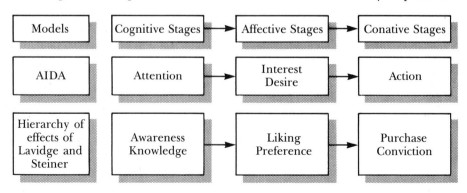

buyer into liking the product (affective elements), and also induce the buyer to try the brand (conative elements). Consequently, an advertising message may have a simultaneous effect on the three attitude components by pushing a buyer into the cognitive, affective, and conative stages.

The progression in the hierarchy is not necessarily unidirectional.[27] For instance, brand preference often follows and seldom precedes the purchase or trial of a product.[28] A consumer may well try a brand he or she was not even aware of, when the brand has been offered as a gift. In the same way consumers may select a brand they have never heard of because in an emergency situation, the brand may have been the only one available at the closest retail outlet.

Attitude Formation and Attitude Change

The Role of Communications in Attitude Formation and Change

A favourable attitude is generally a necessary condition for a consumer to buy a product, at least for repetitive or durable product purchases. Several studies have shown that purchase behaviour can be predicted from the attitude people hold toward the different brands of a product.[29] Therefore, advertisers have a vested interest in building favourable consumer attitudes toward their brands, especially in their target market segments.[30]

Advertisers may pursue several objectives concerning buyers' attitudes. They may try to:

- create favourable buyer attitudes toward a brand, especially for new products introduced in the market,
- change buyers' negative feelings into positive attitudes about the brand,
- reinforce present customers' positive attitudes toward the brand.

To achieve these objectives, advertisers must understand how attitudes develop and know to what extent and how attitudes can be changed.

In order to build favourable attitudes toward a brand, advertisers can follow one of three strategies:

1. They can try to reinforce buyers' positive evaluation of certain brand attributes.
2. They can try to increase the salience of those brand attributes for which customers generally make positive judgements.
3. They can try to decrease the salience of those brand attributes for which buyers generally make negative judgements.

The advertiser of an important fruit juice brand may attempt to show consumers that the brand is high in vitamin content and that consumption of it is very healthy. Thus, the advertiser would try to reinforce the health attribute of the brand (which appeals to the health motivation of consumers). This is an example of the first strategy. Alternatively, the advertiser may try to show that vitamins are not an important factor in fruit juice consumption because vitamins can be found in many other food products. This could be a desirable strategy if consumers perceive the advertised brand as low in vitamins. Then, by trying to decrease the salience of the vitamin content attribute on which the brand is negatively perceived, the advertiser would pursue the third strategy. Or the advertisements could suggest that a good fruit juice should be selected for its taste (an attribute on which a large number of consumers positively rate the brand). In doing so, the advertiser tries to increase the salience of the taste attribute in the fruit juice brand selection process, an example of the second strategy.

Changing unfavourable attitudes into favourable ones is generally a long and difficult communication task. Thus marketers often prefer to launch a new brand to replace a brand for which potential buyers have developed negative feelings. It takes generally less time and fewer resources to build favourable attitudes from neutral attitudes than to change negative attitudes into positive ones.

However, empirical evidence tends to support the proposition that individuals' attitudes are shaped by the information to which they are exposed, group affiliations, and personality. In the same way, changing an attitude implies a change in one or several attitude determinants. Among all these possibilities, an advertiser can only manipulate information through the mass media to influence or change buyers' attitudes. Obviously, consumers' social group affiliations cannot be manipulated, nor can consumers be forced to modify their behaviour. An advertiser can only achieve the goal of changing consumers' attitudes by making advertising as efficient a communication tool as possible.

The direction and attitude change induced by additional information is a function of situational factors and of the source, medium, form, and content of the information.

Situational Factors of the Audience

Substantial evidence suggests that three situational factors favour an attitude change following a communication:

1. When the message is delivered to a homogeneous group of individuals. If the majority agrees with the message content, the communication will have been more effective and have provoked a more important attitude change than if each individual had been individually exposed to the message. If the group majority does *not* agree with the message content, the communication will have been less effective.[31]
2. When the recipient of the communication is publicly involved in the support of the communicator's position. The attitude change in the direction of the communication is likely to be more stable as the individual is supposed to acquire some ammunition against any counterpropaganda to which he might subsequently be exposed.[32]
3. When there is a group discussion. The communication may be more effective than when it is communicated without a discussion.[33]

Advertisers may draw distressing conclusions from these findings. Personal communications allow for a dialogue between communicator and audience, and in communications within a group, group pressure can be exerted on dissident minorities. Such communications are therefore more likely to be effective than impersonal communications delivered to passive groups (such as television advertisements), or to isolated individuals one at a time (such as magazine or newspaper advertisements).

Source-Related Factors

Research findings in psychology suggest that three source-related factors have important implications for the effectiveness of advertising messages: source credibility, attractiveness, and group affiliations.

Effects of Source Credibility. The source of a message is at least as important as the content. Experiments on communication source credibility have shown that a source perceived as credible by a certain audience is likely to generate a more important attitude change than would a source perceived as less credible.[34] In one of these now classic experiments, the same communication was addressed to two groups of individuals.[35] In the first group, the communication was attributed to a highly credible source, and in the second group, to a less credible source. Immediately following the experiment, the subjects who had received the high credibility source message showed significantly larger attitude changes (about 23 percent of net attitude change)[36] than the subjects who had been exposed to the low credibility source (about 6 percent of net attitude change only).

The results are supported on intuitive grounds and probably would not be surprising if the experiment had been stopped at this point. However, after a four-week period, new attitude change measurements were made for the individuals in both groups. It was found that the group that had been exposed to the high credibility source recorded a drop in attitude change from 23 percent to about 12 percent. The second group, which had been exposed to the low credibility source, increased its attitude change to approximately 14 percent. Psychologists have called this phenomenon the *sleeper effect*, meaning that as time elapses, individuals submitted to persuasive communications tended to dissociate the communication content from the source (Figure 9–9).

FIGURE 9–9

Attitude Change Provoked by High and Low Credibility Communicators ("Sleeper Effect")

Source: Hovland and Weiss, "The Influence of Source Credibility on Communication Effectiveness," *Public Opinion Quarterly*, 15 (1951), pp. 635–50.

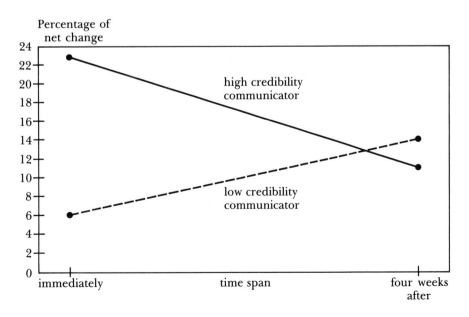

When advertisers want to obtain an immediate effect from an advertising campaign, the use of a credible source is likely to generate more positive results. However, in the medium and long run they suggest that the use and expenses of a credible expert may not be warranted, unless the message and its credible source are constantly associated through frequent repetition of the message.

Effects of Attractiveness of the Message Source. Another determinant of attitude change effectiveness is the perceived source attractiveness for the audience. It was found that a positive attitude change was directly related to the degree of attractiveness of a source for its audience.[37] When a communicator's message is in favour of a subject toward which the audience already has a positive attitude, the attitude toward the communication becomes more positive. Conversely, when an attractive communicator speaks against an object toward which the audience has a positive attitude (or for an object toward which the audience has a negative attitude), the audience's attitude toward the communicator evolves in the negative direction.

Translated into an advertising context, a firm or a communicator may wish to capitalize on a positive image to reduce or change the negative market reactions toward a particular brand.[38] The firm or the communicator may be successful, but they might at least partially lose their positive image in the corresponding target audience.[39]

Effects of the Communicator's Affiliations. Attitude change is related to the way a communicator is perceived by the audience in terms of his or her affiliation to social groups.[40] A study has shown that opinion leaders in a community generally were members of the social groups in which they exercised their leadership.[41] Based on these conclusions, advertisers may, instead of using glamorous movie stars, use people with the same (obvious) social group characteristics as those of the target market. The rationale is that these people are more likely to be identified with an actual opinion leader from the same social group and the same social class than would be a movie star or another prestigious personality.

Media-Related Factors

There exists a considerable amount of market data to which a consumer is exposed and which is channeled through word-of-mouth communications. Because social groups are influenced by their information sources and their past experience with the products and brands, there is only one means by which a firm can gain support of this type of information source. It is for the product's users not to have been deceived. Consumers who have used the product, the brand, or the service must have been satisfied in order to transmit the results of their positive experience and positive product information to other potential buyers.

Then the question of which communication channel is the most effective can be raised. Unfortunately for advertisers, the answer does not make their task easier. As was seen in Chapter 1, interpersonal communications, for example word-of-mouth communications that take place among consumers or with salespeople, are likely to be more effective and persuasive than advertising through the mass media.[42] However, mass media play a more subtle role in transmitting information, if credit is given to the *two-step flow of information theory*.[43] According to this theory, ideas are transmitted through the mass media to the opinion leaders in a social group. Information then flows from these opinion leaders to less active segments of the population. To support their hypothesis, Katz and Lazarfeld were able to show that opinion leaders tend to have a wider exposure to the mass media than the rest of the population.

This theory is extremely appealing to advertisers. If there is a market segment constituted of opinion leaders who are more easily reached through mass media and more prone to be influenced than the rest of the market, an advertiser's task could be substantially simplified. Provided these leaders can be identified and located, advertisers could direct a campaign to this market segment at a relatively low cost. Then this restricted segment of opinion leaders could take charge of transmitting the information to the primary groups in which they exercise their opinion leadership.

Unfortunately, the reality of information diffusion is more complex than this simplified description of the two-step flow of communication theory implies.[44] There are no real opinion leaders who have definite and identifiable characteristics. An individual may be considered by peers as an opinion leader in cars, but not be considered as a leader in food. Another individual may always be asked advice about electronics but will seek the advice of other well-informed people when it comes to subscribing to insurance.

Message/Content-Related Factors

To change an audience's attitudes, a communicator may try to change the cognitive and affective attitude components. Informative messages are designed to change the cognitive elements. Emotional appeal messages try to influence the affective elements.

Informative Advertising Messages.

Two theories attempt to explain how an informative advertising message can influence buyers' attitudes: the *instrumental relation hypothesis* and the *theory of cognitive dissonance*.

Instrumental Relation Hypothesis. This theory relies on the hypothesis that an attitude toward any object or situation is related to the ends to which the object serves, i.e., to its consequences. This is called the *instrumental relation*.[45] According to this assumption, to change an attitude the instrumental value of the attitude must be altered through new beliefs. A study based on this hypothesis has found a curvilinear relationship between an individual's initial attitude and the subsequent attitude change.[46] Individuals holding extreme attitudes changed their attitudes less drastically than individuals holding moderate attitudes.

This theory has implications for determining the best possible message intensity for provoking an attitude change in the direction desired by the communicator. It seems that the answer is highly related to how central the individual's attitude is. If a subject is not very interested in the object of the attitude or the communication content, the message intensities and the corresponding attitude changes are positively related.[47] In contrast, if an individual is highly concerned about the object of the attitude, the relationship may be reversed. That is, the more the position advocated in the communication departs from the subject's position, the less important that attitude change is. Eventually, the message may have an effect opposite to that intended.[48]

What advertising principles can be drawn from these findings? First, it should be determined what a product represents for a consumer and what types of attitudes and attitude strength are involved. If the product does not relate to a consumer's important values or does not involve strong emotive values (salt or bread would be examples), it seems that the best results could be obtained through extreme advertising appeals, or what advertisers generally call *dramatizing* a product. The idea is to induce excitement for the product.

When the product is loaded with symbolic meanings that are highly valued by a consumer (most baby-related products that show some aspect of the highly emotional and valued relationship between a mother and her children would fall into this category), an advertiser should not take positions that depart too sharply from those generally held in the target market. A more effective strategy would be to induce consumers to change their attitudes little by little by making moderate statements rather than dramatic and extreme advertising appeals.

Theory of Cognitive Dissonance. Many persuasive communications rely on mechanisms that can be explained by the theory of cognitive dissonance.[49] This theory is based on two propositions: First, when an individual is exposed to information that contradicts some already assimilated information that constitutes his beliefs, the individual experiences a state of psychological tension or *cognitive dissonance*. Second, an individual who experiences cognitive dissonance tries to reduce the psychological tension. To do so, an individual can change attitudes and make beliefs consonant with the new information just received, the new information can be rejected as being false, or the credibility of the communicator can be challenged. The subject may also seek new information that could reinforce an attitude change or, on the contrary, invalidate the dissonant information.

All advertising messages that rely heavily on superlatives are probably based on this theory. The rationale is to communicate to consumers the idea that they have not been using the best available product on the market. In this case, this information is inconsistent with the attitudes and behaviour of those consumers who do not use the advertised brand. The advertiser hopes that the resulting state of cognitive dissonance that some consumers will experience will result in an attitude change and possibly in the trial of the advertised product. Of course, consumers may also react by rejecting the communication or refusing to believe it.

Emotional Advertising Appeals. An advertiser can try to alter some affective elements of buyers' attitudes by following two essentially different approaches. Fear or negative appeals can be used or pleasant or positive appeals based on consumers' satisfaction can be used. Each approach is effective under different conditions.

Fear Appeal Advertising. The use of fear appeals to change attitudes also relies on the theory of cognitive dissonance. The rationale is to show consumers the negative consequences that may result from not using a product or from using a brand different from the advertised one.

Insurance companies often use fear appeals in their advertisements to show potential customers the tragic consequences that may occur when they are not properly insured. For example, an advertisement may show children left without a means of support because the parents neglected to take out life insurance. The advertiser tries to plunge the consumer into a state of cognitive dissonance by creating a gap between present behaviour (no insurance) and what the consumer probably aspires to be (a good parent). The objective is to induce the non-insured customer to change behaviour and buy life insurance. However, the consumer may reduce dissonance by rejecting the information.

Are messages that use a fear appeal more effective? A study showed that the effects produced by a message based on fear and anxiety were inversely related to the intensity of the fear aroused in the subjects.[50] The relative inefficiency of the fear appeal messages could be explained by the fact that the subjects tend to reduce their anxiety by developing hostile attitudes toward the communication. If this explanation holds, it suggests that a fear-arousing advertising campaign could produce adverse effects for advertisers, especially if the anxiety aroused among consumers passed a certain threshold. Other studies have shown, however, that the messages that aroused the highest level of anxiety were the most effective, provided the communicator could suggest a convincing and plausible solution to reduce their anxiety.[51]

Pleasant Appeal Advertising. The basic principle of pleasant appeal advertising is to try to associate a product/brand with pleasant events, objects, or feelings in the hope that buyers will continue to make the association in the future. Messages relying on humour often try to build on such associations. Unfortunately, there is a lack of research on whether messages relying on such positive appeals are more effective.

Buyers' Attitudes Toward the Advertisements. Research in advertising has shown that the buyers' attitudes toward an advertisement, and especially consumers' affective reactions to the commercial itself, has a mediating influence on brand attitude and purchase intention.[52] A study also found that consumers' attitudes toward the advertisement directly influenced not only brand attitudes, but also increased brand cognitions. The rationale is that the more favourable buyers feel toward an ad, the more receptive they are to the advertising claim.[53] Thus, developing advertisements that are liked and positively evaluated by consumers should be an indirect route toward developing favourable attitudes toward the advertised brand.

Message/Structure-Related Factors

Three message/structure-related factors likely to affect attitudes and attitude changes have been identified: conclusion drawing, the use of one-sided or two-sided arguments, and the order in which the arguments are presented to the audience.

The Level of Inference Built into the Message. Inference level is the extent to which the audience of a communication is free to draw its own conclusions from a message. For instance, an advertiser can give certain facts about a brand in an advertising message and let the buyer conclude that the product must be the best on the market. Or the message might state the conclusion that the advertiser wants potential buyers to draw.

When the conclusion of the message is explicitly drawn, the message tends to be twice as effective as when people are left to draw their own conclusions.[54] This is because when an individual is free to draw conclusions from a message, nothing can prevent the individual from drawing conclusions that are completely different from those intended by the communicator. Individuals have different perceptual mechanisms, different needs and motivations, and are likely to react differently to messages.

Despite these general results, other studies have pointed at three situations in which an implicit message would be more effective than a message with explicitly drawn conclusions. First, when the message is simple and the audience is intelligent, the audience may be irritated by what could be perceived as offensively repetitive statements by the communicator. Second, when the source of the message is not very credible, it is more effective to let the audience draw its own conclusions. Third, when the message deals with personal values or intimate feelings, a communicator who explicitly draws conclusions might be perceived as intruding on an audience's privacy.[55]

One-sided or Two-sided Presentations. Is an attitude change more important or less important when the audience is exposed only to arguments in support of the communicator's position or when a number of counterarguments are also acknowledged and refuted? In advertising, the large majority of advertisements are one-sided. There are some noteworthy exceptions: advertisements by Volkswagen (The Bug), or by Avis ("We are no. 2"), or by UNIVAC (the "other" computer company). A one-sided presentation is generally more effective.[56] Exceptions occur when the communicator and the audience hold opposite stands at the beginning. Hence the use of counterarguments probably gives the appearance of objectivity and greater credibility to the communicator[57] when the audience is well-educated and when the subjects are likely to be subsequently exposed to counter propaganda. Counterarguments may have an immunizing effect, because the communicator has already presented counterarguments with the appropriate rebuttals. Since people are continuously subjected to conflicting advertising messages, it is surprising that advertisers have not made more extensive use of two-sided advertising presentations.

Order of Presentation. Another problem for advertisers is to decide in which order different arguments should be presented to an audience. Should the strongest and most convincing arguments be presented first, in order to arouse the audience's interest and make the best impact while the audience is still attentive, or should they be presented last, to leave the audience with the stronger arguments?

Experiments dealing with two-sided presentations have not led to clear-cut conclusions. The message is equally effective whether positive arguments are presented first or whether they are presented last.[58] When only positive arguments are used, most studies have indicated that the order of the arguments was not a determinant of the message's effectiveness.[59]

What are the conclusions that advertisers can draw from these studies? Given that advertising is not the kind of communication that can benefit from sustained attention and interest from its audience, it may be more appropriate to use the best and more convincing argument first. If they succeed, then the attention and interest of at least a part of the audience may be secured for a short period of time. If the weaker arguments are presented first, a large part of the audience may lose interest and will not pay attention to the more convincing selling points.

Forgetting and Repetition

All information tends to be forgotten as time elapses.[60] This forgetting takes place more rapidly or less rapidly depending on how important and valued the concerned attitude is within the individual's attitude system. In general, it occurs more rapidly if the information is inconsistent with the individual's attitude pattern. This phenomenon has been called *selective retention* by psychologists. Conversely, information is best remembered when it is well integrated and fits well into an individual's present attitude system.

The natural process of forgetting learned information can be overcome by message repetition. The quantity of recalled information varies in relation to the frequency with which a message is repeated[61] and in inverse relation to the time span between consecutive messages.[62]

There seems to be a positive relationship between repetition and attitude change,[63] with the following exceptions:

1. when a message has been repeated a great number of times;[64]
2. when messages are repeated at too-short intervals;[65]
3. when message density (the frequency of all the messages, including competing advertisements) is too high.[66]

These results suggest that to be effective, advertising messages should be repeated, but that there is an upper limit to frequency and repetition. Advertisers have long recognized that one single message is of no use whatsoever for obtaining noticeable effects.

SUMMARY

A simplified description of the effects of advertising on buyer behaviour gives some insight into how advertising works and can influence buyer behaviour. A purchase is a decision made by consumers on their evoked set of brands. In order to purchase a specific brand, a consumer should have a need or a desire to buy the product, perceive the brand as the most likely to fulfill a need or desire, and have the ability and the financial and physical resources to purchase the product.

There are three important dimensions of the purchase process: the effect of advertising on buyer needs and motives, on buyer perceptions, and on buyer attitudes. A motivation is a force underlying a need or desire. Advertising cannot create consumer needs but can only stimulate needs that already exist, even if at the unconscious level.

Buyer perceptions may be described as a series of filters through which information and stimuli from the environment must pass to be integrated into the cognitive structure of the consumer's field of experience. These concepts from social sciences can be applied to consumers to analyze their perceptions of brands (the set of objective and psychological attributes given to a brand by buyers), of price, of purchase risks, and the various elements of the communication process (especially the credibility of a source).

An understanding of the role attitudes play in purchase behaviour enables advertisers to influence or change such attitudes. Attitudes are the tendency for an individual to act positively or negatively toward certain objects, individuals, or events. Attitudes include cognitive, affective, and conative elements.

Advertisers also need an understanding of the attitude formation and change processes. Attitudes can be viewed as a reservoir, the level of which represents the intensity of the attitude, and the nature of its content the positiveness or negativeness of the attitude. The reservoir is fed as new information is received from various sources, among them word-of-mouth, product, past experience, retailers, and advertising. Information is continuously pumped out of the reservoir through forgetting as time elapses.

Advertising communications can change consumer attitudes by applying such theories as the two-step flow of communication, the theory of attitude instrumentality, or the cognitive dissonance theory. Also, the principles relating to the design of more effective messages for changing people's attitudes may help guide the design of the advertising message content and format. The role of message repetition and frequency is of primary importance for advertisers.

QUESTIONS FOR STUDY

1. Think of a major purchase you have made recently. Try to describe the role of advertising in this purchase decision. What was the role of all the other information sources that were involved? Which source had the most influence in your final decision? Be as specific as you can.

2. Find a print advertisement or a broadcast commercial that appeals to the following motivations: a) sex; b) fear; c) anxiety; d) security; and e) social esteem. In each case, show how the appeal is being used and comment on the rationale of using such an appeal.

3. Can advertising create needs? Discuss. Give specific examples.

4. Discuss the concept of a brand image. Select a few advertisements or commercials for a) alcoholic beverages and b) perfumes. For each, try to infer the kind of image you think the advertiser would like the brand to have among consumers. Explain why you think so.

5. Find examples of print advertisements or broadcast commercials that use testimonial advertising and that are based:
   a. on the competence of the source
   b. on the affective "trustworthiness" of the source
   Discuss the rationale for using these types of testimonials in each example.

6. Find specific examples of print advertisements or broadcast commercials that use:
   a. reference groups
   b. opinion leaders
   c. word-of-mouth communication.

7. Find examples of print advertisements or broadcast commercials that try to:
   a. reinforce consumers' positive evaluation of certain product/brand attributes
   b. increase the salience of attributes on which customers make positive judgments
   c. decrease the salience of attributes on which customers make negative judgments
   Justify in each case.

8. Find print advertisements or broadcast commercials in which the message source is a typical member of the social groups of the (probably intended) target audience. Evaluate this approach in this specific context. Justify your answers.

9. Find examples of print advertisements using two-sided arguments. Study the order of the arguments. How would the principles outlined in the text have been applied? Discuss.

10. Find examples of print advertisements or broadcast commercials that:
   a. apply the theory of cognitive dissonance (superlative advertising)
   b. use fear appeals
   Discuss the approach in the specific contexts of the advertisements.

PROBLEMS

1. Your are the manager in charge of advertising for an important department store chain, Canadian Stores, operating in all Canadian cities. In the past, the stores have always tried to develop an image of offering a wide variety of merchandise. However, because of competing stores making similar claims, you are not sure that consumers in the Calgary market still perceive Canadian Stores as the department store where they can get almost every item they possibly would need. As a result, you have decided to analyze the Canadian Stores image in Calgary.
   a. Outline the type of information you would like to obtain from the marketing research department in order to have sufficient information about the store image strategy that you will follow for your next campaign.

b. Show how the results of this study are likely to affect the advertising strategy for the next campaigns.

2. As the advertiser for a medium-sized sports equipment firm, you are considering the following three alternatives for your next advertising campaign:

- use of talents of a national hockey star as an "expert" source;
- use a well-known television star as an "affective" trustworthy source;
- use an "ordinary" actor to play a sportsman in the commercials.

a. How could the concept of the perceptual map be effectively used to select among these three alternatives?

b. How would you conduct a cost-benefit analysis to select the most profitable alternative?

c. On intuitive grounds, which alternative do you think is likely to be the most profitable for the company? Why?

NOTES

1. For more detailed models of consumer behaviour, see G. Kindra, T. Muller and M. Laroche, *Consumer Behavior in Canada*. Toronto: Nelson, 1989; John Howard *Consumer Behavior in Marketing* (Englewood Cliff, N.J.: Prentice-hall, 1989); James F. Engel and Roger D. Blackwell, *Consumer Behaviour* (New York: Holt, Rinehart and Winston, 1990).

2. Thomas S. Robertson, *Consumer Behaviour* (Glenview, Ill.: Scott, Foresman, 1980), p. 2.

3. David Krech, Richard S. Crutchfield, and Eagerton A. Ballachey, *Individual in Society* (New York: McGraw-Hill, 1962), pp. 69–85.

4. Abraham H. Maslow, "A Theory of Human Motivation," *Psychological Review*, 50 (1943), 370–96.

5. Kurt Lewin, *A Dynamic Theory of Personality* (New York: McGraw-Hill, 1935); Joseph Clawson and W. Alderson, ed., *Theory in Marketing* (Homewood, Ill.: Irwin, 1950).

6. K.W. Kendall and D.J. Brown, "Effects of Threatening Advertising and Prior Information on Product Lastings," *Marketing*, ed. Robert G. Wyckham (Administrative Sciences Association of Canada, 1981), pp. 152–57.

7. G. A. Mauser, D. McKinnon, and M. Nash, "The Effects of Taste and Brand Name on Perceptions and Preferences," *ASAC Proceedings* (1977), pp. 4–24.

8. André Gabor and C.W.J. Granger, "Price as an Indicator of Quality: Report on an Equity," *Economica*, 33 (February 1966), 43–47.

9. Henry Joannis, *De l'Étude de Motivation à la Création Publicitaire et à la Promotion des Ventes* (Paris: Dunod, 1966), p. 20.

10. To keep this exposition as simple as possible only two attributes are considered. However, the same principle applies to any number of attributes and to any number of brands.

11. Mathematically, the distance between two points can be represented by the Euclidian distance.

12. René Y. Darmon, "Multiple Joint Space Analysis for Improved Advertising Strategy," *The Canadian Marketer*, 10, no. 1 (1979), 10–44.

13. J.G. Barnes and G.H. Pynn, "A Hierarchical Model of Source Effect in Retail Newspaper Advertising: Research Implications," *ASAC Proceedings* (1975), pp. 5–29.

14. Herbert C. Kelman and Carl I. Hovland, "Reinstatement of the Communicator in Delayed Measurement of Opinion Change," *Journal of Abnormal and Social Psychology*, 17 (1953), 327–35.

15. G.R. Rarick, "Effects of Two Components of Communication Prestige," (paper presented at the Pacific chapter, American Association of Public Opinion Research, Asimolar, California, 1963).

16. Ralph L. Rosnow and Edward J. Robinson, *Experiment in Persuasion* (New York: Academic Press, 1967), pp. 2–3.

17. Bobby J. Calder and Robert D. Burnkrant, "Interpersonal Influence on Consumer Behaviour: An Attribution Theory Approach," *Journal of Consumer*

Research, 4 (June 1977), 29–38; Linda L. Golden, "Attribution Theory Implications for Advertisement Claim Credibility," *Journal of Marketing Research*, 14 (February 1977), 115–17; Robert A. Hansen and Carol A. Scott, "Comments on Attributes Theory and Advertiser Credibility," *Journal of Marketing Research*, 13 (May 1976), 193–97.

18. This may also be the case when a message is approved by a recognized association of experts in the field.

19. H.G. Gordon McDougall, "Cognitive Responses to Advertising Messages: A Diagnostic," *Marketing*, ed. Robert G. Wyckham (Administrative Sciences Association of Canada 1981), pp. 205–15.

20. "Frequency in Broadcast Advertising: 1," *Media/Scope* (February 1962).

21. See, for instance, "Frequency in Print Advertising 1," *Media/Scope* (April 1962); *Recognition Increased with Advertising . . . Dropped when Advertising Stopped* (New York: McGraw-Hill Advertising Laboratory, May 1961); E. Pomerance and H.A. Zeilske, "How Frequently should you Advertise," *Media/Scope* (September 1958), pp. 25–27.

22. George David Hughes, *Attitude Measurement for Marketing Strategies* (Glenview, Ill.: Scott, Foresman, 1971), p. 9.

23. Gary Lilien and Philip Kotler, *Marketing Decision Making: A Model Building Approach* (New York: Harper and Row, 1983).

24. E.K. Strong, *The Psychology of Selling*, 1st ed. (New York: McGraw-Hill, 1925), p. 9.

25. Robert J. Lavidge and Gary A. Steiner, "A Model of Predictive Measurement of Advertising Effectiveness," *Journal of Marketing* (October 1961), p. 61.

26. John R.G. Jenkins, "The Hierarchy of Effects Theory of Consumer Decision Making: A Re-evaluation," *ASAC Proceedings*, ed. J.M. Boisvert and R. Savitt (1978), pp. 139–48.

27. Kirstian S. Palda, "The Hypothesis of a Hierarchy of Effects: A Partial Evaluation," *Journal of Marketing Research* (February 1966), pp. 13–24.

28. Charles K. Raymond, "Must Advertising Communicate to Sell," *Harvard Business Review* (September-October 1965), pp. 148–61.

29. Alwin A. Adenbaum, "Knowledge is a Thing Called Measurement," *Attitude Research at Sea*, ed. Lee Adler and Irwin Crespi (Chicago: American Marketing Association, 1966), pp. 111–26; Henri Assael and Georges S. Day, "Attitudes and Awareness as Predictors of Market Share," *Journal of Advertising Research*, 8 (December 1968), 3–10.

30. S.A. Brown, "An Experimental Investigation of Attitude as a Determinant of Consumer Spatial Behaviour," *ASAC Proceedings* (1975), pp. 5–75.

31. Kurt Lewin, "Group Decision and Social Change," *Readings in Social Psychology*, ed., G.E. Swanson, T.M. Newcomb, and L.E. Hartley, 2nd ed. (New York: Holt, 1952).

32. C.I. Hovland, Evid M. Campbell and T. Brock, "The Effects of Commitment on Opinion Change Following Communication," *The Order to Presentation in Persuasion*, ed. C.I. Hovland et al. (New Haven: Yale University Press, 1957).

33. May Brodbeck, "The Role of Small Groups in Advertising the Effects of Propaganda," *Journal of Abnormal Psychology and Sociology* 52 (1956), 166–70.

34. C.I. Hovland and W. Weiss, "The Influence of Source Credibility on Communication Effectiveness," *Public Opinion Quarterly*, 15 (1951), 635–50.

35. Herbert C. Kelman and Carl I. Hovland, "Reinstatement of the communicator in Delayed Measurement of Opinion Change," *Journal of Abnormal Sociology and Psychology*, 48 (1953), 327–35.

36. Net attitude change means the absolute difference between positive changes and negative changes.

37. P.H. Tannenbaum, "Initial Attitude Toward Source and Concept as Factors in Attitude Change Through Communication," *Public Opinion Quarterly*, 20 (1956), 413–25.

38. Benny Rigaux-Bricmont, "Structure des attitudes du consommateur à l'égard des sources d'information qui l'entourent," *Marketing*, ed. Michel Laroche, Vol. 3 (Administrative Sciences Association of Canada, 1982), pp. 263–75.

39. Benny Rigaux-Bricmont, "Structure des attitudes du communicateur à l'égard des sources d'informations qui l'entourent," *Marketing*, ed. Michel Laroche, (Montreal: Administrative Science Association of Canada, 1982), pp. 263–75.

40. Emmanuel Chéron and Michel Zins, "La théorie de l'attribution: Développements et applications pour le marketing," *Marketing*, ed. Vernon Jones, Vol. 1 (Administrative Sciences Association of Canada), pp. 97–106.

41. Elihu Katz and P.E. Lazarfeld, *Personal Influence: The Part Played by People by People in the Flow of Mass Communication*, (Glencoe, Ill.: Free Press, 1955).

42. P.E. Lazarfeld, B. Berelson, and H. Gaudet, *The People's Choice* (New York: Duell, Sloan and Pearce, 1944).

43. Katz and Lazarfeld.

44. Elihu Katz, "The Two-Step Flow of Communication: An Up-to-Date Report on an Hypothesis," *Public Opinion Quarterly* 21, (Spring 1957), 61–78.

45. Helen Peak, "Attitude and Motivation," *Nebraska Symposium on Motivation* 1955, ed. M.R. Jones (Lincoln: University of Nebraska Press, 1955).

46. E.R. Carlson, "Attitude Change Through Modification of Attitude Structure," *Journal of Abnormal and Social Psychology*, 52 (1956), 256–61.

47. C.I. Hovland and H.A. Pritzker, "Extent of Opinion Change as a Function of the Amount of Change Advocated," *Journal of Abnormal and Social Psychology*, 54 (1957), 257–61; W. Weiss, "The Relationship Between Judgments of a Communicator's Position and Extent of Opinion Change," *Journal of Abnormal and Social Psychology*, 56 (1958), 380–84.

48. Hovland and Pritzker, p. 258.

49. Leon Festinger, *A Theory of Cognitive Dissonance*, (New York: Harper and Row, 1967).

50. I.L. Janis and S. Fishback, "Effects of Fear-Arousing Communication," *Journal of Abnormal and Social Psychology*, 48 (1953), 78–92.

51. Carl I. Hovland, Irvin L. Janis and Harold H. Kelly, *Communication and Persuasion* (New Haven: Yale University Press, 1953), pp. 87–88.

52. Andrew A. Mitchell and Jerry C. Olson, "Are Product Attribute Beliefs the Only Mediator of Advertising Effects on Brand Attitude?", *Journal of Marketing Research*, 18 (August 1981), pp. 318–32. Terence A. Shimp, "Attitude Toward the Ad as a Mediator of Consumer Brand Choice," *Journal of Advertising*, 10 (1981), pp. 9–15.

53. Scott B. MacKenzie, Richard J. Lutz, and George E. Belch, "The Role of Attitude Toward the Ad as a Mediator of Advertising effectiveness: A Test of Competing Explanations," *Journal of Marketing Research*, 23 (May 1986), pp. 130–42.

54. Carl I. Hovland and Wallace Mandell, "An Experimental Comparison of Conclusion-Drawing by the Communication and by the Audience," *Journal of Abnormal and Social Psychology*, (July 1952), pp. 581–88.

55. Philip Kotler, *Marketing Management: Analysis, Planning and Control*, 6th ed. (Englewood Cliffs, N.J.: Prentice-Hall 1988).

56. See C.I. Hovland, A.A. Lumsdaine, and E.D. Sheffield, "Experiments in Mass Communication," *Studies in Social Psychology in World War II*, vol. 3 (Princeton, N.J.: Princeton University Press, 1948), chapter 8; A.A. Lumsdaine and I.L. Janis, "Resistance to Counter-Propaganda Produced by One-Sided and Two-Sided Propaganda Presentations," *Public Opinion Quarterly*, 17 (1953), 311–18.

57. E. Walster, E. Aronson, and D. Abrahams, "On Increasing the Persuasiveness of a Low Prestige Communicator," *Journal of Experimental Social Psychology*, 2 (1966), 325–42.

58. Brian Sternthal, "Persuasion and the Mass Communication Press," (Ph.D. diss., Ohio State University, 1972), chapter 8.

59. H. Gilkinson, S. Paulson, and D. Sinkink, "Effects of Order and Authority in an Argumentative Speech," *Quarterly Journal of Speech*, 40 (1954), 183–92; H. Galley and D. Berlo, "Effects of Intercellular and Intracellular Speech Structure on Attitude Change and Learning," *Speech Monographs*, 23 (1956), 288–97.

60. Ebbinghaus found in 1885 that one-third of the nonsense syllables he memorized were forgotten after twenty minutes and that nearly three-quarters were forgotten after six days. Quoted in James F. Engell, David T. Kollat, and Roger D. Blackwell, *Consumer Behaviour*, 2nd ed. (New York: Holt, Rinehart and Winston, 1973), p. 340.

61. See H. Cromwell and R. Kunkel, "An Experimental Study of the Effect on Attitude of Listeners of Repeating the Same Oral Propaganda," *Journal of Social Psychology*, 35 (May 1952), 175–84.

62. E.K. Strong, "The Factors Affecting a Permanent Impression Developed Through Repetition," *Journal of Experimental Psychology*, 1 (1916), pp. 319–38.

63. "Frequency in Print Advertising: 1," *Media/Scope* (April 1962); "Frequency in Broadcast Advertising: 2," *Media/Scope* (March 1962).

64. "Frequency in Broadcast Advertising: 2," op.cit.

65. Michael Ray and Allan Sawyer, "Repetition in Media Models: A Laboratory Technique," *Journal of Marketing Research*, 8 (1971), 20–29.

66. T. Cook and C. Insko, "Persistence of Attitude Change as a Function of Conclusion Re-exposure: A Laboratory Experiment," *Journal of Personality and Social Psychology*, 9 (1968), 243–64.

CHAPTER

10 *Advertising and the Purchase Decision Process*

Needs and motivations are the starting points of purchase decisions. For a purchase to take place, buyers must experience sufficiently positive attitudes toward the product and the brand and consciously felt needs. When all the elements of the marketing program are properly designed, a buyer will include the advertised brand in his or her evoked set of brands, which is all the brands that are considered for purchase. These elements of the marketing program include designing the product to have the attributes buyers seek, ensuring that the product is available at conveniently located retail stores, and setting a price that buyers perceive as reasonable. This chapter describes the process buyers follow to select a brand from within their evoked set. Emphasis is put on elements of the process that advertisers can influence through a well-designed communication program.

THE PURCHASE DECISION PROCESS

Most purchases imply the decision to buy a product or service. This purchase decision process includes:

1. A goal to be reached (i.e., lessening the tension created by an unsatisfied need or desire).
2. A number of alternatives (i.e., competing products and brands). Products and brands are perceived, evaluated, and compared on the basis of their distinctive attributes and on their ability to satisfy a set of needs. These alternatives also include the non-purchase decision.
3. Some evaluation criteria for choosing the "best" alternative.
4. A state of doubt, arising from the impossibility of possessing all relevant information on the different products and brands. Buyers are always uncertain about how well a given product or brand will satisfy their needs or desires.

Because they must act on the basis of incomplete information, buyers automatically and consciously incur a risk in every purchase and non-purchase decision. The size of the risk buyers perceive depends on the importance of the particular purchase and on the quantity of relevant information about the product category and the competing brands. Potential buyers may act in two ways, depending upon the pressure exerted in the particular purchase situation. They may make an immediate decision based on their present

FIGURE 10–1
*The Purchase
Decision Process*

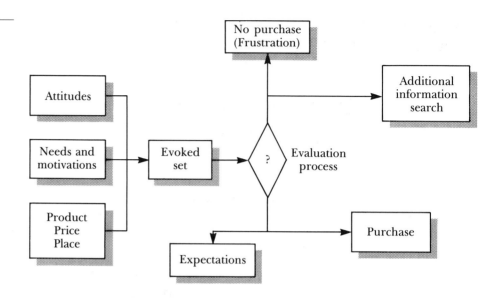

information and buy the product they perceive as capable of procuring the most satisfaction. Or they may delay the purchase to seek additional information by comparison shopping, listening to commercials, making additional calls to sellers or retailers. Or they may inquire about the product among acquaintances, who may be the opinion leaders described previously in the theory of the two-step flow of communications.

When they buy a specific brand, buyers have expectations. This notion of expectation is intimately related to any purchase decision. A consumer who buys a product has developed definite expectations about the consumption of this product. Consumers buy a certain brand because it is preferable to competing brands; they have implicitly or explicitly anticipated that the selected brand will yield more satisfaction than the other brands and that it will respond more appropriately to the relevant set of felt needs. Hence, the amount of satisfaction consumers anticipate they will receive from a certain brand constitutes the *expectations* raised by the selected brand. An overview of consumers' purchase decision process is shown in Figure 10–1.

The Purchase Decision: An Optimization Process

A purchase decision can be considered as an optimization process through which buyers seek the product or the brand that will yield the greatest satisfaction. In order to find which brand will produce the highest utility, buyers compare these brands along attributes they consider as important. The choice process can be considered as the search for the most satisfying trade-off among brands that possess desirable attributes at different levels.

Assume that a buyer judges—wrongly or rightly—that all the brands of one product on the market have exactly the same level of a given attribute. This attribute does not enable the consumer to differentiate among different brands, since it is present in all of them. This attribute is called an *inherent* attribute. Obviously, in this case, to choose a brand, one would have to compare the different brands along other important attributes. For example, a buyer may perhaps think that all the umbrellas on the market are waterproof, whether or not this opinion is technically well-founded. The consumer who perceives this as a fact cannot use the water-resistance attribute to compare umbrellas, since all the brands are perceived as being equal on this attribute.

A corollary of this observation is that brand comparison is possible only when a consumer considers those attributes on which some differences among brands can be perceived. These attributes are *distinctive* brand attributes. Consumers can compare different brands of umbrellas by their colour, style, or durability if they think these characteristics vary from one brand to another.[1]

The Purchase Decision: A Decision Under Uncertainty

A buyer who experiences the psychological tension caused by an unsatisfied need or desire faces a series of decision problems: What product should I buy? Which brand should I choose? These decisions may be described within decision making under uncertainty framework.[2]

As was shown before, consumers run a certain risk in making a decision based on present information because this imperfect information does not enable them to predict exactly which product will procure the maximum satisfaction sought nor which brand really has the qualities desired (or that should be desired).

A certain number of costs are related to the risks taken by buyers. These costs, are, for example, financial losses (if the product does not adequately satisfy all or part of a consumer's needs as it was hoped it would). The costs may also be physical (if, for instance, the realization of the risk endangers the consumer's life) or psycho-sociological (if a wrong purchase jeopardizes a consumer's reputation in one of his social groups, for example). As is shown by curve 1 in Figure 10–2 (next page), these costs are essentially associated with a fast decision (hence with a limited amount of information). They decrease with time, because time has been used by the buyer to gather additional information, thus reducing the risk involved in the purchase.

However, when the buyer waits until more information is gathered before making a decision, costs associated with a delayed decision are incurred.[3] This time, two types of cost are involved. First, there are *psychological opportunity* costs experienced by consumers who are deprived of the product they need and are consequently in a state of psychological tension. As time elapses, this psychological tension becomes more acute and eventually develops into a state of frustration. Second, buyers experience costs associated with the information-gathering effort. They must invest time and energy to visit several retailers, seek out and read advertisements, or inquire for other opinions about the best product to buy. These *delayed decision* costs are represented by curve 2 in Figure 10–2. These costs considerably increase as time elapses. Curve 3 in Figure 10–2 represents the total costs associated with a fast decision and those associated with a delayed decision, at each stage of the decision process. This curve first decreases, reaches a minimum t*C*, then starts to increase. Since buyers want to reduce the total costs associated with the decision as much as possible,

FIGURE 10–2

The Economics of Buyer Purchase Decisions

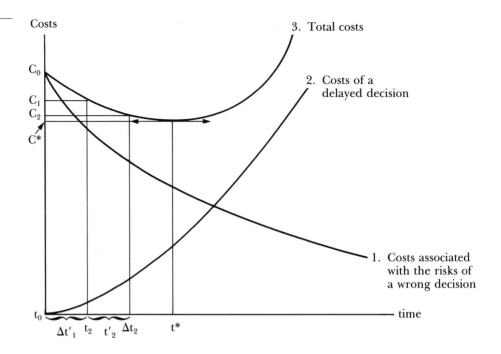

they will seek the t*C* point that represents the best compromise between the costs associated with risky decisions and those associated with information-gathering activities.

Let us assume that a buyer located on the T_0 point experiences some need. Taking an immediate decision means running a risk cost equal to C_0. But this buyer may wait and call on several retailers to compare the product and brands which are offered on the market. This will require a certain amount of time equivalent to Δt_1. While reducing the risk, this visit to different retailers has caused the buyer the inconvenience of waiting and going to several retailers. The risk that has been avoided is so important as to yield a total cost of C_1.

At the end of this round of retailers, however, the buyer is faced with the same problem. Must he make an immediate decision on the basis of present information (with an expected cost of C_1) or must he seek additional information, perhaps this time by consulting different consumer reports? This new search for information, which will require an amount of time equal to Δt_2, will deprive him of the product during this time, will incur the cost of purchasing various consumer reports, but will again enable him to reduce the purchase risk. The buyer will then reach a total cost of C_2, which is smaller than C_1. Consequently, this new step will have been well advised. The process will continue in this manner until the costs involved in a new information search are superior to those of an immediate decision (past the t*C* point). As is shown in Figure 10–2, the buyer must seek information until it is felt (at least intuitively) that a search for additional information will bring about more costs than benefits.

Advertising Implications of the Purchase Decision Process

This view of the role of additional information in consumer purchase decisions has implications for advertisers. An advertisement reaching a potential buyer while the buyer is seeking information will have a greater impact, since the buyer is spared the time and effort needed to seek out this information himself and is less likely to turn to competing brand advertisements to obtain the additional information. In other words, buyers are generally more responsive to different brand advertisements while they are seeking information on these brands. This is why they become a choice target for the advertiser, provided the advertiser can identify and locate them. The strategy that consists of asking consumers to return a coupon at the bottom of a print advertisement is often devised along these principles. Thus, a consumer who is interested and is in an information-gathering stage is asked to return a coupon in order to obtain more information on the product or the brand. Then the advertiser takes advantage of the consumer's having identified him or herself to send a series of informative (and persuasive) messages or to send a salesperson who will try to conclude a sale. This strategy is currently used by life-insurance companies.

A second series of implications that this analysis of the buyer decision process has for advertising is that an advertiser must reduce the buyer's uncertainty about the *distinctive* attributes of the brand. Because a buyer takes only these attributes into consideration when comparing and evaluating brands, an advertiser normally tries to give positive information about the brand's performance on the distinctive attributes. An advertisement about the inherent attributes of a brand is bound to be ineffective. At best, it will be primary advertising for the whole product class, which will also promote the competing brands. This is why an advertiser must know which attributes in the relevant product category are perceived as inherent by the buyer, and what are the distinctive attributes on which the advertising effort should be concentrated.

POST-PURCHASE REACTIONS

Once a purchase is completed, a buyer has acquired a product or a service contract. Beyond the mere possession of the product, the buyer also has undergone some psychological change. The buyer has acquired expectations that go beyond the material possession of this product or this service contract; the buyer expects the products or services to provide the satisfaction he or she was seeking and that motivated the purchase. For goods with a short consumption cycle, consumers can judge if the product meets their expectations by using it immediately. But with durable products with long consumption cycles, consumers cannot tell immediately whether the product will meet their expectations.

A consumer buying a new brand of cereal will know if his or her family likes it and if it is as good as expected by serving it for breakfast the next day. But a consumer who had just bought a new car may use it several weeks, even several months, and still wonder "Is the motor strong enough to last 80 000 km? Will it really resist rust for several years, as promised by the dealer?" and not really be able to answer these questions.

FIGURE 10–3

A Buyer's Post-Purchase Feelings

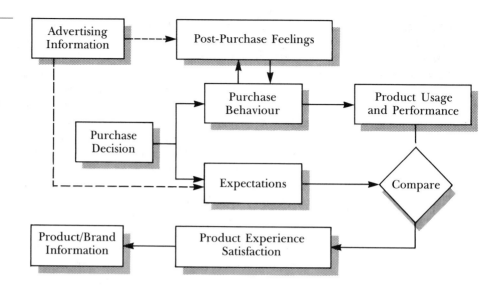

Therefore, a distinction must be drawn between the post-purchase feelings (Figure 10–3), which are essentially experienced during the period of relative uncertainty about the actual instrumental value of the purchased product, and which concern the occasional important and costly purchase; and between the post-usage feelings, when the consumer has evaluated the degree to which a product has met expectations.

Post-Purchase Feelings

Studies have determined that an individual who has just made an important decision experiences post-decisional feelings.[4] In the consumer's case, these are post-purchase feelings. These post-purchase feelings can be explained by the theory of cognitive dissonance (Chapter 9).[5]

With a purchase decision, there are two possible causes of cognitive dissonance for a buyer. One is the risk inherent in all purchase decisions of not having made the best possible decision, since buyers can have only imperfect information on products and brands, as was seen previously. At this stage, the buyer's concern could be expressed as: "Have I bought the product that I should have to satisfy my needs?"

Second, buyers can experience cognitive dissonance because no product on the market exactly fits their ideal brand. Because of this inability to find an ideal product, buyers must compromise and select among the brands closest to the ideal. In making this compromise, they must give up certain desirable brand characteristics for other desirable features the other brands may not have. For example, the consumer in this type of situation may wonder: "Have I done well in choosing a four-door six-cylinder Pontiac Model A? Or should I have bought the Chevrolet Model X that has an eight-cylinder motor, which I could have had with a Pontiac, but only with a coupé?"

As was discussed previously, a subject in a state of cognitive dissonance tries to reduce the dissonance. An individual can become consonant by changing

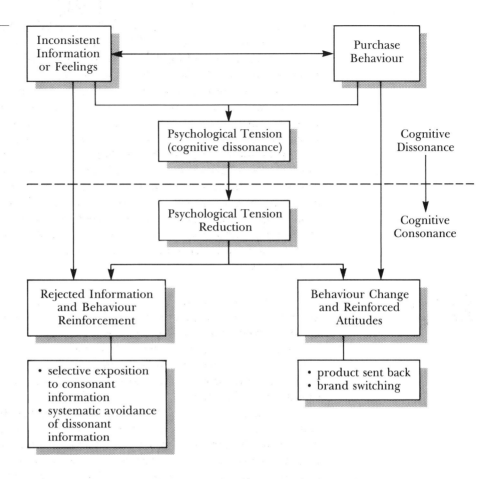

FIGURE 10–4
**The Cognitive
Dissonance Theory**

Inconsistent
Information
or Feelings

Purchase
Behaviour

Psychological Tension
(cognitive dissonance)

Cognitive
Dissonance

Psychological Tension
Reduction

Cognitive
Consonance

Rejected Information
and Behaviour
Reinforcement

Behaviour Change
and Reinforced
Attitudes

- selective exposition
  to consonant
  information
- systematic avoidance
  of dissonant
  information

- product sent back
- brand switching

the behaviour to make it consistent with intimate convictions or may change some cognitive elements to make them more consistent with overt behaviour. Unfortunately, the theory does not enable us to predict which method a subject will choose to reduce the state of cognitive dissonance nor in which situation one way is more likely to be chosen than the other. Behavioural change corresponds to cancelling a purchase if possible or brand switching, in the case of repetitive purchases. A change of opinion can be reached if consumers are exposed to certain information. Thus, the subject may deliberately seek information that confirms the decision and try to avoid information questioning the merits of the choice (Figure 10–4). An experiment found that owners of a new car were more likely to notice and read advertising for the model they had just bought than for the other brands.[6]

The Role of Advertising in Post-Purchase Feeling Reduction

There is no empirical evidence yet to support the contention that advertisers can reduce buyers' post-purchase feelings. Some authors have said that an advertiser should undertake communication programs targeted at new buyers of a product.[7] This could be done, for instance, by sending leaflets on the newly bought products which would demonstrate the wisdom of the consumer's choice. It is not evident that manufacturers would benefit from such programs, however. If a consumer really seeks reasons to justify a choice, then the advertiser has nothing to do because the buyer will rationalize the purchase decision anyway. Also, it must be questioned whether the manufacturer or the retailer is an adequate and sufficiently credible source to reduce dissonance. In an experiment, consumers who just made a purchase received a message stating the merits of their choice.[8] Some were made by mail, others by telephone. The clients who received a letter were less dissonant and developed more favourable attitudes toward the retailer than those who did not receive a letter. However, those who received the telephone communication were more subject to dissonance and developed less favourable attitudes toward the retailer than those who received no communication at all. Thus it is difficult to draw definite conclusions on the usefulness of post-purchase advertising from this experiment.

Post-Usage Feelings

As time elapses, post-purchase feelings give way to post-usage feelings, which are directly tied to a comparison of the product's performance with the consumer's expectations. It is to be hoped that the use of a product enables the consumer to attain a certain level of satisfaction. However, the consumer does not judge the satisfaction obtained through product usage in absolute terms but rather in relation to what was expected of the product. A simple example can illustrate this idea.

A consumer tries a new detergent that has just been launched on the market. Suppose that for some reason, this consumer expects the new detergent to bleach more than the average brand. If after use this proves to be the case, this consumer will experience an average level of satisfaction with the product. If the product is superior to what was expected, the level of satisfaction will increase rapidly. However, if the product registers a performance inferior to what was expected, satisfaction would fall below the normal level.

Suppose now that another consumer expects the new detergent to be very much superior to the average, possibly as a result of advertising claims. As for the previous consumer, the level of real satisfaction will be determined as a function of the difference between expectations and the product's actual performance. Because this time the consumer's expectations are higher, however, actual product performance also needs to be higher in order to produce the same consumer satisfaction level as before! This suggests that advertisers should guard against unduly raising consumers' expectations through exaggerated advertising claims.

Of course, the consumer must have a sufficiently high level of expectation concerning the use of the product or the service for the purchase to materialize. Too high a level of expectation generally lowers the degree of satisfaction obtained by the consumer through consumption of the product. This degree of satisfaction as well as all the information on the product, the brand, and the use of the product, will increase the consumer's knowledge of the product class (i.e., improve the cognitive attitude components). In the same way, the consumer's evaluation of the product and brands during or after usage will improve or worsen attitudes toward the brand through a change in the affective attitude components.

The Role of Advertising in Post-Usage Feelings

An advertising message implicitly or explicitly promises a buyer a certain level of satisfaction through the purchase and consumption of the advertised product or service. In doing this, an advertiser raises a buyer's expectations. Consequently, the product performance will have to be better for the consumer to feel the promised satisfaction. Advertisers who make exaggerated claims about the merits of a product or use deceptive advertisements have a short-term view of their place in the market. It may be easy to raise a buyer's expectations to sell a product, but if the product's performance does not meet these expectations, consumers will inevitably be dissatisfied and will not repeat their purchases.

INTERPERSONAL DIFFERENCES IN PURCHASE SITUATIONS

Personal or Psychographic Factors

The factors that lead to diverse behaviour within a single market segment are personal or psychographic characteristics, social factors, and cultural factors, i.e., a consumer's cultural environment.

Personal or psychographic factors characterize individuals at the psychological level and affect their lifestyles, behaviour, and purchase behaviour. An individual may be impulsive, seek other people's company, act independently, or in a conservative and authoritative manner. These traits affect consumers' personality and influence their needs, motivations, perceptions, attitudes toward risk, and the decision and information processes. Certain consumers behave like energetic entrepreneurs and may be demanding of themselves and of others. An impulsive person wastes little time in seeking and processing information before making a purchase; an extrovert may make purchases that supposedly reflect personality.[9]

Advertisers and other communicators need to know whether consumers can be easily persuaded. In Figure 10-5 (next page), four individuals are exposed to three messages concerning different subjects. Message A uses a fear appeal; B is an emotional appeal message and C is a rational appeal message.[10] Individual no. 1's reaction may be characterized as independent of the communication; he has been easily persuaded, whatever the nature of the appeal used. Individual no. 2 is the least persuasible of the four. Individual no. 3 is likely to be influenced more easily with messages using rational appeals, while the fourth individual is more likely to respond positively to messages based on fear. Persuasiveness is also tied to message characteristics and depends on the subject of the communication, the type of appeal used, the argument provided, or the style of the communication. In this example, persuasibility depends upon the communication.[11]

FIGURE 10–5

*Reactions of
Four Individuals
with Various
Persuasibility
Levels to Three
Communications
(A, B, and C)*

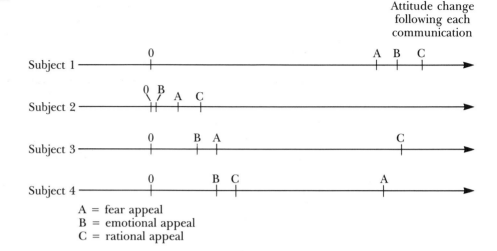

A = fear appeal
B = emotional appeal
C = rational appeal

The question which then arises for advertisers is to know whether they can identify the consumers who can be easily persuaded and who therefore are most influenced by advertising. If the consumers could be identified by easily observable characteristics, it would be easier to locate and reach them. Unfortunately, studies that sought the typical characteristics of persuasible individuals produced few sure conclusions. There is as much empirical evidence to suggest that a person's intelligence and propensity to be persuaded are positively,[12] negatively,[13] or not at all[14] related. The same statement applies to self-confidence.[15] In general, however, women seem easier to persuade than men.[16] Other factors that have been proposed as possible determinants of persuasibility are cognitive needs,[17] ego-defensiveness,[18] authoritarianism,[19] self-esteem,[20] aggressiveness,[21] the need for social approval,[22] and dogmatism.[23]

Thus, people differ as to the ease with which they are likely to accept a persuasive communication and tend to react differently after such a communication. Advertisers cannot, however, meaningfully use this criterion to segment an audience.

Socio-Economic Factors

Socio-economic factors characterize the social groups, formal or informal, structured or not, to which individuals belong, could belong, or would like to belong. These factors are an individual's age, sex, revenue, profession, education, religion, nationality, social class, size of the family, and the state in the family's life cycle. These different characteristics lead to a better comprehension of consumers' behaviour. The needs of a young unmarried male are not those of a middle-aged married woman; the transportation needs of travelling salespeople are not similar to those of sedentary office employees. Education, profession, and social class affect consumers' perceptions and attitudes, just as an individual's income directly influences the brands that are included in the evoked set. Bank employees earning $28 000 a year will probably not include a Cadillac in their evoked set of brands when they consider buying a new car.

Because needs and attitudes differ from group to group, the pressures a group exerts on its members in order to induce them to comply to group norms must also be considered. Thus, if a branch clerk could afford the luxury of a Cadillac through some unexpected good fortune, he or she would probably incur the disapproval of colleagues, neighbours, and members of the same social class.

Cultural Factors

Buyers must also be considered in the context of their cultural environment. Culture includes the knowledge, beliefs, art, ethics, law, customs, language, and all the other habits acquired by a society's members. Like socio-economic factors, these elements also influence behaviour and purchase behaviour. They are perhaps less visible since they are shared by all the consumers in the same market, as well as by the manufacturer and the advertiser. This is perhaps why cultural factors are less recognized by advertisers. However, if advertisers try to address market segments in which the cultural element is not the same for all consumers, an important dimension is without doubt added to the problem of buyer behaviour. As will be discussed in Chapter 16, this is the case when multinational firms must advertise in several countries to several different cultures, or of manufacturers who must, as in Canada, advertise in a bicultural environment.

Within one society, different cultural groups are identified by age, ethnic origin, geographical location, language, and religion. For example, Puerto Ricans in New York, The Pennsylvania Amish, and the Cubans in Miami might be considered as distinct cultural groups within American society. The multicultural dimension of the Canadian market has already been discussed in Chapter 4. These cultural differences highlight the need for advertisers to take them into account.

THE DYNAMICS OF PURCHASE BEHAVIOUR

The Determinants of Purchase Information-Seeking Activities

As we have seen, buyer behaviour is not static; rather buyer behaviour and the information acquisition process can be viewed as a continuous system. To purchase a product or a brand, buyers need a certain level of information about the characteristics and the probable performance of various brands on the market. Pre-purchase information-seeking activities depend on four factors that have an important time dimension (Figure 10–6, next page). Two factors are purchase-situation related: the urgency of the purchase situation and the level of information the buyer has acquired by the time of the purchase decision. The two other factors relate to the type of product and market: the length and regularity of the purchase cycle for a particular product type and the risk perceived by consumers in the purchase situation.

Urgency of the Purchase Situation

The urgency of the purchase situation affects the quantity and quality of information that a buyer has time to acquire before making a purchase deci-

FIGURE 10–6

The Determinants of Pre-Purchase Information-Seeking Activities

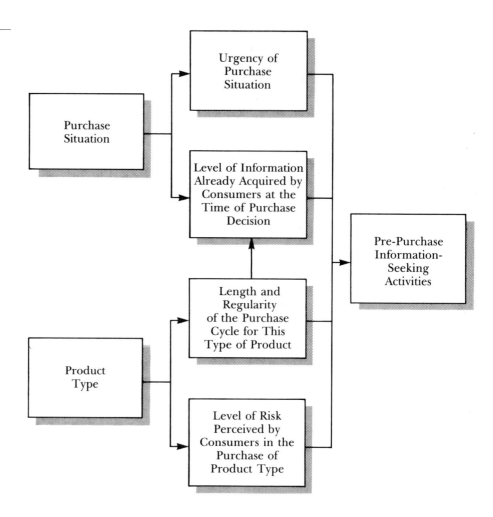

sion. For instance, a consumer who is suffering a severe migraine may go to the nearest drugstore to buy a pain reliever, and thus is acting under great time pressure. Because of this hasty decision, the consumer probably will not buy the same brand he might have if he was seeking a pain reliever for some future headache.[24]

Level of Information Already Acquired

Depending on the extent of market information, a buyer's decision process has differing levels of complexity. A product's characteristics in relation to an individual's past experience determines the level of complexity of the decision process.

Three possible cases can be identified:[25]

1. The consumer is familiar with a product category and knows the characteristics of competing brands. This process is called *routinized response behaviour.*

2. The consumer knows the product category well but not the particular brand. For example, a new brand of pecan pie has been introduced on the market. The process through which the consumer becomes familiar with this brand is called *limited problem solving*.
3. The consumer does not know either the product category or the brand. For example, a newcomer to Canada must learn what a pecan pie is before deciding which brand to choose. Another example is UHT or long-life milk which, at the time it was introduced, represented a totally new concept. This process is called *extensive problem solving*.

The level of information already acquired is directly affected by the length of the purchase cycle, because the rate of information forgetting depends on how frequently a product is purchased.

Length and Regularity of the Purchase Cycle

Purchase situations related to certain needs and wants occur at various frequencies and paces. Frequency is linked to the type of product and market. Based on the regularity and length of the purchase cycle, three types of markets can be identified:

1. *Short purchase cycle markets* are characterized by routine purchase decision processes or by limited problem solving when a new brand is introduced on the market. Most food products, such as coffee, sugar, bread, soft drinks, canned vegetables, and household and beauty care products fall into this category.
2. *Irregular purchase cycle markets* are characterized by products that are purchased more or less regularly. This category of products includes desserts, cookies, cake mixes, aperitif wines, and deluxe food products.
3. *Long or unpredictable purchase cycle markets* include all durable goods, such as cars, household appliances, and furniture. Also in this category are products for which occasions of purchase cannot be predicted, for example, drug products, which most consumers buy only occasionally.

Level of Perceived Risk

In general, the nature of the risk—physical, financial, and/or psychological— as well as the level of the risk depend on the kind of purchase contemplated. Buying a candy bar typically does not involve the same level of risk as buying an expensive second-hand sports car. When buyers perceive a high risk in a purchase situation, they will generally require more information about the brand and the product class before making a decision. The relationship between the size of the risk and the consumer's information research depends, in turn, on the consumer's attitude toward risk.

Brand Loyalty and Brand Switching

The information a buyer has already acquired, the urgency of the purchase, the type of product, and the risk involved interact with one another and determine a buyer's level of pre-purchase information-seeking activities. Once evaluated, this information is used to implicitly rank-order the different brands in the evoked set, and other conditions permitting, the most preferred brand will be purchased.

But for how long will this brand remain the most preferred? Is a buyer likely to switch to another brand at the next purchase? Learning theory may help answer these questions. According to psychologists, learning is the behavioural change resulting from previous behaviour in similar situations.[26] Learning theories postulate a state of tension as soon as a need is felt by an individual, in response to a stimulus in the environment (such as products or ads), which calls for the subject's response (a purchase decision). If the behaviour is rewarded by satisfaction and, consequently, by tension reduction, it is repeated when the need occurs again.

Learning is more likely to take place in short purchase cycle and routinized response behaviour situations. During the short time lag between two consecutive purchase occasions, only a fraction of information has been forgotten, and a substantial amount of additional information has been gained through using the selected brand. At the next purchase occasion, a buyer does not need and generally does not deliberately seek additional information. If the previously selected brand resulted in a positive experience, this buyer remains loyal to the brand with no further reassessment of purchase alternatives. Otherwise, if the preceding purchase has led to a negative evaluation of the brand, or if the buyer has been exposed to and has accepted new information that changed the order of the brands, then the conditions for *brand switching* are met. The buyer will try the new, most positively evaluated brand at the time of the next purchase.

Types of Market Situations and Advertising Implications

Because advertisers control only one of the buyer information sources, they can try to influence buyer behaviour by communicating information when it is needed. To be able to meet advertising objectives, advertisers must understand how buyers' information load varies over time in various types of markets.

Short Purchase Cycle Markets

A buyer's information lead is likely to vary in short purchase cycle markets in the case of low risk products (for instance, candy bars) and of higher risk products (such as fashion items). In both cases, the first purchase is preceded by fairly extensive problem solving. However, for subsequent purchases the buyer has enough information and falls into routinized problem solving or limited problem solving. Depending on the nature of this information, the buyer may be loyal to one brand or to several brands, if each brand is bought for various consumption occasions, or switch to a new brand. However, in a low risk situation, buyers are unlikely to actively search for additional information, contrary to the higher risk situation.

In short purchase cycle markets advertisers may induce buyers who buy competitive brands to switch to the advertised brand, induce new buyers of the product class to try the advertised brand, or convince present users of the advertised brand that they should remain loyal to the brand.

Attracting New Buyers.   To attract new buyers, advertisers should conduct a campaign that shows potential users of the product category that they have some unsatisfied needs of which they may not even be consciously aware and that the advertised brand can best fulfill these needs. The objective is not to create needs that consumers did not experience before. Advertising cannot sell skiing equipment in countries where it does not snow. The problem is, rather, to make consumers aware that they have a problem or need for which they have not found a satisfactory solution. For instance, a consumer may not have consciously recognized the need to combat halitosis, not knowing that products existed to solve this problem. The advertiser for a mouthwash product might show this consumer that their product can solve the problem of bad breath better than any other brand on the market.

Attracting Buyers from Competitive Brands.   To attract buyers from competitive brands, advertisers can create a state of cognitive dissonance. The objective is to show consumers that they are not buying the best product. This can be done by proving that the advertised brand is superior to competitive brands or that the most positive attributes of the competitive brands are not the most important. The goal is to improve buyer attitudes toward the advertised product so as to make it preferable to the brand currently purchased. Advertisers try to encourage buyers who experience cognitive dissonance to reduce it by trying the new brand. In order to be effective, however, advertisements based on this principle should not be deceptive. Otherwise, unsatisfied customers will not repeat the purchase of the brand and will probably go back to their former brand.

Retaining Present Buyers.   To keep present buyers, advertisers attempt to combat the cognitive dissonance that competitors' advertising has created among their customers. They may emphasize arguments that buyers consider important or reinforce the importance of the brand attributes on which the advertisers have some competitive advantage.

Short and Irregular Purchase Cycle Markets

In short and irregular purchase cycle markets, an advertiser can attempt to increase the average consumption rate, i.e., shorten the length of the purchase cycle, or induce buyers to purchase more at each occasion.

Increasing the Consumption Rate.   An advertiser may attempt to influence a buyer's memory by reminding him of the existence of the product and of the brand. This type of advertising is generally called *reminder advertising*. It is especially effective when it is made at the point of purchase. Suppose that a shopper in a supermarket is looking for a dessert and sees a large poster for Jello or a large Pepperidge Farm product display. If this person already tried the brand and has been satisfied with it, the purchase may be repeated. Without this advertisement, the shopper would probably not have thought of buying the product.

Increasing the Purchase Volume.   In this case, an advertiser may suggest new uses for the product. For instance, Kraft often suggests new recipes to consumers, with Kraft cheeses as essential ingredients. A similar result can be obtained if new occasions to consume the product are suggested to potential buyers. For example, an advertisement for cheddar cheese states, "I feel like eating this cheese seven times a day." In both cases, an advertiser tries to increase buyers' information load concerning the possible uses of the products in question.

Long or Unpredictable Purchase Cycle Markets

Long or unpredictable purchase cycle products are the most difficult to advertise. It is practically impossible to identify potential buyers of these products in the market at a given time. This is why an advertiser should make sure that at any given time, potential buyers have a sufficiently positive attitude toward the brand so that they will select it when a purchase occasion arises. The advertiser's role is to give buyers all relevant information in order to build this favourable attitude. The advertiser may also give information that is likely to reduce the risk perceived by buyers when the product is purchased.

SUMMARY OF ADVERTISING'S POTENTIAL FOR INFLUENCING BUYER BEHAVIOUR

Effect on Buyer's Needs and Motivations

The preceding analysis of buyer behaviour points out the possible impact of advertising (a persuasive communication) at three levels: on buyers' needs and motivations, on perceptions and attitudes, and on post-purchase feelings.

Advertising can influence buyer behaviour by being present in the buyer's environment and by suggesting a solution to needs felt either consciously or in a less latent form. If advertising does not really create a need, it can act upon the buyer's emotional equilibrium by responding positively to motivations that would induce the buyer to make the purchase. Or it can decrease the motivations with a negative valence that would prevent the potential buyer from purchasing. In this case, an advertisement will try to show the instrumental value of a product in responding to the buyer's needs (physical and psychological) and, consequently, in easing at least partially the tension caused by these needs.

Effects on Perceptions and Attitudes

An advertisement can try to act upon the buyer's perceptions to create a certain brand image in the market. More generally, advertising can try to cause changes in buyer attitudes and make them more favourable toward the consumption of the advertised brand.

To do this, advertising can provide information (cognitive elements) and/or act upon the affective elements of buyer attitudes. This should eventually result in a buyer's predisposition in favour of the purchase (conative elements). To make these changes, the advertiser can use the following research findings from social psychology.[27]

The Communicator

Manufacturers can identify themselves as the communicator and deliver the message. However, their credibility is weak because they have a visible interest in persuading buyers and inducing them to buy their brand. Manufacturers can also use an intermediary who will "testify" in favour of their product and deliver the advertising message. In this case:

1. The message will be as effective as the source is perceived to be credible. Credibility requires a) expertise (extensive knowledge about the subject of the communication) and b) trustworthiness (motivation to communicate unbiased information).
2. The communicator's credibility has an impact on the immediate effectiveness of the advertisement and seems to be less important in the long run.
3. The message effectiveness is enhanced if the witness first expresses some ideas that are already shared by the audience.
4. The more an advertisement demands an extreme change on the part of its audience, the more the attitude change obtained by the advertiser is likely to be important. However, if the message is too far away from a buyer's initial position and if the "expert" is not credible enough, the attitude change will be less extreme.
5. Some of the communicator's characteristics that are not relevant to the message content can strongly influence the message's effectiveness. For example, an advertising message delivered by a black person—an irrelevant characteristic—could be rejected by people with a racial prejudice.
6. In a more general way, what buyers think of an advertisement can affect their attitudes toward the communicator (the person who delivers the message or the brand).

The Message

1. Advertisers should present only those arguments that are in favour of the product: if the market already holds a favourable attitude toward the brand; if the market is not likely to be exposed to competing advertisements (a fairly unusual case); or when an immediate, albeit temporary, attitude change is sought.
2. Advertisers should present arguments in favour of and against their product if, for example, they want to convince users of another brand to switch to their brand, or if the buyers are likely to be exposed to competing advertisements. A relatively small number of advertisers use this approach, yet it seems very effective.
3. If advertisers decide to use arguments and counterarguments, those presented last are likely to be the most effective.
4. The message is more effective when the conclusions are explicitly drawn, rather than when buyers are left to infer conclusions. The exception to this rule would apply when the market segment targeted by the advertiser is highly intelligent.

5. The effectiveness of emotional versus factual messages depends upon the nature of the target market segment.
6. With advertisements using fear appeals, the effectiveness of the message will increase with the intensity of the provoked fear, provided clear solutions are proposed and provided these solutions are possible and seem plausible to the buyer. Otherwise, the message can have an effect opposite to the one intended.
7. There is no clear evidence indicating the order in which the arguments should be presented in terms of importance.
8. One can reasonably expect some resistance on the part of a buyer to persuasion by an advertisement. It could be, however, that a distracting device simultaneously presented to the audience could decrease the audience's resistance to the persuasive communication.

The Buyer

1. Apparently, buyers seek selective exposure to messages that agree with their positions and avoid information that is inconsistent with their attitudes. Thus advertisers' ideal audience is generally composed of people who are the least likely to listen to their message.
2. The effectiveness of certain messages depends upon the audience's intelligence level.
3. An effective advertisement must take into account the reasons that motivate a buyer's attitudes; these reasons as well as the attitude must be changed.
4. Buyers' personality traits affect their propensity to be persuaded. Women or individuals with low self-esteem can generally be more easily influenced.
5. Buyers' ego-involvement with the advertised product (that is, if the product involves sensitive ideological values) decreases their acceptance of the message.
6. Buyers belonging to certain social groups are probably less influenced than others by an advertising message asking them to violate the norms of these groups.
7. It is easier to change a buyer's privately held opinions (such as opinions on products related to personal problems), than to change an opinion that has been publicly stated (such as opinions on products related to family or social environment).

Persistence of Advertising Effects

1. The effects of an advertising message tend to wear off over time. The effects of a message delivered by a positive source wear off more rapidly than those of an advertisement communicated by a negative source. A complex or subtle message, if it is understood, produces a slower decay of attitude change.
2. Repetition of an advertisement tends to extend its effect over time.

3. An attitude change can increase some time after the advertising message has been received by the audience (sleeper effect).

Effects on Post-Purchase Feelings

Advertising has a potential value in reducing a buyer's dissonant feelings after an important purchase. Although no sure evidence can give advertising a precise role in this area, there are at least theoretical arguments supporting such a role. Consequently, this possibility should be kept in mind in spite of the lack of empirical evidence.

THE LIMITS OF ADVERTISING COMMUNICATIONS

In the description of the potential of advertising communications, the (sometimes very particular) conditions under which an advertisement could be effective give an indication of advertising's limits. Advertising communications' limitations can be grouped into three broad categories: message effectiveness, parallel communication channels, and other elements of the marketing mix.

Advertising Message Effectiveness

An advertising message's effectiveness depends on the communication format, the message content in relation to the buyer's initial attitude toward the advertised product, and the style of the message. These are the variables that have been considered by researchers and that have led to precise conclusions. However, many content as well as format variables remain to be analyzed so that the advertisers can draw useful conclusions for devising their messages. Thus, the length of the message, and whether the message is communicated through pictures, sounds, or words are other types of variables that are important to advertisers and on which few clear cut conclusions have been drawn.

Besides these structural variables that influence advertising effectiveness, one of the greatest limits of advertising is the ability of a message to pass successfully through the selective attention, selective distortion, and selective retention barriers. Of course, even if there are certain useful gimmicks, for example, an appeal to the buyer's interests or the use of mechanical devices to attract the audience's attention, each message is one among hundreds vying for buyers' attention.

Buyer's Parallel Information Channels

Buyers generally do not rely on advertising for information. Indeed, buyers are faced with an information overload coming from different sources. Since they are unable to process all the information they are exposed to, buyers must consciously or unconsciously discard some information and select their information sources. This information overload is one of the principal limits to advertising effectiveness.

As was discussed, an advertising message must compete for the buyer's attention and against advertisements for the competing brands which, of course, generally give contradictory information. Furthermore, an advertisement also competes for the buyer's attention against all other advertisements. If a consumer pays attention to an advertisement for furniture, he or she cannot at the same time consider an advertisement describing the pleasures of a one-week vacation in Acapulco.

In addition, all advertising information received by a potential buyer is only a small part of this buyer's information about the products and brands on the market. Buyers' actions are very much influenced by the social groups to which they belong. First, a buyer's opinions and attitudes are influenced by these groups. Consumers are rewarded when their purchase behaviour complies with the norms of the group and are sanctioned when it does not. Second, a great part of buyers' information originates from their social groups. Advertising through word-of-mouth plays a powerful role in buyer behaviour. According to the two-step flow of communication theory, mass media advertising influences only a small section of the market, which in turn can relay (or not relay) the advertiser's message.

Consequently, advertising is only one information source for the buyer. Unfortunately, for the advertiser, this source is far from being the most effective, since personal communications considerably exceed mass communications in effectiveness. These important limits should be kept in mind when the effectiveness of advertising communications is assessed.

Other Elements of the Marketing Program

Another series of limits to advertising effectiveness can be found in the marketing program. As shown in Figure 10–7, buyer behaviour is far from being influenced only by advertising. The other marketing mix variables are also important: the product, the price, the distribution, and personal selling. As we have seen, advertising for a product is useless if this product is unlikely to respond effectively to some need of the consumer or if it cannot deliver the expected satisfaction. It is also useless to advertise a product if its price does not correspond to what the buyer is ready or able to pay or if this product is not available at the buyer's local retailer.

Several conclusions can be drawn from these various constraints on the power of advertising. First, these constraints have the merit of showing that advertising is not independent from the other marketing tools. As was discussed in Chapter 2, the marketing program is a consistent and integrated plan with precise objectives. All the elements of the marketing program must be in harmony with these objectives. The role as well as the interdependence of the elements of the marketing program are highlighted in Figure 10–7.

Second, this interdependence shows that an advertising campaign must be devised in accordance with the other elements of the marketing program. *Otherwise, it cannot be effective.* Thus, the advertising message can be used only if the product does possess the advertised characteristics (otherwise the advertising would be deceptive, which, as we have already seen, would not be in the manufacturer's best long-run interests). Also, an advertiser cannot devise the campaign without considering the price of the product, which often influences the type and number of consumers who will be tempted by the product. In the same way, a campaign cannot ignore the product's distribution channels, because an advertising campaign must take into account the intermediaries in the distribution channels as well as the right mix of advertising and personal

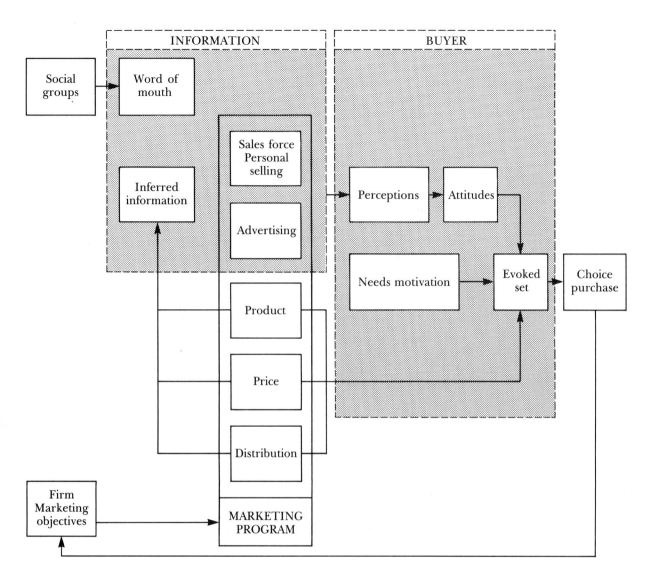

FIGURE 10–7
*The Role of the
Marketing Program
in Influencing Buyer
Behaviour*

selling. This was discussed in Chapter 2, when the pull and push marketing strategies were outlined.

Finally, these constraints have an important impact on the advertiser's work method. Devising an advertising campaign is not the work of a single individual (the advertiser) nor the lonely creation of one artist. It is the task of an entire *marketing team*, for which the marketing program and the marketing objectives are of primary concern. Advertising must be integrated in this program and be given the role that only a mass communication tool can fulfill in a marketing program.

INDUSTRIAL BUYER BEHAVIOUR

Although most of the principles of consumer behaviour apply to industrial advertising, industrial buyer behaviour does have unique characteristics.

Webster and Wind have developed a general model of organizational buyer behaviour.[28] It identifies the important variables in the development of an industrial marketing strategy. The model does not describe any one specific buying situation: rather it brings together in a logical structure the variables known to influence industrial purchasing decisions.

According to this model, organizational buying behaviour is the result of four interrelated variables: the buying centre, buying tasks, organization structure, and buying technology. These variables are in turn influenced by such environmental factors as business fluctuations, governmental regulations, trade unions, and social and cultural values.

The Buying Centre

This concept encompasses all the members of an organization that influence a buying decision. In discharging their duties, members of the buying centre perform the roles of users, buyers, influencers, deciders, and gatekeepers. An individual may occupy more than one role or several persons may share the same role. The purchasing agent is the person who usually places an order (buyer), and may also be the person who informs (gatekeeper) engineers and other production personnel (users and/or influencers) about available sources of supply.

Buying Tasks

The model defines five specific tasks outlined as five stages in a buying decision: identification of a need; establishment of specifications; identification of alternatives; evaluation of alternatives; and selection of suppliers. At each of the five stages of the decision to buy, different members of the buying centre may be involved, different decision criteria are employed, and three different sources of information may be utilized.

Organizational Structure

The formal organizational structure consists of the sub-systems of communication, authority, status, rewards, and work flow. Some of these elements are evident from a company's formal organization chart, but industrial marketers must evaluate customers individually because the relationships among these sub-systems vary from one organization to another.

Buying Technology

The technology a company uses defines its plant and equipment. Its level of sophistication limits those products the company can buy and determines how it will buy them.

The model postulates that industrial buying is a problem-solving process. A problem is created when someone in the organization perceives a discrepancy between the present situation and a desired state of affairs. Although the model provides a useful framework for understanding how an organization behaves in order to solve its buying problems, it must be remembered that all organizational behaviour is human behaviour. Marketing efforts should always aim at the specific individuals who can influence the buying decision. Individual motives are both of a task and non-task nature. Task motives may predominate in most industrial buying situations. All other things being equal, non-task motives such as a pleasing personality, a free lunch, or a gift may influence a buyer to favour a particular source of supply.

SUMMARY

The purchase process is a decision-making process under risk. The selection of one brand over all other brands is a process of optimizing the consumer's utility. This optimization is done under uncertainty, since the buyer does not have perfect information. Buyer decision-making can also be described as a decision process under uncertainty. According to this process, buyers must always choose between making an immediate decision (to buy or not to buy) or delaying this decision to seek additional information, and thus reduce the decision risk. The buyer's post-purchase feelings may also be analyzed in the light of the theory of cognitive dissonance. Advertising has the potential to improve a buyer's post-purchase feelings after an important purchase. A consumer's feelings after product usage can be described in terms of a simplified view of consumer behaviour that takes into account the psychographic, socio-economic, and cultural differences involved in the purchase process. To give a better understanding of the buyer decision process over time, buyers' information loads can be compared to a reservoir that is fed with new information and is drained through forgetting as time elapses. To account for the time dimension of information processing by buyers and to assess the role of advertisers, different types of markets are identified.

QUESTIONS FOR STUDY

1. Consider an important purchase that you have made recently (for instance, stereo equipment, car, furniture, vacation tour). Show how the purchase process you followed was:
   a. an optimization process.
   b. a decision-making process under uncertainty.
   Be specific.

2. Contrast the potential roles of advertising in pre-purchase and in post-purchase situations. Which role is likely to be more effective? Give specific examples.

3. Find examples of advertisements based on the theory of cognitive dissonance. Explain in what respect they apply this theory. Assess how adequately the theory applies to these specific situations.

4. Find examples of advertisements that you think make exaggerated advertising claims. Explain how these advertisements do or do not violate some of the principles discussed in this chapter. Can you suggest to the advertisers responsible for these ads plausible and more effective ways to advertise their products? Be specific.

5. Socio-economic and personality factors are likely to affect all the aspects of the consumer's decision process which was described in chapter 10. Suppose that a Canadian travel agent wants to advertise a ten-day winter

tour to Florida and is considering two possible market segments:
a. higher income and upper-middle-class Canadians living in major Canadian cities;
b. middle-income, lower-middle-class Canadians who are socially mobile and socially active.

6. Show how an important Canadian beer manufacturer should approach advertising a brand:
a. in the Anglophone provinces
b. in the Quebec market

7. Same question as 6, but the manufacturer considers exporting his beer to:
a. Western European countries
b. Eastern European countries
c. Latin America

8. Explain the concept of a consumer's information load. Why is this concept useful to an advertiser? Consider the cost-revenue aspects of the concept, from the consumer's point of view as well as from the advertiser's point of view.

9. How are the concepts of brand loyalty and brand switching related? Explain how these two concepts involve opportunities as well as liabilities for an advertiser.

10. Compare the behaviour of industrial buyers with that of ultimate consumers with respect to:
a. buyer motives and needs,
b. the number of people involved in the decision process,
c. the time it takes to sell the product,
d. the dollar value of the sales.
Draw the corresponding implications for advertising targeted to these two types of market.
Show how the purchase decision of the potential customers in the two market segments is likely to be different. How should or could an advertiser use these differences for designing an effective advertising program?

PROBLEMS

1. a. A consumer is contemplating the purchase of a rather expensive watch. Using Figure 10–10, show how the purchase decision process is likely to differ when the purchase is intended:
   • for the buyer
   • as a gift to a close relative
   b. Does the model apply equally well to both situations? Explain.
   c. Outline plausible advertising strategies for both types of market segments, and contrast the major differences required for communicating with them.

2. a. Find a family who has recently purchased a major durable good, such as an automobile. Through interviews with relevant members of the family, find out to what point the model of industrial buyer behaviour could apply to this purchase process.
   b. In the same way, after interviewing the purchasing agent of a medium- or small-sized firm about the typical decision process in the firm, find out to what point the purchase decision model in Figure 10–10 could be used to explain this process.

NOTES

1. Bent Stidsen, "Aspects of a Theory of Consumer Information Processing," *ASAC Proceedings* (1977), pp. 4–21.
2. Paul E. Green, "Bayesian Statistics and Product Decisions," *Business Horizons* (Fall 1962), pp. 101–9.
3. Peter Thirdell and Harrie Vredenburg, "Individual and Situational Determinants of Prepurchase Information Search: A National Study of Canadian Automobile Buyers," *Marketing*, ed. Michel Laroche (Montreal: Administrative Science Association of Canada, 1982), pp. 305–13.
4. M.T. O'Keefe, "The Anti-Smoking Commercials: A Study of Television's Impact on Behaviour," *Public Opinion Quarterly*, 35 (1971), 242–48; J.G. Greenworld, "Dissonance and Relative vs. Absolute Attractiveness of Decision Alternatives," *Journal of Personality and Social Psychology*, 11 (1969), 328–33; J.W. Brehm and A.R. Cohen, "Re-evaluation of Choice Alternatives as a Function of Their Number and Qualitative Similarity," *Journal of Abnormal and Social Psychology*, 58 (1959), 373–78; J.W. Brehm and A.R. Cohen, *Exploration in Cognitive Dissonance* (New York: John Wiley and Sons, 1962).
5. Leon Festinger, *A Theory of Cognitive Dissonance* (Evanston, Ill.: Row, Peterson, 1957).
6. D. Ehrlick, I Guttman, P. Schönback, and J. Mills, "Post Decision Exposure to Relevant Information," *Journal of Abnormal and Social Psychology*, 54 (1957), 98–102.
7. Leonard LoSciutto and Robert Perloff, "Influence of Product Preference on Dissonance Reduction," *Journal of Marketing Research*, 4 (August 1967), 286–90; Gerald D. Bell, "The Automobile Buyer After the Purchase," *Journal of Marketing*, 31 (July 1967), 12–16.
8. Shelby P. Hunt, "Post-Transaction Communication and Dissonance Reduction," *Journal of Marketing*, 34 (July 1970), 46–51.
9. S.A. Ahmed, "Personality Correlates of Product Purchase Behaviour: A Canadian Experience," *ASAC Proceedings* (1977), pp. 4–22.
10. Ralph L. Rosnow and Edward J. Robinson, *Experiments in Persuasion*, (New York: Academic Press, 1967), pp. 195–204.
11. I.L. Janis and C.I. Hovland, "An Overview of Persuasibility Research," *Personality and Persuasibility*, ed. I.L. Janis and C.I. Hovland (New Haven: Yale University Press, 1959), pp. 1–26.
12. H.H. Hyman and P.B. Sheatsley, "Some Reasons Why Information Campaigns Fail," *Public Opinion Quarterly*, 11 (1947) 412–23; C.E. Siranson, "Predicting Who Learns Factual Information from the Mass Media," *Groups, Leadership, and Men: Research in Human Relations*, ed. H. Guetzhow (Pittsburg, Pa.: Carnegie Press, 1951).
13. H.J. Wegrocki, "The Effect of Prestige Suggestibility on Emotional Attitude," *Journal of Social Psychology* 5, (1935), 382–94; D.W. Cannent, C.G. Miles and V.B. Cervin, "Persuasiveness and Persuasibility as Related to Intelligence and Extraversion," *British Journal of Social and Clinical Psychology*, 4 (1965), 1–7.
14. G. Murphy, L.B. Murphy, and T.M. Newcomb, *Experimental Social Psychology*, (New York: Harper and Row, 1937), pp. 930.
15. Donald F. Cox and Raymond A Bauer, "Self-Confidence and Persuasibility in Women," *Public Opinion Quarterly* (Fall 1964), pp. 453–55; Abe Schuchman and Michael Perry, "Self-Confidence and Persuasibility in Marketing: A reappraisal," *Journal of Marketing* (May 1969), pp. 146–54.
16. I.L. Janis and P.B. Field, "Sex Differences and Personality Factors Related to Persuasibility," *Personality and Persuasibility*, ed. I.L. Janis and C.I. Hovland (New Haven: Yale University Press, 1959), pp. 55–68.

17. A.R. Cohen, "Need for Cognition and Order of Communication as Determinants of Opinion Change," *The Order of Presentation in Persuasion*, ed. C.I. Hovland (New Haven: Yale University Press, 1957), pp. 79–97.

18. I. Sarnoff and D. Katz, "The Motivational Bases of Attitude Change," *Journal of Abnormal and Social Psychology*, 49 (1954), 115–24; D. Katz, C. McClintock, and I Sarnoff, "The Measurement of Ego-Defense as Related to Attitude Change," *Journal of Personality*, 25 (1957), 465–74.

19. L. Berkowitz and R.M. Lundy, "Personality Characteristics Related to Susceptibility to Influence by Peers and Authority Figures," *Journal of Personality*, 25 (1957), 306–16.

20. H. Leventhal and S.I. Perloe, "A Relationship Between Self-Esteem and Persuasibility," *Journal of Abnormal and Social Psychology*, 64 (1962), 385–88.

21. A. Roland, "Persuasibility in Young Children as a Function of Aggressive Motivation and Aggression Conflict," *Journal of Abnormal and Social Psychology*, 66 (1963), 454–61.

22. D.P. Crowne and D. Marlowe, *The Approval Motive*, (New York: John Wiley and Sons, 1964), chapter 8.

23. N. Miller, "Involvement and Dogmation as Inhibitors of Attitude Change," *Journal of Experimental Social Psychology*, 1 (1965), 121–32.

24. Roger M. Heeler and Rolf Seringhaus, "Buyer Behaviour in Emergency Situations," *Marketing*, vol. 2, ed. Robert G. Wyckham (Administrative Sciences Association of Canada, 1981), pp. 133–41.

25. John A. Howard and Jagdish N. Sheth, *The Theory of Buyer Behaviour*, (New York: John Wiley and Sons, 1969), p. 150.

26. Bernard Berelson and Gary A. Steiner, *Human Behaviour: An Inventory of Scientific Findings*, (New York: Harcourt, Brace and World, 1964), p. 25.

27. Adapted from Philip Zimbardo and Ebbe B. Ebbesen, *Influencing Attitudes and Changing Behaviour*, (Reading, Mass.: Addison-Wesley, 1970), pp. 20–23.

28. Frederick E. Webster, Jr. and Yoram Wind, "A General Model for Understanding Organizational Buying Behaviour," *Journal of Marketing*, (April 1972), pp. 12–19.

PART IV

Management of Advertising Programs

The stage has been set for planning an advertising campaign. PART I described the nature and functions of advertising within the overall marketing program. In PART II, the respective roles of the advertiser, the advertising agency, the print and the broadcast media were discussed and evaluated. In PART III, the existing body of knowledge of the decision making process of Canadian consumers was evaluated in the context of communication effects. These sources of information based on social science research are useful to advertisers in all phases of campaign planning.

PART IV shows how to plan the overall advertising program. Setting the advertising objectives and budgets is explained in

Chapter 11. Next the process of developing a creative strategy and effective print and broadcast messages consistent with the objectives is detailed in Chapters 12 and 13. The task of media planning, explained in Chapter 14, enables the advertiser to effectively reach the targeted audience. Finally, the advertiser needs information at each level of campaign planning, as well as for the execution and control of the campaign. The various forms of advertising research are described in Chapter 15.

CHAPTER

11 *Planning the Campaign and Setting Advertising Objectives and Budgets*

An effective advertising campaign takes a step-by-step approach to planning and management. Within the planning process, one of the major decisions is determining the direction and intensity of the advertising effort to achieve overall marketing objectives. This process involves two types of decisions that are interdependent: setting precise and operational advertising objectives, and establishing the size and allocation of the advertising budget.

PLANNING, EXECUTING, AND CONTROLLING AN ADVERTISING CAMPAIGN

The process of developing and managing an advertising campaign comprises the same number of steps, although the duration of each step may vary according to the market, company, and product. A new product may require a longer planning process and involve more participants than a mature product. Also, a firm with little marketing expertise may require a longer planning process than a firm with an advertising department. An advertising agency may play an important role in all phases of the planning process. If a firm is not using the services of an advertising agency, these functions must be performed internally or with the assistance of outside suppliers.

The complete process of planning, executing, and controlling an advertising campaign comprises six major steps (Figure 11–1).

Developing the Fact Book

A fact book is a summary of all relevant facts about a market and a brand or product (Figure 11–2). The fact book should be developed by both the advertising manager and the account executive. It represents the best available information about the industry, the trade, and the advertiser's brand. It is used at all levels in the advertiser's organization to appraise market opportunities and analyze the market in which the brand is to be advertised. The advertising agency often plays a critical role for many firms that lack marketing expertise and rely on the agency for marketing advice.

Company Facts

Information about the history of the company and the history of the product must be included in the fact book to assist the agency personnel who work on

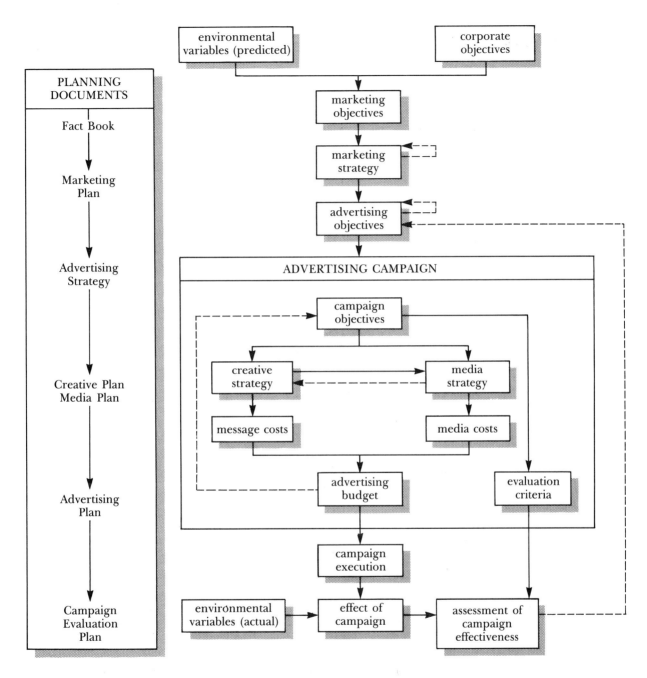

PLANNING DOCUMENTS
Fact Book
↓
Marketing Plan
↓
Advertising Strategy
↓
Creative Plan Media Plan
↓
Advertising Plan
↓
Campaign Evaluation Plan

environmental variables (predicted) → corporate objectives → marketing objectives → marketing strategy → advertising objectives

ADVERTISING CAMPAIGN

campaign objectives → creative strategy → media strategy → message costs → media costs → advertising budget → evaluation criteria

campaign execution

environmental variables (actual) → effect of campaign → assessment of campaign effectiveness

FIGURE 11–1
Planning, Executing, and Controlling the Advertising Campaign

the marketing and advertising programs. For example, Kraft and Electrolux have used flashbacks about the company's history in their advertising to emphasize that their product and service is the same as in the "good old days." Company brochures and other promotional material contain some of these facts to convey that the company has been innovative and successful. Package

FIGURE 11–2
Suggested Outline for the Fact Book

FACT BOOK

A. Company Facts	B. Market Facts	C. Brand Facts
1. History of the company	1. Environmental variables (predicted)	1. Basic characteristics
2. History of the product	2. Market size and trends	2. Current marketing objectives
3. Corporate objectives	3. Segmentation and positioning	3. Current marketing strategy
	4. Channels of distribution	• target definition
	5. Competition	• marketing mix

designs or re-designs may use this information or incorporate some old symbols to convey the same message. It is essential that all agency personnel working on an account understand the company's objectives.

Market Facts

This section of the fact book develops an opportunity analysis for the firm. Major environmental variables—the economic, cultural, legal, or other uncontrollable variables affecting the market—are described first (Chapter 2). The size of the intended market, its predicted evolution, and a thorough analysis of market segmentation must also be included in this section. In particular, the nature and sizes of various market segments, as well as the positioning of competitive brands with respect to these segments should be well documented. For example, in the beer market it is important to know the sizes and nature of the various market segments, how well each competitive brand appeals to these segments, and that the most important characteristics are strength and social image. Information about distribution channels and how they relate to market segmentation and competition should also be included.

Brand Facts

The last section of the fact book should include all relevant information about the brand to be advertised. It describes the brand's basic characteristics: history, evolution, and benefits. Interesting information about the production process, quality control procedures, or a new innovative packaging process should be included here. Current marketing objectives and strategy for the brand are described in detail for the benefit of all individuals working on the marketing and advertising of the brand, particularly an agency's account service group.

Developing the Marketing Plan

Based on a thorough understanding of the market situation and the marketing objectives for a particular brand, a marketing plan must be developed, preferably with the assistance of agency personnel involved in advertising and sales promotion.[1] A study of planning procedures for packaged goods companies showed extensive use of the advertising agency, even by large firms, in developing the marketing plan.[2]

FIGURE 11–3

MARKETING PLAN

A. Summary of Facts (from Fact Book)	B. Problems and Opportunities	C. Marketing Objectives and Strategy
		1. Long-range marketing objectives
		2. Target market
		3. Product policies
		4. Pricing policies
		5. Advertising plan (including sales promotion)
		6. Sales force policies
		7. Distribution policies
		8. Other considerations

D. Plan for Implementation	E. Timetable of Activities	F. Summary of Plan
1. Short-run plan (if necessary)		
2. Timing		
3. Organizational changes (if necessary)		
4. Research activities		
5. Marketing budget		
6. Sales and profit forecasts		

The marketing plan describes the overall marketing strategy that a company intends to follow for a product, i.e., the strategic decisions concerning the target market and the marketing-mix variables (the 4 Ps) as explained in Chapter 2. It also includes some critical implementation issues, such as timing, organizational changes, and information needs, as well as the marketing budget, sales and profit forecasts, and a timetable of activities. Figure 11–3 shows a suggested outline for a marketing plan.

The *summary* of facts highlights major points from the fact book as a result of the opportunity analysis done in the first planning document.

The *problems and opportunities* describe the options open to a company that result from the opportunity analysis in the fact book.

The *marketing objectives and strategy* make up the most important part of the marketing plan. It describes the firm's final decision on the marketing objectives and strategy for the next planning period. Depending on the marketing problem a company faces, these decisions may involve a slight modification to current marketing strategy or a radical departure. First, long-range marketing objectives must be stated clearly and in operational terms. Second, the target market must be defined precisely using information from the opportunity analysis. Finally, decisions on the marketing-mix variables (Chapter 2) are described. It is important to note that the advertising strategy is part of the overall marketing plan, but at this stage of planning, the marketing plan is used as input for developing a more detailed advertising plan.

The *plan for implementation* deals with critical implementation issues. Short-run plans (if any) are described. It may be essential for the plan to be implemented before a certain date because of competitive moves or seasonal or cyclical factors. The plan may also require a re-organization of the marketing function. Research activities that must be undertaken during the next period must be properly planned and funded. The implementation plan also includes a description of the marketing budget and forecasts of sales and profits.

The *timetable of activities* co-ordinates all activities in order to maximize the impact of the marketing plan.

Developing a Preliminary Advertising Plan

The advertising plan is developed within the objectives defined by the marketing plan, in which the role and functions of advertising are defined as one of the marketing-mix variables. In the previous step, decisions are made about which overall marketing strategy is the best course for achieving marketing objectives. The next task for the advertiser and the agency is to develop the advertising component of the marketing mix.

Four steps are involved in this task, which is often done by the agency or the advertising manager. First, precise and operational advertising objectives consistent with the marketing strategy are established. Second, the creative director develops a preliminary creative strategy for translating advertising objectives into an effective message. For example, the marketing strategy of appealing to teenagers to use a fruit-flavoured toothpaste may be translated into a social gathering where good breath is emphasized. Third, the media director develops a preliminary media strategy and a tentative advertising budget. Fourth, a tentative plan for evaluating the effects of the campaign is developed.

Developing the Final Advertising Plan

If the preliminary advertising plan is approved by the agency management or the plans board (Chapter 3), then the agency group working on the account presents the proposed campaign to the advertiser. This presentation will include campaign objectives, creative strategy, media plan, prototype advertisements, research, marketing services, and budget.

If the proposed campaign is approved by the advertiser, the account executive and the advertiser develop the final advertising plan. A suggested outline for the advertising plan is shown in Figure 11–4. The process of developing an advertising plan is an iterative process from the setting of the campaign objectives, the development of an advertising strategy consistent with these objectives, and the setting of a specific budget. If a client does not approve the plan, the process is repeated. Ultimately, the process stops when the agency and the advertiser agree with all of the decisions on objectives, strategy, budget, and control.

The *summary of marketing strategy* highlights the key elements of the marketing plan. These are either developed by the agency for the client or derived from the marketing plan developed by the advertiser.

FIGURE 11–4

*Suggested Outline for
the Advertising Plan*

ADVERTISING PLAN

A. Summary of Marketing Plan	B. Advertising Objectives	C. Advertising Strategy
1. Marketing objectives 2. Target market characteristics 3. Marketing-mix decisions 4. Critical implementation issues		1. Creative strategy and plan • rationale for creative strategy • copy platform • art • research on copy and layout 2. Media plan • target audience • media strategy and rationale • media schedule and costs • media research

D. Other Promotional Activities: Planning and/or Co-ordination	E. Advertising Budget	F. Campaign Evaluation Plan
	1. Appropriation 2. Allocation	

G. Summary of Plan

The *advertising objectives* are derived from the marketing objectives and strategy, and they should be stated in precise and operational terms. The agency helps the advertiser develop sound, realistic, and operational advertising objectives.

The *advertising strategy and plan* is presented in two parts. First, the creative strategy is described with a detailed rationale using facts from the opportunity analysis and research, if available. The creative strategy translates the marketing strategy into an effective message in order to achieve the advertising objectives. The rationale justifies the proposed message in terms of content and format. The two main ingredients of the creative strategy, copy and art, are developed in detail. Findings on pretesting of copy and layout are presented and used to evaluate the proposed creative execution. Planned copy posttesting activities may also be presented.

The *media plan* starts with a description of the target audience derived from the target market defined in the marketing plan. Then the media strategy is presented with a detailed rationale for the various media types and vehicles selected as well as for those rejected. Next, the media plan must contain a media schedule and an evaluation of the media budget. Finally, findings on media research from various sources are presented, as well as planned research activities on the selected media.

Other promotional activities involve such sales promotion techniques as sampling, product demonstrations, and publicity/public relations activities (Chapter 8). All these activities must be properly co-ordinated with advertising efforts and the rest of the marketing mix.

The *advertising budget* section provides the rationale for the advertising appropriation, as well as the allocation to different markets, products, advertising functions, media, and time periods.

The *campaign evaluation* plan provides procedures for ascertaining the campaign's effects and whether the advertising objectives have been reached. This activity is critical for effective management of the advertising function (see Chapter 15).

Executing the Campaign

Once the advertising plan is approved by the advertiser, the account executive, in consultation with the client, co-ordinates the execution of the campaign. Production of advertisements or commercials must be completed in time for the start of the campaign and finished advertisements or commercials must be approved. The final media plan must be developed and approved by the advertiser before orders may be sent to the media for buying space and/or time.

Evaluating the Effects of the Campaign

After the campaign has run, the advertiser must determine if the advertising objectives have been reached. Research on the campaign's effects may be done by the firm's in-house advertising department, an outside research firm, or by the agency research group. Based on the information collected, a campaign evaluation report is written, often by the account executive. A suggested outline for the evaluation report is shown in Figure 11–5. The advertiser decides whether the marketing and advertising elements should be continued or modified or whether the campaign should be completely re-worked for the next period.

The *summary of the advertising plan* states the main elements of the advertising campaign that are relevant to the evaluation. These elements are the advertising objectives (test criteria), the main copy points, and the selected media and vehicles.

The *research methodology* describes the methods used to collect the data and analyze it. Procedures for these tasks are detailed in Chapter 15.

The *results* section evaluates the entire campaign by comparing the research results with the stated campaign objectives. If these activities were planned, results on copy posttesting and on different media and vehicle effectiveness are presented.

FIGURE 11–5

Suggested Outline for the Campaign Evaluation Report

CAMPAIGN EVALUATION REPORT

A. Summary of Advertising Plan	B. Research Methodology	C. Results
1. Advertising objectives	1. Survey method	1. Advertising objectives and campaign effectiveness
2. Advertising strategy	2. Sample	2. Copy posttesting (optional)
3. Other promotional activities	3. Questionnaire	3. Media effectiveness (optional)
4. Campaign evaluation plan	4. Data analysis	

D. Conclusions and Recommendations

The *conclusions and recommendations* summarize the report's main findings and make recommendations on the advertising objectives, the advertising budget, the advertising strategy, the copy and layout of the messages, and the selected media or media vehicles for the next planning period.

SETTING ADVERTISING OBJECTIVES

From the statement of the marketing objectives and the marketing strategy, the objectives assigned to the advertising function are derived. Marketing objectives may be stated in terms of sales, profit, or market shares, but it is a common fallacy to state the advertising objectives in the same terms. Since advertising takes place toward the end of the implementation of the marketing plan, it seems natural to many marketers to relate this activity and that of the sales force to the ultimate sale. But sales are the results of the total marketing effort, including advertising. Would advertising alone "sell" the product to the wrong target market? Would advertising alone "sell" if the product does not meet the needs and requirements of consumers? Would advertising alone "sell" if the price is too high in relation to competitive products? Would advertising alone "sell" if the product were not on the retail shelves? Questions like these may be asked for every aspect of the marketing plan. Only when one is reasonably assured of proper control of the other elements of the marketing mix and of unchanged factors can inferences be drawn about the effects of an advertising campaign on sales volume or market share.

The role of advertising within the marketing mix is twofold:

1. to communicate with the target market, i.e., to inform these consumers about the contents of the marketing mix;
2. to persuade the consumers in the target market that this marketing mix is the best one to satisfy their needs.

Of course, communication takes place in other parts of the marketing mix, and these should be properly integrated with advertising. For example, price level often communicates something about the quality of the product;[3] and the brand name and packaging may provide information about the product. But the main task of communicating with the mass market is usually assigned to advertising.

Therefore, advertising objectives should be defined in terms of communication goals. This requires a sound understanding of how consumers process commercial and non-commercial information, and how this affects their decision process.

In addition, advertising objectives should be defined as precisely and completely as possible in order to help managers find the means to meet these objectives, as well as to assess whether the advertising campaign has been successful. Properly defined advertising objectives should help in efficiently managing this function. A clear understanding of what advertising can or cannot do and how it contributes to the attainment of sales, profit, and market share objectives, should ensure and protect the means for carrying them out, which is the advertising budget.

Statement of Precise and Operational Advertising Objectives

The statement of precise and operational advertising objectives must include the "five Ts":

1. the *target audience(s)*, which is the group(s) of individuals to whom the communication is directed;
2. the *theme(s)* of the campaign;
3. the *task(s)* of the communication, which is the campaign's intended effect(s) on the target audience;
4. the *time horizon* during which the communication task is to be accomplished;[4]
5. the *test criteria*, which will be used at the end of the time horizon to evaluate the campaign's effectiveness.[5]

A good example of a precise and operational objective is the following:

To increase awareness of Brand X milk-based drink among teenagers and young adults aged 18 to 24 from the present 10 percent unaided recall of Brand X to a desired 50 percent, within one year, by associating it with sports events, and presenting it as the drink of winners.

In this example, the five ingredients have been properly specified in operational terms:

Advertising Campaign Objectives
TARGET AUDIENCE: teenagers and young adults aged 18 to 24
THEME: the drink of winners in sports events
TASK: increase awareness of Brand X milk-based drink from the present 10 percent to a desired 50 percent.
TIME HORIZON: one year
TEST CRITERION: unaided recall of Brand X

Defining the Target Audience

The audience that is to receive the communication is derived from the target market identified in the marketing strategy. If this target market has been identified in precise and operational terms, and if it represents a unique segment of the market, then the target audience is quite similar to the target market.

If the market is comprised of different segments to which the same product is being offered, it may be more efficient to specify the advertising objectives in terms of a *primary target audience* and a *secondary target audience*. This is particularly important when the communication tasks and themes differ from one group to the other. When the differentiation is pronounced, different advertising campaigns may be used, as is often the case for products advertised to different cultural groups like the French and English markets in Quebec, the French markets in Nova Scotia, or the English markets in Toronto, Calgary, and Vancouver.[6]

The communication task may require a more precise definition of the target audience than the target market identified in the marketing plan. Again, one may introduce a primary target audience, a secondary target audience, and so on. For example, the target market for Milk Mate, a liquid milk modifier, may be defined as families with children aged three to sixteen.[7] In this case, the child is the user of the product and influences the parent's purchase decision. Or the primary target audience may be only children aged three to sixteen, and the advertising appeal may be "a tasty and fun drink." The secondary target audience may be parents with children aged three to sixteen, and the advertising appeal may stress convenience and nutrition.

Introducing the Theme of the Campaign

In developing the product's marketing strategy some differentiating measure(s) may have been selected, and one of the functions of advertising is to communicate this feature to the target audience. The basic theme(s) of the campaign must be based on the marketing strategy for the product.

For example, take the following statement: "to convince parents of children of ages three to sixteen that Wonder Juice is the ideal drink to serve their children, because it is very nutritious and has a taste children always love." Here the strategy is to appeal to parents on the basis of good nutrition for their children, as well as ease of getting them to drink the juice.

Defining the Communication Task and the Appropriate Test Criteria

The statement of advertising objectives must clearly identify one or several communication tasks to be accomplished by the campaign within the time horizon specified. It is critical to define the main communication task, in order to select the type of campaign to be used, as well as the appropriate test criteria. Table 11–1 elaborates on advertising campaigns that are appropriate for selected communication tasks and target audiences.

If *brand awareness* is the selected communication task, the target audience may be all users of the product category; the type of campaign used may be an attention-getting campaign with teasers, a good slogan, or a catchy jingle, with the objective of increasing the number of users who remember the brand name from 5 percent to 30 percent. A brand awareness survey, using either aided or unaided recall, can determine the campaign's success. The advertisement for British Columbia (Figure 11–6) falls into this category.

If the selected communication task is *knowledge of brand attributes*, the target audience may be all the users who are aware of the brand name. The type of campaign used may rely on product demonstration, repetition of the brand's main attributes, or a catchy jingle or slogan, for example, "When it rains, it pours" (Morton Salt), or "When you care enough to send the very best" (Hallmark cards). An appropriate test criterion for the campaign's success may be aided or unaided recall of copy. The advertisement shown in Figure 11–7 emphasizes knowledge of brand attributes.

If *brand liking* is the selected communication task, the target audience may be consumers who are aware of the brand and its main attributes. The type of campaign used may be competitive, with both argumentative copy and image building techniques like endorsements or group identification, in order to induce consumers to include the brand in their evoked set. Appropriate test criteria may be attitude or image changes from 15 percent to 25 percent, as well as evoked set identification. Brand liking is the main objective of the Heineken advertisement (Figure 11–8).

TABLE 11–1 SOME EXAMPLES OF RELATIONSHIPS AMONG TASK, TARGET AUDIENCE, TEST CRITERIA, AND TYPE OF CAMPAIGN

Related behavioural dimensions	Task of the communication	Example of primary target audience	Type of advertising campaign	Test criteria
Cognitive— the realm of thoughts	Awareness ↓	All users of product category	Attention-getting (teasers, slogan, jingle, humour)	Brand awareness (aided or unaided recall)
Ads provide information and facts	Knowledge ↓	Users aware of brand	Learning (repetition, description, demonstration)	Recall of copy
Affective— the realm of emotions	Liking ↓	Users aware of brand attributes	Competitive (argumentative, reason why, endorsements)	Attitudes or images; evoked set
Ads change attitudes and feelings	Preference ↓	Buyers of competive brands	Agressive (comparative, argumentative, status, testimonials)	Preference ranking
Conative— the realm of motives	Conviction ↓	Present buyers of the brand	Reminder (reinforcements, image, new uses)	Intention to purchase
Ads stimulate or direct desires	Purchase	Buyers of major brands	Value-oriented (specials, price deals, rebates, co-operative, direct-mail)	Sales figures (with proper control)

Source: Adapted from Robert J. Lavidge and Gary A. Steiner, "A Model for Predictive Measurement of Advertising Effectiveness," *Journal of Marketing* (October 1961), p. 61.

Courtesy American Marketing Association

If the selected communication task is *brand preference*, the target audience may be buyers of a competitor's brand. The type of campaign used may be aggressive, with comparative ads, argumentative copy, or the use of testimonials to confer status or glamour on the product. An appropriate test criterion is a measure of preference ranking to determine if improvements of preferences are taking place as a result of the campaign. The Dairy Bureau advertisement (Figure 11–9) attempts to develop consumers' preference for butter.

If *brand conviction* is the selected communication task, the primary target audience may be present buyers of the brand. The advertising campaign may be a reminder type of campaign, with a soft-sell approach to reinforce the brand image or to suggest new uses of the brand or new occasions to consume it. The appropriate test criterion may be changes in intention to purchase the brand. The advertisement in Figure 11–10 attempts to create brand conviction.

In a situation where there is proper control of other marketing elements, the selected behavioural task may be brand purchase. The type of advertising campaign used may be value-oriented and stress reduced prices, price deals, rebates, or use co-operative or direct mail advertising. Assuming proper con-

FIGURE 11–6

The object of this advertisement is to create awareness of British Columbia as a spring vacation spot, particularly among U.S. tourists.

Courtesy Tourism British Columbia

FIGURE 11–7

This advertisement uses an intriguing headline and illustration to demonstrate the fact that the Volvo is a safe car.

Courtesy Volvo Canada

trol of other marketing elements, the appropriate test criterion may be the changes in sales volume. The advertisement for Intellivison (Figure 11–11) calls for consumers to act immediately.

Specifying Test Criteria in Operational Terms

As was seen, the selection of test criteria is based on the communication task, i.e., on the campaign's intended effects on the target audience. To properly assess the effectiveness of the advertising campaign, both the present or pre-campaign levels of the test criteria *and* the desired or post-campaign levels of the test criteria must be stated.

In the example of Brand X milk-based drink, the test criterion was "unaided recall of Brand X." Before the campaign, unaided recall of Brand X was 10 percent of the target audience, and the campaign aimed at unaided recall of Brand X to be 50 percent at the end of the time horizon. Such benchmarks, which are related to the budget decision, provide advertisers with direction in designing the campaign and control over the campaign's effectiveness. If advertising is viewed as an investment—as part of the marketing effort—a realistic, quantified, and written goal may be considered an estimate of the return on that investment.

Effects of the Campaign on Other Behavioural Dimensions

Once a communication task has been selected and the campaign designed accordingly, the effects are felt at all levels of the hierarchy of effects model. An examination of these effects can help pinpoint weaknesses in the campaign. For example, an advertisement may be noticed but consumers may have difficulty remembering the brand name or cannot associate a brand name with the brand's main attributes.

FIGURE 11–8

This advertisement for Heineken uses very little copy because the product is already well-known to beer drinkers. The illustration and the copy suggest to the reader that Heineken should be part of their evoked set of brands.

Courtesy Amstel Brewery Canada Ltd.

"A Heineken: that's exactly what I had in mind!"

FIGURE 11–9

This advertisement attempts to develop a preference for butter instead of margarine by emphasizing butter's natural process and taste.

Courtesy Dairy Bureau of Canada

Butter is easy to make.

Imitations aren't.

MARGARINE

Naturally, the choice is up to you.

Nutrition Division, Dairy Bureau of Canada

A simplified example of how this type of analysis can help pinpoint problem areas and be used to design future campaigns is provided in Figure 11–12. The two campaigns both advertise the same product and have awareness as the major task of the campaign. Suppose both campaigns are equally effective in increasing brand awareness to 50 percent of all users of the product category. One possible weakness of A is in translating brand knowledge into brand liking, while for B, it is in the link between brand awareness and brand knowledge.

Avoiding Common Pitfalls of Campaign Planning

If developed properly, operational advertising objectives include the five Ts: the **T**arget audience(s), the **T**ask(s) of the communication, the **T**hemes(s) of the campaign, the **T**ime horizon, and the **T**est criteria to be used at the end of the time horizon to determine the effectiveness of the campaign.

Critical as they are, these ingredients are often ignored in practice. One study of 135 campaigns created by 40 agencies showed that almost none of these agencies really knew or could know if their campaigns were really successful. The most common pitfalls in stating the objectives and in relating the proof of success to the stated campaign objectives were:[8]

1. In the statement of objectives:
   a. failure to state them in quantifiable terms (99 percent);
   b. failure to recognize that, in most cases, a sales increase is not a proper advertising objective (24 percent);
   c. failure to identify the advertising audience (16 percent);
   d. use of superlatives, which are unmeasurable (2 percent).

This advertisement for the Royal Bank is attempting to convince the reader that it offers the best services. The Royal Bank is well-known to the public, so the emphasis is on its superior services.

Courtesy The Royal Bank of Canada

This newspaper advertisement for Intellivision uses an unusual layout to attract readers' attention. The offer of two cartridges is good only for two months, so quick action is required to take advantage of it.

Courtesy Mattel Canada Inc.

2. In relating the "proof of success" to the stated objectives:
   a. with awareness as objective, success was stated in terms of sales (68 percent)
   b. with a new image as objective, success was stated in terms of readership or inquiries (35 percent)
   c. with several objectives stated, success was mentioned only in relation to one of them (45 percent)

The failure to state the advertising objectives properly is related to a lack of understanding of the role of advertising in general and advertising objectives in particular. For example, the client's misconception that advertising alone will increase sales or market share may cause an agency to present a campaign and its result in these terms. This attitude is unfortunate, because if advertising does not "deliver" right away, the temptation is great to change agencies, switch campaigns, or cut the advertising budget. In all cases, the effects of that decision may spell more problems for the brand.

DEVELOPING THE ADVERTISING BUDGET

The advertising budget is a detailed plan specifying how the total amount of money allocated to advertising is to be spent within a planning period. The total sum to be spent on advertising within the same period is called the advertising *appropriation*. Thus, the budget decision includes the appropriation plus a scheme detailing how much is to be allocated to various media and other

FIGURE 11–12
*Analysis of Two
Alternative
Advertising
Campaigns*

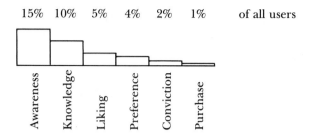

Before the campaign

15%   10%   5%   4%   2%   1%   of all users

Awareness Knowledge Liking Preference Conviction Purchase

After the campaign

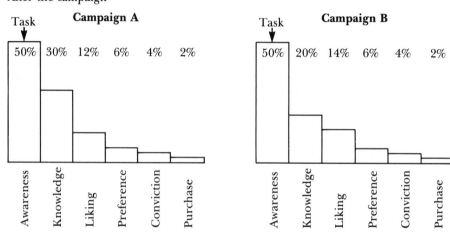

Task → **Campaign A**

50%   30%   12%   6%   4%   2%

Awareness Knowledge Liking Preference Conviction Purchase

Task → **Campaign B**

50%   20%   14%   6%   4%   2%

Awareness Knowledge Liking Preference Conviction Purchase

advertising functions, to sales territories, to different products, to different time periods, and so on.

It must be re-emphasized that all the major decisions are interrelated, and that the advertising budget is directly affected by decisions made on objectives, creative, media, and others. The planning process is an *iterative* process within the planning period and among successive periods. The involvement of senior managers, product managers, and advertising agency personnel is critical in order to maximize the effectiveness of these planning procedures.[9]

*Factors to
Consider in
Developing the
Advertising
Appropriation*

Before the methods for determining the appropriation are described, it is important to understand the conditions or constraints under which the appropriation is set. The two general types of constraints are external and internal.

External Constraints

Four factors related to a market situation affect the size of the advertising appropriation:

The Stage in the Product Life-Cycle. The amount of the advertising budget spent on a product varies with the stage in the product's life-cycle. A brand at the introductory or the growth stage requires more spending in relation to sales than a product at the maturity or decline stages (Chapter 2).

The Target Market.   The size and composition of the target market affects the size of the appropriation and allocation to sales territories and market segments. Canadian markets tend to be widely dispersed and heterogeneous, thus the pattern of population density and the multicultural nature of Canadian consumers present a great challenge to advertisers. Advertisers' solutions to this problem have included:

- regional or cultural campaigns, as in Quebec and Ontario, or in both French and English;
- phased product introduction, by market, region, or segment;
- use of such lower cost media as newspaper or radio;
- segmenting the market to obtain smaller homogeneous targets who can be reached by low cost media.

Competitors' Strategies.   Competitors' strategies should be taken into account when the advertising appropriation is determined. The same level of spending would not have the same effect if no one is advertising or if all major competitors are spending heavily on advertising. A small hamburger chain, for example, Harvey's, would be hard-pressed to match the $35 million in media space and time that McDonald's spent in 1989.[10] Such large, marketing-oriented companies as General Foods and Procter & Gamble often choose fragmented markets to introduce new products with heavy advertising spending, and often prefer television as the advertising medium. Small- and medium-sized companies emphasize other variables in the mix, like pricing, display, and service, or use other media like radio, billboards, or transit advertising.

Environmental Variables.   Environmental constraints may affect a company's ability to advertise. Poor economic conditions may force advertisers to cut their appropriations, as during a recession. Laws or voluntary self-regulation may force advertisers to avoid certain media, or to limit the extent of their advertising, like the Tobacco Products Control Act for cigarettes.[11] Cultural norms may prohibit or discourage the use of certain media for advertising such products as contraceptive devices or guns.

Internal Factors

The most important internal factors affecting the budget decision are the nature of the marketing mix and of the organization.

The Nature of the Marketing Mix.   All decisions concerning the marketing-mix variables affect the size of the appropriation. If the product concept is clearly differentiated from the competition, the size of the appropriation would be lower than if differentiation is to be created by the advertising campaign. The role of advertising within the *promotional mix* affects the size of the appropriation. It will be higher for a pull strategy than for a push strategy. With a pull strategy, the role of advertising is to build interest in the brand, so that consumers will recognize it in retail stores, especially in self-service stores. The relationship between price and the advertising appropriation must also be considered. Higher prices lead to higher *unit profit margins*, thus allowing higher advertising appropriation per unit. This is not true for the total profit, which depends on the level of price elasticity. A high level of brand loyalty decreases price elasticity, and a heavily advertised brand may command a higher price. Otherwise, a lower price may lead to higher profits and higher total appropriation. For example, in 1989 John Labatt spent $45 million, but the advertising cost per case was low. Therefore, the relationship between advertising appropriation and unit profit margins depends on the level of price elasticity of the target market.

The Nature of the Organization. Several organizational factors may affect the size of the appropriation. First, the size of the company and its financial strength will limit the amount to be spent in advertising. The objectives and organizational structure of the company and its style of management affect the decision on the degree of advertising support to be given to a new or an unsuccessful brand.[12] Some managers are willing to take some risks to ensure the success of a new brand, while others are more cautious and would tend to take conservative action. The degree of influence of the advertising agency, as well as the confidence of senior managers in the ability of the agency's account service group may also affect the size of the appropriation. The account executive can ascertain the relationship among advertising objectives, strategy, and budget and thus advise the advertiser on the amount to spend on the forthcoming campaign. The final determination of the appropriation may or may not be influenced by this recommendation, depending on the relationship between advertising and agency personnel.

Methods for Determining the Advertising Appropriation

Setting the advertising appropriation implies formal or intuitive knowledge of the relationship between the amount spent on advertising and its contribution to the advertising objectives. Traditionally, three types of methods are used to determine the advertising appropriation: naive methods, economic models, and objective and task methods.

Naive Methods

Several naive (simplistic) methods are used to set the advertising budget.

Affordable Budget. The method of the *affordable budget* is a rudimentary procedure and consists of spending any amount of advertising in excess of an acceptable profit margin. In a study conducted among a cross-section of Canadian companies, it was found that 20 percent used the affordable method.[13] A related method is the *arbitrary method*, and the amount spent is arbitrarily based on what is spent on a similar product or some other rationale. By these methods, a company would only by pure chance be spending the optimal amount. More likely, the company would be spending too little or too much. With an affordable budget, an increase in the appropriation may, in conjunction with the rest of the marketing mix, lead to higher profits to absorb the increased spending. With the arbitrary method, a company spends wastefully, "just in case advertising works."[14] In the same study, it was found that the arbitrary method was used by 10 percent of Canadian companies.[15]

Adjustment of Last Year's Budget.   Another naive method consists in making adjustments to what was spent last year using one of the above methods. Again, the rationale is to look at results achieved in terms of sales or market share, and decide to spend more or less with the expectation that sales will follow the direction of the advertising budget. About 25 percent of Canadian companies indicated that they used this method.[16]

Percentage of Sales Methods.   Some advertisers spend a certain percentage of past sales or of future sales on advertising, ignoring that, in theory, advertising should contribute to generating sales. This is a reverse approach, since sales determine the advertising expenditures. The main advantage of this method is its simplicity and its intuitive attractiveness to managers who think in terms of contribution to profits and not in terms of market demand. This method is similar to the cost-plus approach often used for pricing, instead of the more logical demand-based approach. Thus the method suffers from the same weaknesses, since the appropriation would be an optimal amount only by chance.

In highly turbulent markets, such a method can do considerable damage to a brand if past sales were at a peak or in a trough, or if sales forecasts were too optimistic or too pessimistic. In the same study, the method of percentage of future sales was used by 33 percent of Canadian companies. The corresponding figure for the method of percentage of past years' sales was 20 percent.[17]

Instead of using sales figures, another related method consists of setting the advertising appropriation as a percentage of past or future profits. This method magnifies the same drawbacks, since profits fluctuate more than sales.

Still another related method is setting a fixed sum per unit for advertising. For example, an appliance manufacturer would set eight dollars per refrigerator to be used for advertising and a brewery would set two dollars per case. The total appropriation would be obtained by multiplying the fixed sum per unit by the anticipated sales in units or cases. The problems with this method are the same as with the others, but it is often used for its intuitive appeal, particularly in dealing with distributors, for example, in co-operative advertising programs. In the same study, the method of unit anticipated sales was used by 11 percent of Canadian companies. The corresponding figure for the method of unit past years' sales was 10 percent.[18]

Competitive Relationship Methods.   Some advertisers determine the advertising appropriation by looking at the amount their competitors spend; they rely on the wisdom of the industry. What they are really doing is following the industry's collective ignorance, and they fail to take advantage of a weapon that could help them gain an advantage over competitors. In addition, competitors may vary widely in size, follow different promotional strategies, or even marketing strategies. For instance, can and/or should a small- or medium-sized firm match the amount spent by the largest competitor? The same study revealed that 3.3 percent of Canadian companies match what the competition spends, and another 1 percent spend an amount greater than the competition.

A variant of this method is to spend more than a firm's share of the market to maintain or improve market share. For new products, a company's share of advertising expenditure should be twice the projected market share.[19] The method does recognize that advertising expenditures precede sales and may be considered an investment in market share, if the rest of the marketing program is also effective. Nevertheless, companies should not use this rule of thumb unless all the other competitive factors are considered. About 10 percent of Canadian companies use this method.

Economic Models

An economic model for determining the advertising appropriation should take five elements into account (Figure 11–13).[20]

The first two elements characterizing the advertising expenditure-sales relationship are: the *marginal rate of advertising effectiveness* at various levels of advertising expenditure, which specifies the slope and curvature of the function; and the *market potential* (at a given time), because whatever the amount spent on advertising, sales cannot exceed this upper asymptotical limit. The relationship between advertising expenditures and sales is represented in the first diagram in Figure 11–13.

The importance of advertising carry-over effects should also be taken into account in determining the advertising budget.[21] Thus, a third element, the *carry-over effect rate* of an advertising dollar over subsequent periods, should be included as well as the *discount rate*, a fourth element that is used to discount the future income stream of the advertising investment at its present value. These two new elements are essential in establishing the relationship represented in the second diagram of Figure 11–13, which relates advertising to the resulting long-run sales flow estimated at its present value.

The fifth element that should be taken into account in a theoretical model for setting the advertising appropriation is the *gross margin rate* prevailing at various sales levels for the company considered. This leads to an estimate of the relationship in Figure 11–13 between advertising and gross contribution to profits. By subtracting the amounts invested in advertising (represented by the 45° line in the third diagram), from the gross contribution to profits, the fourth relationship can be derived. This is the relationship between advertising expenditures and net profits. This relationship has the highest significance for an advertiser, because it shows the optimal advertising expenditure level (B*) that should be selected to maximize the company's long-run net profits.

Limitations of the Economic Model.   Several strong assumptions are embedded in the economic model. One is that the shape of the advertising/sales relationship is not greatly affected by media-mix decisions and creative decisions. In reality, this is not the case. Another assumption is that this model does not explicitly take account of the interdependence between advertising and other marketing mix variables. For example, a change in price may affect

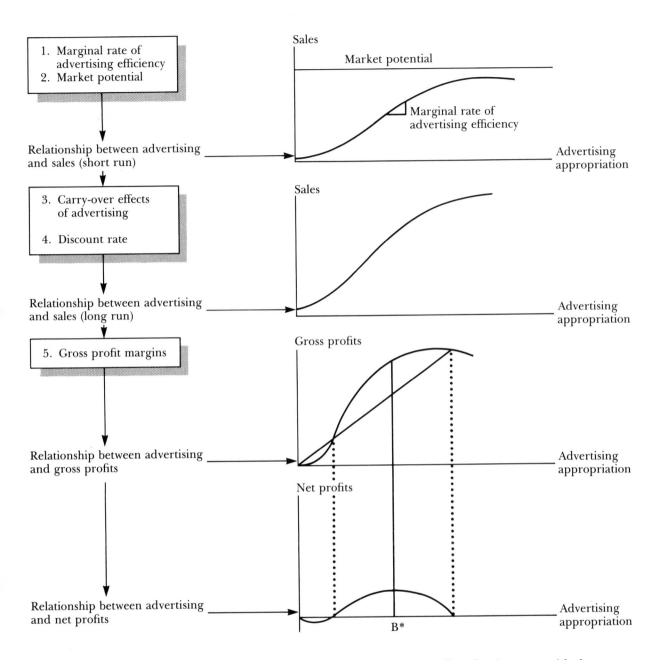

1. Marginal rate of advertising efficiency
2. Market potential

↓

Relationship between advertising and sales (short run)

Sales

Market potential

Marginal rate of advertising efficiency

Advertising appropriation

↓

3. Carry-over effects of advertising

4. Discount rate

↓

Relationship between advertising and sales (long run)

Sales

Advertising appropriation

↓

5. Gross profit margins

↓

Relationship between advertising and gross profits

Gross profits

Advertising appropriation

Net profits

↓

Relationship between advertising and net profits

B*

Advertising appropriation

FIGURE 11–13
A Theoretical Model for Determining the Advertising Appropriation

the market potential and have a carry-over effect that interacts with the carry-over effect of advertising. Also, the model does not explicitly incorporate the effect of competition on the overall advertising effort. Finally, when several products of the same company are advertised, the model does not explicitly take into account the joint effect of advertising across all products. Nevertheless, despite these drawbacks, there are numerous practical approaches for determining the appropriation using the economic model.

Some Practical Approaches Using the Economic Model. Several attempts have been made to include many or all of the various elements in a practical method for determining the optimal advertising appropriation. Examples are the method proposed by Vidale and Wolfe,[22] the DEMON model[23] used by the BBD&O (U.S.) advertising agency to estimate the advertising budgets at the introduction of new consumer products, and the adaptive control method.[24] All these methods share a common characteristic: they attempt to measure all or part of the relationship between advertising expenditures and sales in order to derive the optimal advertising appropriation. These procedures and models require a sophisticated level of mathematical training in order to be fully understood. In the Canadian study, econometric models were found to be used by 6.5 percent of companies. About 4 percent of Canadian companies indicated that they used other quantitative methods.[25]

Objective and Task Method

As was emphasized earlier, an advertising campaign should contribute to the realization of precise marketing objectives, which in turn help realize a company's general objectives, given the marketing manager's predictions about environmental variables. From these objectives, an advertising manager derives the means necessary to meet them. These means include the advertising message content and format and the media selected to convey the message to the relevant market segments. Decisions about the structure and format of the message depend on the media selected and are guided by a *communication model*, such as the hierarchy of effects model, and by the selected *communication task* indicated in the advertising objectives. This process is represented in Figure 11–14. These advertising tools involve costs that indicate the size of the budget needed to meet the advertising objectives.

This method of determining an advertising budget is known as the *objective and task method*. For an advertising campaign to be effective and profitable, advertisers should select objectives so that costs warrant their pursuit. This is why it is always necessary to reassess the objectives in the light of costs whenever a harmonious equilibrium has not been reached between expected returns and costs. This is represented in Figure 11–14 by the feedback loop from approval of budget to the campaign objectives.

Procedures to measure an advertising campaign's effectiveness are typically designed to control the whole advertising process. From such an evaluation, the advertising strategy can be reassessed for the following period (year), because market penetration, the level of consumer awareness, or consumer attitudes achieved at the end of the current campaign can then be measured. This is represented in Figure 11–14 by the feedback loop from campaign evaluation to advertising strategy.

The objective and task method is a logical method that allows advertisers to start from desired objectives and to follow a logical procedure. Its greatest strength is that efforts are made to determine the level of advertising appropriation that can best attain advertising objectives. It also forces advertisers to

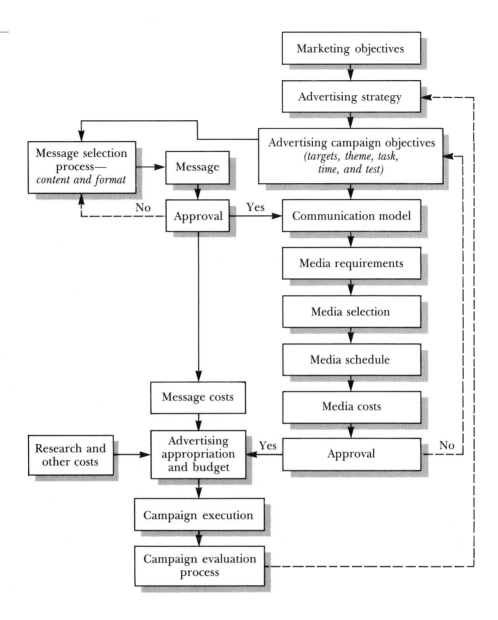

FIGURE 11–14
Objective and Task Method for Setting the Advertising Appropriation

think through the whole process and acquire experience and competence in carrying out this difficult but rewarding process. An advertiser would be less likely to concur with John Wanamaker's statement that about 50 percent of his advertising budget is wasted, but he doesn't know which half! The same study found that 40 percent of Canadian companies used the objective and task method.[26]

When asked how he advises clients on budgeting effectively, Peter Swain, president of Media Buying Services in Toronto, reported:

Our methods vary with advertisers. The ideal circumstance is to work on a task method: define the objectives for a given point in the campaign, then determine the necessary budget.

Our primary concern should be to determine the needs. The more exactly we can pinpoint . . . needs and objectives, the more effectively we can use the budget to fulfill those objectives. When inflation takes a bigger chunk of our budget dollars, we may have to downscale objectives or decrease spending.

Hopefully . . ., we will see a lot more advertising research on the advertiser's part. That's necessary because if we can predict effectively the value of the shift produced by advertising, we can judge whether increasing media costs are worthwhile. I suspect if we took this approach, we'd see that some of the increase in costs is quite reasonable.[27]

Objective and Task Method and Payout Planning. With promising products, it may be advisable to plan the marketing and advertising effort over three years. The advertising effort would be higher in the earlier years, when awareness for the product has to be built, than in later years when preference would be the task. Since media costs are often higher in the earlier years, it may be better to invest in advertising early in a product's life cycle in order to improve the new product's chances of success.

The objective and task method may be used to estimate the advertising appropriation for each year of the three-year plan. The campaign objectives are set in terms of a communication model, and the criteria for approving the media costs are based on the long-term marketing objectives. If the estimated costs are still too high, a reassessment may have to be made of the campaign objectives.

A hypothetical example of a three-year payout based on the objective and task method is provided in Table 11–2. In the first year, the task of the campaign is to increase awareness of the brand name from 10 percent to 50 percent. Based on the target market and the type of approach to be used, several media are selected. The total appropriation is then estimated to be

TABLE 11–2 **A HYPOTHETICAL EXAMPLE OF A THREE-YEAR PAYOUT PLAN**

Year	Projected sales ($)	Market share	Price ($)	Distribution coverage	Communication task	Advertising appropriation ($)	Share of three-year advertising budget	A/S
1	5 000 000	10%	50	10%	50% awareness from 10%	2 100 000	42%	42
2	9 000 000	15%	45	30%	60% knowledge from 20%	1 600 000	32%	18
3	14 000 000	25%	35	60%	40% preference from 20%	1 300 000	26%	9
Total	28 000 000					5 000 000	100%	

$2 100 000. The total appropriation for the three-year period is thus estimated at about $5 million for projected sales of $28 million. Of that amount, 42 percent is spent the first year; 32 percent and 25 percent the second and third year, respectively. The effect of such a spending pattern is to strongly support the brand when it needs it most, and to improve its chances of becoming a leading brand in its product category. It represents an investment in market share and in long-term profits.

Allocation of the Appropriation: The Advertising Budget

In the process of developing the appropriation, some consideration may or may not have been given to how it is to be spent. The advertising budget must, however, provide this information, including allocations by advertising function, by medium and time period (schedule), by sales territory, and by product.

By Advertising Function

The appropriation must cover all advertising activities, and allocations must be made for four categories of expenses. These are as follows:

1. Total media allocation used to buy time or space in various media. These costs are roughly 70 to 90 percent of the appropriation.
2. Message production costs, which may be up to 15 percent or 20 percent of the appropriation.
3. Research costs when research is used at any point in the development of the campaign (consumer, media, copy, and effectiveness research). These costs vary from zero to 15 percent of the appropriation.
4. Administrative overhead costs, including contingencies.

By Medium and Time Period (Schedule)

Decisions must be made on the allocation of total media expenditures to the various *media types*—newspaper, magazine, radio, television, direct mail, and other media. For instance, an advertiser may allocate 30 percent of the media budget to magazines, 20 percent to radio, and 50 percent to television. With each type of medium, allocation of expenditures is made according to media vehicles, which are the individual magazines or newspapers, television or radio stations, and the television shows during which the commercials will be broadcast. A media budget for magazines can be split equally among three vehicles, i.e., *Chatelaine*, *Homemaker's*, and *Reader's Digest*. (See Chapter 14.)

The *media schedule* is worked out for each media vehicle. This schedule provides all the details about the issues of the magazines or newspapers, the days, and the time of the day at which each advertisement will appear or will be broadcast. The schedule also gives indications about the *media options* (the number of colours for print advertisements, the size of the advertisement or length of the commercial, the position of the advertisement in the vehicle).

By Sales Territory

This task complements the previous one, since this allocation represents another breakdown of the total media budget. It concerns the disparities among sales territories in terms of penetration, sales potential, message appropriateness, and media availability. For example, how do you allocate the media budget according to the French and English markets in Montreal; the English, Italian, and French markets in Toronto; the English markets in Vancouver, Toronto, and Halifax? This allocation must answer such questions as sales potential, how well a brand is doing, how effective the message is to each group, and availability of media and differences in viewing patterns.

By Product

When an advertising appropriation has been developed for a whole line of products, the budget must specify the amount allocated to each product in the line. Three types of allocation are possible:

1. A *proportional* allocation is made according to the share of each item in the total dollar volume of the line. New additions to the line may receive little advertising support other than the promotional value of the family name. An often used method is a small display of two or three low-selling items (receiving a small allocation) within the advertisement for the best-selling item.
2. A *concentrated* allocation is made to the best sellers in the line, in the hopes that increased spending on these items will create more goodwill toward the family name that will carry over to the items.
3. An *unbalanced* allocation is made in favour of low-selling items with good potential. Some advertising support is withdrawn from the best sellers for new items with fast growth potential. This is equivalent to the investment spending method used with the objective and task method.

SUMMARY

Planning, executing, and controlling an advertising campaign involves a six-step approach: develop the fact book; develop the marketing plan; develop a preliminary advertising plan; complete and approve the advertising plan; execute the campaign; evaluate the campaign's effects.

Within this process, two critical and interrelated tasks are undertaken: setting the objectives of the advertising campaign, and developing the advertising appropriation and budget. These are difficult tasks, but they are essential steps in planning, executing, and controlling the advertising function. If its existence is not properly justified, advertising is bound to suffer in times of economic slowdown.

Precise and operational advertising objectives must specify five ingredients (the five Ts): the **T**arget audience, the **T**heme of the campaign, the **T**ask of the communication over the **T**ime horizon, and the **T**est criteria for determining the effectiveness of the campaign.

The advertising budget includes the total appropriation as well as the exact allocation of the appropriation. Methods for determining the appropriation include naive methods, economic models, and objective and task methods. Allocation of the appropriation may be made according to advertising functions, media, time periods, sales territories, and products.

Decisions on the advertising objectives and budget are difficult ones for most situations. Since they are closely related to each other and to the creative and media decisions, it is important that these two tasks be done properly. It may take several iterations between objectives and budget to arrive at a satisfactory set of decisions, but the overall campaign will be more consistent and effective. The client and the agency service group will gain useful insights that will make future campaign planning more efficient.

QUESTIONS FOR STUDY

1. "My only concern is whether or not I will sell more if I advertise." Comment.

2. Find some examples of print advertisements for each of the communications tasks in Table 11–1. Justify your choices.

3. Is it reasonable to expect advertisers or agencies to be able to state precise and operational objectives? If this is not done, who is most likely to be affected? Explain your answer.

4. Relate the following fictitious slogans to the hierarchy of effects model of Table 11–1. Justify your choice.
   a. "The best ice cream in all of creation"
   b. "The newest show on earth" (an amusement park)
   c. "Help that counts" (personal computers)
   d. "Mr. Salad's best friend" (dressing)
   e. "Be at your best" (designer clothes)

5. Discuss under what conditions the percentage of sales methods may be a reasonable method for determining the size of the appropriation. What are the major risks in relying on it?

6. "Your share of advertising dollars should be equal or greater than your share of the market." Comment.

7. "The objective and task method is much too difficult for most advertisers or agencies to use." Do you agree with this statement?

8. Does it make sense to spend a much larger proportion of the appropriation on one or two items in a product line, rather than on the rest of the line? Explain.

9. "You cannot properly plan advertising expenditures because you never know how the market will respond to the creative approach of the campaign." Do you agree with this statement? Explain your answer.

10. "Advertising objectives must be stated in operational terms in order to plan the campaign effectively." Do you agree with this statement? Explain what form the statement of advertising objectives should take, and how they affect the other campaign decisions, i.e., creative, media, budget, and research.

PROBLEMS

1. Select a product with a low awareness level, and develop some advertising objectives and an advertising appropriation. Assume that your market is situated in an urban area, and that radio would be the best medium for that product. Indicate *all* the steps you would go through using the objective and task method for the appropriation. Indicate also *all* the information you would need to complete this job.

2. By using the data in the Surelock Homes case, develop an advertising appropriation using all the naive methods and the objective and task method. Make sure that you are documenting all calculations.

NOTES

1. Kenneth E. Bowes, "Develop Marketing Plan, with or without Agency, Before Trying to Devise Ad Budget," *Marketing News*, March 18, 1983, Section 2, p. 17.
2. Stanley E. Stasch and Patricia Lanktree, "Can Your Marketing Planning Procedures be Improved," *Journal of Marketing* (Summer 1980), pp. 79–90.
3. Deborah J. Nicholls and John P. Liefeld, "The Price (Brand)-Perceived Quality Relationship: Further Evidence," *The Canadian Marketer* (Fall 1973), pp. 21–24; see also Thomas E. Muller, "Price Awareness in the Supermarket," *Marketing*, ed. James D. Forbes, vol. 4 (Administrative Sciences Association of Canada, 1983), pp. 238–46.
4. Russell H. Colley, *Defining Advertising Goals for Measured Advertising Results* (New York: Association of National Advertisers, 1961).
5. Ibid; see also Stuart H. Britt, "Are So-Called Successful Advertising Campaigns Really Successful," *Marketing Management and Administrative Action*, ed. S.H. Britt and H.W. Boyd, Jr., 3rd ed. (New York: McGraw-Hill, 1973), pp. 553–64.
6. G.H.G. McDougall, "Canadian Theme Appeals in Advertising," *Marketing 1978*, ed. J.M. Boisvert and R. Savitt (Administrative Sciences Association of Canada, 1978), pp. 178–88.
7. "Grenadier Chocolate Company Limited," *Canadian Problems in Marketing*, eds. B. Little, J.R. Kennedy, D.H. Thain, and R.E.M. Nourse, 4th ed. (Toronto: McGraw-Hill Ryerson, 1978), pp. 501–7.
8. Britt, p. 562.
9. Stasch and Lanktree, pp. 79–90.
10. "Ad cutback not what it seems," *Marketing*, March 26, 1990, p. 2.
11. James G. Barnes, "Advertising and the Courts," *Canadian Business Review* (Autumn 1975), pp. 51–54.
12. Lionel A. Mitchell and Peter M. Banting, "Organization Structure and Factors Influencing Advertising Activities," *Marketing*, ed. James D. Forbes, Vol. 4 (Administrative Sciences Association of Canada, 1983), pp. 220–29.
13. Lionel A. Mitchell, "Common Approaches to Budgeting Advertising: The Wheel of Advertising," *Developments in Canadian Marketing*, ed. Robert D. Tamilia (Administrative Sciences Association of Canada, 1978), pp. 30–31.
14. André J. San Augustine and William F. Foley, "How Large Advertisers Set Budgets," *Journal of Advertising Research* (October 1975), pp. 11–16; "The Mackenzie Salt Company," *Canadian Problems in Marketing*, ibid., pp. 320–26.
15. "The Langton Company," *Canadian Problems in Marketing*, ibid., pp. 318–20.
16. Louis Desjardins and Michel Laroche, "A Study of Current Advertising Budgeting Practices of Cana-

dian Advertisers and Agencies," Working paper #88–014, Concordia University.

17. Ibid.

18. Ibid.

19. Ibid.

20. James O. Peckham, "Can We Relate Advertising Dollars to Market Share Objectives?", *How Much to Spend for Advertising?*, ed. Malcolm A. McNiven (New York: Association of National Advertisers, 1969), p. 30.

21. Kenneth A. Longman, *Advertising* (New York: Harcourt Brace Jovanovich, 1971), p. 18; for threshold effects, see F.W.A. Bliemel, "Are Thresholds of Advertising Response Substantial," *Linking Knowledge and Action*, vol. 4, ed. James D. Forbes (Administrative Sciences Association of Canada, 1983) pp. 1–10; "Advertising Thresholds in Canadian Markets: A Cross-sectional Analysis of Management Estimates," *Management Education: Its Place in the Community*, vol. 5, ed. Sheila Brown (ASAC, 1984), pp. 31–40.

22. M.L. Vidale and H.B. Wolfe, "An Operations-Research Study of Sales Response to Advertising," *Operations Research* (June 1957), pp. 370–80.

23. David B. Learner, "Profit Maximization Through New Product Marketing Planning and Control," *Applications of the Sciences to Marketing Management*, ed. Frank M. Bass, Charles W. King, and Edgar A. Pessemier (New York: John Wiley and Sons, 1968), pp. 151–67.

24. John D.C. Little, "A Model of Adaptive Control of Promotional Spending," *Operations Research* (November 1966), pp. 1075–97.

25. Desjardins and Laroche, op. cit.

26. Ibid.

27. Michael Hallé, "Computers Can Help Agencies Save Costs, Increase Efficiency," *Marketing*, February 25, 1980.

CHAPTER

12 Developing a Creative Plan

After the advertising appropriation decision, the next important aspect of planning an advertising campaign is the development of the creative strategy and plan. The creative plan addresses the problem of translating the communication task specified in the campaign objectives into effective advertisements using specific themes and slogans for the campaign. The planning process of an advertising campaign, and the creative and media plans should be developed at about the same time. It is nearly impossible for an agency's account executive or an art director to determine the advertising message content and format unless they know what type of media will be used. The design of a 30-second TV commercial has quite different considerations and constraints than a four-colour full-page advertisement in a national magazine. Consequently, the creative people should be informed of media decisions as soon as possible.

In the same way, the content of the message has obvious media implications. For instance, if product demonstration is an important ingredient in the advertising creative plan, television would almost certainly be used. High-quality image advertising is best conveyed by four-colour advertisements in prestige national magazines.

This chapter describes how advertisers can develop effective advertising messages.

THE ADVERTISING CREATIVE PROCESS

Advertising Message Creation

Developing the creative plan implies the steps listed in Figure 12–1. The whole creative process must start with an understanding of potential consumer behaviour and consumers' motives, knowledge, perceptions, attitudes, and buying habits with respect to the advertised product category. Then advertisers should select the advertising message content. This set of decisions is aimed at determining *what* should be said to potential buyers to induce them to purchase the advertised brand. The next set of decisions attempts to answer *how* the message should be put to woo potential buyers in the most effective way. Once these decisions on the structure and format of the advertising message are resolved, the television or radio commercials or print advertisements are produced.

The task of deciding what to say is essentially the responsibility of the account executive, who is assisted by the agency's creative department, marketing executives, and research people working for the agency or the client. The decisions about the message structure and format—the words, images, and sounds used to convey the message—are the responsibility of the agency's creative department.

FIGURE 12–1
Developing the Creative Plan

1. Understanding of potential buyer behaviour with respect to product category and brands:
   • motives, needs, benefits
   • attitudes
   • perception, knowledge
   • buying habits

↓

2. Message content decisions: *What* should be said to potential buyers to motivate them to buy the brand?

↓

3. Message structure and format decisions: *How* should be said to be as effective as possible?

↓

4. Advertising message production:
   • print advertisements
   • radio commercials
   • TV commercials

Creativity in Advertising

One of the simplest definitions of creativity is "the ability to formulate new combinations from two or more concepts already in the mind."[1] Although this definition may seem simple, the act of creating never is. Advertising creation is generally the result of hard work, sweat, and persistence. Advertising creative people who get inspired ideas that turn out to be great ideas is part of Madison Avenue folklore and bears little resemblance to reality.

What is needed to create a good and effective advertisement? Two ingredients are essential: people who are truly creative, and a creative process that involves a method and discipline. Various studies have tried to identify the common characteristics of highly creative people.[2] Such characteristics are that creative people share a boundless curiosity. They are interested in practically every aspect of life, read a lot, and want to understand everything. They also are imaginative and capable of conceptual fluency; they can generate many original ideas within a short period of time. They are empathetic, that is, able to feel what others are feeling. Their sense of humour is better than average, they tend to be more enthusiastic and less authoritarian than others, and they generally show a high degree of independence of judgment. People with this mix of qualities are a necessary but not sufficient ingredient for designing successful advertisements.

The Creative Process

The other prerequisite to successful advertising design is method and discipline in the creative process. Authors do not agree on the role and/or mechanisms of the creative process. Some describe the process of generating original ideas as one in which "talent plays a leading part in that which is known as association of ideas";[3] "the most [that] can honestly be said is that it usually includes some or all of these phases: orientation, preparation, analysis, hypothesis, incubation, synthesis, and verification."[4] Others see the creation process as being "as definite as the production of Fords."[5] The truth lies between these two extreme points of view. There are certain steps that promote the creative process. Frank Alexander Armstrong describes five steps: assessing the situation, defining the problem, using the subconscious, holding an idea-producing session, and using judgment in selecting ideas.[6]

Assessing the Situation

The creative process should start with a clear understanding of the problem, the goals to be attained, and all the relevant facts. In an advertising context, a clear understanding of the marketing objectives, the market situation, the marketing strategy, and the brand's marketing mix is the starting point for designing an advertisement. Susan Kastner, vice president and creative director at the Benton and Bowles advertising agency in Toronto, thinks that in order to create more effectively, the part of the marketing process that should be worked at hardest is "definitely the preparation for the creative, the planning, getting the marketing scene cold and clear."[7] To illustrate the point, Susan Kastner gives the example of Procter & Gamble, her agency's largest client: "When you have your marketing data and your strategy, then you can feed them into your creative."[8]

Defining the Problem

In this phase of the creative process, the problem is clearly understood and defined. It is practically impossible to solve a vaguely defined problem. In an advertising context, identification of the marketing and advertising objectives that specific advertisements should contribute to achieve, as well as the main constraints, are the second step to perform.

Using the Subconscious

Creative people involved in the design of an advertisement should give the subconscious time to work on the problem. Working in a rush and under severe time pressure may prevent this step from taking place.

The Idea-Producing Session

Once the subconscious has had time to work, the conscious mind can be put back to work to produce ideas. This can be done in a systematic way, either by an individual or in group sessions, known as brainstorming sessions.[9] The procedure is usually to gather a group of five to ten people. The problem is stated to the group, and each participant generates as many ideas as possible in a freewheeling discussion. At this stage, no criticisms are made, and all ideas, even the wildest, are encouraged, recorded, and considered.

Selecting the Best Idea

Once a large number of ideas have been generated, the best one is identified. The probability of finding a good idea out of a pool of ideas is greater when one starts with a large pool. All kinds of input are considered in order to find and refine ideas to arrive at the best possible selling advertisement or commercial.

Although the creative process depends on the individual talents of the creative staff, research plays an important role. This is also recognized by Susan Kastner, who asserts that to create more effective advertisements, research should be used "every step of the way. Research, to know your market, to discover how consumers view your product. Research during the making of the commercial to ensure the message is being produced more effectively, and research the ad after production to make sure you continue to say the right thing . . . Research is absolutely indispensable."[10]

The Advertising Creation Budget

The ideas generated during the creative process are tried out and pretested on consumers. When many ideas are generated and many advertisements created and tested, the odds increase that the idea chosen is a very good one. But as an agency spends more time and resources to create and test alternate advertisements, costs also increase. Thus a compromise must be reached on the number of advertisements an advertising agency should create for its clients. The problem with advertising creation is that advertising agencies may lack the motivation to create the optimal number of advertisements. Indeed, it has often been said that expenditures on advertising creation are probably too small in comparison with media expenditures. Two reasons may account for this. One is that many advertising managers do not see advertising creating expenditures as yielding concrete results. The quality of advertisements may be improved, but how can message quality be measured? In contrast, money spent on the media can buy more advertisements or more time for the advertiser. Right or wrong, the latter often seem to be more concrete and profitable expenses to an advertising manager. The second reason can be found in the compensation structure of advertising agencies. When an agency is compensated with a 15 percent commission on media billings, the creation costs are supported by the agency. At present, the costs of creating and pretesting advertisements typically run around 5 percent of the advertising budget.

This problem has been analyzed in a study which showed that agencies generally create too few advertisements for pretesting.[11] Advertisers thus do not necessarily get a good advertisement, but only the best out of the small number of advertisements created. It concluded that agencies should devote more of the advertising appropriation to creating more advertisements, at the expense of the media budget. As much as three to five times more than what is presently spent (i.e., at least 15 percent of the advertising budget) should be allocated to advertising creation. These conclusions suggest that advertising creation—although it is often recognized a critical part of the advertising process—may not get its fair share of the advertising dollar.

Decisions about the advertising message content are influenced the most by the marketing and advertising objectives. For instance, when an advertiser decides to convince new buyers of a product category that the advertised brand is superior in a certain respect, this sets the stage for the type of message content that should be used. The type of product being advertised also gives more or less flexibility as to what can be said. For instance, a music lover's choice of a specific brand of stereo equipment may be influenced by the quality of sound, the power, the physical appearance, and the controls available. Each points at a possible advertising appeal. The list of possible advertising claims, however, becomes more limited when it comes to advertising a specific brand of gin, for instance. Advertising agencies develop specific creative styles and approaches that dictate the kind of advertising message content to be created and produced.

Advertising approaches can be classified according to the situation and considerations involved.[12] One convenient classification is based on the nature of the appeal, whether the advertising is argumentative or suggestive. Although the border between these two types of advertising may be difficult to draw with precision, it is nevertheless convenient. *Argumentative advertisements* give specific and explicit reasons for buying a product and a particular brand.[13] The selling argument can be based on rational grounds, but this definition does not preclude the selling argument from arousing such emotions as pleasure or fear. The distinctive feature of this type of advertising is that it explicitly uses arguments to sell the product or service.[14] *Suggestive advertising* does not explicitly state any rationale for buying the product or brand.[15] It appeals directly to consumers' emotions and feelings and conveys a certain product or brand image.

Argumentative Advertising

Argumentative advertising may be approached in one of three ways: according to the target group to be reached, consumers' underlying motivations, or the unique selling proposition.

The Target Group Approach

This approach uses as a basic advertising appeal the specification of the consumer group to which the product or service is intended. A well-known example of this type of advertisement is Pepsi-Cola's claim: "For Those Who Think Young." Other examples are advertisements which identify the brand with target groups with certain needs such as the Kodak copier advertisement (Figure 12–2): "People who rely on copying for a living." Here the advertiser is attempting to have consumers associate the brand with a specific target audience profile: people who are striving for excellence. Some advertisers have criticized the target group approach as dogmatic,[16] since in general it gives little or no justification of the brand's appropriateness for the targeted group of consumers. In Pepsi's advertisement, no justification can be found as to why people who think young are likely to prefer Pepsi-Cola. In the Kodak

example, this is tempered by the implicit endorsement from the professionals
(Kwik Kopy).

However, the target audience approach has often been effective, especially
when it associates a product or brand with a certain reference group. For
instance, the association between beer and sports fans has been a favourite
theme of the Canadian beer industry; it attempts to associate beer drinking
with a certain lifestyle. All those who are—or like thinking of themselves as—
sports fans may develop a favourable attitude toward the brand, which becomes
an additional symbol of what they are or would like to be associated with.

This approach, however, has major limitations. Some advertisers argue
that associating a brand with its target group may be a desirable marketing
objective but a poor advertising theme.[17] The argument is that there is no
motivating element in the statement of the company's marketing objectives
that may induce consumers to actually buy the brand. This approach also does
not differentiate the advertised brand from its competitors, who can make the
same claim. This is why many advertisers would favour the motivation or the
differential product advantage approaches.

The Motivation Approach

The motivation approach is more commonly used since it provides a framework that is useful for many situations or product categories. This approach
has two major steps.[18] The first is the selection of some basic psychological
element of buyer behaviour involved in the purchase of the specific product

and brand. This element may be a specific benefit, a motivation, or even an inhibition that prevents some consumers from buying the brand or the product category. This psychological element will then be the prime target of the advertisement. Starting from this *abstract* definition and specification of the psychological element, an advertiser will then try to find the *concrete* elements that can best arouse or evoke in consumers' minds the selected satisfaction or motivation. The second stage of the selection process leads to the choice of a specific theme for the advertisement and/or the whole advertising campaign. It specifies the content of the advertising message.

Selection of the Basic Motive. To illustrate the process of selecting the best possible psychological element of the consumer purchase decision that advertising can influence, Lewin's theory briefly outlined in Chapter 8 can be used. It will be recalled that consumers are subjected to various forces or motives related to the purchase of a certain product and/or brand. The forces that induce the consumer to buy the brand are motives with a positive valence. Others tend to prevent a consumer from purchasing the product, and these are motives with a negative valence. Hence, any purchase decision can be viewed as a situation of conflict that involves motives with both positive and negative valences. No purchase decision can occur as long as the negative forces override the positive ones. Moreover, the number and strength of the positive and negative forces implied in a purchase decision create psychological tension for the consumer.

Examples of Non-Purchase Situations. Consider two examples of a purchase situation. One involves great financial risk and psychological tension and consequently, high consumer ego-involvement, such as the purchase of a microwave oven. The other situation involves the purchase of a product characterized by lesser tension and consumer ego-involvement, such as the selection of a brand of automatic dishwashing detergent.

With the microwave oven purchase, consumers may be submitted to forces or motives that induce them to buy the product, for instance, the time saved by fast cooking, especially for households in which both spouses work outside the home, and the convenience of quick defrosting of frozen food. Other positive motives might include a consumer's pride in possessing up-to-date appliances (social motives) or the pleasure of having a well-equipped and modern kitchen. Other factors prevent many households from indulging in the purchase of a microwave oven, for instance, the relatively high price of this equipment, the health hazards that may result from exposure to microwaves, or the fact that these ovens sometimes cook food unevenly. In some households, limited kitchen space or a relatively limited range of usage occasions may also be constraining factors. Figure 12–3a represents this conflictual situation, which often results in a non-purchase situation.

Alternatively, let us consider the psychological elements involved in purchasing an automatic dishwashing detergent. Because fewer financial and psychological risks are involved and the product is purchased more frequently, fewer negative forces with less strength are involved. Thus, the relative price

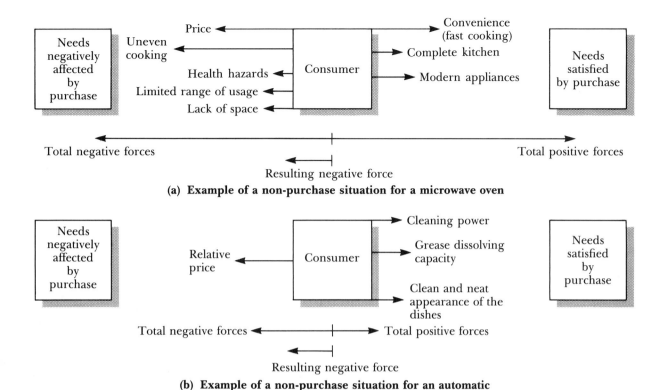

(a) **Example of a non-purchase situation for a microwave oven**

(b) **Example of a non-purchase situation for an automatic dishwashing detergent brand**

FIGURE 12–3

Examples of Two Non-Purchase Situations

for this brand may be the main negative valence force. However, among the positive motivations, which may induce the consumers to buy the brand, one may find for instance the cleaning power of the detergent, its capacity to dissolve grease and perhaps its ability to give spot-free cookware. This situation is depicted in Figure 12–3b. In this example, the decision is a non-purchase situation because the negative motives result in stronger forces than the positive ones.

Possible Advertising Actions. What can advertisers do to change a non-purchase situation? The advertiser can pursue three different types of action (as well as any combination of these three actions simultaneously) that start from a given non-purchase situation (Figure 12–4a).

An advertiser may try to increase satisfaction to a point at which the resulting force would change direction, i.e., where the consumer would lean toward a purchase decision (Figure 12–4b). This is what has been attempted in the advertisement for Smith Corona (Figure 12–5). By highlighting the large number of features of this typewriter, the advertiser has tried to increase the consumer's satisfaction of the good result obtained through brand usage and to induce the consumers to buy a Smith Corona typewriter.

The advertiser may bring a new satisfaction into the picture, i.e., a motive that was not felt before by the consumer with regard to this type of product

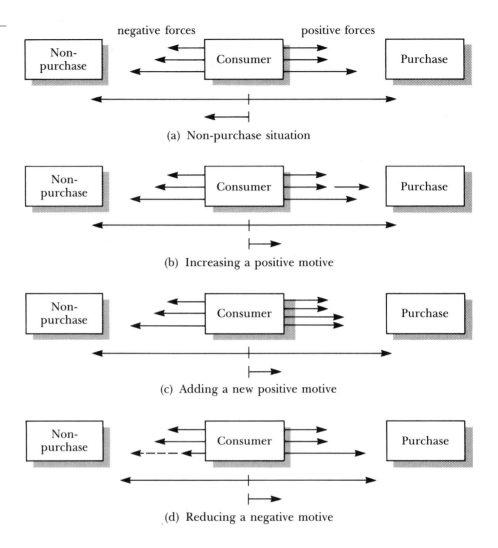

FIGURE 12–4
Possible Advertising Actions

(a) Non-purchase situation

(b) Increasing a positive motive

(c) Adding a new positive motive

(d) Reducing a negative motive

(Figure 12–4c). For instance, advertising featuring a toy added in a package of cereal tries to add extra satisfaction that could induce a child to insist on buying a certain brand. As an example, this approach is used in a more subtle way in the Neutrogena advertisement (Figure 12–6): The promise is to give Neutrogena cleanliness in addition to the mildness of a facial cleansing cream.

Finally, in order to achieve the same results an advertiser could choose to suppress (or reduce) a negative valence motive which prevents the purchase decision from taking place (Figure 12–4d). For instance, in the case of the microwave oven, the advertiser could select to suppress or reduce one of the major constraining forces, such as the uneven cooking argument. This is the approach followed by the Saran Wrap advertisement (Figure 12–7) which demonstrates how the Saran Wrap will behave in comparison with "cheap wraps."

PLATE I

All the elements of this
advertisement as well
as the selected colours
convey a luxurious
atmosphere for this
brand.

Courtesy Jaguar
Canada Inc.

V12 POWER. CONTINENTAL FLAIR.

THE JAGUAR XJ·S CONVERTIBLE

Whether its electronically-controlled roof is in place or retracted, this Jaguar is pure motoring elegance for all seasons. Aesthetically and aerodynamically, the XJ-S Convertible symbolizes Jaguar's dedication to the pursuit of automotive perfection.

Beneath its seductively graceful hood resides a power plant that is the evolutionary result of over 20 years of V12 engineering and racing refinement. It is Jaguar's 5.3 litre, fuel-injected, 12-cylinder May head engine. It is powerful.

whisper quiet, and dependably responsive.

Jaguar engineered, road and race-proven handling systems include power-assisted rack and pinion steering, an advanced anti-lock braking system, and fully independent fore and aft suspensions, with anti-dive geometry, to provide longitudinal stability under heavy braking conditions. You can unleash the power of this cat—confident that you will never relinquish the tether.

The driver and passenger compartment is

a synthesis of Jaguar virtues. Classic Jaguar instrumentation is clear and easy to read at a glance. In seating and in positioning of controls and gauges, attention to ergonomics is immediately evident. Lustrous, burl walnut veneers, supple Connolly leathers, and a veritable host of electronic amenities assure your complete motoring comfort.

All new Jaguars are protected by an exclusive Club Jaguar membership, which includes no-cost scheduled main-

tenance, 24-hour emergency service, and other valuable benefits for the full three-year or 60,000 km warranty period.

Whether you choose the XJ-S Convertible or the inimitable XJ-S Sports Coupe, you are assured of unique elegance and stirring performance. For more information, contact your nearest Jaguar dealer or send your business card to Jaguar Canada Inc., Communication Services, Indell Lane, Bramalea, Ontario L6T 4H3.

JAGUAR

A BLENDING OF ART AND MACHINE.

PLATE II

The illustration of the
Via advertisement
conveys the idea of
friendliness and a
social event in a relaxed
atmosphere when
travelling on Via trains.

Courtesy Via Rail
Canada Inc.

"We met some super people!"

"Everyone on the train was so friendly. Interesting, too! The meals were delicious, and the VIA™ staff took such good care of us. For us, VIA's the best way to see the country in good company. In fact, we're already thinking about doing it again!"

VIA offers you hundreds of destinations, plus a choice of fares and hotels to suit every budget. Ask about our value-packed VIA Canada Tour packages, VIA Getaways and Canrailpass. Then join the many travellers who've made VIA the natural choice... it's a unique way to see a great country, and meet fascinating people!

Take the train. There's nothing quite like it!™

*Registered trademark of VIA Rail Canada Inc. ™Trademark of VIA Rail Canada Inc.

PLATE III

The main idea of this
advertisement is
expressed graphi-
cally. The cellular
phone is so light that
it can be lifted by a
balloon.

Courtesy NEC
Canada, Inc.

Introducing a somewhat lighter cellular phone.

At 14 ounces light, 2.3 inches narrow, 7.2 inches short and a mere inch thin, the NEC
Portable Phone may be the easiest way to carry a conversation. It can go from a car to a
boat to a pocket in seconds. And with a talk time of 80 minutes (or 18 hours standby) and
digital clock with automatic wake-up features, there's only one smart thing to do. Pick up the
phone. For more information and where to buy an NEC Portable Phone, call **1-800-363-2847**.

NEC

 C&C Computers and Communications

INTRODUCING A WHOLE NEW CLASS OF SEDAN: WORLD CLASS.

The totally new 1991 four-door Regal.

Only its competitors will experience some discomfort. The Regal Sedan is built to further enhance Buick's reputation for quality – a reputation that is growing by leaps and bounds.

It is stylish and sophisticated. And it comes with an impressive list of standard features like air conditioning, four-wheel power disc brakes and four-wheel independant DynaRide suspension. Plus an even more impressive list of available features, including: ComforTemp climate control with dual temperature controls, compact disc player with Concert Sound and steering-wheel-mounted radio controls. Also available is a powerful 3800 tuned-port, fuel-injected V-6 – a Buick exclusive.

The new Regal Sedan is in a class by itself: world class.

BUICK REGAL
The Buick Touch

PLATE V

Although it is not
recent, this ad is an
excellent example of
the selective use of
colour. The black
and white photograph
behind the coloured
product package con-
veys a personalized
feeling to the adver-
tised product.

Courtesy Kimberly-Clark
of Canada Ltd., 1975

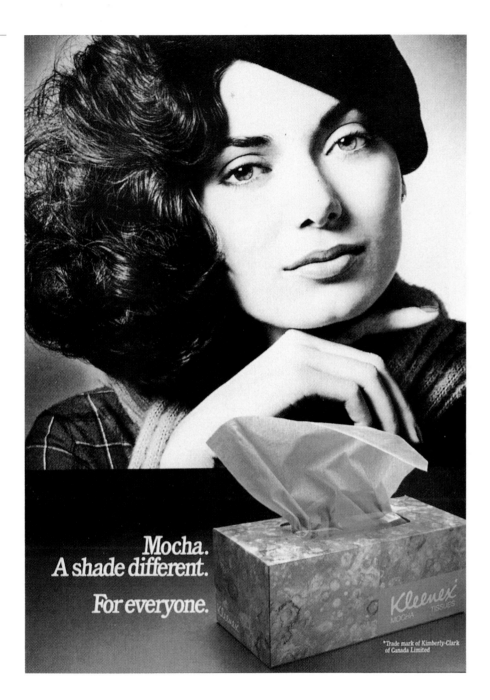

PLATE VI

This ad highlights the contrast of the busy life of business travellers (painting) with the relaxed Air France traveller (photograph).

Courtesy Air France

THE FINE ART OF FLYING
by Segui.

"Mucha Gente" by Antonio Segui. In sympathetic tribute to the business traveller, the Argentinian painter Segui dedicated his work to the new Air France Terminal at the Charles de Gaulle Airport in Paris. Voted the most innovative of its kind today, it promotes the ease of passage and quickness between all of our connections to the world. Another demonstration proving that we go to all lengths so that you won't have to.

FIGURE 12–5
By enhancing the large
number of features of this
typewriter, the advertiser
increases the positive
motivations for buying
the product.
Courtesy Smith Corona
Corporation and RSH & S
Advertising, Inc.

FIGURE 12–6
The main thrust of this
advertisement is to offer
a new benefit beyond the
usual satisfaction of using
the cleansing lotion.
Courtesy Professor Pharmaceutical Corp.

FIGURE 12–7
The Saran Wrap advertise-
ment uses a pictorial demonstration to try to change
consumers' perceptions of
a drawback of using plastic
wrap for microwave cook-
ing: it might melt over the
food.
Reprinted with the permission
of the copyright owner
DowBrands Canada Inc.
All rights reserved.

The Basic Motive Selection Procedure.   Given that all the forces affecting a purchase decision are potential candidates for advertising actions, the problem
arises of selecting the best one. There are several steps an advertiser can follow
to select a good psychological element for building an advertising campaign.

An exhaustive list can be drawn of all the positive and negative valence
motives involved in the purchase of the product category. This list should not
be based on the advertisers' common sense alone. Motivation research, focus
group interviews, and in-depth interviews are research methods and techniques that can help advertising researchers to develop the list. Research
should supplement whatever knowledge marketing and advertising managers
have of consumer behaviour concerning the purchase of their product category
and brands.

To select the psychological element on which an advertising action could
have the greatest effect, advertisers can apply a number of criteria and considerations to every possible motive involved in the purchase decision.

When a purchase decision involves both a product category purchase decision and a brand selection decision, then an advertiser should select a psychological element that can simultaneously influence the two interrelated
decisions. This is the case with innovations or with most infrequently purchased
durables, for example, microwave ovens. In such cases, advertisers can use the
following criteria:

1. The selected motive, either positive or negative, should be strongly felt by
   individual consumers. If the selected psychological element is a strongly
   felt motivation that can be enhanced or a very serious constraint that can
   be removed or substantially decreased, then chances that the advertisements will affect individual consumer behaviour are greater. If a motive
   that is not strongly felt is selected, even assuming that the advertisement is

effective, it may not be sufficient to change the direction of the resulting forces toward a purchase decision.

2. The selected motive should be felt by a large proportion of consumers in the target market segment; the appeal should be relevant and effective not just for a small proportion of consumers but for the entire target audience. Obviously, it would not be very effective to select an appeal that can have an effect on only a fraction of the audience. This is especially true when the advertiser tries to remove or reduce a force inhibiting a purchase decision. If the negative force is not presently felt by a significant proportion of the market segment, then advertising may obtain results opposite to the intended goal, by revealing to the majority of the market segment the existence of a negative argument. For instance, assume that a large proportion of potential microwave oven buyers were not aware that microwave ovens can produce uneven cooking. If an advertiser builds an advertising campaign on this argument, not only may it be ineffective with a large proportion of the market segment that did not feel this was a problem before, but it may also inform this part of the market that uneven cooking may be a drawback with this product.

In addition to the above criteria, other considerations should be added so that not only the general product category is bought but also the *advertised brand*. Obviously, it is not efficient to induce consumers to buy a microwave oven if they end up selecting a competing brand. The motive selected should meet two other criteria.

1. The advertising claim used to enhance a motivation or reduce an inhibition should be specific to the brand and should not be applicable to the competing brands. In the Saran Wrap example, the product feature that promises resistance to heat is a distinctive feature of Saran Wrap that cannot be claimed by competing brands.
2. The claim must be true. This may seem obvious, but to keep the same example, it would have not been possible for Saran Wrap to use this appeal if the product could not effectively resist heat.

Another determinant of the basic psychological element choice process is the kind of psychological tension that is aroused by the purchase decision. When the purchase of the product involves several powerful positive and negative forces, it is generally preferable to reduce or eliminate an element constraining the purchase of the brand, rather than trying to add a new motivation to buy. The latter action would still increase the overall psychological tension of the purchase decision, while the former action has a tendency to reduce the tension and to make it easier for the consumer to purchase the brand. (See Figure 12–8.)

Selection of a Specific Advertising Theme. Once a basic motivating force of the consumer purchase decision has been selected, the next step is to select the advertisement theme. The advertisement theme is defined as the concept that concretely and effectively evokes in a consumer's mind the positive or

FIGURE 12–8

Psychological Tension as the Result of Different Advertising Actions

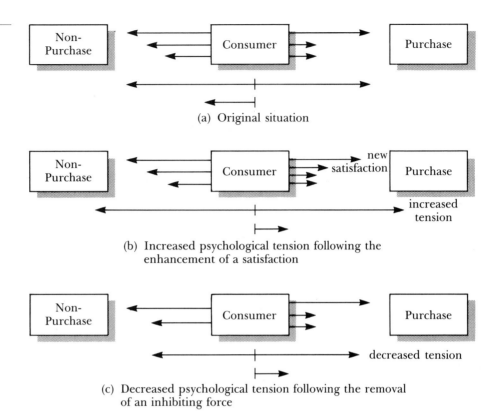

(a) Original situation

(b) Increased psychological tension following the enhancement of a satisfaction

(c) Decreased psychological tension following the removal of an inhibiting force

negative psychological element that the advertiser has chosen. At this stage, it must be decided what should be said to consumers in order to act upon the selected motive. This step is essential, because consumers are not likely to understand abstract psychological language but only concrete facts and words. There are several ways advertisers can translate general abstract psychological elements into concrete information and statements:

Direct Description of the Satisfaction. The first possibility is to give a concrete description of the satisfaction that can be derived from using the brand. For instance, an advertiser for a toothpaste may have selected as the motivating force parents' fear that their children may not have healthy teeth. The solution is to describe this satisfaction by demonstrating that with Toothpaste X, children will be kept away from the dentist. In the Avon advertisement, reproduced in Figure 12–9, the satisfaction of looking younger with Avon skin Perfector is directly described.

Inferring the Satisfaction. Two methods of inferring the selected satisfaction can be used.[19] First, an advertiser may try to infer the selected satisfaction by describing the product and/or brand action, and let consumers deduce the satisfaction that can be derived from using a brand. In the toothpaste example,

FIGURE 12–9

The satisfaction of looking younger is evoked by calling upon the consumer's imagination.

Courtesy Avon Canada Inc.

FIGURE 12–10

This advertisement stresses the Italian taste of the spaghetti sauce. The red, white, and green background represents the Italian flag.

This advertisement has been provided by Thomas J. Lipton Inc.

A recipe for homesick Italians.

an advertiser could state, "Toothpaste X fights cavities in youngsters' teeth." This approach is illustrated in the Ragu' advertisement (Figure 12–10). In this advertisement, the satisfaction is the authentic Italian taste of the spaghetti sauce. Instead of directly stating the motivation: "Use a sauce that has the authentic Italian taste," the message says: "A recipe for homesick Italians." From the message, the consumers will infer "therefore the Ragu' spaghetti sauce must taste like real Italian sauce."

An advertiser can also try to further imply the selected satisfaction by describing a product feature that will result in a certain consequence, which in turn will yield the selected consumer satisfaction. Thus, an advertiser for toothpaste may state: "Toothpaste X contains sodium fluoride, an effective decay preventive agent." From this consumers might conclude "therefore it should protect against cavities" and, consequently, "my kids' teeth would stay healthy." This approach is illustrated in the Crest advertisement (Figure 12–11).

Another example is the advertisement for Star Kist (Figure 12–12), which features a product characteristic: it is packed in Canada. Hence, consumers, who are also instructed that Canada has the toughest standards in the world, will or should conclude that this must be a high quality product (the resulting consequence), and that it would be tasty and safe to use (the underlying consumer satisfaction).

Any approach that evokes the benefits a brand can bring to consumers has its merits and its drawbacks. Directly describing the satisfaction is typically more abstract and generally less credible than the two other approaches.

FIGURE 12–11

Consumers who read only the headline in this advertisement have to make a two step deduction in order to infer the underlying satisfaction to be found from the product usage: healthy teeth. Note also that this advertisement is built upon a fear appeal.

Courtesy Procter and Gamble Inc.

FIGURE 12–12

This is an example of an advertisement that requires some reasoning from the readers.

Courtesy Star Kist Foods Canada Inc.

However, it is easier to communicate to the market, because it is likely to be correctly understood by consumers; they cannot be led astray in the stream of deductive statements they need to make to understand the satisfaction they can derive from this brand.

However, the second and especially the third inductive approach are more concrete because they directly relate to the product. Thus, they are more likely to be believed, because the message is more fact- and product-feature oriented. Unfortunately, many consumers may not correctly deduce the proper satisfaction, or even worse, could derive quite different conclusions from those intended. It is conceivable, for instance, that with the Star Kist advertisement some readers may conclude that since it is packed in Canada it is a local and cheaper product.

Selecting the proper theme or advertising claim for an advertisement and for the advertising campaign should be done according to how well each possible theme meets the following criteria: its likelihood of being properly understood by consumers, how brand specific it is, and how believable and how acceptable to consumers it is. Because the theme will be translated into specific advertisements and commercials, other criteria should include how well each advertisement concept lends itself to being easily and powerfully expressed by the agency's creative department.

The Before-After Demonstration. The advertising concept can often be best conveyed by showing or demonstrating the results of the product. One particular instance of product demonstration is to show the situation before and after product usage, and consequently, the substantial improvement in the consumer's situation and satisfaction which has resulted from product con-

FIGURE 12–13

Before and after adver-
tisements are often
used for drugs and
pharmaceutical
products.

Courtesy Smith &
Nephew Inc.

sumption. The approach has often been used by advertisers of drugs, pharmaceutical products, and cosmetics. In this case, advertisers dramatically
emphasize the difference between the situations before and after the advertised
product has had its effects. This approach is illustrated in the advertisement
reproduced in Figure 12–13.

Comparative Advertising. Another approach for evoking product satisfaction
is to make direct comparisons with competing brands. This style of advertising
is relatively recent, at least on the scale at which it is presently used. A substantial
proportion of advertising can now be classified as comparative advertising.
Figures 12–14 and 12–15 show two examples following two different
approaches. Olivetti undertakes a systematic comparison of its personal computer features with those of its identified competition—IBM, Apple, and
Xerox. Note that only the characteristics for which Olivetti is better or equal
to competitors have been retained. The Toyota advertisement indirectly
alludes to the competition by stating that they are part of the "Big Three,"
without specifying who the "Other Two" are.

Sometimes, though, when using comparative advertising, an advertiser
concedes some superiority to a competitor, capitalizing on the two-sided pre-

FIGURE 12–14

This is a typical example of comparative advertising in which product features are compared with those of the main competing brands (see table in the upper right corner).

Courtesy Olivetti Office Canada Inc.

Building a better personal computer than IBM, Apple and Xerox wasn't easy. Thanks for waiting.

We know what you're thinking. How could Olivetti have developed a better computer than the rest?

The answer—in a word—is experience.

Since we introduced the world's first desktop model, in 1965, we've continued to market a variety of mini and microcomputers to a wide range of users.

Incorporating our experience and the latest technological advances—like our true 16-bit microprocessor.

And today the M20 proves that dollar for dollar, we've built the most powerful personal computer on the market.

Just look at the comparison chart.

The M20 has 100% more mass storage than a Xerox 820. Its 512K memory is twice as memorable as the Apple III's.

And it outperforms IBM right across the board.

It's easy to use, too, because the M20 teaches you about itself. One step at a time.

So you can handle most any application. Electronic spread sheets. Accounting. Data entry. Technical. Word processing. Communications. Scientific.

	OLIVETTI M20 PERSONAL COMPUTER	IBM PERSONAL COMPUTER	APPLE III PERSONAL COMPUTER	XEROX 820 PERSONAL COMPUTER
True 16-bit microprocessor*	YES	NO	NO	NO
Standard memory	128K	64K	128K	64K
Maximum memory	512K	256K	256K	64K
Expandability	5 extra expansion slots in sample configuration**	No extra expansion slots in sample configuration**	4 extra expansion slots in sample configuration**	No expansion slots
Diskette storage (per drive)	320K	160K	140K	92K
Mass storage (per drive)	11MB hard disk	None	5MB hard disk	None
Display capability	High-resolution B/W or high-resolution colour	High-resolution B/W or colour	High-resolution B/W or colour	High-resolution B/W
Built-in screen graphics	YES	NO	NO	NO

*Defined as 16-bit microprocessor with 16-bit bus.
**Sample configuration means system includes display, dual-disk drives, printer and RS 232C communicator. NOTE: Chart based on manufacturers' information and configuration available as of December, 1981.

Our exclusive disk-based operating system will make things easier and more productive still.

By managing the entire system, while providing a constant HELP function and more.

There's also a high-contrast colour screen, plus built-in software and growth capabilities.

And for a compatible letter printer, look no further than your Olivetti typewriter.

Finally, the M20 is backed by service that has satisfied Canadians for over 25 years.

Just call your nearby Olivetti branch or authorized dealer, to see how the M20's performance can help you outperform the competition.

Or return our coupon today.

olivetti
Olivetti outperforms you know who. Again.

I'd like to find out all about the M20 personal computer
☐ Please call me and arrange a demonstration.
☐ Please send me additional literature.

Name
Company_____ Title
Address
Postal Code_____ Telephone

To:
Mr. Paul Manina
Olivetti Canada Ltd.
1390 Don Mills Road
Don Mills, Ontario M3B 2X3
Telephone: (416) 447-3351

---

sentation discussed in Chapter 9. For example, recall Avis's advertisement: "We are number 2, so we try harder." Research on the effectiveness of comparative advertisements has led to mixed results. As will be discussed in Chapter 17, some authors have found comparative advertisements to be more effective under certain circumstances, particularly for shopping goods[20] or for relatively unknown or small market share brands.[21] However, comparative advertising has also been found to be sometimes offensive[22] and less credible than non-comparative advertising.[23]

Testimonial Advertising. In order to translate concretely the basic motivation, advertisers can also use some credible source to testify for the product claim. This approach capitalizes on the concept of source credibility discussed in

FIGURE 12–15

In this type of advertisement, comparison is made with other makes, from unnamed companies. This type of comparison may be less credible than comparisons that explicitly name competing brands.

Courtesy Toyota Canada Inc.

Chapter 9. The testimony may be provided by a celebrity who will most likely be viewed as a competent expert by consumers. When a famous hockey player makes a statement about ice skates, he is more likely to be believed. Chanel has used Catherine Deneuve to advertise its No. 5 perfume, and she is certainly a credible expert for beauty care products.

The testimony can also be that of "ordinary" people, meaning people very similar to the target market segment. Here the rationale is to build the advertisement on the concepts of the two-step flow of communication and interpersonal influence. This type of advertising is shown in Figure 12–16 for L'Oreal, in which a maturing woman testifies that she has discovered an effective way to cover her grey hair.

Should an advertiser use a celebrity, an expert, or a typical consumer? It has been suggested that the perceived risk involved should be the main criterion. Thus, when the risks associated with the purchase of a product are psychological and/or social, advertisers should use celebrities to endorse the product (this would be the case of Catherine Deneuve endorsing a perfume). When the risk is financial or physical, the expert endorser may be more effective. For products involving low risks, advertisers should use a typical consumer, as in the advertisement of Figure 12–16.[24]

The Unique Selling Proposition Approach

The unique selling proposition (USP) approach is similar to the motivation approach. The difference is that emphasis is put on finding advertising appeals that can provide consumers with benefits specific to the advertised brand. This

A typical consumer testifies on the product's qualities.

Courtesy Cosmair Canada Inc.

"I have finally discovered a simple way to gently cover my gray hair: Avantage from L'Oréal."

Gently covers gray hair.

AVANTAGE

L'ORÉAL

With Avantage, L'Oréal has created a simple way to cover gray hair.
■ AVANTAGE is a creme haircolour lotion that covers the gray gently yet efficiently. It is ready to use without mixing: simply apply like your favorite shampoo.

■ AVANTAGE contains no peroxide, no ammonia. Non-permanent, it gradually washes out in 5 or 6 shampoos so you never ever have roots.
■ AVANTAGE. The gentle way to cover gray and to recapture the natural colour of your hair.

approach has been advocated by the Ted Bates advertising agency. A USP may be defined as follows:[25]

A USP is a memorable set of words promising a unique benefit no one else can promise or does promise. The set of words must answer the consumer's basic question: "What benefit will I get from buying your brand that I won't get from buying other competitors' brand?" In other words, "Why is your brand superior?" The USP is a memorable set of words that sum up the unique reward or benefit. This must be explicit.

FIGURE 12–17

Examples of USPs

Courtesy Backer Spiel-
vogel Bates Advertising

1. Product-oriented USPs:

M & Ms:
"The Milk chocolate melts in your mouth—not in your hands."

Wonder Bread:
"Helps build strong bodies 12 ways."

Shredded Wheat:
"100% whole wheat—0% sugar

Hefty Trash Bags:
"Tough enough to overstuff."

Kal Kan Cat Food:
"So rich in nutrition, it's like getting a multi-vitamin in every can."

Halls Mentho-Lyptus Cough Tablets
"Vapour Action"

2. Consumer End-Benefit USPs:

Sanka:
"Drink Sanka and be at your best—always."

Panasonic:
"Just slightly ahead of our time."

Figure 12–17 gives examples of successful USPs developed by the Ted Bates agency (now Backer Spielvogel Bates Advertising). USPs are product-oriented when they emphasize a benefit provided by a product feature; some are consumer end-benefit USPs when they directly describe the benefit.

Another characteristic of this approach is that once an effective USP has been developed, it should be kept indefinitely, or at least as long as the claim remains a USP. This may be difficult to apply in practice because many people directly associated with a campaign get bored with the theme, and get the false impression that any consumer in the market must be as bored as they are with the brand advertising.

The Ted Bates agency has a five-step procedure for developing effective USPs:

1. *Total immersion in the clients' business.* All the agency personnel who work on the account—account executives, creative people, media and research groups—must be thoroughly familiar with the marketing mix, policies, and history of the product or brand to be advertised.
2. *Conduct additional research.* When all the information needed to develop an effective USP is not available, then the agency's research department conducts its own research, especially by using such qualitative techniques as focus groups.
3. *Strategic development and evaluation.* All product positioning strategies are enumerated and evaluated carefully. This includes a translation of all the possible strategies into ad concepts or statements and into rough ads or storyboards. Research can provide additional insight into the value of the different ad concepts.

4. *Develop an approved strategy.* The formal written strategy is prepared for client approval and then serves as the basis for providing the creative group with guidelines on writing and producing the advertisement.
5. *Create and test the USP.* The actual phrasing of the USP is developed and formally evaluated with qualitative and quantitative research techniques.

Suggestive Advertising

All the advertisements that have been discussed so far attempt to give consumers a rationale, an argument, or a reason why they should buy a certain product or brand. In contrast, suggestive advertising is not concerned with emphasizing some product features or consumer benefits but with building a positively valued brand image in the target market segment. The objective is to ensure that consumers will have developed sufficiently positive attitudes toward the advertised brand and that they will consider purchasing it whenever the need or the occasion arises. Such an approach is best when the brands in a certain product category are fairly similar, since there is no strong physical product differentiation on which to build effective USPs or to use as a basic selling argument. Such product categories include perfumes, most beauty care products, or alcoholic beverages. In such cases, the idea is to attribute a specific personality to the brand in order to cater to specific market segments. This type of advertising is also called *emotional* or *mood* advertising, as it appeals to emotions, often aesthetic emotions, and creates a special mood or atmosphere. David Ogilvy, a leading advertiser, is a well-known advocate of this approach.[26]

There isn't any significant difference between the various brands of whisky, or cigarettes, or beer. They are all about the same. And so are the cake mixes and the detergents, and the margarines. The manufacturer who dedicates his advertising to building the most sharply defined personality for his brand will get the largest share of the market at the highest profit. By the same token, the manufacturers who will find themselves up the creek are those shortsighted opportunists who siphon off their advertising funds for promotions.

Examples of suggestive advertising are illustrated by the Jaguar advertisement in Plate I and the Via advertisement in Plate II.

Manufacturers of beverages, jewelry, fragrances, jeans, financial services, cars, food/fast food, airlines/tourism, film/cameras are often using mood or image advertising.[27]

According to research carried by a leading advertising agency, mood advertising can be very effective in terms of brand awareness and recall.[28] (See Table 12–1.)

Although mood advertising seems not to fare as well on consumer motivation and attitudes, it should be kept in mind that it is generally not intended to bring strong or immediate product persuasion.

In order to build a suitable image, prestigious individuals are often used. The eye-patched character in the Hathaway shirt advertisement (Figure 12–18) is a case in point. Usually, however, celebrities are used in order to "transfer" their personalities to a brand.

TABLE 12–1 EFFECTIVENESS OF MOOD ADVERTISING IN COMPARISON WITH OTHER TYPES OF ADVERTISING APPROACHES

Scores on:	Mood	Hard Sell	Celebrity	Slice-of-Life
Clutter/Awareness; *Brand Recall*				
Above average	40%	37%	41%	46%
Average	30	28	21	25
Total Acceptable	70	65	62	71
Attitude/Motivation				
Above average	31%	37%	41%	49%
Average	23	28	21	19
Total Acceptable	54	65	62	68

Source: Jo Marney, "Good, Good, Good, Vibrations," *Marketing*, April 25, 1988, p. 12.

In *Confessions of an Advertising Man*, David Ogilvy gives his approach to advertising creation:[29]

1. What you say is more important than how you say it. Two hundred years ago Dr. Johnson said, "Promise, large promise is the soul of an advertisement." When he auctioned off the contents of the Anchor Brewery he made the following promise: "We are not here to sell boilers and vats, but the potentiality of growing rich beyond the dreams of avarice."
2. Unless your campaign is built around a great idea, it will flop.
3. Give the facts. The consumer isn't a moron; she is your wife. You insult her intelligence if you assume that a mere slogan and a few vapid adjectives will persuade her to buy anything. She wants all the information you can give her.
4. You cannot bore people into buying. We make advertisements that people want to read. You can't save souls in an empty church.
5. Be well-mannered, but don't clown.
6. Make your advertising contemporary.
7. Committees can criticize advertisements, but they cannot write them.
8. If you are lucky enough to write a good advertisement, repeat it until it stops pulling. Sterling Getchel's famous advertisement for Plymouth ("Look at All Three") appeared only once, and was succeeded by a series of inferior variations which were quickly forgotten. But the Sherwin Cody School of English ran the same advertisement ("Do You Make Mistakes in English?") for forty-two years, changing only the type face and the colour of Mr. Cody's beard.
9. Never write an advertisement which you wouldn't want your own family to read.

FIGURE 12–18

The famous eye-patched character is a distinctive feature of the brand.

Courtesy Hathaway Division of Warnaco of Canada

10. The image and the brand. It is the total personality of a brand rather than any trivial product difference which decides its ultimate position in the market.
11. Don't be a copy cat. Nobody has ever built a brand by imitating somebody else's advertising. Imitation may be the "sincerest form of plagiarism," but it is also the mark of an inferior person.

THE MESSAGE FORMAT DECISION

Although in the process of translating advertising objectives into a specific advertising message the creative group of the advertising agency is involved, it is essentially the responsibility of the agency's marketing and account executives to find out *what* should be said to consumers. This section concerns the question of *how* to say it, i.e., what is the best combination of words, images, and sounds that will effectively convey the idea to the target market segment. This task is the main responsibility of the creative group at the advertising agency. It is now that the purely creative part of the advertising process begins. The rest of this chapter focuses on some basic principles that creative people follow in translating a message content into effective advertisements and commercials.

Principles for Creating Advertising Messages

In order to design effective advertising messages, advertisers may follow four simple and widely accepted principles:

Principle 1. An advertiser should try to communicate the message content as quickly as possible.

The rationale is that the contact time between the consumers and a specific advertisement or commercial is often extremely short. For example, posters are seen in a glance as are magazine and newspaper advertisements. Hidden camera tests have revealed that when readers are leafing through the pages of a magazine, the average ad has less than half a second to get their attention.[30] The time constraint is somewhat less stringent for broadcast commercials. If the message can be delivered during the first few seconds or even fractions of a second during which the consumer is exposed to it, this could make the difference between an effective advertisement and what could have been an ineffective message. At the other extreme are advertising messages that try to attract consumers' attention through means not directly related to the message or the advertised product. The rationale is to try to arouse consumers' interest (the fourth advertising creation principle) and then try to sell the product. Such advertisements strictly follow a hierarchy of effects sequence. They are likely to be much less if at all effective than messages that attempt to deliver the complete story at once and within the shortest possible period of time. Look at the Volkswagen advertisement in Figure 12–19. A mere glance is sufficient to grasp a somewhat complex idea. Because of its size (full page) and its simplicity it can effectively deliver the message in the shortest possible time.

Principle 2. All the communication elements of the advertising message should help express the idea selected as the campaign theme.

Whatever the medium, an advertising message is made up of a number of communication elements, and all of these communication elements convey information to consumers.

The *verbal message* is constituted of the written words in a print advertisement or the spoken and/or written words in a telecast commercial. *Visual elements* are the illustrations, the photograph, the graphical representation on a print advertisement, or the part of an advertising scenario that can be seen on a television screen. The *audio elements* are the sound effects and the music that are used in most broadcast commercials. Finally, the *general ambiance* or *atmosphere* of an advertisement or commercial also says something about the brand and/or the company to consumers. Because all these elements of the advertising message convey information, effective messages are those in which all the elements communicate all or part of the *same* idea or message.

For instance, a consumer watching a television commercial receives a visual message conveyed by the pictures. Simultaneously, the verbal message is spoken by an announcer, and the background music conveys another message. The advertisement would be much less effective if each element tried to convey unrelated meanings or contradictory meanings. If each communication ele-

FIGURE 12–19

This award-winning full-page advertisement expresses consumers' frustration with the energy crisis.

Courtesy Volkswagen Canada Inc.

Or buy a Volkswagen.

ment conveys different messages, none of the messages reaches its objectives and confusion may result.[31] In the Volkswagen advertisement in Figure 12–19, the visual and verbal elements complement each other to convey the same idea: "If you do not want to kill yourself paying outrageous gas bills" (expressed by the drawing), "buy a Volkswagen" (which constitutes the written headline).

Principle 3. If the medium permits, advertisers should try to convey as much of the message as possible with visual elements.

The rationale is that non-verbal communications are always more effective than verbal communications. What people do attracts more attention than what people say. Comedians know that the effect of a humorous reply can be "killed" if at the same time another actor starts moving on the stage. Teachers generally find it difficult to keep their students' attention when someone leaves the classroom during a lecture. These are examples of attention to verbal elements being distracted by visual elements. If, in spite of Principle 2, the visual and the verbal elements do not contribute to the communication of the same idea, the visual elements can be expected to be the strongest.[32] In the Volkswagen advertisement, the largest portion of the message is communicated by the drawing. The illustration is roughly equivalent to a statement that says: "If you think of killing yourself because you cannot afford outrageous gasoline bills . . ." The reader notices how much more effectively and rapidly the drawing delivers this idea. Only four words are needed to complete the sentence.

Sometimes an entire message can be expressed through visual elements. These are likely to be the most effective messages from a communication point of view. The NEC advertisement in Plate III delivers the entire message through the picture: "The NEC portable phone is so light that it can be lifted by a balloon." The only word that would be needed to complete the message is the brand name: NEC.

In a multicultural country like Canada, completely non-verbal advertising has the incomparable advantage of requiring the creation of one advertising message that can simultaneously be understood by both French and English speaking consumers.[33]

Principle 4. Advertisers should try to arouse consumers' interest as quickly as possible. This principle is a corollary of Principle 1. The classic hierarchy of effects model that suggests buyers' attention should be attracted first, before their interest can be aroused, may not be the most efficient advertising procedure. The rationale is that interested consumers will naturally pay more attention to the advertising message. In the Volkswagen advertisement, readers who are concerned (and therefore interested) about the soaring costs of energy and who are actively looking for new ways to save on gas are most likely to pay attention to the advertisement. Moreover, *because* they are interested, their attention will more likely be attracted by a message linked to energy savings. There is a strong tendency for people's attention to be attracted to what interests them.

The Atmosphere of Advertising Messages

Another dimension important to the visual and non-verbal elements of the advertising message is the ability to create an ambience or an atmosphere that is loaded with meaning for consumers. The atmosphere created by an advertising message strongly influences the personality or image that consumers will assign to the advertised brand.

Influence of the Non-Verbal Elements

The setting in which products are used, the type of people who are shown in the illustration, the way they are dressed, how they look, and what they do, give quite different personalities to an advertised brand. For instance, compare Plate IV and Figure 12–20. The Buick Regal advertisement evokes an atmosphere of luxury and class by using sober pictures and copy, and emphasized by the phrase "World Class." The Hyundai Sonata advertisement evokes the

FIGURE 12–20

The good value appeal is suggested through an ambiance of outdoor activities of upper-middle class people (suggested by the horse riding party).

Courtesy Hyundai Canada Inc.

TREND UPSETTER.

Driving a car that shows how smart you are seems to be a growing trend. Especially for Hyundai owners.

The 1990 Sonata, putting it plainly and simply, is the best value in mid-size cars today. And the reasons are just as plain and simple.

The Sonata has more interior room than any car in its class and that includes the Honda Accord and Toyota Camry. It also offers the biggest standard engine in its class and a new V-6 option.

Sonata also offers Free Regular Scheduled Maintenance - parts and labour - for 3 years or 60,000 km, whichever comes first. That gives you a pretty good

idea of how confident Hyundai is in Sonata's inherent quality. You won't find this level of confidence among our competition.

Our new 3 year /60,000 km comprehensive warranty is among the best in the business, and it's made even better by a 5 year/100,000 km warranty on major components.

All the standard features on Sonata that other cars offer as options add to what many automotive journalists consider to be the best value on the road today.

So if you've been wanting for the right mid-size car to come along, be part of the growing trend. Head for your Hyundai dealer

The 1990 Hyundai Sonata.

HYUNDAI
Cars that make sense.

atmosphere of casual albeit above-average people, who are sports fans and like outdoor activities.

Objects, situations, or product usage scenarios also project a certain image as does the typeface used for the headline and the copy. But more important, beyond each specific detail the general atmosphere evoked determines what personality consumers will attribute to the brand.

As was discussed in Chapter 1, consumers decode and interpret communication symbols through their fields of previous experience, knowledge, and their present situation and their aspirations for the future. As pointed out by Maurice Borts:

This means that the content of an ad is often evaluated by potential consumers in terms of how well the messages fit in which the receiver's needs—current lifestyle and values. As a consequence, it is possible that the identical message would be interpreted differently by various individuals.[34]

For example, a well-dressed and elegant man in an advertisement could evoke to some people high class, expensive, quality products. However, other people could infer from the same advertisement an image of a brand for snobbish, idle people. Thus marketers should ensure that the proper interpretation of the advertisement's symbols be made by the target market segment.

The meaning of the symbols used in advertising messages is likely to evolve over time. For instance, failing to dress models according to the current fashion may have a positive or negative interpretation by consumers and an effect on the brand image.

Borts gives the following objectives for properly administering non-verbal messages:

- they reinforce the planned communication and do not unintentionally create conflicting messages;
- they replace or support word messages that lack credibility or which cannot be adequately presented in words;
- communication barriers such as legal constraints, bilingual considerations, or the resistance that consumers build up against commercial communication can be circumvented.[35]

The Use of Humour

Humour is an important element that advertisers have often used to increase the effectiveness of their messages and that gives a unique atmosphere to an advertisement. However, the effectiveness of humour in advertising is still a subject of controversy in the advertising industry. There are as many examples of successful humorous advertising campaigns as examples of outright failures.

Humour is difficult to define, and there are many kinds of humour, some of them eliciting at best a smile, others triggering outbursts of laughter. Moreover, humour is not universal. An advertisement may be considered humorous by some and offensive or silly by others. One study using analytical techniques found eight types of humour in advertising.[36]

Some advertisers use empirical research to support their belief that humorous advertising may be more effective. Such studies suggest that humour tends to build a positive mood, enhance source credibility, and increase readership level. One study[37] reached the conclusion that humour was most effective when used to promote brands that had already achieved a certain level of recognition among consumers in a market: "Humour out-performed the use of celebrities and 'real people' in commercials for established brands but it can impede communication and hinder conviction for a product that has not had the opportunity to build a reputation and image."[38] Two reasons may explain these results. First, new product advertising generally has a lot of information to convey and the facts can be lost because the audience's attention is distracted by the humorous aspect of the story. Second, humorous advertising may project the image of a not too serious company. This effect is neutralized if the company is well established and taken seriously. However, it can have a quite

FIGURE 12–21

This advertisement uses humour to communicate and reinforce a selling point that otherwise might seem exaggerated.

Courtesy Kraft General Foods Canada Inc.

negative impact on new product advertising, which may be rejected by consumers as "not serious." As Figure 12–21 illustrates, humour emphasizing a selling point can be effectively used by Miracle Whip, which is a well-known brand in the Canadian market.

Other arguments suggest that humour should be used with caution, since it may distract the audience from the main point of the advertisement. Furthermore, as already mentioned humour is sometimes very personal and a humorous advertising message may often not be understood by some people in the audience. Thus, advertisers should try to avoid subtle wit, which may be lost on many consumers. For example, some readers may not pay attention to the spelling of the word "beans" in the Melitta advertisement and may miss the humorous intent of the advertiser.

FIGURE 12–22

In this advertisement, the humour results exclusively from a play on the word "beans."

Courtesy Melitta Canada Inc.

After experiencing the taste of these new gourmet blends, other coffees become has beans.

When you love coffee you know the difference the quality of the beans and the balance of the blend can make to the taste. That's why you'll truly appreciate these new gourmet coffees from Melitta. Four exceptional blends created with only the richest Arabica beans.

Experience the rounded smoothness of German Premium Style. The rich, full-bodied flavour of Vienna Premium Style. The complex, yet delicate flavour of Blue Mountain Style that makes this blend so special. And the distinctive tang of Café Noir Espresso. One taste and you won't settle for anything less.

Melitta is Coffee Perfection.

A review of the literature on the effectiveness of humour in advertising suggested the following generalizations:

1. Humorous messages attract attention.
2. Humorous messages may detrimentally affect comprehension.
3. Humour may distract the audience, yielding a reduction in counterargumentation and an increase in persuasion.
4. Humorous appeals appear to be persuasive, but the persuasive effect is at best no greater than that of serious appeals.
5. Humour tends to enhance source credibility.
6. Audience characteristics may confound the effect of humour.
7. A humorous context may increase liking for the source and create a positive mood. This may increase the persuasive effect of the message.
8. To the extent that a humorous context functions as a positive reinforcer, a persuasive communication placed in such a context may be more effective.[39]

Thus, advertisers should exercise judgment when using humour as an advertising tool.

SUMMARY

Developing the creative plan should start with an understanding of potential consumer behaviour and consumers' motives, knowledge, perceptions, attitudes, and buying habits. The creative process continues with a series of decisions about the message content, the message structure and format, and about message production. Creativity has been defined as the "ability to formulate new combinations from two or more concepts already in the mind." The creative process typically follows a sequence: assessing a situation, defining the problem, using the subconscious, generating ideas, and selecting the best idea. The advertising creation budget is often underestimated in many instances.

Concerning message content, advertising can follow an argumentative or a suggestive approach. Argumentative advertising may concentrate upon the target group, or on consumers' motivations. In the latter case, care should be given to the choice of a powerful, generally felt motivation, and on the choice of powerful arguments to enhance this motivation. The before/after demonstration, or comparative or testimonial advertising can be used affectively to communicate the advertising messages. Another possible approach to argumentative advertising is the choice of a Unique Selling Proposition (USP).

Concerning the message format, a number of principles can be followed for communicating the advertising message effectively. The influence of non-verbal elements and the use of humour have been stressed.

QUESTIONS FOR STUDY

1. Find a few examples of print ads that use:
   a. the target group approach
   b. the motivation approach
   c. the USP approach
   d. the suggestive approach
   Compare them in terms of communicative effectiveness.

2. For which type(s) of product and/or service are the following techniques best suited? Why?
   a. comparative advertising
   b. use of humour
   c. testimonial by celebrities
   d. testimonial by "ordinary" people

3. Find examples of print ads that in your opinion do not follow the creative principles given in the text. What test(s) could you do to confirm (or contradict) your opinion?

4. With a few examples of print advertisements, show how the different visual, verbal, and atmosphere elements all tend to convey a basic advertising message.

5. Find several advertisements using humour. Compare them in terms of the type of humour, the extent of their reliance on humour, and their effectiveness in communicating the advertising message. Evaluate each advertisement.

6. Find print advertisements in which the underlying consumer benefits are:
   a. directly described
   b. inferred
   Discuss their relative communication effectiveness. Give reasons.

7. Find examples of advertising claims aimed at:
   a. increasing some motivation
   b. reducing some fear
   Try to find the rationale for using these types of appeals.

8. USP advertising tends to stress a product feature, while the motivation approach tends to stress a consumer benefit and may be more in line with the marketing concept. Discuss.

9. In order to be effective, an advertising message should bring the consumers along a hierarchy of effects model like AIDA. First the message should attract attention. Then, it should arouse consumers' interest. Next, it should create desire, and finally, it should sell (action). Discuss.

10. Find examples of print advertisements in which all the elements do not tend to convey the same message. Give the reasons for your assessment.

PROBLEMS

1. Secure an interview with the advertising executive and/or manager of an important advertiser. During this interview, determine
   a. what underlying creative approach is generally followed and the reasons why;
   b. how the creative aspects fit into the overall advertising strategy and in the marketing strategy of the product/brand;

c. what the manager's opinions are about the use of humour, comparative advertising, and testimonials for advertising the firm's products and/or brands.

2. Find two print advertisements (if possible, for the same product category): one in which you think that all the elements tend to convey the same idea; one in which you think that inconsistent or conflicting meanings may be conveyed by the different channels.

    Show each advertisement to different people, varying the length of exposition (5, 10, 15, 30 seconds), and then measure what people recall and have understood.

    Do the results confirm your hypothesis? Discuss.

NOTES

1. John W. Macfale, *Creativity and Innovation*, (New York: Reinhold Publishing, 1962), p. 5.
2. W. Gordon, *Synectics: The Development of Creative Capacity*, (New York: Harper and Row, 1961); G. Steiner, *The Creative Organization*, (Chicago: University of Chicago Press, 1965).
3. Alex F. Osborn, *Applied Imagination*, rev. ed. (New York: Scribner's, 1957), pp. 110–14.
4. Ibid., p. 115.
5. Jane Webb Young, *A Technique for Producing Ideas*, 4th ed. (Chicago: Advertising Publications, 1960), p. 15.
6. Frank Alexander Armstrong, *Idea Teaching*, (New York: Criterion Books, 1960), pp. 139–44.
7. Michael Hallé, "Creative Is Not Really Creative Unless It Sells," *Marketing* (July 1980), pp. 9–12.
8. Ibid., p. 10.
9. Osborn, p. 84.
10. Hallé, p. 12.
11. Irwin Gross, "The Creative Aspects of Advertising," *Sloan Management Review*, (Fall 1972), pp. 83–109.
12. Kenneth A. Longman, *Advertising*, (New York: Harcourt, Brace, Jovanovich, 1971).
13. H. Munro and David Taylor, "Assessing Information Content in Advertisement," *Marketing*, ed. Sheila Brown (Montreal: Administrative Science Association of Canada, 1984), pp. 202–11.
14. John P. Liefeld, "The Informativeness of Print Advertising," *Marketing*, ed. Thomas Muller (Montreal: Administrative Science Association of Canada, 1986), pp. 328–37.
15. Lise Héroux, "Informational and Non-Informational Advertising Appeals: The Bauer and Cox Hypothesis Reviewed," *Marketing*, ed. Thomas

Muller (Montreal: Administrative Science Association, 1986), pp. 338–47.
16. Longman, pp. 187–88.
17. Henri Joannis, *De l'Etude de Motivation à la Création Publicitaire et à la Promotion des Ventes*, (Paris: Dunod, 1965).
18. Ibid., p. 113.
19. Ibid., p. 176.
20. Gordon M.C. McDougall, "Comparative Advertising: Consumer Issues and Attitudes," *Contemporary Marketing Thought*, ed., B.A. Greenberg and D.N. Bellanger, (Chicago: American Marketing Association, 1977), pp. 286–91.
21. Edwin C. Kackleman and Subhash C. Jain, "An Experimental Analysis Toward Comparison and Non-Comparison Advertising," *Advances in Consumer Research*, 6 (Ann Arbor, Michigan: Association for Consumer Research, 1979).
22. Terence A. Shimp and David C. Dyer, "The Effects of Comparative Advertising Mediated by Marketing Position of Sponsoring Brand," *Journal of Advertising*, 8 (Summer 1978), pp. 13–19.
23. Philip Levine, "Commercials that Name Competing Brands, *Journal of Advertising Research*, 16 (December 1976), pp. 7–14; R. Dale Wilson, "An Empirical Evaluation of Comparative Advertising Messages: Subjects' Responses on Perceptual Dimensions," *Advances in Consumer Research*, ed. B.B. Anderson, 3 (Ann Arbor, Michigan: Association for Consumer Research, 1976), pp. 53–57.
24. Jo Marney, "Testimonial Ads: Real People vs Celebrities," *Marketing*, 13 (September 1982), pp. 10–12.
25. Bob Jacoby, "Ted Bates: The USP Agency" (Speech delivered to Ted Bates Management Representa-

tives, New York Management Reps, unpublished document 1981).

26. David Ogilvy, *Confessions of an Advertising Man*, (New York: Atheneum, 1964).

27. Jo Marney, "Good, Good, Good, Good Vibrations," *Marketing*, April 25, 1988, p. 12.

28. Ibid., p. 12.

29. Ogilvy, p. 93.

30. Jo Marney, "Gotcha! (and Now that We Have Your Attention . . .)", *Marketing*, February 22, 1988, pp. 14–18.

31. Maurice Borts, "Power of the Unspoken Word," *Marketing*, 3 (December 1979), p. 20.

32. Benny Rigaux-Bricmont, "Implicit Attributes in Perceptual Mapping of Ads," *Marketing*, ed. Alain d'Astous (Montreal: Administrative Science Association of Canada, 1989), pp. 247–58.

33. Borts, pp. 23–23.

34. Ibid., p. 20.

35. Ibid., pp. 23–24.

36. Mervin D. Lynch and Richard C. Hartman, "Dimensions of Humour in Advertising", *Journal of Advertising Research*, 8 (December 1968), pp. 39–45.

37. David Ogilvy and Joel Raphaelson, "Research on Ad Techniques that Work—and Don't Work," *Marketing News*, 17 (September 1982), p. 2.

38. Ibid., p. 2.

39. Brian Sternthal and C. Samuel Craig, "Humour in Advertising," *Journal of Marketing*, 37 (October 1973), pp. 12–18. American Marketing Association.

13 *Developing Effective Advertisements and Commercials*

The principles and concepts described in Chapter 12 apply to the creation of all types of advertising messages, regardless of the media through which they are carried. This chapter deals with specific creative aspects of print advertisements and broadcast commercials. The first section shows how the visual, verbal, and atmosphere elements of a print advertisement are blended to communicate the selected advertising message effectively. The second section is devoted to the creation and production of broadcast commercials, with a specific emphasis on television commercials.

CREATING PRINT ADVERTISEMENTS

The principles of print advertisement creation are depicted in Figure 13–1, which shows how the visual, verbal, and ambience elements can be combined into a unique piece of artwork.

The Visual Elements in Print Advertisements

The visual elements of a print advertisement must fulfill two basic functions. First, they must ensure that the advertised product, service, or brand can be recognized quickly by the public, if possible at a glance. For some products, this is a relatively easy task. It may be sufficient that the product, the brand name, or the package be easily visible in an advertisement. Other products are more difficult to identify quickly. How can a brand of carpets be advertised by depicting a luxuriously furnished living room with the advertised carpets, and make sure that readers do not assume that furniture or decoration services are being sold? This problem is shared by advertisers of household cleaning products and of services in general. To convey the idea of the product and/or service being advertised, the art and expertise of talented photographers and artists are needed.

Second, the visual elements should express as much as possible of the message content. The expression of this task depends on the kind of message to be communicated. Figure 12–19 showed how the visual elements could express a substantial portion of the message and Plate III showed how they could express it all.

The illustration in a print advertisement often represents the product itself or part of the product if a special feature must be emphasized. Often, picturing the product in use or ready for use adds a suggestive dimension and interest and life to the advertisement. Consumers' satisfaction with product usage or ease of use may be effectively demonstrated in a illustration. To do so, the art

FIGURE 13–1

*The Basic Elements
of Print
Advertisements*

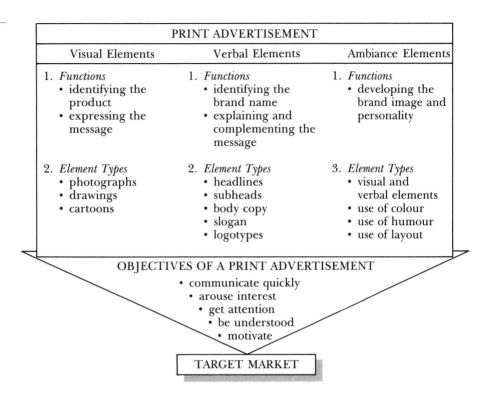

director and the creative team use the combination of people, symbols, and objects that best communicate the basic message content.

Visual elements may be classified into photographs, drawings, and other types of artwork. Advertising experts disagree over the relative merits of these various types of visual elements for effectively conveying the advertising message. Each has its merits and drawbacks, depending on the advertising situation.

Photographs

Photographs lend realism, appeal, and credibility to an advertisement. Whenever advertisers want to depict real-life situations, the use of photographs is almost mandatory. Photographs are used to advertise product categories for which the visual element is important, such as food or fashion items. In Plate V, the photograph lends realism to the Kleenex advertisement as does the photograph of the advertisement in Figure 13–2.

The vividness of photographs make them an excellent way of capturing readers' attention. Such advertisers as David Ogilvy unconditionally favour using photographs in print advertisements:

Over and over again research has shown that photographs sell more than drawings. They attract more readers. They deliver more appetite appeal. They are better remembered.

They pull more coupons. And they sell more merchandise. Photographs represent reality, whereas drawings represent fantasy, which is less believable.[1]

Drawings

Because dramatic photographs have become ubiquitous in print advertisements, many advertisers resort to other techniques to make their advertisements more original and striking. Drawings have the advantage of standing out by contrasting with the more common photograph advertisements. When properly used, they create a special mood that will enhance a product image. In the Bye-the-Sea advertisement reproduced in Figure 13–3, drawings are used to show some views of St. Andrews-By-the-Sea as a background for presenting the product.

Other Types of Artwork

Paintings, cartoons, abstract drawings, and any other forms of illustration also convey a special atmosphere or meaning to a print advertisement. A painting used to advertise a cologne or beauty product can project an image of exclusivity, elegance, and fantasy. In the Air France advertisement shown in Plate VI, a painting by Antonio Segui is skillfully used to make a selling point. Because they are not often used in advertising, cartoons attract readers' attention and create a light, humorous, and casual atmosphere, as in the Participaction advertisement reproduced in Figure 13–4.

In the final analysis, the choice of a specific type of visual element should depend on the product advertised, the communication objectives, and the message content. Therefore, these different types of illustration should be

FIGURE 13–4
This cartoon-like
illustration conveys a
casual atmosphere
and lends a light
humorous tone to
this advertisement.

Courtesy Participaction

evaluated on a case-by-case basis and be chosen to best fit the mood and the message to be conveyed by the advertisement.

The Verbal Element in Print Advertisements

The verbal elements of a print advertisement serve to identify the brand, to sign the advertisement, and to supplement the visual message. Readers cannot properly identify the brand being advertised unless it is written in the advertisement or on an illustration of the package. As with the NEC advertisement (Plate III), even where the visual elements could express the whole message, it is still necessary to identify the brand name in writing.

However, in most instances the message cannot be fully expressed by visual elements alone, and verbal elements are needed to complete the message. The verbal part of the message should complement the illustration, so as to convey the entire message content to the reader.

The verbal elements that can be used in a print advertisement are the headline, a subhead, the body copy, a slogan, and a logotype. Each verbal element fulfills a specific role and function.

The Headline

Headlines are the most conspicuous verbal elements of a print advertisement. They are often the only elements of an advertisement that are read, since many readers just glance at advertisements and go on to the next page. Therefore, it is essential that the headline work with the visual element to convey the message in a striking, interesting manner.

A prerequisite for a headline is that it attract readers' attention. At the same time, the headline must also arouse interest, so readers will want to read the body of the advertisement. Furthermore, a headline must "discriminate" among potential readers and retain only those who would be likely to be interested in the product advertised. It can do this by directly identifying the

FIGURE 13–5

This advertisement directly addresses an almost universal fear among women: the signs of aging on the skin.

Courtesy L'Oreal Plenitude/Cosmair Canada Inc.

FIGURE 13–6
This advertisement's headline directly promises a consumer benefit—assertion of a definite personality type—with product usage.

Courtesy Coty Division of Pfizer Canada Inc.

FIGURE 13–7
This headline promises a reward—special cooking—with Jenn-Air Ovens.

Courtesy Jenn-Air Co.

consumers in the targeted audience or by addressing a concern common to the target market segment. For instance, the L'Oreal advertisement reproduced in Figure 13–5 indirectly identifies a perceived target audience—aging women. The headline plays on the notion that Plénitude is a mosturizing cream that is effective against the signs of aging.

The headline should complement the illustration of the print advertisement, not repeat it. A test advertisers often carry out is to hide the illustration and show only the headline to people who have not seen the ad before. If the reader can understand the whole message, the copy is inefficient. The reader may test this principle on the Volkswagen advertisement in Figure 12–19. Without the illustration, the written part—"or buy a Volkswagen"—does not convey the whole message. The whole message can only be fully understood when the visual and the verbal elements are put together.

The Headline's Information Content. Headlines can be used in several ways. One way is to make the headline an implicit or explicit statement of a promised reward to the consumer. Extensive research has shown that this approach is quite effective. The reward should represent the satisfaction of a conscious consumer need or desire resulting from use of the product. Headlines can also stress the informational value of the body copy and therefore present the consumer with a reward that is not directly related to product consumption. The advertisements reproduced in Figures 13–6 and 13–7 give an example of each type of reward appeal. The Coty advertisement suggests that using Exclamation is to make a statement about one's personality. In Figure 13–7, the headline promises a reward that bears no direct obvious relation with the use of the advertised product: The reward (a special experience) may become true . . . after some experience with the product.

Headlines can be direct or indirect. Direct headlines present the product or product feature in an informative, straightforward manner. For instance, the headline in the Water Pik advertisement (Figure 13–8) directly states the product brand name along with one highly desirable product feature: it is

FIGURE 13–8
One product particularity is emphasized in the headline: it is indispensable.

Courtesy Teledyne Water Pik

indispensable. Headlines that present a product in a vivid, interesting manner are more likely to attract consumers' attention, as with the American Express Gold Card advertisement reproduced in Figure 13–9.

Indirect headlines convey interesting information but do not pertain directly to the advertised product. As an example, the advertisement for Actiprofen reproduced in Figure 13–10 is designed to stimulate consumers who are prone to headaches to read about the new scientific breakthrough. The brand name is only identified in the fourth paragraph of the body copy.

To be effective, this advertisement must be read in its entirety, and the headline is created to achieve that purpose.

The Headline's Syntax. To communicate effectively in the shortest possible time span, attract consumers' attention, and arouse interest, the headline should be as short as possible. Every word in the headline should convey the right meaning to consumers. Some authors argue that it is always desirable to include the key words that are most likely to attract readers' attention, such as *announcing, new, now, at last, reduced, free, how to, how, why, which,* and *wanted.*[2] Such words can make a headline more striking and attention grabbing.

Headlines tend to follow one of several patterns. They can resemble a news headline, by announcing a new product discovery or by providing readers with some interesting and novel product information. It should also remain as specific as possible, since a vague headline is not interesting. An example of a news headline is given in the Tide advertisement reproduced in Figure 13–11.

Another interesting way of presenting a headline is by using the "how to" approach. Such headlines suggest that the rest of the advertisement will pro-

FIGURE 13–9
This headline plays on a consumer's fear—losing face—if not covered by the Gold Card Purchase Protection Plan.
Courtesy American Express Canada. Gold Card® and Purchase Protection Plan℠ are trademarks owned by the American Express Company.

FIGURE 13–10
As with any other indirect approach, the problem described can often be solved by other means than the advertised brand.
Courtesy Sterling Drug Ltd.

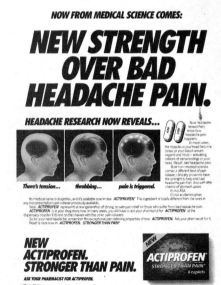

FIGURE 13-11
This headline presents new product information and reinforces the illustrations.

Courtesy Procter and Gamble Inc.

vide the reader with a means of achieving a desirable objective. Advertisements employing the "How you can" approach are more personal, since they are addressed directly to the reader.

Attention can also be attracted by asking a question which raises a problem and excites the reader's curiosity. It is hoped that readers will feel compelled to look at the rest of the advertisement to find the answer. A question can also be purely rhetorical when the answer is self-evident. The question allows for a more striking presentation of the message. This is shown in the Maclean's advertisement in Figure 13–12.

Headlines can also be expressed in the imperative form. This type of headline is generally used when immediate action is sought from the consumer. However, it tends to be less interesting than other approaches and in some instances may be less effective.

The different approaches to content and headlines can be combined, as is demonstrated in Table 13–1.

Selecting a Headline. How is an effective headline designed? There are no strict rules to follow to achieve an effective headline; an advertiser must rely on common sense and intuition to select the most effective headline for a specific advertising situation.

Nonetheless, the probable effectiveness of a headline can be assessed by evaluating the concept according to the following criteria:

1. Does the headline attract a reader's attention?
2. Is it clearly understood? Does it convey the message in a straightforward, unambiguous way?

TABLE 13–1 **TYPES OF CONTENT AND SYNTAX IN HEADLINES**

Type of Headline	Type of Headline Content	
	Direct	Indirect
News Headline	Introducing the Protected Curl from L'Oreal (L'Oreal)	The six year molar may be the most important tooth in his mouth and the most vulnerable (Aim)
"How to" Headline	How your hair can have beautiful body language (Enhance)	How to prove to your mother-in-law that her son's in good hands (Hershey's Cocoa)
Question Headline	Hotdog know how? Maple Leaf's got it! (Maple Leaf)	Are you ready for your next great romance? (Silhouette Special Editions)
Command Headline	Watch good skin happen—Wash with Noxzema every day (Noxzema)	Learn how beautiful a little self-confidence can make you (Mary Kay)

FIGURE 13–12
What news-minded person would not want to have an answer to the question?

Reprinted by permission from *Maclean's*

FIGURE 13–13
Without the subheads, the headline cannot be understood. The subheads are used here to complete the message.

Courtesy Minolta Business Equipment Canada Ltd.

3. Does it identify the target audience either directly or by addressing a specific problem faced by this target audience?
4. Does it avoid banality and vagueness?
5. Does it properly supplement and is it consistent with the other elements of the advertisement, visual and verbal?
6. Does it effectively demonstrate how the product can satisfy some consumer need, or does it lead toward such a demonstration?

The Subheads

The main headline may not be enough to make a point, but only attracts readers' attention. In these cases advertisers can explain the meaning of the headline in a subhead, which can develop a point raised by the headline or give additional information designed to reinforce the advertisement's main point. The Minolta advertisement reproduced in Figure 13–13 gives a good example of effective use of subheads. Here the headline identifies the brand and the subheads elaborate on the meaning of the headline.

The Body Copy

A headline and a visual element may be enough to drive home the point of the advertisement, and lengthy elaboration is unwarranted. The advertisements for Volkswagen (Figure 12–19) the NEC Portable Phone (Plate III) or the Smirnoff ad (Figure 13–14) are cases in point. In some instances an advertiser may want to communicate additional product advantages or factual information about the product, as in the advertisement for butter shown in Figure 13–15. Or the advertisement can elaborate on the theme announced by the headline.

FIGURE 13–16
The body copy con-
stitutes one of the
essential elements
of this advertise-
ment and provides
potential customers
with a substantial
amount of technical
information.

Courtesy Subaru Auto
Canada Ltd.

FIGURE 13–17
In this "reason why"
copy, the advertiser
gives consumers argu-
ments why they should
stay at Ramada hotels
when they travel.

Courtesy Ramada
Canada Ltd.

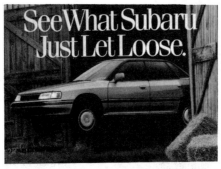

Advertisers usually resort to a written text or body copy to present more detailed selling arguments. The body copy may be quite lengthy, as for products that contain many technical features, for example the advertisement for the New Subaru Legacy (Figure 13–16).

Few readers will likely read the body copy of this advertisement, unless they are interested potential customers for this type of car. Therefore, this message is targeted at a limited market segment of people who want to buy a car and are seeking the type of information the copy provides. This example shows that the existence and length of copy depend on the nature of the product, as well as on the communication objectives of the advertisement.

Types of Body Copy. The type of body copy varies according to the nature of the appeal used for the advertisement. Copy that gives consumers good reasons to buy a product is known as "reason why" copy. The Ramada advertisement (Figure 13–17) is a good example, because it gives the readers the reasons why they should consider patronizing the Ramada hotels.

Advertisers may try to make a sales pitch more appealing by using humour in the body copy. For technically advanced products, descriptive copy provides a more elaborate description of the product than is possible in the headline or illustration. Testimonial advertising is another popular technique and was illustrated with the Pampers and Kelly advertisements in Chapter 9 (Figures 9–7 and 9–8).

Body copy can also take the form of a dialogue or a narrative text. The text should be interesting, precise, and well-written, because consumers will not otherwise be motivated to read lengthy copy.

Writing the Copy. As with headlines, there is no precise set of standards that determine good body copy. The copy should aim at brevity and clarity, but not at the expense of additional information or persuasive arguments. It should be interesting, specific, concise, easy to understand, and believable. It should never be vague or use unconvincing terms, as this would decrease the advertiser's credibility. Advertisers must strive to bolster a sales pitch with concrete examples and convincing arguments.

Just as in headline creation, the best tool to effective copy writing lies in advertisers' assessment of how best to meet the communication objectives for a particular situation. Therefore, much is left to the individual creator's common sense, intuition, and imagination.

Slogans

Slogans are somewhat like headlines, with a few differences. They may last for several years, throughout an entire advertising campaign, are intended to produce a lasting impression, and sum up the recurring theme of an advertising campaign. Examples are "Kentucky fried chicken is finger lickin' good" or "Drink Coca-Cola."

Good slogans are easy to remember. They are usually short, concise, and contain an inner rhyme, rhythm, or alliteration. A slogan such as "I like Ike," although not used in an advertising context, is striking and produces a lasting impression. There is no miracle recipe for creating effective slogans, however. Perhaps more than any element of print advertisement, they rely on the creator's stroke of genius. Slogans should, however, meet two standard requirements: they should be memorable, and they should effectively sum up the theme of the advertising campaign.

Logotypes

A logotype "derives from the Greek *logos*, meaning speech or word. Thus, logo strongly suggests a legible entity, e.g., a company's name. Visually, such a company name may simply be represented in a particular type style—hence, logotype.[3] According to this definition, the name Ramada at the bottom of Figure 13–17 is a logotype. The concept of logotype may be extended to any non-verbal symbol used to identify a brand. Thus the red box in the same advertisement, which is used as a symbol for the company, can be considered part of its logotype.

Like a slogan, the logotype should be memorable and become associated in consumers' minds with the advertised brand. If a brand name is written in a distinctive manner, this style is considered a logotype, in that it identifies the company. Tourists who see a Coca-Cola sign written Hebrew or Arabic will recognize the brand, even though they do not know either language. The purely non-verbal elements of the sign give added identity to the brand name and make it more readily identifiable by consumers. A logotype should not clash with the product image but serve to enhance it.

The Atmosphere Conveyed by Print Advertisements

The purpose of creating a certain ambiance or atmosphere with a print advertisement is to convey a specific personality or image to the brand that is consistent with the brand positioning strategy. As was seen in Chapter 12, all the visual and verbal elements in an advertisement generate an image. In Chapter 9, it was seen how specific characters, media vehicles, and consumption scenarios featured in the advertisement tend to convey definite images to a brand. Advertisers should try to control these elements and use them to confer the right image on the advertised product. To meet this objective, they can rely on intuition, experience, or on formal research techniques.[4]

It has been suggested that every detail of an advertisement contributes to brand image formation and that consequently, advertisers should try to control every detail of print advertisements so as to convey the desired brand image. Specific elements of an advertisement also convey a definite atmosphere. These include humour, as well as colour and the advertisement layout, which are exclusive characteristics of print advertisements.

The Use of Colour

In recent years, colour advertisements have gained wider usage; most magazine advertisements and an increasing number of newspaper advertisements are now run in colour. Colour can be used effectively to attract attention, make representations with complete fidelity, emphasize some part of the message, suggest abstract qualities, and create pleasant first impressions or prestige for the product, service, or advertiser, in readers' memories.[5]

Studies on the value of colour advertisements indicate that colour tends to increase the readership rate, enhance the prestige of the brand or the advertiser, and increase the retention rates for visual images among consumers. One study conducted by Daniel Starch on more than 25 000 advertisements in various product categories in national magazines showed that four-colour advertisements were noticed more often in comparison with black and white or even two-colour advertisements, regardless of the advertisements' size. The results of this study are shown in Figure 13–18.[6]

Because colour advertising rates are substantially higher than rates for black and white advertisements, the question arises whether colour is really worth the extra cost. According to Starch, because four-colour rates are only 46 percent above black and white rates for half-page advertisements, and about 35 percent for one-page advertisements, four-colour advertisements seem to warrant the increased advertising costs.

Colour can be effectively used to attract readers' attention or to highlight certain parts of an advertisement. For example, the Seiko advertisement in Plate VII, where only the product is in colour on a black and white background, was designed to focus on the product package.

Like any element of the advertisement, colour creates a certain mood. An advertiser should be well aware of the meaning of colour in order to make it enhance the atmosphere of the advertisement.

When food is being advertised, colour represents a definite advantage, since it appeals to consumers' senses. Using just the right colour is important;

FIGURE 13–18

The Effectiveness of Colour Advertisements According to the Starch Study.

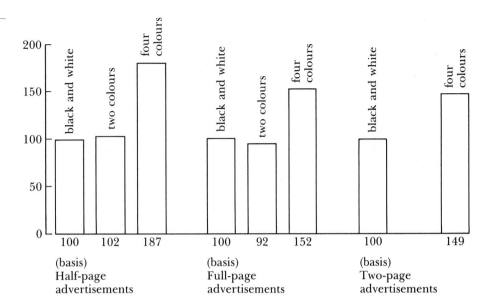

	Half-page advertisements			Full-page advertisements			Two-page advertisements	
	black and white	two colours	four colours	black and white	two colours	four colours	black and white	four colours
	100	102	187	100	92	152	100	149
	(basis)			(basis)			(basis)	

otherwise, the food in an illustration could look artificial and unappetizing. Colour also carries a great deal of symbolic information. For instance, cool colours are associated with relaxation and warm colours convey excitement. Also, colour preferences vary considerably according to cultural background, which is an important factor for a company that advertises on an international scale as will be discussed in Chapter 16. Indications about the symbolic value of colours are reproduced in Figure 13–19.[7]

Unfortunately, the scant research conducted in this area provides little conclusive evidence on the symbolic meaning of various colours. Therefore, the advertising creator must once again rely on artistic evaluation to choose colours that are consistent with the mood of the advertisement.

Layout

A layout is a working drawing showing how the various parts of an advertisement—the headline, subheads, illustration, copy, picture captions, trademarks, slogans, and logotype—fit together. Layouts generally fulfill two purposes. First, they are blueprints showing how the various elements of an advertisement must be placed in relation to one another; it is a guide for the artists and copywriters to show what is required to develop effective artwork.

Second, and more importantly, the layout is often responsible for conveying the feeling or mood of the advertisement and thus has a psychological and symbolic function. Different positions, weights, and organization of the various elements of an advertisement may suggest completely different atmospheres and convey very different brand images.

The most important features of a good layout are: interesting composition and balance, variety, simplicity, and intelligent positioning of the different units.

FIGURE 13–19

The Symbolic Value of Colour

Source: Walter Margulies in *Media Decisions*, reproduced in Douglas Johnson, *Advertising Today*, (Minneapolis: Paradigm Publishing International, 1978) p. 103.

What Colors Should You Use?

Reaction to color, says Walter Margulies, is generally based on a man's national origin or race. For example, "warm" colors are red, yellow and orange: "these tend to stimulate, excite and create an active response." Those from a warmer clime, apparently, are most responsive to these colors.

Violet and "leaf green," fall right on the line between warm and cool. Each can be one or the other, depending on the shade used.

Here are some more Marqulies observations:

Red Symbol of blood and fire. A runnerup to blue as man's "favorite color", but it is the most versatile. i.e., it's the hottest color with highest "action quotient." Appropriate for Campbell's Soups, Stouffer's frozen foods and meats. Conveys stong masculine appeal—shaving cream, Lucky Strike, Marlboro.

Brown Another masculine color, associated with earth, woods, mellowness, age, warmth, comfort. i.e., the essential male: used to sell men anything (even cosmetics), for example, Revlon's Braggi.

Yellow High impact to catch consumer's eye, particularly when used with black—psychologically right for corn, lemon or sun tan products.

Green Symbol of health, freshness—popular for tobacco products, especially mentholated. i.e., Salem, Pall Mall menthol.

Blue Coldest color, with most appeal, effective for frozen foods (ice impression): if used with lighter tints becomes "sweet"—Montclair cigarettes, Lowenbrau beer, Wondra flour.

Black Conveys sophistication, high-end merchandise or used to simulate expensive products: good as background and foil for other colors.

Orange Most "edible" color, especially in brown-tinged shades, evokes autumn and good things to eat.

Composition and Balance. Arranging the various visual and verbal elements of a layout may seem like a simple task but in fact it is not. The visual elements should be positioned dramatically to avoid monotony and attract attention. Therefore, the visual elements should be of unequal sizes. This is a basic principle in art and photography. An advertisement in which the space was divided into four equal rectangles, for instance, could seem monotonous and consequently not command attention. The advertisement in Plate VIII has a less conventional, more exciting layout.

Variety. Variety can be generated through such devices as dramatic use of colour (see the advertisement in Plate IX), blank space (such as in Figure 13–20), or different typefaces.

FIGURE 13-20
The use of the white space in this advertisement highlights the product and contrasts with the yellow of the sun flowers.

This advertisement has been provided by Monarch Fine Foods, a division of Thomas J. Lipton Inc.

ONE GOOD SPREAD DESERVES ANOTHER...

BECEL LIGHT.

Canadians are spreading the good example: Becel Margarine. That's because Becel is an excellent way to help your family eat heart-smart. Becel has 55% polyunsaturates and 29% saturates. And because Becel is made of sunflower oil, it has a natural, delicate taste. It's the heart-smart way to spread a good example.

Becel Light has all the goodness of Becel Margarine with half the fat and calories. It's the light way to eat heart-smart. (Not available in Quebec.)

becel

BECEL TAKES YOUR HEALTH TO HEART.

Simplicity. Cluttered layouts should be avoided. An illustration is best understood when it is kept simple. Only elements which add force to the communication should be kept. Plate X is an example of a layout that might be considered too crowded.

Positioning of the Units in the Layout. The first illustration of Figure 13–21 (page 346) shows the visual path followed by the eye as it scans an advertisement. The eye does not always follow this path, however, but may be drawn to other interesting points. The point at which this happens most frequently is called the optical center or focal point. It is located one-third of the way down from the top of the illustration, at the intersection of the vertical and horizontal lines, in illustration 2. The area surrounding this point, as shown in illustration 3, is the most frequently noticed by readers. Therefore, the most important element of an advertisement, usually the product, should be positioned in this very visible area.

Although advertising art directors or artists may find these guidelines useful in creating print advertisements, no principle can replace talent; creativity blended with communication abilities and common sense should yield effective advertising layouts.

Evaluating Print Advertisements

Once a print advertisement has been created, it must be formally evaluated before it can be accepted by the client. The objective is to ensure the advertisement meets some basic qualities, from a communication as well as from a marketing point of view. To make such an assessment, criteria and a formal procedure to test the advertisement should be set up.

FIGURE 13–21
*Visual Path and
Focal Point.*

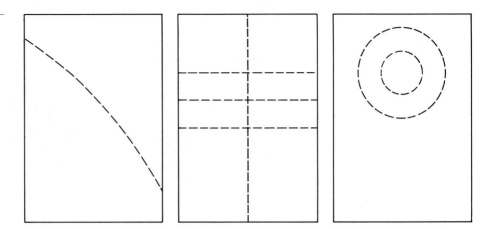

Criteria for Evaluating Print Advertisements

A list of criteria for evaluating and selecting print advertisements has been proposed by Joannis.[8] This list gives a good idea of what an advertiser's concerns should be when an advertisement is created. Three criteria concern the advertisement's psychological effectiveness; two criteria concern its communicative effectiveness, and two criteria concern its marketing consistency.

PSYCHOLOGICAL EFFICIENCY CRITERIA.

Is the message powerful and distinctive? Is the motive or the satisfaction to which the advertisement appeals important to consumers? Does the message properly differentiate the brand from competitive products?

Is the message properly understood? Has the advertiser avoided making coding errors?

Does the message fit consumers' psychological background? Can the message be perceived by consumers as relating to their experience, culture, concerns, and psychological environment? Is it likely to be rejected? Does it go against consumers' moral, cultural, or aesthetic values?

COMMUNICATION EFFECTIVENESS CRITERIA.

Can the message be quickly perceived and understood by the consumer? Can consumers understand the meaning of the advertisement at a single glance (in this case, it has a high communicative value), or should the consumer be required to think in order to grasp the advertisement's meaning?

Is the message graphically powerful? Does the advertisement copy, the illustrations, and the advertisement layout powerfully communicate the idea that the advertiser wants to convey to consumers?

MARKETING CONSISTENCY CRITERIA.

Can the message be adapted to other types of media? Can the advertisement's appeal be easily adapted to other media if they must also be used for the advertising campaign?

Is the message consistent with other marketing constraints? Can the message be easily adapted to other promotional means (point-of-purchase advertising, posters, or displays)?

Research Evidence for Evaluating Print Advertisements

Formal research methodology for pretesting advertisements in relation to each criterion is discussed in Chapter 15. Past research, however, can also give clues as to what types of advertising format options have proved most effective.

Readership scores of 137 advertisements in the *American Builder* were found to be explained mainly by such factors as the size of the advertisement, the size of the illustration, and the number of colours. These were better explanatory variables than some message content variables.[9] A similar but more extensive study involved 1070 advertisements that appeared in *Life* magazine over a six-month period.[10] Here again, a substantial proportion of the variance in the reading scores provided by Starch was accounted for by such factors as the size of the advertisement (the scores were higher for a double page than for a single page, greater for a horizontal half page than for a vertical one), and the number of colours. Advertisements with photographs scored higher than advertisements without visual elements. The scores had a tendency to drop sharply once the copy contained more than 50 words. It was also found that the brand or headline prominence in the advertisement had little or no effect.

Such results should not be considered as absolute truths, and they are highly situation dependent. It is somewhat artificial to consider each individual element of an advertisement separately. An advertisement is a whole that is greater than the sum of its parts, and it would be misleading to judge each element without considering the entire advertisement. These findings should be considered only as indications of general trends.

Creating Other Types of Print Advertisements

Although most of the principles discussed above also apply to outdoor and transit advertising, additional constraints must also be considered because of the special conditions in which the message must be conveyed to the audience.

Outdoor Advertising

Because consumers are likely to be exposed to an outdoor poster for only a short period of time, the principle of quick message delivery is more imperative than for magazine or newspaper advertising. Whether an advertiser designs new copy or adapts the copy already written for other media (as usually happens for national multi-media advertising campaigns), the problem is to simplify the copy as much as possible yet still make it powerful.

The copy should meet three basic requirements. First, the product and the brand should be attention-grabbing, which requires the use of bright colours. Second, the illustration should deliver as much of the message as possible. Third, headlines should be as short and unambiguous as possible. No other element should appear on the poster, because consumers might become confused about the message.

Transit Advertising

Interior bus advertisements should follow about the same creation principles as magazine advertisements. But for outdoor car signs, the creation principles for outdoor advertising apply. The major difference between the two types of advertising lies in the horizontal format of bus signs, which requires a different layout.

Print Advertisement Production

After approval of the creative elements of the print advertisement, the production process begins. Print production has developed into a highly complex and technical process. Therefore, while it is neither possible nor even necessary that most advertising managers be versed in all the technical subtleties of this field, they must have at least a hands-on knowledge of its different phases in order to evaluate the costs, constraints, and opportunities in the production process. (See Appendix 2.)

As shown in Figure 13–22, the print advertisement production process can be divided into three stages. First the original plates for the advertisement are produced. Then this plate must be duplicated, especially if the advertisement is to be carried by several different publications. The third and final stage is the actual printing of the advertisement.

The original plate can be produced through a variety of techniques, depending on the type of print media that carries the advertisement, the quality and nature of the advertisement, the printing process, and other factors. One of the first decisions a producer must make are those concerning the different type styles for the advertisement's verbal elements. Next, the type must be

FIGURE 13–22

Outline of the Print Advertisement Production Process

CREATION

1. Define the creative strategy
2. Develop the advertisement concept
3. Develop, revise, refine the advertisement layout and copy
4. Evaluate the production costs

PRODUCTION

1. *Produce the plate*
   - select the type style
   - set the type
   - produce photographic plates for drawings and illustrations
2. *Duplicate the plates*
   - select the duplication process
3. *Printing*
   - select the printing process

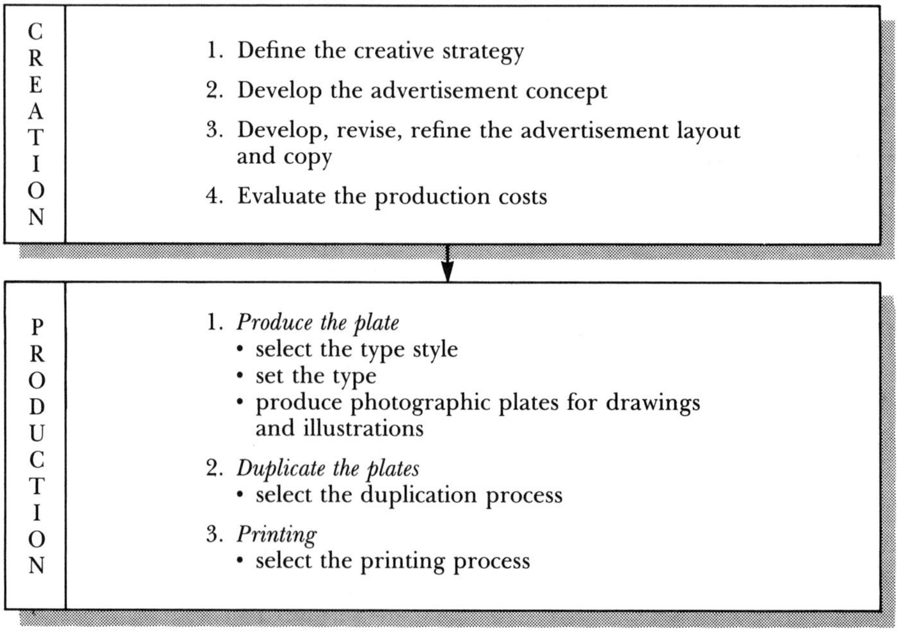

set. Mechanical typesetting methods such as linotype or monotype are being replaced by newer, more efficient techniques that consist in exposing the text on photo-sensitive paper or film. If the advertisement contains an illustration, drawing, or photograph, this visual element will have to be etched on a separate plate. With colour advertisements, one plate must be designed for each colour. A full-colour advertisement needs four plates, one for each of the basic colours: red, blue, yellow, and black. These plates are then superimposed, creating the impression of numerous different shades, as is illustrated in Plate XI.

Several different publications may carry the same advertisement. This requires making a mould of the plate, either as a stereotype or as a more expensive, higher quality electrotype.

The printing process involves transferring the image of the advertisement from a press onto paper. The three most commonly used printing techniques are letterpress, gravure, and offset.

CREATING BROADCAST COMMERCIALS

Special Characteristics of Broadcast Commercials

The creation of broadcast commercials has some basic differences from print advertisements. These differences derive from the presence of other channels of communication: the audio element, a unique time dimension, and the particular medium/audience interface that broadcast media have developed.

The Audio Elements in Broadcast Commercials

A broadcast message contains an audio element not present in print advertisements. For television commercials, the audio elements are added to the three other communication channels of verbal, visual, and ambience that characterize print advertisements. For radio commercials, they are a substitute for visual elements. Thus, the presence of audio elements changes the nature and effectiveness of the communication. When properly used, audio elements tend to increase a communication's effectiveness. There is typically a higher level of message retention among an audience exposed to a broadcast commercial, since a verbal message tends to be remembered better than the text in a print advertisement.

The Time Dimension of Broadcast Commercials

Whereas space is the limiting constraint for print advertisements, broadcast commercials are limited by time. The broadcast creator's problem is to deliver a message effectively in a brief period, usually 15, 30, or 60 seconds. Although these periods are often much longer than the amount of time that many readers of print advertisements devote to a single ad, the trend toward shorter, 30-second commercials (for obvious cost reasons) has caused the "commercial clutter" phenomenon. Television commercial time is filled with many 15-second and 30-second commercials, hence the increasing need for advertisers to vie aggressively for viewers' attention.

A second time-related difference lies in the relative control an advertiser has over the audience while the commercial is aired. Readers of a print advertisement are subjected to selected exposure to the selling arguments, since they may glance at some parts of an illustration, ignore others, and read only part of the text. With television or radio commercials, listeners are sequentially exposed to the various points, and advertisers have more control over the exact content of the message delivered.

The Consumer/Broadcast Media Interface

As most advertisers know, people frequently talk or engage in other activities while watching television. Audiences' low involvement in broadcast media is one manifestation of selective attention barriers that people use to screen out what they do not want to hear. Furthermore, Festinger found that people tend to argue mentally with commercials that are at variance with their own ideas, and that this counter-argumentation was listeners' attempt to resist commercial persuasion.[11] Consequently, this particular consumer/broadcast media interface tends to counterbalance the effectiveness of the audio elements.

Creating Television Commercials

Television's popularity and highly concentrated audiences make the medium an extremely powerful communication tool. This is why companies allocate an increasing amount of their advertising dollars to television. Because of its four parallel communication channels—visual, audio, verbal, and ambience—television commercials are a more complete communication device. All the elements of every channel should be selected to communicate the desired message. This is represented in Figure 13–23.

The Functions of the Television Commercial Elements

Visual Elements. The functions of the visual and verbal elements of a television commercial are closely related. As with print advertisements, the visual elements are assigned the function of expressing as much of the advertising message as possible. However, because of the relatively longer period of time to be filled by a commercial, advertisers are not limited to one major selling argument, as is the case for print advertisements. Depending on the duration of the commercial and the nature of the advertised product, advertisers can make several selling points. Nonetheless, the visual elements should highlight the product and the brand, either to demonstrate its use or simply to make consumers aware of the package so that they would recognize the brand at a store. This is why a product or brand should be identified as early as possible during the television commercial. The visual elements, together with the verbal elements and the script, constitute the television commercial's scenario.

Verbal Elements. The verbal elements—the script of the commercial scenario—are used to explain, reinforce, and complement the visual elements in order to communicate the advertising message effectively. Visual elements are needed to identify the brand name properly. As in print advertisements, this function can be performed in conjunction with written headlines, slogans, and logotypes.

TELEVISION COMMERCIAL			
Visual Elements	Verbal Elements	Audio Elements	Ambiance Elements
1. *Functions* • Express the message • Demonstrate and present the product/brand	1. *Functions* • Explain and supplement the message • Identify the brand name	1. *Functions* • Deliver the message • Increase the realism and attractiveness of a commercial • Distract from counterargumentation	1. *Functions* • Develop brand image and personality
2. *Element Types* • Commercial • Storyboard	2. *Element Types* • Copy • Written headlines, slogans, logotypes	2. *Element Types* • Voices • Sound Effects • Background music • Jingles	2. *Element Types* • Visual, verbal, audio • Colour • Humour • Pace

OBJECTIVES OF A TELEVISION COMMERCIAL

• get attention
• arouse interest
• communicate effectively
• be understood
• motivate

TARGET MARKET

FIGURE 13–23
Elements of a Television Commercial

Audio Elements.   Audio elements in broadcast commercials fulfill three main functions: they deliver the verbal message, increase the message effectiveness through higher realism and attractiveness, and create a "distracting" element to reduce consumers' counter-argumentation during a commercial. Background music, sound effects, and jingles can be effectively used to achieve these three functions.

Ambiance Elements.   Advertisers can build the proper atmosphere in a commercial that will generate the desired brand image and personality. All the visual, verbal, and audio elements are likely to suggest symbolic interpretations, and the use of colours, the use of humour, as well as the pace of the commercial may create quite different moods.

Developing the Storyboard

A storyboard is the counterpart of a layout for print advertisements. It is a set of pictures or frames that describe each scene or movement during the

FIGURE 13-24

**Storyboard for
a Television
Commercial**

*Courtesy Marketing
Magazine*

commercial. At the bottom of every frame are indications about the copy,
sound effects, and music that correspond to the scene. A storyboard is a detailed
screenplay for a television commercial. A sample storyboard is shown in Figure
13-24.

Once an advertiser has described the main claim that will be emphasized
in the commercial and for other related selling arguments, the approach to

the commercial must be selected. There are a finite number of ways a commercial can be presented on television. The main categories for television commercials are as follows:[12]

Story Line. A commercial that tells a story; a clear, step-by-step unfolding of a message that has a definite beginning, middle, and end.

Problem-solving. Presents the viewer with a problem to be solved and the sponsor's product as the solution to that problem. Probably the most widely used and generally accepted example of a TV commercial.

Chronology. Delivers the message through a series of related scenes, each one growing out of the one before. Facts and events are presented sequentially as they occur.

Special Effects. No strong structural pattern. Strives for and often achieves memorability through the use of some striking device, for example, an unusual musical sound or pictorial technique.

Testimonial. Also called "word-of-mouth" advertising, it uses well-known figures or an unknown "man in the street" to provide product testimonials.

Satire. A commercial that uses sophisticated wit to point out human foibles, generally produced in an exaggerated style. Parodies on James Bond movies, "Bonnie and Clyde," "Hair," and the like.

Spokesperson. The use of an on-camera announcer who talks. Talk may be fast and hard sell or more personal, intimate sell.

Demonstration. Uses some physical apparatus to demonstrate a product's effectiveness. Analgesic, watch, and tire commercials employ this approach heavily.

Suspense. Somewhat similar to story line or problem-solution structures, but the build-up of curiosity and suspense to final resolution is given a heightened sense of drama.

Slice-of-life. A variation of problem-solution. Begins with a person at the point of, and just before the discovery of, an answer to a problem. Heavily used by detergent manufacturers.

Analogy. Offers an extraneous example, then attempts to relate it to the product message. Instead of delivering a message simply and directly, an analogy uses one example to explain another by comparison or implication. "Just as vitamins tone up your body, our product tones up your car's engine."

Fantasy. Uses caricatures or special effects to create fantasy surrounding product and product use: "Jolly Green Giant," "Hostess Munchies," "Tetley Tea Men," "Max Headroom."

Personality. A technical variation of the spokesperson or announcer-on-camera, straight-sell structure. Relies on an actor or actress rather than an announcer to deliver the message. Uses a setting rather than the background of a studio. The actor plays a character who talks about the product, reacts to its use, or demonstrates its use or enjoyment directly to the camera.[13]

Selecting the Audio Elements

Because of their special importance for television commercials, audio elements should be selected carefully and should match the kind of story selected as a support to the sales pitch. Most important is the kind of voice selected to announce the product, the sound effects, the background music, and the jingles. These bring life and realism to broadcast advertisements.

The Announcer's Voice. The selection of the proper voice can decide the success of a commercial, and a certain type of voice can give the right brand image or suggest the right product usage situation for the target market segment. There are ten voice styles for broadcast commercials, listed in Figure 13–25.[14]

A voice suitable for advertising a price cut at a discount store cannot be used to advertise expensive perfumes. Not only the voice itself, but also the tone of the voice, its nuance, the accent, and the emotion are loaded with information that is deciphered by the consumers and associated with the advertised brand.

Sound Effects. There is a hierarchy of sound effects for use in a television commercial. Some sounds have an obvious raison d'être in a commercial because they are expected to be heard as the commercial unfolds. Their use is a question of realism. For instance, the roaring of cars passing on a highway, the noise of a lawn mower being demonstrated, the pop of a champagne cork, or the hiss sound of a spray can are natural complements to the verbal part of the advertising message. At a higher level, an advertiser can make effective use of sounds to say something about the product or the brand. For instance, a car door being slammed with a solid sound suggests a sturdy, well-built automobile; the fizz of sparking natural water suggests that brand's thirst-quenching property; the crunch of a biscuit evokes freshness. At a more subtle level, sounds can build symbolic meanings around a brand and can be instrumental in brand image creation. The sound of a zipper closing during a commercial for a diet drink evokes the ability of the product to help consumers stay thin (so that they can close the zippers without difficulty). Although nothing is said about the zipper, consumers clearly deduce the meanings.[15]

Thus, decisions about the choice and selection of sound effects are important because of the direct and symbolic information they convey to consumers.

The Use of Music. Advertisers must decide what role music should play in the overall advertising message. Should the selling proposition be put into music (in this case, the music line is called a jingle), or should the music be assigned the role of setting a background to supplement the message? Should the music attract the listener's attention, or should it go unnoticed as an atmosphere-creating device? Should the music be already familiar to the consumers, or should it be created especially for the commercial? What instruments should be used?

PLATE VIII

In this advertisement, the eye is attracted first by the unusual illustration which visually conveys the theme and directs the eye from left to right and down to the headline, the body copy, and the logo; in addition, the use of "white" space is very effective

Courtesy British Airways. Advertising agency Saatchi & Saatchi.

Someone up there is looking after you.

No matter where your business takes you, rest assured that British Airways people will smooth the way with superb service and the most convenient connections round the world. It's simply because of our unique training program in the finer points of looking after our passengers . . . among other things.

BRITISH AIRWAYS
The world's favourite airline.

The Art
of Relaxation

Clean, flowing lines. A shape contoured for comfort. An array
of colors pleasing to the eye. With controls that direct the
warm water's caress with just a touch of the fingertips.
This is true relaxation, an art made possible by
Acriform. And with our full line of acrylic
whirlpool baths, never has it been
so elegantly expressed.

acriform

ACRIFORM ENGINEERING INC., 395 MULOCK DRIVE, P.O. BOX 327, NEWMARKET, ONTARIO L3Y 4X7 (416) 898-5511

PLATE X

This type of layout uses a simple device of image and word association to convey its message of exercise and proper diet.

Courtesy Participaction

BILLY NEWTON DAVIS' BIKE.

BILLY NEWTON DAVIS' 'POWER' PASTA.

BILLY NEWTON DAVIS.

PARTICIPACTION MAKES PERFECT.

Left is yellow only;
right is red only.

Left is yellow and red; top right is blue only; bottom right is yellow and blue.

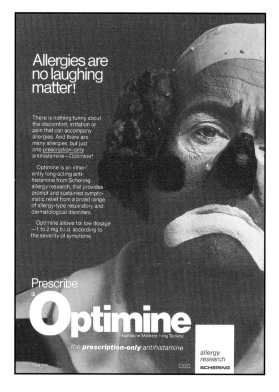

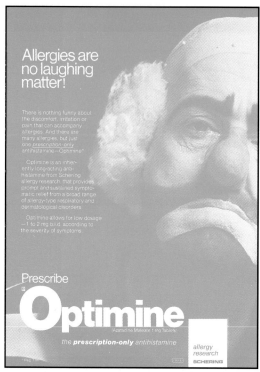

Top is blue and red; bottom left is yellow, red, and blue; bottom right is black only.

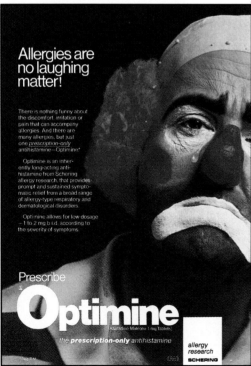

Top left is black, yellow, and blue; bottom left is black, yellow, and red; the right is in full colour (as in Plate XI), red, blue, yellow, and black.

FIGURE 13–25

Types of Voices in Commercials

Source: Adapted from Douglas Johnson, *Advertising Today* (Minneapolis: Paradigm Publishing International, 1978), pp. 105–6.

Straight Voice-of-Print Very objective, non-emotional voice of a news announcer. Appeals particularly to men and is best suited to bank, financial institutions, car, truck, automobile accessories, sports event tickets, gasoline, insurance commercials.

Disk Jockey Announcer: Young, modern voice using casual and often confidential tone. Appeals to young people and is best suited for commercials on fashion clothes, musical happenings, music stores, hair care products.

Beery Announcer. Bass or baritone voice often used to announce beer or cigarettes, automobiles, or trucks. The leadership tone of the voice is effective in influencing men.

Pound-Pound, Hard-Hitter, Fast-Talker Announcer. Very assertive voice often used in discount store or second-hand car commercials.

Folksy Announcer. Use of regional pattern of speech and accent. Each best fits the area where it is typical or can be used as a symbol of the area.

Cosmetic Voice: Often used as a voice-over in television (without the announcer being seen) to advertise perfume and cosmetics. Generally sexy, low, husky voice.

Impersonator Voice. Imitation of the voices of such well known actors as Humphrey Bogart, Gary Cooper, or Mae West. If not carefully checked, this may involve legal complaints. Has high attention value.

Character Voice. Overacting of certain stereotypes (such as the henpecked husband or the rich dowager) depending on the screenplay of the commercial.

Personality, Star, Celebrity. These are actual celebrities used in testimonial commercials.

Real People. Untrained, natural voices of ordinary people used for certain types of testimonial commercials.

Music lends uniqueness and interest to a commercial. Depending on the effects being sought, music can be used either as background or as a jingle generally sung off screen. Whenever music is used as background, an advertiser can use *stock music*. Stock music is already orchestrated music corresponding to various moods advertisers want to create. This music can be acquired at a reasonable cost from stock music companies. Or original music especially composed and recorded for a given commercial by an independent contractor may be used. This is certainly much more costly than stock music, but if a commercial is to be aired many times over an extended period, the high cost of original music may be warranted.

Jingles fulfill a purpose quite different from that of background music. They help consumers identify a brand immediately, create almost constant presence, express the personality of the brand, product, and/or company, get a new brand across to a market quickly, and help keep a brand name or a slogan in people's memory.[16] An effective jingle can unforgettably associate in consumers' minds a brand name with a short advertising message. Thus, a jingle sets to music either the slogan for the advertised brand or lyrics written usually by the advertising agency.

Advertisers have several options for selecting music. Original music composed especially for the jingle can be used. Composing fees would have to be considered before choosing this option. A popular song could also be used. The advantage of this option is that the public is already familiar with the tune and can memorize the jingle more quickly, with less message repetition. However, in this case advertisers must pay fees to the copyright owners. For songs in the public domain there is no fee to pay, but neither is there any guarantee that the song is not being or will not be used by other advertisers.

Evaluating Television Commercials

What makes a good and effective television commercial is somewhat hard to define. Creating a television commercial is as much an art as a science, and depends on such intangible and qualitative aspects as aesthetic values, emotional appeals, or credibility. But because of the high stakes involved in television advertising, advertisers have often tried to define the criteria that could help them to assess the quality of television commercials. Some general criteria are:

Do the visual elements powerfully convey the message?   Pictures are a powerful means of communication. Often, a single visual element can replace a lengthy description. Vivid pictures yield better results, attract more attention, increase reach, are most remembered by consumers, and generally make for a better advertisement. Striking pictures, if used judiciously, always reinforce the advertising message.

Has the commercial been kept simple?   Typical television viewers are relaxing, and their concentration level is usually quite low. Thus they will reject subtle, complex, or muddled commercials. Therefore, the virtues of simplicity must once again be emphasized. The most powerful messages are always clear and straightforward.

Does the commercial make the best possible use of motion?   A static picture will not hold viewers' attention. Fast-moving pictures generate interest in the commercial.

Does the commercial demonstrate the use of the product?   Television is the best medium for product demonstration, especially for household and food products.

Is the commercial entertaining?   Entertainment can make a commercial more lively and interesting. It should, however, be subordinated to the advertisement's communication objectives. It should not distract the audience from the main objective of the commercial, which is to convey certain product advantages and/or promote the product.

Is the commercial credible?   Credibility is an essential prerequisite for any form of effective communication. Television advertising bears no exception to this rule. Commercials must avoid any kind of double talk, vague expressions, and inadequately backed claims that could ruin the sales presentation. In television advertising, this task becomes more complicated, because all the elements—setting, decor, acting, situation, language—must combine to create authenticity.

Although a great deal of research has been conducted, scientific advances made in the field of television advertising are not being applied sufficiently in practice. David Ogilvy and Joel Raphaelson of Ogilvy and Mather, a Chicago-based advertising agency have deplored this lack of scientific attitude among advertising creators: "Advertising could achieve better results if more people who create it would take the time to learn which techniques are most likely to work."[17] Among the techniques that yielded above-average results in changing brand preferences, they found:

- problem solution;
- humour (when pertinent to the selling proposition);
- relevant characters (personalities, developed by the advertising, who become associated with the brand);
- slice-of-life (enactments in which a doubter is converted);
- news (new products, new uses, new ideas, new information);
- candid camera testimonials and demonstrations.

Commercials using celebrities were not found to be very effective. One explanation proposed was that "such messages focus attention on the celebrity rather than on the product."[18]

Other findings reported were:

- cartoons and animation are effective with children, but below average with adults.
- commercials with very short scenes and many changes of situations are below average.
- "supers" (words on the screen) add to a commercial's power to change brand preference, but the words must reinforce the main point.
- commercials that do not show the package, or that end without the brand name, are below average in changing brand preference.
- commercials that start with a key idea stand a better chance of holding attention and persuading the viewer. When you advertise fire extinguishers, open with the fire.

Television Commercial Production

A television commercial may start with a great concept and a clever storyboard, only to be spoiled by inadequate casting, poor lighting, amateurish filming, or any one of a hundred flaws in the production process. This is why production is a crucial stage in the development of a commercial and special care must be taken to ensure that nothing goes wrong. The production process for television commercials is divided into three stages, as is shown in Figure 13–26 (next page). The first stage involves the decisions that must be taken before the

FIGURE 13–26

Outline of Television Commercial Production

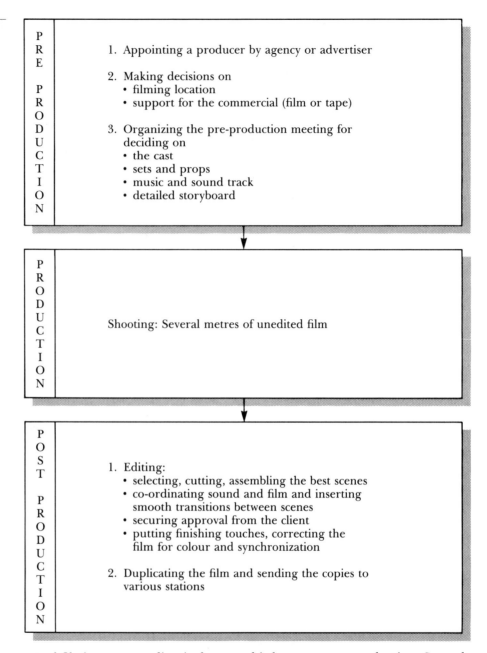

P R E P R O D U C T I O N	
	1. Appointing a producer by agency or advertiser
	2. Making decisions on • filming location • support for the commercial (film or tape)
	3. Organizing the pre-production meeting for deciding on • the cast • sets and props • music and sound track • detailed storyboard

P R O D U C T I O N	
	Shooting: Several metres of unedited film

P O S T P R O D U C T I O N	
	1. Editing: • selecting, cutting, assembling the best scenes • co-ordinating sound and film and inserting smooth transitions between scenes • securing approval from the client • putting finishing touches, correcting the film for colour and synchronization
	2. Duplicating the film and sending the copies to various stations

actual filming or recording is done, and is known as preproduction. Second, the storyboard is enacted and recorded on film or tape. Finally, the film is edited and submitted to the advertiser for approval. This last stage is post-production.

Preproduction.   Once a storyboard has been drafted and approved by the creative director of the advertising agency, the producer is summoned to oversee the actual production before the commercial is aired. The producer must decide on a studio or location in which the commercial will be shot. Then, a preproduction meeting is called, which is perhaps one of the most important stages of the entire production process. This meeting decides the schedule and the shooting: casting, music, sound effects, sets and props, lighting, camera angles, and other technical details. Nothing should be overlooked during this meeting, and the producer should set everything straight before the shooting. Even a minor snag noticed too late could result in time delays and costly overruns.

Production. Since all of the important decisions have already been made at the preproduction level, shooting merely involves recording the commercial according to the detailed and precise instructions contained on the storyboard. Usually, the time allotted for filming each scene is kept to one day because of the high cost of labour, studio time, and actors. Since an agency can ill afford a mistake that would force it into costly retakes, several versions are taken on each scene, and even superfluous scenes are sometimes added. For a typical 30-second spot, 600 to 900 metres of 35 mm film may be exposed, while only 15 metres will end up in the final commercial. If the commercial contains several different settings, the scenes are not filmed sequentially, for reasons of cost and efficiency.

Postproduction. What finally comes out of the studio is an unfinished product: several meters of film or tape, bearing a set of unrelated sequences. This rough copy is taken to the editor, who edits and cuts the film, selects the takes, recasts, improves, co-ordinates, and assembles the pictures into a coherent commercial. The film editor is in charge of the final stage of production. The creative department and the producer decide the content of an ad, but the editor makes their conception bear fruit and delivers the finished product, which can be aired once the client's approval is received. (See Appendix 2 for more information on the technical aspects of television commercial production.)

Creating Radio Commercials

Creating radio commercials bears some similarities to television commercial creation, but also a number of major differences. The first obvious difference is that radio commercials lack the visual elements of television. However, it would be wrong to conclude that radio commercials are nothing but the sound track of a corresponding television commercial. For television, the maximum amount of information must be conveyed through visual elements, and audio elements are used to supplement, reinforce, and make explicit the message to be communicated to the target audience. For a radio commercial, the audio elements are the only means available for conveying the message. Consequently, the sound track of a radio commercial is likely to be substantially different from that of television. The radio commercial communication process is represented in Figure 13–27 (next page).

In a given market, radio audiences are much more fragmented and segmented than television audiences. Depending on the types of programs and music aired, radio stations cater to audiences that vary according to age, social

FIGURE 13–27
Elements of a Radio Commercial

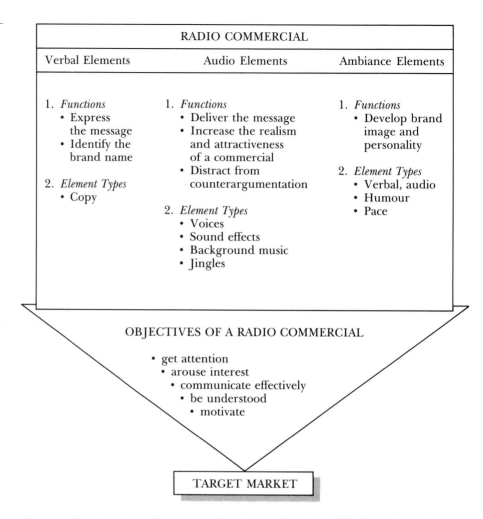

RADIO COMMERCIAL		
Verbal Elements	Audio Elements	Ambiance Elements
1. *Functions* • Express the message • Identify the brand name 2. *Element Types* • Copy	1. *Functions* • Deliver the message • Increase the realism and attractiveness of a commercial • Distract from counterargumentation 2. *Element Types* • Voices • Sound effects • Background music • Jingles	1. *Functions* • Develop brand image and personality 2. *Element Types* • Verbal, audio • Humour • Pace

OBJECTIVES OF A RADIO COMMERCIAL

• get attention
• arouse interest
• communicate effectively
• be understood
• motivate

TARGET MARKET

class, and education. Consequently, it may be desirable for advertisers to develop radio commercials built not only on the product to be advertised but also according to the different market segments reached by different kinds of stations.

Unlike television audiences, which are more homogeneous in their watching time and related activities while watching, radio audiences may be in different states of mind depending upon the time of the day and on the type of activity of the listener at the time the commercial is aired. For instance, radio listeners are not equally receptive when listening to a car radio while on the way to work, as when they listen to a portable radio while relaxing on a beach. Copywriters must take these considerations into account when developing a radio commercial for a certain brand.

Copywriters have much more freedom in developing a radio commercial than a television commercial. They are not constrained by the practical feasibility and/or the costs of developing the visual elements. With only words and sounds to manipulate, copywriters are limited only by their imagination. There are several types of radio commercials. Live or recorded commercials are the most common.

Types of Radio Commercials

Live Commercials. The copy is prepared to be read "live" by a station personality or an announcer. Live commercial scripts are generally prepared in advance. They run about 100 to 120 words per minute so they can be read at a normal pace. Among other advantages, such messages tend to be more credible because they are read (and indirectly endorsed) by local personalities; they also are less costly than pre-recorded scripts. However, they cannot take full advantage of the audio elements, such as background music, jingles, or sound effects. They cannot rely on carefully selected voices and controlled diction of the message. This is why advertisers often prefer to use recorded commercials.

Announcer Delivery. This type of commercial is much like a live commercial, but the script has been pre-recorded. Sound effects, background music, jingles, careful voice selection—all the audio elements—can be controlled, and the commercial can be revised until it fully satisfies the advertiser's requirements.

Musical Commercials. Jingles and musical commercials can effectively associate a brand name with a slogan or a selling argument. All the characteristics of using music in television commercials also apply to the development of good musical radio commercials.

Dialogue Commercials. Dialogue makes a radio commercial more lively and interesting. This approach also lends itself to the use of humour, which can enhance the positive image of a brand.

Testimonial Commercials. The testimonial approach uses either real people or celebrities.

Basically the same criteria for evaluating the effectiveness of commercials apply for radio and television commercials, but the entire communication is carried by the sound. A good radio commercial should entice consumers with interesting informative content, provide a lively soundtrack, and depict believable situations. The message should be kept simple, be repeated for added force, and the announcer should use short words and sentences so that the message is understood by consumers with the low level of concentration typical of radio listeners.

Radio Commercial Production

Radio production is simpler and less expensive than television. With a live recording, the production stage is almost nonexistent, since the agency merely has to supply radio stations with a script. However, if the commercial is to be recorded, the production stage is necessary.

The production of a radio commercial is straightforward. The advertiser appoints a director who selects a recording studio and a cast. The director may hire professional actors to read the script, musicians to play the music, or composers. Rehearsals may be held before the actual recording. Then the sound track and the music are prepared in a studio on separate tapes. The various elements are mixed at a later stage, yielding the master tape. After several such recordings have been made, the best is chosen and is duplicated, either on tape or on records. The commercials are then sent to various stations to be aired.

SUMMARY

With print advertisements the visual, verbal, and atmosphere-creating elements should be selected so as to be consistent and should help convey the basic advertising message to consumers. The visual elements are the most powerful in communicating to the market. They include photographs, drawings, or other kinds of artwork. Verbal elements should complete the message and supplement it. They include the advertisement headline, the subheads, the body copy, the slogan, and the logotype. In addition to the visual and verbal elements of an advertisement, which tend to create a particular atmosphere and build a certain brand image, other elements are powerful in ambience content. They include the use of colour or black and white, and the layout for an advertisement. There are several criteria for evaluating print advertisements, as well as considerations that apply to outdoor and transit advertising.

Broadcast commercials have unique audio, time, and consumer/medium interface characteristics. To develop effective commercials, advertisers must design a creative storyboard and make intelligent use of the announcer's voice, sound effects, and music. Although advertisers need not be versed in all the technical subtleties of producing commercials, they must have at least a hands-on knowledge of the different phases of production in order to evaluate the costs, constraints, and also opportunities inherent in the production processes of the different media.

QUESTIONS FOR STUDY

1. Find two recent advertisements, one in a magazine, one in a newspaper. Using the criteria for print advertisement evaluation given in the text, evaluate these advertisements.

2. What is the most important part of a print advertisement? Advertisers' opinions vary; some say it is the headline, others, the illustration: still others suggest that the whole concept is important, regardless of the type of advertisement. Discuss these viewpoints. What is your view? Elaborate with specific examples.

3. List all the elements of a print advertisement that, in your opinion, lead to image formation and/or atmosphere. Give specific examples.

4. List all the elements in a broadcast commercial (i.e., television and radio) that tend to convey some brand image.

5. Some advertisements have no illustration, only lengthy copy. Under what circumstances do you think such advertisements can be effective (if at all)?

6. In what way is it increasingly difficult or easy to create television commercials?

7. Select a few print advertisements from a magazine. Study and compare their layouts. If possible, find the rationale for each one.

8. For what kind of products might the use of a jingle be more appropriate? List some of the advantages and drawbacks of using jingles in a) radio commercials and b) television commercials.

9. After reading Appendix 2, define the following terms: typography, roman, sans-serif, script, typesetting, handsetting, pica, em, monotype, photo-typography, photo-text, monophoto.

10. After reading Appendix 2, define the following terms: letterpress, gravure, offset, photo-engraving, half-tone engraving, electrotype.

PROBLEMS

1. A group of accounting students at a university have set up a small non-profit organization to help individuals and small organizations figure their income tax. They have been given by a government agency a small budget to advertise in the local newspapers and on the local radio. Because of their limited resources, this group of students turns to you to ask you to write the advertisements (print and broadcast). You are free to select the creative approach you think is best, and you are responsible for the total creation and eventually the production of these advertisements.

2. Select a print advertisement in a magazine. Using the same concept as this advertisement a) write a radio commercial and b) create a television commercial storyboard for this same campaign, but using radio and television as the basic media.

NOTES

1. David Ogilvy, *Confessions of an Advertising Man*, (New York: Atheneum, 1964), p. 146.
2. John Caples, *Tested Advertising Methods*, rev. ed., (New York: Harper and Row, 1961), chapter 3.
3. Hans Kleefeld, "Symbol or Logo—What's the Difference," *Marketing*, 3, January 1983, p. 18.
4. René Y. Darmon, "Multiple Joint Space Analysis for Improved Advertising Strategy," *Canadian Marketer*, (Fall 1979), pp. 10–14.
5. Thomas B. Stanley, *The Technique of Advertising Pro-duction*, 2nd ed., (New York: Prentice-Hall, 1954), p. 59.
6. Daniel Starch, *Measuring Advertising Readership and Results*, (New York: McGraw-Hill, 1956), p. 59.
7. Walter Margulies, "Media Decisions," reproduced in J. Douglas Johnson, *Advertising Today*, (Chicago: Science Research Associates, 1978), p. 103.
8. Henry Joannis, *De l'Etude de Motivation à la Création Publicitaire et à la Promotion des Ventes*, (Paris: Dunod, 1965), pp. 285–87.

9. Dick Warren Twedt, "A Multiple Factor Analysis of Advertising Readership," *Journal of Applied Psychology*, (June 1952), pp. 207–15.

10. Daniel Diamond, "A Quantitative Approach to Magazine Advertisement Format Selection," *Journal of Marketing Research*, (November 1968), pp. 376–87.

11. Leon Festinger and Nathan Maccoby, "On Resistance to Persuasive Communication," *Journal of Abnormal and Social Psychology*, 4 (1968), pp. 248–52.

12. Albert C. Book and Norman d. Cary, *The Television Commercial: Creativity and Craftsmanship*, (New York: Decker Communications, 1970).

13. Ibid., p. 210.

14. Johnson, pp. 105–6.

15. Example given in Johnson, p. 108.

16. Ibid., p. 109.

17. David Ogilvy and Joel Raphaelson, "Research on Ad Techniques That Work—and Don't Work," *Marketing News*, 17, September 1982, p. 2.

18. Ibid., p. 2.

14 *Developing a Media Plan*

The role of the media director is to efficiently deliver an advertiser's message to a target audience. This is an enormous task, since a staggering amount of information on the markets, the media, and consumers' media habits must be processed. Also, the task of selecting media types, media vehicles and options, and developing a media schedule is extremely complex.

Computers can help media planners handle the information available and can suggest media selection and schedules by applying statistical and mathematical models. These decision tools are still being perfected, however, and media planners must use a great deal of individual judgment in working with them.

An understanding of the media planner's tasks is needed in order to arrive at the most efficient media schedule given the advertising objectives and the advertising budget. Media planning is conducted in the general context of corporate, marketing, and advertising planning. Thus, it is important that media planners understand fully the objectives and strategies developed at higher levels. Advertising objectives and the advertising appropriation are the constraints within which the media director must work. Figure 14–1 (next page) outlines the media planning process.

The media director translates the advertising objectives into *media objectives* and strategies by using all information pertaining to the communication process, including the advertising message developed by the creative director. The media objectives in turn guide the selection of *media types* and *media vehicles*, i.e., a specific magazine, newspaper, radio station, or television program. Then a detailed *media schedule* is developed. It indicates when, where, and how long each message is going to run. At any stage in this process the media planner may conduct research to get additional information for effective decision making. This planning process culminates in the *media plan* (Figure 14–2, next page). Since media planning is part of the overall campaign planning, the media plan is ultimately incorporated into the advertising plan. Nevertheless, a separate media plan is useful early in the planning process because it helps determine the overall appropriation. It is also necessary to know very early which vehicles are selected, since lead times, particularly for prime-time television, may be quite long.

DEVELOPING MEDIA OBJECTIVES

The purpose of media objectives is to select the best possible media for reaching the advertising objectives for the selected target audience(s), the list of key market(s), the task of the communication, the creative execution of the message, and the advertising appropriation.

FIGURE 14–1 ———————
The Process of
Developing the
Media Plan

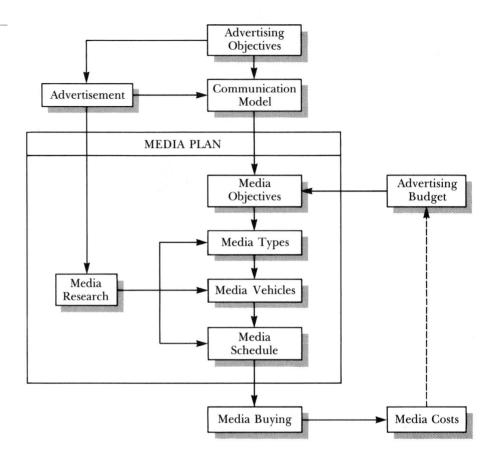

FIGURE 14–2 ———————
Suggested Outline for
the Media Plan

MEDIA PLAN

A. Media Objectives: Select the best media for:	B. Media Selection: Translate objectives into:	C. Media Schedule and Budget
1. Target audience(s)	1. Reach/Frequency/ Continuity/Intensity/ Impact levels	1. Media schedule
2. Key markets		2. Media budget
3. Communication task	2. The best media types	
4. Creative execution	3. The best media vehicles	
5. Advertising budget constraint		

D. Media Research

The media planner must make sure that the message reaches the right people at the right time, but in such a way as to ensure that effective communication takes place. The first task is most commonly associated with media directors, but the second is often as important in identifying the best conditions under which actual communication of the message (the work of the creative group) is to take place. Media objectives must thus reflect these two tasks.

Making Decisions about the Target Audiences

As explained in Chapter 11, the advertising objectives define the main target audiences of the campaign.

The media director must take into account the target audiences in the statement of advertising objectives and select the advertising media according to the different sizes of the audiences. To do so, a *weighting system*[1] is used that gives secondary and tertiary audiences lower weights than primary audiences. An example of the application of audience weights for a magazine is given in Table 14–1. The weight levels are determined by the media director based on judgment and past experience with each audience's level of interest in the advertised product.

TABLE 14–1 **NUMERICAL APPLICATION OF THE AUDIENCE WEIGHTING SYSTEM**

Consumer magazine A (readership: 200 000) Advertisement for a women's perfume			
	Audience	Weight	Weighted audience
Primary target audience Women 18–45	100 000	1.0	100 000
Secondary target audience Men 18–45	50 000	0.5	25 000
Tertiary target audience Teenagers 14–18	40 000	0.3	12 000
	Total adjusted audience		*137 000*

Target audiences should be defined as precisely as possible in terms of demographic, economic, and psychographic variables. When a target audience is defined in the advertising objectives, the task of the media director is a little easier, but it still may be necessary to apply weights according to the values of the various subgroups. For example, a subgroup of individuals or families who are heavy users of frozen pizzas should have a higher weight for advertising that product than light users, particularly if marketing objectives call for market share gains rather than market development. This second group of weights may be called demographic, economic, or psychographic weights depending on the variable(s) used to form the subgroups. Weights may also be derived from research data, either primary research or such syndicated sources as the PMB product profile studies and A.C. Nielsen.[2]

Target audiences have media usage habits that determine the use of certain media types or vehicles, if they are to be reached effectively. This section deals not with audience profiles of various media, which are used in the media selection process, but with factors called *media imperatives*. This term has been used mainly for magazines, but in fact it may be applied to any medium. A medium imperative calls for the media director to seriously consider using a particular medium because a substantial proportion of the target audience are heavy users of the medium *and* light users of the other media. For example, a large proportion of well-educated, high-income consumers watch very little television but read several magazines regularly. Thus these consumers may not be reached if magazines are not selected.

Making Decisions About the Key Markets in Which to Advertise

When a campaign is to run in several sales territories, it is necessary to develop the means for allocating the advertising effort among various territories. This is often a marketing strategy decision, and the allocation among territories may be spelled out in the marketing plan. Such decisions may be in the form of marketing objectives, such as increasing penetration of the brand in territories with low or medium penetration or increasing market share in territories with high penetration.

Whatever options an advertiser selects, it is necessary to establish priorities for allocating the media budget. Media directors often use market weights and/or brand development indices to translate marketing objectives into an operational allocation to territories.

Market weights may be used to account for behavioural differences among various markets. For example, consumers in some territories may have historically been quite disposed toward a brand, while in others they have been neutral or unaccepting. An advertisement for a brand may not be noticed and accepted to the same extent by consumers in all the markets. Market weights take these differences into account, consistent with the selected marketing strategy. Applying the weights may lead to a decision *not* to advertise in some markets.

Brand development indices (BDI) identify markets with low penetration and markets with high penetration. The BDI is an index of per capita sales of a brand in a given market compared to the national figure. An example of calculation of BDIs is provided in Table 14–2. In this example, the brand is doing very well in Nova Scotia, Quebec, and Manitoba, and poorly in Alberta and British Columbia. Based on the advertiser's marketing objectives, weights

TABLE 14–2 **A HYPOTHETICAL EXAMPLE OF CALCULATING BRAND DEVELOPMENT INDICES**

Territories	(A) Distribution of brand volume	(B) Distribution of households	BDI = 100 A/B
Nova Scotia	5.0	3.7	135
Quebec	35.0	28.5	123
Ontario	35.0	39.0	90
Manitoba	6.0	4.7	128
Saskatchewan	4.0	4.2	95
Alberta	6.0	8.3	72
British Columbia	9.0	11.6	78
	100.0	100.0	

may be derived to account for these differences. In the case of BDI, the behavioural variable used is past purchase. Thus, weights derived from BDI are a special type of market weights.

Taking the Creative Execution into Account

Media planners must take into account the type of message created by the creative group and assess the requirements of the creative execution in terms of media types, media vehicles and media options, as well as the interactions among the message, the audiences, and the media types or vehicles.

Some creative approaches may require a specific medium. For example, an advertisement demonstrating a product in use may require television, or an advertisement with a jingle may require radio or television. Certain creative approaches may require a special editorial environment to be most effective, for example, an advertisement for sports equipment is to be aired during a sports program. Another example would be a testimonial advertisement using a specific actor or cartoon character shown during a film featuring the actor or character.

Creative execution may require certain media options that would eliminate some media types or vehicles. For example, an advertisement requiring perfect colour reproduction would be best suited to magazines.

There may be interdependencies among the message, the audiences, and the media types or vehicles, since the same message may have very different effects if seen on television or in a magazine, or even on two different television programs when the audience predispositions are different. It is extremely difficult to account for those differences, but an experienced and knowledgeable media director can identify the most important interdependencies and weight them accordingly.

Taking the Communication Task into Account

The communication task set out in operational terms in the statement of advertising objectives is the critical element of the campaign. One task of the media director is to translate the advertising objectives into operational media objectives. This is a difficult step to undertake, but with experience the media director can develop reliable estimates. Some previous media objectives were concerned with maximizing the probability of exposure to the medium. Here the concern is with the various steps involved in communicating the message, from exposure to the message to conviction about the brand. The media director does not supersede the work of the creative group but complements it by ensuring that the target audience is exposed to that message at the right time, in the right place, and with enough repetition to ensure that the communication task is completed.

To illustrate the relationship between the communication task and media objectives, a hypothetical example has been constructed in Figure 14–3, using the framework introduced in Chapter 11, Figure 11–4. Assume that the brand is new. If increased awareness of the brand is the campaign objective, it may be estimated that 40 percent of the target audience should be exposed to the advertising message at least four times. Thus, the number of total exposures to the message may be calculated as follows: if the number of individuals in

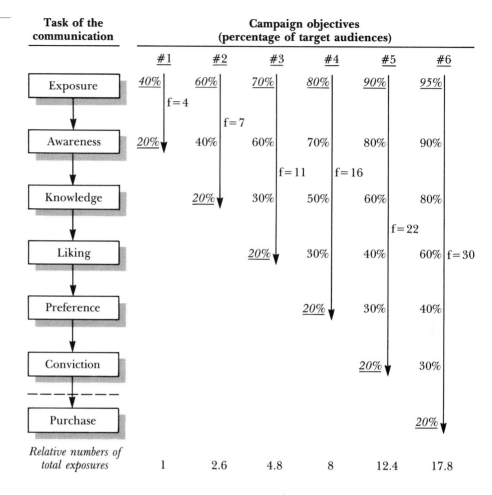

FIGURE 14-3

Hypothetical Example of the Relationship between Communication Task and Total Number of Exposures Required

Task of the communication

Campaign objectives (percentage of target audiences)

	#1	#2	#3	#4	#5	#6
Exposure	40%	60%	70%	80%	90%	95%
Awareness	20%	40%	60%	70%	80%	90%
Knowledge		20%	30%	50%	60%	80%
Liking			20%	30%	40%	60%
Preference				20%	30%	40%
Conviction					20%	30%
Purchase						20%

f = 4, f = 7, f = 11, f = 16, f = 22, f = 30

Relative numbers of total exposures

1	2.6	4.8	8	12.4	17.8

the target audience is 100 000, the number of exposures should be:

100 000 × 40 percent × 4 exposures/person = 160 000 exposures

This information in turn is used in the media selection process.

Similarly, if increased knowledge about the brand is the selected communication task, it may be estimated that at least 60 percent of the target audience should be exposed to the message at least six times. This level of repetition may be necessary to ensure that copy claims about the brand are learned by the targeted number of individuals, which is 20 percent of the target audience. The required number of gross exposures may be calculated as 420 000, i.e., 2.6 times the required number for increased awareness.

The same reasoning may be made for increased liking, preference, conviction, and purchase. As shown in Figure 14–3, the relative number of total exposures required are, respectively, 4.8, 8, 12.4, and 17.8 times the required number for increased awareness of the new brand.

In practice it is often difficult to estimate the various numbers used in this example. The media director may derive these estimates from a variety of sources. First, there is a body of knowledge about learning, motivation, and attitude change that can help a media director evaluate the effect of a message on the various communication steps. The media director's past experience, particularly with similar campaigns, represents a more or less accurate estimate of the "response function" of the target audience. Research data on the target audience, and/or the product category, and/or the advertised brand, and information on the effectiveness of past campaigns for the brand, may be very useful if all the communication steps have been included in the test.

It must be emphasized that this exercise, however scarce the data available, is a necessary step in ensuring that the advertising objectives are guiding the media objectives.

Taking the Advertising Appropriation into Account

In general, the media director develops the media plan within the overall media appropriation. As explained in Chapter 11, the total advertising budget is based on the marketing and advertising objectives for the brand. Thus the role of the media director is to find the most effective media plan for this budget, i.e., one that meets these objectives.

The budget may affect the work of the media director in two ways. First, the size of the advertising appropriation may preclude the use of some media types or media vehicles. The most obvious example is television, which requires a very large budget, because of the costs involved. Second, if the budget allows for volume buying or for frequency or continuity buying of certain vehicles, the media planner may obtain significant discounts, thus allowing for more time and/or space to be bought. Similar reasoning may be used when lower rates can be negotiated, for example, for buying network television.

Writing Precise and Operational Media Objectives

The development of media strategies should start with well-defined, operational media objectives that take account of target audiences, key markets, creative execution, communication tasks, and the advertising appropriation.

For example, the media objectives derived from the advertising objectives in Chapter 11 may be as follows:

Advertising objectives
To increase the awareness of Brand X fruit-based drink among teenagers and young adults aged 18 to 24 from the present 10 percent unaided recall of Brand X to a desired 50 percent within one year, by associating it with sports events, and presenting it as the drink of winners.

Media objectives
To maximize message frequency among teenagers and young adults aged 18 to 24 in metropolitan Toronto, Montreal, Vancouver, Ottawa-Hull, and Winnipeg by selecting media types and vehicles compatible with creative execution and media appropriation and reaching at least 50 percent of the audience.

With such objectives, the media director still has leeway in developing an efficient media plan. In so doing, the media director works closely with the creative director and the account executive. But before developing a complete media strategy, the media director must collect a staggering amount of information, a great deal of which is available through direct computer access.

PLANNING THE MEDIA STRATEGY

In the process of developing a media plan, the media director must deal with several types of media and media vehicles. In order to make the appropriate selection of media types and vehicles, some general concepts are used. These include reach, frequency, gross rating points, intensity, continuity, and impact.

Reach/Frequency Levels and Gross Rating Points

The concepts of reach and frequency apply to one or a combination of media vehicles, or to a media type.

Reach

Reach (R) is usually expressed as a percentage of the target audience exposed *once* to one or several vehicles. It is a measure of *unduplicated* audience, and thus represents the percentage of different units of the target audience exposed to the vehicle(s). For example, in Figure 14–4 the target audience is composed of 500 000 units (e.g., individuals, families, or firms). Medium or Vehicle A has a total audience of 300 000 units but only 200 000 belong to the target audience. Thus the reach of A is 40 percent (200 000 / 500 000). Similarly, B has a total audience of 200 000 units, but only half are members of the target audience. Thus, the reach of B is 20 percent.

If there is no duplication of the target audience members by A and B, i.e., the 200 000 units of A are different from the 100 000 of B, then the reach of A and B is 60 percent (300 000 / 500 000).

On the other hand, if 75 000 units of the target audience are exposed to *both* A and B, then the number of units reached by A and B is 225 000 (300 000 less 75 000). Thus, the reach of A *and* B is 45 percent (225 000 / 500 000).

From this example, it is evident that information on duplications between pairs of vehicles is important for estimating the reach of any pair of individual vehicles. If the information is not available, it may be assumed that duplication is random. For example, if A reaches 40 percent of the target audience, 60 percent are not reached by A (let us call this group A̸). Since B reaches 20 percent of the target audience, the possibility that those who are not reached by A are reached by B is A̸ x B = 12 percent (20 percent of 60 percent). In this case the reach of A *and* B is 52 percent (40 percent plus 12 percent).

This method may be generalized to more than two vehicles. For example, if we have three vehicles with the following individual reaches and their complements:

A:	50%		A̸:	50%
B:	40%		B̸:	60%
C:	30%		C̸:	70%

the net reach of A, B, *and* C is calculated as follows:

$$\text{net reach} = A + A̸ \times B + A̸ \times B̸ \times C$$
$$= .50 + .50 \times .40 + .50 \times .60 \times .30 = .79 \text{ or } 79\%$$

FIGURE 14–4

Illustration of the Reach and Frequency Concepts

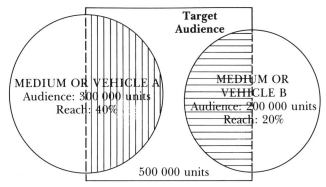

(a) The reach of two media or vehicles without duplication is 60 percent—the sum of the reaches of A and B. The frequency of A and B is 1.

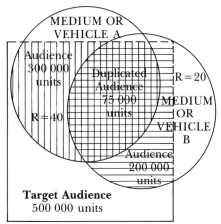

(b) The reach of two media or vehicles with duplication is based on the unduplicated audience of A and/or B—45 percent. The frequency of A and B is 1.3.

When information is available on duplication between pairs of vehicles, there are some methods available to calculate the net reach of the schedule such as the Agostini method[3] (see question no. 3 at the end of this chapter). Other methods use specific statistical distribution such as the beta-binomial.[4] A simple example of the latter is the TELPAK program for television scheduling developed by Marshall Rice to be used with this book and a standard microcomputer.[5]

Frequency

Frequency is the number of times a member of the audience is reached by one or several vehicles. This concept is closely associated with the reach concept (Figure 14–4). If there is no duplication between A and B, and all 200 000

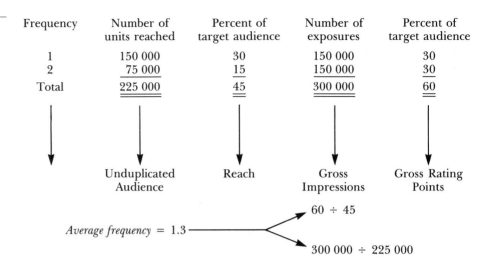

FIGURE 14–5

Relationships among Reach, Frequency, GRP, Net and Gross Impressions

Frequency	Number of units reached	Percent of target audience	Number of exposures	Percent of target audience
1	150 000	30	150 000	30
2	75 000	15	150 000	30
Total	225 000	45	300 000	60
	Unduplicated Audience	Reach	Gross Impressions	Gross Rating Points

Average frequency = 1.3 →

60 ÷ 45

300 000 ÷ 225 000

units of A and all 100 000 units of B are reached once, then the frequency of A and B is one.

If there is duplication between A and B, with 75 000 units exposed to both, then we have the frequency distribution indicated in Figure 14–5. Because of the duplication, 300 000 impressions were received by 225 000 units. Thus, each unit was reached an average of 1.3 times.

The average frequency is useful to know as an overall measure for the media or vehicles selected, but it is equally important to use the *frequency distribution*. This is because one may expect an individual who has been exposed eight times to an advertisement to be at a higher level in the communication hierarchy than one who has been exposed only once. The TELPAK computer program provides a frequency distribution for television.

The frequency distribution may be used in two ways. The numerical example in Table 14–3 will be used for illustrative purposes.

First, one may establish a minimum level of frequency necessary to move the average member of the target audience to accomplish the communication task stated in the advertising objectives. The minimum number of exposures within a four-week period may be set at four to move the prospects from awareness to knowledge. Thus a weight of zero may be assigned to prospects with less than four exposures and a weight of one to those with a frequency of four or more. This gives an effective reach of 38 percent and an average frequency of 6.7, to be compared with a reach of 85 percent and a frequency of 4.0 for the whole distribution.

If the previous method is considered too severe, one may weight the frequency levels according to their utility to the media director. Prospects with a frequency of one, two, or three may have moved toward the advertising goal and may be won over in the next campaign. Prospects with a frequency level of five and higher may have moved beyond the advertising goal, and thus may contribute to the marketing goal. Thus, the level of four exposures is indexed

TABLE 14-3 FREQUENCY DISTRIBUTION AND EFFECTIVE REACH

Frequency	Percent of audience	Cumulative reach (%)	Frequency weighting schemes equal weights	minimum frequency	response function
1	20	85	100	0	50
2	15	65	100	0	65
3	12	50	100	0	85
4	8	38	100	100	100
5	7	30	100	100	105
6	5	23	100	100	110
7	4	18	100	100	115
8	4	14	100	100	120
9	3	10	100	100	125
10+	7	7	100	100	135
	85		↓	↓	↓
		Effective reach	85%	38%	73%
		Average frequency	4.0	6.7	4.9
		Effective GRPs	340	255	358

at 100, and frequency levels of less than four at less than 100, and those of five and over at more than 100. Using the example in Table 14–3, one finds an effective reach of 4.9, again to be compared with 85 percent and 4.0 for an equal weighting scheme. This is called *response function weighting*.[6]

Gross Rating Points (GRP)

The gross rating points concept has been developed to take into account the fact that some people may be exposed to the same vehicle more than once or exposed to more than one vehicle. Developed initially for television, the concept has found acceptance in the other media. Gross rating points may be derived in three different ways:

From Gross Impressions.   *Gross impressions* are the sum of all audiences of the selected media vehicles, including duplications. For example, in Figure 14–4, the gross impressions for A and B are 300 000 (200 000 plus 100 000). Viewed differently in Figure 14–5, the gross impressions of A and B are 300 000, i.e., 150 000 for the people exposed once to A or B, plus 150 000 for the people exposed to both A and B. Gross rating points may be defined as gross impressions as a percentage of the target audience—here 60 percent (300 000 / 500 000).

From Ratings and Coverages.   The *rating* is expressed as the percent of TV or radio households that are tuned, on the average, to one time period (e.g., one quarter-hour) of a particular program. A similar concept in print media is called *coverage*, i.e., the percent of members of a target audience who read an average issue of the publication. Gross rating points may be defined as the sum of individual ratings and coverages of the selected media vehicles. For example, in Figure 14–4, the gross rating points are 60 percent (40 percent plus 20 percent).

From Reach and Frequency. Since the concepts of rating and coverage are special cases of the reach concept in broadcast and print media, it may be said that gross rating points are the sum of the individual reach of each vehicle. Since the reach of a set of vehicles is the percentage of unduplicated audience, gross rating points may be defined as the product of reach and average frequency (Figure 14–5).

Thus, one has the following relationship for a given set of vehicles:

$$GRP = REACH \times FREQUENCY$$

Application Exercise: Using the data given in Problem 1, calculate in three different ways the GRPs of each schedule of magazines.

The GRP Concept and Media Planning

The GRP concept is extremely useful in media planning, since it represents an operational measure of the campaign objectives. It can be used in many different markets, since it takes into account different competitive situations, rate structures, and fragmentation situations. Because of these properties, GRPs may be used for planning by allocating them to different markets according to a desired weight schedule and then calculating the desired number of announcements and insertions. This method is extremely useful for television and print media but difficult to use for radio, because of the complex interplay of reach and frequency, and the various rotation plans available. For radio, the accepted method is to first state the desired R/F levels, and then calculate the GRPs in each market and compare them in order to check for imbalances in market weighting.

Allocation With Equal Weights. Assume that an advertiser is faced with five markets of equal importance but with varying situations. Each market is to receive 100 GRPs (Table 14–4). In market A, the average vehicle (spot or issue) has a reach (rating or coverage) of 10 percent, because there is heavy competition among the various media in market A. By contrast, in market E, the corresponding reach is 50 percent, because there is little competition among its media. In market A the media planner will need ten spots or inser-

TABLE 14–4 **THE USE OF GRPs IN PLANNING TELEVISION OR PRINT MEDIA**

Market	GRPs/market	Coverage/issue or rating/spot (%)	Number of spots/ insertions required
A	100	10	10
B	100	20	5
C	100	25	4
D	100	33	3
E	100	50	2

tions in order to obtain 100 GRPs, while in market E the media planner will need only two.

All spots or issues in each market may not have the same individual reach figures, but the principle of allocation is the same. The allocation of 100 GRPs may actually be made among four vehicles according to various patterns, as in Table 14–5, which illustrates how to calculate the reach of a set of vehicles. Table 14–4 does not provide the reach of the ten spots in market A or the two spots in market E, although they may be estimated with the assumption of random duplication, or with actual measures of duplication in calculating reach and frequency levels in each market. Analysis of the examples in Table 14–5 leads to two observations:

1. Reach for a set of vehicles is higher than the highest reach of individual vehicles. Thus, if high reach is sought out by the media director, it is better to select vehicles with high individual reach.
2. Frequency increases as the number of vehicles increases, and the range of individual reaches decreases, assuming that there is a fair amount of duplication among vehicles. Thus, if high frequency is sought, it is better to select many vehicles with a low reach.

Allocation Strategies With Unequal Weights. Table 14–6 illustrates the various allocation strategies which may be used by the media director, who is faced with five markets of different sizes and concentrations of heavy users of the product category. Three different strategies may be used to allocate the 380 GRPs to the five markets:

Proportional Allocation Strategy. This strategy consists in allocating the total GRPs according to the relative sizes of the markets. This is done in column 4 of Table 14–6 (i.e., the same distribution as in column 2). If the primary targets are the heavy users in each market, then the number of effective gross impressions may be calculated, as shown in column 5 (col. 3 × col. 4). This strategy leads to the delivery of 2 530 000 gross impressions to heavy users.

TABLE 14–5 **HYPOTHETICAL EXAMPLES OF R/F LEVELS FOR VARIOUS VEHICLE SELECTIONS WITH 100 GRPs**

Markets	Reach of each vehicle (%)				R/F levels for the selected vehicles	
	V1	V2	V3	V4	Reach (%)	Frequency
1	25	25	25	25	68.4	1.46
2	40	20	20	20	69.3	1.44
3	40	30	30		70.6	1.42
4	50	30	20		72.0	1.39
5	60	20	20		74.4	1.34
6	60	40			76.0	1.32
7	80	20			84.0	1.19
8	100				100.0	1.00

TABLE 14–6 **HYPOTHETICAL EXAMPLE OF THE EFFECTS OF THREE MEDIA STRATEGIES**

Target markets	Size	Heavy users	Proportional allocation strategy		Profile-matching strategy		High-assay strategy	
			GRPs %	Heavy users* (000s)	GRPs %	Heavy users* (000s)	GRPs %	Heavy users* (000s)
Halifax	300	100	30	30	17	17	0	0
Montreal	1000	900	100	900	156	1404	130	1170
Toronto	1500	1000	150	1500	173	1730	250	2500
Calgary	500	100	50	50	17	17	0	0
Vancouver	500	100	50	50	17	17	0	0
Total	*3800*	*2200*	*380*	*2530*	*380*	*3185*	*380*	*3670*

*Number of effective gross impressions (on heavy users).

Profile-Matching Strategy. This involves allocating the total GRPs according to the relative sizes of the primary target audiences. This is done in column 6 of Table 14–6 (i.e., the same distribution as in column 3), and the resulting number of effective gross impressions is shown in column 7 (col. 3 × col. 6). This strategy leads to the delivery of 3 185 000 gross impressions to the heavy users. It is clearly superior to the proportional allocation strategy, since it focuses directly on the primary target audience. The first strategy would use general media and waste a large amount of gross impressions outside of the primary target audience, and this would not contribute to the advertising objectives. In contrast, the profile-matching strategy, which is the one most commonly used, relies on information about demographic, economic, and psychographic profiles of both the users of the product category and the various media. Its name refers to the matching of these two profiles.

High-Assay Strategy.[7] This consists in allocating the total GRPs first to the market with the "richest" collection of heavy users, in the same way a gold miner starts mining a vein with the highest assay of ore. This is done in columns 8 and 9 of Table 14–6. Here it is assumed that all 380 GRPs cannot be allocated to Toronto, and that 250 GRPs is the maximum. This leaves 130 GRPs to be allocated to the next best market—Montreal. Thus, this strategy leads to the delivery of 3 670 000 gross impressions to heavy users. The high-assay strategy is clearly superior to the previous two strategies. It requires the availability of very specialized media vehicles allowing the media director to precisely target heavy users in order to minimize wasted circulation. This strategy is commonly used by media directors who want to select the best metropolitan area (under key markets) subject to the budget constraint.

Continuity and Intensity of the Campaign

The concept of *continuity* is related to the overall pattern of advertising exposures over the time horizon of the campaign. As defined, it only affects the distribution of advertising weights over time. Changes in campaign continuity do not greatly affect the media budget, assuming that everything else stays

FIGURE 14–6

Difference in
Continuity for Two
Campaigns with
1200 GRPs

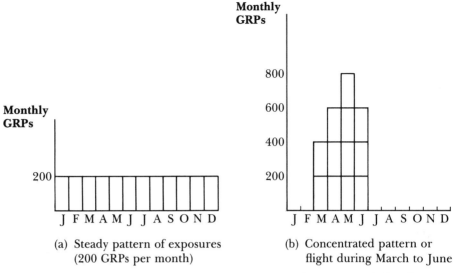

(a) Steady pattern of exposures
    (200 GRPs per month)

(b) Concentrated pattern or
    flight during March to June

constant. For example, Figure 14–6 has two different patterns of distributing 2400 GRPs. The first one is a steady campaign using 200 GRPs per month for 12 months. The advantage of a steady campaign is that the product is advertised regularly and the effects are accumulated over time, minimizing forgetting between exposures.[8] The second pattern shown in Figure 14–6 is a concentrated pattern, also called a *flight* when concentrated in one medium, in which the whole campaign runs from March to June. The rationale of a concentrated pattern of exposures is to try to bring a large number of consumers through several steps in the hierarchy of communication effects until the advertising objectives have been reached.

There are, of course, a variety of distribution patterns of the total effort, over the time horizon, and across media types or vehicles. These are described in detail in the scheduling section, but from the media strategy viewpoint a decision must be made on the type of continuity most likely to contribute to the advertising objectives.

Unlike the continuity concept, which implies different options for allocating the same total effort, the level of intensity of the campaign can have a great impact on the advertising budget. *Intensity* may be defined as the average monthly GRPs over the time horizon. Figure 14–7 illustrates this point. Campaign A has an average intensity of 200 GRPs per month, while campaign B with the same pattern of continuity has an average intensity of 100 GRPs per month. Thus the media budget for A is likely to be much larger than that for B. If one starts with a given media budget, the implication is that increased intensity can only be accomplished by lowering the cost per GRP. For example, whole regions or provinces may be excluded, the sizes of messages may be reduced, some media options cancelled, spot may be substituted to network time, and fringe to prime time. Again, a strategic decision must be made on the desirability of increased intensity versus size, options, media types, and media vehicles.

FIGURE 14–7

*Difference in
Intensity Levels for
Two Campaigns with
the Same Pattern of
Continuity*

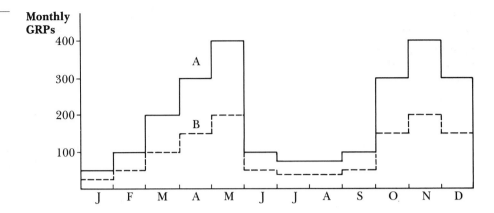

Impact of the Campaign

Another important strategic decision relates to the desired impact of the campaign. *Impact* refers to all the physical characteristics of the advertisement that may increase its effectiveness given a basic creative execution. Examples of these characteristics, often referred to as *media options*, are:

- size of the messages in terms of the number of lines in a newspaper, the number or fractions of pages in a magazine, or the number of seconds in a radio or a television program;
- the shape of the advertisement, as in free-form;
- the number of colours in a print advertisement;
- a preferred position in the vehicle;
- some degree of exclusivity or dominance in the vehicle, as in multiple-page and/or pop-up advertisements or sponsorship of a radio or television program.

All decisions relate to an advertiser's desire, as expressed in the campaign objectives, to establish the brand name in a leadership position in the market by impressing both consumers and distributors. The impact of the advertisement may then improve the image of the brand and give it a favourable market position.

Increasing the impact of the campaign leads to an increase in the cost per GRP and a decrease in the intensity of the campaign in the context of a fixed media budget. A decrease in intensity will in turn lead to lower reach and/or frequency levels.

In the same way as there is a trade-off between reach and frequency for a given GRP level (intensity), there is a trade-off between intensity (measured in level of GRP) and impact (measured in cost per GRP) of the campaign for a given advertising budget. Thus, the two important formulas of media planning are:

$$ADVERTISING\ BUDGET\ =\ INTENSITY \times IMPACT$$
$$INTENSITY\ \qquad\qquad =\ REACH \times FREQUENCY$$

For example, given a fixed media budget, doubling the size of a print advertisement leads to a large decrease in intensity (since more dollars are spent for each insertion), which in turn leads to a decrease in reach and/or frequency of the campaign.

SELECTION OF THE MEDIA TYPES

Based on the media objectives and the decisions on the previously developed dimensions, media types are selected. This selection process is based on media characteristics, competitive analysis, and campaign requirements.

Media Characteristics

Each medium has strengths and weaknesses (Table 14–7), which were outlined in Chapters 5 to 8. Each medium has a given profile of its audience, in particular in terms of light use of the medium.[9] Thus, comparison of various media types according to these characteristics and their suitability for the product category and/or brand to be advertised may lead to a rejection or combination of some of these media types. For example, radio may be rejected for a new disposable razor, if demonstration and package identification are important, and newspaper may be rejected for a food product if good colour reproduction is important. Media may be combined to increase reach or according to the media imperative concept. Thus television and magazines, or television and radio are often used together. In particular, radio may be used as a low-cost extension of a television commercial by using the mind's ability to relive a commercial from hearing the audio component of that commercial, once it has been registered in long-term memory. This is called *image transference*.

TABLE 14–7 **MAIN STRENGTHS AND WEAKNESSES OF MAJOR MEDIA TYPES**

Medium	Strengths	Weaknesses
Radio	• high frequency • high selectivity • flexible (coverage and time) • affordable to small businesses	• fragmentation (low reach) • clutter • short life of message • limited availability in major markets • background medium
Television	• complete communication • high reach and frequency • flexible (geographic and creative) • high prestige and credibility	• high absolute costs (time and production) • fragmentation • short life of message • long lead time • heavy regulation
Daily newspapers	• high reach • broad coverage • flexible (geographic, lead time, creative) • high reader interest • high frequency potential • affordable to small businesses • well-researched (NADbank)	• poor colour reproduction • low audience selectivity • low passalong rate • national coverage is difficult/expensive

TABLE 14–7 **MAIN STRENGTHS AND WEAKNESSES OF MAJOR MEDIA TYPES (continued)**

Medium	Strengths	Weaknesses
Community newspapers	• high local reach • broad local coverage • flexible (geographic, lead time, creative) • high reader interest • very affordable to small businesses	• poor colour reproduction • low audience selectivity • low passalong rate • national coverage very difficult/ expensive • low frequency
Consumer magazines	• highly selective • high passalong rate • high-quality reproduction • well-researched (PMB) • long life • high prestige and credibility	• little flexibility (lead time, geographic) • low penetration • high cost of production • low frequency • clutter
Other periodicals	• extremely selective • high-quality reproduction • high reader interest • long life • high prestige and credibility	• little flexibility • low penetration • high production costs • low frequency
Outdoor	• high reach & frequency • geographic flexibility • long life of message • high message impact	• short message • no selectivity • long lead time • high production costs
Transit	• high reach & frequency • high readership • low cost per thousand	• no selectivity • long closing dates • high production costs
Direct response	• highest selectivity • flexible (creative, coverage) • high degree of control	• high relative cost • no editorial support • low response rate
Specialty	• high selectivity • long life • high interest	• high cost • short message

Competitive Analysis

Since most advertisers are competing with other advertisers for consumers' attention, it is important to analyze what competitors' media decisions are. This analysis may affect an advertiser's media selection process at two levels.

Media Types Used by Competitors

The types of media used by most competitors in the same product category *may* be an indication of their effectiveness. This point should be thoroughly investigated since, if true, it may require that an advertiser use the same types of media. The rationale may be in terms of traditional media usage or in terms of information processing needs.

First, the medium may be heavily used by the selected target audience for the brand and thus may be the best one for carrying the advertisement. This does not, however, guarantee exposure to an advertisement, especially if it has to compete with similar ones.

Second, a medium may not be heavily used by the target audience but the probability of exposure to the advertisement by the target audience may be high because of consumers' *overt* information search at the time of purchase. For example, a couple looking for a new car may look at several consumer magazines because this medium has traditionally been used by car manufacturers. Similarly, since retailers often use newspapers for advertisements, these may be consulted by consumers looking for specials in food, hardware, and appliances. Thus, the advertiser may be able to capitalize on this learned overt behaviour in order to improve exposure to an advertisement. Of course, the message still must compete with similar messages, and many factors may determine its effectiveness, such as marketing-mix dimensions, creative execution, and clutter.

Competitive Campaign Intensities

The extent of advertising in a given medium by competitors may not be matched by small-budget advertisers, who cannot afford the level of intensity of large advertisers. Thus, many small-budget advertisers try to achieve high intensity within a *limited period* or in a *limited media mix*.

With the first strategy, media planners may advertise heavily during flights in order to achieve a high initial impact and break the barrier of heavy competitive advertising. This situation is illustrated in Figure 14–6, in which a steady pattern may not be able to break through the clutter, while a four-month flight may make a lasting impact with memorable creative. On the other hand, forgetting between flights may be a serious problem, and flighting may carry additional expense since some discounts (e.g., for continuity) may be lost. Thus the length and frequency of flights should be selected carefully (Figure 14–8).

With the second strategy, the media planner may select to advertise in one medium only during the time horizon or to use a few flights, one for each medium. *Media concentration strategy* is used when a large proportion of the target may be reached with one medium (Figure 14–8). In this case, it makes sense to use the entire media appropriation in that medium and to try for increased frequency and/or impact to move these prospects up the communication ladder. In addition, continuity of advertising may bring some media discounts and lower the unit cost of exposure. But if one medium is insufficient to reach a large proportion of the target audience, the media planner may decide to divide the media budget among two or three media and use the flighting technique for each one (Figure 14–8). If two or three flights cover the same period, the first strategy applies (Figure 14–8a). If these flights are used sequentially to cover a large portion of the campaign's time horizon, this is called *media-mix dominance strategy* (or media alternation strategy). This

FIGURE 14–8
*Comparison of
Flighting, Media
Concentration,
and Media-Mix
Dominance Strategies*

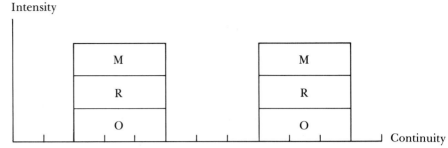

(a) Two three-month flights with a three-month hiatus
    using magazines (M), outdoor (O), and radio (R)

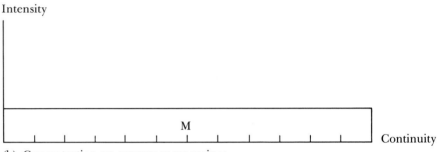

(b) Concentration on consumer magazines

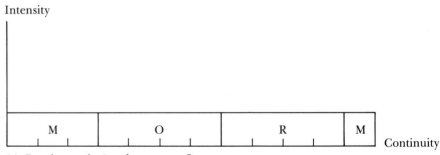

(c) Dominance in (or alternance of) consumer
    magazines (M), outdoor (O), and radio (R)

strategy shares some of the problems of the flighting strategy in terms of
forgetting and media discounts.

***Campaign
Requirements***

The objectives of the campaign as translated into media terms influence the
selection of media types. Budget constraints may influence the choice of media
types at several levels:

*   the size of the budget may preclude the use of such media as television, even
    if one of the previous strategies is used.

- the allocation of the budget among media types must rely on some form of inter-media cost comparison. Because costs and audiences are not standardized across media types, this is a difficult task to accomplish. The most commonly used measure of media efficiency is the cost per thousand impressions introduced in Chapter 5, which is

$$CPM = \frac{unit\ cost\ of\ a\ message}{audience\ size\ (in\ 000s)}$$

The media objectives require different levels of reach and/or frequency. A *reach dominant strategy* requires the use of a variety of media types selected according to the individual reach of the target audience and the corresponding CPM. Consideration can also be given to frequency levels when several media mixes are equally attractive. A *frequency dominant strategy* requires that a few media be used in order to reach the same prospects many times. The selection may be based on minimum reach levels and the corresponding CPM.

The nature of the communication task as well as the creative execution may lead to a preference for some media types, based on an assessment of the communication environment and the principles developed in Chapters 9 and 10.

To conclude, it is essential that a detailed rationale be given in the media plan both for the *selected* and the *rejected* media. It is important to state why certain types were selected, and how the media budget was allocated among the media. It is equally important to state why the other media were not selected.

SELECTION OF THE MEDIA VEHICLES

The next step after the selection of the media types to be used in the campaign is the selection of actual media vehicle(s) within each type. For example, if the consumer magazine medium was selected, which consumer magazine(s) should be used? Similarly, if television was selected, which television program(s) should carry the commercial?

The selection of media vehicles is based on the campaign requirements, the characteristics of each vehicle, and cost comparisons among vehicles.

Campaign Requirements and Vehicle Characteristics

Creative Execution and Media Options

The media director must look at the creative execution of the message and its requirements in terms of media options. Some vehicles may thus be eliminated because some options are not available or cannot be negotiated satisfactorily. Examples of such options are flexform, spectacolour, and split run. In addition to these special services, some vehicles may have restrictions that are listed in *CARD* under the heading "mechanical requirements." These restrictions may affect the decision to select a vehicle.

Target Audiences and Key Markets

The media director must consider a vehicle's ability to reach the target audience(s) specified in the media objectives. *Demographic and psychographic* profiles of the vehicle must be compared with the target audience to determine the vehicle's ability to achieve the objectives. Also, the audience's *geographic* distribution must be compared with the key markets specified in the media objectives, in order to assess the vehicle's ability to deliver audiences in the key markets. Some vehicles are more selective than others in reaching specific groups defined by demographic, psychographic, or geographic variables, and thus may be more efficient on a relative cost basis (as will be seen later in the chapter).[10] Thus, this factor is related to the campaign's reach targets, as defined in the media objectives, with respect to the definition of the target audience(s) and the selection of key markets.

Enhancing the Communication Task

The media director must consider several factors related to the communication task. The vehicle's *editorial environment* is evaluated in terms of the message and the target audiences. The degree of the target audience's interest in the editorial may promote proper communication of the advertiser's message through exposure and other steps in the communication hierarchy. The degree of interest in the editorial may be obtained by looking at the trend in circulation figures of the vehicle. Increased circulation indicates that interest in the vehicle is high, and vice-versa. Another factor that may hamper the communication process is the amount of clutter, the number of advertisements competing for attention. Thus, the media planner may prefer a particular vehicle because it offers a better opportunity for a message to be noticed. If a vehicle must be used for other reasons, it may be necessary to use preferred positions in the vehicle. The effect of clutter can be lessened if a campaign has been highly successful in the past, and the advertisement is recognized by the audience. Finally, the time of exposure to the message may be quite important for some products, because the target audience may be in the right frame of mind for buying the product category. Food advertisements usually appear before the weekly shopping trip, advertisements for movies and/or restaurants toward the end of the week, or commercials for snack foods during early to late evening television programs.

Discount Structure

Media planners must compare the discount structures offered by different vehicles. This factor considerably complicates the selection task, since a vehicle that has a high relative cost without any discount may become very attractive with one or several discounts (e.g., volume or continuity). The discount structure is thus heavily influenced by decisions on the levels of frequency, intensity, and continuity. When one or several of these factors are emphasized, it is relatively easy to take advantage of discounts. When reach is emphasized, this task is more difficult, since it is often better to use several vehicles.

Availability

The media director must verify the availability of certain vehicles. For example, a certain magazine may not be distributed in a key market, or a particular program may be completely booked by the time media planning is done.

Since many popular vehicles, particularly in television, radio, and outdoor, are booked well in advance, it is important to begin the vehicle selection process as soon as possible. Sometimes a large agency may book blocks of time in advance to ensure that these time periods are available to their clients. Of course, this is a risky strategy if all time periods are not used by these clients, and it is often not recommended. An agency may, however, use this strategy to attract good clients by guaranteeing popular programs.

Impact

Media planners must take into account the use of each vehicle by competitors in order to determine which vehicle(s) to use and to what extent. The considerations here are similar to those used to select media types. If one vehicle must be used because of the audience's characteristics, then consideration must be given to improving the message's chances of being noticed, e.g., a cover position or near some particular editorial matter. In this case, decisions on the advertisement's impact in a particular medium may influence the selection of the vehicle(s), and vice versa.

Budget Constraint

The vehicle selection process is constrained by the budget allocated to each media type. Thus, some vehicles may be eliminated if the budget is insufficient for certain vehicles because their absolute cost is too high.

Vehicle Cost Comparisons

The absolute cost of using a particular vehicle with or without any discount is available through the various rate cards discussed in Chapters 5, 6 and 7. The absolute cost is often not a valid measure for comparing vehicles within a given type of media, because different vehicles have different audience sizes, space sizes, and so on. Thus, various relative cost measures have been developed in order to compare various vehicles within a given medium.

Even though the CPM measure is used for all media types, it cannot be used to compare vehicles in different media types, since there is no widely accepted definition of a unit across media types. For example, is a one page, four-colour bleed advertisement in a magazine the same unit as a 1000 line, black and white advertisement in a newspaper, or a 30-second prime time commercial? A similar question arises with respect to the definition of the audience for the message.

Within a particular medium, it is possible to minimize these problems by using the same definition for both units and audiences. Nevertheless, these measures suffer from the lack of standardization across vehicles. For example, although most broadsheets have adopted the CNU system, a major problem in comparing newspapers is still a lack of standardization of space sizes and circulation figures, especially between broadsheets and tabloids. A numerical example is provided in Tables 14–8 and 14–9 for three Toronto newspapers with different formats, and using the circulation figures for the primary market only.

TABLE 14–8 **CALCULATION OF THE PAGE COST FOR NEWSPAPERS***

Newspaper	Number of columns (1)	Depth (2)	Line Rate (3)	Page Cost (1) × (2) × (3)
Globe and Mail	6	308 MAL	$16.98 (Ont.)	$31 379
Toronto Star	6	308 MAL	$14.71 (M-F)	$27 184
Toronto Sun**	6	200	$ 5.00 (M-F)	$ 6 000

*For simplicity, the calculations are based on the transient rate only.
**The Toronto Sun did not adopt the CNU format.

TABLE 14–9 **CALCULATION OF THE MILLINE RATE AND THE CPM FOR NEWSPAPERS***

Newspaper	Circulation in thousands (1) (designated market)	Line Rate (2)	Milline rate 1000 × (2)/(1)	Page cost (3)	CPM for one page (3)/(1)
Globe and Mail	249.100	$16.98 (Ont.)	$68.17	$31 379	$125.97
Toronto Star	411.043	$14.71 (M-F)	$35.79	$27 184	$ 66.13
Toronto Sun	252.022	$ 5.00 (M-F)	$19.84	$ 6 000	$ 23.81

*For simplicity, the calculations are based on the transient rate only.
Source: Adapted from *CARD* (June 1990), pp. 20–21.

Newspapers

For newspapers, what unit of space should be used to compare them? Two measures have been widely used, the milline rate and page costs.

Milline Rate. If the unit of space is 1000 lines, black and white, and the audience is the circulation figure (in 000s), then the CPM definition is identical to the milline rate introduced in Chapter 5. Calculation of the milline rates for the three Toronto newspapers is done in Table 14–9. Thus, although the *Star* has a line rate 13 percent lower than that of the *Globe and Mail*, its milline rate is 47 percent lower. On the other hand, the *Globe and Mail* has a much larger circulation outside the primary (or designated) market, and on a national basis its milline rate would be much lower than for its primary market. Circulation figures do not indicate the actual audience of the newspaper in terms of how many different people read each copy (i.e., readers per copy), and the members of the target audience who read that newspaper. If the information is available, more meaningful measures of milline rates may be used. But a serious problem remains with this definition: would a 1000-line advertisement in the *Sun* be equivalent to 1000 lines in the *Star*? The answer is obviously no, since the same advertisement in the *Sun* would occupy more than 83 percent of the page, while in the *Star* it would occupy 54 percent of the page.

Page Costs and CPM. Media buyers prefer using one newspaper page as the unit of space. The calculations for the page costs and CPMs are provided in Tables 14–8 and 14–9. For newspapers with the same standardized format, the two definitions lead to the same relative measures: 68.17 / 35.79 = 125.97 /

66.13. The significant difference is between broadsheets and tabloids. The milline rate for the *Sun* is about 55 percent of the rate for the *Star*, while in terms of CPMs (per page), the ratio is now 36 percent. For the milline rate, a more meaningful measure of the CPM is derived by using the number of people in the target audience who read the newspaper, whether or not they have bought it, to divide the page cost.

Magazines and Other Periodicals Cost Comparisons

For magazines and other periodicals, the unit of space commonly used is one page, four colours. The audience figure may be either the circulation figure or the total readers, including both primary readers (members of the subscribing or purchasing household) and secondary readers. Alternatively, the total readership is obtained by multiplying the circulation figure by the number of readers per copy. A better measure of audience is derived from the previous analysis of members of the target audience and their geographic distribution.

A similar analysis may be made by changing the unit of space to one page black and white or by adding the premium cost for bleed to the cost of the one page, four-colour unit. Table 14–10 provides examples of CPM calculations for selected consumer magazines and for both black and white and four-colour bleed pages. It must be emphasized here that this comparison of CPMs is only one factor in the selection process of the vehicle, which includes the other considerations mentioned previously.

Radio Cost Comparisons

For radio, the unit of time often used to compare vehicles is the cost of one minute of commercial time. Care should be taken in using the same classification in calculating and comparing CPMs for radio. Ideally the audience factor should be the number of listeners who belong to the target audience(s).

Media planners use another measure of efficiency based on the GRP system. The *cost per rating point* (CPRP) is useful for comparing vehicles or combinations of vehicles, that is, alternative radio scheduling units. It is calculated by dividing the cost of the scheduling unit by the GRPs delivered by that unit. For one vehicle, the CPRP is defined as:

   CPRP = cost per time unit / rating

For more than one vehicle, the CPRP is defined as:

   CPRP = cost per schedule / total GRPs of schedule

Since it is difficult to use the GRP concept for selecting radio vehicles, the accepted practice is to base the radio schedule and vehicle selection on reach and frequency targets. These alternative selections may then be compared in terms of GRPs and CPRP, and the decision is based on this information and other cost comparisons.

Television Cost Comparisons

For television, the unit of time most often used to compare vehicles is the cost of one 30-second block of commercial time. One must ensure that the same

TABLE 14-10 **SELECTED CONSUMER MAGAZINES: COSTS AND CPM COMPARISONS**

English Publications	Circ.	Page 4/C Bleed Rate $	CPM $	Page B/W Bleed Rate $	CPM $	Rates Effective
Best Wishes	143 712	12 406	86.33	9 098	63.31	11/89
Canadian	119 922	10 850	90.49	8 680	72.39	11/89
Canadian House & Home	100 994	7 460	73.87	5 968	59.09	1/90
Canadian Geographic	218 397	7 725	36.37	5 795	26.53	4/90
Canadian Living	558 531	18 056	32.33	15 345	27.47	1/90
Canadian Workshop	121 945	5 600	45.92	4 450	36.49	1/90
Chatelaine	1 010 152	29 200	28.91	22 785	22.56	1/90
City & Country Home	88 589	8 045	90.81	6 140	69.31	2/90
Cottage Life	72 610	4 885	67.28	4 100	56.47	1/90
Country Estate	83 752	6 775	106.95	5 060	79.37	1/90
Crafts Plus	116 163	3 400	29.27	2 600	22.38	9/89
Destinations	331 200	12 395	37.42	9 110	27.51	1/90
Domino	331 200	16 295	49.20	11 985	36.19	1/90
enRoute	139 585	12 400	88.83	10 540	75.51	2/90
Equinox	168 340	8 830	52.46	6 315	37.51	1/90
Flare	214 291	10 770	50.26	8 045	37.54	1/90
Globe & Mail Broadcast Week	331 200	4 236	12.78	2 545	7.68	11/89
Goodlife Magazine	270 659	15 660	57.85	12 840	47.44	9/89
Great Expectations	149 612	8 370	55.94	6 120	40.90	1/90
Harrowsmith	152 258	7 105	46.66	5 255	34.51	1/90
Hockey News (Cdn. edition)	110 147	2 575	23.37	1 975	17.93	9/89
Homes	87 909	5 800	65.97	—	—	11/89
Homemaker's (Eng)	1 600 054	20 800	12.99	17 680	11.04	1/2/89
Images Magazine	320 000	14 425	46.07	12 261.25	38.31	2/90
Legion Magazine	494 385	10 473.75	21.18	8 891.40	17.98	2/90
Leisure Ways (Ontario)	499 728	8 600	17.00	6 800	13.60	1/90
Maclean's	600 000	22 950	38.25	17 920	29.86	1/90
Marquee	400 000	10 710	26.77	8 575	21.43	2/90
MTL Montreal	61 323	3 850	75.01	2 915	56.80	1/90
Network	150 000	6 700	44.66	5 975	39.83	1/90
New Mother	163 275	16 480	94.80	12 385	75.85	1/90
Outdoor Canada	134 979	7 600	55.56	6 450	47.78	2/90
Pet's Magazine	60 967	4 400	72.17	3 560	58.39	1/2/90
Photo Life	64 064	6 950	108.48	5 175	80.77	11/88
PrimeTime	760 000	14 840	19.52	11 875	15.62	1/90
Reader's Digest	1 306 000	24 456	18.72	19 565	14.98	1/90
Saturday Night	110 153	7 250	65.81	5 065	45.98	1/90
Select Homes & Food	123 313	8 650	70.14	6 920	56.12	1/90
Small Business	105 106	8 809	83.81	7 109	67.63	1/90
Starweek Magazine	803 081	15 205	18.93	9 340	11.63	1/90
Sunday Sun TV-Tor.	464 798	6 762	14.54	4 526	9.73	1/90
Sunday Sun TV-Cal.	96 381	1 641	16.68	1 023	10.39	12/89

Source: Canadian Media Directors' Council Media Digest, 1990/91, pp. 54–56.

time classification for calculating CPMs is used. The audience factor may be calculated in terms of viewers or households tuned to a program. Again, the closer the definition of the audience factor to that of the target audience(s), the more useful the CPM measure.

CPRP is often used in television to compare the cost of various vehicles or combinations of vehicles. Since the GRP concept is widely used in television planning, the CPRP concept is the logical measure of efficiency. The TELPAK program provides the cost per rating point for a TV schedule.

When the information is available, ratings and GRPs may be broken down into demographic or psychographic subgroups and/or weighted according to primary, secondary, and tertiary target audiences.

Out-of-Home Cost Comparisons

For outdoor and transit, the unit of space used may be the daily showing according to a given GRP level. Thus the cost per unit may be calculated by converting the monthly cost on a daily basis. For outdoor or transit the CPM definition may be stated as:

CPM = daily cost / daily circulation (000s)

As for other media, circulation figures may be weighted according to various subgroups in the target audiences.

Conclusions

Based on the budget allocated to a specific media type, media planners must consider both qualitative and quantitative factors when selecting vehicles. The environment for communicating the message must be favourable, through decisions on media options, editorial, level of clutter, timing of exposure, and competitive use of vehicles. The right audience must be selected at the lowest possible cost, and the selection is affected by market coverage, unit rates and discounts, availability, and vehicle cost comparisons weighted by the target audiences. Once the selection process is completed, the media planner must justify the choice of vehicles. Each vehicle must have a rationale.

DEVELOPING THE MEDIA SCHEDULE AND BUDGET

After the media vehicles are determined, the final step in developing the media plan is the *media schedule*. The media schedule is a calendar indicating how and when the selected vehicles are to carry the advertisement over the campaign's time horizon.

The scheduling strategies are based on the selected communication task and the media planner's knowledge about the various steps in the communication process:

- consumer motivations and the proper timing of response to the advertisement when the prospect is in the right frame of mind, e.g., a beer spot during the early fringe on television;
- consumer perceptions, consumer attitudes, and the proper placement and spacing of a series of advertisements to improve attention and learning (and minimize forgetting), and its effects on the attitudes of consumers;
- the dynamics of purchase behaviour and the influence of purchase cycles on the media scheduling strategy.

FIGURE 14-9

Six Basic Types of Scheduling Strategies

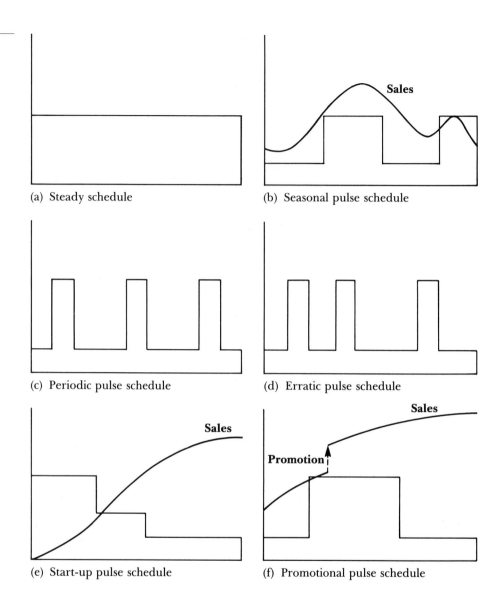

(a) Steady schedule

(b) Seasonal pulse schedule

(c) Periodic pulse schedule

(d) Erratic pulse schedule

(e) Start-up pulse schedule

(f) Promotional pulse schedule

Media Scheduling Strategies

Several schedules may be compatible with the media objectives and strategy for frequency and continuity. There are six types of scheduling strategies (Figure 14-9):[11]

Steady

This strategy consists in using a vehicle regularly in order to produce an even flow of exposures and increase the effect of the message (Figure 14-9a). The critical problem here is inter-exposure time. If it is too large, some forgetting may take place.[12] Reducing this interval of time may, however, only be done by increasing the size of the budget or reducing the size or length of the message. This type of scheduling strategy is usually applied to products that are well known and have a constant probability of purchase across the campaign's time horizon.

Seasonal Pulse

This strategy consists in timing the advertising to precede or coincide with the sales pattern. Thus, the media schedule will have heavy advertising just before or during the high-sales periods. The advantage of this strategy is high impact. It reaches prospects when they are gathering information and making decisions to buy a product (Figure 14–9b). Examples of products with seasonal pulse strategies are lawn mowers, toys, and moving companies. The problem with such a strategy is that considerable forgetting may take place during the off-season period, depending on the length of each period.[13]

Periodic Pulse

This strategy consists in placing short pulses or flights at regular intervals during the time horizon (Figure 14–9c). These flights may not necessarily be related to seasonal patterns. This strategy is used when the effects of each flight can be sustained without too much forgetting and consumers need to be reminded regularly of the product. Such strategies may be used for well-known brands like Coke or Pepsi, or for food products like cheeses and snack foods. When the creative execution uses approaches that tend to wear out rapidly, like humour, this strategy can restore the message impact by allowing some forgetting to take place.

Erratic Pulse

This strategy is similar in principle to the periodic pulse strategy, except that the flights are not spaced regularly (Figure 14–9d). It may be used to take advantage of specific market conditions, or because the purchase cycles are irregular, or to modify purchase cycles. Products that may use such a strategy are desserts, aperitif wines, turkeys, and cranberry sauce. The difficulty with this strategy lies in determining the intervals between flights.

Start-up Pulse

This strategy consists in advertising heavily when a new product is introduced in order to stimulate adoption and trial (Figure 14–9e). It is used for new consumer products and services as well as for new models of automobiles and other durable products.

Promotional Pulse

This strategy calls for heavy advertising during a promotional campaign, such as sampling and couponing (Figure 14–9f). This type of pulsing is designed to increase the target market's response to the promotional tool by encouraging trial, repeat purchase, or multiple purchases.

Media Scheduling Models

Traditionally, the media selection problem has been solved with a sequential approach. The advertising budget is first split among the different types of media. For instance, an advertiser may decide to allocate 60 percent of the advertising budget to print media and 40 percent to broadcast media. Then, within each class of media, the budget is further split among media vehicles. Finally, the media schedule is worked out for each media vehicle. The media schedule also specifies the media options that have been selected. Nonetheless, even if it were possible to make optimal decisions at each different decision level (i.e., budget allocation among media types, media vehicles, media options), this procedure would not lead to an overall optimal media schedule. Optimizing each part of a system is not the same as optimizing the entire system. Thus a better approach is to derive an optimal media schedule immediately.[14]

Media Selection Through Mathematical Programming

The media selection problem is an optimization problem (i.e., maximization of profits, sales or exposure value) under constraint (the advertising budget, the maximum and minimum number of insertions that should or could be made in each media vehicle). Therefore, it was one of the first problems operations researchers tackled when they turned to marketing problems. The application of linear programming was first proposed in 1961.[15] Unfortunately, when these techniques were first applied to media selection, the problem was grossly oversimplified. Most relationships are not linear. Moreover, the principle of diminishing marginal returns applies in many circumstances, and an optimal solution implies that the media vehicles and the media schedule should be determined simultaneously. Several of these methods have now been improved, and the problem is normally solved through mathematical programming rather than linear programming. Such methods determine the media schedule, which maximizes either the total number of media exposures of the schedules or sales or profits.

Among such models, one of the most complete to date is MEDIAC.[16] In principle, MEDIAC is an interactive computer system where a manager interacts with a model on the conversational mode. The purpose of this model is to determine the media schedule that maximizes a firm's profits for a given advertising budget. A marketing manager supplies basic data about the audience and the cost structures of each advertising media vehicle, and also judgmental estimates on the appropriateness of each advertising vehicle for the advertiser's purpose. The system yields output on the best media schedule. In addition, the model user can change basic estimates and assess the impact of the proposed schedule.[17]

Other types of models utilize the minimization of the cost per GRP or of the CPM, and software programs that have been developed for microcomputers and can be implemented at a very little cost.[18]

High Assay Method

This method consists of making a purchase in the media vehicle that is the most profitable for a given period.[19] The profitability of the media vehicle purchase is assessed in terms of a given criterion, for instance, the media insertions that yield the best results per dollar spent. Then, taking into account the effect of this first purchase on the duplicated audiences with all other available media vehicles, and on the costs of subsequent purchases in the media vehicle (because of quantity discounts), the second best purchase is made, and so on. This procedure is continued until a certain objective has been met for a given period of time.[20] Typically, this objective is a function of several variables, among them the number of potential customers and the product life-cycle stage of the brand.

Simulation Models

Other authors have solved the media selection problem through simulation[21]. The effect of a given media schedule is simulated on a fictitious population that is a small-scale representation of the actual target market segment. The most likely effect of a given advertising schedule on this simulated market segment is estimated and then inferred to the whole population of interest.[22]

The actual use of media models for the purpose of scheduling is still somewhat low according to a study surveying media decision-makers in both companies and advertising agencies.[23] However, as low-cost methods (such as the one utilizing the CPM rule) are being implemented, it is expected that these methods will become more common.[24]

Media Schedule and Budget

The media *schedule* must include a list of all the vehicles that were selected and regrouped according to the various media types; the amount of time or space to be bought in each vehicle, with the indication of the various media options selected; and the dates when the advertisements are to appear.

A useful document that accompanies and summarizes the schedule is called a *blocking chart*. An example of a completed blocking chart is reproduced in Figure 14–10 (next page).

The final media *budget* indicates how much money is allocated to each vehicle and each key market. Often, a detailed expenditure statement by month or quarter is also provided.

MEDIA BUYING

Once the media schedule has been prepared, the actual execution of the media plan is the responsibility of media buyers. Since media buying is a complicated and time-consuming task, many agencies use different specialists for print, television, and radio. Thus, the media service group represented in Figure 3–5 (page 62) has a television time buyer, a radio time buyer, and a print buyer. These specialists may be assisted by estimators in preparing, negotiating, and controlling the various buys.

Media buyers have an important role to play in three areas. They have to interpret the work of the media planner in making decisions on actual buys or in finding a suitable replacement if a particular vehicle is not available. Often, in the course of negotiation, it is too late for the buyer to consult the media planner when some problems arise.

They are skilled in negotiating with media representatives for better rates, favourable positions, and any other factors that will enhance the message's

FIGURE 14–10

Example of a Blocking Chart

With the kind permission of Cadbury Beverages Canada Inc. on behalf of Cadbury Limited, owner of the trademark Cadbury's Dairy Milk and Cadbury's Thick Dairy Milk

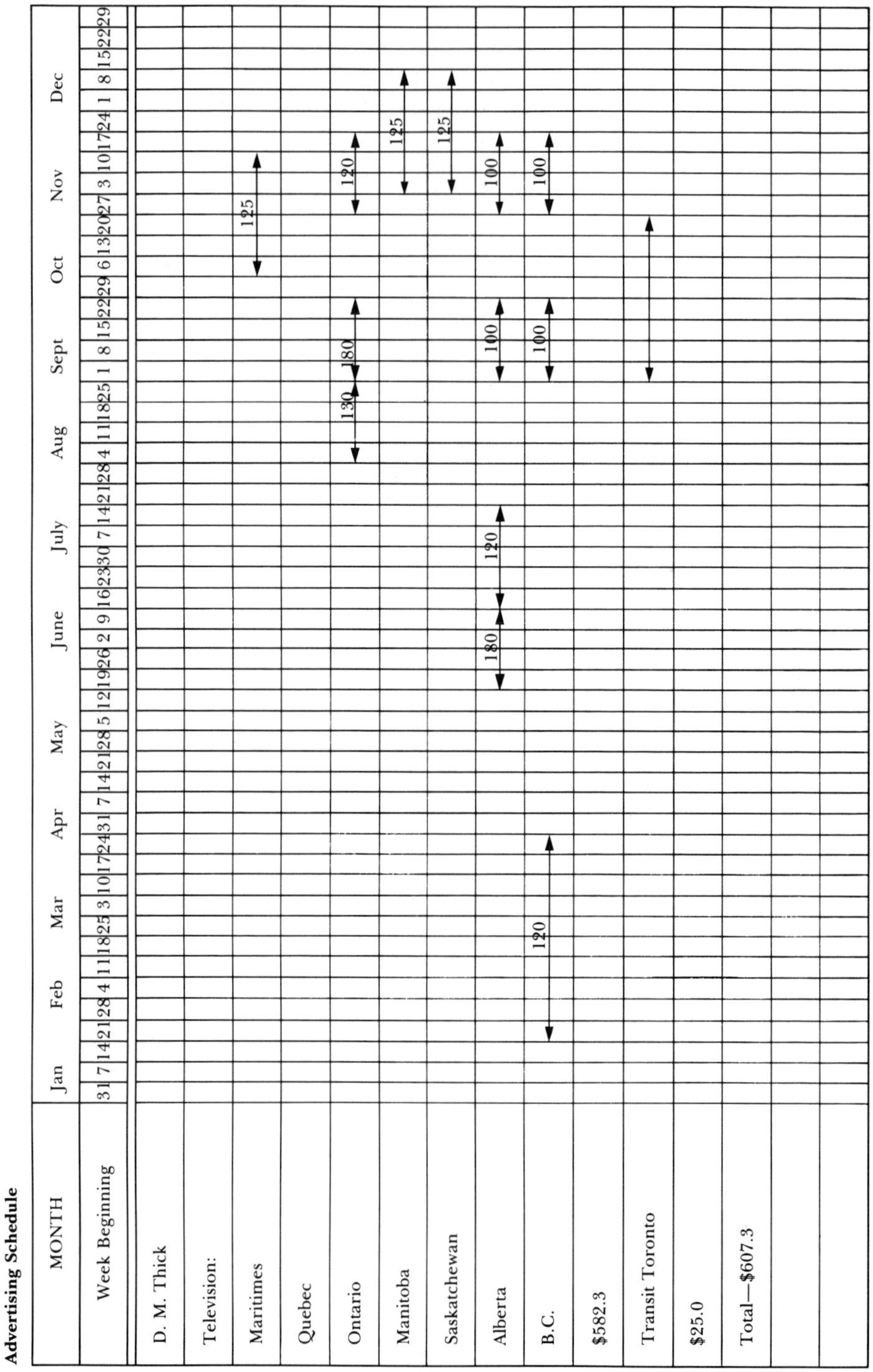

Advertising Schedule

MONTH	Jan	Feb	Mar	Apr	May	June	July	Aug	Sept	Oct	Nov	Dec
Week Beginning	31 7 14 21 28	4 11 18 25	3 10 17 24 31	7 14 21 28	5 12 19 26	2 9 16 23 30	7 14 21 28	4 11 18 25	1 8 15 22 29	6 13 20 27	3 10 17 24	1 8 15 22 29
D. M. Thick												
Television:												
Maritimes										125		
Quebec												
Ontario								130 80		120		
Manitoba											125	
Saskatchewan											125	
Alberta						180	120		100		100	
B.C.		120							100		100	
$582.3												
Transit Toronto									100			
$25.0												
Total—$607.3												

effectiveness within a given schedule. In doing so, they stretch the efficiency of the media budget.

They have to make tactical decisions during the campaign, when schedule changes are required by a competitor's move, a shift in the editorial environment of the vehicle, or anything else that can affect the media schedule.

The process of media buying follows five steps:

• gathering all the relevant information about the campaign and the media plan;
• requesting submissions from the media representatives of each vehicle;
• evaluating each submission and, if necessary, requesting more information or another submission;
• negotiating the media purchase and signing a contract;
• reporting the total schedule.

Once the media buying has been completed, the agency or advertiser must control or verify that the advertisement or commercial has been run. Most print media vehicles provide the agency with a tear sheet, which is a copy of the page in which the advertisement appeared. For broadcast media vehicles, the usual practice is an affidavit from the station or network that the commercial was aired. Otherwise, suitable replacements must be negotiated at no extra cost to the advertiser.

SUMMARY

The development of a media plan is a difficult and complicated task. Since most advertising dollars go to purchasing media time or space, it must be done efficiently.

The development of the media plan starts with the advertising objectives, which are in turn reworked and stated as media objectives. These are developed in terms of target audiences, key markets, creative execution, and the selected task of the communication within various constraints.

The media strategy for achieving these objectives is designed around such basic planning dimensions as reach, frequency, continuity, intensity, and impact of the campaign, and some relative cost measures. The strategy involves selecting the media types and media vehicles consistent with the media objectives and the decisions on the previous dimensions.

The sequence an advertisement or commercial appears in the selected vehicle is called the media schedule. Six basic scheduling strategies may be used: steady, seasonal, periodic, erratic, start-up, and promotional pulses. Some mathematical models developed in the last 30 years can help media planners process the huge amount of information available and arrive at an optimal schedule. Nevertheless, they are still being refined, and are not in widespread use. Computers, however, are heavily used in media departments for many basic operations, and it is likely that in the future, some of these models will gain acceptance by media planners.

Once the media schedule has been prepared, the task of media buying and verification is undertaken.

1. Find some examples of advertisements where the creative execution had a great influence on the choice of media types and/or vehicles. Explain your choice.

2. Explain the concepts of reach and frequency and their usefulness in the media planning process. When would high reach be more important than high frequency as a media strategy?
Give some examples of campaigns:
   a. with high reach and low frequency
   b. with low reach and high frequency
   c. where both reach and frequency are important

3. The Agostini method for calculating net reach is based on the following formula:

$$NR = 100 \frac{A}{TA} / \left(1 + \frac{KD}{A}\right)$$

where NR = net reach of all vehicles
      A = sum of the audiences of all vehicles
   TA = target audience
      D = sum of all pairwise duplications
      K = Agostini's constant of 1.125

   a. Calculate the net reach for five magazines, with the following information:

Magazine	Net reach of each magazine	Duplication with			
		B	C	D	E
A	12%	13 000	14 000	15 000	16 000
B	16%	—	12 000	13 000	14 000
C	20%		—	15 000	16 000
D	24%			—	14 000
E	28%				—

The size of the target audience is 250 000.

   b. Calculate the net reach for the five magazines using the assumption of random duplications.

4. Discuss the advantages and disadvantages of the flighting strategy, the media concentration strategy, and the media-mix dominance strategy. Give a numerical example of each, assuming that you have a media budget of $300 000 for a chain of jewellery stores in your province.

5. How do the media decisions of competitors affect those of
   a. a chain of supermarkets
   b. a French restaurant owner
   c. a toy manufacturer

6. Give some detailed examples of campaigns for each one of the six basic media scheduling strategies.

7. Select three consumer magazines and explain how you would use the main factors in vehicle selection described in this chapter.

8. Explain the CPM concept in the context of the main media types: television, radio, newspapers, magazines, out-of-home, direct mail. Compare all the major vehicles in your area using the CPM concept and using the most common unit of space in each medium: one page/four colours, 1000 lines/black and white, 30-second prime time television, 60-second prime time radio, 100 GRP.

9. What are the main advantages and disadvantages of using media models in planning the media plan? Why are so few of them used in practice?

10. Explain when and why weekly newspapers are considered for a media plan. In a market with more than one daily newspaper, how would you go about selecting the vehicle(s) to include in your media plan?

PROBLEMS

1. You are given a magazine budget of $140 000. Your target group is defined as women 25 to 49, English-speaking, and with a household income of $35 000 and more (total target group population: 1 404 000). You have narrowed the choice down to four magazines: *Canadian Living*, *Chatelaine*, *Homemaker's*, and *Reader's Digest*, and that 10 different schedules would satisfy your budget requirement, as indicated in the accompanying table:

One Issue Reach	Canadian Living 30.6%	Chatelaine 32.6%	Homemaker's 22.2%	Reader's Digest 24.9%	Schedule Cost $	Reach %
	(Number of insertions for each magazine in the corresponding schedule)					
Schedule #1	10	0	0	0	140 550	67.4
2	0	7	0	0	137 655	61.2
3	0	0	8	0	138 626	43.0
4	0	0	0	7	144 831	48.2
5	2	3	2	0	141 310	72.8
6	4	2	2	0	144 830	74.5
7	0	2	3	2	146 630	70.4
8	3	2	0	2	136 670	74.7
9	4	4	0	0	146 480	72.5
10	6	2	0	0	136 160	71.3

With this information, calculate for each schedule the CPM, GRP, average frequency, and gross impressions. Determine the best schedule for each of the following media objectives: maximize reach, maximize frequency, minimize CPM, maximize gross impressions, maximize reach for a minimum frequency of 3, and maximize frequency for a minimum reach of 50.

2. Given the following information, put together the best possible TV buy and then explain your choice of programming.

	CFTO	CITY	CHCH	CBLT
Program	Academy	Laverne/MASH	Event TV	Early News
Cost	1025.00	945.00	1750.00	800.00
GRP	8	7	11	5
CPR	128.13	135.00	159.09	160.00
Audience	232 200	199 100	431 000	199 000
CPM	4.41	4.75	4.06	4.02
Program	Late News	Late Movies	Saturday Sports	Journal/Late News
Cost	525.00	405.00	100.00	700.00
GRP	3	3	2	4
CPR	175.00	135.00	50.00	175.00
Audience	140 000	71 800	74 000	145 600
CPM	3.74	5.64	1.35	4.81
Program	Burnet/News	Sunday Movies	Renovating Home	Disney
Cost	1025.00	405.00	100.00	800.00
GRP	8	3	1	7
CPR	128.13	135.00	100.00	114.29
Audience	449 800	94 700	7 800	268 600
CPM	2.28	4.28	12.82	2.98

Client: Paint company
Target: Homeowners 25 years and over
Market: Toronto
GRP Obj.: 30
Budget: $4 000.00

Present the result of your work in the form of a media plan.

NOTES

1. Tony Jarvis, "Time to Play the Weighting Game," *Marketing*, June 22, 1981, pp. 52–53; see also L. Van Esch and R.A. Powell, "Preference for Choice and Its Applications to Marketing," *Marketing*, vol. 4, ed. James D. Forbes (Administrative Sciences Association of Canada, 1983), pp. 351–59.
2. *Canadian Media Directors' Council Media Digest, 1989/90*, pp. 75–96.
3. J.M. Agostini, "How to Estimate Unduplicated Audiences," *Journal of Advertising Research* (March 1961), pp. 11–14; see also H.J. Claycamp and C.W. McClelland, "Estimating Reach and the Value of K," *Journal of Advertising Research* (June 1968), pp. 44–51; R.A. Metheringham, "Measuring the Net Cumulative Coverage of a Print Campaign," *Journal of Advertising Research* (December 1964), pp. 23–28.
4. Robert S. Headen, Jay E. Klompmaker, and Jesse

E. Teel, Jr., "Predicting Audience Exposure to Spot TV Advertising Schedules," *Journal of Marketing Research* (February 1977), pp. 1–9.

5. John D. Leckenby and Marshall D. Rice, "A Beta Binomial Network TV Exposure Model Using Limited Data," *Journal of Advertising*, Vol. 14, No. 3 (1985), pp. 25–31.

6. Jarvis, p. 53.

7. William T. Moran, "Practical Media Decisions and the Computer," *Journal of Marketing* (July 1963), pp. 26–30.

8. Hubert A. Zielske, "The Remembering and Forgetting of Advertising," *Journal of Marketing* (January 1959), pp. 239–43.

9. Gary A. Mauser, "Segmenting Media Usage: A Case of Methodological Triangulation," *1976 Proceedings* (Administrative Sciences Association of Canada, 1976), Section 5, pp. 221–27.

10. S.A. Ahmed and J.R. Kennedy, "Factor Analytic Search for Television Programs," *1976 Proceedings* (Administrative Sciences Association of Canada, 1976), Section 5, pp. 1–9; S.A. Ahmed, "Prime-time TV Viewing Correlates," *1975 Proceedings* (Administrative Sciences Association of Canada, 1975), Section 4, pp. 1–7.

11. Kenneth A. Longman, *Advertising* (New York: Harcourt Brace Jovanovich, 1971), pp. 371–72.

12. Zielske, pp. 239–43.

13. Ibid.

14. E. Brian Bimm and Allan D. Millman, "A Model of Planning TV in Canada," *Journal of Advertising Research* (August 1978), pp. 43–48.

15. Frank M. Bass and Ronald T. Londsdale, "An Exploration of Linear Programming Method in Media Selection," *Journal of Marketing Research* (May 1966), pp. 179–88.

16. John D.C. Little and Leonard M. Lodish, "A Media Planning Calculus," *Operations Research* (January-February 1969), pp. 1–35.

17. Ibid.

18. Yvan Boivin, "Media Planning with the CPM Rule," in *Marketing, vol. 10*, ed. Alain d'Astous (Administrative Sciences Association of Canada, 1989), pp. 39–47; Yvan Boivin, "Simple and Complex Rules for Allocating Budget Between Media," *Canadian Journal of Administrative Sciences*, vol. 4:1, pp. 97–111.

19. William T. Moran, "Practical Media Decisions and the Computer," *Journal of Marketing* (July 1963), pp. 26–30.

20. Note that this method does not lead to media schedule optimization because the algorithm may find a local but not the global optimum.

21. *Simulatics Media-Mix: Technical Description* (New York: The Simulatics Corporation, October 1962).

22. Dennis Gensch, *Advertising Planning: Mathematical Models in Advertising Media Planning* (Amsterdam: Elsevier Publishing, 1973).

23. Gordon McDougall and Gerald Simpson, "Media Planning in Advertising: the Practitioner's Viewpoint," *Marketing 77*, ed. G.H.G. McDougall and R. Drolet (Administrative Sciences Association of Canada, 1977), pp. 91–98.

24. Marshall D. Rice and Christopher Kubas, "Estimating the Audience of Canadian Television Advertising Schedules," *Canadian Journal of Administrative Sciences*, Vol. 5:1 (1988), pp. 75–80.

CHAPTER

15 *Advertising Research in Canada*

Although judgment plays an important part in the analysis and solution of many advertising problems, advertisers also have at their disposal analytical tools that range from simple procedures to sophisticated decision systems. Advertisers should and must bring original and creative thinking to rigorous scientific analysis.

Thus, advertising communications, like any element of the marketing mix, is elaborated from a precise knowledge of consumers. Because of the high costs involved, advertising communications must be efficient. It costs only a fraction of a cent to reach a potential customer with an advertising message, but a large number of potential customers must be reached several times in order to move them up the hierarchy of effects.

Because of the potential competitive advantage that an efficient advertising campaign can give a firm, no elements of the advertising communications program can be neglected. This is why they have been the object of formal research by advertisers and advertising agencies. Research projects can be either systematic and recurrent, such as those which are periodically undertaken on the audiences of media vehicles, or occasional, when they are carried out every time a new advertising campaign is planned. This chapter briefly describes the means available to advertisers and agency personnel to obtain and analyze advertising data. Then the various types of advertising research for different types of advertising decisions are detailed.

ADVERTISING RESEARCH METHODS

The nature of research in advertising includes obtaining information relevant to the decision-making process. The information seeker may be the advertising manager, the account executive, the copywriter, the creative director, or the media director. Of course, advertising research is a special application of marketing research and uses many of the standard marketing research techniques and methods. Nevertheless, some types of advertising research, for example copy testing and research on media habits, are carried out by organizations separate from the traditional market research organizations.

Source of Advertising Data

Advertising data may be collected on a regular basis in order to control the effectiveness of various campaigns or flights, or data may be collected through *ad hoc* research in order to assist in a precise advertising decision. Advertising data come from different sources. They come from *secondary sources* when they have already been collected for purposes other than those of the advertising manager. Advertising data come from *primary sources* when they have not been collected before and are collected for a particular need of a marketing advertising unit.

Internal Secondary Sources

Companies collect information on their customers in the normal course of business transactions. The internal accounting system, the customer relations department, and the company sales force may all provide valuable information on customers' characteristics, their geographic and demographic distribution, and their reactions to packaging and advertising.

External Secondary Sources

Several media organizations collect data regularly on the viewing or reading habits of consumers, as well as demographic and psychographic information. Examples of external secondary sources are the Print Measurement Bureau (PMB), the Newspaper Marketing Bureau, and the Bureau of Broadcast Measurement studies. Secondary sources of information are among the least costly for a company to obtain.

Primary Sources of Advertising Data

Primary source data are collected for a specific purpose. In other words, it is information that has not already been collected or is not readily available. Thus researchers must design a specific project for collecting the desired data. This type of advertising research is generally expensive. Some companies organize "home-panel" or ongoing tracking studies, and market research studies are also carried out at intervals. Primary data may be collected through observation, experimentation, and surveys.

Observation. This is the most elementary data collection procedure. It consists solely of observing consumer behaviour. Obviously, what can be observed is only overt behaviour. No indication is given about thoughts, opinions, and deeper attitudes of the observed subjects. Researchers often use recording devices, such as cameras and tape recorders and conceal the recording devices.

Experimentation. When a researcher attempts to infer a causal relationship between two sets of events, the most appropriate research method is experimentation.[1] For instance, if a researcher wants to find out which advertising budget level has the greatest effect on sales, a causal relationship is implied between advertising and sales. The experiment should show the nature of the relationship, its direction, shape, and amplitude. In practice, sales are likely to vary because of factors other than the variable under investigation. This is difficult to use in practice.[2]

Experimentation has had only limited application to advertising problems. There are serious problems in setting up experimental designs where environmental variables can be manipulated by the researcher,[3] since advertising decisions are made in a complex environment.

Surveys. Because each advertising campaign is different, surveys are the most widely used technique for collecting information. The principle of a survey is to interview individuals or other units by means of a questionnaire. The respondents are often consumers. In most cases, advertisers want to ask consumers about their past or present behaviour, their buying intentions or intended buying behaviour, as well as their perceptions, preferences, attitudes, and opinions. Because interviewing all the consumers in a market segment would not be practical and is too costly and time consuming, only a sample of the whole population is selected and interviewed. If the sample of respondents has been drawn according to statistical procedures, the probability that the sample has the same characteristics as the whole population can be calculated. Each step in a market survey involves the risk of committing various errors. Some types of error can, to a certain extent, be controlled. Other types can be avoided only through the expertise of the researcher.

The steps a researcher follows in conducting a market survey are shown in Figure 15–1. Once a marketing or advertising problem has been identified and has been properly translated into a research problem, the objectives of the research study should be stated clearly. Then, to design the survey, decisions must be made in three fundamental areas: the questionnaire, the sample, and the survey method. In designing the questionnaire, the researcher is concerned with the question: *Which* information should the respondents be asked? The sampling procedure involves the question: To *whom* should the information be asked? The survey method is directed to the question: *How* should this information be obtained? Of course, the decisions concerning the survey design cannot be made independently. All the questions must be answered with the other questions in mind, in order to arrive at a coherent survey design.

The Questionnaire. A questionnaire is characterized by the number of questions, the content and wording of each question, as well as by the sequence of questions a respondent is asked. The wording of the questions depends on the survey medium. Some questions involve sensitive issues and may require the use of various projective techniques to elicit accurate and truthful answers.[4] The principle of projective techniques is to induce a respondent to reveal deep personal feelings by making a third person answer instead. The third person bears the responsibility for the opinion expressed, not the respondent.

Sampling. To obtain an adequate sample, the ideal universe to be studied should be properly and carefully defined, as well as the operational universe that will be used. Then the sampling frame, the sampling method, and the sample sizes are determined.[5]

The *ideal universe* is composed of all the individuals or sampling units that possess the information the advertising researcher wants to collect. However, advertising researchers must settle for an *operational universe*, which is a more practical definition of the individuals who can be interviewed. For instance, a razor blade advertiser may define its ideal universe as all the male adults living

FIGURE 15–1

Major Steps to be Completed in a Typical Advertising Survey

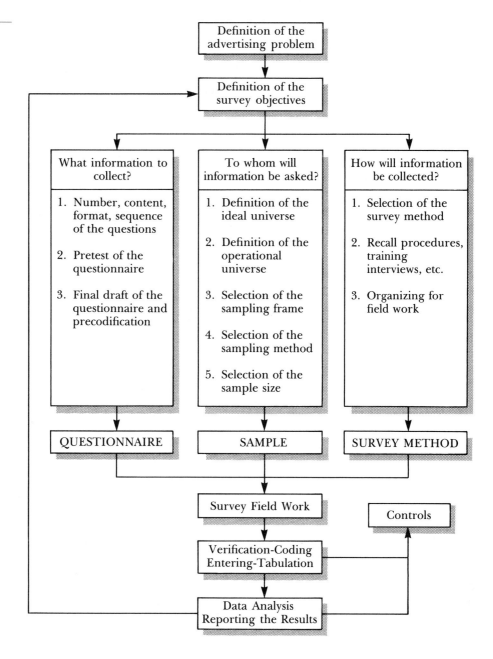

in the Calgary metropolitan area (CMA). As it may be too difficult to identify all these individuals, the advertiser may define its operational universe as all the male adults living in the metropolitan area whose households are listed in the telephone book.

The next step is to obtain a *sampling frame*, which is a list of the units to be interviewed. This could be a list of households, individuals, or any other unit.

In the preceding example, the sampling frame would be constituted by the names under each household listed in the telephone directory of the CMA, excluding all firms, organizations, and public administrations. By identifying all the male adults in each household, an advertising manager car sample an operational universe.

At the same time as the decision to use a given sampling frame is made, the researcher must also decide which *sampling method* to follow. A sampling method is generally related to three criteria: the objectives of the survey, the quality and costs of the available sampling frames, and the costs of interviewing the selected sample units. If the research is exploratory, there is no need to draw a simple random and representative sample of the population. However, if the survey objective is to estimate a population parameter, for example, the mean number of units of a certain brand consumed by households, the method to use is simple *random sampling*. The researcher draws the desired number of units in the sample, following certain random procedures.

The sampling plan must also specify the sample size. A sample size is chosen on the basis of the results to be achieved, the sampling method to be selected, the expected rate of non-response, and the size of the research budget. The sample size should be adjusted so that the number of completed questionnaires yields the desired level of precision in the results.

Survey Methods. The advertising researcher must decide which method will be used to collect data—a personal, telephone, or mail survey. The selection of the survey method depends on the type of information to be collected and the costs involved weighed against the expected benefits of the study.

The *personal interview* is the most adequate data collection procedure when lengthy explanations must be given or when it is important to ascertain whether respondents correctly understand a question or what has been asked of them. Response rates are generally higher for personal interviews than for any other type of survey, but a major drawback is the cost.

Telephone interviews are less expensive than personal interviews. However, respondents are sometimes reluctant to give personal data or even talk over the telephone to a so-called interviewer that they do not know and see in person. Telephone interviews are best suited for short questionnaires that do not deal with personal or sensitive issues.[6]

Mail surveys are generally selected as a survey method when cost constraints are very important. A mail survey is used when it is essential that a simple random sample be used and when the research budget does not allow for personal or telephone interviews. Like telephone surveys, questionnaires used for mail surveys should be short enough to keep the non-response rate as low as possible and at the same time obtain data as accurate and complete as possible.[7, 8]

Recently, new research technologies have been developed using improvements of such methods as WATS telephone centre interviewing, cathode-ray tube (CRT) interviewing machines in shopping centres, or in the home through a two-way cable system. Since we are experiencing an information revolution, one may expect the introduction of other forms of survey methods.

Advertising Decision Models[9]

A model is a simplified replication of the real world. An advertising model presents an advertising phenomenon from which the less important or irrelevant variables have been deleted and which retains the most relevant aspects of the real world for the purpose of the model user.

Two types of marketing models have proved very helpful in solving advertising problems: optimization and simulation models. With an _optimization model_, an advertiser provides basic data, which are the model's parameters, and the system yields the values of the decision variables that maximize a certain criterion variable, for instance, what advertising budget would maximize profits.[10] _Simulation models_, as their name implies, simulate the real world. Thus, a marketing manager can manipulate this simulated environment to test the effects various decisions would have on such other variables as sales, profits, or market share. For instance, how would sales be affected by a 10 percent increase in the advertising budget?

The ADBUDG system decision model is designed to help advertisers select the proper level of advertising expenditure. An advertiser makes a series of judgments about expected sales territory responses to different levels of advertising expenditure. These estimates are processed through a computer-based model that assesses the underlying profit response functions to advertising and estimates the corresponding optimal advertising budget for maximizing profits.[11]

The same problem can be solved with a simulation model. In this case, the population of Canada is simulated by means of a sample of fictitious individuals. With PERCEPTOR, expected market performance for a new product can be predicted. Information collected during the pre-test stage of new product development becomes the input data. The system predicts the long-run market share that the new product idea could capture.[12]

These are only a few examples of a new generation of advertising models that have been designed for decision-makers. With the greater use of time-sharing and mini-computers, these management tools will likely become available to more medium- and small-sized firms.

ADVERTISING RESEARCH AVAILABLE IN CANADA

Marketing and advertising research activities grew from the need of the full-service advertising agencies early in the twentieth century for information needed to solve marketing and advertising problems. In 1929, Warren Brown, president of National Publicity, created the first Canadian marketing research department. In 1932, Ethel Fulford and Associates was founded in Toronto as the first independent research firm. In 1943, it became known as Canadian Facts Ltd. Four other independent firms were created by 1945: Elliott-Hayes, which became Elliott Research, the Canadian Institute of Public Opinion, which became the Gallup Poll of Canada, A.C. Nielsen of Canada, and International Surveys.[13]

To help advance the discipline, practice, and professional standards of advertising research, several organizations were created. The Canadian Advertising Research Foundation is a non-profit organization supported by advertisers, advertising agencies, and media. Its objectives are to develop new research

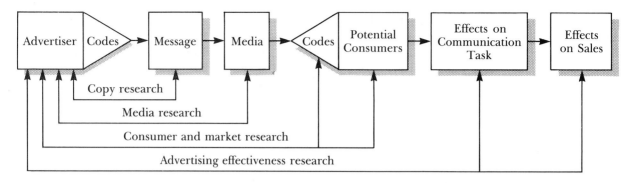

FIGURE 15–2

Major Types of Advertising Research Undertaken by or for Advertisers

methods and techniques, to analyze and evaluate existing methods and techniques, and to establish research standards. One useful booklet it distributes is "Media Research Standards and Full Consultation Procedures and Requirements."[14] Several advertising agencies have adopted nine principles of copy testing called PACT (Positioning Advertising Copy Testing).[15] Two other professional organizations assist members in improving the quality of research: The Professional Market Research Society and the Canadian Association of Market Research Organizations.

Depending on the stage of the planning process, there are four main types of research on which advertising decisions rely. Following the order in which an advertiser plans a campaign (which is the reverse of the order in which the communication takes place), they are: market and consumer research, media research, copy research, and advertising effectiveness research (Figure 15–2).

Marketing and Advertising Research Methods

Qualitative Methods

These methods are motivation research, focus groups, in-depth interviews, attitude scaling, and/or projective techniques. Studies are usually carried out on small samples of consumers drawn from the target market. The objective of *motivation research* is to unveil motives that are often hidden or buried in the consumer's subconscious mind and that may explain purchasing behaviour patterns.[16] However, the diagnosis phase that should follow analysis of the psychological material gathered from in-depth interviews with consumers requires more expertise than that possessed by amateurs. The relatively small sample sizes, sometimes as few as 50 people, cast doubt on the reliability of such research studies' findings.

Focus groups are made up of about 10 to 15 individuals who are similar to the product target group. The group leader elicits responses from the group members in a non-directive manner.[17] Focus groups may be used for new concept testing, brand name selection, brand image, and package testing.

In-depth interviews are conducted with one representative individual at a time by a trained interviewer who probes the individual's reactions to a new concept, a prototype new product, a brand name, or a new package. As with motivation research, this method is quite expensive and only provides directions for further analysis and research.

Attitude scaling and *projective techniques* can be administered much more quickly and cheaply. Both may be done through a self-administered questionnaire. With attitude scaling, an introduction describes the concept, mentions the brand name, or asks respondents to look at the prototype product or package accompanying the questionnaire. The respondent is then asked both closed and open-ended questions. With projective techniques, indirect questioning provides more accurate answers. Individuals are asked to assume the identity of another person, like a neighbour, a character in a drawing (as in the Thematic Apperception Test, or a balloon test), or in a verbal statement. Respondents are then asked to record their reactions to the material provided, or to make a statement in answer to a question based on, or included in, the material.[18]

Quantitative Methods

This type of study uses market surveys with structured questionnaires and multiple choice questions that can be easily pre-coded. The surveys are taken on larger samples drawn from the entire population of potential or actual customers in order to draw conclusions about the whole population. These types of research studies provide input into the development of the marketing plan and help define the target market more precisely.

Quantitative research may be conducted either by the advertiser's research department or by an outside supplier, which may be the research group of an advertising agency or a private research house.

Omnibus Studies.   Another alternative is for an advertiser to participate in an omnibus study, in which advertisers share the cost of research. First introduced by Canadian Facts, several companies now offer this service which has the following characteristics:

1. Each client contributes a number of questions (which form the basis for the fee), and gets the results of these questions and a specified target group (e.g., the over 50).
2. All aspects of the survey are done according to professional standards, and a large sample size (several thousand) is obtained on a regular basis.

Monitoring Services.   Information on the nature and extent of competitive advertising is very useful in the planning stages. For example, an outside supplier may specialize in providing estimates of national advertising expenditures for companies or brands. This is done by monitoring advertising in daily newspapers, weekend supplements, consumer magazines, farm publications, radio and television stations, and by estimating the expenditures for space and time by brand and company. Results are published monthly and sent to subscribers. Additional information an advertiser requires may also be obtained on a custom basis. Advertisers can purchase scripts of radio commercials and photographic story boards from research houses that specialize in monitoring and recording competitive creative activity in the broadcast media.

Media Research Methods

The object of media research is to analyze the media exposure habits of consumers in various market segments. Advertisers use the results to select the most appropriate media vehicles for reaching selected market segments.[19] The management of many media vehicles often sponsor such studies in order to identify their audiences' socio-economic characteristics or purchasing habits. The objective is to furnish media representatives with arguments to help them sell advertising space or time to potential advertisers.

Print Media Research

The object of print media research is to measure audiences and readership, to determine the profile of print media readers, and to correlate the profiles with consumption patterns. Research may be done by media, co-operative associations, or individual vehicles.

Daily Newspapers. Data on daily newspapers are collected on a regular basis by the Audit Bureau of Circulations (ABC), the Canadian Daily Newspaper Publishers Association (CDNPA), and the Newspaper Marketing Bureau.

The Audit Bureau of Circulations is an association of over 4000 advertisers, advertising agencies, and publishers in seven countries, including Canada. Its objectives are 1) to issue standardized statements of circulation and other data reported by members; 2) to verify these figures; and 3) to disseminate them, without opinion. To be eligible for ABC membership, a publication must have at least 70 percent paid circulation. ABC publishes a number of reports, including the *Canadian Newspaper Circulation Factbook*, which includes circulation figures by individual newspapers, countries, and major markets for dailies (and by province for weeklies).

The Canadian Daily Newspaper Publishers Association represents 84 daily newspapers and about 88 percent of the total circulation of Canadian dailies. It provides extensive research support to the industry, including the *cost estimator*, which is a computer system for on-line costing of newspapers' advertising schedules.

The Newspaper Marketing Bureau represents 50 daily newspapers in order to promote newspapers as viable national advertising vehicles. The Newspaper Audience Databank (NADbank) is an integrated source of newspaper audience information, as well as an extensive source of product usage information available through on-line computer access. It contains readership data for 53 newspapers in 33 major Canadian markets, with a wide range of demographic information for both weekday and weekend newspapers. It is based on a sample of over 27 000 interviews.

Magazines. Data on magazines are collected on a regular basis by the Audit Bureau of Circulations (ABC), the Canadian Circulations Audit Board (CCAB), Magazines Canada (MC), and the Print Measurement Bureau (PMB).

The role of ABC for magazines is similar to that of daily newspapers. The CCAB audits business publications as well as several large controlled-circulation consumer magazines. MC's objective is to promote the use of magazines as an advertising medium, and it collects and publishes research data on magazines.

Print Measurement Bureau. The Print Measurement Bureau is a non-profit organization of advertisers, advertising agencies, and magazine publishers. It was established in 1971 to provide readership data on consumer magazines. The first PMB study was conducted in 1973 with 20 consumer magazines. The next two studies were conducted every three years and each added questions on product usage, general media habits (for cross media comparisons) and psychographics. Participating magazines contribute about 60 percent of the total cost of the study. Since 1983, PMB has been conducting annual studies with about 6000 interviews, and publishing annual reports by combining the data for two years, i.e., a sample size of about 12 000. About 77 consumer magazines and business publications participated in the 1990 study.

The PMB reports contain data on readership of consumer magazines, with demographic subgroups, duplications of readership, and accumulation of audience; exposure to major media for selected demographics; and qualitative readership data on reading occasions, editorial interest, and others.

In addition, the PMB product profile study measures purchasing and usage of 1006 product categories covering some 21 product fields, as listed in Table 15–1 (pages 412 to 413). The data contain usage information on products or services (light, medium, or heavy users), demographics, psychographics, and media habits covering 77 magazines plus all other major media for cross-media comparisons. The subscriber to the study receives the standard published information (on microfiche) on the product categories requested. In addition, the subscriber may, through computer access, conduct additional analysis on the data by cross-classification of product usage with media habits or psychographic information. For example, one may want to find the media habits of heavy users of decaffeinated coffee and their type of lifestyle. The information is useful not only for developing the marketing and advertising plans, but also for the media planner and the creative director. For instance, if such a heavy user plays tennis several times a week, this may suggest to the creative director to set the creative execution on a tennis court or to use a known tennis player in the television commercial.

Magazines may also use the results from these studies to sell advertising space to major advertisers. For example, the *Maclean's* advertisement reproduced in Figure 15–3 uses results from a PMB study to show that its magazine delivers 2.5 million readers and quality readership with 4 readers per copy, and an average reading time of 65 minutes.

FIGURE 15–3
Advertisement for Maclean's using the results of a PMB study to show that it is a superior vehicle with 2.5 million readers and quality readership with four readers per copy, 2.6 occasions, and 65 minutes reading time.

Courtesy Maclean's

Other Print Media. Organizations representing other print media are attempting to develop similar types of data on individual vehicles. PMB studies include other *general* media such as outdoor and transit, as well as visits to shopping malls, which may assist the media planner in comparing major media.

Community newspapers are audited by CCAB, as well as the Canadian Community Newspapers Association (through the Verified Circulation Paid

Program and the Verified Circulation Controlled Program), and in the province of Quebec by the ODC (Office de la distribution certifiée).

Outdoor traffic circulation is measured every year for one-quarter of the boards in Canada by the Canadian Outdoor Measurement Bureau. Similar studies are conducted for transit audiences in major markets by means of a camera mounted in cars and buses and analyzed later for calculating traffic (pedestrians and cars) and exposure to a board. COMB provides quarterly circulation reports, which is accessible on-line.

Nevertheless, for many advertisers and media planners, more and better data are necessary, and it is likely that additional research will be done by media organizations or individual media vehicles.

TABLE 15–1 **TYPES OF PRODUCTS INCLUDED IN THE 1989 PRODUCT PROFILE STUDY**

Section	Index	Questions
01	MEDIA: Daily Newspapers, Radio, TV, Local Community Newspapers	35
02	STORES: How often shop at different store type(s)?	17
03	WOMEN'S PRODUCTS: Cosmetics, Cosmetic Brands, Face Care, Fragrances, Toiletries, Feminine Hygiene, Women's Clothing, Hair Removal, Hair Colouring	71
04	MEN'S PRODUCTS: Shaving, Men's Clothing	1
05	PERSONAL CARE: Skin Care, Oral Hygiene, Bar Soaps, Skin Care Products, Deodorant, Hair Care, Other Personal Products, Remedies, Glasses/Dentures, Shaving (Hair Removal)	73
06	FOOD: Food Shopping, Food, Condiments and Spreads, Cooking and Baking, Baking, Snacks and Confectionery	135
07	BEVERAGES: Coffee, Tea, Milk, Soft Drinks, Other Beverages	37
08	OTHER PACKAGED GOODS: Children's Products, Cat Food, Dog Food, Laundry Products, Household Products	50
09	LEISURE ACTIVITIES: Participation, Attendance, Pay TV, Eating Out, TV Sports	67
10	AUTO PRODUCTS: Driving, Ownership/Type/Price, Maintenance, Gasoline/Fuel Types	31
11	RECREATIONAL EQUIPMENT/FARM:	12
12	HOME/IMPROVEMENTS/PRODUCTS: Home, Improvement/Maintenance, Telephone/Communications, Major Appliances, Small Appliances, Tools and Equipment, Television, Use of VCR/Commercial Deletions, Radio/Stereo, Home Electronics, Cameras, Films, Batteries, Flashlights, Personal Goods, Tableware	115
13	GIFTS: Gift Giving, Value of Gifts	22
14	TRAVEL: Pleasure/Vacation: Accommodation; Trips to Canada, U.S., Other, Travel Agents/Bookings, Car Rental	46

Section	Index	Questions
15	TRAVEL: Business Trips: Transportation; Trips to Canada, U.S., Other	34
16	FINANCIAL: Bank Services, Loans, Investments, Auto, Bank Machines, Value, Insurance, Credit Cards/ Travellers Cheques	55
17	MISCELLANEOUS: Mail Order Club, Books and Magazines, Lotteries	9
18	BEVERAGE/ALCOHOL: Beer, Liquor, Fortified Wine/ Vermouth/Aperitifs, Wines, Coolers	64
19	TOBACCO PRODUCTS: Cigarettes, Cigars/Cigarillos, Pipe Tobacco	15
20	BUSINESS PURCHASING: Company Type, Size, Operations, Banking; Expansion, Individual's Purchase Involvement—Finance, EDP, Office Equipment, Services, Facilities, Distribution, Maintenance, Vehicles, Property	43
21	PSYCHOGRAPHICS: Products/Pricing/Advertising, Principles/Values/Aspirations/Likes/Dislikes/Attitudes	74
	Total	1006

Courtesy PMB Print Measurement Bureau

Broadcast Media Research

The object of broadcast media research is often to produce estimates of Canadian audiences and program ratings, as well as to determine the audience composition of broadcast media and correlate it with consumption patterns. Research may be done by syndicated rating services, media associations, or individual vehicles or networks.

Radio. Data on radio audiences are collected on a regular basis by the Bureau of Broadcast Measurement (BBM) and the Radio Bureau of Canada (RBC).

Bureau of Broadcast Measurement. The BBM is a non-profit organization of advertisers, advertising agencies, and broadcasters. It was founded in 1944 to survey radio audiences and to provide estimates of the audiences to its members. The mandate of the BBM was enlarged about a decade later to include television audiences.

BBM radio reports are based on the results of a personal diary survey normally conducted during three consecutive weeks and averaged over the three-week period. Audience estimates are calculated by projecting diary information to the total population and according to age, sex, and language subgroups. The fall survey covers all subscribing stations, the spring one most medium and large markets, and the summer one covers 14 major markets in alternate years.

For the purpose of a BBM radio or television survey, the whole of Canada, except the Yukon and the Northwest Territories, is divided into 370 sampling cells. Within each sampling cell, a random sample is drawn from a list of telephone households in cities and towns. Each household is then called, using bilingual operators where necessary, in order to obtain a list of persons living at that address. The actual number of selected households is designed to provide a *sampling frame* containing a sufficient number of names for all the BBM surveys in one year. This number is currently over one million.

Each radio diary sample is then randomly selected from the sampling frame. The sampling method is to select respondents from a random starting point within each of thirteen demographic subgroups in each sampling cell. Finally, each individual in the sample receives a diary by mail with a monetary incentive to gain co-operation. This diary contains a brief demographic questionnaire, and a daily log to record radio listening by quarter hour, every day for seven days. When completed, the diary is mailed back to the BBM. A reminder card is sent in order to increase the response rate, which averages 50 percent. A sample page of a radio diary is reproduced in Figure 15–4. A sample of a BBM radio report is provided in Figure 15–5.

FIGURE 15–4

Sample Page from a BBM Radio Diary

Courtesy BBM Bureau of Measurement

TUESDAY	②		DAYTIME		
	TIME	STATION		WHERE LISTENED	
		CALL-LETTERS	AM	FM	At home	Away from home
01	5.00-5.15AM					
02	5.15-5.30					
03	5.30-5.45					
04	5.45-6.00					
05	6.00-6.15					
06	6.15-6.30					
07	6.30-6.45					
08	6.45-7.00					
09	7.00-7.15					
10	7.15-7.30					
11	7.30-7.45					
12	7.45-8:00					
13	8.00-8.15					
14	8.15-8.30					
15	8.30-8.45					
16	8.45-9.00					
17	9.00-9.15					
18	9.15-9.30					
19	9.30-9.45					
20	9.45-10.00					
21	10.00-10.15					
22	10.15-10.30					
23	10.30-10.45					
24	10.45-11.00					
25	11.00-11.15					
26	11.15-11.30					
27	11.30-11.45					
28	11.45-12.00					
29	12.00-12.15PM					
30	12.15-12.30					
31	12.30-12.45					
32	12.45-1.00					
33	1.00-1.15					
34	1.15-1.30					
35	1.30-1.45					
36	1.45-2.00					
37	2.00-2.15					
38	2.15-2.30					
39	2.30-2.45					
40	2.45-3.00					

TUESDAY	②		EVENING		
	TIME	STATION		WHERE LISTENED	
		CALL-LETTERS	AM	FM	At home	Away from home
41	3.00-3.15PM					
42	3.15-3.30					
43	3.30-3.45					
44	3.45-4.00					
45	4.00-4.15					
46	4.15-4.30					
47	4.30-4.45					
48	4.45-5.00					
49	5.00-5.15					
50	5.15-5.30					
51	5.30-5.45					
52	5.45-6.00					
53	6.00-6.15					
54	6.15-6.30					
55	6.30-6.45					
56	6.45-7.00					
57	7.00-7.15					
58	7.15-7.30					
59	7.30-7.45					
60	7.45-8.00					
61	8.00-8.15					
62	8.15-8.30					
63	8.30-8.45					
64	8.45-9.00					
65	9.00-9.15					
66	9.15-9.30					
67	9.30-9.45					
68	9.45-10.00					
69	10.00-10.15					
70	10.15-10.30					
71	10.30-10.45					
72	10.45-11.00					
73	11.00-11.15					
74	11.15-11.30					
75	11.30-11.45					
76	11.45-12.00					
77	12.00-12.15AM					
78	12.15-12.30					
79	12.30-12.45					
80	12.45-1.00					

Please check (✓) box if you did *not* listen at all today ☐

FIGURE 15–5

Sample Page from a BBM Radio Report

Courtesy BBM Bureau of Measurement

CFMX–FM
TORONTO/COBOURG

BBM SUMMER 1990 ETE

CENTRAL AREA–TIME BLOCKS — TRANCHES HORAIRES–REGION CENTRALE

	TOTAL TOUS 7+	WOMEN-FEMMES 18+	18/49	18/44	18/34	18/24	25/54	25/49	25/34	35/64
WEEKLY CUME (00)	2110	1071	456	325	135	24	544	432	111	648
WEEKLY CUME (%)	6.2	7.2	4.6		2.4	1.2	6.1	5.4	3.0	9.3
TOTAL HOURS (000)	1602	877	332	163	61	9	374	323	51	521
SHARE OF WKLY HRS	2.5	2.8	1.7	1.0	.6	.2	2.3	2.2	.8	3.6
AVG. WEEKLY HOURS	7.6	8.2	7.3	5.0	4.5	3.8	6.9	7.5	4.6	8.0
AVERAGE ¼ HOUR AUDIENCE IN HUNDREDS ('00)										
1. STANDARD										
500A- 100A MO-FR	116	61	21	11	4	1	24	20	4	35
500A- 100A SA-SU	111	66	31	13	5	1	33	30	4	43
700A- 700P MO-FR	136	74	23	12	5	-	28	23	5	43
700A- 700P SAT	141	90	37	9	7	1	43	35	5	58
700A- 700P SUN	143	82	45	22	6	2	45	43	5	63
2. RATE CARD										
600A-MDNT MO-SU	123	68	26	12	5	1	29	25	4	41
600A-NOON MO-SU	119	67	24	14	7	1	28	24	6	36
NOON - 600P MO-SU	143	80	28	9	4	-	32	28	3	53
600P-MDNT MO-SU	107	56	25	14	3	-	28	25	3	35
3. REQUESTED										
600A-MDNT MO-FR	125	67	22	12	4	-	26	22	4	38
600A-1000A MO-FR	101	49	17	11	4	1	19	16	4	23
1000A- 300P MO-FR	143	78	23	12	7	-	28	23	7	43
300P- 800P MO-FR	146	84	28	13	3	-	33	28	3	55
800P-MDNT MO-FR	99	48	19	12	2	-	23	18	1	27
600A-NOON MO-FR	120	64	20	12	6	1	24	19	5	32
NOON - 600P MO-FR	140	78	24	10	4	-	27	24	4	47
600P-MDNT MO-FR	113	58	23	14	3	-	28	23	3	36
NOON - 100P MO-SU	144	72	25	11	6	-	28	25	6	49
300P- 500P MO-FR	163	95	25	9	3	-	29	25	3	58
500P- 600P MO-FR	119	74	28	10	-	-	34	28	-	55
600P- 800P MO-FR	143	78	32	19	6	-	38	32	6	52
600A- 900A SAT	64	49	10	6	6	4	8	6	3	21
900A- 530P SAT	159	98	41	10	7	1	50	41	6	65
600P- 800P SA-SU	125	71	47	18	10	-	47	47	10	51
800P- 900P SAT	93	49	37	20	10	-	37	37	10	27
900P-MDNT SAT	64	43	16	10	-	-	16	16	-	16
600A- 900A SUN	70	44	8	7	-	-	13	8	-	29
900A- 500P SUN	156	93	55	25	8	2	54	53	6	71
800P-MDNT SUN	78	40	19	10	-	-	20	19	-	25
600A- 600P SAT	132	84	33	9	6	1	40	32	5	53
600A- 600P SUN	134	79	41	19	5	2	41	40	4	59
CUMULATIVE AUDIENCES IN HUNDREDS ('00)										
1. STANDARD										
500A- 100A MO-FR	1835	947	392	273	107	13	459	379	94	580
500A- 100A SA-SU	1249	695	277	181	69	11	342	266	58	407
700A- 700P MO-FR	1572	829	367	248	87	13	422	354	74	509
700A- 700P SAT	872	492	161	77	59	11	218	150	48	263
700A- 700P SUN	720	425	191	136	51	11	201	180	40	275
2. RATE CARD										
600A-MDNT MO-SU	2100	1061	445	315	125	24	534	421	101	648
600A-NOON MO-SU	1436	778	325	217	85	24	371	301	60	474
NOON - 600P MO-SU	1474	774	298	198	64	11	379	286	53	481
600P-MDNT MO-SU	1306	617	237	149	65	13	269	224	52	334
3. REQUESTED										
600A-MDNT MO-FR	1825	937	381	263	96	13	448	368	83	580
600A-1000A MO-FR	921	497	233	141	44	13	254	220	31	294
1000A- 300P MO-FR	967	521	207	155	55	-	276	207	55	330
300P- 800P MO-FR	1196	598	230	140	43	-	274	230	43	364
800P-MDNT MO-FR	857	412	155	88	43	13	186	142	30	254
600A-NOON MO-FR	1159	618	273	165	54	13	309	260	41	382
NOON - 600P MO-FR	1105	605	226	146	35	-	286	226	35	365
600P-MDNT MO-FR	1163	542	187	110	55	13	219	174	42	294
NOON - 100P MO-SU	695	368	150	95	40	-	183	150	40	242
300P- 500P MO-FR	732	385	111	81	25	-	140	111	25	214
500P- 600P MO-FR	511	309	106	41	5	-	131	106	5	175
600P- 800P MO-FR	780	355	136	88	33	-	161	136	33	207
600A- 900A SAT	220	168	32	22	22	11	35	20	10	63
900A- 530P SAT	703	378	136	67	49	11	193	125	38	210
600P- 800P SA-SU	342	183	106	51	19	-	106	106	19	137
800P- 900P SAT	127	55	43	20	10	-	43	43	10	33
900P-MDNT SAT	136	87	21	10	-	-	21	21	-	21
600A- 900A SUN	199	123	29	19	-	-	39	29	-	72
900A- 500P SUN	562	323	167	111	41	11	166	156	30	216
800P-MDNT SUN	228	104	29	11	-	-	37	29	-	51
600A- 600P SAT	840	471	136	67	49	11	193	125	38	248
600A- 600P SUN	660	388	167	111	41	11	176	156	30	260

	MEN-HOMMES 18+	18/49	18/44	18/34	18/24	25/54	25/49	25/34	35/64	12/17	WKG WOM FEM TRAV	F. H. W.CH. F. R. A. EN
WEEKLY CUME (00)	936	517	390	179	32	537	486	148	565	38	391	124
WEEKLY CUME (%)	6.7	5.3		3.2	1.5	6.2	6.3	4.1	8.4	1.3		
TOTAL HOURS (000)	715	390	266	84	2	436	388	83	467	7	316	160
SHARE OF WKLY HRS	2.6	2.0	1.5	.8		2.5	2.4	1.1	3.5	.2	1.9	2.9
AVG. WEEKLY HOURS	7.6	7.5	6.8	4.7	.5	8.1	8.0	5.6	8.3	1.7	8.1	12.9
AUDITOIRES MOYENS PAR ¼ D'HEURE EN CENTAINES ('00)												
1. STANDARD												
500A- 100A MO-FR	54	29	21	7	-	32	29	6	34	1	19	11
500A- 100A SA-SU	45	25	15	5	-	29	25	5	31	-	31	14
700A- 700P MO-FR	61	34	26	7	-	36	34	7	38	1	25	14
700A- 700P SAT	51	24	19	9	-	29	24	9	31	-	43	16
700A- 700P SUN	60	38	18	1	-	43	38	1	49	-	38	23
2. RATE CARD												
600A-MDNT MO-SU	54	30	20	6	-	33	30	6	36	1	25	13
600A-NOON MO-SU	51	26	18	8	-	28	26	7	32	1	22	8
NOON - 600P MO-SU	62	37	26	5	-	40	37	5	42	-	34	20
600P-MDNT MO-SU	50	26	17	5	-	32	26	5	35	-	19	11
3. REQUESTED												
600A-MDNT MO-FR	57	31	22	6	-	35	31	6	38	1	21	12
600A-1000A MO-FR	51	26	18	8	-	26	26	8	33	1	13	3
1000A- 300P MO-FR	64	39	29	8	-	40	39	7	39	1	30	14
300P- 800P MO-FR	61	30	24	4	-	34	29	4	41	-	26	21
800P-MDNT MO-FR	50	28	15	6	-	37	28	6	37	1	11	6
600A-NOON MO-FR	55	29	21	9	-	30	29	8	33	1	19	6
NOON - 600P MO-FR	62	37	27	5	-	39	37	5	41	-	29	18
600P-MDNT MO-FR	54	27	18	5	-	35	27	5	39	-	14	11
NOON - 100P MO-SU	72	47	37	8	-	50	47	8	50	-	32	16
300P- 500P MO-FR	68	41	30	5	-	43	40	4	47	-	33	19
500P- 600P MO-FR	44	16	13	3	-	20	16	3	24	1	20	22
600P- 800P MO-FR	62	25	23	4	-	32	25	4	43	-	21	23
600A- 900A SAT	15	-	-	-	-	2	-	-	13	-	12	-
900A- 530P SAT	60	30	23	13	-	35	30	13	33	-	48	18
600P- 800P SA-SU	55	33	18	-	-	36	33	-	41	-	47	18
800P- 900P SAT	44	24	17	12	-	30	24	12	22	-	37	17
900P-MDNT SAT	22	15	14	12	-	15	15	12	4	-	10	6
600A- 900A SUN	26	13	7	3	-	15	13	3	20	-	6	-
900A- 500P SUN	63	41	21	-	-	48	41	-	54	-	48	32
800P-MDNT SUN	38	23	8	3	-	24	23	3	28	-	24	2
600A- 600P SAT	48	22	17	9	-	26	22	9	28	-	39	14
600A- 600P SUN	55	34	17	1	-	40	34	1	45	-	36	22
AUDITOIRES CUMULATIFS EN CENTAINES ('00)												
1. STANDARD												
500A- 100A MO-FR	790	412	321	133	32	420	380	101	483	38	340	108
500A- 100A SA-SU	536	295	213	80	-	331	295	80	353	13	239	61
700A- 700P MO-FR	664	312	255	124	32	312	280	92	374	19	288	108
700A- 700P SAT	362	187	145	61	-	222	187	61	243	13	189	31
700A- 700P SUN	295	149	107	8	-	173	149	8	229	-	173	50
2. RATE CARD												
600A-MDNT MO-SU	936	517	390	179	32	537	486	148	565	38	380	124
600A-NOON MO-SU	633	367	287	155	16	392	352	139	367	19	304	83
NOON - 600P MO-SU	687	348	249	96	16	376	332	80	424	13	273	88
600P-MDNT MO-SU	603	331	222	75	-	362	331	75	401	26	200	72
3. REQUESTED												
600A-MDNT MO-FR	790	412	321	133	32	420	380	101	483	38	330	108
600A-1000A MO-FR	411	233	192	84	-	253	233	84	243	13	195	54
1000A- 300P MO-FR	427	165	137	46	16	168	149	30	224	19	143	93
300P- 800P MO-FR	525	253	191	77	16	260	237	61	309	13	212	65
800P-MDNT MO-FR	419	212	132	36	-	243	212	36	297	26	141	55
600A-NOON MO-FR	522	285	228	108	16	290	269	92	302	19	230	68
NOON - 600P MO-FR	487	205	154	46	16	220	189	30	293	13	180	83
600P-MDNT MO-FR	535	271	192	67	-	303	271	67	350	26	168	60
NOON - 100P MO-SU	314	153	111	33	-	185	153	33	224	13	134	64
300P- 500P MO-FR	348	161	121	38	16	168	145	22	207	-	121	50
500P- 600P MO-FR	189	90	62	19	-	103	90	19	129	13	92	45
600P- 800P MO-FR	366	162	111	39	-	185	162	39	244	-	103	53
600A- 900A SAT	52	-	-	-	-	12	-	-	43	-	45	-
900A- 530P SAT	308	175	133	61	-	198	175	61	197	13	151	31
600P- 800P SA-SU	160	86	56	-	-	101	86	-	110	-	102	35
800P- 900P SAT	72	30	23	12	-	42	30	12	42	-	43	23
900P-MDNT SAT	49	23	16	12	-	23	23	12	19	-	10	11
600A- 900A SUN	77	30	19	8	-	43	30	8	60	-	20	-
900A- 500P SUN	239	112	76	-	-	135	112	-	181	-	153	50
800P-MDNT SUN	124	48	19	8	-	51	48	8	79	-	43	7
600A- 600P SAT	351	175	133	61	-	211	175	61	231	13	164	31
600A- 600P SUN	272	127	84	8	-	150	127	8	206	-	163	50

SONDAGES BBM SURVEYS (CANADA)

Since 1986, the BBM has been offering some *Radio Product Measurement* information collected using the same procedure as for the audience data, but a methodology based on an independent sample and a unique questionnaire. RPM-II released in 1989 contains information on media usage, product purchases and retail patronage by category and specific chains.

In addition to the standard reports, the BBM data may be accessed directly in order to interrogate it or to perform some specific operation of interest to the member. Finally, the BBM may undertake proprietary studies requested by a member.

Other Radio Sources.   Birch Radio is a U.S. company which provides radio audience and product usage information for the Toronto markets.

The RBC is a non-profit association of commercial radio broadcasters set up to promote radio as an advertising medium. Each year it publishes a fact book containing a summary of the latest available radio statistics. More detailed information is available without charge to advertisers and agencies from the RBC's Marketing Data Centre, which also contains a library of over 20 000 indexed commercials and related sonic material.

Television.   Data on television audiences are collected on a regular basis by the Television Bureau of Canada (TVB), the BBM, and A.C. Nielsen.

TVB.   The TVB is a non-profit organization set up by the television industry to promote the use of television as an advertising medium. Each year it publishes *TV Basics*, a fact book that contains the latest available information on television. A data bank of statistics on television is also available to advertisers and agencies. The videotape library contains over 25 000 domestic and international commercials indexed by category.

Bureau of Broadcast Measurement.   The BBM television surveys follow the same methodology as for the radio surveys. Both network and individual television market surveys are conducted. Each network survey is issued as a series of 36 one-week reports. On the other hand, each television market survey is taken over two or three weeks, and the total number of weeks surveyed for each market is as follows:

17 weeks: Toronto, Montreal, Vancouver
11 weeks: Halifax, Quebec City, Ottawa, Kitchener, London, Winnipeg, Calgary, Edmonton
 9 weeks: Windsor, Hamilton, Victoria
 6 weeks: all other markets

The BBM television diary is similar to the radio diary, and a sample page is reproduced in Figure 15–6. Information on cable television is also included in the brief questionnaire. A sample page of a BBM television report is provided in Figure 15–7.

As for radio, the BBM data may be accessed directly, and proprietary studies may be done for a member.

A.C. Nielsen of Canada.   A.C. Nielsen of Canada is a privately owned company that provides television audience estimates, program ratings, and special analysis services. It issues two reports. The *Nielsen Television Index (NTI) Network Report* covers all Canadian networks for 52 weeks per year. The *Nielsen Broadcast Index (NBI) Local Market Report* measures station audiences per quarter hour in 42 designated market areas and covering from 6 to 16 weeks depending on the size of the market.

FIGURE 15–6
Sample Page from a BBM Television Diary

Courtesy BBM Bureau of Measurement

24 **TUESDAY DAYTIME**

	TIME	TV SET ON	TV SET OFF	NAME OF PROGRAM	STATION CALL LETTERS OR NAME	CHANNEL NUMBER		1	2	3	4	5	6	7	8
6A 01	**6.00-6.14AM**						01								
02	6.15-6.29						02								
03	6.30-6.44						03								
04	6.45-6.59						04								
05	**7.00-7.14**						05								
06	7.15-7.29						06								
07	7.30-7.44						07								
08	7.45-7.59						08								
09	**8.00-8.14**						09								
10	8.15-8.29						10								
11	8.30-8.44						11								
12	8.45-8.59						12								
13	**9.00-9.14**						13								
14	9.15-9.29						14								
15	9.30-9.44						15								
16	9.45-9.59						16								
17	**10.00-10.14**						17								
18	10.15-10.29						18								
19	10.30-10.44						19								
20	10.45-10.59						20								

								1	2	3	4	5	6	7	8
21	**11.00-11.14**						21								
22	11.15-11.29						22								
23	11.30-11.44						23								
24	11.45-11.59						24								
25	**12.00-12.14PM**						25								
26	12.15-12.29						26								
27	12.30-12.44						27								
28	12.45-12.59						28								
29	**1.00-1.14**						29								
30	1.15-1.29						30								
31	1.30-1.44						31								
32	1.45-1.59						32								
33	**2.00-2.14**						33								
34	2.15-2.29						34								
35	2.30-2.44						35								
36	2.45-2.59						36								
37	**3.00-3.14**						37								
38	3.15-3.29						38								
39	3.30-3.44						39								
40	3.45-3.59						40								

With the *diary method*, the sampling procedure followed by A.C. Nielsen is also a two-step procedure. First, some areas are defined as measurement cells. The sampling frame is drawn from telephone directories, and a sample of households is selected, with the possibility of selecting a household which has participated in one or two past surveys and has agreed to participate again. The sample must contain less than half of such respondents. The others are selected randomly from the sampling frame.

FIGURE 15–7

Sample Page from a BBM Television Report

Courtesy BBM Bureau of Measurement

EDMONTON BBM SUMMER 1990 ETE 4

TIME BLOCKS TRANCHES HORAIRES	EXTENDED MARKET – MARCHE ETENDU								12/17	2/11	TOTAL 2+ TOUS		FULL COVERAGE AUDIENCE (000) AUDITOIRES DANS RAYONNEMENT (000)								
	WOMEN FEMMES				MEN HOMMES						EM FC %	EM AUD (000)	2+	18+	WOMEN FEMMES				MEN HOMMES		

(Table of audience data by station: ALL STNS, CBXFT, CBXT, CFRN, CITV, KHQ, KREM, KXLY, OTHERS — across time blocks:)

- MO-FR 700P– 800P
- MO-FR 700P–1100P
- MO-FR 800P–1000P
- MO-FR 1000P–1015P
- MO-FR 1000P–1100P
- MO-FR 1015P–1100P
- MO-FR 1100P–1130P
- MO-FR 1130P–MDNT
- MO-FR MDNT – 200A

SONDAGES BBM SURVEYS (CANADA)

As mentioned before, the sample contains households who are sent a diary with some monetary incentive. Here all individuals in the household participate in the study by recording the station call letters, channel number, and program name when the set is on. When completed, the diary is mailed back to A.C. Nielsen. A reminder card is sent to increase the response rate, which is around 50 percent. A sample page of a Nielsen diary is reproduced in Figure 15–8. Sample pages of an NTI Network Report and of an NBI Local Market Report are reproduced in Figures 15–9 and 15–10 (page 418).

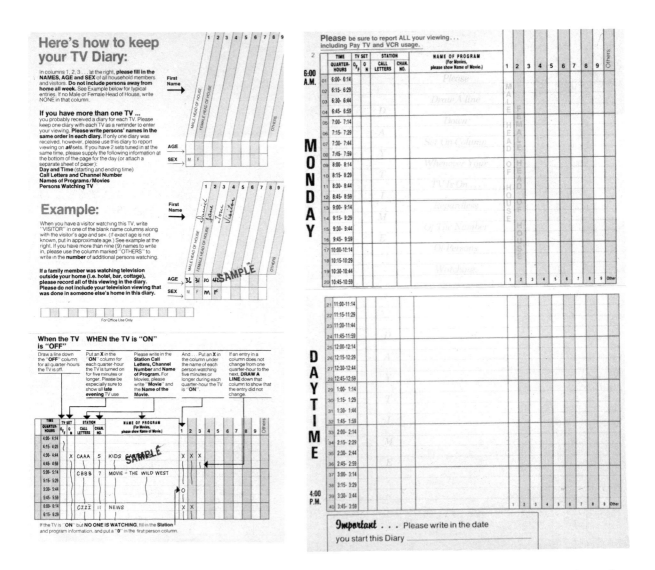

FIGURE 15–8

Instructions and Sample Pages from a Nielsen Television Diary

Courtesy Nielsen Media Research

In addition to its regular reports, Nielsen publishes a series of supplementary reports and may conduct some special analysis services, such as audience duplication studies, viewer preference studies, and audience fragmentation studies.

The *people meter* is a new system of electronic audience measurement which has been under study in Canada for many years, although it was introduced successfully in the United Kingdom several years ago. After extensive pretesting, two systems were introduced in the United States in 1987, and one in Canada in 1989 by A.C. Nielsen. With such a system, advertisers are able to have information on the actual audience of any segment of a particular program and commercial, instead of the general program viewership provided by the diary method. The system consists of a panel of families who have agreed to co-

FIGURE 15-9

Sample Data from a Nielsen NTI Report

Courtesy Nielsen Media Research

ALPHABETICAL LISTINGS
ALL NETWORKS COMBINED

PROGRAM/EMISSION SEASON-TO-DATE AVG MOY A CE JOUR #TELE/DIFF	NET RES	DAY(S) JOUR(S)	START DEBUT	DUR MIN	# STNS	AVERAGE MINUTE AUDIENCE/AUDITOIRE MOYEN PAR MINUTE(000)																
						HHLDS/FOYERS				VIEWERS/TELESPECTATEURS						WOMEN/FEMMES					
						TOT	<30	30-55	55+	2+	18+	18-34	18-49	25-54	55+	18+	18-34	18-49	25-54	55+	WKG TRA
... CE SOIR S-T-D/M-A-J 77	R-C	AV/MO 4	6.00P	30	18	325 / 292	139 / 106	93 / 104	93 / 82	488 / 449	428 / 398	91 / 105	211 / 219	231 / 233	176 / 142	232 / 210	57 / 53	113 / 104	120 / 117	96 / 76	102 / 95
A TOUTES ALLURES	R-C	THU/JEU	11.00A	60	18	121	68	31	22	148	97	43	62	49	30	57	33	42	33	10	29
ACTION REACTION S-T-D/M-A-J 80	Q-S	AV/MO 5	5.00P	30	9	153 / 120	81 / 45	47 / 50	24 / 24	259 / 192	244 / 179	42 / 35	83 / 68	97 / 79	136 / 88	149 / 104	16 / 15	45 / 38	56 / 44	89 / 55	54 / 44
ADDERLY S-T-D/M-A-J 2	GLBL	THU/JEU	7.30P	60	9	130 / 152	46 / 49	51 / 44	34 / 60	198 / 245	174 / 212	49 / 63	85 / 109	65 / 111	72 / 73	93 / 94	15 / 23	51 / 52	48 / 50	31 / 36	41 / 43
ADV.LITTLE KOALA S-T-D/M-A-J 2	GLBL	SAT/SAM	6.30A	30	9	IFR / 61	27	IFR	IFR	61	42	21	33	33	9	34	19	29	29	5	19
ADVENTURES-PRINCE S-T-D/M-A-J 6	YTV	SAT/SAM	7.00A	30	2	IFR / IFR															
ALIENS IN THE FAMILY S-T-D/M-A-J 9	YTV	THU/JEU	8.30P	30	2	45 / IFR	7	34	3	72	56	51	52	36	4	24	22	22	15	2	13
ALL DAY BEST OF MUCH	MM	MON/LUN	12.00N	240	1	85	23	21	41	104	87	64	81	68	4	37	25	32	33	4	31
ALL DAY BEST OF MUCH	MM	MON/LUN	5.40P	20	1	88	29	8	50	132	123	83	88	38	34	55	34	39	12	16	33
ALL DAY BEST OF MUCH	MM	MON/LUN	9.40P	20	1	73	35	26	12	148	141	63	87	37	54	77	23	39	17	38	27
ALL DAY BEST OF MUCH	MM	TUE/MAR	8.00A	240	1	IFR															
ALL MY CHILDREN S-T-D/M-A-J 74	CBC	AV/MO	1.00P	60	36	458 / 445	197 / 218	172 / 153	90 / 75	602 / 561	508 / 498	182 / 174	280 / 267	244 / 217	191 / 199	364 / 382	139 / 155	214 / 221	181 / 168	122 / 139	133 / 140
ALL THE BEST OF MUCH	MM	MON/LUN	12.00M	240	1	IFR															
ALL THE BEST OF MUCH	MM	MON/LUN	5.40A	20	1	IFR															

FIGURE 15-10

Sample Data from a Nielsen NBI Report

Courtesy Nielsen Media Research

NBI PROGRAM AVERAGES/
SECTION MOYENNES DES EMISSIONS NBI   TORONTO/HAMILTON   JANUARY/JANVIER 1990

DESIGNATED MARKET AREA/MARCHE DESIGNE

PROGRAM/EMISSION STATION DAY/JOUR TIME/HEURE	METRO AGGLO HHLDS % FOYERS				MULTI-WEEK AVERAGES MOYENNE MULTI-HEBDO							TOTAL VIEWERS/TELESP					WOMEN/FEMMES					MEN/HOMMES				TNS ADO	CHD ENF	NUMBER OF 1/4 HOURS AVERAGED		
	TOR R%C	TOR S%P	HAM R%C	HAM S%P	R%C	JA90	JA89	NO89	MR89	CAB		2+	18+	18-34	18-49	25-54	TOTAL	18-34	18-49	25-54	WKG TRA	TOTAL	18-34	18-49	25-54	12-17	2-11	1	2	3
STAR TREK MUTV SAT 6:00PM	3	8	5	13	4	10	22X	18	10	75		2	2	1	3	3	2	1	2	2	3	3	1	3	4	1	4	4	4	
STARS-HOCKEY CKCO SAT 3:00PM	<<		<<		<<																								4	
STARTNG-SCRTCH CHCH SAT 6:30PM	1	4	7	17	2	5	7	3	5	83		1	1	1	1	1	1		1	1	1	2	1	1	1	1	1		2	2	
STARTRK NXTGEN CITY SAT 5:00PM	4	17	4	13	4	15	20X	28	19	92		4	4	6	5	5	3	6	4	3	4	5	7	7	7		3	4	4	
STARTRK NXTGEN MUTV SAT 7:00PM	3	9	6	14	4	12	17X	15	10	86		3	3	2	3	4	3	1	3	4	4	2	2	3	4	3	3	4	4	
STELLAR AWARDS WKBH SUN 9:00PM	<<		<<		<<	6	4	6																				8		
STREET CENTS CBLT SAT 10:00AM	1	6	<<		1	5		3	5			1	1	1	1		1	1	1			1	1	1	1	2	1	2	2	
STREET LEGAL CBLT FRI 8:00PM	10	24	4	9	11	25	11X	15	15	75		6	7	3	2	4	9	4	4	6	10	5	1	1	2	2	2	4	4	
STREET LEGAL CKVR FRI 8:00PM	1	3	<<		1	2	2X	2									1	1	1	1	1							4	4	

operate and have a special device attached to their television set. The device is a small box with a series of buttons on top (Figure 15–11). Each member of the family is given a code and is required to press the appropriate button when starting to watch television and every time he or she leaves the room and comes back. The box records automatically the channel number at small intervals and the codes of the members watching the program. During the night the information is transmitted by telephone line to a central computer and the data can be tabulated instantly. At a later phase, it is planned to link the

FIGURE 15–11

Nielsen's People Meter

Courtesy Nielsen Media Research

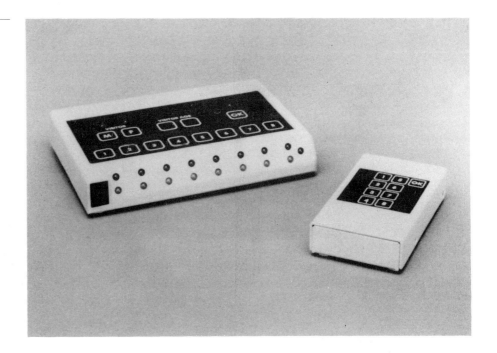

audience data to purchases of products using the new scanner technology at the retail level, by means of a type of debit card containing the code of the family. This new technology has replaced the diary method, in major markets where the NTI is based solely on People Meter data. The challenge for advertisers will be finding means of dealing efficiently with this information explosion.

Copy Research

Advertising research that provides information on the creative part of the campaign is called copy research. In effect, it represents creative research since all creative aspects, including execution, may be tested. Depending on the information required from copy testing, one must differentiate between strategic and executional research. *Strategic copy testing* is used to differentiate between two or more creative strategies. In this case an advertiser wants to ensure that a message has the intended effect on consumers, i.e., the communication task of the campaign as developed in Chapter 11. *Executional copy testing* is used to differentiate between two or more executions of the same creative strategy. These tests determine whether the message is correctly understood by consumers, whether it has good attention value, and whether the theme of the message is remembered correctly.

Copy testing may be conducted before a message is finally selected for an advertising campaign, either to select the best message from several possibilities or to make any minor changes before the campaign is actually run. These are called advertising copy pretests.

Copy testing carried out after the message has actually run is a *posttest*.[20] The objective is to assess the effectiveness of each message in the actual environment in which it will appear and as consumers will see it within the media vehicle and among competitive messages.

Copy Pretesting

Pretesting of a message is becoming more common as advertisers realize it is better to identify weaknesses in the message before it is produced.[21] Three types of pretesting methods may be used: indirect or projective questioning, direct questioning, or laboratory tests.

Projective Techniques or In-Depth Interviews. The projective techniques for copy testing are similar to those for market and consumer research.[22] Here the researcher is interested in the reactions of selected individual(s) to the proposed creative execution of an advertising message. Often, the message is in the initial stages of development, i.e., rough sketches, animatics, or storyboards. The respondent is asked third-person reactions to the whole message or to the headline or the slogan. Test methods include (cartoon-type) balloon tests, sentence completion tests, Thematic Apperception Tests (TAT), and word association tests.

In-depth interviews may also be used to pretest copy. A trained interviewer probes an individual's reactions to a message and its components (the headline, subheads, body copy, and slogan). The message may be a rough sketch, a radio commercial, or a storyboard. Because of the depth of probing, the pretest provides a detailed qualitative evaluation of the message's effects. Weaknesses in the copy are identified and interpreted, thus pointing toward some improvements. This method is expensive, however, and the results are based on a small, often non-random, sample of consumers. The cost varies between $100 to $400 per interview.

Direct Questioning Methods. Copy pretesting may also be done by asking a selected group of individuals a series of questions. The groups may be small for focus group testing, or large for mall or theatre testing. The questioning may be unstructured or structured.

Focus Groups. Focus groups usually involve 10 to 15 individuals with the demographic characteristics of the brand's target group. These individuals are brought together in a room equipped with one-way mirrors and audio-visual equipment. A trained moderator defines the areas for informal exchange among the participants.[23] The stimulus for the group may have one of the following formats:

- Showing one advertising message in rough or finished form. A finished advertisement is always superior for reliable results.
- Showing a series of unrelated advertising messages with the test message "buried" in the series.
- Showing several versions of the same advertising message.
- Showing a whole package with some editorial matter and the test message(s) placed within it.

For print, this method is called the *portfolio test*, and each portfolio resembles a newspaper or magazine.

Group members are then asked to comment on what they have seen or heard or read. They may also be asked to choose one or several brands in a display, and explain their choice.

Depending on the complexity of the procedure, a focus group interview takes between one and two hours. At least two focus groups should be run on the same procedure in order to minimize a chance occurrence that may distort the results.

Several focus groups may also be used to test different versions of the same message. Instead of showing all the versions to the same group, each group is exposed to a different version within the same procedure. If the groups are properly matched, each version may be pretested for major flaws. It is also advisable to have two groups per version, as mentioned before. The cost of this method varies from $1000 to $2000 per group.

Mall Tests. Mall tests or *ad hoc* commercial testing are conducted with respondents intercepted in shopping malls and plazas, and recruited according to certain demographic characteristics. They participate in an interview that may involve showing some advertising messages and commenting on them. This kind of test also has drawbacks. The population sampled may be biased because of the neighbourhood in which the mall is situated or the kind of people it attracts. In addition, the interview must be short since most respondents are intercepted while on a shopping trip. On the other hand, this method is relatively inexpensive, can accommodate large samples, and gives fast answers to copy problems. Safeguards may be taken to ensure proper coverage of the target group and to improve the accuracy of the data obtained.

One example of a mall test is the Dadson Compare Test, which uses two groups for testing a commercial: one test group and one control group. A series of questions on attitudes toward the product and on intention to buy the product are asked of individuals in the control groups. They are not shown the commercial. The test group is shown the commercial and then asked the same battery of questions. Differences between the two groups' responses are measured and analyzed. The cost of such a method is about $2000 per group.

Theatre Tests. Theatre tests are conducted with a large group of people selected according to demographic characteristics, who have agreed to go to a theatre at a certain time to preview a television program. The time period may be during lunch time on weekdays, or in the evening, or during the weekend. The television program shown contains commercials to be pretested. After the program is played respondents are asked to answer a questionnaire designed to assess the effects of the test commercial, and how it achieves the advertiser's communication task. A theatre test is relatively expensive, however, takes place in an artificial setting, and tends to measure only verbal communication elements. Nevertheless, it is a useful diagnostic tool for copy testing.

The best known theatre test in Canada is the *Clucas method*, which can be used for both rough and finished commercials. About 100 respondents are randomly selected and asked to go to an auditorium one evening to view a 25-minute program.

Laboratory Techniques. This type of advertising copy pretesting is not commonly used in Canada but it may become more popular as improvements are made. In the laboratory type of experiments consumers are exposed to a message and their reactions observed, recorded, and measured with sophisticated equipment. What these instruments measure is still being debated, and the techniques of measurement are still being developed. Some of these techniques involve the use of the following devices:

The *eye-movement camera*[24] records the path of eye travel as a respondent looks at a message. It can test layout or determine if and how the copy is read.

Pupilometric devices measure a respondent's pupil dilation as a message is shown. These changes may be correlated to the attention level and emotional responses of the respondent, but more work is needed to validate the technique.[25]

The *psychogalvanometer* measures the level of perspiration on the hand of the respondent, which is correlated with interest in the message. Here, too, more development is needed to validate the technique.[26]

Electroencephalographs (EEGs) measure brain wave activities as a respondent views the message.[27] Its use is still limited.

Voice-pitch analysis is a computer analysis of changes in voice pitch of a respondent reacting verbally to viewing a message. It is assumed that voice pitch correlates with emotional reaction to the message.[28]

A *tachistoscope* is a device for varying the length of exposure to a message and then measuring the rate of perception and comprehension of the advertising message. It allows advertisers to test a message for its effectiveness in gaining attention and registering the brand name in the context of quick exposure, as for outdoor, or with high clutter in magazines or television. Of all the laboratory techniques, this is probably the most commonly used.

The *Facial Action Coding System* (FACS) consists in recording respondents' facial expressions as they view a commercial. From the subtle muscle movements recorded by the camera are identified various emotions generated by different parts of the commercial.

Copy Posttesting

There are three basic methods of testing copy after the message has appeared in print or broadcast media: the day-after-recall (DAR) method, the Starch recognition method, and the split-run method.

Day-After-Recall. The day-after-recall (DAR) method is used to test television commercials and it may be used to test radio commercials. The day after a commercial is first aired, a telephone survey is conducted with about 150 randomly selected target group members who saw the commercial. They are asked to recall and repeat the commercial's main messages and to indicate what they liked or disliked. Results are then compared to norms developed for each product category. Reporting of results is usually fast. One drawback is that only recall of verbal communication elements is available. Because the test is usually done on one exposure only, it does not measure the effects of multiple exposures.

Starch Method. The Starch recognition method was developed in 1921 by Daniel Starch. It measures the degree to which a print advertisement is seen and read.[29] The method uses a through-the-book or recognition technique for a particular issue of a publication, after a suitable waiting period to give readers the opportunity to read the issue. This period varies from two days for a daily publication to three weeks for a monthly one. Starch uses a minimum of 100 readers per sex, who are sampled according to the target audience's geographic and demographic distribution.

Interviewers carry a copy of the test issue, coded according to the list of advertisements to be tested and the starting point of the interview. Each interviewer is assigned a different starting point to minimize the order effect. To minimize boredom, no more than 90 items are tested with one respondent. The interviewer follows the same procedure with each respondent who meets the quota requirements, who has read or looked through the particular issue of the publication, and who agrees to co-operate. With the issue at hand, and starting from the assigned page, the interviewer turns the pages and asks a series of questions about each advertisement to be studied, such as seeing and reading the headline, the illustration, the brand name, the signature, and the copy blocks.

For each advertisement the respondent is classified as follows:

1. *Ad-as-a-Whole: A "Noted" reader* if the respondent has previously seen this advertisement; *an "Associated" reader* if the respondent also saw or read some part of the advertisement that clearly indicated the brand or the advertiser; *a "Read Most" reader* if the respondent read half or more of the written material in the advertisement.
2. *Copy blocks. A "Read Some" reader* if the respondent read some of the copy.
3. *Headline, slogan, signature, or illustration.* The appropriate item is checked if the respondent saw the illustration or the signature or read the headline or the slogan.

After all advertisements have been tested, the interviewer ends the interview by asking some basic demographic data for cross-tabulation purposes.

Data from all interviews are compiled and analyzed and a report is sent to all subscribers. This *Starch Readership Report* contains the following items:

1. A labelled issue of the magazine that is a copy of the study issue with labels affixed on the tested advertisements and that contains the percentage of some group of readers (e.g., male adults) in each of the previous categories. A sample of a labelled advertisement is provided in Figure 15–12 (next page).
2. A summary report listing the summary readership figures for all tested advertisements and arranged according to the product category and inser-

FIGURE 15–12

Sample Page from a Labelled Issue of a Starch Report. The Results are Given for Male Readers.

Courtesy First Brands Corporation

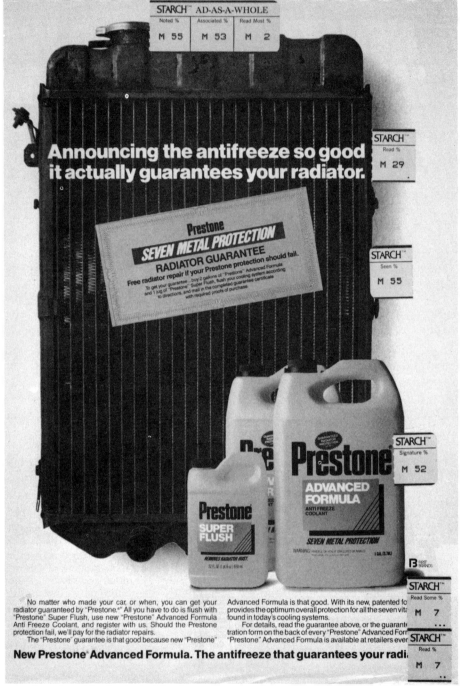

tion size. Also included in the report are the advertisement rank in the issue according to the number of readers, and readership indexes based on the issue median.

3. Adnorm data reports containing figures for two years of the study publication. These are used to compare results with a norm for a similar advertisement (in size and colour).

These numbers may be interpreted along the following lines: the "noted" score may relate to attention to the advertisement; the "associated" score may relate to recognition of the brand name, i.e., the source of the message; the "read most" score may relate to interest or involvement in the message. The pattern among this set of numbers for this advertisement and for competitive ones may be useful for pinpointing copy or layout problems.

The Starch readership service is a reasonable and relatively inexpensive test of an advertisement, particularly the copy elements, in an actual environment.

By analyzing results across a number of advertisements and campaigns, the researcher may be able to determine actionable trends and principles, which are then communicated to the creative director.[30] But the method does have methodological weaknesses in terms of sampling and measurement. In particular, the "recognized" advertisement may have been seen in previous issues or in other magazines. This potential for overstatement should be kept in mind when using this method.

Split-Run Method. The split-run method is a controlled experiment in which one version of an advertisement is printed in half the issues of a publication, and the other version in the other half. Many parts of the advertisement's copy may be tested with this method. Each advertisement contains some form of offer calling for a response from the reader. Each advertisement is coded in order to trace the responses and to determine which one generated the largest number of responses.

This method is used with newspapers and magazines and will come into use in broadcast media when dual cable systems become more common. This method is ideally suited to direct mail where many variations are possible.

CAMPAIGN EFFECTIVENESS RESEARCH

The fourth type of research that advertisers undertake concerns the effects of an advertising campaign after the campaign has been executed. These effects may be tested by using various research designs. In addition, the advertising researcher needs to know what to measure and when to measure them.

Effectiveness Research Designs

Depending on the research budget and the complexity of the sampling procedure, the research designs are based on the number of measurement points and the use of a control group. There are four simple research designs.

The first design uses a single group after the campaign has run and is the least expensive. However, there is no benchmark to which results can be compared, unless the information is available by other means. It is often used to check consumers' reactions to the campaign, but as mentioned in Chapter 11, this is often not sufficient.

The second design uses two groups after the campaign has run, with one group exposed to the campaign and one control group not exposed to it. The main assumption is that both populations had the same level of the measured variable(s) before the campaign started and that environmental conditions were the same during the campaign. This design has the merit of isolating the effect of the campaign from other effects, for example, from distribution or competitive advertising.

The third design also uses two groups, one before the campaign starts and the other after it has run. The main problem with this design is that the effects of the campaign often cannot be isolated from the effects of such other variables as distribution or competitive advertising, even when the same measures are made of the other brands. Nevertheless, this design is often preferable to the previous one.

The fourth design uses four groups and combines the advantages of the previous two designs. Two populations are identified, one of which is to be exposed to the advertising campaign. Then one group is selected in each population before the campaign starts. After the campaign has ended, another group is selected in each population. The differences between both groups represent the changes that would have taken place without the campaign. The effects of the campaign are measured by subtracting the changes recorded in the control groups to those recorded in the test groups. Because it involves four groups of respondents, this design is the most expensive of the four.

Testing the Effectiveness of the Campaign

Depending on how the advertising objectives have been stated, advertisers measure the effects of an advertising campaign on intermediate variables, such as consumer awareness, brand recall, brand preference, attitude toward the brand, or when possible, on the end variable, which is sales. It may be useful here to review Table 11–1 for the relationship between objectives and advertising effectiveness research.

Research into the communication effects of advertising attempts to measure how effectively a campaign has moved consumers up the first two levels of the hierarchy of effects—the cognitive and affective levels. The cognitive level involves effects on brand awareness and knowledge of brand attributes. The affective level involves effects on variables such as liking and preference and is generally much more difficult to test. Some advertisers try to measure the effects of advertising on sales. In terms of the hierarchy of effect model, these advertisers are only interested in the conative stage of consumer behaviour. Methods that directly measure the advertising-sales relationship include experiments, econometric methods, and mathematical models. But, as was mentioned, sales are the result of many factors besides advertising (including each of three other Ps on the marketing mix), and the effect of advertising on sales has not yet been satisfactorily established.

Objectives with Cognitive Variables

When advertising campaign objectives are expressed in terms of such cognitive variables as awareness or recall of copy, advertisers may use a syndicated service, participate in an omnibus study, or conduct a special research project often by using telephone interviewing.

Awareness. If the communication task is to change brand awareness, the test criteria may be top-of-mind recall, unaided recall, share-of-mind recall, or aided recall. *Top-of-mind recall* of a brand is the percentage of individuals mentioning this brand as the first one that comes to mind. *Unaided recall* of a brand is the percentage of individuals mentioning this brand when asked to name all brands of which they can think. *Share-of-mind recall* of a brand is the percentage of all brands mentioned unaided. It may also be obtained by normalizing unaided recall scores. Finally, *aided recall* of a brand is the percentage of individuals indicating that they have heard of a brand when presented with a list of brand names. For any of these measures, the result is generally compared with the target defined in the statement of advertising objectives.

If an advertiser wants to measure whether a campaign has had a strong impact and in what media, research questions are intended to determine advertising awareness, either unaided or aided. An unaided measure would be to ask if the respondent has heard, seen and/or read any advertising message for a product category, and if yes, for which brand(s). An aided measure would be to ask if the respondent has heard, seen, and/or read any advertising for Brand X. In both cases, follow-up questions ask which of a list of media the advertising messages appeared in.

Knowledge. If the communication task is to increase knowledge about the brand's attributes, test criteria may ask for recall of copy points, brand identification, believability, importance, and exclusiveness of copy claims. *Recall of copy points* measures the amount and type of information about the brand that the respondent remembered. It measures only what the respondent can remember from the advertising campaign, and thus does not measure the full extent of the communication, e.g., changes in the amount of information about the brand due to the campaign. The latter may be done by measuring *brand identification* before and after the campaign, i.e., how much a respondent knows about a particular brand.[31] For a communication to be effective, the source must be credible and the respondent must *believe* the claims made in the copy. Otherwise, even if the claims are learned by the respondent, they may not be used in the latter stages leading to purchase.

Two other measures testing copy claims may shed some light on the communication's effectiveness during the campaign. The *saliency or importance* of the copy claims can be measured when the advertiser aims at positioning the brand along dimensions that are important to the respondent. Also, among the important claims a respondent remembers are some that are common to competitive brands, and some that are particular to the advertiser's brand. It is the *exclusiveness* of the advertiser's copy claims that should be measured.

Objectives with Affective and/or Conative Variables

When the advertising campaign objectives are stated in terms of affective and/or conative variables, such as attitudes or preference ranking or trial, advertisers tend to use a custom-designed research project, often with personal interviews. Three types of information may be collected.

Liking.   If the communication task is stated in terms of brand liking, the test criteria measure attitude and attitude change as well as inclusion in the evoked set or brand satisfaction. By recording *attitudes* toward the brand, advertisers determine if the brand is viewed positively by the target market. *Attitude change* measures the campaign's effect on the target market's attitude toward the brand and is a better measure of the communication's persuasiveness. Measuring inclusion of the brand in consumers' *evoked set*[32] is an important indication that the brand has been properly positioned, for brands in the evoked set have a much higher chance of being purchased.[33] Measuring *brand satisfaction* helps advertisers determine problems with the brand or if the product is unsatisfactory in view of the copy claims.

Preference.   If the task of the communication is brand preference, the test criteria measure attitude or preference ranking. Here an advertiser wants to know if the brand is the most liked or preferred brand among all major competing brands. *Preference ranking* may be measured by asking a straight ranking of the brand, or by making pairwise comparisons. Changes in the brand position before and after the campaign is often a good measure of the effectiveness of the advertising strategy.

Conviction.   If the task of communication is in terms of conviction or trial, the test criteria measure intention to buy or to try the brand. *Intention to buy* may be measured by asking the degree of intention to purchase the brand within a specific period. Another measure may be in terms of probability to purchase that brand. A third measure may be to ask to indicate the brand(s) to be bought in the next 10, 20, or 100 purchases of the product category. *Trial* may be asked directly and the length of time should be consistent with the length of the campaign. More important are the reasons for trial or non-trial of the brand, which may indicate how the campaign affected the trial rate. This is particularly important for a new product, a new service, or an idea such as energy conservation.[34]

Measuring the Wearout Factor

Studies have shown that television commercials have an initial effect on the audience, but with subsequent exposure to the same commercial, attention, recall, and liking level off and ultimately decline.[35] This phenomenon is called wearout.

To reduce wearout, advertisers have used three strategies to enhance attention to the message and thus its effectiveness. First, the inter-exposure time is increased to allow some forgetting to occur, particularly with humorous commercials. However, since frequency declines, the exposure value of the campaign is reduced. Second, multiple executions of the message are used to maintain frequency and allow some forgetting of each execution to take place. This strategy is quite expensive, however, since the cost of production is increased by multiples of the number of executions. Third, attention to the message can be increased by dominating the media environment and lowering the level of clutter. This strategy is also expensive, since the impact of the campaign must be increased.

Television commercial wearout can occur even if these strategies are used.[36] Thus, careful consideration is necessary to weight the benefits of various strategies against the additional costs, and more research on the wearout factor is needed.

Tracing the Effects on Sales

As was mentioned in Chapter 11, a natural inclination is to judge the results of an advertising campaign in terms of sales. Several kinds of research may be conducted to determine the relationship between sales and other variables. This section provides a general overview of various approaches to the problem of tracing the effects of advertising on sales.

Researchers can study the *evolution* of a previous variable and compare it to sales figures of the product. The problem with this method is that sales may be affected by other factors during the same time period, and it is risky to attribute the changes in sales figures to advertising. A better procedure is to gather information on such other factors as price, competitive advertising, and distribution coverage, and to relate sales to all the relevant factors, including advertising.[37] Techniques such as multiple regression analysis may be used.

Another variable in relating advertising to sales is the *time*: when does an advertising campaign take effect and for how long (the carry-over effect). These effects were discussed in Chapter 11, in the context of economic models of budget setting. Techniques that may be used here are spectral analysis of time series[38] and econometric techniques.[39]

Still another category of research includes all *controlled experiments* in which the advertising component is manipulated while other factors are left reasonably constant. This method is useful mainly when an advertiser is interested in the *short-term effect* of advertising on sales. One example of such a study involved placing advertisements in daily newspapers in six cities. In each city, two matched samples of home delivery routes were selected, one test group and one control group. About 30 hours after delivery of the morning newspaper, about 200 housewives in each of the two matched groups and the six cities were personally interviewed. On the average, researchers found that the group exposed to the advertisement purchased 14 percent more of the test brand than the control group. It was also found that although most advertisements did produce some positive results, three out of 31 advertisements actually produced negative results.[40]

This method can be used by broadcast media with a dual cable system covering the same market, thus controlling for many variables. Other forms of controlled experiments are split-run tests, direct-mail experiments, and tests of retail advertising based on short-term deals, specials, and rebates, as well as for market tests in which the advertising effort or strategy is manipulated across various test markets.

SUMMARY

Advertising research is an integral part of the advertising plan. Advertisers can use general sources of information for advertising decision making, as well as the standard methods for obtaining and analyzing information.

Various kinds of research are done at each stage in the planning, execution, and control of the campaign. Market or consumer research may be either qualitative or quantitative. Media research is used to measure audiences as well as exposure patterns to media types and media vehicles. Media information is available from syndicated services, media or industry associations, or through custom studies.

Copy research is useful in determining whether the message has been properly designed by the creative group and properly understood by the target audience. Methods for copy research involve projective techniques, in-depth interviews, direct questioning, laboratory techniques, and post-testing techniques.

The effectiveness of the campaign as set out in the campaign objectives may be assessed in order to control the budget. Various research designs may be used. Depending on the communication task, emphasis may be put on cognitive measures (awareness), affective measures (attitude), or conative measures (trial). There are several methods available for determining the effect of advertising on sales.

QUESTIONS FOR STUDY

1. "Research is the last thing I want to include in my advertising budget." Do you agree? Comment.

2. Compare the Nielsen and BBM services for television media research. Evaluate the research methodology of these two companies, particularly their sampling procedures.

3. What are the problems associated with the use of sophisticated laboratory equipment for copy testing?

4. What are the strengths and weaknesses of the day-after-recall method for copy testing?

5. Why is it so difficult to measure the extent of the effects of an advertising campaign in the field?

6. Explain what each of the Ad-As-A-Whole Starch scores measure and compare them. How would you use them, and which one would you use most often? Answer the same question for the other types of scores, i.e., copy blocks, headlines, slogan, signature, and illustration.

7. What are the advantages and disadvantages of pretesting advertisements? Answer the same question for posttesting. Compare the two methods.

8. What should be the relationship between the advertising research group and the creative group? Between the research group and the account service group? What do you see as potential conflicts, and how can these be avoided?

9. Should research on campaign effectiveness be part of every advertising plan? Comment.

10. Is copy testing a necessary research activity for each advertising campaign? Explain.

PROBLEMS

1. Assume that you are the advertising manager of Camelback, a moving company in your town, and that you are advertising on radio during May and June in order to increase awareness of your name during the heavy moving season. You have to develop a complete research program in order to evaluate the effects of your campaign. Write a campaign evaluation plan along the lines described in Chapter 11, including the choice of the survey method, the sampling methodology, and the questionnaire that you will be using.

2. An insurance company wants to estimate the market potential for a new kind of life insurance it contemplates selling in the Maritimes. The ideal universe is defined as all the households in the Maritimes that have not yet subscribed to a life insurance policy. Because he wants to obtain a certain precision level in the results, the company statistician tells the marketing manager that for a probability sample he should get about 1000 answers. Which survey methods would you recommend (i.e., telephone, mail, or personal survey)? Why? What are the problems likely to be encountered with each method?

NOTES

1. For a discussion of experimental designs, see, for instance, Donald T. Campbell and Julian C. Stanley. *Experimental and Quasi-Experimental Designs for Research* (Chicago: Rand McNally and Co., 1963).
2. See, for instance, Seymour Banks, *Experimentation in Marketing* (New York: McGraw-Hill, 1965).
3. Thomas E. Muller, "Information Load at the Point of Purchase: Extending the Research," *Marketing*, ed. Michel Laroche (Administrative Sciences Association of Canada, 1982), pp. 193–202.
4. Stanley L. Payne, *The Art of Asking Questions* (Princeton, N.J.: Princeton, N.J.: Princeton University Press, 1951).
5. Sampling is discussed in great detail in Morris H. Hansen, William N. Hurwitz, and William G. Neadown, *Sample Survey Methods and Theory*, vol. 2 (New York: John Wiley and Sons, 1953).
6. Douglas J. Tigert, James G. Barnes, and Jacques C. Bourgeois, "Research on Research: Mail Panel Versus Telephone Survey in Retail Image Analysis," *The Canadian Marketer* (Winter 1975), pp. 22–27.
7. Ibid.
8. Ethical problems in marketing research have been discussed, for instance, by George S. Day, "The Threat to Marketing Research," *Journal of Marketing Research* (November 1975); George S. Day and Adrian B. Ryans, "The Changing Environment in Marketing Research in Canada," *Problems in Canadian Marketing*, ed. Donald N. Thompson (Chicago: American Marketing Association, 1977), pp. 203–22.
9. A more complete treatment is given in David B. Montgomery and Glen L. Urban, *Management Science in Marketing* (Englewood Cliffs, N.J.: Prentice-

Hall, 1969); and Philip Kotler, *Marketing Decision Making: A Model Building Approach* (New York: Holt, Rinehart and Winston, 1971).

10. Roger G. Calantone and Donald H. Drury, "Advertising Agency Compensation: A Model for Incentive and Control," *Management Science* (July 1979), pp. 632–42.

11. John D.C. Little, "Models and Manager: The Concept of a Decision Calculus," *Management Science* (April 1970), pp. 466–85.

12. Glenn L. Urban, "Perceptor: A Model for Product Positioning," *Management Science*, 21 (April 1975), 858–71.

13. Jo Marney, "Beyond the Six Ps of Market Research," *Marketing*, April 25, 1983, p. 8.

14. Canadian Advertising Research Foundation (Toronto).

15. "Twenty-one Ad Agencies Endorse Copy Testing Principles," *Marketing News*, February 19, 1982, pp. 1, 9.

16. George H. Smith, *Motivation Research in Advertising and Marketing* (New York: McGraw-Hill, 1954); Rena Bartos and Arthur S. Pearson, "The Founding Father of Advertising Research: Ernest Dichter: Motive Interpreter," *Journal of Advertising Research* (June 1977), p. 4.

17. Keith J. Cox, James B. Higginbotham, and John Burton, "Applications of Focus Group Interviews in Marketing," *Journal of Marketing* (January 1976), p. 79; Bobby J. Calder, "Focus Groups and the Nature of Qualitative Marketing Research," *Journal of Marketing Research* (August 1977), pp. 353–64.

18. Mason Haire, "Projective Techniques in Marketing Research," *Journal of Marketing* (April 1950), pp. 649–56.

19. An interesting approach can be found in Deirdre Grondin, "The Media Preferences of Anglophone and Francophone Canadian Consumers: an Expectancy Value Model," *Marketing*, ed. Thomas E. Muller (Administrative Sciences Association of Canada, 1986), pp. 348–60.

20. There are also a number of important academic studies concerned with the analysis of the *contents* of advertisements. See John Liefeld, "Profile of a Database for the Content Analysis of Canadian Print Advertising," *Marketing*, ed. Jean-Charles Chebat (Administrative Sciences Association of Canada, 1985), pp. 211–20; Richard W. Pollay, "Twentieth Century Magazine Advertising: Determinants of Informativeness," *Written Communica-*

tions (January 1984), pp. 54–77; John P. Liefeld, "The Informativeness of Print Advertising," *Marketing*, ed. Thomas E. Muller (Administrative Sciences Association of Canada, 1986), pp. 328–37; Karen A. Blotnicky and Nathan D. Kling, "Advertising in Canadian Women's Magazines: a Study of Subjective Ad Strategies Across Product Types," *ibid.*, pp. 361–70; Benny Rigaux-Bricmont, "Implicit Attributes in Perceptual Mapping of Ads," *Marketing*, ed. Alain d'Astous (Administrative Sciences Association of Canada, 1989), pp. 247–58.

21. Mark Lowell, "Pretests Taking the Lead," *Creativity* (Spring 1980), pp. 27–28.

22. Haire, pp. 649–56.

23. Cox et al.; Calder pp. 353–64.

24. Norman H. Mackworth, "A Stand Camera for Line-of Sight Recording," *Perception and Psychographics* (March 1967), pp. 119–27.

25. Roger D. Blackwell, James S. Hensel, and Brian Sternthal, "Pupil Dilation: What Does it Measure," *Journal of Advertising Research*, 10, no. 4 (1970), 15–18.

26. "Psychogalvanometer Testing Most Productive," *Marketing News*, June 16, 1978, p. 11.

27. Herbert E. Krugman, "Brain Wave Measures of Media Involvement," *Journal of Advertising Research*, 11, no. 1 (1971), 3–9.

28. "Voice Analysis May Give Insights into Consumer Advertising Attitudes," *Product Marketing* (April 1977), pp. 14–17.

29. For outdoor posters, Starch uses a port-a-scope, which shows a poster with varying threshold levels, from one to five seconds. The respondent is questioned after each of the three exposures.

30. Robert G. Blunden, T.K. Clarke and M. Eileen MacDougall, "A Simple Method for Predicting Starch Scores by Microcomputers," *Marketing*, ed. Sheila Brown (Administrative Sciences Association of Canada, 1984), pp. 41–50; Karen Blotniky and June A. MacDonald, "The Effects of Informative Ad Strategies on Starch Measures of Ad Effectiveness for Men and Women: An Exploratory Study," *Marketing*, ed. Ronald E. Turner (Administrative Sciences Association of Canada, 1987), pp. 38–47.

31. John A. Howard, *Consumer Behavior: Application of Theory* (New York: McGraw-Hill, 1977), pp. 46–49.

32. Ibid., p. 32.

33. Jacques E. Brisoux and Michel Laroche, "Evoked Set Formation and Composition: An Empirical Investigation in a Routinized Response Behavior

Situation," *Advances in Consumer Research*, ed. Kent B. Monroe, Vol. 8 (Chicago: Association for Consumer Research, 1980), pp. 357–61; see also Michel Laroche and Jacques E. Brisoux, "A Test of Competitive Effects in the Relationship Among Attitudes and Intentions," *The Changing Marketing Environment: New Theories and Applications*, ed. Ken Bernhardt et. al (Chicago: American Marketing Association, 1981), pp. 213–16.

34. Gordon H.G. McDougall, "Cognitive Responses to Advertising Messages: A Diagnostic," *Marketing*, ed. Robert G. Wyckham (Administrative Sciences Association of Canada, 1981), pp. 205–15.

35. Bobby J. Calder and Brian Sternthal, "Television Commercial Wearout: An Information Processing View," *Journal of Marketing Research* (May 1980), pp. 173–86.

36. Ibid, p.186.

37. N.K. Dhalla and S. Yuspeh, "Forget the Product Life-Cycle Concept," *Harvard Business Review* (January-February 1976), pp. 102–12; see also the discussion in Kenneth G. Hardy, "Procedures and Problems in Evaluating Sales Promotions," in *Marketing*, vol. 4, ed. James D. Forbes, (Administrative Sciences Association of Canada, 1983), pp. 142–50.

38. C.W.J. Granger and M. Hatanaka, *Spectral Analysis of Economic Times Series* (Princeton, N.J.: Princeton University Press, 1964).

39. Richard E. Quandt, "Estimating Advertising Effectiveness and Some Pitfalls in Econometric Methods," *Journal of Marketing Research* (May 1964), p. 60; Kristian S. Palda, *The Measurement of Cumulative Advertising Effects* (Englewood Cliffs, N.J., Prentice-Hall, 1964); Eben Otuteye and Kristian S. Palda, "Testing for Causality Between Aggregate Advertising and Consumption in Canada," *Marketing*, ed. Ronald E. Turner (Administrative Sciences Association of Canada, 1987), pp. 226–35.

40. Leo Bogart, B. Stuart Tolley, and Frank Orenstein, "What One Little Ad Can Do," *Journal of Advertising Research*, 10 (August 1970), 3–13.

P A R T V

Advertising and the Canadian Economy

Throughout this text, the role played by advertising in the marketing programs of Canadian consumers and industrial and non-profit organizations has been discussed from the viewpoint of Canadian advertisers. An overview was provided of the workings of advertising in the Canadian environment, of advertising's role in the marketing program and of the tools and techniques available to advertisers to fulfill their communication tasks.

In the fifth part of this text, a broader perspective will be taken: advertising in an international setting will be considered in Chapter 16, and the effects of advertising on the Canadian economy and society will be investigated in Chapter 17.

16 *International Advertising*

The preceding chapters have been essentially concerned with advertising in the Canadian environment, targeted at Canadian buyers. Of course, as an institution advertising is not restricted to this country. It is a worldwide institution, although it has its own specificities in various parts of the world. Because nowadays Canadian firms must increasingly have a global vision of their operation, it is essential for Canadian manufacturers to have a basic understanding of international advertising, and to understand the major issues faced by manufacturers when they must advertise to foreign markets. Especially, Canadian manufacturers should understand how to address foreign consumers effectively if they want to sell them their goods and services. As with communicating with the domestic markets, they should know which advertising message, themes, and media are likely to be the most effective in various international settings. To do so, they should recognize which elements in the environment are likely to be the most important and must be taken into account when designing the international advertising plan. This chapter is devoted to a brief discussion of these issues and of the specific aspects of international advertising. It discusses the importance of international advertising, considers major issues in international advertising, and briefly discusses the planning process for international advertising campaigns.

IMPORTANCE OF INTERNATIONAL ADVERTISING

International advertising can be defined as advertising sponsored by firms selling their products or services to markets located in other countries, and targeted at those markets. International advertising is gaining in importance as a result of increased international trade and exchanges over the years.

Present Trends in International Relations

At the beginning of the 1990s, international relations and international trade are characterized by two trends which have a significant impact upon international advertising.

First, is a definite trend toward increased national identity consciousness. Many people, cultural groups or subgroups tend to assert—sometimes very strongly—their national identity and request or fight for their *political* independence or autonomy. These cultural groups operate sometimes within countries, like the Quebecers in Canada, the Basques in Spain, the Azeris in the Soviet Union, or the Albanians in Yugoslavia. Sometimes they are countries which strive for independence from larger political blocks. This is the case of the Eastern European countries. This trend toward national identity consciousness calls for more market segmentation along such dimensions as language, culture, or values held by these national groups. Such segmentation should be recognized and accounted for by marketers who want to communicate with these markets effectively.

A second trend seems to go in a somewhat opposite direction: countries and nations tend to associate and form *economic* free trade zones. The European Economic Community and the USA-Canada free trade agreements are two cases in point. These associations are formed to enhance international trade and to build larger markets for the firms of each participating country. This trend pushes toward the globalization of marketing, and consequently advertising activities. The world is getting smaller every day as a result of faster transportation means, increasingly sophisticated communication devices such as satellite communications, or telecopying machines. Fast and easy communications facilitate transactions on a worldwide basis. As a result of this trend, national economies are becoming more and more interdependent. This trend pushes toward the globalization of advertising campaigns. Some marketers may want to advertise to the global market rather than to specific countries.

Importance of International Trade in Canada

International marketing plays an important role in the Canadian economy. More than 20 percent of the Canadian Gross National Product (GNP) is accounted for by exports of Canadian goods and services to foreign countries. In the United States, only about 10 percent of the GNP is constituted by exports.[1] This suggests that Canada relies on foreign trade to a greater extent than other countries, and consequently must actively compete in foreign markets. Canada exports over $125 billion and imports over $116 billion worth of goods and services. Most of this trade is with the United States (about 70 percent), and to a lesser extent with the European Economic Community, and Japan.[2] This relative importance of foreign trade in the Canadian economy underscores the need for Canadian marketers and advertisers to apply their know-how on the international scene.

Importance of Advertising Worldwide

Advertising plays an important role worldwide. This can be illustrated by a few figures. Global advertising expenditures have been estimated at about $268.1 billion in 1988. Experts estimate that this amount could reach $780 billion in the year 2000.[3] These expenses increase at a substantial rate in most countries, following the lead of the evolution of global advertising in the United States. It is interesting to note that the U.S. has been a world leader in advertising: not only is it the country spending the most on advertising in absolute dollar value, but it is also the country with the highest percentage of the GNP spent for advertising and advertising expenditure per capita.[4]

Table 16–1 on page 440 gives the countries with the highest and the lowest advertising expenditures as a percentage of their GNP.[5] As could be expected, advanced countries account for a larger proportion of advertising expenditures than countries with developing economies. There is a clear correlation between advertising expenditures and economic development (although it is not clear whether the two are linked by a causal relationship).

TABLE 16–1 **ADVERTISING AS A PERCENTAGE OF GNP FOR SELECTED COUNTRIES AND PER CAPITA**

The First			The Last	
Country	**%**		**Country**	**%**
United States	2.4		Pakistan	0.3
Switzerland	2.2		Mexico	0.3
Finland	2.1		India	0.3
New Zealand	2.0		Zambia	0.2
Spain	1.9		Kenya	0.2
Netherlands	1.8		United Arab Emirates	0.1
United Kingdom	1.7		Qatar	0.1
Australia	1.7		Morocco	0.1
Israel	1.5		Kuwait	0.1
Dominican Republic	1.5		Jordan	0.1
Canada	1.4		Indonesia	0.1
Japan	1.4		People's Republic of China	0.1
South Africa	1.4		Taiwan	—
Bolivia	1.3		Saudi Arabia	—
Jamaica	1.3		Oman	—
Chile	1.2		Lebanon	—
Costa Rica	1.2		Bahrain	—

Source: World Advertising Expenditures (New York: Starch INRA, Hooper and International Advertising Association, 1988), pp. 14–15.

Table 16–2 gives the countries which spend the most per capita on advertising, in decreasing order. The United States leads the list with $397.11 US per inhabitant.[6] Not surprisingly, the first 14 countries of the list are developed countries from North America, Europe, and Asia.

International Marketing and Advertising

For many Canadian firms, entering and succeeding in capturing foreign markets are essential for sustaining growth and profitability. Consequently, they must devise international marketing programs, of which international advertising is only one part. As is also the case for domestic advertising, international advertising cannot be meaningfully considered in isolation from the total international marketing program and from the specific international environment. However, in an international setting advertising can play an even more significant role. For instance, advertising may often be the only representative of a company abroad. Even more than for domestic markets, advertising is likely to be the only vehicle of a company's image and reputation. More importantly, advertising is probably the most cost-effective method for communicating with consumers in foreign markets.

MAIN ISSUES IN INTERNATIONAL ADVERTISING

Many concepts that have been discussed in the preceding chapters also apply to international advertising. Several issues, however, are specific to advertising in an international setting. In this section, some of the most important aspects

TABLE 16–2 **PER CAPITA ADVERTISING SPENDINGS IN SELECTED COUNTRIES (1985)**

Country	1988 Population (in million)	1988 Ad Expenditures (in millions)	1988 Per Capita Expenditures (in U.S. $)
United States	254.9	118 050	480.2
Finland	4.9	1 766	357.2
Switzerland	6.6	1 973	301.5
Japan	122.4	34 471	281.6
Canada	26.1	6 059	232.2
United Kingdom	57.0	12 076	211.8
Australia	16.5	3 475	210.6
West Germany	61.1	11 750	192.5
Norway	4.2	762	181.2
Sweden	8.4	1 494	178.8
Netherlands	14.8	2 563	173.7
France	55.9	6 937	124.2
Belgium	9.9	1 173	119.0
Israel	4.4	525	118.1

Source: World Advertising Expenditures, 23rd edition (Mamaroneck, N.Y.: Starch INRA, Hooper and International Advertising Association, 1989), pp. 14–15.

specific to international advertising will be discussed, especially whether multi-cultural advertising campaigns should be standardized or not, the important role of international environment (and especially, cultural and legal environments) for devising effective international advertising campaigns, and finally the specific problem of consumers' perceptions and image formation of international brands and multinational companies.

The Standardization of Multicultural Campaigns

There are arguments for and against standardized multicultural advertising campaigns.

Arguments for Standardized Multicultural Campaigns

Market Similarities. It is feasible to standardize a multicultural campaign when consumers' similarities are greater than their differences, and when evolutionary trends in various societies point toward increasing similarities and uniformities rather than to increasing differences.[7] One author states that with a universal appeal such as "better life for people and families," "to be beautiful," or "mother and child," a standardized campaign can be effective in any market. Nationalistic tendencies cannot be ignored but improved international communications, travel and work mobility, and the simultaneous launching of new products make standardized advertising more feasible and desirable.[8]

In his discussion about standardization in European Economic Community (EEC) advertising, an author states that different advertisements for the same product cannot be justified because trends in consumption habits across countries are more important than truly "national" trends. These trends in consumption habits are: 1) differences in habits are decreasing due to changes in the possession and availability of goods and services; 2) Europeans live in increasingly similar conditions; 3) as trade barriers drop, convergence of consumption habits is favoured by individuals. Furthermore, increased international communication (especially television) and mobility in work and travel make it more desirable to repeat a consistent advertising theme.[9] This author also points out that company mergers and product standardization lead the way to advertising standardization, that nonstandardization in advertising contradicts the philosophy of a united European market, and that in the arts, national boundaries are less important, and point to a convergent world style. "If there is no belief in advertising that can pass over all boundaries, then neither should we manufacture goods which pass over all boundaries."[10]

Other market and environmental factors favour standardization, but "the question of advertising approaches cannot be considered realistically in isolation from other elements of a company's marketing 'mix' in each market, including its product line, packaging, pricing, distribution system, sales force, and other methods of promotion."[11] Significant cost savings create pressures for standardization, especially in product design. These savings may be so great that although sales may decrease in some markets, profits will increase. Some companies can save millions of dollars by standardizing their advertising.[12]

A study analyzed lifestyles in twelve countries according to five dimensions (activities, interests, opinions, basic characteristics, and demographics), as well as media usage, product use, and orientation toward promotion. It found a high correlation between the level of product usage, which was used as the common element cross-nationally, and various lifestyle characteristics. For example, heavy beer drinkers in Canada, the U.S., and Mexico are similar enough that a common campaign could be developed. Attitudes, interests, opinions, and values may also be universal, regardless of social class, occupation, product usage, or culture.[13]

Advertising Consistency. The second factor that favours standardization is the advisability of consistent dealings with customers. Aside from the increasing cross-border flow of tourists, businesses, and communications, many companies sell to such multinational customers as industrial users and wholesalers, who either buy centrally or co-ordinate buying. Also, professional and technical groups are homogeneous enough to warrant a standardized approach.

Improved Advertising Planning and Control. The third factor, improved planning and control, is particularly important in the context of increasing social and economic convergence and decreasing trade barriers. Finally, as an expert points out, good ideas are hard to find and, once found, usually have universal appeal, for example, Avis's "We Try Harder" theme.[14]

Arguments against the Standardization of Multicultural Campaigns

One argument against standardization holds that cross-national differences, especially legal, cross-cultural, or other environmental differences, are too great to allow the development of effective standardized campaigns.[15]

Legal Differences. The most obvious barriers to transferring an effective advertisement to another country are the legal restrictions on advertising. In some countries, comparison advertising is illegal (Table 16–3), as are certain forms of promotion. Regulations involving free samples, contests, and sweepstakes (some countries forbid straight lotteries), and two-for-one or other reduced-price deals vary from nation to nation.

TABLE 16–3 **THE LEGALITY OF COMPARATIVE ADVERTISING IN 30 MAJOR COUNTRIES**

Essentially Illegal		Relatively Minor Legal Restrictions			Relatively Major Legal Restrictions			
		with relatively minor self-regulatory restrictions		with relatively major self-regulatory restrictions		with relatively minor self-regulatory restrictions		with relatively major self-regulatory restrictions
Belgium	NU/O	Canada	SU/O	Australia	MU/—	Austria	NU/O	Argentina	NU/O
France	NU/O	Ireland	MU/+	Denmark	SU/—	Brazil	MU/O	Japan	NU/O
Italy	NU/O	Sweden	MU/O	Hong Kong	MU/O	Chile	MU/+	Korea	NU/—
		United Kingdom	SU/O	India	MU/+	Germany	MU/O	Mexico	MU/O
		United States	SU/O	Philippines	NU/—	Finland	MU/O	Switzerland	MU/O
				South Africa	MU/O	Greece	NU/O	Trinidad & Tobago	MU/+
				Spain	MU/+	Malaysia	MU/O		
						Netherlands	MU/+		
						Norway	MU/O		
Total	3		5		7		9		6

SU = significant use (4)   NU = no use (9)   MU = minor use (17)   O = no change (20)
+ = change favouring CA (6)
– = change hampering CA (4)

Sources: J.J. Boddewyn, "Comparison Advertising: Regulation and Self-Regulation in 55 Countries." International Advertising Association, New York (January 1983), p. 8: J.J. Boddewyn and Katherin Morton, *Comparison Advertising: A Worldwide Study* (New York: Hastings House, 1978), p. 120.

A recent survey sponsored by the International Advertising Association (IAA) revealed that legal restrictions were obstacles to international advertising. Advertisers may use foreign languages in most countries. However, there are restrictions according to the kind of medium. 91 percent of the 46 countries that participated in the survey allow foreign languages in print ads, 91 percent in direct mail, 85 percent in outdoor advertising, 84 percent in sales promotion material and 72 percent in cinema commercials.[16] About 25 percent of the responding countries, however, restrict foreign language ads to media targeted to foreign-speaking consumers. In addition, 22 percent of the surveyed nations forbid the use of foreign-made productions and foreign talents in advertising, while another 39 percent partially restrict the use of foreign material and artists' models. Concerning advertising agency regulations, 75 percent of the responding countries allow full foreign ownership of advertising agencies, but often require prior approval by the government.[17]

Several reasons may explain these restrictions and regulations. They include economic considerations, nationalistic and culture preservation preoccupations, consumer protection, the need to prevent misleading advertising and national sovereignty considerations.

Even in instances where regulations are standardized, however, administration of the laws may vary. In Germany, for example, comparative claims are legal, with major restrictions requiring proof of claims. Interpretation of the laws is very strict, however. A statement that "Brand X is better for your dog" can be interpreted as a comparative claim even if no other brand is mentioned.[18] In general, relatively poor countries such as Spain have fewer and less strictly enforced controls, while relatively rich countries have more controls and stricter interpretations.

In addition to legal controls, many countries have self-regulatory bodies. Most of these bodies have adopted at least the statement of basic principles and the rules (Articles 1 to 18) of the International Code of Advertising Practice (revised 1973), which has also been accepted by the International Chamber of Commerce. One study found that countries with a central self-regulatory body generally have a relatively high level of advertising expenditures, active consumer groups, and government controls on advertising.[19]

Cultural Differences. In addition to legal and self-regulatory codes, international advertising practices are restricted by unwritten codes. Culture has a considerable impact upon consumer behaviour, and consequently is a key factor in international advertising. Culture refers to the set of values and beliefs which are learned and passed on from one generation to the next, and that evolve slowly over time. Besides the material elements of culture which are characterized by technological know-how and the economic organization of a society, culture also affects the meaning, function, and role of social institutions in a foreign country (such as the family, the church, the political system). Cultural codes are unwritten, but strictly observed by the individuals sharing the same culture. For instance, in Japan, direct confrontation is discouraged by traditional values, and decorum in competitive behaviour is preferred. As a result, Japanese advertising refrains from comparative claims, open attack, and aggressive advertising. In Switzerland comparative advertising is considered a kind of in-fighting, and business people tend to unite against foreign competition.

Another barrier to cross-cultural advertising is "the silent language".[20] This refers to differences in cultural frames of reference, which enable the receiver of a communication to determine what is significant and/or relevant. Some of these differences are:

- The concept of time. For example, in Arab countries, a mechanic feels pressured when asked to repair a car before a specific date and may respond by slowing down or stopping work.
- The language of "personal space," or the meaning of the distance people maintain between themselves when speaking to each other. This distance may be greater with Northern Europeans than with North Americans.
- The language of things (since possessions have different meanings). An advertising theme for a washing machine in Canada where it is an essential good often put out of view of guests could not be used in Mexico, where it is a luxury good, often displayed in the living room as an indication of high social class.[21]
- The language of colours. Colour may have different meanings in different countries: a product with a green package might be accepted in Mexico and become a failure in Egypt. For each of these countries, green is a national colour, but differences in behaviour proceed from the attitudes toward its commercial use. A product with a green package might also be a failure in Malaysia because green is associated with the jungle and, therefore, with sickness. White, often associated to joy and wedding in Western countries is the symbol of death and mourning in the Orient.
- Friendship. In some countries friendships form more slowly, last longer, and involve real obligations, in contrast to North America.
- The language of agreements. For example, unstated, unwritten agreements may be the norm in some countries.

In a study comparing the British and the Americans, one author states that the manner of communication in advertising is "firmly anchored to cultural norms and often says more about a society's psyche than the more obvious stereotypes of content."[22]

Culture may affect perceptions of colours and sounds, cognitive and affective processes, evaluative behaviour, and learned motives. A study of the *attribution of responsibility* (i.e., under which conditions are people responsible for an event) involving Mexican-American, Black, and Anglo subjects, found the cultural factor highly significant.[23]

These results may contradict the assumption that there is a common appeal in the philosophy that "everyone wants a better life for oneself and one's family." What people want may be universal but what people perceive they can control or get may not be universal. It is the latter that determines whether "wants" are translated into behaviour.

Culture also affects the criteria consumers use to evaluate products.[24] One Canadian study found significant differences in the effectiveness of English advertisements dubbed into French and English advertisements adapted as to presenter, working, setting, and/or structure. The study did conclude, however, that with these significant adaptations, the campaign could be transferred.[25]

A Few Examples of International Advertising Cultural Blunders. Examples of advertising campaigns that have failed to properly account for cultural differences, or have been considered as offensive by some cultural groups are numerous, and they encompass all parts of the world:

- In Germany, Maxwell House met with little success with its advertising campaign: "Great American Coffee." It turns out that Germans do not think much of American coffee.[26]
- In Brazil, the Campbell Soup Company had to reduce the scale of its canned soup operations after experiencing severe losses. Advertising research revealed that Brazilian housewives felt that they were not fulfilling their role as homemakers if they served their families a soup they did not make themselves. As a result, the extra-large cans of Campbell soup with the familiar red and while label had to be withdrawn from this market.[27]
- In South-West Asia, United Airlines had a hard time adjusting to and accounting for the local culture when it took over the Pacific routes from Panamerican Airways a few years ago: First, the map inserted into United Airline's promotional brochure left out one of Japan's main islands. Second, a magazine ad campaign which was run with the theme: "We know the Orient" listed the names of Far Eastern countries below pictures of local coins. Unfortunately, the coins did not match up with the countries. Third, a concierge service for first class passengers had concierges wearing a white carnation, the oriental symbol of death.[28]
- In Nigeria, an advertisement featured a Nigerian praising a glass of beer by holding it in his left hand—a sign of homosexuality in this country. In this country again, a Renault car advertisement featured a platinum blonde sitting next to the driver. This was perceived by local consumers as not very respectable and created a feeling of shame.[29]
- An advertising campaign run in African countries for a perfume used a backdrop of rain in order to evoke a clean, cool, and refreshing atmosphere. However, this is a symbol of fertility for Africans, which in many cases conveyed the meaning that this perfume was effective against infertility.[30]
- In Canada itself, McDonald's recently ran an advertisement in which Ali Baba (a Muslim) was used to promote bacon cheese burgers. (A campaign intended to be fun, according to a company vice president.) Of course, the Muslim religion strictly forbids eating pork or any product of pork, and the ad was reported to have offended many Muslims (there are about 98 000 Muslims in this country).[31]

Other Environmental Differences. Other arguments against the standardization of advertising relate to market factors. Effective commercials offer a vital promise that fits the needs and desires of the audience. One can distinguish three categories of commercials: those that establish product benefits (overcome unfamiliarity or doubt, or create primary demand by emphasizing a product, not a brand); those that establish brand superiority; and those that promote unique features. These categories are stages related to the degree of market development.[32] One could conclude, then, that markets at different levels of development (as measured, for example, in terms of a product's life cycle) need different advertising strategies that correspond to differing levels of awareness, knowledge, liking, preference, and/or conviction.

In addition, differences in the level of economic and industrial development may necessitate the development of separate campaigns. Underdeveloped countries have relatively low literacy rates and low per capita income. Low literacy rates make a campaign based on visuals preferable or even necessary. Low per capita income may mean that the relative cost of a given product is higher than in North America. This may change the way a product is evaluated by consumers and make a purchase more risky. This makes it more difficult to influence consumers with a campaign that is suitable for countries where the relative cost is lower.

Advertising National Specificities: The Japan Example. All the legal, cultural, and environmental characteristics for a country tend to shape advertising in that country. It is not surprising, therefore, that substantial differences exist among advertising approaches, institutions, and practices across countries, which tends to limit the possibilities of international advertising campaign standardization. Let us illustrate this point by examining the case of a specific country: Japan.[33]

In order to properly understand the world of advertising in Japan, one must have a solid understanding of the cultural dimensions of the Japanese society. These, in turn, affect the behaviour of consumers at different stages of their life-cycles, as well as the organization of the business and economic structures. Advertising in Japan is still relatively underdeveloped compared to many industrialized countries. As a percentage of GNP, total advertising expenditures are about 1.4 percent, compared to 1.4 percent in Canada and 2.4 percent in the United States.

Institutional Particularities. Distribution in Japan is extremely complex and cumbersome. On a per capita basis there are twice as many retailers and wholesalers as there are in North America. Japanese companies tend to have larger sales forces to reach these distributors, and also because they put more emphasis on push strategies.

Concerning Japanese advertising agencies, some agencies are among the largest in the world. However, they do not have the influence that North American agencies have on their clients. There is an enormous concentration in the agency business, with the largest agency, Dentsu, having about 25 percent of the market, and the second largest, Hakuhodo, having 12 percent of the market. By comparison, the largest agency in Canada has about 2 percent of net advertising revenues, and a similar situation exists in the United States. On the other hand, advertising agencies in Japan are basically media brokers working on commission, from which they derive almost all of their revenues. Very little creative work is done within the traditional agency, with the bulk of the creative effort done in-house or by creative boutiques. The agency acts more as a facilitator of the creative function of the campaign. In that sense, none of the agencies function as a true full-service agency for their clients, but more like a media buying service. There is also a complete lack of client/agency partnership, which is one of the reasons most agencies have multiple clients for the *same* product category. Thus, there is no such thing as account conflict for Japanese agencies.

Another unusual situation is that the media themselves have enormous power over the agencies: they can impose the use of a particular agency on the client. For example, it is common for one agency to handle the buying of space for Kirin beer in Newspaper A, and another to handle the buying for the *same* brand in Newspaper B, and so on. This situation also helps explain the multiple client situation and the lack of account conflicts.

Very little advertising research is done by clients, and almost none by agencies. The most common indicator of success is sales increases, which can be deceiving since several product categories have been growing according to natural market development, as consumption is stimulated by economic growth. Japanese branches of American advertising agencies are minor players in Japan, unlike the situation in Europe, where they are among the largest in most countries. This situation has not changed even after creating a partnership with some Japanese agencies.

Media Particularities.   With a population five times that of Canada, and half that of the United States, the media markets in Japan are highly concentrated with 33 markets compared to 205 in the USA. Thus advertising in Japan is highly cost efficient. Television has the largest share of net advertising revenues, 35 percent compared to 30 percent for newspapers. The opposite is true in Canada and the USA where the percentages for television are in the 17 to 27 percent range. One of the major reasons for this situation is that television in Japan is a relative bargain compared to North America, with CPMs about 50 to 67 percent of Canadian or U.S. CPMs.

The top five magazines in Japan are comic books, and cover a wide range of subjects, for example economics. Newspapers in Japan tend to be national with a huge circulation, over 10 million copies daily for the top ones. These newspapers have a great deal of credibility and prestige. Some also publish an English condensed edition essentially for prestige reasons.

Cultural and Creative Particularities.   The Japanese language relies heavily on the Chinese kenji characters, which are pictograms. This makes creativity a very difficult and challenging art in Japan, more so than in Canada. In addition, creativity must account for a number of cultural and social factors specific to Japan. For instance, Japanese women tend to be less involved with the broadcast media than their North American counterpart, and they listen very little to radio (45 minutes compared to over 3 hours). On the other hand, they tend to be more positive toward advertising: they find it more enjoyable.

Most successful brands tend to have huge market shares because of the "follow the leader" syndrome. The majority of commercials tend to be very short, i.e., 15 seconds, and there is a high level of clutter. There is no comparative advertising in Japan, since traditional Japanese values tend to discourage direct confrontation, instead stressing decorum in business rivalry. In fact, a direct reference to a competitor's brand in a truthful comparative advertisement may appear to injure the competitor's reputation and be considered tortuous by all. The cultural norm is to "respect each other's face," as "losing face" is a major blow to a Japanese. This explains why there is an industry-wide agreement to ban comparative advertising, as well as puffery.

Japanese consumers do not respond to argumentative advertising, but rather to emotional advertising. They like their commercials to be gentle, moody, suggestive, entertaining, to appeal to the right (symbolic) side of the brain, rather than the left (logical) side. Thus many creative approaches used in commercials tend to be rather unexpected, use style, have a strong artistic presence, and make the people who created them, as well as the client, very proud. Typically, the brand or the product would not be mentioned until the end of the commercial. This makes creating commercials in Japan extremely challenging and requires an extraordinary understanding of the audience and of the product.

Another factor has been referred to as the "iceberg principle of advertising in Japan": Japanese consumers do not like to be told the whole story; instead they like to be told 20 percent of the story, and to imagine the remaining unseen 80 percent. A large number of advertisements use westerners, either well-known personalities (e.g., actors, singers) or unknown individuals often with blond hair and blue eyes, who may appear neutral, and who do not lend themselves to social categorization.

The Japanese make a clear distinction between their "public persona" and their "private persona." A commercial must respect this distinction, and the creative director must separate the social (accepted) conduct that can be shown in advertisements from the private thoughts not divulged in public. Testimonials are not used any more in Japanese advertising since they are not considered effective.

Finally, Japanese can use humour to advertise products that Canadians or Americans would talk only very cautiously about. For instance, "one hemorrhoid-preparation commercial features a man in an outlandish costume, his trousers around his ankles, sitting on a toilet and whining about pain."[34] Another ad for a toilet-bowl cleaner is shot from inside the toilet "so you can watch a wife urge her husband to stick his head inside the bowl to see how clean she got it." In an other advertisement for a tampon, a famous Japanese actress is dressed up as a tampon.[35]

All these particularities of the Japanese advertising would practically prohibit the use of an advertising campaign that would appeal, for instance, to a Western audience. Even building a campaign that would fit the two cultures would be an extremely difficult task that should be carried out with the utmost care.

Standardization? It Depends.

Several criteria determine whether uniform advertising is appropriate.[36] One is the type of product. A standardized appeal is effective with products that

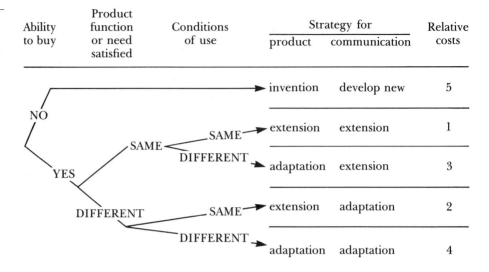

FIGURE 16–1

Product/Communication Alternatives in International Markets

Ability to buy	Product function or need satisfied	Conditions of use	Strategy for product	Strategy for communication	Relative costs
NO			invention	develop new	5
YES	SAME	SAME	extension	extension	1
		DIFFERENT	adaptation	extension	3
	DIFFERENT	SAME	extension	adaptation	2
		DIFFERENT	adaptation	adaptation	4

have a universal selling point and that are sold primarily on an objective basis (according to physical characteristics).

The homogeneity (or heterogeneity) of markets, the characteristics and availability of media, and the types of advertising agency service available should also be considered. For example, if only poor agency service is available, standardized advertising developed elsewhere may be the most attractive alternative. Government restrictions, trade codes, industry agreement, and ethical practices may preclude standardization. Tariffs on artwork and printed matter may eliminate the cost advantages of centralized production.

The organization of a multinational firm determines whether the implementation of a standardized campaign is possible. For example, tight central control makes implementation easier, while a firm operating through independent, non-exclusive agents, or through licenses may have more difficulties. Implementation is the important element. The question is not only whether an effective cross-national or cross-cultural campaign can be developed, but also whether the firm is capable of imposing such a campaign.[37]

The standardization of product and communication strategies depends on three key factors.[38] The first is the *product* itself, defined in terms of consumer needs satisfied. The second is the *circumstances* under which the product is used (including consumers' ability to buy and their preferences). The third is the *cost* of any changes, should nonstandardization be necessary. The strategic product/communication alternatives are represented in Figure 16–1.

International Product, Company, or Brand Images.

Because the products and the brands are made in foreign countries, consumers tend to develop images that are affected by the country of origin of the brand or product. In addition, the brand image and company images are also affected by the fact that they are either multinational or foreign companies. This is an additional dimension that should be taken into account in international marketing.

Country-of-Origin Product/Brand Images

When consumers evaluate a product or a brand, they use an array of cues such as the price, the brand name, the store, the package, the label, or any information they may have on the product.[39] For products manufactured abroad, and often advertised as foreign origin products, this is an additional cue which is likely to affect a consumer's evaluation of the brand. Consequently, it becomes imperative for international advertisers to understand the nature of the cue's impact, especially if it becomes an asset or a liability to the brand.[40] For instance, Germany has developed over the years a strong reputation for its engineered products. German products are often associated with precision, high engineering quality and design, and durability. In this case, it may be profitable for a German car manufacturer like Volkswagen to capitalize on the German origin of the car in its advertising. Alternatively, if a country does not possess a strong or a positive image as a producer of certain goods, it may decide to play down the country-of-origin in its advertising.[41] This strategy has been followed by the Japanese beer, Kirin, for entering the U.S. market. Kirin is Japan's best selling beer, and the world's number three brand. However, it is not known in the North American market, and the Japanese have not yet built a reputation as beer manufacturers in the United States. Consequently, Kirin has entered an agreement with Molson Breweries of Canada Ltd. and the Market Importing Company (Molson's U.S. marketing company), and now, Kirin is brewed in Canada at Molson's breweries. The strategy was to build on the Canadian company's reputation to put the beer in a favorable light.[42]

International Company Images

Many foreign companies seem to fear that because of trade deficit and of incentive to protect national economies, foreign consumers may turn their backs to foreign products and buy only national products. This phenomenon is increasing as many companies have become multinationals operating in every part of the world. There are over 15 000 such companies in the United States alone, and Canada itself controls several multinational companies (for instance, Alcan, Abitibi, Canadian Pacific, Canada Packers, Domtar, Noranda, and Northern Telecom). This is why recently many corporations have felt the need to advertise in foreign markets and try to convince foreign consumers that they are good "world citizens." According to a corporate ad consultant, companies have stepped up their advertising with the message, "We're thinking global and are concerned about your society and welfare. We're giving jobs to your country."[43] In addition, these companies have increased their donations to cultural, educational, or other non-profit causes in the countries in which they operate. The advertisement run by Toshiba in the United States and reproduced in Figure 16–2 likens the Japanese president of Toshiba America (with headquarters in Wayne, New Jersey) to Bruce Springsteen, in an attempt to bridge the gap between Japan and the western world.[44] Internationalism has become a fashionable theme in advertising, as is also

FIGURE 16–2
Toshiba America's
president is shown in
a Bruce Springsteen
stance to show the
company's commit-
ment to its new head-
quarters in New Jersey.

Courtesy Toshiba America
Consumer Products, Inc.

FIGURE 16–3
For Honeywell, which
uses technological
know-how from several
countries, customers
are more important
than computers.

Courtesy Honeywell Ltd.

shown by the Honeywell advertisement in Figure 16-3: "Honeywell Bull computers combine the best of American, French, and Japanese technology."[45]

THE INTERNATIONAL ADVERTISING PLANNING PROCESS

The international advertising planning process is outlined in Figure 16–4. The
various steps are similar to those of a domestic advertising campaign plan, but
there are some important differences, too, especially concerning the approach
and the ways to carry those steps.

Understanding the International Advertising Environment

Understanding the environment in the foreign countries in which advertising
will be run is an essential prerequisite to designing a successful advertising
campaign. As was already discussed in the preceding section, it would be
practically impossible to make good decisions on the various aspects of the
advertising plan without understanding thoroughly:

- the structure of the foreign markets, and especially their competitive
  structures;
- the institutional particularities of those markets, especially the distribution
  channels, and the advertising agencies that are available, as well as the way
  these institutions operate;
- the media available in those markets;
- the legal constraints operating in these markets;
- the cultural dimensions affecting those markets (probably the most difficult
  part of this knowledge acquisition step).

FIGURE 16–4
*The International
Advertising Planning
Process*

1. Understanding the International Advertising Environment

2. Specifying the International Advertising Strategy

3. Selecting the International Advertising Agency

4. Creating the International Advertising Message

5. Selecting International Media

6. Implementing and Controlling International Advertising

Table 16–4 (on pages 454 and 455) provides a comparison of 22 countries in terms of advertising practice, media penetration, and restriction on TV advertising.[46] As can be seen, this environment can vary substantially from one country to the next. Obviously, an advertising manager should investigate other relevant aspects of the international environment that may be important to the marketing of the product.

Specifying the International Advertising Strategy

Canadian marketers must devise appropriate promotion policies for foreign markets. Different external constraints influence the pull and push strategies adopted for each foreign market. In particular, the types of distribution systems available in each country determine whether personal communication or advertising are more desirable. The availability and costs of reaching consumers through mass media[47] also determine the degree of reliance on a pull strategy. For instance, in countries where several languages are spoken (e.g., India), it is difficult to develop an efficient promotional strategy.

The relative costs of the two types of communication have a great effect on the promotional mix. In developing nations, where labour is cheaper, the promotional mix is based more on personal selling than in industrialized countries.

As for the domestic advertising plan, the international advertising plan cannot be properly designed if clear objectives of what advertising should accomplish in the overall international marketing program has not been carefully and precisely defined.

Selecting the International Agency

The decision is often between hiring an international agency or a local agency. The principle to guide the decision should be determining which agency can best meet the advertising objectives, taking into account the costs, as well as all

TABLE 16–4   CONCISE GUIDE TO ADVERTISING IN 22 COUNTRIES

	Austria	Australia	Belgium	Brazil	Canada	Switzerland	Germany	Spain	Ireland	France
Total advertising expenditure 1979 Local Currency	7 900 Million A.S.	1 482 Million Dollars	9 500 Million Francs	50 700 Million Cruzeiros	3 008 Million Dollars	981 Million Francs	10 786 Million D. Marks	64 800 Million Pesetas	45.1 Million Punts	17 400 Million Francs
Total expressed as a % of Gross National Product	0.88%	1.46%	0.3%	0.95%	1.16%	0.6%	0.8%	0.5%	0.6%	0.83%
Breakdown of Advertising Expenditure by principal media. %										
TV	16.5	30.3	12.8	42.0	16.6	12.1	9.6	33.0	32.1	9.5
National Press	25.3	10.6	31.0	22.5	*	55.9	48.1	29.4	32.6	17.5
Regional Press		29.4	10.8		28.6	NA	NA		7.9	
Magazines/Periodicals	In Other	7.6	28.7	9.5	17.9	32.0	18.4	16.9	1.5	21.1
Trade & Technical		2.6			19.1	NA	*		*	
Radio	6.5	8.8	1.2	16.0	11.4	0	3.3	12.3	9.9	6.5
Cinema	0.3	1.6	1.2	0.5	O	NA	0.8	1.9	*	1.0
Outdoor	4.2	9.1	14.3	3.5	6.4	NA	3.6	6.5	6.0	9.3
Other	47.2	NA	NA	6.0	*	NA	16.2	NA	*	35.2
Proportion of households with TV sets	91%	96%	93%	54%	97%	84%	85%	95%	85%	92%
Proportion of households with colour TVs	44%	75%	50%	30%	81%	53%	62%	30%	32%	33%
Number of TV channels accepting advertising/sponsorship	2	50	None but RTL Luxembourg is received	89	95	3	2	2	2	2
Advertising time in 24 hour period. Approximate minutes	20	154	62 (RTL)	360	216 Per Channel	60	40	85	85	48
Restrictions on TV advertising	No tobacco, hard liquor; regulated drugs and foods. Restrictions on children's advertising	No cigarettes	No tobacco, alcohol	No alcohol, cigarettes, cigars, until 9 PM	No cigarettes, liquor. Regional restrictions on beer and children's advertising.	No alcohol, tobacco, drugs, politics, religion.	No cigarettes, religion, charities, narcotics, prescription drugs, children's advertising, cures.	No tobacco, hard drinks.	No tobacco, contraceptives, religion, politics.	Many categories are excluded, alcohol, margarine, slimming products, tobacco products, etc.
	+ DM, –AC, PC	– DM, PC PC	– DM, PC, +AC	+ DM, AC, PC	+ DM, PC, –AC	– DM, AC, PC	+ DM, –AC, PC	– DM, AC, PC	– DM, AC, PC	+ DM, AC, –PC

Note: NA = not available. * = insignificant amount. O = medium not used. DM = direct mail. AC = agency commission. PC = production cost.

Source: From William J. Hawkes' presentation at the International Marketing Workshop AMA/MSI, March 1983, of A.C. Nielsen Company material. Reprinted by permission of A.C. Nielsen Company.

TABLE 16-4 continued

	Great Britain	Greece	Italy	Japan	Mexico	Netherlands	New Zealand	Portugal	Argentina	Sweden	United States	South Africa
Total advertising expenditure 1979 Local Currency	2 219 Million Pounds	3 735.6 Million Drachmas	1 186 Billion Liras	2 113 Billion Yen	9 660 Million Pesos	3 825 Million Florins	195.5 Million Dollars	1 462.5 Million Escudos	1 028 Billion Pesos	2 004 Million Kronor	49 690 Million Dollars	290 Million Rands
Total expressed as a % of Gross National Product	1.34%	0.32%	0.35%	0.95%	0.36%	1.29%	1.12%	0.2%	1.27%	0.46%	2.1%	1.8% (G.D.P.)
Breakdown of Advertising Expenditure by principal media. %												
TV	22.1	46.4	19	35.5	65.0	5.0	25.4	55	24.6	0	20.5	19.3
National Press	48.0	27.8	24	31.0	8.0	46.9	0	29	42.3	36	4.2	35.3
Regional Press					NA	8.7	48.1			41	25.1	4.1
Magazines/Periodicals	22.3	20.0	53	5.3	4.0		6.6	16	15.7	16	5.9	16.3
Trade & Technical			NA	In "other"	1.0	3.6	NA	NA		0	3.4	6.5
Radio	2.4	4.6	4	5.0	15.0	0.7	8.2	NA	9.0	1	6.6	12.0
Cinema	0.8	NA	NA	In "other"	4.0	0.3	1.2	NA	1.4	5	0	2.1
Outdoor	4.4	1.1	NA	In "other"	2.5	6.1	0.3	NA	6.1	NA	1.1	4.4
Other	NA	NA	NA	23.1	0.5	28.7	10.2	NA	0.9	NA	33.2	26.5
Proportion of households with TV sets	94%	95%	96%	98%	43.8%	97%	95%	NA	86%	93%	98%	
Proportion of households with colour TVs	65%	5%	27%	96%	None	65%	70%	NA	18%	71%	83%	18.4%
Number of TV channels accepting advertising/sponsorship	1	2	2 + Many private stations	93	15	2	2	2	38	None	728	1
Advertising time in 24 hour period. Approximate minutes	80	120	27 excluding private stations	230	12 Hour/station	30	260	30	10 Hour/channel	—	Voluntary code: hour/station	24
Restrictions on TV advertising	No contraceptives, cigarettes, politics, gambling, religion or charities	No cigarettes, ethical drugs	No jewels, furs, newspapers, magazines, cigarettes, gambling, clinics and hospitals	No overstatement comparison with competitors, sensual messages on commercial films	No liquor before 10 PM	No tobacco, political, religion. Special legislation for pharmaceuticals, sweets, alcohol	No cigarettes, alcohol, feminine hygiene products, contraceptives, politics	No tobacco, gambling, liquor only after 9 PM. Restrictions on medicines	No use of foreign words or slang. No attitudes against morals. No misuse of country symbols	—	No tobacco, contraceptives, fortune tellers	No Sunday advertising, no spirits, wine, beer, cigarettes after 9 PM except Sunday. No "sensitive" products
	−DM, +AC, PC	−DM, PC, +AC	−DM, PC, +AC	−DM, AC, PC	−DM, PC, +AC	+DM, AC, −PC	+DM, AC, +PC	−DM, PC, +AC	+DM, AC, +PC	−DM	+DM, AC, PC	−DM, AC

the legal constraints that may be imposed upon the decision by the local governments. Obviously, this decision is linked to the type of campaign being considered. If a standardized approach is followed, an international advertising agency may be warranted. However, if the campaign is non standardized and should closely account for the specificities of the local culture, a local agency may have an edge over an international organization. Table 16–5 gives the 50 Top Agency Groups in the World in 1989.[48]

TABLE 16–5 **WORLD'S TOP 50 AD AGENCY GROUPS IN 1989**

Rank	Agency	Gross Income* 1989	Billings* 1989
1.	Dentsu Inc.	$1 316.4	$10 063.2
2.	Saatchi & Saatchi Advertising Worldwide	890.0	6 049.9
3.	Young & Rubicam	865.4	6 250.5
4.	Backer Spielvogel Bates Worldwide	759.8	5 143.2
5.	McCann-Erickson Worldwide	715.5	4 772.3
6.	Ogilvy & Mather Worldwide	699.7	4 828.0
7.	BBDO Worldwide	656.6	4 550.0
8.	J. Walter Thompson Co.	626.4	4 407.5
9.	Lintas: Worldwide	593.3	3 957.6
10.	Hakuhodo Inc.	585.5	4 449.2
11.	DDB Needham Worldwide	552.9	4 095.4
12.	Foote, Cone & Belding Communications	510.9	3 413.9
13.	Grey Advertising	498.9	3 267.4
14.	Leo Burnett Co.	483.8	3 245.5
15.	D'Arcy Masius Benton & Bowles	471.5	3 803.1
16.	EWDB Worldwide	381.0	2 702.3
17.	Publicis-FCB Communications B.V.	358.8	2 405.4
18.	N W Ayer Inc.	210.5	1 398.2
19.	Bozell Inc.	190.7	1 400.0
20.	RSCG	175.3	1 234.3
21.	Tokyu Agency	156.2	1 259.4
22.	Dai-Ichi Kikaku	155.8	1 053.0
23.	Daiko Advertising	152.1	1 214.1
24.	Chiat/Day/Mojo	150.0	1 060.0
25.	Lowe International	137.8	918.6
26.	Wells, Rich, Greene	132.5	885.0
27.	Scali, McCabe, Sloves	127.0	870.1
28.	TBWA Advertising	123.7	827.0
29.	Ketchum Communications	117.8	915.7
30.	Asatsu Inc.	113.9	837.3
31.	Yomiko Advertising	100.3	753.5
32.	Ross Roy Group	97.7	651.1
33.	I&S Corp.	94.7	770.2
34.	MPM Propaganda	83.9	220.7
35.	Asahi Advertising	82.9	509.4
36.	BDDP	79.2	527.9
37.	Cheil Communications	64.0	247.5

TABLE 16–5 **WORLD'S TOP 50 AD AGENCY GROUPS IN 1989**
(continued)

Rank	Agency	Gross Income* 1989	Billings* 1989
38.	Nihon Keizaisha Advertising	56.3	337.3
39.	W.B. Doner	52.1	381.0
40.	Clemenger/BBDO	52.0	325.1
41.	Hill, Holliday, Connors, Cosmopulos	51.6	344.0
42.	Chuo Senko Advertising	50.6	376.4
43.	Armando Testa Group Worldwide	50.2	349.4
44.	Sogei Co.	49.2	300.2
45.	Orikomi Advertising	47.5	435.8
46.	Oricom Inc.	45.1	173.0
47.	Admarketing Inc.	44.9	252.0
48.	FCA! Group	42.3	281.7
49.	Man-Nen-Sha Inc.	42.2	550.4
50.	Telephone Marketing Programs	40.5	270.0

*Figures are in millions, unless otherwise noted.

Source: "Agency Income Report," *Advertising Age*, March 26, 1990. Reprinted with permission. Copyright Crain Communications Inc., 1990.

Creating the International Advertising Message

The message will essentially be affected by the decision to use a standardized or a non standardized approach to advertising. As was discussed in the preceding paragraphs, this decision is highly dependent upon the specific environment, and especially upon cultural factors. In any case, the importance of understanding cultural factors for designing effective messages that will be understood and accepted by foreigners should be underscored.

Selecting International Media

The media selection for a foreign advertising campaign can be constrained by media availability and effectiveness for reaching the target audience. Media availability and usage is highly dependent upon the country's stage of economic development, its political and social system, as well as by its legislation. For instance, television has a low penetration rate in some countries which have not reached a high level of economic development. Print media cannot be very effective in those countries with a substantial level of illiteracy. In some countries, the movie theatre provides a powerful advertising medium. Movie theatre advertising provides all the advantages of television advertising, plus the fact that the message is delivered to a captive audience which has less opportunity for distraction than the typical television viewing situation.

Because of all these differences, it may not be surprising that the mix of media typically used may vary considerably from one country to another. For instance, about 55 percent of European advertising is spent in print media compared to about 28 percent in Latin American countries.[49] In the latter countries, 38 percent of advertising goes through television versus only 12 percent in Europe, where television stations are often government owned and where television advertising is either not allowed or severely restricted.[50]

Implementing and Controlling International Advertising

As for domestic advertising campaigns, international advertising should be controlled after the campaign has been seen in order to assess whether it has reached its objectives. The major difference here is the additional difficulty of assessing the campaign's effects when the campaign has been seen in a foreign language and has reached a market with a different culture than that of the executives of a parent company. Because of these additional difficulties, special care should be given to the control aspects of the international advertising campaign, as a cultural advertising blunder as those reported above may have important and often lasting effects.

SUMMARY

International advertising is becoming more important in the world economy as international relations and trade undergo major changes. As many people throughout the world achieve political independence and assert their national and cultural identity, they often enter economic association with other countries to facilitate economic growth and international exchanges. This trend is especially felt in Canada where exports account for about 20 percent of the Gross National Product.

One of the main issues in international advertising is whether it is feasible and/or desirable to standardize the campaign across countries. Certain authors argue that it may be possible to standardize a multinational campaign when consumers' similarities are greater than their differences. Others point out that it is advisable to make consistent dealings with customers, and that standardization facilitates and improves campaigns' planning and control. There are, however, important barriers to multinational campaign standardization. Legal constraints are likely to vary from country to country, and the laws as well as administration of the law and its interpretation can vary from one country to the next. Even more importantly, cultural factors may prevent standardization. Language, the concept of time, the language of personal space, of things, and of colours can, if improperly used, convey the wrong meaning to the target audience. Examples of advertising mistakes that fail to account for such differences have been provided in this chapter. Other environmental specificities include the level of economic development, or the market structure. Advertising particular characteristics were illustrated on the Japanese advertising case. A second major issue in international advertising is related to consumers' perception of foreign products/brands and companies.

Finally, this chapter concluded with a brief outline of the international advertising planning process. This process includes the understanding of the international advertising environment, specifying the strategy, selecting the advertising agency, creating the message, selecting the media, and implementing and controlling the international advertising campaign.

QUESTIONS FOR STUDY

1. Contrast the standardized and non standardized approach to international advertising. Provide specific examples.

2. Why is it so important for international advertisers to understand the specific aspects of international advertising?

3. Explain the major trends that tend to increase the level of international trade and advertising throughout the world. In your opinion, is this trend likely to continue over the next 25 years? Why?

4. What are the major arguments for standardizing international advertising campaigns? Provide examples.

5. Same question as 4, but for non-standardization of advertising campaigns.

6. Assume that you contemplate running an important advertising campaign for a brand of soap addressed to European countries. Would you use a standardized or non standardized campaign? Why? Be as specific as you can.

7. Same question as 6, but the product is road building equipment, and the market is the whole world.

8. Select any two countries with different cultures. How are these cultural differences likely to affect the advertising campaigns of a foreign manufacturer of:
   a. frozen food products
   b. small household electric appliances
   c. industrial products

9. Outline the major steps in building an international advertising campaign. Discuss the major differences from a domestic advertising campaign.

10. Discuss the major particularities of Japanese advertising. Which differences can be attributed to culture? Religion? Geography? Explain.

PROBLEMS

1. Take a few issues of a Canadian general magazine and a few issues of a general magazine from a different country of which you know the language. Through a content analysis of advertisements contained in those magazines, what can you say about the major differences and similarities. Can you explain them?

2. Through library research, try to list the major specificity of mainland China's advertising. (Use as an example the case of Japanese advertising discussed in this chapter.)

NOTES

1. Statistics Canada, *Summary of Canadian International Trade*, December 1987.
2. Statistics Canada, Ibid.
3. "U.S. Outspends the World in Ads," *Marketing News*, February 2, 1988, p. 15.
4. "Strong Spending: Foreign Ad Budgets Again Beat U.S.," *Advertising Ages*, March 28, 1988, p. 6.
5. *World Advertising Expenditures*, (New York: Starch INRA, Hooper and International Advertising Association, 1988), pp. 14–15.

6. *World Advertising Expenditure*, 20th Edition, (Mamaroneck, N.Y.: Starch INR, Hooper and International Advertising Association, 1988), pp. 7–17.

7. P.C. Lefrancois and G. Chatel, "The French Canadian Consumer: Fact or Fancy?" *New Ideas for Successful Marketing*, ed. J.S. Wright and J.L. Goldstucker (Chicago: American Marketing Association, 1966), pp. 706–15.

8. Arthur C. Fatt, "The Danger of 'Local' International Advertising," *Journal of Marketing*, (January 1967), pp. 60–62.

9. Erik Elender, "How International Can European Advertising Be?" *Journal of Marketing* (April 1965), pp. 7–11.

10. S. Watson Dunn, ed., *International Handbook of Advertising* (New York: McGraw-Hill 1964), p. 71.

11. Robert D. Buzzell, "Can You Standardize Multinational Marketing?" *Harvard Business Review* (November-December 1967), p. 102.

12. Ibid., p. 102–13.

13. Joseph T. Plummer, "Consumer Focus in Cross-National Research," *Journal of Advertising* (Spring 1977), pp. 5–15.

14. Buzzell, op. cit., pp. 102–13.

15. Arthur C. Nielson, Jr., "Do's and Don'ts in Selling Abroad," *Journal of Marketing* (April 1959), pp. 405–11.

16. J.J. Boddewyn, "International Advertisers Face Government Hurdles," *Markting News*, May 8, 1987, p. 20.

17. Ibid., p. 21.

18. J.J. Boddewyn and K. Morton, *"Comparison Advertising: A Worldwide Study* (New York: Hastings House, 1978).

19. J.P. Neelankavil and A.S. Stidsberg, *Advertising Self-Regulation: A Global Perspective* (New York: Hastings House, 1980).

20. E.T. Hall, "The Silent Language of Overseas Business," *Harvard Business Review* (May-June 1960), pp. 87–98.

21. E. Dichter, "The World Customer," *Harvard Business Review*, 40 (July-August 1962), pp. 113–22.

22. Stephen J.F. Unwin, "How Culture Affects Advertising Expression and Communication Style," *Journal of Advertising* (Spring 1974), p. 24.

23. J. Lipton and R. Garza, "Responsibility Attribution Among Mexican-American, Black and Anglo Adolescents and Adults," *Journal of Cross-Cultural Psychology* (September 1977), pp. 259–72.

24. R. Green, W. Cunningham, and I. Cunningham, "The Effectiveness of Standardized Global Advertising," *Journal of Advertising* (Summer 1975), pp. 25–30.

25. Dunn, p. 71

26. S. Watson Dunn, "Effect of National Identity of Multinational Promotional Strategy in Europe," *Journal of Marketing*, 40 (October 1976). p. 51.

27. *Business Week*, "Brazil: Campbell Soup Fails to Make It to the Table," October 12, 1981, p. 66.

28. John R. Zeeman, "Service—The Cutting Edge of Global Competition: What United Airlines Is Learning in the Pacific," Presentation delivered at the Academy of International Business, Chicago, Ill., November 14, 1987.

29. Irene de Bretteville, "African Advertising Expands," *World Press Review* (February 1984), p. 48.

30. Ibid.

31. *The Gazette*, "Muslims Cheesed Off by Ad Showing Ali Baba Eating Bacon," February 10, 1990.

32. S. Watson Dunn, ed. International Handbook . . . op. cit., p. 71.

33. Michel Laroche, "Unique Practices in Japan: A Cultural Explanation," Unpublished paper, undated.

34. Damon Darlin, "Japanese Ads Take Earthiness to Levels Out of this World," *The Wall Street Journal*, Tuesday, August 30, 1988, p. 11.

35. Ibid.

36. G.E. Miracle, "International Advertising Principles and Strategies," *MSU Business Topics* (Autumn 1968), pp. 29–36.

37. D.M. Peebles, J.K. Ryans, and I.R. Vernon, "Coordinating International Advertising," *Journal of Marketing* (January 1978), pp. 28–34.

38. Warren J. Keegan, "Multinational Product Planning: Strategic Alternatives," *Journal of Marketing* (January 1969), pp. 58–62.

39. D.A. Schellink, "Determinants of Country of Origin Cue Usage," *Marketing*, ed. Alain d'Astous (Montreal: ASAC), 1989, pp. 268–75; Marjorie Wall, John Liefeld, and Louise Heslop, "Impact of Country of Origin Cues and Patriotic Appeals on Consumer Judgments: Covariance Analysis," in *Marketing*, op. cit., pp. 297–305.

40. Nicolas Papadopoulos, "Made in Canada, Eh?: A Cross-National View of Canadian Products," *Markting*, ed. Ronald Turner (Montreal: ASAC), 1987, pp. 196–203; Louise A. Heslop, John Liefeld, and Marjorie Wall, "An Experimental Study of the Impact of Country of Origin Information," *Marketing*, op. cit., pp. 179–185.

41. D.A. Schellink, "An Exploratory Study Into the Impact of Country of Origin as a Cue in Product-Choice," *Marketing*, ed. Thomas Muller (Montreal: ASAC), 1986, pp. 181–90.

42. Joe Agnew, "Japanese Beer from Canada: Kirin Pushes for Larger U.S. Market Shares," *Marketing News*, January 18, 1988, pp. 1–2.

43. William Weathersby, Jr., "We Are the World," *Public Relations Journal*, (September 1988), p. 32.

44. Ibid., p. 33.

45. Ibid., p. 34.

46. William J. Hawkes, Presentation at the International Marketing Workshop, AMA/MSI, March 1983.

47. Erdener Kaynak and Lionel A. Mitchell, "A Study of Comparative Media Usage in Canada, the United Kingdom, and Turkey," *Developments in Canadian Marketing*, ed. Robert Tamilia (Montreal: ASAC), 1979, pp. 131–2.

48. "Agency Income Report," *Advertising Age*, March 26, 1990.

49. World Advertising Expenditures, Starch INRA, Hooper (New York: Mamaroneck, 1988), pp. 8–9.

50. Ibid., p. 31.

CHAPTER

17 Economic and Social Effects of Advertising

Critics and advocates of advertising all too often rely on impressions rather than facts. Of course, assessing the economic and social effects of advertising is difficult, and the complex issues involved are far from being resolved. This chapter discusses the effects of advertising on the economy and society, and examines the protections against abuses from unethical advertising practices that are available to Canadian consumers. Figure 17–1 outlines some possible negative and positive effects of advertising.

THE ECONOMIC EFFECTS OF ADVERTISING

The main economic consequences attributed to advertising concern the following: consumers' information load; the process of new product development and/or product proliferation; consumer prices, through its impact on distribution costs and market competition; business cycles; and the media and media

FIGURE 17–1

Possible Effects of Advertising on the Economy and on Society

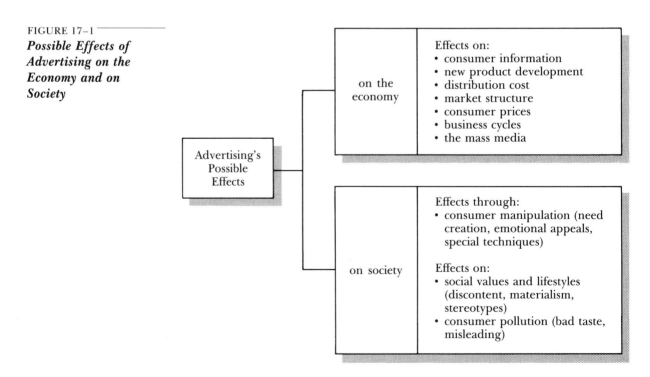

economics. These issues can be grouped into three categories (Figure 17–2). The first two—that advertising provides consumers with product and service information and enhances the new product development process—are often advanced by advocates of advertising as proof of its positive economic function. If properly fulfilled, these roles of advertising would tend to benefit the consumer. Critics of advertising argue that advertising results in increased consumer prices, through the two above mentioned effects on distribution costs and on the market competitive structure. Thus, if this latter argument is

FIGURE 17–2

The Controversy on the Economic Effects of Advertising

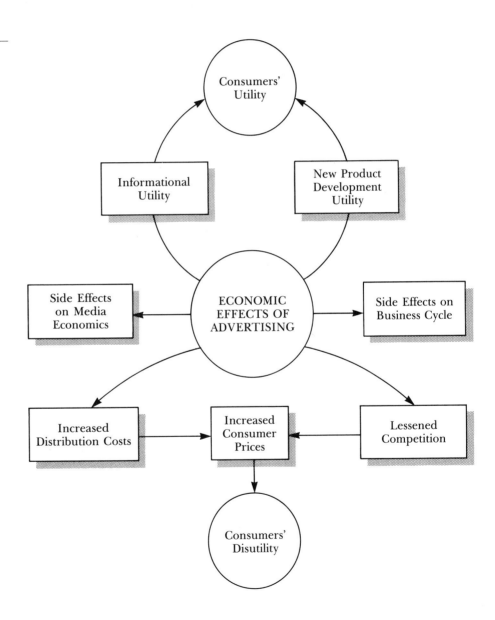

true, advertising would also involve some disutilities to consumers. The third category is based on the fact that advertising has two important "side effects" that indirectly impinge upon consumers' welfare. They are called side effects because they do not directly affect the marketing process but have consequences for business cycles and the economics of the various media.

<table>
<tr><td>

***Advertising and
Consumer Utility***

</td><td>

Advertising and Consumers' Informational Utility

Even the most vocal critics admit that advertising's objective is to provide consumers with information about products and services. The dream of classical economists, who conceived of perfect and free information available to all consumers, bears little resemblance with the reality of the market. As was shown in Part 3, consumers look for information to make better choices and to reduce the risks of their purchase decisions. Advertising is such an information source and should fulfill the essential role of providing information on the products and services available in the marketplace.

</td></tr>
</table>

One important way in which advertising can meet this informational objective is to build brand awareness and favourable brand images. Brand names constitute an investment for a manufacturer, because consumers can expect a certain quality level associated with a specific brand name. The role of a brand name is more important for products that involve high risks for consumers and also for products whose quality consumers are not technically competent to assess directly, especially before they use the product. Thus, a well-known brand name has high informational value and an economic raison d'être. Consequently, when advertisers build a brand name or a brand image, they also build a name that has some informational value for consumers. They are then committed to delivering a product quality that is consistent with advertising claims and consumers' expectations.

Therefore deceptive advertising or advertising claims that induce consumers to make suboptimal choices constitute a disutility for these consumers and is not in a company's best long-term interests. If advertising fails to provide consumers with relevant information, it is ineffective. Although critics and advocates of advertising might agree with these statements, they may disagree over what constitutes relevant information. Some economists define such information as objective information about the technical features and/or the physical characteristics of the brand.

According to critics, only informational advertising should be permissible while so-called persuasive advertising should be banned. For instance, one critic wrote: "At the point where advertising departs from its function of informing and seeks to persuade, it tends to become a waste of resources."[1] Similar claims can be found in other works.[2,3] However, it has been shown that the informative-persuasive advertising dilemma is a false dichotomy.[4] Based on the concepts of information theory, "if advertising critics really believe that persuasive advertising should not be permitted, they are actually proposing that no advertising be allowed, since the purpose of advertising is to persuade."[5] On another distinction between low versus high information content advertising, one may argue that the quantity of information in a message cannot be meaningfully measured independently from the quality or usefulness of the information, which in turn, is essentially individual specific. Advertisements with a high information content for one consumer may have a low information value for another. Thus, marketers who recognize that consumers use several dimensions, some objective, others subjective, to evaluate brands, would broaden the definition of what constitutes relevant information to include any information that consumers process to help them make a purchase decision.

In the same vein, economists who perceive the consumer as close to the ideal rational economic man argue that advertising designed to create certain moods or to associate products with certain lifestyles or activities is completely void of information content. In contrast, marketers have long recognized that consumer behaviour is essentially rational but is also affected by psychological, social, or cultural values, and that such motives are at least as powerful as economic motives in the consumers' logic. These marketers would argue that mood or lifestyle advertising adds to consumers' utility, since consumers buy not only physical products but also the set of meanings attached to the products.[6] The quarrel between advocates and critics of advertising can be traced to both groups' disagreement over this extended concept of a product. However, if consumers find additional value and utility in these meanings, the role of advertising should be to establish such meanings through mood or lifestyle advertising and to communicate them to the market.

Advertising and New Product Development

Advertising—and sometimes only advertising—can efficiently inform consumers about new products and innovations. If such a convenient and relatively inexpensive device were not available for communicating the existence of new products or new ideas to potential buyers, the new product development process would be seriously impaired. Without advertising, the large number of product improvements and innovations that characterize our economy might not have been possible.

Critics of advertising challenge the role of advertising in providing consumers with real new product utilities. They argue that by focusing on inconsequential product features, advertisers attempt to differentiate products in ways that are not beneficial to the consumer. Marketers would answer such criticisms by saying that as long as a market segment responds positively to a certain product with specific advertised features, *knowingly and in the absence of any deceptive advertising claim*, then these consumers find some real value and satisfaction in the brand they purchase. Since what constitutes value to one customer may be worthless to another, one should guard against imposing one's value judgments on a market or on society. This endless quest for meaningful product differentiation is a powerful economic catalyst. Because firms always try to find and promote products with differential advantages, meaningful innovations often—if not always—reach the marketplace.

When properly used by companies that refrain from deceptive or exaggerated claims, advertising fulfills an essential economic role. It provides consumers with informational utility, keeping in mind that consumers need not only objective information but also meanings, moods, and subjective information. This information is often built into brand names. Consumers are also provided with utility derived from innovations that try to cater to consumer needs and desires in order to secure competitive advantages.

Obviously, there are costs attached to all these benefits. It is often difficult to find the limits between "informative" and "non-informative" advertising. In addition, non-informative advertising (as perceived by consumers) is likely to be ineffective and constitutes an economic waste. Moreover, product differentiation may be pushed to a point at which the differences do not warrant introducing a new product on the market. Much of the controversy between critics and advocates of advertising lies in their view of what constitutes "informative advertising" and "value to the consumer." Much of the difference lies in the implicit assumption made by advertising critics that consumers are "rational economic individuals," while marketers and advertisers view consumers as rational beings motivated not only by economic forces but also by psychological, social, and cultural values.

Advertising and Consumer Disutility

Among the most vocal critics of advertising are economists who advance the argument that advertising increases the prices paid by consumers for goods and services. They suggest two broad types of mechanisms through which consumer prices could increase as the result of advertising: increased distribution costs and/or lessened competition, and concentrated market structures.

Advertising and Distribution Costs

Critics of advertising claim that advertising expenditures are a waste of economic resources and that advertising expenses are often a substantial part of the good sold. Consequently, in the end consumers pay for these additional selling expenses, since the selling price must recover these costs if a company is to make a profit. This argument has been extended to all the promotional devices marketers use to enhance consumer sales.

Although this argument may seem to carry some weight, it must be seriously qualified. First, two underlying assumptions in this criticism of advertising do not always hold. The first assumption is that marketers always use a cost-oriented pricing strategy (such as cost-plus pricing). This is not always the case. If a demand-oriented pricing approach is followed—and assuming that advertising expenses could be suppressed without decreasing the demand for a product—then any cost reduction would not be passed on to consumers but would increase the company's profits.

The second assumption is that advertising has no definite impact on sales and that marketers could do without it at no extra cost. Obviously, this assertion is at variance with what has been discussed previously. Advertising fulfills an important information function in a marketing program. If advertising were not used for this essential marketing information function, marketers would have to use something else, such as personal selling, and the information cost would be transferred to other marketing expense accounts. Moreover, these costs would probably increase dramatically, because only advertising can efficiently perform certain tasks of mass communication.

While the argument that advertising increases the retail price of goods rests on two questionable assumptions, there are strong arguments that suggest the contrary—that advertising can decrease the unit distribution cost of products. This idea is conveyed by the upper part of Figure 17–3, which shows how the unit cost of a certain product varies at different levels of output and sales. The unit cost has been split between production and advertising cost. The (M) curve presents the typical U-shaped manufacturing cost curve. As economies of scale are felt, the unit manufacturing cost drops and then increases as diseconomies of scale are involved. The lower part of the diagram represents the sales response function to advertising expenditures. Thus, if no advertising expenditures were made, the firm could probably sell a certain quantity S_0 (although a small one) because of the effects of the other elements of the marketing mix. It can be seen on the upper part of the diagram that at the S_0 sales level, the unit cost of the product could be C_0.

FIGURE 17–3

Unit Cost of a Product and Different Output/ Sales Levels

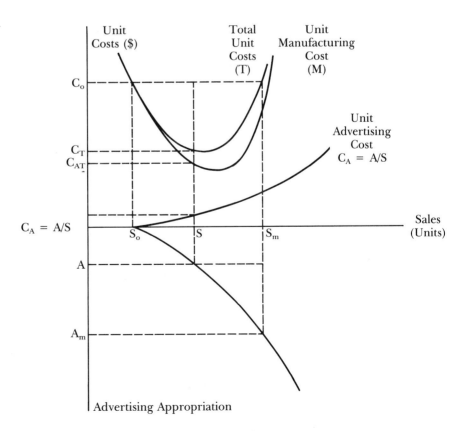

Now consider what happens when this firm decides to spend some money on advertising (for instance, A). These additional advertising costs should be added to the manufacturing costs. The unit advertising costs at various sales levels are represented by the curve (C_A). This curve starts at S_o and increases at an increasing rate ($C_A = A/S$), because the sales response gets smaller for successive equal additional increments of advertising expenditures, which is the result of the law of diminishing marginal returns. The (T) curve is the vertical summation of the manufacturing and advertising costs that are needed at the different contemplated sales levels. When the firm spends A on advertising, the *total unit cost* of the product drops from C_0 to C_T. The reason becomes evident when Figure 17–3 is considered: advertising can increase demand so that the economies of scale that are now possible result in a decreased average manufacturing cost (from C_0 to C_M) that is still larger than the additional advertising cost per unit (C_A).

It may also turn out that advertising does result in an increased total unit cost. This may happen if the resulting sales level falls at the right of S_M (i.e., if the advertising expenses are larger than A_M) for one of three reasons:

1. The firm continues to stimulate demand for the product when production is close to capacity (with very high marginal manufacturing costs). This happens when the firm overspends on advertising.
2. The demand for the product cannot be stimulated any more, because the market is saturated or close to the saturation level (i.e., the sales curve is in its flat part). Here again the firm has overspent on advertising.
3. For some reason, advertising is ineffective.

All three cases may occur as the result of marketers making inefficient use of advertising dollars. They constitute marketing mistakes that marketers try to avoid. Nevertheless, the inefficient use of tools and techniques is not restricted solely to advertising, or even marketing. It can also be present in the other elements of the marketing mix (such as personal selling or pricing policies) or in other aspects of the firm's management (financial or personnel management).

To sum up, advertising can result in a consumer price increase when 1) marketers follow a cost-oriented pricing strategy and 2) marketers use advertising dollars inefficiently by overspending and/or conducting ineffective advertising campaigns.

Advertising and Market Structure

That advertising leads to higher consumer prices and higher profits through market concentration is a more subtle argument. Economists have studied this problem theoretically and empirically, and although there is no clear evidence in either direction, this argument can be substantiated more than the preceding one. Figure 17–4 illustrates these hypothetical market mechanisms.

Overview of the Model. According to economists, advertising can lead to market concentration and to higher consumer prices. At first glance this pro-

FIGURE 17–4
*Model of the Effect
of Advertising on
Market Structure*

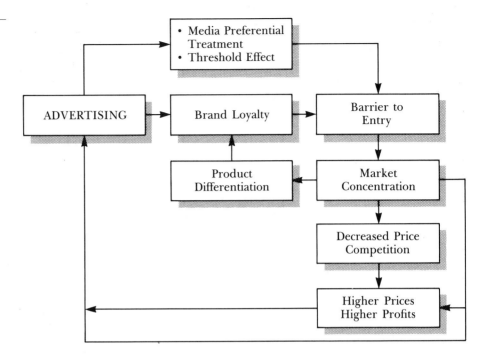

cess resembles an endless loop. In other words, advertising leads to market concentration, which leads to more advertising, and so on. The upper part of the loop, which represents how advertising could lead to market concentration, is believed to be a barrier to market entry. Such barriers are said to exist when a new company finds it difficult to enter a market and compete with well-entrenched firms.

There are three ways in which advertising can give a company differential advantages that may constitute a barrier to entry by new competitors. One is that advertisers can build brand loyalty. Economists argue that new competitors may find it very difficult to break the loyalty that consumers have developed to well-established brands. Loyal customers are essentially satisfied consumers, and breaking loyalty patterns is a difficult endeavour. A second way is that advertisers can gain preferential treatment from the media that could not be obtained by a smaller newcomer. A third way is that there is a threshold effect for advertising before it can be effective. Thus the large resources required to overcome this handicap may discourage a new competitor from entering the market.

As shown in Figure 17–4, barrier to entry eventually leads to market concentration, which means that a small number of competitors share a substantial part of the market. Market concentration leads to lower competition and decreased price competition. The rationale of this assertion is that when only a small number of large competitors share a market, that is, when a market has an oligopolistic structure, a price decrease initiated by any manufacturer is likely to be immediately matched by competitors. Consequently, there is no incentive to compete on prices. Lack of price competition usually means higher prices for consumers and larger profits for the manufacturer.

As can be seen in Figure 17–4, three feedback loops tend to perpetuate and even accelerate this process. First, market concentration can lead to product differentiation. Because firms in a concentrated industry do not compete on prices, they differentiate products that are essentially similar in their primary function by artificially altering some secondary attributes. From an economic point of view, product differentiation is not a bad strategy when it better serves the differentiated needs of consumers. However, if this process is pursued to an extreme, it can result in an artificial proliferation of brands. As was pointed out by Neil Borden, an expanding set of product options can be disadvantageous for consumers when they involve only minor differences over existing brands that add little to consumers' real utility.[7] In this case, it can be argued that a large number of brands increases distribution costs and makes consumer buying more difficult and less efficient. But the objective of product differentiation is to build brand loyalty by increasing consumers' preferences for a specific set of product attributes, and brand loyalty is a major cause of barrier to entry.

Second, lack of price competition in a concentrated industry leads not only to product differentiation but also to advertising competition to promote the artificial differences of a product. If the additional advertising costs are passed on to consumers, then this competition may lead to higher consumer prices and certainly to more advertising.

Third, higher prices and profits are believed to lead to increased advertising expenses because manufacturers have an incentive to promote highly profitable items more aggressively.

Analysis of Some Key Relationships. The preceding argument rests on hypothesized relationships, some of them real and well documented and others not as well established. Some of the relationships of the model are quite controversial.

Advertising and Preferential Treatment from the Media. Although theoretically correct, this advantage does not seem to materialize in practice and at best seems a rather weak relationship. (This relationship is analyzed fully later in this chapter, in the discussion of the effect of advertising on media economics.)

Advertising and Brand Loyalty. Advertising plays an important role and function in establishing brand names and in establishing a close relationship between the brand name and consumers' expectations of a certain level of quality. When advertisers spend large amounts of money on advertising, they want to build some brand loyalty for products or brands by promising something unique, usually the assurance of a certain quality level. If advertising is aimed at building brand loyalty, industries with the largest advertising expenditures would show the most stable market shares. Although market share stability does not necessarily imply brand loyalty, since a large amount of brand switching can take place with relatively stable market shares,[8] brand loyalty should definitely result in stable market shares. A study carried out a few years ago showed an *inverse* relationship between these two variables.[9] From a marketing point of view, these findings are not surprising when one considers that in a heavily advertised market, consumers of a certain brand who are exposed to advertising that induces them to remain loyal to the brand are also exposed to advertisements that induce them to switch brands. Consequently, the hypothesized direct relationship between advertising and brand loyalty does not have conclusive support from empirical data.

Advertising and Market Concentration.   If advertising leads to market concentration, one could observe an association between advertising levels and market concentration. In other words, those spending the most on advertising should be the most concentrated industries. Most empirical studies that have attempted to test the existence of this relationship have reached contradictory conclusions. Some studies have concluded that no significant relationship existed.[10,11] Other studies have reached the opposite conclusion.[12] These conflicting results may find at least some partial explanation in the substantial difficulties that researchers face when they have to operationally define and measure such concepts as industry, industry advertising, and market concentration. Industries are generally defined according to the Standard Industry Classification (SIC). Unfortunately, this classification for which industry data are available has somewhat arbitrary boundaries that do not always suit the purposes of researchers. Industry advertising is typically measured by the advertising to sales ratio (A/S), which reflects the percentage of industry expenditures devoted to advertising. Here again, this ratio may be a poor indicator of the level of advertising, because it is highly dependent on the type of product characterizing each industry. Furthermore, it does not take into account past advertising effort (carry over effects). Finally, market concentration is often measured by the concentration ratio. This ratio measures the market share held by the four largest competitors in an industry.[13] This widely accepted measure of industry concentration is also highly dependent not only on industry definition but also on its variability when firms or brands are considered as the competitors in an industry.

The inconclusive evidence for a relationship between the amounts spent on advertising and the level of industry concentration suggests that if the relationship exists, it is not as strong as some economists have believed.

Market Concentration and Increased Prices.   Although economic theory shows that market concentration leads to higher consumer prices, in at least two situations this may not necessarily be true. For instance, when a firm enters a market on a local or regional basis and competes with national firms by catering to local needs better than a national firm can, it becomes quite feasible for a newcomer to enter a highly concentrated market and to compete on price with well-entrenched companies. In addition, buyers in a concentrated industry can form an association in order to negotiate better prices from the concentrated industry. This tendency has been noted, especially in the distribution channels of consumer products.[14] Consequently, here again, even if there exists a relationship between market concentration and increased prices, it may not be as strong as is shown in Figure 17–4.

Advertising and Profits.   There is stronger empirical evidence to support a positive relationship between advertising expenditures and profitability across industries.[15] A study concluded that industries with the largest advertising expenditures had profits approximately 50 percent in excess of other industries.[16] Although the results may be explained by the barriers to entry created by large advertising outlays, the association does not necessarily imply causation. If there is a causal relationship, no conclusion can be safely drawn as to which direction the causation runs, that is, whether advertising leads to higher profitability or if profitability leads to more advertising, as is suggested by Figure 17–4. It may also be the case that advertising expenditures and profitability are both positively or negatively related to a third extraneous variable.

Product Differentiation and Brand Loyalty.   One basic objective of the strategy of product differentiation is to build customer loyalty by better meeting consumers' needs and desires than any other brands. Although few empirical studies have been made in this area, it seems reasonable to conclude that when product differentiation is substantial enough and corresponds to actual differences in customers' needs, product or brand loyalty can be and is created. As was noted, few economists argue against this type of product differentiation. They instead challenge the concept of product differentiation when it is based on immaterial product characteristics, which leads to a proliferation of nearly identical brands. It is also reasonable to assume that the brand loyalty created by such secondary features is not as strong and thus can be broken more easily, especially as new, similar brands appear on the market.

In conclusion it can be said that Figure 17–4, which summarizes the argument that advertising increases consumers' prices through increased market concentration, should not be considered as a definite causal model but as suggestive of some plausible market mechanisms. Although this model embodies some real and theoretically true relationships, these relationships may not be as strong and prevalent as they seem. More empirical research is needed before conclusions can be drawn on all the issues involved.

Advertising and Retail Price Competition.   It has been noted[17] that with a single exception, empirical studies reporting that advertising increases price sensitivity looked at consumer prices,[18] and studies reporting that advertising decreases price sensitivity examined factory prices.[19] Advertising has also been positively associated to factory price levels[20] and negatively to consumer price levels.[21]

A study conducted in the United States compared the prices of eye examinations and eyeglasses in states that permit advertising versus those that do not. After allowing for possible differences in income and socio-demographic characteristics of the various populations, it concluded that the prices paid by consumers for these products and services were on average $4.43 cheaper in those states where advertising was allowed.[22] These results can be explained by theories about the role of retailers as links between manufacturers and consumers.[23] Retailers may price highly advertised products in such a way that they earn a lower gross profit margin than on unadvertised products (such as private label brands).

Two reasons may account for this pricing behaviour. First, advertised brands have a higher turnover rate than less advertised products, and this tends to keep down the retailer's inventory cost per unit. Because retailers often use a cost-plus approach to set their prices, one can expect lower retail selling prices and retail gross margins for advertised brands. Retailers may "prefer a quick nickel to a slow dime."[24] Second, highly advertised brands are often used by retailers as loss leaders. The rationale for using advertised brands rather than less known brands as loss leaders is that consumers are more likely to know the prices of such brands and should be able to use those prices as benchmarks to compare the prices charged by competing retailers. According to some authors:

Both of these factors increase the probability that a price cut on advertised brand will bring more customers into the store (where they may also buy other items . . . perhaps at higher gross profit margins) than a price cut on unknown unadvertised brands.[25]

If only the differences in unit sales and in retail prices between advertised and unadvertised brands are considered, the value of advertising would be underestimated. Actually, the differences between manufacturers' prices are very pronounced and relevant to an evaluation of advertising's contribution to profitability. Because retailers are willing to cut their profit margins to provide consumers with low prices, part or all of these differences are not felt at the consumer's level.

Economic Side Effects of Advertising

Advertising also has important side effects. They are called side effects in the sense that they only indirectly affect consumers' utility. Advertising may also affect business cycles and the economics of the mass media.

Advertising and Business Cycles

Advertising is believed to have a negative impact on business cycles. An economic analysis reached the conclusion that advertising expenditures had a tendency to follow the same pattern as business cycles,[26] because advertisers tend to increase advertising when the economy is booming and to curtail advertising expenditures when sales are weak. Some advertisers determine their advertising expenditures by applying a fixed percentage to their sales. Even those advertisers who do not follow such rigid rules may take into account the current sales level to decide how much to spend on advertising. From a theoretical point of view, the opposite practice should prevail: advertisers should reduce advertising expenditures when they foresee a booming economy and increase advertising budgets in periods of economic recession, to try to alleviate the extremes of business cycles. Although the practice seems to contradict theory, even if advertising has a negative impact on economic cycles, this effect is probably relatively small in comparison with major determinants of business cycles.[27]

Advertising and the Mass Media

A large part of the amount spent on advertising (about 75 percent) is used to buy advertising space and time. These amounts collected by selling advertising space and time are a major—and sometimes the sole—source of income for the mass media. The remaining 25 percent is devoted to production and administrative costs. It has been estimated that in Canada about 60 percent of the cost of periodicals, about 70 percent of the cost of newspapers, and practically 100 percent of the cost of radio and television are covered by advertising revenues.[28] When consumers buy a product (which includes some advertising cost), they also buy, in addition to the satisfaction directly derived from the consumption of the product, the possibility of watching a TV or radio program or a substantial reduction in the price of a favourite magazine or newspaper. If we could imagine a world without advertising, other means of financing the mass media would have to be found. In the final analysis, consumers would have to pay the bill, either through direct radio or TV taxes and duties, as is presently done in some European countries, and higher prices for each issue of newspapers and magazines, or through additional taxes. Thus, consumers recover a great amount of the money spent on advertising through media attendance (watching TV, listening to radio, reading newspapers and magazines), at a substantially reduced cost.

It has been argued that the financial support advertisers give to the mass media is not without a social cost, since advertisers try to exercise control over the media contents. This control can reduce a medium's freedom to report some anti-business news or articles and programs that may have a negative impact on large advertisers. There certainly is a danger of pressure being exerted by important advertisers. It may also be argued, however, that it is better to have pressure exerted on the media by several advertisers whose interests often conflict than to have the mass media under the sole control of government. Governments are run by political parties whose objectives, motives, and interests are more obvious and definitely more homogeneous than those of various businesses.

It has also been argued that through rate schedules the media could favour large advertisers at the expense of small advertisers. The media generally do offer large discounts to volume purchasers, but the allegation of discriminatory pricing practices does not hold. For instance, many time slots on television that are not sold in advance are offered to all advertisers at substantial discounts, regardless of the advertiser's total commitment. This is why smaller advertisers can also purchase time slots at substantially reduced prices.[29] Thus the present pricing structure does not appear to give a substantial differential advantage to large advertisers.

Conclusions on the Economic Effects of Advertising

The model in Figure 17–2 indicates that advocates of advertising stress two broad types of economic benefits to consumers, i.e., that advertising fulfills the useful role of providing information to consumers and of enhancing new product development.

Critics point to the upward pressure advertising may exert on prices as the result of increased distribution costs or because of lessened competition. Here again, critics and advocates of advertising are likely to disagree on where the limits stand between what is truth and what is speculation.

Advertising does have desirable and undesirable economic effects. The real problem is to assess whether the benefits of using advertising are worth the economic costs. One answer is that advertising plays a role no other communication tool can fulfill as efficiently. From an economic point of view, if it were possible to get rid of advertising, the costs would certainly be much higher than the cost of keeping—and at the same time trying to refine and improve—this economic institution.

As a conclusion to a speech try to answer "Why Over $109.8 Billion Was Spent on Advertising in America Last Year" Joseph De Deo, President of Young and Rubicam Europe stated:

> . . . A director of advertising at Procter and Gamble, the largest single advertiser in the U.S., long ago gave the answer, very succinctly, for all American businesses when he said: "Advertising makes a sale more frequently, with more impact and less expensively than any other method. If there were a better method, we would use it." And they would—count on it.[30]

THE SOCIAL EFFECTS OF ADVERTISING

Critics of advertising who are concerned with the impact this economic institution has upon our social life stress two main arguments for questioning the relevance of advertising for our social well-being (Figure 17–5). One is that advertising manipulates consumers. The second is that advertising has undesirable social effects on lifestyles, values, and culture.

Does Advertising Manipulate Consumers?

Lecture ▽

This argument can be examined by emphasizing various aspects of the advertising communication process. Advertising has been accused of having the immediate effect of manipulating consumers by creating needs. At the level of the message, advertising could manipulate its audience by intensively appealing to emotions. Critics view the use of appeals based on sex, fear, or love as attempts to manipulate consumers by making extreme appeals to their emotions. Other social critics view advertising as manipulating through its use of tools and techniques that seek to influence consumers at a subconscious level. Motivation research and subliminal advertising are cases in point. Finally, advertising has also been considered as manipulating such persuasible audiences as children.

Can Advertising Create Needs?

Critics of advertising have argued that advertising can create needs among consumers and induce them to buy products that they do not otherwise want. They picture advertisers as unscrupulous individuals who persuade consumers to buy against their will products and services that do not or cannot bring any satisfaction. The view that advertising can create some kind of irresistible desire and can change otherwise intelligent consumers into robots that advertisers can manipulate is far removed from the real world of advertising communications.

FIGURE 17–5

**Questions Raised by
Social Critics of
Advertising**

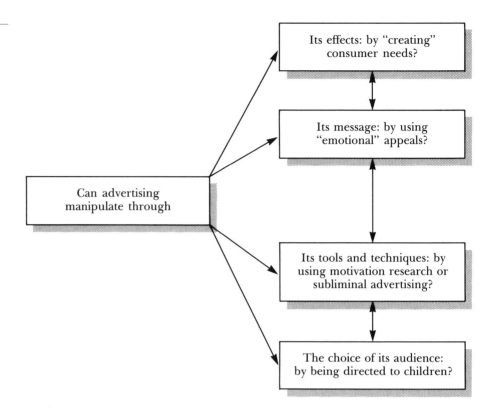

At this point it should be asked whether advertising experts can cause consumers to purchase products they do not need. "Need" is a relative concept, since psychological needs can be as important as and sometimes more important than physical needs. What is considered a necessity by one individual may be trivial to another; a necessity in one society may be a luxury in another. For instance, vacuum cleaners and refrigerators are considered by Canadians as necessities. However, such items are unaffordable luxuries for many African villagers.

Statistics show that between 35 and 80 percent of new products introduced into the market are rejected by consumers.[31] A well-known example is the Edsel automobile, which was introduced by the Ford Motor Company in 1957. This pioneer of the automobile industry lacked neither promotional funds, expertise in engineering, or sophistication, but the Edsel proved to be a monumental failure.

This particular case has been analyzed from many different angles. The results of all available analyses point to one fundamental fact: the company tried to sell a product for which there was absolutely no need or desire at the time. This point cannot be over-emphasized. Vast amounts of money spent on advertising and publicity to promote a given brand of cigarettes will not persuade a strongly committed non-smoker to smoke.[32]

What then is the value of advertising? Why promote a product if consumers cannot be induced to purchase it? Is advertising a useless endeavour? Much to the contrary. As was shown throughout this text, advertising exerts a powerful influence on consumer behaviour. However, rather than creating needs, advertising stimulates existing needs. That is, it arouses latent needs that consumers do not feel strongly or consciously.

From a marketing standpoint, viewing advertising as creating needs negates the marketing concept. While these critics see manufacturers as making up products, and then creating the need for the product, marketers know the process goes in a reverse order. The marketer first recognizes, identifies, and discovers unsatisfied consumer needs in order to design products and services that are wanted and are acceptable to the consumers.

Should Advertising Use Emotional Appeals?

Rationality. Those who contend that advertising manipulates often point at the extensive use advertisers make of emotional appeals, especially for household or beauty care products. They imply that advertising should use only rational appeals, such as economy, or provide consumers with objective information about the physical characteristics of the product. Consider an advertiser faced with the problem of advertising a beauty care or grooming product. Obviously, this advertiser could advertise the product's price, its chemical ingredients, or any other objective characteristic of the product. But how would that relate to the profound motives of most people when they make such purchase decisions? Most buyers of beauty care or grooming products use such products in order to look attractive, to feel better, or for other emotional reasons.

When advertisers promise people that they will look more attractive if they use the brand, the advertiser attempts to use the same language the consumers probably use when they contemplate making such purchases. As was emphasized, consumers make choices and purchase choices (and the more so for products and services that have strong psychological and social meanings), by using a large number of criteria and dimensions, emotional as well as economic and objective. In other words, what economists or social critics label emotional appeal is what marketers call making a sales presentation that uses the consumers' logic and language. For marketers, even highly emotional motives are considered rational, because buyer behaviour is rational behaviour. The problem of many critics can often be traced to their denial of rationality to anyone who does not use their own value judgments and behaviour standards!

Puffery. Another dimension to this problem is whether it is legitimate for advertisers to promise greater attractiveness or to hint at irresistible success with the opposite sex if their products are purchased. Advertisers are often guilty of such puffery. Some critics would view these as outright deceptive claims, and in some ways, they are right. It is true that advertisers do not and cannot believe that their brand of detergent can fulfill a consumer's life. The real question is whether people can be deceived by such puffery.

Language is full of exaggeration, even if one ignores advertisements. Who has not been "terribly sorry" for some cigarette ashes falling on a carpet? Or who has never expressed "profound sympathy" to a neighbour who is experiencing some painful event? To highlight this point further, think of the cards that people send to their families and friends to celebrate the main events of their lives. From these cards one can draw a good sample of dramatized overstatements and could conclude that this type of language has become part of our culture. In the same way, people have become accustomed to advertising's inflated language and have learned to somewhat discount the hyperbole that is part of advertising. Such advertisements are effective not because they slightly exaggerate, but because they appeal to the right motivation.

Does Advertising Use Powerful Tools and Techniques?

The tools and techniques at the disposal of advertisers are far from perfect; they have only a limited effect even when they are properly used. Two common charges are that advertisers manipulate consumers into buying unwanted products and services through motivation research and subliminal advertising.

Motivation Research. The objective of motivation research is to unveil motives hidden or buried in consumers' subconscious mind. Such unconscious motives may explain purchasing patterns. Prune consumption has been reported to be associated in consumers' minds with old age and parental authority, or the purchase of a convertible car was subconsciously thought of as a substitute for a mistress.[33] When motivation research techniques were introduced, one author, Vance Packard, objected strongly to the manipulation of consumers. In the *Hidden Persuaders* he wrote:

People's surface desires, needs, and drives were probed in order to find their points of vulnerability. Among the surface motivating factors found in the emotional profile of most of us, for example, were the drive to conformity, need for oral stimulation, yearning for security. Once the points of vulnerability were isolated, the psychological hooks were fashioned and baited and placed deep in the merchandising sea for unwary prospective customers.[34]

However, motivation research soon revealed its limitations. The interpretation of the extensive psychological material gathered from consumers' in-depth interviews required more expertise than that of the personnel commonly working with the data. The relatively small sample sizes, with sometimes as few as 50 people, cast serious doubts on the findings of such research studies. Motivation researchers reached very different conclusions from an analysis of the same data. Even assuming that the interpretation of the data was correct, a substantial gap had to be filled before research results could be translated into "manipulative" and "effective" advertising campaigns.

For these reasons, motivation research has not lived up to its promise of being the advertiser's panacea. Today, it is mostly used as a first step in the qualitative research process that generally leads to the formulation of hypotheses about consumer behaviour that must be tested through large-scale surveys.

Subliminal Advertising. The effect of subliminal advertising, in which advertising messages are shown so fast that they fall below consumers' perceptual threshhold, is extremely limited. However, some critics have raised strong objections to its use on ethical grounds and have also attributed to advertisers the power of manipulating consumers through subliminal messages. Given the lack of positive evidence about its effectiveness and uncertainty about the ethical issues involved, subliminal advertising is not likely to become an actual advertising technique. An extensive review of the relevant literature concluded, "In general, the literature of subliminal perception shows that the most clearly documented effects are obtained only in highly contrived and artificial situations. These effects when present are brief and of small magnitude . . . These processes have no apparent relevance to the goals of advertising."[35]

From the evidence at hand, accusing advertisers of having at their disposal tools and techniques for manipulating consumers at a subconscious level overestimates grossly the power of these techniques. As has been seen, advertisers have only limited tools and techniques to deal with what is extremely complex and heterogeneous human behaviour. Accusing advertisers of being able to manipulate consumers reveals a fundamental misunderstanding of the advertising process and of consumer behaviour as well.

Are Children More Persuasible?

More serious is the argument that advertising induces children to desire objects that parents cannot afford or may not wish to give to their children. This has been a relatively recent concern with the increased presence of television and cable TV in North American homes. A study conducted in Canada concluded that children in homes with cable television watch more television and do more of that watching alone than children whose homes receive only conventional television.[36] This has led the province of Quebec to pass laws forbidding advertising directed at children and has also motivated formal research in the United States and Canada.

Are children especially persuasible through advertising? If so, until what age? Until they are 13 years old, as specified by Quebec law? One study conducted showed that toy advertising influenced children's choices, especially during the Christmas season.[37] Thus the effectiveness of advertising cannot be doubted. However, it also shows that the effects of advertising on children are relatively limited. Advertising increased by only 5 percent the quantity of toys and games chosen by children as Christmas presents (only for those items that were heavily advertised during the Christmas season). One other interesting fact is this: the increase was not related to the children's age, which was 7, 9, and 11 years. Another study arrived at identical conclusions and suggests that the effects of advertising on children may have been overestimated.[38] According to their results, children develop sceptical attitudes and defense mechanisms against advertising messages at an early age.

That children develop defense mechanisms against advertising was also demonstrated in a study which showed that children can detect the persuasive intent of an advertising message.[39] Furthermore, once a child can detect this intention, he reacts against the persuasion. According to the authors, a child capable of detecting a persuasive intent is less influenced by advertising because he places less confidence in it, likes the advertisement less, and tends to make less purchase demands.

Furthermore, the ability to recognize persuasive intent is directly related to a child's age. In the previous study, this ability was found in 53 percent of all first-graders, 87 percent of all third-graders, and 99 percent of fifth-graders. This has two implications for advertising: Since fifth-graders can be no more influenced than adults, the legal limit of 13 years of age is perhaps too high. Moreover, the ability to detect persuasive intent is directly related to age. However, for Jean Piaget, age represents two things:[40] maturity and acquired experience. Thus, isolating a child from advertising may delay the formation of the mechanisms through which he resists advertising persuasion. Some children, however, may be badly in need of these mechanisms in the first stages of adolescence. A study showed that a child's behaviour and attitudes are affected by advertising.[41] Furthermore, children who have the best chance of obtaining whatever they desire are the most affected. This suggests that advertising is more effective with children who know their parents are likely to give in to their demands. Another study points out that, just like adults, children are subject to advertising saturation effects. Thus, after a certain number of repetitions of the same commercial, the advertising effects would become negative.[42]

Thus research conducted in this field seems to conclude that the efficiency of advertising aimed at children, while real, has been somewhat exaggerated. Children perceive at quite an early stage the persuasive intent of an advertisement, develop perceptual mechanisms against it, are subject to the same saturation as adults, and are more influenced if they know parents are likely to give in to their demands. However, this does not mean that thay are fully inoculated against the persuasive intent of advertising.

Another interesting question is whether children exert pressure on parents and whether they give in. One study found only a slight correlation between five to ten year olds' attempts at exerting influence and the actual instances in which parents have given in to such pressure, when the age factor was not considered.[43] However, when age is considered, it was found that childrens' attempts to pressure parents decrease with age, and the instances in which parents give in to their children's demands increase with age. This phenomenon seems quite normal, since parents lend more judgment to their children as they grow older.[44] Parents often given in to their child's preferences when they lack other criteria on which to base their decision.

A study examined the influence of children on the choice of a particular brand of cereals.[45] Their findings suggest that mothers who cared a lot about their children were less likely to buy the cereals their children wanted than mothers who were less centered on their children. This conclusion suggests that mothers who care about their children's well-being buy what they deem best for their child rather than buying what the child wants.

These studies, although incomplete, point out that in general parents do not give in to pressure exerted by their children and that this pressure decreases as the child gets older. The role of parents as educators, particularly their role in informing their child's buying habits, must be underlined. However, a child is not always "a gullible agent working unknowingly for the manufacturer," who is used by the advertiser to influence parents. A child usually has more judgment than some people think. According to a study, children may show interest in advertisements directed at adults when they are concerned about the advertised product. Moreover, they can remember the product brands much better than their parents can.[46]

A child is not only an "agent" but also a consumer, who often disposes of limited purchasing power. In order to use this purchasing power in an intelligent way, a child needs and is entitled to relevant information provided by advertising.

Does Advertising Have Negative Social Effects?

There is a high level of subjectivity in this area of assessment of advertising effects, because it is related to social values, lifestyles, and tastes, and to our social and economic system.[47] Contradictory points of view can be quite legitimately held about the role and effects of advertising depending on one's values and views of what society is or should be. There is no one truth in this controversy over advertising because it is not a controversy over facts but over value systems.

There are two aspects of the argument over the possible negative social effects of advertising. First, some critics see advertising as a force that negatively affects our values and lifestyles. Other critics, without necessarily granting such power to advertising, deplore its "polluting" effects and argue that it undermines aesthetic and intellectual values.

Does Advertising Affect Values and Lifestyles Negatively?

Advertising has been accused of unduly raising the expectations of economically deprived segments of our society and of enhancing materialistic values. Others point out that it promotes undesirable social stereotypes, for example, the stereotyping of women.

Advertising, Social Discontent, and Materialism. The process through which advertising is seen to lead to consumer discontent and/or materialism is outlined in Figure 17–6. By making consumers aware of products and services and by inducing them to buy, advertising encourages consumers to desire products that they would not even dream of if they were not advertised. If a consumer cannot financially afford the advertised and desired product, advertising can lead to frustration and discontent. This problem is more acute for consumers who are not affluent and who must cope with many advertising stimuli.

If consumers can afford to buy the advertised products, critics argue that advertising fosters materialism. Materialism refers to excessive importance

FIGURE 17–6

Possible Effects of Advertising on Consumers' Discontent or Materialism

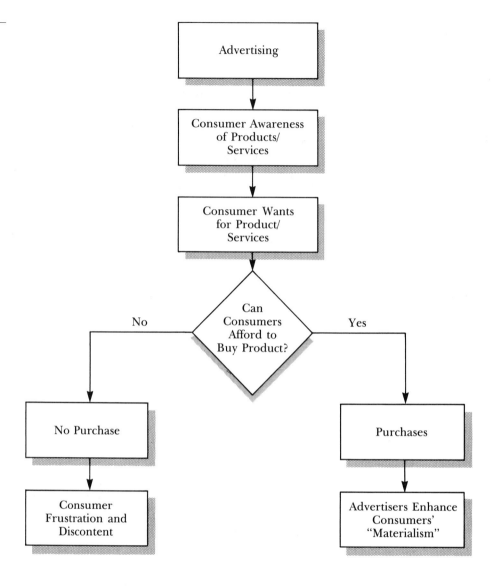

given to material welfare as compared to such non-material values as love, freedom, and intellectual development.

Following this line of thought, advertising involves negative social effects by the mere fact of generating consumer wants. This proposition is related to the charge that advertising can create unwarranted needs and wants. As has been pointed out, "Much of the criticism that advertising sells people things they do not need is directed more at the fact that people buy things the critic does not think they should want."[48] Thus, if consumers are considered to be adults who should enjoy freedom of choice, this argument does not hold unless one believes that wants are legitimate when they originate from the individual and are not induced by such external forces as advertising. This view emanates from the economic theory that resource allocation should serve consumers and should maximize consumers' satisfaction; it should not be in the hands of persuaders or advertisers. This view of our society is somewhat naive. Advertising is only one stimulus that consumers receive about products and services. Even if consumers—financially deprived or not—could be completely isolated from advertising, they would see expensive cars in the streets, they could see displays of fine foods in supermarkets or luxury clothes in stores, see well-off people consuming all kinds of goods that they sometimes could afford, and sometimes not. Consequently, although the argument of consumer discontent and materialism may be valid, it cannot be attributed to advertising alone. The criticism should be more adequately addressed to our society and our economic system, which favour and are built on mass consumption. Advertising is part of the system because it is an institution designed to serve this society and this economic system. However, if the value system on which society is built or its economic system are responsible for people's discontent or materialism, it is useless and misleading to attack an institution that is only one of its logical consequences; the debate should focus instead on the roots of the problem rather than on its symptoms.

Those who blame advertising for being the result of our economic system should remember that whatever the social and political system, advertising must play a part because it fulfills essential economic functions. For example, long before the "perestroïka", the U.S.S.R. reintroduced advertising:

Thanks to well-organized advertising, the consumer can more rapidly find the goods needed by him, purchase them with a smaller expenditure of time, and select the goods according to his taste . . . This function of advertising not only reflects the new relation of the consumer, care about the population, and its needs, but it also has important economic significance. It creates the precondition for a more economic and rational use of material goods which are created by society, and permits a more satisfied consumer.[49]

The report of the Prairie Provinces Royal Commission on Consumer Problems and Inflation commented:

Though advertising has long been regarded by the Russians as the result of sinful capitalist aggression for markets, the overwhelming requirement for information for the consumer simply forces the acceptance of this solution.[50]

Those who are satisfied with our economic system do not always view consumer discontent as an evil. Of course, if discontent is the chronic state of a consumer with low economic status, it is certainly regrettable. But instead of hiding goods from the sight of the poor, a more logical approach to the problem is to improve their economic welfare until they can afford these products. Here again, this is a social problem that goes well beyond the effects of advertising. Moreover, the proponents of our economic system argue that consumer discontent in not so extreme cases may be an economic catalyst, since major innovations and inventions have evolved from consumer discontent.

As for the third relationship in Figure 17–6, which specifies that consumers who want and purchase goods pursue materialistic goals, it can be argued that people often buy products to pursue non-materialistic goals. For instance, one may purchase products as gifts to express love or esteem, or books and records for intellectual development. In our society, consumption has become one of the most natural ways by which one achieves even non-material goals. Here again, the argument implies a condemnation of the Western way of life, which relies heavily on mass consumption.

The argument that advertising leads to consumer discontent and materialism can be differently appreciated by the proponents and critics of advertising. However, as advertising is an institution of the free enterprise economic system, it tends to foster the values and principles on which this society is built. But it is only one and probably not the strongest of the forces that shape values and culture. The divergent views about the social effects of advertising often point to different beliefs about what society should be.

Advertising and Stereotypes. Advertising messages sometimes feature "slices of life"; they picture consumers in various roles and situations, as they are—or supposedly are—in their daily lives. Inasmuch as advertising assigns definite roles to various types of individuals, such as minority groups or women, it can promote or perpetuate certain stereotypes. This is true of any mass communication. This argument against advertising originated in the United States when minority groups, particularly blacks, accused advertisers of picturing them in low status roles. Since the 1970s advertisers have used "integrated" advertising, which portrays blacks in higher status roles.[51]

More recently, women's associations have charged that advertisers portray women in limited and traditional roles, such as housewives, clerks, or secretaries, and seldom in higher occupational levels. As put by Robert Oliver, then president of the Canadian Advertising Advisory Board:

If advertising does help perpetuate such stereotypes, does it, in the process, erect one more psychological barrier to human freedom? To the degree that it does, is this aspect of advertising not a negative social force? Do some advertising portrayals by their very nature constitute an affront to women?[52]

These questions have led to a number of studies in the United States[53] and in Canada. A 1971 study of 729 advertisements in eight general interest magazines concluded that feminists were at least partially justified in saying that women were not portrayed in the variety of roles they actually play in American society. Most frequently, women's roles were stereotyped as follows:

• Women do not make important decisions.
• Women need men's protection.
• A woman's place is in the home.
• Men regard women essentially as sex objects.[54]

Subsequent studies[55,56] showed that between 1959 and 1971 the stereotypes of women were unchanged, except for a substantial decrease in the number of women portrayed as sex objects.[57]

In a cross-cultural study involving 2977 general interest magazine advertisements carried out in 1975 and involving the U.S., Canada (French and English), the U.K., and France, it was found that women are not caricatured in magazine advertisements as useless, decorative sex objects any more than men. Female decorative models outnumber male models in such advertisements because women's clothing and beauty products are more heavily advertised in magazines. It was found that in Canada, discrimination in advertising role portrayal focuses more on social class than sex; for example, blue collar workers are severely underrepresented.[58] Finally, a study involving 861 advertisements in eight magazines published in 1981 suggested that "although the portrayal of women in traditional roles had declined, their projected image continues to be narrow and limited."[59]

Thus there is empirical evidence to suggest that advertisers have lagged behind in portraying women in new roles. One explanation could be that advertisers fear to arouse negative reactions from audiences if they use a so-called liberated type of advertising. However, one study conducted in 1976 by the Task Force on Women and Advertising sponsored by the Canadian Advertising Advisory Board concluded that the fear that such advertising would lack impact and arouse negative reactions is unwarranted. On the contrary, such messages tend to be more successful than the traditional type of message.[60] These results were confirmed to a large extent by another study.[61] Similar conclusions were reached by a study on integrated advertising in the United States, which found that such advertising tended to have positive effects on black audiences, and a neutral impact on white audiences.[62]

One might question whether advertising should promote new ideas and/ or fight undesirable social stereotypes or should communicate effectively with markets. As the role of women in society changes, it is normal and probably more efficient for advertisers to picture women in new roles. Note that the Canadian Advertising Foundation has published some guidelines about sex-role stereotyping which have been already endorsed by the major advertising assocations in this country.[63] Advertisers should not be geared to the past but should reflect the values and lifestyles of the market rather than represent what society could or should be. As the task force on women reported:

. . . At the same time, today's woman becomes irritated by advertising that shows women and men in an exaggerated and unrealistic way. For maximum effectiveness, the advertisers must understand the reality of today's women and ensure that the portrayals of both women and men are genuine (or reflect that reality).[64]

Does Advertising Have "Polluting" Effects?

Advertising is omnipresent. If all or part of what consumers see or hear in commercials and advertisements offend their feelings or aesthetic values, then advertising can be considered a polluting agent. Commercials are often criticized for being too loud, repetitive, or boring, for overusing sex or fear appeals, or emphasizing sensitive product classes, such as products that some consumers would not like to see openly advertised or even talked about, for example, personal hygiene products, drugs, or alcoholic beverages. Also criticized are commercials that insult consumers' intelligence, use unpleasant or stupid jingles, or carry messages that are dishonest or misleading.[65]

Advertising and Bad Taste. Taste is not universal. What is considered good taste by some individuals may be viewed as stupid or offensive by others. This is true of advertising as of anything else. Rock music may be considered sheer noise by classical music lovers. All gourmets do not favour the same dishes, and the list could go on. Consequently, it is inevitable that advertising messages are diversely evaluated and judged by various segments of the market.

Not all advertising to which the public is exposed is conceived and created by responsible professionals. Some advertising is also the work of individuals with the unfortunate marketing philosophy of selling at any cost. These people have typically little concern about the aesthetic value of their advertisements. It is true that a certain percentage (it is hoped a small one) of advertisements fall into the latter category, but this is sufficient to give the entire advertising industry a poor image. Just as a single misdeed can spoil an individual's reputation for exemplary behaviour, a few poorly conceived advertisements can give advertising a reputation of bad taste, in spite of a substantial proportion of well-conceived and responsible advertisements.

Consumers may see bad taste in some advertisements as the result of what has been called "imperfect segmentation."[66] Because the media cannot perfectly match advertisers' desired target audience, some consumers may see or hear what is not intended for them. Messages that are designed specifically for certain market segments may be considered silly or offensive by others. As was pointed out:

. . . To the extent that pinpoint accuracy cannot be accomplished, we must logically expect some messages to fall on the "wrong" ears. Or, what is the same thing, we will encounter messages so compromised by the "general" nature of the audience that they are very likely to offend with their blandness. It is particularly true of our general media—television and general appeal printed media—that a pinpoint matching of messages and tastes is very nearly impossible.[67]

The question concerning stereotypes applies to the taste or aesthetics of advertisements: Should advertisers be concerned with and try to promote good taste, or should they be interested only in the long-run efficiency of their communications with the market? Evidence suggests that very pleasant and very unpleasant advertisements are more effective than those in between.[68] Obviously, the two objectives can be somewhat reconciled. Shouldn't a lawyer take into account the laws or the facts of a case when delivering an effective address to the court? Can't an architect design a masterpiece and still meet the functional constraints for the building? In the same way, advertisers should reconcile art and marketing communications. Their responsibility is to translate selling arguments into words and images that are likely to induce consumers to buy what the economy has produced for them.

Truth in Advertising. The charge that advertising is dishonest and tells lies or only half-truths is often raised. Although the public may tend to put all advertisements in the same category several situations should be recognized. Some advertisements may constitute outright lies, for instance, claiming that a product does things that it cannot do, or is made of substances it does not contain, or has characteristics it does not possess. In such cases, there is an obvious and deliberate intent to deceive and mislead consumers to get them to buy the advertised product, whether or not the product can provide the promised satisfaction. All professional advertisers vigorously condemn such practices. Besides the fact that such practices are illegal, advertisers who subscribe to the Canadian Code of Advertising Standards are not likely to indulge in unethical practices.

The argument of half-truth is more subtle. Advertisers of two competitive products might both claim that their respective products are the best or the first. Some advertisers might also claim that their product is, for example, unbreakable. Besides exaggeration, which dramatizes the product and would not deceive most consumers, advertisers could claim the superiority of their product by referring to specific functions or characteristics, or to a specific usage occasion, or they could use a different product category than that used by a competitor making a similar claim. Sometimes there are subtle and very technical arguments involved in these claims that are impossible to explain in a short commercial. Obviously, in such cases consumers receive imperfect information, but it is not possible for an advertiser in a 30-second commercial or in a half page ad to give all the facts. Consequently, advertisers must exercise judgment as to what should be said to consumers. It is only logical that the facts or aspects of the product that give a differential advantage over competitive products would be emphasized.

In the same way, claiming that a product is unbreakable seems to be an outright exaggeration. There is no such thing as an unbreakable product, provided the proper destructive means are employed. An unbreakable watch would not resist a streamroller. What the advertiser's claim generally means is that a product is unbreakable under normal and typical usage conditions. Here again, because of time and space constraints and because of the need to sustain consumers' attention and interest for extended periods, advertisers are obliged to use short-cuts that may seem to be, if not pure lies, at least overstatements or part-truths. Do consumers really need to know that an unbreakable watch could not actually resist a streamroller?

Conclusions on the Social Effects of Advertising

In general, it can be said that advertising's effects on consumer behaviour have been somewhat overestimated. Advertising cannot create consumer needs. It can stimulate latent needs, perhaps unconsciously felt by the consumers, but does not manipulate consumers.

Whether advertising has undesirable social effects on value systems, lifestyles, on social discontent, whether it is deceptive, or in bad taste, or perpetuates undesirable stereotypes, are more complex issues to assess. There are a number of situations ranging from a minority of outright deceptive and unprofessional advertisements, which are vigorously condemned by the advertising industry, to well done, professional, and sometimes artistic advertising.

Thus the quality of advertising should not be the subject of unwarranted generalizations. Another important conclusion is that the quarrel between critics and advocates of advertising often rests on a criticism or a defense of the social and economic system and values that are based on free enterprise and stress mass consumption.

Advertising is a tool, and a tool is never good or bad in itself. Rather, those who handle the tool can make good or bad use of it. In the same way, critics should address many of their questions to our social system, which uses advertising as one of its efficient and logical institutions.

CONSUMER PROTECTION

We have seen that it is extremely difficult to assess the true impact of advertising on the economy and on our social and personal lives. The mechanisms through which advertising exerts its influence are complex, and every argument that can be advanced for or against advertising can be matched by counter-arguments. This leads to the question how consumers are and should be protected against the potential abuses of advertisers and against advertising that they judge offensive or in bad taste. Consumers can find some protection through the law, by the self-regulation of the advertising industry, and they can also protect themselves.

Legal Protection

In Canada consumers have some legal protection. Parts of the Criminal Code forbid, at a penalty, the publishing of outright falsehoods. However, because the advertising process is so complex, it is often difficult to ascertain what exactly constitutes a falsehood. Since consumers have failed so far to bring pressure to bear on attorneys-general to have charges laid under the provisions of the Criminal Code, there is no body of case law on which to rely. The lack of misleading advertising cases tried under the Criminal Code may be due to the extent of federal and provincial legislation restricting advertising content in Canada.

Nevertheless, under the various sales of goods acts, consumers have recourse against manufacturers when products do not perform as specified. As stated in the report of the Prairie Provinces Royal Commission on Consumer Problems and Inflation, this is of limited value:

First, just what it was said the good in question would do, and under what conditions, is not usually easy to establish in sufficiently precise terms to secure a judgement in the consumer's favour. Second, and much more important, it is usually too costly to obtain recourse in view of the expected recovery. The law, then, contains only limited attempts to grapple with potential abuses in advertising, and such legal enactions as there are have experienced only very limited application and enforcement.[69]

Most provinces find it more efficient to enforce consumer legislation that is more specific about the acceptability of product and service representation. Canada does not have a body similar to the U.S. Federal Trade Commission, which can order advertising campaigns to be stopped without going through full criminal proceedings against the advertiser. However, there are a number of Canadian federal and provincial regulations that deal with advertising. Although much of the legislation deals with broadcast advertising, some laws, such as the Competition Act and the provincial consumer protection acts, deal with any form of advertising.

What characterizes the Canadian legislation about advertising is the great number of laws and bills both at the federal and the provincial levels that attempt to constrain the work of advertisers. As was pointed out, ". . . there are possibly more active curbs and constraints on advertising and marketing in Canada than in any other business-oriented society."[70] This legislation is changing and growing rapidly, which made the same author write: "If Canada's past is any forecast of its future, then governments, crown corporations, trade associations, and consumerists will soon make yesterday's controls look archaic and mild."[71]

Federal Government Regulations[72]

The main pieces of federal legislation dealing with advertising are listed in Figure 17–7.

One of the most important pieces of federal legislation concerning advertising is the Competition Act (see Figure 17–8, on pages 490 to 492).

The Competition Act does not require advertisers to clear advertisements prior to publication. Moreover, advertisers have the option to use the so-called program of compliance. According to this program, advertisers may submit advertising material to the Marketing Practices Branch of the Bureau of Competition Policy of the Department of Consumer and Corporate Affairs. Advertisers are then notified whether action will be taken on the material submitted.

FIGURE 17–7
Federal Legislation Affecting Advertising

FEDERAL ACTS

Broadcasting Act (Sections 5, 8, 8a, 8c, 16)

Regulations: 9) Advertising Generally
10) Liquor, Beer, Wine, and Cider Beer, Wine, and Cider Advertising Criteria
11) Food and Drugs, Proprietary or Patent Medicines

Circulars
Clearance of Food and Drug Commercials
Food Advertising
Registration Procedures for TV Commercials

Canadian Human Rights Act
Competition Act
Consumer Packaging & Labelling Act
Copyright Act
Criminal Code
Department of National Revenue— Customs and Excise Tariff item 99221-1, Schedule C, June 30, 1972
Food & Drug Act
Hazardous Products Act
Income Tax Act (Section 19)
National Trade Mark & True Labelling Act
Official Languages Act
Textile Labelling Act
Trade Marks Act

36. (1) No person shall, for the purpose of promoting, directly or indirectly, the supply or use of a product or for the purpose of promoting, directly or indirectly, any business interest, by any means whatever,

(*a*) make a representation to the public that is false or misleading in a material respect;

(*b*) make a representation to the public in the form of a statement, warranty or guarantee of the performance, efficacy or length of life of a product that is not based on an adequate and proper test thereof, the proof of which lies upon the person making the representation;

(*c*) make a representation to the public in a form that purports to be

(i) a warranty or guarantee of a product, or

(ii) a promise to replace, maintain or repair an article or any part thereof or to repeat or continue a service until it has achieved a specified result

if such form of purported warranty or guarantee or promise is materially misleading or if there is no reasonable prospect that it will be carried out; or

(*d*) make a materially misleading representation to the public concerning the price at which a product or like products have been, are or will be ordinarily sold; and for the purposes of this paragraph a representation as to price is deemed to refer to the price at which the product has been sold by sellers generally in the relevant market unless it is clearly specified to be the price at which the product has been sold by the person by whom or on whose behalf the representation is made.

(2) For the purposes of this section and section 36.1, a representation that is

(*a*) expressed on an article offered or displayed for sale, its wrapper or container,

(*b*) expressed on anything attached to, inserted in or accompanying an article offered or displayed for sale, its wrapper or container, or anything on which the article is mounted for display or sale,

(*c*) expressed on an in-store or other point-of-purchase display,

(*d*) made in the course of in-store, door-to-door or telephone selling to a person as ultimate user, or

(*e*) contained in or on anything that is sold, sent, delivered, transmitted or in any other manner whatever made available to a member of the public,

shall be deemed to be made to the public by and only by the person who caused the representation to be so expressed, made or contained and, where that person is outside Canada, by

(*f*) the person who imported the article into Canada, in a case described in paragraph (*a*), (*b*) or (*e*), and

(*g*) the person who imported the display into Canada, in a case described in paragraph (*c*).

FIGURE 17–8

Abstract from the Competition Act

Source: Department of Justice Canada Competition Act (Ottawa: 1986).

Reproduced with the permission of the Minister of Supply and Services Canada, 1990.

Television advertising of food, drugs, cosmetics, health devices, beer, and wine comes directly under the control of the Canadian Radio-Television and Telecommunications Commission (CRTC). Radio and television broadcast regulations required that the Food and Drug Directorate, Health Protection Branch, Health and Welfare Canada, pre-clear all drug, cosmetic, health devices, and broadcast advertising. They also require that all food broadcast advertising be pre-cleared by the Department of Consumer and Corporate Affairs. The CRTC sets technical standards, such as 12 minutes of advertising per hour, prohibits subliminal advertising, and sets standards for good taste. It is also involved in licensing stations and setting regulations for programming.[73]

The CRTC together with the provinces review liquor, wine, and beer advertising; each province has a liquor control board with a different set of standards for the amount and kind of liquor, beer, and wine advertising that can appear in all media. Some provinces do not allow any liquor advertising. In addition, all commercials to be aired on the CBC require preclearance.

(3) Subject to subsection (2), every one who, for the purpose of promoting, directly or indirectly, the supply or use of a product or any business interest, supplies to a wholesaler, retailer or other distributor of a product any material or thing that contains a representation of a nature referred to in subsection (1) shall be deemed to have made that representation to the public.

General impression to be considered

(4) In any prosecution for a violation of this section, the general impression conveyed by a representation as well as the literal meaning thereof shall be taken into account in determining whether or not the representation is false or misleading in a material respect.

Punishment

(5) Any person who violates subsection (1) is guilty of an offence and is liable

(*a*) on conviction on indictment, to a fine in the discretion of the court or to imprisonment for five years or to both; or

(*b*) on summary conviction, to a fine of twenty-five thousand dollars or to imprisonment for one year or to both. R.S., c. C-23, s. 36; 1974-75-76, c. 76, s. 18.

Representation as to reasonable test and publication of testimonials

36.1 (1) No person shall, for the purpose of promoting, directly or indirectly, the supply or use of any product, or for the purpose of promoting, directly or indirectly, any business interest

(*a*) make a representation to the public that a test as to the performance, efficacy or length of life of the product has been made by any person, or

(*b*) publish a testimonial with respect to the product,

except where he can establish that

(*c*) the representation or testimonial was previously made or published by the person by whom the test was made or the testimonial was given, as the case may be, or

(*d*) the representation or testimonial was, before being made or published, approved and permission to make or publish it was given in writing by the person by whom the test was made or the testimonial was given, as the case may be,

and the representation or testimonial accords with the representation or testimonial previously made, published or approved.

Punishment

(2) Any person who violates subsection (1) is guilty of an offence and is liable

(*a*) on conviction on indictment, to a fine in the discretion of the court or to imprisonment for five years, or to both; or

(*b*) on summary conviction, to a fine of twenty-five thousand dollars or to imprisonment for one year or to both. 1974-75-76, c. 76, s. 18.

Double ticketing

36.2 (1) No person shall supply a product at a price that exceeds the lowest of two or more prices clearly expressed by him or on his behalf, in respect of the product in the quantity in which it is so supplied and at the time at which it is so supplied,

(*a*) on the product, its wrapper or container;

FIGURE 17–8
Continued

Provincial Government Regulations

The main provincial laws that deal with advertising are listed in Figure 17–9 on page 493.

Various provincial consumer protection and trade practices acts affect advertising in all media in that they deal with "representations made . . .," and "paid messages . . .," when outlining laws on misleading advertising and trade practices.[74]

Some Possible Effects of Canadian Legislation

These laws and bills constraining advertising in Canada are the result of a long history during which pieces of legislation have been added over the last few decades. Presently, the control of Canadian advertising is characterized by "fragmental law and piecemeal regulation."[75] What have been the effects of this legislation on advertising in Canada?

(*b*) on anything attached to, inserted in or accompanying the product, its wrapper or container or anything on which the product is mounted for display or sale; or

(*c*) on an in-store or other point-of-purchase display or advertisement.

Punishment

(2) Any person who violates subsection (1) is guilty of an offence and is liable on summary conviction to a fine not exceeding ten thousand dollars or to imprisonment for one year or to both. 1974-75-76, c. 76, s. 18.

Definition of "scheme of pyramid selling"

36.3 (1) For the purposes of this section, "scheme of pyramid selling" means

(*a*) a scheme for the sale or lease of a product whereby one person (the "first" person) pays a fee to participate in the scheme and receives the right to receive a fee, commission or other benefit

(i) in respect of the recruitment into the scheme of other persons either by the first person or any other person, or

(ii) in respect of sales or leases made, other than by the first person, to other persons recruited into the scheme by the first person or any other person; and

(*b*) a scheme for the sale or lease of a product whereby one person sells or leases a product to another person (the "second" person) who receives the right to receive a rebate, commission or other benefit in respect of sales or leases of the same or another product that are not

(i) sales or leases made to the second person,

(ii) sales or leases made by the second person, or

(iii) sales or leases, made to ultimate consumers or users of the same or other product, to which no right of further participation in the scheme, immediate or contingent, is attached.

Pyramid selling

(2) No person shall induce or invite another person to participate in a scheme of pyramid selling.

Punishment

(3) Any person who violates subsection (2) is guilty of an offence and is liable

(*a*) on conviction on indictment, to a fine in the discretion of the court or to imprisonment for five years or to both; or

(*b*) on summary conviction, to a fine of twenty-five thousand dollars or to imprisonment for one year or to both.

Where pyramid selling permitted by province

(4) This section does not apply in respect of a scheme of pyramid selling that is licensed or otherwise permitted by or pursuant to an Act of the legislature of a province. 1974-75-76, c. 76, s. 18.

FIGURE 17–8
Continued

Some authors have questioned the benefits of Canadian advertising legislation. For instance, "Whenever regulations fail to specify adequate models of audience behaviour [and the authors demonstrate they do], the quality of regulation will suffer. Such questionable quality in the face of increasing government costs suggests that the answer to the question: 'It is worth it?' is a simple: 'No'."[76]

However, despite the need for simplification and unification of Canadian advertising laws, the regulations have decreased the amount of advertising that is in poor taste or misleading. In addition, the complexity of Canadian law might have been a factor in inducing Canadian advertisers to develop stricter codes of ethics. By adhering to such codes, advertisers can stay within the limits of the law. Enforcement of advertising legislation has given way to new advertising practices, i.e., comparative advertising and corrective advertising.

Comparative advertising[77] has been encouraged by the Federal Trade Commission since 1972. The underlying assumption of the legislator was

FIGURE 17–9 ———————
*Provincial Legislation
Affecting Advertising*

PROVINCIAL ACTS

Alberta
The Unfair Trade Practices Act
Credit and Loan Agreements Act
Liquor, Beer, and Wine
    Advertising Regulations

British Columbia
Trade Practices Act
Consumer Protection Act and
    Regulations
Closing Out Sales Act
Motor Dealer Guidelines
Liquor, Beer, and Wine
    Advertising Regulations

Ontario
Business Practices Act
Consumer Protection Act
Human Rights Code
Regulation 128 (Credit Advertising)
Liquor Control Act

Quebec
Charter of the French Language
Regulations—Language of
    Business and Commerce
Consumer Protection Act
Regulation—Children's Advertising
Lotteries Act
Broadcast Advertising Tax Act
Agricultural Products and Food Act
Liquor, Beer, and Wine
    Advertising Regulations
Pharmacy, Professional Advertising
    Regulations
Roadside Advertising Act
Quebec Class Actions Act

Saskatchewan
Consumer Products Warranties Act
Cost of Credit Disclosure Act
Liquor, Beer, and Wine
    Advertising Regulations

Manitoba
Consumer Protection Act
Trade Practices Inquiry Act
Liquor, Beer, and Wine
    Advertising Regulations

New Brunswick
Consumer Product Warranty and
    Liability Act
Cost of Credit Disclosure Act

Nova Scotia
Consumer Protection Act
Liquor, Beer, and Wine
    Advertising Regulations

Prince Edward Island
Business Practices Act
Consumer Protection Act
Highway Advertisements Act
Liquor, Beer, and Wine
    Advertising Regulations

Newfoundland
Trade Practices Act
Consumer Protection Act
Exhibition of Advertisements Act
Liquor, Beer, and Wine
    Advertising Regulations

that naming competing brands would oblige advertisers to be more truthful about their claims. This was followed in 1976 by guidelines issued by the Federal Department of Consumer and Corporate Affairs concerning comparative advertising.

Ever since, advertisers have had mixed reactions about this form of advertising. Some argue that comparative advertising gives better information to the consumers. Critics charge that it confuses consumers and increases scepticism about advertising or that such advertising benefits the competitors named in the advertisements. Research in the United States[78] and in Canada[79] has failed so far to show clear consumer benefits from comparative advertising.

Advertisers may use corrective advertising as a defence for misleading representations. Misleading advertisements must be the result of an error, reasonable precautions must have been taken to prevent the error, and the corrective advertisement must be placed immediately and so as to reach the same audience as effectively.[80]

In the United States, corrective advertising is used by the courts as a sanction against advertisers convicted for misleading advertising. Because an advertisement can be established as misleading only after its publication, corrective advertising is needed to deprive advertisers of these "immoral" gains, as well as to rectify consumers' false information. In view of its possible future application to the Canadian scene, there are five unresolved issues about corrective advertising:[81]

1. What objectives can corrective advertising effectively pursue?
2. Does misleading advertising have long-run effects on consumers, in order to justify the need for corrective advertisements?
3. Can consumers be "inoculated" against corrective advertising by actions of the firm?[82]
4. What is the optimal time lag between the false and the corrective advertisements?
5. What should be the best duration, budget, copy, and media to run corrective advertisements?[83]

Unfortunately, few of these questions have been answered, which reinforces the point that U.S. and Canadian advertising legislation is built on belief rather than fact.[84]

Clearly, some advertising legislation is needed in order to prevent abuse by unscrupulous advertisers. A large body of laws is in force in Canada, but it is largely piecemeal legislation, and is not necessarily based on sound consumer and advertising research.

Protection Through Industry Self-Regulation

Canadian advertising agencies and advertisers have set up codes of conduct that are designed to keep high standards of ethics in the profession. These codes have been developed through a consensus reached among advertisers, advertising agencies, the media, government departments, and the Consumers' Association of Canada. Although these codes are adhered to on a voluntary basis, once they are endorsed by the various industry bodies, they take on a different status. Because all national media associations subscribe to these codes, they agree that if the Advertising Standards Council finds an advertisement that does not conform to the code, and if the advertiser refuses to withdraw or amend this advertisement, the media are notified and must stop its distribution.[85] Figure 17–10 lists the main self-regulatory codes in force in Canada.

One of the most important self-regulation codes is the Canadian Code of Advertising Standards (Figure 17–11). The code is written in clear and concise

FIGURE 17–10

Industry Codes Regulating Advertising

Courtesy Canadian Advertising Foundation

INDUSTRY CODES

Broadcast Code for Advertising to Children
Canadian Code of Advertising Standards
CBC Advertising Standards
Code of Consumer Advertising Practices for Cosmetics, Toiletries and Fragrances
Code of Consumer Advertising Practices for Non-Prescription Medicines
Direct Marketing Code of Advertising for Horticultural Products
Guidelines for the Use of Comparative Advertising in Food Commercials
Guidelines for the use of Research and Survey Data in Comparative Food Commercials

Pharmaceutical Advertising Advisory Board Code of Advertising Acceptance
Telecaster Committee of Canada Guidelines
Television Code of Standards for the Advertising of Feminine Sanitary Protection Products

The Advertising Standards Council are independent, autonomous bodies, founded and funded by advertisers, advertising agencies and media through the Canadian Advertising Foundation.

FIGURE 17–11

The Canadian Code of Advertising Standards

By permission of the Canadian Advertising Foundation

Advertising's Self-Regulatory Process

The Canadian Code of Advertising Standards was originally sponsored by the Canadian Advertising Advisory Board. First published in 1963, it was revised and republished by the CAAB in 1967.

This latest edition was developed by the Copy Standards Committee.

Since 1967, this Code has been supplemented by several other industry Codes, an on-going process. These Codes are administered by the Advertising Standards Councils and le Conseil des normes de la publicité. The Council in Toronto handles all national advertising complaints and complaints from the Ontario region, when these concern English-language advertising; complaints from Quebec, and all national French-language complaints, are handled by le Conseil in Montreal.

Across the country Regional Councils — in the Atlantic Provinces (Halifax), Manitoba (Winnipeg), Saskatchewan (Regina), Alberta (Calgary and Edmonton), and British Columbia (Vancouver) — handle local advertising complaints in their respective areas. All Councils include representatives from all three sectors — advertiser, media, and advertising agency — as well as public representatives, many of whom are nominees of the Consumers' Association of Canada.

Advertisers, their agencies and the media have agreed that all broadcast commercials directed to children and that English-language televised commercials for feminine sanitary products should be cleared by special committees of the Council prior to station acceptance. (The CRTC has made adherence to the Broadcast Code for Advertising to Children part of a station's licensing agreement). Scripts and storyboards are checked by Council staff, but a final approval number is not given until the finished commercial has been reviewed by the Council's Clearance Committee, which includes public representatives.

A PAAB Code of Advertising Acceptance applies to advertisements for pharmaceutical products appearing in the health-services magazines — directed to doctors, dentists, hygienists, nurses and pharmacists. Such messages must also be approved before media acceptance. Because these messages are often highly technical, they are not cleared through the Advertising Standards Council but by the Commissioner of the Pharmaceutical Advertising Advisory Board of which the ASC is a member.

Role and Responsibilities of Council

The Advertising Standards Council and the regional Councils, which include public and business representatives, are autonomous bodies within their area, established and funded by advertisers, media and advertising agencies, to enforce codes of standards adopted voluntarily by the advertising community, and to

(i) Work with industry and consumer bodies in developing, updating, administering and publicizing industry standards and codes of ethics, and to initiate related research.

(ii) Review and resolve complaints regarding advertisements and, where necessary, initiate such complaints.

(iii) Provide advice to individual advertisers and agencies on laws, regulations, standards and codes affecting advertising.

(iv) Issue position papers and advice on matters of social concern related to advertising's self-regulatory process.

(v) Maintain contact with government, educators and other public interest groups regarding self-regulation.

How to Complain

If you see or hear advertising carried by Canadian media that you feel contravenes one of the industry Codes, write to the Advertising Standards Council nearest you. (The Councils, of course, have no control over advertising carried by non-Canadian media.) If it is a print advertisement, it helps if you can enclose a copy of the advertisement; with a broadcast message, give the station, approximate time, the name of the product, etc. If you have a complaint form or coupon to fill out, fine; if not, just say why you think the message contravenes the Code.

The addresses of the various Councils are listed on pages 13 and 14 of this folder.

What Will Happen?

Your complaint will be acknowledged and reviewed. If it appears the Code has been violated, Council staff will get in touch with the advertiser directly. In most cases corrective action follows. Where the advertiser or complainant disagrees with staff findings, the matter may be referred to the full Council. If Council sustains the complaint, the advertiser is notified, and asked to amend or withdraw the advertising. Generally, this closes the matter. Regardless of whether the complaint has been sustained or not, you will be notified of the outcome.

Occasionally an advertiser will refuse to take corrective action. The Council then notifies the media involved, or will sometimes ask that a bulletin be sent to all association members of those media, indicating that this message, in Council's judgement, contravenes the Code. In effect, this means media will not accept the message in its existing form.

Background

In adopting this Canadian Code of Advertising Standards, the participating organizations are fully conscious of the dynamic role advertising plays in the Canadian economy.

Advertising is a communication channel that benefits both the buyer and the seller. Consumers benefit through easy access to low-cost information on the availability or prices of goods and services and news of improved or new products and services; sellers through advertising expand their markets and find new ones.

In an agro-industrial economy such as ours, advertising also contributes very directly to the country's economic well-being. By stimulating sales it helps to provide jobs and to pay wages, taxes and dividends; by helping sustain and level out the mass production process it often contributes to lower unit costs and stability of employment.

FIGURE 17–11
Continued

As advertising volume increases, so does the responsibility of the industry to the Canadian consumer and the community. The average citizen is now exposed daily to an estimated several hundred advertising messages. It is therefore important that advertising be prepared in ways that respect the taste and values of the public at large. In a society that recognizes the equality of the sexes, advertising should also reflect an awareness of and a sensitivity to this reality and to other human rights issues.

Through the adoption of this Code of Advertising Standards, the participating organizations undertake to apply high ethical standards to the preparation and execution of Canadian advertising. It is their desire and intention to make advertising more effective by continuing to raise the standard of advertising excellence and by ensuring integrity in advertising content.

This Code in no way replaces any existing standards which have been meant to meet the individual needs of media and association groups in Canada. The various Code clauses are supplementary to those standards and to federal, provincial and municipal regulations affecting advertising. (See listing of Federal and Provincial legislation at the back of this booklet).

Communications regarding the interpretation and application of the Code should be addressed to Advertising Standards Council, 350 Bloor Street East, Suite 402, Toronto, Ontario, M4W 1H5 or le Conseil des normes de la publicité, 4823 ouest, rue Sherbrooke, suite 130, Montréal, Québec, H3Z 1G7.

Definition of Advertising

For the purpose of this Code, advertising is defined as any paid communication, addressed to the public or a portion thereof, for the purpose of influencing the opinion or behaviour of those addressed.

The various clauses in the Code apply to all such messages (with the exception noted below) in all media, and to all components thereof.

Exception:
The ASC does not rule on election campaign advertising, partly because of the constraints of time and partly because such messages are usually highly subjective, reflecting a candidate's or party's point of view. This exclusion does not extend to advertising by government departments or by crown corporations.

Authority and Scope of the Code

The Code deals with **how** products or services may be advertised, **not** with **what** may be advertised. Thus, the authority of the Code and the jurisdiction of the Council are over the content of advertisements and do not include, in any way, the right to prohibit the promotion of legal products or services or their portrayal in circumstances of normal use.

The Code

Public confidence exerts an important influence upon the effectiveness of advertising, just as it affects any other communication process in a democratic environment. So directing advertising practices toward meriting and enhancing such confidence is both socially responsible and an act of practical self-interest.

This Code of Standards, which has been approved by all participating organizations, is designed to help set and maintain standards of honesty, truth, accuracy, and fairness in the marketplace.

Since products and values in the marketplace are constantly changing, the Advertising Standards Council will periodically review the Code and where it seems appropriate will recommend proposed revisions to the Copy Standards Committee. The principles underlying the Code and more detailed descriptions of its application are presented in the Manual of General Guidelines for Advertising.

No advertisement shall be prepared or knowingly accepted which contravenes this Code of Standards.

The clauses should be adhered to in letter and in spirit.

1. Accuracy, Clarity

(a) Advertisements may not contain inaccurate or deceptive claims or statements, either direct or implied, with regard to price, availability or performance of a product or service. Advertisers and advertising agencies must be prepared to substantiate their claims promptly to the Council. Note that, in assessing the truthfulness of a message, the Council's concern is not with the intent of the sender or the precise legality of the phrasing. Rather the focus is on the message as received or perceived, that is, the general impression conveyed by the advertisement.

(b) Advertisements may be deceptive by omission of relevant information.

(c) All pertinent details of advertised offers should be clearly stated.

(d) Disclaimers or asterisked information should be so located and large enough as to be clearly visible.

2. Disguised Advertising Techniques

No advertisement shall be presented in a format which conceals its commercial intent. Advertising content, for example, should be clearly distinguished from editorial or program content. Similarly, advertisements are not acceptable if they attempt to use images or sounds of very brief duration or physically weak visual or oral techniques to convey messages below the threshold of normal human awareness. (Such messages are sometimes referred to as subliminal).

3. Price Claims

(a) No advertisement shall include deceptive price claims or discounts, unrealistic price comparisons or exaggerated claims as to worth or value. "Regular price", "suggested retail price", "manufacturer's list price", and "fair market value" are misleading terms when used by an individual advertiser to indicate a savings — unless they represent prices at which a reasonable number of the item was actually sold within the preceding six months in the market where the advertisement appears.

(b) Where price discounts are offered, qualifying statements such as "up to", "xx off", etc., should be in easily readable type, in close proximity to the prices quoted, and, where practical, regular prices should be included.

(c) Prices quoted in Canadian media in other than Canadian funds should be so identified.

4. Testimonials

Testimonials must reflect the genuine, reasonably current opinion of the endorser and should be based upon adequate information about or experience with the product or service advertised. This is not meant to preclude, however, an actor or actress presenting the true experience of an actual number of users or presenting technical information about the manufacture or testing of the product.

5. Bait and Switch

The consumer must be given a fair opportunity to purchase the goods or services offered at the terms presented. If supply of the sale item is limited, this should be mentioned in the advertisement. Refusal to show or demonstrate the product, disparagement of the advertised product by sales personnel, or demonstration of a product of superior quality are all illustrations of the "bait and switch" technique which is a contravention of the Code.

6. Comparative Advertising

Advertisements must not discredit or attack unfairly other products, services or advertisements, or exaggerate the nature or importance of competitive differences. When comparisons are made with competing products or services, the advertiser must make substantiation available promptly upon the request from the Council.

7. Professional or Scientific Claims

Advertisements must not distort the true meaning of statements made by professionals or scientific authorities. Advertising claims must not imply they have a scientific basis they do not truly possess. Scientific terms, technical terms, etc., should be used in general advertising only with a full sense of responsibility to the lay public.

8. Slimming, Weight Loss

Advertisements shall not state or imply that foods, food substitutes, meal replacements, appetite suppressants, creams, lotions or spe-

language and avoids legal jargon. In sixteen articles, it covers such important issues as false or misleading advertising, subliminal advertising, false price claims, testimonials, bait and switch, unfair disparagement, guarantees, imitation, safety, superstition and fears, and advertising to children and minors.

Concerning the efficacy of such self-regulation, Robert Oliver, President of the Advertising Standards Council wrote:

. . . Because members of the business community, whether signatories of the code or not, are generally supportive of the self-regulatory concept, this "weapon of least resort" is rarely needed—in my memory, over the last fifteen years less than a half-dozen times with a national advertiser, and no more than twice a year with retail advertisers or advertisers from abroad. But without this resource, we could be helpless to cope with the out-and-out fraud artist or those advertisers who were firmly convinced that because their advertising was perhaps legal it was therefore necessarily ethical . . .[86]

FIGURE 17–11
Continued

cial devices will enable a person to lose weight or girth except in conjunction with a balanced, calorie-controlled diet; and reference to the part played by such a diet shall be so located and large enough to be clearly visible.

9. Guarantees

No advertisement shall offer a guarantee or warranty, unless the guarantee or warranty is fully explained as to conditions and limits and the name of the guarantor or warrantor, or it is indicated where such information may be obtained.

10. Imitation

No advertiser shall deliberately imitate the copy, slogans, or illustrations of another advertiser in such a manner as to mislead the consumer. The accidental or unintentional use of similar or like general slogans or themes shall not be considered a contravention of this Code, but advertisers, media, and advertising agencies should be alert to the confusion that can result from such coincidences and should seek to eliminate them when discovered.

11. Safety

Advertisements shall not display a disregard for public safety or depict situations which might encourage unsafe or dangerous practices, particularly when portraying products in normal use.

12. Exploitation of Human Misery

Advertisements may not hold out false hope in the form of a cure or relief for the mental or physically handicapped, either on a temporary or permanent basis.

13. Superstition and Fears

Advertisements must not exploit the superstitious, or play upon fears to mislead the consumer into purchasing the advertised product or service.

14. Advertising to Children

Advertisements to children impose a special responsibility upon the advertiser and the media. Such advertisements should not exploit their credulity, lack of experience, or their sense of loyalty, and should not present information or

illustrations which might result in their physical, mental or moral harm. (See also Broadcast Code for Advertising to Children and the Quebec Consumer Protection Act, Bill 72).

15. Advertising to Minors

Products prohibited from sale to minors must not be advertised in such a way as to appeal particularly to persons under legal age and people featured in advertisements for such products must be, and clearly seen to be, adults under the law.

16. Taste, Opinion, Public Decency

As a public communication process, advertising should not present demeaning or derogatory portrayals of individuals or groups and should not contain anything likely, in the light of generally prevailing standards, to cause deep or widespread offence. It is recognized, of course, that standards of taste are subjective and vary widely from person to person and community to community, and are, indeed, subject to constant change.

Protection Through Consumer Action

Consumers should practice self-protection against forms of advertising that for any reason they feel are dishonest or in bad taste. Consumer groups can also influence new legislation.[87] Consumers can take an active part in consumer associations by reporting offenders. Other actions include:

- Avoiding any advertising that is considered offensive. Consumers can stop watching a commercial, do something else during the time certain commercials are aired, or turn the page of the magazine in the case of a print advertisement.
- Failing to buy products the advertising of which they do not approve. Because advertisers generally do not want to lose customers, even a small drop in market share or sales volume may produce a change in advertising messages if advertisers have been made aware that their message offends a small portion of their audience.
- Comparing sources of information, i.e., not only watching competitive advertisements but also consulting social sources (peers, neighbours, and family members).
- Contacting the advertiser directly and protesting. In the case of collective actions, this form of protest can even go as far as publishing research results that disprove the advertiser's claim or that denies the claim, in the case of an outright lie.

In a free market society consumers generally have their way, because they can select the goods they want. They decide the success or failure of all the products in the marketplace. Consequently, responsible advertisers have a vested interest in helping consumers make responsible and well-informed choices.

SUMMARY

Advertising has always been an area of disagreement among economists, marketers, sociologists, and the public. There is little empirical evidence to support the various arguments that advertising has positive or negative economic and social effects. It has been claimed that advertising affects a consumer's load of information or the new product development process, increases the distribution costs of goods, alters the market structure, affects consumer prices or business cycles, and has a negative impact on the mass media. Part of the controversy between proponents and critics of advertising can be traced to the underlying views of what constitutes relevant information to be given to consumers and to the acceptance of a policy of product differentiation. As for the effect of advertising on consumer prices, no definite conclusions can be safely drawn given present research. Nevertheless, advertising fulfills a function in our economy that no other communication tool presently can.

Among the social criticisms of advertising are charges of consumer manipulation (need creation, the use of emotional appeals, or of special techniques working at the subconscious levels), of affecting social values and lifestyles by enhancing consumer discontent and materialism, or by promoting undesirable stereotypes, and of polluting consumers' environment with misleading or offensive advertisements. Critics have a tendency to overestimate the power of advertising. Although negative social effects can sometimes be attributed to advertising, critics often indirectly attack the economic system of free enterprise and/or the society of mass consumption that is promoted by this economic institution.

Various protections are available to Canadian consumers, in particular the federal and provincial regulations, industry self-regulations, and the protection that consumers can secure through their actions and behaviour.

QUESTIONS FOR STUDY

1. Take a recent issue of a magazine or newspaper and find some advertisements that you think are deceptive. Explain why and in what way they are deceptive. Propose some corrective actions that could be taken by the advertisers.

2. Answer question 1, using advertisements that you think are in bad taste.

3. Take a sample of about ten advertisements from a recent issue of a magazine and analyze what kind of stereotypes they promote. Are they desirable or undesirable stereotypes? Speculate what they might be considered 10 to 20 years from now.

4. Take some advertisements from a few recent issues of a magazine. Analyze the type of information provided about an advertised product or service. How much information is objective and how much is emotional appeal? Can you find a pattern according to the type of product being advertised? In your opinion, can these emotional appeals be justified for some or all of these advertisements?

5. Try to imagine and describe our society if for some reason all kinds of advertising were suddenly banned.

6. Should advertisers try to promote consumers' tastes or change their general attitudes by promoting more desirable images of minority groups? Justify your answer.

7. In what way is it possible to say that a country has the kind of advertising it deserves?

8. Is advertising moral, immoral, or amoral? What should advertising be? Explain.

9. Does advertising increase or decrease consumer prices? Explain in detail.

10. Is the role of advertising to inform or to persuade consumers? Why? Be specific.

PROBLEMS

1. Select one current issue of a national magazine and an issue of the same magazine published twenty years ago. Make a comparative analysis of the advertisements in both issues with respect to:
   • role stereotyping
   • the use of testimonials
   • the use of emotional appeal advertising
   • deceptive/bad taste advertisements
   What may explain the changes you have observed (if any)? Up to what point can the results you have obtained be generalized? Why?

2. Using library research, try to estimate the role advertising should/could play in a:
   a. capitalistic economy
   b. socialist economy
   c. developing economy.

NOTES

1. Richard Caves, *American Industry: Structure, Conduct, Performance*, (Englewood Cliffs, N.J.: Prentice-Hall, 1964), p. 102.
2. Roger Leroy Miller, *Economic Issues for Consumers*, (St. Paul, Minn.: West Publishing Company, 1975), p. 35.
3. Ivan Preston, *The Great American Blowup*, (Madison, Wis.: University of Wisconsin Press, 1975), p. 281.
4. Shelby D. Hunt, "Information vs. Persuasive Advertising: An Appraisal," *Journal of Advertising*, 5, no. 3 (Summer 1976), 5–8.
5. Ibid., p. 6.
6. Raymond A. Bauer and Stephen A. Greyser, "The Dialogue that Never Happens," *Harvard Business Review*, 50 (January-February 1969), 122–28.
7. Neil H. Borden, *The Economic Effects of Advertising*, (Chicago: Richard D. Irwin, 1942), p. 609.
8. Frank M. Bass, "The Theory of Stochastic Preference and Brand Switching," *Journal of Marketing Research*, 11 (February 1974), 1–20.

9. Lester G. Telser, "Advertising and Competition," *Journal of Political Economy*, (December 1964), pp. 537–62.
10. Ibid.
11. Jules Backman, *Advertising and Competition*, (New York: New York University Press, 1967), pp. 90–94.
12. H.M. Mann, J.A. Henning, and J.W. Meeham, Jr. "Advertising and Concentration: An Empirical Investigation," *Journal of Industrial Economics* (November 1967), pp. 34–45; Lee E. Preston, "Advertising Effects and Public Policy," *Proceedings of the AMA 1968 Fall Conference*, (Chicago: American Marketing Association, 1968), pp. 563–64.
13. Paul D. Scanlon, "Oligopoly and 'Deceptive' Advertising: The Cereal Industry Affair," *Antitrust Law & Economic Review*, 3 (Spring 1970), p. 100.
14. John K. Galbraith, *American Capitalism: The Concept of Countervailing Power*, (Boston: Houghton Mifflin, 1956), p. 117.

15. William S. Comanor and Thomas A. Wilson, "Advertising Market Structure and Performance," *Review of Economics and Statistics* 49 (November 1967), pp. 423–40.

16. Ibid. p. 440.

17. Paul W. Farris and Mark A. Albion, "The Impact of Advertising on the Price of Consumer Products," *Journal of Marketing*, 44 (Summer 1980), pp 17–35; see also James M. Ferguson, "Comments on 'The Impact of Advertising on the Price of Consumer Products'," *Journal of Marketing*, 46 (Winter 1982), pp. 102–5; Paul W. Farris and Mark S. Albion, "Reply to 'Comments on "The Impact of Advertising on the Price of Consumer Products"'," *Journal of Marketing*, 46 (Winter 1982), pp. 106–7.

18. D.R. Wittink, "Advertising Increases Sensitivity to Price," *Journal of Advertising Research*, 17 (April 1977), pp. 39–42; G.J. Eskin, "A Case for Test Marketing Experiments," *Journal of Advertising Research*, 15 (April 1975), pp. 27–33; J.J. Eskin and P.H. Baron, "Effect of Price and Advertising in Test-Market Experiments," *Journal of Marketing Research*, 14 (November 1977), pp. 499–508; V.K. Prasad and L.W. Ring, "Measuring Sales Effects of Some Marketing Mix Variables and Their Interactions," *Journal of Marketing Research*, 13 (November 1976), pp. 391–96.

19. Comanor and Wilson, J.J. Lambin, *Advertising Competition and Market Conduct in Oligopoly Over Time*, (Amsterdam: North-Holland Publishing Co., p. 425.

20. R.D. Buzzell and P.W. Farris, "Marketing Costs in Consumer Goods Industries," Marketing Science Institute, Report No. 76–111 (August 1976); P.W. Farris and D.J. Reibstein, "How Prices, Ad Expenditures and Profits are Linked," *Harvard Business Review*, 57 (November-December 1979), pp. 173–84.

21. L. Benham, "The Effect of Advertising on the Price of Eyeglasses," *Journal of Law and Economics*, 15 (October 1972), pp. 337–52; J. Cady, "Advertising Restrictions and Retail Prices," *Journal of Advertising Research*, 16 (October 1976), pp. 27–30; R.L. Steiner, "Does Advertising Lower Consumer Prices?" *Journal of Marketing*, 37 (October 1973), pp. 19–26; R.L. Steiner, "Learning from the Past-Brand Advertising and the Great Bicycle Craze of the 1980s," *Advances in Advertising Research and Management*, Proceeding of the annual conference of the American Academy of Advertising, ed. Ste-

ven E. Permut (1978), pp. 35–40; R.L. Steiner, "A Dual Stage Approach to the Effects of Brand Advertising on Competition and Price," *Marketing and the Public Interest*, ed. John F. Cady, Marketing Science Institute, Report No. 78–105, (Boston, 1978), pp. 127–50.

22. Benham, p. 340.

23. R.L. Steiner, "Toward a New Theory of Brand Advertising and Price" (Paper presented at the annual meeting of the American Academy of Advertising, March 1977); Steiner, "Does Advertising Lower Consumer Prices?" and "A Dual Stage Approach," p. 148.

24. P.W. Farris, "Advertising's Link with Retail Price Competition," *Harvard Business Review*, (January-February 1981), pp. 40–44.

25. Mark S. Albion and Paul W. Farris, "The Effect of Manufacturer Advertising on Retail Pricing," Marketing Science Institute, Report No. 81–105, (December 1981), p. 3.

26. Julian L. Simon, *Issues in the Economics of Advertising*, (Urbana, Ill.: University of Illinois Press, 1970).

27. Ibid.

28. *The Financial Post*, November 1978, Section 5. Fritz Machlup, *The Production and Distribution of Knowledge in the United States*, (Princeton, N.J.: Princeton University Press, 1962), p. 265.

29. David M. Blank, "Television Advertising: The Great Discount Illusion, or Tony Panda Revisited," *Journal of Business*, (January 1968), pp. 10–38.

30. Joseph E. De Deo, "Why Over $109,800,000,000 Was Spent on Advertising in American Last Year." New York: Young and Rubican Inc., undated.

31. David S. Hopkins, New Product Winners and Losers, (New York: National Industrial Conference Board, 1980); *Management of New Products* 4th ed., (New York: Booz, Allen and Hamilton, 1968), p. 8.

32. Harold Kassarjian and Joel B. Cohen, "Cognitive Dissonance and Consumer Behaviour," *California Management Review*, (Fall 1965), pp. 55–64.

33. L. Edward Scriven, "Rationality and Irrationality in Motivation Research," *Motivation and Marketing Behaviour*, ed. Robert Ferber and Hugh G. Wales, (Homewood, Ill.: Richard D. Irwin, 1958), pp. 67–70.

34. Vance Packard, *The Hidden Persuaders*, (New York: Pocket Books, 1957), p. 30.

35. Timothy E. Moore, "Subliminal Advertising: What You See Is What You Get," *Journal of Advertising*, 46 (Spring 1982), pp. 27–47.

36. James G. Barnes, "Television Viewing Patterns of Children and Adolescents in Cable and Non-Cable Households," (Paper presented at the European Marketing Academy Conference, Grenoble, France, 1983).

37. Thomas S. Robertson and John R. Rossiter, "Short-Run Advertising Effects on Children: A Field Study," *Journal of Marketing Research*, 13 (February 1976), pp. 68–70.

38. Scott Ward, Daniel Wackman, and Ellen Wartella, *Children Learning to Buy: The Development of Consumer Information Processing Skills*, (Cambridge, Mass.: Marketing Science Institute, 1975).

39. Thomas S. Robertson and John R. Rossiter, "Children and Commercial Persuasion: An Attribution Theory Analysis," *Journal of Consumer Research*, 1 (June 1974), pp. 13–20.

40. Jean Piaget, *The Psychology of the Child*, (New York: Basic Books, 1969).

41. Marvin E. Goldberg and Gerald J. Gorn, "Children's Reactions to Television Advertising: An Experimental Approach," *Journal of Consumer Research*, 1 (September 1974), pp. 69–75.

42. Gerald J. Gorn and Marvin E. Goldberg, "Children's Television Commercials: Do Child Viewers Become Satiated Too", (McGill University working paper, 1976).

43. Scott Ward and Daniel Wackman, "Children's Purchase Influence Attempts and Parental Yielding," *Journal of Marketing Research*, 9 (August 1972), pp. 316–19.

44. W.D. Wells, "Children as Consumers," *On Knowing the Consumer*, ed. J.W. Newman, (New York: John Wiley and Sons, 1966).

45. L.A. Berey and R.W. Pollay, "Influencing Role of the Child in Family Decision Making," *Journal of Marketing Research*, 5 (February 1968), pp. 70–72.

46. Mark Lowell, "Advertising to Children: An Issue Where Emotion is Getting in the Way of Objectivity," *Marketing*, 4 June 1975.

47. Richard W. Pollay, "The Distorted Mirror: Reflexions on the Intended Consequences of Advertising," *Journal of Marketing*, 50 (April 1986), 18–36; Morris B. Holbrook, "Mirror, Mirror, on the Wall, What's Unfair in the Reflexions on Advertising," *Journal of Marketing*, 51 (July 1987), 95–103; Richard W. Pollay, "On the Value of Reflexions on the Values of the Distorted Mirror," *Journal of Marketing*, 51 (July 1987), 104–110.

48. Charles J. Dicksen, Arthur Kroeger, and Franco M. Nicosia, *Advertising Principles and Management Cases*, 6th ed., (Homewood, Ill.: Richard D. Irwin, 1983), p. 569.

49. D. Kurnin, "Iz Opyta Sovetskoi Torgovloi Reklamy," *Sovetskaia Torgovlia*, (February 1958), pp.46–47, quoted in Marshall I. Goldman, "Product Differentiation and Advertising: Some Lessons from the Soviet Experience," *Speaking of Advertising*, (Toronto: McGraw-Hill, 1963), pp. 352–53.

50. Prairie Provinces Royal Commission, *Report on Consumer Problems and Inflation* (1968), p. 254.

51. Thomas F. Pettigrew, "Complexity and Change in American Racial Patterns: A Social Psychological View," *Daedalus*, (Fall 1965), p. 974.

52. *Women and Advertising: Today's Messages—Yesterday's Images*, Report of the Task Force on Women and Advertising, (Toronto: Canadian Advertising Advisory Board, November 1977), p. 2.

53. Alice E. Courtney and Sarah Wernick Lockeretz, "A Woman's Place: An Analysis of the Roles Portrayed by Women in Magazine Advertisements," *Journal of Marketing Research*, 8 (February 1971), pp. 92–95.

54. Ibid.

55. Louis C. Wagner and Janis B. Banos, "A Woman's Place: A Follow-up Analysis of the Roles Portrayed by Women in Magazine Advertisements," *Journal of Marketing Research*, 10 (May 1973), pp. 213–14.

56. M. Vankatesan and Jean Losco, "Women in Magazine Ads: 1959–71," *Journal of Advertising Research*, 15 (October 1975), pp. 49–54.

57. Ahmed Belkaoui and Janice Balkaoui, "A Comparative Analysis of the Roles Portrayed by Women in Print Advertisements: 1958, 1970, 1972," *Journal of Marketing Research*, 13 (May 1976), pp. 168–72.

58. Peter W. Pasold, "Role Stereotyping in Magazine Advertising of Different Countries," *ASAC Proceedings*, ed. J.R. Brent Ritchie and Pierre Filiatrault (1976), pp. 41–50.

59. Gurprit S. Kindra, "Comparative Study of the Role Portrayed by Women in Print Advertising," *Marketing*, ed., Michel Laroche, vol. 3, (Administrative Sciences Association of Canada, 1982), pp. 109–18. See also Robert G. Wyckham, "Female Stereotyping in Advertising," *Marketing*, ed. James Forbes (Montreal: Administrative Science Association of Canada), 1983, 102–112; Roger J. Calantone, Dick Pope, and Jacques Picard, "Attitudes Towards Women's Roles Portrayed in Advertising Messages," *Marketing*, ed. Sheila Brown (Montreal:

Administrative Science Association of Canada), 1984, 91–100.

60. *Women and Advertising*, p. 5.

61. John V. Petrof, Elie Sayegh, and Pandelis I. Vlahopoulos, "Publicité et Stéréotypes des Femmes," *Marketing*, ed. Michel Laroche, vol. 3 (Administrative Sciences Association of Canada, 1982), pp. 238–46. See also Robert G. Wyckham, "Female Stereotyping in Advertising," *Linking Knowledge and Action*, ed. James D. Forbes, vol. 4, (Administrative Sciences Association of Canada, 1983), pp. 371–82.

62. James Stafford, Al Birdwell, and Charles Van Tassel, "Integrated Advertising—White Blacklash," *Journal of Advertising Research*, 10 (April 1970), pp. 15–20.

63. Canadian Advertising Foundation, *Sex-role Stereotyping Guidelines*, Toronto: Canadian Advertising Foundation (July 24, 1987).

64. *Women and Advertising*, p. 17.

65. See, for instance, Philip H. Love, "Entertainment in the Midland," *Omaha World Herald*, 24 November 1968, p. 11; E.S. Turner, *The Shocking History of Advertising*, (Baltimore, Penguin Books, 1965).

66. Ronald R. Gist, *Marketing and Society: a Conceptual Introduction*, (New York: Holt, Rinehart and Winston, 1971), pp. 401–2.

67. Ibid. p. 402.

68. John Treasure and Timothy Joyce, *As Others See Us*, (London: Institute of Practitioners in Advertising, 1967).

69. Prairie Provinces Royal Commission, Report on Consumer Problems, pp. 266–67.

70. Ralph S. Engle, "Advertising and the Law," *Advertising in Canada*, ed. Peter T. Zarry and Robert D. Wilson, (Toronto: McGraw-Hill Ryerson, 1981), pp. 369–442.

71. Ibid., p. 369.

72. Reproduced from the Canadian Advertising Advisory Board, "Laws and Regulations Package," (Toronto: February 1980).

73. "Laws and Regulations Package," (Toronto: Canadian Advertising Advisory Board, 1980).

74. Ibid. p. 2.

75. D. Alyluia, "The Regulation of Commercial Advertising in Canada," *Manitoba Law Journal*, 5 (1972–73), pp. 97–200.

76. Robert W. Sweitzer, Paul Temple, and John H. Barnett, "Political Dimensions of Canadian Advertising Regulation," *The Canadian Marketer*, 10 (Fall 1979), pp. 3–8.

77. W.L. Wilkie and Paul W. Farris, "Comparison Advertising: Problems and Potential," *Journal of Marketing*, 30 (October 1975), pp. 7–15.

78. T.E. Barry and R.L. Tremblay, "Comparative Advertising Perspectives and Issues," *Journal of Advertising*, 4 (1975), pp. 15–20; P. Levine, "Commercials That Name Competing Brands," *Journal of Advertising Research*, 16 (December 1976), pp. 7–14; V.K. Prasad, "Communications Effectiveness Comparative Advertising: A Laboratory Analysis," *Journal of Marketing Research*, 13 (May 1976), pp. 128–37; R.D. Wilson, "An Empirical Evaluation of Comparative Advertising Messages: Subjects' Responses on Perceptual Dimensions," *Proceedings*, Fall Conference, Association of Consumer Research (1975), pp. 53–57.

79. Gordon H.G. McDougall, *Comparative Advertising in Canada*, Monograph, (Ottawa: Consumer Research Council, 1976); Gordon H.G. McDougall, "Comparative Advertising: Consumer Issues and Attitudes," *Proceedings*, Fall conference, American Marketing Association (1977), pp. 286–91; Gordon H.G. McDougall, "Comparative Advertising in Canada: Practices and Consumer Reactions," *The Canadian Marketer*, 9 (1978), pp. 14–20.

80. Robert G. Wyckham, "Corrective Advertising," *The Canadian Marketer*, 10 (1979), pp. 24–28.

81. Robert F. Dyer and Philip G. Kuehl, "The Corrective Advertising Remedy of the FTC: An Experimental Evaluation," *Journal of Marketing*, (January 1974), pp. 48–54; Michael B. Mazis, "An Experimental Evaluation of a Proposed Corrective Advertising Remedy," *Journal of Marketing Research*, (May 1976), pp. 178–83. See also A.J. Faria and Pete Mateja, "Consumer Attitudes Towards Corrective Advertising," *Linking Knowledge and Action*, ed. James D. Forbes, vol. 4 (Administrative Sciences Association of Canada, 1983), pp. 102–12.

82. H. Keith Hunt, "Effects of Corrective Advertising," *Journal of Advertising Research*, (October 1973), pp. 15–22.

83. Wyckham, p. 26.

84. A.J. Faria and Pete Mateja, "Consumer Attitudes Toward Corrective Advertising," *Marketing*, ed. James Forbes (Montreal: Administrative Science Association of Canada), 1983, 102–12.

85. Robert G. Wyckham, "The Advertising Standard

Council: A Critical Examination," *Marketing*, ed. J.C. Chebat (Montreal: Administrative Science Association of Canada), 1985, 346–55.

86. R.E. Oliver, letter dated July 21, 1983 to the authors.

87. J.D. Forbes, "Influence Groups in Canadian Consumer Policy Formulation," *The Canadian Marketer*, 10 (Fall 1979), pp. 27–32.

C A S E S

1. ROMEX INDUSTRIES[1]

Vince Pietrantonio ran a highly unusual but successful business selling disposable diaper seconds in Mississauga, Ontario. It was June 1986, seven months after operations began. Certain opportunities along with Vince's ambition were forcing him to make decisions which could have a profound impact on the future of his business.

Disposable Diaper History

Disposable diapers were introduced in the United States in 1956 as an alternative to reusable cloth diapers. Eliminating the hassle of laundering, keeping the baby drier, and providing better comfort were the main features of disposable diapers. In 1956 less than 1 percent of the billion diaper changes in the United States were done with disposable diapers. In 30 years, times had certainly changed.

The Canadian disposable diaper industry had grown to record annual sales of $320 million. The basic disposable diaper was made up of a plastic shell with a cellulose lining for absorbency and was either secured to the baby by pinning or through the use of adhesive tape.

Children up to the age of two years wear diapers. Thus three sizes had been developed: newborn, medium (toddler over 11 pounds), and large (over 23 pounds). As one may suspect, diaper usage decreased with age. Newborns used about ten diapers a day while the older large children could use as many as seven diapers a day. There were additional variations that were available: daytime versus nighttime usage; elastic or non-elastic legs; and patterned (e.g., denim) versus traditional white.

Company Background

In the production of disposable diapers, mistakes were inevitable. Blemishes, missed or overtrimming and missing adhesive tape caused the diapers to become "seconds." In the case of a "second," no brand name could be used, yet the product was comparable in function and in quality. These "seconds" were packed into corrugated cardboard boxes of 100 and sold to people like Vince at a reduced price. In Vince's case, he purchased his seconds from a leading generic brand diaper manufacturer in the area. He acted as a middleman reselling the diapers in the boxes to the bargain-conscious public.

Vince's outlet was unusual. He rented a 100 square metre space in a public storage area on Royal Windsor Drive in Mississauga for $200 per month. Though usually used for storing cars or equipment, Vince used the area to store his diapers. Locating within this public storage area made it difficult for some customers to find him but once found they often returned.

Even more unusual were Vince's hours of operation—9:00 A.M. to noon each Saturday. The three employees he hired for $5.00 per hour worked an additional half hour before opening and after closing to tidy up the warehouse. His only other "people" expense was for unloading a truckload shipment of diapers. Two people were paid $30.00 to offload the twice monthly shipment of seconds.

No matter how unusual it was, people came to Vince's warehouse every Saturday. The big attraction was his prices. For newborn, medium and large, he charged 8, 14, and 17 cents per diaper respectively. This compared to 24 and 33 cents per diaper for medium and large "name" brands and 20 cents per diaper for a medium-size generic brand. Vince's cost for the diaper seconds was roughly 60 percent of his selling price. He only sold lots of 200 diapers. This meant that people bought two boxes of medium and large diapers as compared to just one box of newborn diapers.

Each week about 150 lots of diapers were sold. In describing the people who bought the diapers, Vince said "Obviously they have a family but by this I mean that they have two or more children. I would say that the people who come here are budget-conscious probably earning $30 000 per year or less as a family. You would probably call them 'blue-collar'."

Vince's single biggest expense after the diapers was promotion. His primary vehicle was a newspaper ad (See Exhibit 1). To place the ad for two days in the local edition of The *Toronto Star* cost him $325, in the local edition of The *Toronto Sun* $225 and in the *Oakville Beaver* $125. In this way he blanketed his target area.

Besides world-of-mouth promotion, his other vehicles were the three portable signs that were placed around the storage area each Saturday morning to direct people to his outlet. Vince didn't even have a sign in the window of his outlet—for the rest of the week it looked like any other storage unit.

EXHIBIT 1   *Newspaper Ad*

Problems and Opportunities

Vince made a very nice second income from this business and wanted to open a second outlet on the other side of Toronto—probably in the Oshawa area. His only problem was a lack of supply. In the normal production process a manufacturer made just so many seconds (they were in the qual-

ity diaper business after all). The seconds that were produced had to be shared between Vince and a person operating a similar business in the Hamilton area. The second person had an "inside" position and so got more than half the seconds and his choice of sizes. As it was, Vince often ran out of the newborn size and could not get a larger allotment. As well, he occasionally ran out of the medium and large elasticized diapers. Elastic diapers were more popular than the plain kind.

There were other makers of disposable diapers but under the terms of the verbal contract Vince had, if he approached another diaper company for seconds he would be cut off by his current supplier.

Vince was concerned about a new operation which had opened two miles away from him in Mississauga. This company sold first quality diapers bearing the "Smiles" brand name at prices that were comparable or slightly lower than his own. It had opened two months earlier and so far he had not noticed any appreciable decline in business. Rather than being reactive, Vince wanted to take a proactive stance and meet this challenge head-on but he did not know what he should do.

Finally, Vince was approached by a Toronto based company called Northern Cosmetics. This company produced shampoos, cleaners, liquid soaps, deodorizers, and colognes and was looking for someone to help push their line of products. Two factors made this offer unusual: 1) there was no brand name associated with the products; and 2) the products were sold in four litre containers. The selling price was about $10.00 per container which was a considerable saving over buying the product in stores. There was a smaller 75 ml personal size available but Northern did not want to push it.

Vince's problems with this were many. Could he offer the products in his current outlet or would he have to use a different approach? How should he price this product? Which products should he stock? What kind of promotional program should he use?

Conclusion

Of course, Vince's main concern rested with his original business. He thought that he was doing a pretty good job running the company but he felt that there could be room for improvement. His other problems and opportunities just compounded the number of decisions he would have to make in the next few weeks.

---

2. NEW BRUNSWICK OPTICAL COMPANY (NBO)[1]

The retail optician is in the business of selling and fitting glasses, with sales and service being the primary functions at this level. Fitting glasses includes two processes: grinding the lens and edging it to the frame size. Grinding involves changing the rough lens to meet the exact specifications of the doctor's prescription. The optician also carries a variety of commonly required lenses known as stocked lenses. A simple edging process, fitting the lens to the frame, is all that is required before the sale of a stocked lens. Lenses that must be ground are sent to an operation that specializes in this process and there is usually a four- to-six-day wait. The edging, on the other hand, usually takes place on the premises of the store and constitutes part of a service package available to the customer. Other features of this package include the service of fixing broken lenses or making adjustments to the frames.

The owners of New Brunswick Optical, located in downtown Moncton, are Mike James and Arthur Mitchell. For the past ten years these men have operated a successful retail optical store. Both men are in their late forties and have been associated with this business for many years. Mike James is more technically qualified than his partner, but Arthur has an excellent approach in sales. Mike acquired his technical abilities the hard way—as an apprentice to an optician in a small town in New Brunswick. Mike prides himself on this experience, for it has provided him with a thorough understanding of the technical requirements for the business. The partners appear to complement each other's strengths and weaknesses. Both men are community-oriented and well-respected business people.

New Brunswick Optical is an independent optical dispensary that competes with three other independent companies in a market influenced by a fully integrated optical chain. This chain enjoys all the usual economies of scale and operates right across Canada. The chain owns its own manufacturing operation for frames and lenses as well as a grinding company. There is little question that this company has a considerable competitive advantage. Both the independents and the chains have existed successfully for a number of years.

Mike and Arthur feel that good competition is healthy for the business, and except for the past eight months business had been good. As the partners saw it, any potential threat to NBO would be from the chain operation with its large financial and marketing resources. NBO had been witnessing a sales slump, which began to worry Mike and Arthur. They knew they were losing customers somewhere. Neither of the men were able to identify any visible reason why sales were so low as compared to last year. They asked a friend and local consultant to discuss the issue with them at a meeting in their office.

The conversation went as follows:
Consultant: Well, gentlemen, what has happened in the last six or eight months that would cause your sales to go down the way they have?

James: We really cannot pinpoint the exact factors. There does not seem to be anything visible or concrete enough to deal with.

Mitchell: Things are pretty much the way they have always been. Our service is strong and one of our best assets. Our buying policies and business procedures have really not changed much in the last five or six years. And these have been successful years, but this current slump is very frustrating.

Consultant: Have you raised your prices any in the past six or eight months? This could account for a decline in sales.

Mitchell: We watch our prices pretty carefully but only make changes when we feel that it is necessary to stay with the prices of our competitors. We don't feel we are higher or lower than local prices.

Consultant: What kind of factor is price when it comes to buying glasses?

James: It is a factor, but the service and sales are more important than price. As I mentioned, price tends to be stable across the board in Moncton. Sure we may lose some customers on the basis of price, but we also gain some customers who are dissatisfied with prices elsewhere.

Consultant: How much do glasses sell for or what would a typical pair of glasses cost?

James: The range varies between about $45 to $60 for traditional frames including lenses and this price climbs to about $100 or $110 for fancy imported glasses that require special professional work.

Consultant: At what price do the majority of your sales take place?

Mitchell: Well, we tend to sell glasses more in the range of about $45 to $55—the more common frames and lenses.

Consultant: You mentioned this issue of service. Could you explain what you mean by that?

Mitchell: Our idea of service is a number of things. Good, efficient service is the most important part of our business and we think we offer it quite well. Efficient service to us means you meet the customer well, you are polite and courteous, you understand the nature of his or her particular prescription, and you are able to fill it in the way the optometrist has outlined. We can usually offer three- or four-day service for grinding a lens, and

for servicing requiring edging we can do it in as little as two days. Another dimension to this issue of service is the fact that we get to know our customers and their particular optical needs. We frequently serve the whole family and often get to know them by name, and they often return to us for their next pair of glasses. This kind of service builds strong customer loyalty.

Consultant: Is there any other technical aspect of this service that you offer?

Mitchell: Yes, there is, and it is very much a part of what we're talking about. A good deal of technical skill is required in edging the lens to the frame and seeing that the glasses are properly adjusted to the bridge of the nose. We also strive to be very courteous and approachable.

Consultant: What kind of role does the optometrist play in the business? Is he a source of customers for the optician?

Mitchell: Well, there's no question that he's a source of customers for the optician. However, we feel that no particular optician has a unique relationship with the optometrist. We feel that there is probably an equitable distribution of customers from the optometrist to the various retail outlets. A patient in the optometrist's office might ask the optometrist where he could fill his prescription, and the optometrist generally gives him the names of two or three opticians in town who are reputable. And again, it gets back to the reputation and the service provided by the optician.

Consultant: So you don't feel necessarily that the proximity to the optometrist's office is a factor?

Mitchell: No, I don't.

Consultant: You really do stress the importance of service at the retail level, don't you?

Mitchell: It's very much an integral part of our operation.

Consultant: How do you deal with a new customer, say a 28-year-old banker, when he comes into your store with prescription for new glasses?

Mitchell: Well, that's simple. We usually let him browse around a little and then approach him to assist him.

Consultant: What do you think is uppermost in his mind at this time?

James: I'd say finding frames and ensuring we fit him properly.

Consultant: What segment of the market do you feel you best serve? The older, more conservative people?

James: There is no question about that. Many of our customers are older and have been coming here for years.

Mitchell: I sometimes find myself perplexed by the younger customer who insists on trying on every style in the store.

Consultant: Do you think that consumers will ever come to own more than one pair of glasses? Say, one for the office and one for leisure wear?

James: I don't know. I never really thought about that!

The consultant jotted down a note and asked the next question.

Consultant: Is there a lot of competition in this business?

Mitchell: Well, the competitive position here in Moncton is considerably stable. There are, as I mentioned before, three or four independents and one main chain store that has branches across Canada. There has not been any indication that the chain store is interested in putting us out of business, though.

Consultant: Is there anything that the competitors are doing that you're not doing, particularly the large chain store?

James: The other independent stores are pretty much the same as we are in terms of their business activity. They also stress good service and customer relationships. The chains, on the other hand, are able to save money in their purchasing because of their size. Also, the chains are more integrated than we are, and frequently we buy products from companies they own. As well, at the other end of the scale, they own the companies that grind and edge the lenses. The other concern that we have with respect to competitors is, of course, their advertising and promotion, particularly their television advertising.

Consultant: With respect to competition, have the chain stores got the same kind of personal service that you people feel is so important in your business?

James: Well, it's difficult to say.

Mitchell: Well, my feeling is that we are able to establish a little more personalized service, being a smaller operation.

Consultant: How much promotion do you have in your store? Do you advertise on television or radio?

James: In the past we've relied pretty much on word-of-mouth for our promotion and advertising. That is, a friend telling a friend about our service and their satisfaction in dealing with us. As you can see, we have some point-of-purchase displays that are attractive and help promote our frames. We use modern display cases that are well maintained and well lit. As for advertising on television or radio, the cost is somewhat prohibitive in this area and the other companies have not made a practice of using this medium for communication. However, lately the chain store has been doing some advertising on television.

Consultant: What do you see as the impact of this television advertising on the optical business?

James: We see television advertising by the chain as benefiting us all in some respects. A consumer, after a particular ad, may be motivated to get his glasses updated or purchase new frames, and he may or may not elect to go to the company advertising at that time. And that's about it.

Consultant: Are there any other implications to the advertising on television?

Mitchell: Mike and I have been noticing the content of the ads recently and we have discovered that the ads are projecting a lot of foreign products; foreign import frames with names like Pierre Cardin, deLaurenti, and Mr. Muir are products being used in these ads. Some of the manufacturer's representatives have brought these to us and tried to sell them to us but we have resisted them and elected to maintain traditional styles from Canadian manufacturers. We believe that this is what the consumer wants. We really feel that this business of tinted lenses and fancy glasses is a fad. The cost, too, of advertising is quite prohibitive to the independents. We also feel that promotion, that is, advertising on television or radio, detracts somewhat from the professional nature of our business.

Consultant: Do you feel that the promotion on the part of the chain stores is taking away some of your business and contributing to your problem of a sales slump?

James: Well, they could be getting some of the new business that normally would be coming our way.

Mitchell: I don't know. It seems to me that all this sales promotion is doing is making people buy these new frames and fancy styles.

Consultant: We're talking about sales volume. We're not talking about margins, are we?

James: Yes, you're right. The number of people coming into the store is down. The margins have remained constant. Our costs have gone up marginally but we're not talking about that as much as we're talking about the number of people coming in our door.

Consultant: Well, gentlemen, what is it that the customer walking through your door should be getting and is not getting? Do you really understand what the customers want from their purchase of glasses? Have you over-emphasized service? Are you too traditional in your outlook? What will be the impact on your operation if the chains continue to advertise on television?

---

[1]This case was written by Peter B. McGrady, Lakehead University.

---

3. AERO-TAXI[1]

Situation Summary

Gaetan Belanger, spokesman for Aero-Taxi, was looking forward to the airline's expanding scheduled services. If all goes well, according to Mr. Belanger, Aero-Taxi will offer flights to New York by September 1988. Yet it was already Labour Day, and few people had ever heard of Aero-Taxi; furthermore, the airline was neither listed in the Montreal Yellow Pages nor in the Montreal telephone directory. One confused potential client wishing to fly on Aero-Taxi between Montreal and Maniwaki called up Air Canada for information, only to be told that Maniwaki had no airport. Yet Aero-Taxi had been offering scheduled passenger service to Maniwaki since the spring, and the small airline had plans of expansion.

The Montreal-based airline had recently inaugurated scheduled flights linking Montreal and Quebec City and Hull (the latter being an alternative airport serving the Ottawa/Hull region). The fourth destination selected was Maniwaki (also in the Ottawa/Hull/Gatineau area) partly because that community put up the advertising budget.

Regulatory and Competitive Environments

In 1978, the U.S. Congress enacted the Airline Deregulation Act. Whereas the airline industry had previously been heavily regulated by the Civil Aeronautics Board, on January 1, 1985 the latter ceased to exist as the sector became officially deregulated. This facilitated the entry of new airlines into the industry, with an unprecedented freedom to control product, price, place, and promotion. Over 125 new airlines sprouted up across the U.S. where competition rather than legislation became the regulator of the industry. However, over 120 of these new airlines failed within their first few years of operation.

On January 1, 1988, the liberalization of Canadian skies took place. During the spring of 1988, the Department of Transport in Ottawa granted a license to Aero-Taxi to provide scheduled passenger services. When Aero-Taxi began scheduled flights in Spring 1988, its goal was to nibble at the market shares of existing carriers.

Between Montreal and Quebec City, Air Canada had been flying for half a century. Between

1974 and 1988, Air Canada used only jet service on that route, but to be more competitive, on March 27, 1988, Air Canada inaugurated Dash 8 turboprop service between Montreal and Quebec City, using its Air Canada Connector, Air Alliance. Air Alliance is 75 percent owned by Air Canada, the remaining 25 percent belonging to the Deluce family of London, Ontario. The airline's head office is in the old hangar of Nordair Metro, in Quebec City.

Canadian Airlines International (les Lignes Aériennes Canadien International) became another major player in the Montreal-Quebec City market, on March 27, 1988, when having acquired 31 percent of Quebecair, it gave its own CP designation to Quebecair, marketing "Inter-Canadian" flights as a partner of Canadian Airlines International. Canadian Airlines International also marketed flights of Nordair Metro, another new airline.

A small but growing independent airline also having established a market presence between Montreal and Quebec City is Air Atonabee Ltd., operating as City Express. Its owner, Victor Pappalardo, was previously VP Marketing for Nordair Canada Ltd. He left his job and for $2 million he bought the existing small airline. He purchased a second-hand Canadian-built Dash 7 from Arkia Israel Inland Airways. With an agressive advertising campaign, Pappalardo quadrupled traffic levels of his predecessor in one month. His strategy was to concentrate on attracting passengers who would otherwise not fly, as opposed to fighting for a share of the existing market.

Positioning and Marketing Objectives

In contrast to City Express, which was more interested in expanding market size as opposed to expanding market share, Aero-Taxi was ready to meet its competitors head on and erode their market share. According to Gaetan Belanger, general manager, Aero-Taxi hopes to attract people who would normally fly on other airlines. How? Lower airfares and added convenience, such as a shuttle between the city centre and the airport. An earlier market survey had identified market demand for such service.

Executives of Aero-Taxi wanted the airline to be perceived as a convenient carrier with competitive prices. In developing its marketing mix, Aero-Taxi chose to undercut prices of major airlines such as Air Canada, but was cautious *not* to position itself as the carrier with the lowest fares.

The marketing objectives of Aero-Taxi were:
a. to persuade present users to remain loyal;
b. to attract users of other airlines and possibly of other modes, to switch to Aero-Taxi;
c. to create a positive image for potential passengers and stimulate latent demand.

Targeted Markets

1. *Business Travellers:* General Manager for Aero-Taxi, Gaetan Belanger, specified "businessmen and women" as being a primary component of Aero-Taxi's clientele. Business travellers are the least price sensitive as their tickets are usually paid for by a business, and are tax deductible.
2. *Government Personnel:* Serving the capital city, Aero-Taxi's clientele included a segment of government people travelling on business or pleasure.
3. *Residents of Ottawa and Surrounding Areas:* Mr. Belanger called these "weekend travellers." It has been found that low prices will stimulate latent demand among less frequent price-elastic flyers.
4. *Travel Agents:* These are an important distribution channel of airline tickets.

Advertising Strategy

Rather than allocating much money on an advertising budget, Aero-Taxi's advertising expenditures were kept to a minimum. The airline would benefit from (free) publicity to a certain extent; yet no advertising agency was selected, no mass media campaign prepared. Aero-Taxi did not even list itself in the directories of all the communities it served.

Media Objective and Media Execution

The goal was to build a positive image, maximizing reach while minimizing costs. Aero-Taxi opted to have posters printed.

Advertising Strategy

An airline's advertising may reflect different elements. Sometimes emphasis is on the *product*.

Air Ontario (Air Canada Connector) is advertised as soon to have 37-passenger Dash 8 service on all routes.

Air Alliance (Air Canada Connector) uses exclusively what is advertised as a "fleet of state-of-the-art Dash 8 aircraft . . . Business travellers will appreciate the wonderful comfort that the 37-seat Dash 8 provides."

Many Quebecair destinations were served by Boeing 737 jets until the mid-1980s. These aircraft had in the vicinity of 130 seats, most of which often flew empty. The strategy of Inter-Canadian, once it took over Quebecair routes, was to use smaller airplanes. The use of smaller aircraft reduces costs, and allows an increase in the frequency of flights, thus providing added convenience to the consumer, as stressed in a popular newspaper ad emphasizing three flights daily. In a bold black print on a white background, it read:

Sept-Iles—Montreal
Sept-Iles—Quebec
6:45
15:00
19:40
Inter Canadian

Another alternative is for an advertising campaign to stress *price*. A newspaper ad for Air Canada showed: Sept-Iles—Montreal $159.

In the same newspaper, the following appeared:

Sept-Iles—Montreal
$99
Inter-Canadien

Wardair, meanwhile, advertised its seat sale:

Pick a spring month
Pick a sale price
Pick up the phone fast

Many airlines concentrate their ads on *place* instead. Canadian Airlines International launched a campaign with slogans such as "From Gaspe to Calgary," "From Natashquan to Amsterdam," and "From Mont-Joli to Fiji."

Aero-Taxi's next projected frontier was to be the New York to Montreal market, already served by Air Canada, Eastern, Delta, CSA, LOT-Polish Airlines, Air Maroc, Lan Chile, and Aerolineas Argentinas.

Delta Air Lines has run the following ad to open up the Canadian market to its U.S. readers:

CANADA
Feel the Ambiance of Another World
Without Going Far From Home
Delta to Canada

Another strategy is to advertise a *promotion*. Small airlines affiliated with the major ones (e.g., Air Alliance being an Air Canada Connector) have an advantage of participating in promotions of the larger corporations. Air Canada, for example, was able to advertise that it would offer 1800 Aeroplan points for each Air Alliance flight flown between March 27 and May 15, 1988. A total of 40 000 points would entitle a passenger to a free ticket to Europe. This puts the small independent firms such as Aero-Taxi at a disadvantage.

Question
In view of the current situation, develop a promotional program for Aero-Taxi.

---

[1] This case was researched and written by Leo-Paul Dana, McGill University.

---

4. CBUR-AM[1]

Monica Graydon, Public Relations and Promotions Director at CBUR-AM (a Burloak, Ontario radio station) was reading a letter she had just received from a disgruntled listener. (See Exhibit 1.) It was May, 1988, and it had been her task, as head of the two-year-old promotion department, to implement a plan to increase the number of station listeners. While her efforts had succeeded in a 40 percent increase in listenership, the letter writer accused the station of abandoning its loyal "alternative" radio audience. She leaned back in her chair, a cup of coffee in one hand and a pencil in the other, and stared out the window. She was reviewing the situation and wondering how she should respond to the listener's complaint.

The Radio Industry

In the province of Ontario, there were 106 AM and 72 FM stations. 99 percent of all homes had a radio capable of receiving both AM and FM signals. In Burloak, there were 19 AM and FM radio stations broadcasting. Listeners, however, had a greater choice of stations as signals spilled over from Hamilton, Oshawa, Oakville, Guelph and Buffalo, New York. Thus the actual number of competing stations in the Burloak market was close to 30.

Of course, many of these stations appealed to small segments of the population. In the FM market, the three biggest stations were CPAL-FM, Z97, and CMOR-FM. CPAL-FM broadcast at 101.3 MHz and was founded on September 10, 1961. It played adult oriented rock. Z97 (CJKZ-FM) was founded on June 26, 1975. Broadcasting at 97.3 MHz, the station played progressive rock. CMOR-FM opened its doors on October 10, 1963 and broadcast at 103.7 MHz. Its format was contemporary popular and middle-of-the-road music. There were eight FM stations in the Burloak market.

In the AM market, the three biggest stations were CKYK-AM, CPAL-AM and CBUR-AM. CPAL-AM broadcast at 750 KHz and was founded in 1942. It played top 40 and progressive rock. CKYK-AM was founded on February 28, 1963. Broadcasting at 1230 KHz, the station played top 40 hit music. CBUR-AM which broadcast at 1510 KHz was described as having a progressive alternative rock format.

For all radio stations, the only source of revenue was advertising dollars. While a radio station had different rates for different times of the day, and the length and number of commercial time spots purchased, the key factor which determined the amount charged for commercial air time was

TABLE 1 **COMPARISON OF ADVERTISING RATES AND AUDIENCE SIZE FOR SELECTED BURLOAK RADIO STATIONS**

Station	Audience Size	Rate for a 60-Second Commercial*
CPAL-FM	1 200 000	$430
CJKZ-FM	800 000	$250
CMOR-FM	650 000	$155
CKYK-AM	1 100 000	$415
CPAL-AM	650 000	$200
CBUR-AM	540 000	$150

*Commercial to be broadcast in peak listener time period of 5 A.M. to 10 A.M.

the size of the audience listening. (Table 1 presents a comparison of advertising rates and audience for the major Burloak radio stations.) The more people listening at a given time of day, the more charged for a commercial to be broadcast at that time. As well, the larger the audience of a radio station, the more potential advertisers there were for that station. In other words, a station with an audience of 100 000 might have 1000 potential advertisers. A station with an audience of 200 000 might have 3000 potential advertisers. It was in a station's best interest to increase the size of its audience.

Radio station costs were more or less fixed. A station had to pay 2 percent of its gross revenue to record companies as a royalty for playing their music. All personnel, both on-air and management, were paid a straight salary. All stations had a small advertising/promotion budget which was used to generate awareness for the radio station itself. There were also the standard overhead charges for rent, heat, electricity, etc. The final cost was the upkeep, maintenance, and purchase of equipment. This figure could not be easily projected as technology was rapidly changing in radio. In the last few years, compact disc technology had been introduced. Though undetermined, there would be other technologies that radio would have to acquire in the future.

Company Background

The beginnings of CBUR-AM can be traced to COOL-FM and COOL-AM. COOL-FM, broadcasting at 106.3 MHz, was founded on January 16, 1962. Seven and a half years later, on July 16, 1969, COOL-AM began broadcasting. In the early days, the station was an almost incidental part of COOL-FM. In fact, it was a single turntable in the FM control room.

By the "disco" age of 1976, COOL-AM had built a sizeable audience around a gimmick—it had only blond announcers. But COOL-AM was going nowhere fast. To hear COOL-AM, you had to live within a mile of the transmitter. Why? Because the 23-metre transmitter was in a valley and the 857 watt signal could not escape.

Late in 1976, the station changed its call letters to CBUR-AM and still nothing happened. The big news was in Buffalo, New York where station WBUF-AM broadcasting at 1530 KHz was eating into the Burloak radio market. The Canadian Radio and Telecommunications Commission (CRTC) did not welcome the American instrusion and scouted around for a station broadcasting near the same frequency. Their intention was to allow that station to broadcast with increased power to block out the Buffalo signal. The closest station was located at 1510 KHz—CBUR-AM.

With permission from the CRTC, the signal was boosted to 5000 watts and a new 300-foot tower was built in July, 1977. A new programming director was hired. He was quoted by the *Burloak Star* as saying "We will be playing the music people can't find on the other stations." Thus was born a free form, alternative format that was to become CBUR's hallmark. In those early days, the music varied from classical to contemporary, from pop to punk, from dirge to dance. But this format worked and soon CBUR-AM had a loyal following that some writers described as a "cult" phenomenon.

There still remained one serious problem. One writer put it this way: "You could get the signal loud and clear in some parts of the city, but not in others—and never consistently. In my house, on a sunny day and with the wind blowing north-east, CBUR beamed into the kitchen but never into the office adjoining—a mere six feet further east."

To fix that problem, the station needed a further investment from the owners. However, the owners were having problems of their own. On May 10, 1980, the owners declared personal bankruptcy. Their holdings, including the radio station, were placed into receivership by the Supreme Court of Ontario. At that time, there was a real danger that the CRTC would revoke the station's license. A plea from one of the announcers for listener support brought in 6200 letters and 150 000 names on petitions to "save the feeling in radio." CBUR-AM might have been a cult phenomenon but their listeners were as loyal as a family.

Laurentide Corporation which owned seven radio stations in Alberta, one in Montreal and a television production company, purchased COOL-FM and CBUR-AM for $2.2 million. The corporation was also willing to invest more money in the company. COOL-FM became CETH-FM and switched from broadcasting disco to ethnic/multi-cultural programming. As well, the old station headquarters were abandoned for a new location atop a shopping mall. By now, the CBUR-AM had an audience of 200 000. While the station appealed to a broad spectrum of people, the typical listener was between the ages of 18 and 34, single or married with no children, well-educated and looking for something different or exciting in his or her music. In fact, one person described them as people "with a look all their own."

Like the previous owners, Laurentide ran into cash problems during the recession of 1981–82. Rumours circulated that CBUR-AM was for sale and that a new programming format was being considered. "The station would go country." "A heavy metal format was being discussed." "An oldies programming consultant was being consulted." "A group of born-again Christians were on the case." "An all-talk format was a strong likelihood as was a 'black' format." The newspapers were full of stories.

The eventual purchaser was Scotsman Communications—a media conglomerate. It owned five television stations, ten radio stations, and five cable television services. When Scotsman took over on January 1, 1983, it informed management that it wanted the station to generate more revenue by attracting a larger audience. It was looking for a return on its $3 million investment.

The first step was initiated by Scotsman when it invested more money to have CBUR's signal broadcast from the Railway Tower in Burloak. A 50 000-watt signal coming from the tower increased the potential listenership for the station. Almost immediately after going on the Tower on January 1, 1984, ratings doubled. About 400 000 people were tuning into CBUR's signal. Advertising rates were increased somewhat and revenues improved.

In early 1985, CBUR's major competitor, CKYK-AM, went over 1 000 000 listeners. At that moment, CKYK-AM doubled its advertising rate. A staff person explained that "a national advertiser used to buy commercial time on the top three or four stations. In 1985, we were fourth in the market but for some products appealing to our audience we were considered third. When CKYK doubled their rates, national advertisers could only afford to buy commercial time on two stations. CBUR was sometimes shut out."

By 1986, revenue for CBUR was growing at 2.8 percent per year while revenue for Scotsman Communications was growing at 7.7 percent per year. Scotsman made it clear that station revenues would have to increase. CBUR needed to broaden its listenership. Management felt that it could follow one of two paths. It could modify its blend of music to meet a more mainstream audience or it could develop a promotion department to get more awareness for the station and hopefully more people tuning in. Management chose the latter approach.

A promotion department was set up in 1986. With a limited budget, the department used publicity to generate as much awareness as possible. In the first year, the department was able to get one article per week published in a Burloak newspaper about the station. They also used a promotion vehicle known as the "Rock 'n' Roll Party"—a program for high schools, colleges, and universities that brought together an on-air personality with songs for dances or campus pubs. The radio station sponsored a talent search called "Ontario Backroads" which gave air-play to aspiring new artists.

What little advertising money was available was channelled into television commercials. Advertising the "Feeling in Radio" that could be found at CBUR, the commercials depicted typical people doing typical things while listening to CBUR. According to Monica, who had been hired to direct the newly formed promotion department, "there was an image that our listeners dressed strangely, had strange hair cuts, did strange things. All we did was show average people enjoying the station."

The Problem for CBUR

The campaign was successful and listenership grew by 40 percent. But then the letter from the listener crossed Monica's desk. The station had made every effort to remain loyal to its basic audience. "Where else could a listener hear Bauhaus, Skinny Puppy, The The, Moev, Comsat Angels, Killing Joke, and The Cure?", she thought to herself. "We may have eliminated some of the extremes in the music we play, but we are still very innovative."

As she thought about the competition, she realized that they had changed their musical programming somewhat in the last year. Other people had told her that CKYK-AM and even CPAL-AM were beginning to play songs that used to be heard only on CBUR-AM. As the more commercial stations began playing new music, CBUR-AM would sound more like them. Monica could understand how a listener would be misled into thinking that the station had become commercial.

The dilemma had always been to increase the number of listeners while not alienating the loyal audience. Was the letter writer correct? In the push to expand the audience, had CBUR-AM abandoned its loyal audience? If it had, how could they win them back? If they hadn't, how could they change the misperception? After all, there was a rule of thumb that for every 1000 people who had an opinion, one person would write to the station. If more letters came in, there could be a real problem.

Finally, she felt compelled to respond to this letter. What should she say? How should she say it? The coffee cup was empty. Realizing she would have to sleep on the matter, she turned off the light and left her office. Tomorrow she would have to take some action.

EXHIBIT 1   *The Listener's Letter of Complaint*

Dear Sir:

Several years ago I tuned in CBUR-AM and listened to a plea to help save the feeling in radio. I recall hearing that unless we did something, CBUR-AM was gonna go the way a lot of the other stations have gone. The crunch was coming. We had seen it happen before and it was time for we the listeners to mobilize. We organized petitions, wrote letters to newspapers and placed calls to station management. I was proud to be part of that movement.

Well sir, I've been scammed, ripped off and taken for a ride. Call it what you will but CBUR-AM has gone the way of a lot of other radio stations. We need more airplay for fresh young groups just starting. Sure, "Ontario Backroads" does support local talent on CBUR but what about the rest of the shows?

Any true CBUR listener can't help but notice the drastic change in CBUR's programming. The recent departure of two of my favourite announcers has all but confirmed my beliefs that the true feeling has gone from CBUR.

Well, it's time to mobilize once again, this time to bring back real radio to Burloak. I am telling my friends to once again organize petitions, write letters to newspapers and to place calls to station management. I want the old CBUR-AM. I want you to bring the true feeling in radio back.

Yours Sincerely,

Wes Reagan
Vineland

5. SMITHFIELD-BLUME[1]

In June 1981, the advertising agency of Smithfield-Blume Ltd. was retained by the Ontario Rutabaga Producers' Marketing Board (ORPMB) to develop a new promotional campaign for Ontario Rutabagas. This was a fairly unusual account for the medium-sized agency which specialized in agribusiness. The average Smithfield-Blume client had a promotional budget of $2 million. The firm's clients included fertilizer, chemical, feed, and seed producers. They also handled a few other industrial accounts, the largest of which was the $3 million Warren ("Windows to the World") Window account.

The agency was established in 1952 by Simon J. Smithfield, a former sales representative for Massey Ferguson. Smithfield had started by working with equipment accounts, but as the business prospered and the staff expanded, the firm moved into other areas of agribusiness and industrial products. The agency remained fairly conservative in its approach. Smithfield's own specialty was slogans, but the real agency emphasis was on "quality" promotion designed to inform customers. Though Smithfield himself had no formal marketing training, he was a great believer in hiring account executives with a marketing background because he recognized that ad executives couldn't work in a vacuum:

"We have to work on behalf of the client! We have to look at their strategy or help them develop one. Otherwise they may as well toss their money down a rat hole for all the good a flashy ad campaign will do! What's more, we gotta have the guts to tell them their ideas stink! We owe them that honesty!"

This philosophy was still at work at Smithfield-Blume though Smithfield had retired. Though the agency dealt mainly with agribusiness accounts, Smithfield had never been in favour of hiring only those with an agricultural background: "Too narrow-minded! If he grew up on a hog farm in Simcoe, then basically he thinks he has the last word on hogs! In this business you need a wide range of experience and a quick, open mind."

Most of S-B's junior ad men came right out of university. One of the latest additions was Ted Banner, a graduate of Agribusiness at the Ontario Agricultural College. Ted had been with S-B for two years. He learned fast and was quite ambitious. To date, his greatest success had been the brochure for Farnum Feed. On the basis of his past performance, S-B executives felt he was ready to take on the ORPMB account.

Ted realized that this was his big chance at S-B. The ORPMB account totalled around $150 000, and he planned to make the campaign a real landmark. First, however, he knew he must do his homework, so he carefully studied all the background material he had collected on the ORPMB.

Rutabaga Industry in Canada

Canadian Rutabagas were originally used as feed for sheep which were bound for New England markets in the mid-1800s. In those days, rutabagas were turnips. The sheep buyers themselves tried the vegetable and ordered more for their own consumption. These early turnips were a far cry from the sweeter tasting turnip developed in the 1930s and known as the Laurentian. This variety became known officially as rutabaga in 1967. It is large and globular in shape, with yellow flesh

and a purple top. Usually it is waxed to preserve it during shipping and storage. Rutabagas vary in size from one to three pounds and cost anywhere from 16 to 25 cents a pound.

Ontario is the centre for Canadian rutabaga production, though some Canadian competition comes from Quebec and P.E.I. The Ontario industry supports 130 growers plus a number of shippers and packers. In 1978, the farm value of rutabagas in Ontario was $4.9 million, making it eighth highest for vegetables grown in Ontario. Rutagabas reach the consumer by way of the following channel: Farmer → Packer → Shipper → Wholesaler → Supermarkets and Fruit and Vegetable Stores.

A large share of the Ontario rutabaga crop is shipped to the United States; in fact, rutabagas account for approximately 15 to 20 percent of the value of all fresh and processed vegetables exported to the U.S. from Canada. Rutabagas are also grown in the U.S. but Ontario rutabagas are considered superior. Since there is no tariff on these rutabagas, they can compete effectively in price with those grown in the U.S.

Past Promotional Efforts

Prior to the establishment of the ORPMB, exporters had belonged to the Ontario Rutabaga Council (ORC) which co-ordinated promotional efforts on their behalf. The ORC had overseen a promotional program of sorts since 1973, but had been unable to plan ahead because of uncertainty of future budgets. In 1978 and 1979, the ORC had $30 000 as a result of contributions from members. They used this budget, mainly in the United States, to promote rutabagas to housewives as a unique and different vegetable. Most rutabagas are consumed south of the Mason Dixon Line and east of the Mississippi River, and the ORC felt that the main competition in this area comes from white turnips and turnip greens; hence, their program of differentiating the rutabaga.

To formulate their promotional program, the Council hired the advertising agency of J.B. Cruikshank Ltd. The agency presented a promotional mix consisting of magazine ads, press releases for radio and newspaper, a TV film, and film clips for home economics—all of which were developed around the persona of "June Conway," the fictional resident home economist for the ORC.

The magazine ads appeared in Woman's Day and Family Circle magazines during the months of November (the beginning of the holiday season in the U.S.—the peak period of rutabaga consumption) and April (the end of the U.S. turnip season). These full-page ads stressed new uses and recipe ideas, and featured a sample recipe and picture. They mentioned, but did not stress nutrition, and they included a free write-in offer of a rutabaga recipe book. The agency reported that this phase of the program had received a "reasonable response" of 1000 requests per month.

Other aspects of this promotional program included press releases for radio and TV film. The agency hoped the radio releases would be aired in the late morning or early afternoon on women's shows. The television film, produced at a cost of $14 000 and titled "Everything You Wanted to Know About Rutabagas—But Didn't Know Who to Ask" was distributed upon request to cable TV channels for use at their convenience. The agency felt "this scheduling gave the film excellent exposure without necessitating that the ORC pay for this air time." The film highlighted the growing of rutabagas and their nutritional value, and included attractive recipe ideas. In addition to this, a new filmstrip entitled "The Ontario Rutabaga in the Kitchen" was distributed to school home economists.

The TV film, like the magazine ads, included a write-in address for recipes, but response here was not as high as for the magazines. Mr. Cruikshank explained "this doesn't indicate less interest, but rather that media viewers are less likely to copy an address down and mail for more information than those who see advertisements in a magazine or newspaper." Mr. Cruikshank further reported that "by use, the film appears successful. All ten prints are booked through May 1979." He encouraged the new board to increase the number of film prints and increase the number of school film clips available. Board member Fred Hunsberger supported this idea, especially the proposal to increase the number of school film clips available. He felt that "we have to let those kids know what a good value tur—rutabagas are. If we get them early on, we've got them for life."

Current Situation

Board President, Clyde Carson, was not as excited about Cruikshank's suggestion as was Fred. He had recently seen a publication entitled "Report on the New England Market for Canadian Rutabagas" which documented a decline in rutabaga consumption in that area. Further research revealed that per capita, rutabaga consumption had been declining seriously for the past 20 years, and growers were reducing their acreage or leaving the industry altogether. In 1980, the board president, Clyde Carson presented the board with these depressing statistics and suggested a new "marketing strategy" like that discussed at an agribusiness seminar he had recently attended. As expected, Clyde ran into heavy opposition from other board members who did not understand what a marketing strategy was and who were more interested in increasing their production levels. Fred Hunsberger was particularly adamant about keeping their current promotional program:

"Clyde, we're already telling 'em about all the vitamins and offering free recipes. Now what woman wouldn't jump at a free recipe? And that June Conway is a mighty fine woman! The way she talks about those rutabagas just makes my mouth water. And the kids are sure to like the film. I sure would have been pleased to see films when I was in school! That TV cable film is doing the job too. Booked solid all last year. It looks real classy to have our own TV film. Just a fluke that consumption is down. People don't know when they're well off these days. You wait! The old values will come back soon and people will see that turnips—uh—rutabagas are good solid food!"

Clyde persevered and finally got the board to agree to a large-scale study of the North American rutabaga market. The project involved two stages. The first stage was to obtain rutabaga awareness and usage information from 2000 Canadian and 6000 U.S. households. More detailed information was obtained in the second stage on usage, attitudes, and preferences from 300 households in Canada and 800 in the U.S. Based on the report, Clyde had convinced the Board that a drastic overhaul was needed. The first thing they had done was to find a replacement for J.B. Cruikshank Ltd., the ad agency responsible for "Everything You Always Wanted to Know About..." Fred Hunsberger had insisted that Smithfield-Blume be hired as a replacement because: "That's a classy outfit! I knew old Sim when he was with Massey and I'll never forget his big "Keep Pace With Case" campaign. That's what we need. A catchy slogan! It will turn the tide in a few weeks. Look at the milk people. My grandkids won't stop singing 'Thank you very much milk.' Drives me crazy but they say it sells the milk. Why not tur—rutabagas too? Of course, we'll keep June Conway."

Clyde didn't argue with Fred though he privately felt that perhaps Smithfield-Blume was not the best choice and questioned the usefulness of a slogan. Fred, on the other hand, thought that S-B's familiarity with agriculture would be an asset. The two men planned a meeting with S-B's account man.

Research Project Results

Ted Banner sat at his desk in the office of Smithfield-Blume. In front of him were various documents and folders containing background and past promotional programs of the ORPMB. On top of the pile was a report entitled "Consumer Analysis of the North American Rutabaga Market," the report which presented the results of the Board's large-scale survey done in 1980. Ted knew that this report had to be the basis of his recommendations for the board. In preparation for his initial meeting with Clyde Carson and Fred Hunsberger, Ted looked through the report and summarized the main points.

Common Product Names The report revealed that the product is called by many different names including rutabaga, swede, swede turnip, and turnip. In the U.S., 78 percent of consumers referred

to the product as a rutabaga compared to only 20 percent in Canada.

Awareness and Frequency of Use Consumers were placed in one of six categories depending on their awareness and frequency of rutabaga use (see Exhibit 1). The first category is relatively small and contains people who are not aware of rutabagas. The second category contains people who are aware of rutabagas but never purchased one. This group is relatively small in Canada but large in the U.S. The third group contains people who have not purchased a rutabaga in the last 12 months. These are probably "lapsed users" who have discontinued use of the product. This is a relatively small group.

The last three groups are classified as current rutabaga users and account for 64 percent of Canadian consumers and 31 percent of American consumers. The heavy user segment accounts for 16 percent of Canadian consumers and 3 percent of American consumers.

User and Non-User Profiles Analysis of the above groups in terms of demographic characteristics revealed some distinct profiles. In Canada, rutabaga usage tends to be highest among older consumers, consumers who live in rural areas and small communities, French-speaking Canadians, families whose female head is either a homemaker or retired, and families whose male and female heads have less education. U.S. results are very similar, with rutabaga usage being highest among older consumers, lower income families, families whose male and female heads have less education, single family households, and blacks.

Vegetable Purchase Criteria Consumers in the study were asked to rank six possible purchase criteria. The highest ranking criteria were quality, nutritional value, and taste preference. Price and time needed to prepare the vegetable were of some but lesser importance. Rutabaga users consistently ranked price higher than taste preference. Non-users ranked taste preference ahead of price.

Consumer Attitudes Consumers in both countries responded to a series of statements designed to measure attitudes toward a number of issues related to vegetable and rutabaga usage. The following attitudes emerged:

1. Consumers feel they are eating about the right quantity and variety of vegetables, but a sizeable group think they should eat more and a greater variety. This is particularly true for the non-user segment.
2. Rutabagas are not considered expensive in relation to other vegetables, but consumers stated that large price increases could cause some reduction in consumption. (The price in local supermarkets varies from nineteen cents to twenty-five cents per pound.)
3. A large percentage of consumers increased purchases of rutabagas when on special. Most consumers felt that rutabagas were seldom "featured" items at their stores.
4. Most consumers felt that rutabagas are not conveniently located, nor attractively displayed, and frequently not available at their stores.
5. A large percentage of consumers felt that rutabagas are generally too large for the size of their families. They indicated an interest in pre-sliced, ready-to-cook rutabagas or, especially in the U.S., ready-to-serve rutabaga casseroles.
6. Most consumers judge product quality by external appearance and many felt that the rough, black or brown spots on the exterior of the rutabaga indicated inferior quality.
7. Many consumers commented on the difficulty of preparing a rutabaga.
8. Most consumers have little information on the nutritional value of rutabagas and would like more.

Reasons for Non- and Lapsed Users Both non-users and lapsed users listed not liking the taste as the main reason for non-use. The second most frequent reply given by non-users was that they didn't know how to cook or prepare them. Lapsed users listed several secondary reasons: too much trouble to prepare, too hard to cut, poor quality, and a preference for more nutritious vegetables.

Purchase and Use

Rutabaga users were asked about their purchase and use of the product. Their responses indicated that:

1. approximately one-half of all users decide to purchase the product after entering a store;
2. almost all purchases are made in supermarkets;
3. the most popular methods of preparation are boiled and mashed;
4. less than 30 percent of all users serve the vegetable raw;
5. the vegetables consumers consider close substitutes for rutabagas are carrots and squash;
6. most consumers consider the rutabaga as an ordinary everyday dish;
7. over 80 percent of all current users indicated that they were using rutabagas just as often or more often than five years ago;
8. most consumers obtain recipe ideas from magazines and newspapers.

Ted's Reaction

After thoroughly studying the background information and the research report, Ted knew that the problem he faced was far more complex than he imagined. His telephone conversations with Clyde Carson indicated that Carson was aware of the severity and complexity of the problem, but Carson hinted that other board members expected a "magic-cure-all" along the lines of the famous "Keep Pace with Case" campaign of a few years earlier. Ted knew he would need to call on all his tact as well as his past marketing background in order to come up with a campaign for the rutabaga board. He knew the program must take into consideration various promotional tools and their cost (see Exhibit 2). His first task would be to develop a set of recommendations based on the rutabaga report.

EXHIBIT 1 *Rutagaba Market Segments, United States and Canada, 1980*

Percent of Population Market Segments	Canada	United States
Non-user, not aware	11	14
Non-user, aware	16	40
Lapsed user (not used in past year)	8	14
Light users (less than 4 times a year)	23	19
Medium users (5 to 12 times a year)	25	9
Heavy users (more than 12 times a year)	16	3

EXHIBIT 2 *Selected Advertising Rates*

NEWSPAPERS

Toronto Star	½ page colour ad run once a month for nine months, $6600 per entry
Globe and Mail	⅛ page colour ad in Wednesday's food section for nine months, $1440 per entry
Local Papers	½ page colour ad, $510 per entry

MAGAZINES

Chatelaine	½ page black and one colour ad run for one edition, $10 130 English edition and $3400 French edition

RADIO

Toronto Stations	One 60-second morning announcement, $160 on FM, $170 on AM
Local Stations	One 60-second morning announcement, $24 on FM, $31 on AM

TELEVISION

CTV	One 30-second announcement during day-time (noon to 7 P.M.), $2000; during prime time (7 P.M. to 11 P.M.), $6600
CBC	One 30-second announcement during day-time, $1000; during prime time, $6500

---

[1]Copyright 1981 by Thomas F. Funk. This case was prepared by Jane G. Funk and Thomas F. Funk, University of Guelph.

---

6. ZEST[1]

The first major assignment for Mr. George Mann, the new brand assistant for Zest, was to plan the 1986 Canadian sales promotion campaign. Mr. Mann, a recent business school graduate, joined Procter and Gamble (P&G) in the summer of 1985 and worked closely with Peter McTeer, the brand manager for Zest. He spent his first three months on various tasks involving Zest, one of five bar soaps sold by P&G (Zest, Ivory, Coast, Safeguard, and Camay). Mr. Mann knew that Mr. McTeer was concerned about the sales performance of Zest which had lost share in recent years. One reason for the decline was that competing brands, partic-

ularly Irish Spring, were outspending Zest in the sales promotion area.

Mr. Mann conducted an extensive review of the sales promotion activities of Zest and competing brands. The review involved a detailed analysis of the results of the 1984 campaign and the year-to-date results for 1985 by region and by time period. All of the Zest promotion activities were assessed in terms of volume shipped and market share to determine their cost effectiveness. Based on this analysis, and after a number of meetings, it was decided to increase the sales promotion budget for Zest to $1.2 million for 1986. Mr. McTeer then asked Mr. Mann to plan the sales promotion campaign for 1986 and focus on three decisions: 1) the amount allocated for trade allowances versus consumer sales promotions, 2) the specific sales promotions to be used, and 3) any new promotions to be tried. Mr. Mann wanted to design the best plan possible to increase Zest's sales. He also had a personal objective of introducing new, but speculative promotions which would show his creative ability. However, speculative promotions would have to be justified on the basis of cost effectiveness. With these thoughts in mind, he began reviewing the material he had analyzed.

Company Background

Procter and Gamble was one of the most successful consumer goods companies in the world. The company operates in 26 countries and had sales of $13.6 billion and net earnings of $635 million in 1985. The Canadian subsidiary contributed $1 billion in sales and $49 million in net earnings in 1985. This was an increase in sales of $60 million but a decline in net earnings of $11 million over 1984. The profit decline was attributed to increased spending by the firm on a number of new product introductions and line extensions. The subsidiary was recognized as a leader in the Canadian packaged goods industry and its consumer brands led in 13 of the 16 categories in which the company competed. P&G products can be found in nine out of ten Canadian homes.

While worldwide company sales had been more than doubling every ten years, the Canadian subsidiary's growth was even more rapid. In the past five years sales had doubled on both a dollar and a unit basis. P&G executives attributed the company's success to a variety of factors including: 1) dedicated and talented human resources, 2) a reputation for honesty that won them the trust and respect of their suppliers and customers, 3) prudent and conservative management that encouraged thorough analysis prior to decision making, 4) innovative products offering superior benefits at competitive prices, and 5) substantial marketing expertise.

P&G had three operating divisions, organized by product type: Bar Soap and Laundry Products (brands include Ivory, Camay, Zest, Tide, and Bounce); Personal Care Products (brands include Crest, Head and Shoulders, Secret, Scope, Pampers and Luvs); and Food and Household Cleaning Products (brands include Crisco, Duncan Hines, Joy 2, Cascade, Spic and Span, Comet and Mr. Clean). Each division had its own Brand (or Advertising) Management, Sales, Finance, and Product Development line management groups. These groups reported directly to the General Manager of the operating division. The three General Managers reported to the President of P&G. The divisions used centralized staff departments for other services.

The Advertising Department was formed in 1930 when P&G initiated its brand management system. This system allowed P&G to aggressively market several brands in the same product category by assigning the marketing responsibility for each brand to a single Brand Manager. He or she leads a brand group that includes Assistant Brand Managers, and/or Brand Assistants, depending on the dollar volume and marketing complexity of the product. This group planned, developed, and directed the total marketing effort for its brand.

The Bar Soap Market

On a unit basis, the bar soap market had grown 2 percent per year for the past ten years and was expected to continue at this rate. For 1985 the total unit market was estimated at approximately 1 600 000 statistical cases* and P&G's share was 46 percent, up from 41 percent in 1975.

The bar soap market could be divided into four segments: complexion (beauty), refreshment/

---

*One statistical case or unit equals 540 ounces of soap. This figure is used by A.C. Nielsen, the research company, to determine shares of the various brands of bar soaps. Because bar soaps are sold in different sizes it is necessary to use a common measure to determine share. One ounce equals 28.3 grams. One statistical case would be equivalent to approximately 153 bars of soap weighing 100 grams each.

deodorant, all-purpose/price, and liquid. P&G was well represented in each of these segments (Exhibit 1). While these segments were quite distinct in terms of product characteristics, there was no strong correlation between segments and family income or family size. As well, while one family member might prefer a brand from one segment, another might prefer a brand from another segment. Consequently, families typically had multiple brands from different segments in the home at any one time.

The traditional complexion bars, Camay and Dove, drew largely from a female target, particularly for face washing. The major refreshment/deodorant bars (Zest, Coast, Dial, and Irish Spring) tended to be used for showering and bathing. While usage of these bars were skewed to the male market, women also liked the strong fragrances in these bars, associating fragrance with cleanliness and refreshment. The all-purpose

EXHIBIT 1 **BAR SOAP MARKET**

	1985[a]	1980	1975
Total Market (Statistical Cases)[b]	1 600 000	1 410 000	1 265 000
P&G Share	46%	43%	41%
By Segment (Share) (%)			
All Purpose Bars			
Ivory*	23.0	20.5	19.6
Other	23.8	23.6	19.5
	46.8	44.1	39.1
Beauty Bars			
Camay*	5.4	6.5	7.2
Dove	6.9	6.3	6.3
Caress	—	—	.4
Lux	Restaged	5.2	7.3
Palmolive	3.2	4.9	6.0
	15.5	22.9	27.2
Deodorant Bars			
Zest*	11.2	13.2	13.5
Safeguard	.9	1.0	1.1
Lifebuoy	2.0	3.5	5.3
Dial	5.3	6.8	7.0
	19.4	24.5	26.9
Refreshment Bars			
Coast*	5.2	1.3	—
Irish Spring	5.0	6.4	6.8
Fresh	.9	.8	—
Shield	.9	—	—
	12.0	8.5	6.8
P&G Share—Deodorant/Refreshment	17.3	15.5	14.6
Deodorant/Refreshment (total)	31.4	33.0	33.7
Liquid Soaps	6.3	—	—

[a] Preliminary estimates for 1985.
[b] One statistical case or unit equals 540 ounces of soap.
* P&G Brand

Source: Company Records

segment, which was dominated by Ivory and also included private label and store brands, tended to be used by the whole family. Ivory, in particular, had a family appeal, as parents felt it could be used with very young children.

The Refreshment/Deodorant Segment

Zest competed with all brands in the bar soap market but particularly with Dial and Irish Spring in the deodorant/refreshment segment. The total share of this segment had declined from 33 percent in 1980 to 31.4 percent in 1985 in spite of the introduction of three new brands. Share loss had also occured in the beauty segment, while gains had been achieved in the all-purpose segment and with liquid soaps.

Irish Spring, a Colgate-Palmolive brand, currently held a 5 percent share of the bar soap market in 1985. The brand had experienced share losses each year since 1980, including the first half of 1984. However, in the second half of 1984, a new, more aggressive strategy was adopted by the brand manager for Irish Spring. The brand was restaged, accompanied by a new "Richer Lather, Fresher Clean" advertising campaign and significant increases in sales promotion expenditures. In the second half of 1984, Irish Spring experienced sales increases of 7 percent compared to the same period in 1983.

In the first half of 1985, Irish Spring continued with heavy advertising and sales promotion efforts. Advertising expenditures for the July 1984 to July 1985 period were estimated at $1 million. Substantial trade allowances were offered, a bonus pack was introduced (three for the price of two), and a $0.50 coupon was offered through newspaper ads. This "triple" promotion, plus the advertising support resulted in Irish Spring's share indexing at 111 percent for the first half of 1985 (11 percent more sales than the first half of 1984). Exhibit 2 details the competitive activities for Zest, Irish Spring, and Dial for the first half of 1985.

Zest's other major competitor in the deodorant market, Dial, held 5.3 percent of the total market in 1985. Dial had also experienced share declines in recent years and was pursuing a more aggressive strategy to alter the situation. Dial had been restaged and was currently running an "Improved Deodorant Protection" advertising campaign as well as extensive sales promotions in the form of trade allowances (Exhibit 2). It was

EXHIBIT 2 COMPETITIVE PERFORMANCE OF ZEST, DIAL, AND IRISH SPRING FIRST HALF, 1985

	Zest	Dial	Irish Spring
Share	11.2(98)[a]	5.3(102)	5.0(111)
% off Carload Allowance[b]	6.6(127)	11.2(121)	15.1(113)
Share of Weighted Co-op[c]	12.8(90)	7.5(59)	14.1(120)
Share of Display[d]	13.8(103)	14.2(66)	13.3(105)

[a] Index versus a year ago. For example, Zest's share of 11.2% for the first half of 1985 was at 98% compared to the first half of 1984.

[b] A straight trade allowance. When Zest offered a trade allowance, on average the price to the retailer was discounted by 6.6%. If the regular price to the retailer was $70.00 per case, the average discount would be $4.62 per case. It was estimated that Zest was sold "on deal" about 60% of the time and both Dial and Irish Spring were sold "on deal" about 80% of the time.

[c] A trade allowance for co-op advertising. For bar soap manufacturers the expenditure results in a brand like Zest being featured in the weekly newspaper ad for a supermarket. Co-op share is the percentage of times that Zest was featured in a given time period. For the first half of 1985, Zest was featured 12.8%, Dial 7.5% and Irish Spring 14.1%. A.C. Nielsen samples newspapers and counts the number of times each brand is mentioned, then determines the respective percentage mentions.

[d] A trade allowance for display space. The bar soap manufacturers provide the retail store with an allowance to obtain extra shelf space or superior shelf position. A.C. Nielsen conducts a periodic store audit and measures the amount of shelf space devoted to each bar soap brand.

Note: On the basis of the above data and other competitive information, it was estimated that total trade promotion expenditures for Irish Spring for 1985 would be approximately $1 000 000 and for Dial approximately $900 000. Consumer promotions for 1985 for Irish Spring were estimated at $300 000 and for Dial at $280 000.

estimated that Dial's advertising expenditures for 1985 would be approximately $800 000.

The net effect of these competitive activities for the first half of 1985 was that Zest's share was marginally down (index at 98), Dial's share was slightly up (index at 102), and Irish Spring's share was higher (index at 111). Brand managers at Procter and Gamble, while concerned, wondered if the cost of these competitive activities wasn't seriously affecting the profitability of Irish Spring and Dial. All three companies probably faced similar cost structures (Exhibit 3), but it was estimated that the increased marketing expenditures of Dial and Irish Spring were likely to reduce their profit margins. Regular prices to the trade were similar for all three brands. In 1985, the regular price for a case of the complexion size of Zest (36 packs of four bars at 95 grams each) was $72.70, or approximately $0.51 per bar. This would be equivalent to a statistical case selling for $81.31. Because of the competitive activities, it was predicted that none of the major brands would increase prices in 1986.

EXHIBIT 3 **COST STRUCTURE FOR AN AVERAGE BAR SOAP (%)**

Manufactured cost	57
Distribution	7
Selling and General Administration	5
Marketing Expenditures*	17
Profit	14
	100

* Includes advertising, trade and consumer promotion and brand management expenses.

Note: It was estimated that the manufactured cost, distribution, and selling and general administration expenses (69%) consisted of variable costs of 41% and fixed costs of 28%.

Source: Company records.

Zest

Zest was launched in Canada in 1958 and was the second leading brand in the bar soap market. Zest's market share peaked in 1978 at 14 percent and since then the share had declined slowly but steadily to the current 11 percent. Share losses could be traced to increased competition both in the number of brands and the intensity of promotion competition in the deodorant/refreshment segment, price competition in the all-purpose segment, and the development of the liquid soap segment. While Zest had lost share, unit sales had shown less decline due to the moderate market growth. For example, in 1980 the brand shipments totalled 186 000 statistical cases (13.2 percent share). The current estimate for 1985 was 179 000 cases (11.2 percent share) which was below the target of 184 000 cases.

The brand's share performance differed dramatically in different water hardness areas. Zest's share strength was in the hard water regions (i.e., South-Western Ontario and Manitoba/Saskatchewan) where the product had significant rinsing superiority versus ordinary soaps because it was a synthetic detergent bar, not a soap. This was evidenced by a lack of soap film which occurred with the competing brands. In addition, Zest provided a lighter "airier" lather and its volume of lather was superior to other brands. In soft water regions, competitive brands did not leave a film and the primary benefit of Zest was not as relevant. The product formulation had not been changed in 18 years. Estimates for 1985 were that Zest's shares across Canada would be: Maritimes (7.4 percent), Quebec (5 percent), Ontario (12.7 percent), Manitoba/Saskatchewan (30.6 percent), Alberta (16.4 percent) and British Columbia (6.6 percent). The brand was sold in three sizes, Super (200 grams), Bath (130 grams) and Complexion (95 grams), which represented 12 percent, 42 percent, and 44 percent of Zest sales respectively.

Zest's 1985 Marketing Plan

Zest's long term strategy was to maintain its leading share position in the deodorant/refreshment segment and its number two position in the bar soap category. The 1985 objectives were to attain market share of 11.5 percent and unit sales of 184 000 statistical cases. This was to be accomplished through: 1) maintenance of effective media/copy support, 2) superior display prominence and greater advertising emphasis in hard water regions, 3) continued development of the soft water regions with a new copy strategy, and 4) maintenance of existing sales and consumer promotion support. Zest was positioned nationally as the bar soap that provided superior rinsing and lathering benefits for the whole family's bathing needs. The purchase target continued to be women 18 years of age and over.

Advertising Strategy

Zest's 1985 advertising strategy was to convince consumers that Zest was a unique bar which provided a superior feeling of freshness and cleanliness versus ordinary soap. Zest continued the theme of "Clean Plus" which had been run since August 1983.

Zest's media strategy was to efficiently maximize reach against women 18 years of age and older. Spending was aligned to brand development which meant that a proportionally greater amount was spent in the hard water regions and was skewed seasonally in accordance with brand consumption. To maintain historical reach levels of 60 percent over a 52-week schedule the advertising budget was set at $775 000, a 12 percent increase over the last year's spending. The advertising budget translated to an expected spending level of $4.16 per statistical case.

Promotion Program

Zest's promotion objective in high brand development (BD) regions was to increase usage and trial among current users. In low brand development regions, Zest's promotion objective was to increase usage among infrequent and light users.

The promotion strategy was based on considerable analysis of the successes and limitations of past years' promotions programs, competitive activity, and current objectives. A significant portion of the promotion budget was allocated to trade events which included allowances, support for co-operative advertising, and support for display prominence. The 1985 promotion plan budgeted for seven allowance events in high BD markets, three of which provided additional funds to induce superior display. These events ran for four-week periods (Exhibit 4). One interesting aspect of the trade allowances was that two events with similar offers did not yield similar expected volumes. In general, expected sales were affected by promotion offers, as well as other marketing activities, competitive activities, seasonal buying habits, and general economic conditions. In low BD markets, the plan called for five allowance events, four of which included display monies.

In line with 1985 objectives, a trial-oriented sampling program was initiated in July in Alberta. This program distributed 100g samples through a household drop in cities with the hardest waters. This program was supplemented with a September sampling program distributed on bottles of Scope, another P&G product. The distribution of samples was expected to reach 30 percent of Alberta households.

A bonus pack program was instituted in 1985 which gave consumers four bars for the price of three. This April event was run across all high BD regions. An October mailed coupon program was run in all high BD markets and in the Maritimes and B.C. This event represented an expansion over the previous year in which the Prairies were excluded from couponing events. One additional November coupon event was run in low BD regions and distributed on Zest packages.

Total promotion spending was set at $1 000 000 in 1985 up 5 percent from the previous year. It was expected that 103 000 statistical cases would be sold through allowance programs which represented about 56 percent of forecasted sales at an estimated cost of $9.77 per case.

Early 1985 Results

Mr. McTeer and Mr. Mann were not encouraged by the first half results of the 1985 program. Zest sales were lagging forecasts by 3 percent and it appeared that annual sales would be closer to 179 000 statistical cases, not 184 000 as targeted. They discussed these matters on a number of occasions and based on their review and analysis decided that the sales promotion budget should be increased by 10 percent for 1986 to $1.2 million. This decision was approved in principle at a

EXHIBIT 4 **1985 ZEST PROMOTION PROGRAM AND SCHEDULE**

Month	Area		Expected Statistical Cases Sold On Deal (000)	Dollar Cost Per Stat Case	Total Cost (000)	Expected Cases Sold/ Dollar Cost
January	HBD-ONT	allowance–6.84/SC	4.8	5.77	27.70	.83
	HBD-PRA	allowance–5.00/SC	3.8	4.84	18.40	.78
March	LBD	allowance–9.55/SC	6.4	9.33	59.70	.69
	HBD	allowance–6.11/SC	23.2	6.09	141.30	3.81
	HBD	Bonus Pack (4/3)			267.00	—
April	LBD	allowance & display–8.47/SC	3.3	8.03	26.50	.41
	HBD	allowance & display–6.04/SC	9.4	5.78	54.30	1.62
June	LBD	allowance & display–7.53/SC	3.3	7.24	23.90	.46
	HBD	allowance & display–5.57/SC	8.0	5.34	42.70	1.50
July	ALTA.	sampling–test			19.60	—
August	LBD	allowance & display–8.49/SC	5.5	9.16	50.40	.60
	HBD	allowance & display–5.57/SC	16.6	6.20	102.90	2.68
September	ALTA.	sampling–test			10.50	—
October	LBD	coupon–on pack			45.00	—
	HBD	coupon–on pack			75.00	—
November	HBD	allowance–8.33/SC	4.2	7.50	31.50	.56
	LBD	coupon–on pack			12.30	—
December	LBD	allowance–5.19/SC	1.6	4.94	7.90	.32
	HBD-ONT	allowance–6.84/SC	8.0	6.86	54.90	1.17
	HBD-PRA	allowance–5.00/SC	4.7	5.02	23.60	.94
TOTAL SPENDING					1095.10	

Note: Low brand development regions (LBD) encompass B.C., Quebec, and the Maritimes. High brand development regions (HBD) encompass the Prairies and Ontario. The allowance events include money for reduction in the case price and for co-operative advertising. Some events provide additional monies to induce display prominence. The value of the offers are reported in dollars per statistical unit to facilitate comparison across events.

budget meeting when the Zest brand review was held. The task of allocating the budget remained. They discussed several options including increasing trade allowances to become more competitive with Irish Spring, using more consumer promotions in soft water areas where share was low, and offering fewer, larger trade allowances or more, smaller trade allowances.

Finally, Mr. Mann wanted to bring some fresh if not creative approaches to his assignments. However, he had to be cautious in the use of new programs. First, his proposals might not get past the budget committees and he would have to redo his plans and secondly, promotion plans were expected to achieve reasonable revenue goals. Using tried and true programs had the advantage that they would achieve a relatively certain return for Zest.

Sales Promotions
At a general level, Mr. Mann knew that sales promotions could accomplish a number of objectives.

For consumers, objectives include encouraging more usage and purchase of larger-size items or multiple purchases, getting non-users to try the product, and attracting users of competitors' brands. For retailers, objectives include encouraging the retailer to carry new items, carry higher levels of inventory and related items, offsetting competitive promotions, building the retailer's brand loyalty, and gaining entry into new retail outlets. For the sales force, objectives include encouraging support of a new product, encouraging more sales calls, and stimulating sales in off-season.

The key was to match the objectives with the right blend of the myriad of sales promotion tools at his disposal. The tools included coupons (certificates that entitle the bearer to a stated saving on the purchase of a particular product), price packs (includes offers to consumers of multiple units in a pack with a special price, such as four for the price of three), premiums (merchandise offered at a relatively low cost or free as an incentive to purchase a particular product), samples (offers of a free amount or trial of a product to consumers), refunds or rebates (certificates attached to the product which can be redeemed by the consumer for a stated amount), and contests or sweepstakes (offers of a chance to win a prize by submitting an entry). As well, sales promotions could be directed at the trade and included point-of-purchase displays, co-op advertising allowances, and trade allowances (offer of money off on each case purchased during a stated time period).

The Decision

While knowledge of the general sales promotion tools and objectives was useful, Mr. Mann had to make some specific decisions. With this in mind he jotted down a few notes:

- One of a brand assistant's key responsibilities must be to establish the appropriate mix between trade allowances (in the form of straight trade allowances, co-op advertising allowances, and display allowances) and consumer promotions (direct to consumer spending) for an effective, balanced promotion plan.

- Both Irish Spring and Dial had substantially increased their trade allowances in 1985. Mr. Mann was not certain how the trade would react if the allowances for Zest were not increased.

- A major benefit of consumer promotions such as bonus packs (e.g., four for the price of three) or coupons (e.g., $0.30 on pack) was that the consumer received the entire savings. That is, there was a direct, visible reduced price for the consumer. On the other hand, trade allowances might be passed on to the consumer but this was not guaranteed. Zest had been fortunate in the past in that every $1.00 provided in trade allowances resulted in a $2.00 saving to the consumer because supermarkets had also reduced their margin (in the hope of generating more sales). This was not always true for the competition. In fact, in the first half of 1985, Zest offered a number of trade allowances with an average discount of 6.6 percent. Supermarkets who took advantage of this trade allowance also reduced the price to the consumer resulting in an average saving to the consumer of 12.9 percent off the regular price. Irish Spring offered trade allowances with an average discount of 15.1 percent which translated into consumer savings of 18 percent. Dial offered trade allowances of 11.2 percent which resulted in consumer savings of 13.1 percent.

Next Mr. Mann worked out some details on the three major sales promotion vehicles. Trade allowances would probably be the major vehicle. While the breakdown to the different types of trade allowances had to be considered (e.g., what promotion of the funds to be given as straight trade allowances versus co-op advertising allowances and/or display support allowances), Mr. Mann was more concerned about the percentage of the budget that should be allocated to trade allowances in total. He recognized that the consumer promotions were, in a sense, a supplement to the trade allowance structure.

Three possible coupon programs could be run and specific costs and anticipated results were calculated (Exhibit 5). Finally, two different in-store merchandising events were considered. Bonus

EXHIBIT 5 **ALTERNATIVE COUPON PROGRAMS**

	FSCI[a]		In-Ad[b]		Direct Mail[c]	
Face Value ($)	.40	.50	.40	.50	.40	.50
Redemption (%)	5	6	1	1	11	13
Cost ($000)	95	125	55	64	209	313
Cost/Redemption ($)	.56	.62	.59	.68	.53	.64
Expected Statistical Cases Sold on Deal (000)	19	24	20	20	34	44
Cost/Stat Case ($)	5.00	5.21	2.75	3.20	6.15	7.11

[a] A free-standing coupon insert (FSCI) is a coupon and ad pre-printed on heavy paper and inserted loose into a newspaper or magazine. These estimates are based on national coverage delivered in newspapers.

[b] An in-ad coupon is a coupon contained in a weekly supermarket newspaper advertisement. The consumer would clip the ad from the newspaper and present it to the cashier of the supermarket who ran the ad. These estimates are based on national coverage delivered in newspapers.

[c] A direct mail coupon is a coupon delivered by mail to households. The usual method is for a series of coupons from a number of advertisers to be delivered in one envelope. These estimates are based on coverage to approximately 40% of households.

EXHIBIT 6 **IN-STORE MERCHANDISING EVENTS**

	Bonus packs[a]		PAD[b]	
	Regional HBD Mkts.	National	Regional HBD Mkts.	National
Cost (foregone profit in $000)	240	310	0	0
Artwork ($000)	9	9	5	5
Added Factory ($000)	0	0	108	143
Total Cost	249	319	113	148
Expected Cases Sold on Deal (000)	20	27	18	25
Cost/Stat Case ($)	12.45	11.81	6.28	5.92

[a] Bonus packs are two or more units sold on a "buy two or more, get one free" basis. These estimates are based on the complexion size (95 grams) where the consumer buys four bars and gets one free.

[b] Pre-assembled displays are specially prepared displays which involve minimum effort on the part of store personnel to set up the display.

packs and pre-assembled displays (PAD) (Exhibit 6). The PAD idea was new and was the result of considerable thought and effort by P&G executives. A major problem with the bar soaps was the difficulty in obtaining interesting, inexpensive displays. It takes a store clerk very little time to construct an end-of-aisle or special display of laundry soap, or soft drinks, or potato chips. However, because of the shape and size of bar soaps,

stores were very reluctant to devote time to putting up end-of-aisle displays. The PAD concept addressed this problem. The display (Exhibit 7 provides an illustration of a PAD) was self-contained and all store personnel had to do was to cut/slit open the box and place it at the end of the aisle. While this was a unique selling feature of the brand, Mr. Mann wondered whether the cost (approximately) of $6.00 per statistical case would translate into sufficient sales to be profitable. While the forecast sales were based on the results of a small test market, Mr. Mann was concerned that the consumer would not be receiving a direct incentive (e.g., price pack, coupon) to purchase the product. With these thoughts in mind, Mr. Mann began developing the plan.

EXHIBIT 7 *PAD Display*

---

[1]This case was prepared by Gordon McDougall, Wilfrid Laurier University, and Douglas Snetsinger, University of Toronto.

7. EXPRESS AIR CANADA CARGO[1]

Situation Summary

The most recent and most expensive form of transportation is air freight, and it has experienced the fastest growth. Rapid technological progress in the industry has made it difficult to predict how air freight will compete against other modes of transportation. So far, high cost has limited air freight to the shipment of perishable goods, fashions, and industrial products of high unit values. However, increased transportation costs may be more than offset in the long run by reduced inventory, storage, and packaging costs.

In 1989, Canadian Airlines International announced its intention to take over Wardair Canada Ltd. The result would be a major airline, serious competition for Air Canada for the first time. Pierre Jeanniot, president of Air Canada, was sitting in his office on the twenty-sixth floor of Place Air Canada. The 56-year-old silver-haired executive had moved to Montreal from France at the age of 13. He had first started working for Air Canada in 1955, when it was still known as TCA (Trans-Canada Airlines). In those days, according to Jeanniot, the airline "did not have to go and advertise." Over the years, the airline's services became increasingly consumer-oriented, especially when Jeanniot became Senior Vice President of Marketing in 1979. Simultaneously, advertising gained importance.

A decade later, the time had come to review the advertising strategy of the airline's cargo division. By the late 1980s, the airline industry was giving increasing importance to the freight sector. The October 1988 issue of *Business Aviation* (a magazine widely read by airline management) had a special feature article describing freight as "the gravy that doesn't talk back," easy to handle and yet highly lucrative.

Express Air Canada Cargo had been widely acknowledged as one of the most profitable divisions of Air Canada, and the airline was expanding its cargo handling capacity, as Jeanniot positioned Air Canada to grow into a world-class airline.

Yet the 1987 Air Canada Report admitted to declining yields in its cargo division: "Yields were down, especially on overseas routes, attributable to intense price competition brought on by the more extensive cargo capacity offered by other carriers, primarily on wide-bodied passenger aircraft and combination passenger and freighter aircraft."

Competitive Environment

Murray Sigler, President and Chief Operations Officer of Canadian Airlines International, described cargo as an untapped resource for the airline. Air freight represents $200 million of the firm's annual revenues; Sigler wanted to increase this by setting up a special marketing unit for cargo. One option being considered domestically was door-to-door marketing, to test a courier type of service. Although growth in the domestic air freight market in Canada was faster than in the U.S. market, Canadian Airlines was especially interested in the U.S. market which was already ten times the size of its Canadian counterpart. Its plan was to erode Air Canada's market share.

For the first time, Canadian was seriously looking to penetrate the U.S. market, where Air Canada previously had the advantage! Furthermore, Canadian Airlines International, by exercising its purchase options, could double its fleet by 1993. Sigler's goal was to make Canadian the top airline in Canada.

Positioning

Airlines may position themselves according to the following grid:

	Leisure	Business
Passenger	1	2
Cargo	4	3

A major segment of the traffic of Eastern Airlines, and most of the traffic of Provincetown Boston Air is comprised of leisure passengers (box 1).

Air Canada prefers to position itself in box 2 with the business passenger as the primary target. Express Air Canada Cargo, division of Air Canada, falls into box 3 with Federal Express and Zantop. The heavy cargo users are, of course, industrial users, and advertising is, therefore, business to business.

The Market

In Canada, the annual freight market for shipments over seventy pounds was $700 million in 1988, and growing by 15 percent annually. The worldwide air freight market was projected to be $18 billion U.S. in 1988, with the fastest growth being in Europe and the Far East (15 percent to 20 percent).

Advertising Objectives

Although all the Canadian companies together carried only 45 percent of all the international cargo coming in and out of Canada, Air Canada alone dominated 75 percent of the domestic freight market. Yet Canadian Airlines International was definitely making a strong market presence, and its advertising campaigns were aggressive. Airline officials remembered watching Air Canada's market share in domestic passenger service tumble from 80 percent to below 50 percent. They did not want this to happen in the freight sector as well, especially now that the airlines in Canada were typically taking the position of wanting to increase the importance of air cargo as a percentage of company operations. In 1988, cargo accounted for about 10 percent of revenues of airlines in Canada, but most were hoping to reach 20 percent in the near future. Therefore, a major objective of Express Air Canada Cargo was to protect its market share.

More specifically, advertising objectives of Express Air Canada Cargo included: 1) induce present users to remain loyal, using more of the services offered more often if possible; 2) to invite users of competitors' services to try Air Canada; 3) to persuade new potential shippers to try Air Canada's brand of air cargo service.

Target Markets

Air Canada passenger services were primarily targeted to business travellers. Surplus capacity was then made available for leisure travellers. The services of its freight division, i.e., Express Air Canada Cargo, were targeted to individual users, manufacturers, distributors, importers, exporters, handling agents, other businesses, and consumers.

Advertising Strategy

In 1989, Air Canada's target market was primarily the business passenger. In contrast, Eastern Airlines was catering largely to the holiday-maker. Rather than spending all its efforts in fighting for market share, Eastern chose instead to concentrate on increasing market size on some of its routes where competition was minimal.

Media Objective and Execution

Express Air Canada Cargo wanted to build a positive image and maximize its reach. Whereas other airlines focused on various elements of its marketing mix, Express Air Canada Cargo put emphasis on its product.

Express Air Canada Cargo attempted to increase and maintain awareness via media with ideal reach/frequency. When advertising business to business, trade journals are very important.

A typical 2400 line ad by Air Canada ran 12 columns by 200 lines in two colours (red and white since 1965). This would be seen in on-line newspapers by 7 637 870 readers, and in off-line newspapers by up to 877 544 readers. Industrial advertising in a publication of the freight-forwarding industry is more focused to fewer readers, but these are more likely to be purchasers, i.e., well targeted and cost efficient.

In 1989, the national advertising campaign of Express Air Canada Cargo included three-, two-, and one-page ads in trade publications. This was aimed at industrial users, freight forwarders, etc.

Express Air Canada Cargo also advertised in magazines such as *Time* and *Maclean's* and newspapers such as the *Financial Post* and the *Financial Times*.

Creative Strategy

In industrial advertising, the advertiser is trying to appeal to a buyer with expertise about specialized needs. Express Air Canada Cargo ran a full-page ad with the following caption in bold red letters:

THE PROFESSIONALS KNOW THE VALUE OF PRICELESS CARGO

Below the caption was a black and white illustration of cargo being loaded aboard one of Air Canada's Boeing 747 Combi passenger/cargo airliners. The ad appeared in *Air Cargo World*, a monthly trade journal with a circulation of 24 160, and with 88 percent of its readers reportedly involved in purchasing decisions.

Another ad reflected technical information in *Time* magazine (appeared April 24, 1989).

Put our fleet behind your sales

Air Canada Cargo can be a vital asset to your company, because we understand not only *your* needs, but those of your clients as well. And we really care about our role in making your business a success.

We put the resources of Canada's largest air freight operation behind your business.

Our Same-Day Service is the most dependable way to send time-sensitive goods.

Our service is available between most places Air Canada serves in Canada and the U.S., Bermuda, Bahamas and the Caribbean. With a guarantee that your shipment is on the flight of your choice.

Markets in Europe? Our transatlantic flights leave more often to more European destinations than any other airline in Canada. We're also adding four new international destinations this year: Birmingham, Nice, Zagreb and Athens.

And with the help of our interline partners, we can serve just about any market in the world.

Every day, Air Canada Cargo has nearly 500 departures worldwide, with a total capacity of 1300 tonnes (2.9 million pounds). That's a lot of people with a lot of experience taking care of your business.

Call your local Air Canada Cargo office for details

Be up there with the best

In the same magazine, Canadian Airlines International placed a highly creative ad. On one page was an illustration of a panda with wings flying like an angel on a white background. As the reader flips the page, the following is explained: "IT'S EASY. When the Government of China loans giant pandas to Canadian zoos, they make the easy choice. If we can make pandas fly, imagine what we can do for you. Canadian Air Cargo."
Air Canada passenger flights have always transported freight. After World War Two, the airline acquired all-cargo Bristol 170 freighters, to expedite shipments. However, as pointed out by David Roy, spokesman for Express Air Canada Cargo advertising, virtually negligible resources were invested in advertising Air Canada freight services until 1978. A decade later, the importance of advertising had reached an unprecedented extent due to airline deregulation and expansion of the competition (Exhibit 1).

For the 1990s, Express Air Canada Cargo would have to come up with a new advertising plan.

EXHIBIT 1 *Selected Advertisements Specialized in Air Cargo*

Air France Express: Money back guarantee.

American West Airlines Cargo: We've got the whole country wrapped up.

CAAC–The National Airline of the People's Republic of China: When trading with China, be sure to ship your cargo by China's national carrier.

China Airlines Cargo, Taipei, Taiwan, Republic of China: We make sure there are no unscheduled breaks along the way. As far as we are concerned, every cargo shipment on China Airlines is as precious as gold and as delicate as tropical fish.

Delta Air Cargo: With 3900 daily flights to over 240 cities, we can take a load off your mind.

Fast Air: The all-cargo Chilean airline.

Federal Express: Out of all the air express companies in America, only one had landing rights in Japan.

Finnair: Lower rates don't mean much if you can't find your cargo.

Flying Tigers: We're taking care of business.

Iberia Cargo: Ships to Spain.

Japan Air Lines Cargo: Cross a shallow stream as carefully as a deep one. Get your lantern before it grows dark.

KLM Cargo: KLM has spent millions improving its cargo network. Too bad the freight won't be there long enough to enjoy it.

Korean Air Cargo: Fast Class.

Lan Chile Cargo: How do you make a chicken go 600 mph without losing feathers? Where cargo is second to none.

Lufthansa: (Illustration of airplane full of automobiles) It's amazing what aerodynamics can do for a car . . . If Lufthansa can get Cadillac moving at 750 miles an hour, imagine what it can do for you.

Nippon Cargo Airlines: Whether they are tiny pearls or big cars, NCA handles them all in one fashion.

Northwest Cargo: We can think of only one other carrier who's made a bigger commitment to cargo than we have. Noah. (Illustration of Noah's ark.)

Qantas Cargo: Upper decks down under.

Southern Air Transport: The uncommon carrier.

Trans World TWA Cargo: Box launch.

US Air Cargo: US Air passengers come in all shapes and sizes. (Illustration of dog, chicks, computer, apples, plants, and frozen fish.)

United Airlines: We also carry passengers.

Zantop International Airlines Inc.: CV-640, DC-6, L-188, DC-8.

---

[1]This case was researched and written by Leo-Paul Dana, McGill University and Ecole des Hautes Etudes Commerciales.

---

8. PRESSDENT[1]

Mr. Robert Goulet, president of the Certalab Company of Laval, and two of his associates, Mr. Lalande and Mr. Schiller, met this afternoon to discuss the company's marketing strategy. These three businessmen developed a toothpaste dispenser in the form of a pump container which is rapidly gaining the favour of the Canadian consumer. The product, sold initially in Quebec, was introduced successively into Ontario, the Maritimes, and Western Canada. In less than a year Pressdent captured 8 percent of the toothpaste market. Currently, it is attacking foreign markets—in particular the U.S. market, starting with Southern California.

According to Mr. Goulet, the launching of the product was a success in Canada, sales having greatly exceeded all expectations. At the present time Pressdent is available in two sizes (225 ml and 150 ml) and three flavours (mint, regular, and bubble gum). The product is targeted at consumers who are interested in a high-quality product which successfully prevents cavities.

For toothpaste, the growth of sales can mostly take place at the expense of the market share of existing brands. Consequently, a negative reaction is to be expected from multinational corporations such as Procter and Gamble and Colgate. It is Mr. Goulet's opinion that by the year 1987 tubes of toothpaste will disappear from the market.

History

The idea of toothpaste in a container with a pump mounted on the top was born as the result of an experiment by young Nathalie Goulet, aged 11. She tried to put a tube of toothpaste into a pump container. Mr. Goulet observed her, found the idea to be original, and discussed it with his friends. Jacques Lalande, who had worked a number of years for different pharmaceutical companies, seemed particularly interested in this new concept. After numerous discussions on the possibility of commercial production the two businessmen decided to join together and each contribute $4000 for a preliminary study.

In the spring of 1981, they retained the services of the Avril Marketing firm which made a study of 200 housewives. The results of the preliminary test were favourable. Manufacturers of toothpaste were then approached in order to determine if they had the ability to develop a high-quality product which would appeal to consumers. The difficulty lay not in deciding which ingredients to use but rather in the order in which they should be mixed to obtain the texture best suited to the use of the pump.

Four months later, Mr. Goulet and Mr. Lalande concluded that the project was feasible and that the idea was worth the risk of a large investment. It was then that Ronald Schiller, an accountant and friend of Mr. Goulet, decided to join the group. The financial forecast was re-examined and the initial investment was fixed at $100 000 per partner. In addition, they had to obtain financing for $250 000. They prepared the budget estimates for the first year, a cash flow evaluation, and a detailed marketing program. These three documents were presented to various banks in support of the request for financing. After a serious evaluation of the company's financial situation and the market possibilities of the product, the National Bank agreed to advance the necessary funds.

At the beginning of August 1981, everything was ready for the start-up. The contract for making toothpaste was awarded to Polylab. The plastic containers were made in Quebec, the pump came from the U.S., because there were no Canadian producers available. The company entered into negotiations with brokers in food products in Montreal and Toronto. It explored the Ontario market and signed a contract with an important American distributor.

Mr. Goulet, who owned an advertising agency, undertook the production of television commercials. The budget for the introduction of the product was set at $200 000 for 683 messages in the four principal cities of Quebec (Montreal, Sherbrooke, Trois-Rivières, and Quebec). The partners decided to reserve radio time even though the product was not yet being distributed on a large scale. October 16 marked the beginning of the advertising campaign; on this date it was estimated that 60 percent of the distribution points had been covered. The break-even point was fixed at 250 000 units for the first year. Initially, Certalab was to engage in distribution, but since that time the owner of Polylab, Mr. Robert Vachon, and Certalab have joined together to form Certalab International with Ronald Schiller as president. This new international subsidiary is to be concerned specifically with the American market.

It was agreed to penetrate the American market by starting in California and then moving east as the popularity of the product warranted expansion. In California the product is sold on consignment in the large food chains and in drugstores. All merchandise not sold after a month can be returned to Certalab by the retailer.

Marketing Strategy

The company hopes to capture 20 percent of the Canadian market within two years. To accomplish this it plans to spend $500 000 to $600 000 per year for advertising on television and in the print media. The total cost of the planned introduction in Canada will be $1 500 000, $1 000 000 of which will be spent on advertising. In Canada the sales objective for the first year will be 450 000 units.

The potential market in California has been evaluated at $90 000 000. During the first year the company would like to obtain at least 3.5 percent of the market.

Strategy for the First Year

The advertising campaign in Canada emphasizes the container rather than its contents. Canadian television commercials demonstrate the disadvantages of the conventional tube (losing the cap, wasted toothpaste, etc). The total cost of this advertising campaign is over $800 000. According to Ron Schiller, this amount constitutes the minimum required for the large chains to agree to distribute the product. The advertising expenditures are allocated as follows: $400 000 in Quebec, $350 000 in Ontario and Western Canada, and $50 000 in the Maritimes.

The advertising campaign in the U.S. was undertaken in collaboration with an American company, the RAM Group of New York, which has close relations with regional distributors like Crown BBK of Los Angeles. Crown BBK is responsible for the launching of the marketing program for Pressdent in Southern California. Mr. Goulet presented them with an idea for an advertisement that seemed too different. It was modified along the lines of their recommendations, and the filming took place in Quebec using Quebec film stars. The theme of the advertising campaign is the prevention of cavities and economy of use, with emphasis on economy. The advertising states that the Pressdent container gives three times as many brushings as a tube holding the same amount of toothpaste. The campaign officially started on June 14, and the commercial will be aired for a period of ten weeks. The campaign concentrates on the Los Angeles and San Diego areas, where it is judged that the ads will reach 14 000 000 viewers. The cost of the campaign is over $500 000; of this amount $350 000 is for television commercials and $150 000 is for discount coupons. The break-even point for the California region is 400 000 units. The company has made certain that the product will be available in 80 percent of the retail stores (drugstores and supermarkets) before the beginning of the advertising campaign.

In the course of this first year of operation great importance has been attached to public relations. Mr. Goulet has hired staff to promote the product among the trade and consumers. In addition, numerous articles have been written in newspapers and magazines with the purpose of arousing the interest of the public.

Regarding distribution, the company has contacted food brokers and large chain stores. Currently, there are seven distributors in Canada and two in the United States. Distribution in the U.S. is made through two subsidiaries of Crown BBK, namely Clorox Soft Soap and Vidal Sassoon.

Effectiveness of the Launching of the Product

Canada. In May, 1982, sales were 30 percent higher than anticipated. At the present time the volume of sales has passed 750 000 units, and from now until the end of the year at least 2 000 000 more units are expected to be sold.

In Quebec, between October and December, 300 000 units were ordered by wholesalers and drugstores, 50 percent more than predicted. In February Pressdent had already captured 14 percent of the market. However, despite this resounding success certain difficulties were encountered. In the first place, the pump made by the American manufacturer did not exactly meet the specifications of the company, and because of the flat bottom of the container a certain amount of toothpaste was lost to the user. The company was therefore obliged to redesign the container. In the second place, there were problems of vandalism in the supermarkets and drugstores. The button which activates the pump was not enclosed in the container and there was no protective exterior cap. As a result, simply by pressing the push-button vandals could spread toothpaste over the store shelves. Thus, it was necessary to block the push-button and cover it with a plastic cap. Finally, in May the company decided to change suppliers when it learned that one pump in five was defective.

In Ontario, the product did not sell as well as anticipated, because there was no advertising to make the product known to consumers. Also, Dominion did not wish to participate in the price promotion as Certalab had suggested. Since the consumers did not know that the high price of

Pressdent was offset by an economy of use amounting to three times that of an ordinary tube of toothpaste, they did not think it was a wise purchase. Because of the bad experience of Dominion, the other supermarket chains in Ontario did not wish to sell the product.

United States. The introduction of the product in California was a success. However, Procter and Gamble questioned the truth of the advertising for Pressdent. According to them, it is false advertising to claim that with the same volume of dentifrice the liquid dentifrice of Pressdent gives three times as many brushings as a regular toothpaste. Faced with the possibility of legal action the company is considering the question. It is now being studied at Laval University in Quebec.

The *Canadian Consumer* magazine published the results of a test which was conducted in mid-April. Their conclusion was that the Pressdent container of 225 ml gives 450 brushings while the same amount of ordinary toothpaste gives 340 brushings, a ratio of only 1.32 to 1. On the other hand, while they are not yet definitive, results from Laval University seem to more closely approximate those of Certalab. Consequently, at this stage one cannot predict what will happen as a result of Procter and Gamble's objections.

Perspectives for the Future

Marketing managers must prepare for a period of ferocious competition in the dentifrice market during the next few years. As a result, there will be diminished profits for producers and lower prices for consumers.

In Europe there has been a rapid increase in sales of toothpaste in aerosol containers, and Mr. Goulet feels that the European experience will recur in North America. Nevertheless, his company is in the process of preparing a new advertising campaign and, to this end, is negotiating for the right to use the Schtroumffs or Smurfs in the commercials aimed at children.

Question

Taking into account the experience acquired in the Quebec, Canada, and California markets, pre-pare an advertising plan for 1983; justify your recommendations.

Appendix 1   *Chronological Summary of the Launching of Pressdent*

October 1981:	In Québec, distribution of the product in drugstores and supermarkets. More than 10 000 units are sold before the advertising campaign even begins.
November 1981:	Dominion orders 50 000 units for sale in Ontario. The order must be delivered February 1, 1982.
February 1982:	Distribution to retail stores in the principal cities of the Maritimes.
February 1982:	Delivery of 50 000 units to Dominion (Ontario).
March 1982:	Introduction of the product into Western Canada, principally Vancouver.
April 1982:	Beginning of the California offensive in the Los Angeles and San Diego areas. The official launching is to be supported by an advertising campaign.
May 1982:	A businessman from the West Indies approaches Certalab. He requests samples to show to West Indian enterprises which might be interested in the distribution of Pressdent.
May 1982:	Negotiations in progress for the sale of a franchise in Japan.
May 1982:	Negotiations in progress for the sale of the product in England and Italy.
May 1982:	Mr. Goulet announces that Certalab will produce two new products, a Pressdent travel kit and a dishwashing detergent.

June 1982:	In California the product is introduced into Los Angeles and San Diego.
July 1982:	Pressdent is distributed throughout Southern California. Its introduction into Northern California is now being planned.
August 1982:	Pressdent is sold in the Barbados, Trinidad, St. Vincent, and Curaçao.

Appendix 2   Characteristics of the Dentifrice Market

Market Segmentation. The dentifrice market can be divided into three segments:

The "family" segment is 60 percent of the market. It is composed of consumers who are primarily interested in preventing cavities. The important brands targeting this segment are Crest and Colgate.

The "cosmetic" segment consists primarily of teenagers who attach a great deal of importance to white teeth and fresh breath. This segment represents about 20 percent of the global market. Some of the most popular brands are Aim, Aqua Fresh, and Close Up.

The "specialized" segment is comprised of consumers with special problems, such as sensitive teeth, smokers, etc. It includes brands like Topol, Sensodyne, and Pearl Drop.

The Canadian Market. The potential Canadian market is over $83 000 000. Until a few years ago there was a stable market whose growth was due solely to an increase in the size of the population. The appearance of a dentifrice in gel form plus cavity prevention and dental hygiene campaigns organized by schools and dentists have produced an upheaval in the market. Also, it is worth noting that there is a tendency toward the regionalization of national brands. Certain brands have a very large part of the market in particular regions of Canada, which could mean that in the future marketing managers will have to be content with diminishing national sales.

The United States Market. The population of the United States is much more concerned with hygiene than that of Canada. The potential U.S. market is evaluated at $1 billion. Two regions are particularly promising: the state of New York with 18 percent of the total population, and Southern California with 13 percent.

Appendix 3   Conclusions of the Marketing Study Made by Avril Marketing (Spring, 1981)

Crest: 47 percent of sales
Colgate: 18 percent of sales

Brand loyalty is more or less rigid. We have seen this with the appearance on the market of Aqua Fresh, Close Up, and Ultra Brite.

The first element in the decision to purchase is taste (61%), while the second is related to fluoride (36%).

Seven out of ten persons are willing to try a new mint-flavoured dentifrice.

Two-thirds of the purchasers do not know the price of their dentifrice.

60 percent of 200 women interviewed admitted that taste is their first criterion for the selection of a dentifrice.

Elements favoring the product concept are:
–less waste, less loss of dentifrice	21%
–like it, a very good idea	22%
–more practical, easier to use	18%

Other advantages cited:
–cleaner than a tube
–good taste
–faster
–better looking than a tube
–tube crumples, ugly
–with fluoride, it is better
–better for children
–mild toothpaste, not harsh
–more hygienic

Qualities wanted in a dentifrice
–taste/flavour	44%
–freshness, good breath	17%
–fluoride	21%
–reduces cavities	15%

Summary Report of the A.C.C. (Association of Canadian Consumers)—April, 1982

General Evaluation

Liquid dentifrice is a new formula to solve an old problem. It is claimed that dentifrice in a bottle equipped with a pump is more aesthetic and permits more brushings at a low cost. The pump is not entirely convenient to use. It must be replaced on the bottle by hand; however, Pressdent is more economical than ordinary toothpaste.

Test

A selected number of persons applied Pressdent and a regular dentifrice to a toothbrush three times. The weight of each toothbrush before and after each application plus the density of the two kinds of dentifrice enabled us to calculate the volume of each application. Lastly, using the weight and the volume, we calculated the price per application.

Convenience of Use

Pressdent has a single disadvantage; it is necessary to replace the pump after each application.

Economy

Pressdent is about 20 percent cheaper than ordinary toothpastes. Replacement bottles will cost even less.

Recommendation

We recommend Pressdent because it is economical.

---

[1]This case was written by Jacques Boisvert and Helen Lafrenière of H.E.C. in Montréal and translated from French by Elaine Petrof.

---

9. THE CANADIAN CATTLEMEN'S ASSOCIATION[1]

Carolyn McDonnell was preparing for the Fall 1982 meeting of the Canadian Cattlemen's Association. She knew that at the meeting she would be expected to report on the progress of the beef promotion program and outline her advertising plan for the coming year. Producers at the meeting would want to know if the campaign was beneficial to the Canadian beef industry. Ms. McDonnell believed that advertising was at least part of the answer to the beef industry's problem of flagging consumer demand; however, some producers were skeptical. One of her responsibilities at this meeting would be to convince producers that continued financial support of the promotion campaign would be necessary to achieve its goals.

Background to the Campaign

Through the 1970s, the Canadian Cattlemen's Association and the Beef Information Centre were being pressured by producers and producer organizations to develop a high profile advertising campaign for beef similar to the milk, poultry, and pork campaigns. In 1979-80, members of the Alberta Cattle Commission and the Ontario Cattlemen's Association felt strongly enough in favour of advertising to start their own television and newspaper campaigns. Carolyn McDonnell did not believe that these producer organizations were approaching the problem in the best way. Since little was known about the effectiveness of advertising beef, she felt they may be wasting their advertising dollars.

During 1979, the CCA and the BIC commissioned a study to evaluate the benefits of a major advertising campaign to the beef industry. The results were received in August, 1980. The case in favour of promotion includes only two broad arguments. The first is based on evidence that for beef, as for similar products, promotion appears to have been effective. Advertising campaigns which were investigated included those of the Alberta Cattle Commission, the Ontario Cattlemen's Association, the Pork Producers' Marketing Boards of several provinces, the Ontario Turkey Producers' Marketing Board, the Ontario Chicken Producers' Marketing Board, the Ontario Egg Producers' Marketing Board, and the Ontario Milk Marketing Board. Representatives of these organizations were convinced that their promotion had been at least partially effective in accomplishing the desired objectives. However, none of their campaigns had been properly evaluated by an objective outside market research organization.

Other campaigns investigated included a television advertising effectiveness test carried out by the Beef Industry Council in the U.S. The test indicated some positive advertising effectiveness in that beef consumption declined by about half as much in cities exposed to the advertising as in cities where there was no advertising. During the course of the test, national beef consumption was falling. In addition to this evidence, a 1972 British study found improved consumer attitudes and possible increased beef sales in areas where advertising was done. These improvements, however, appeared to be short-lived. Several months after the advertising program concluded, a survey of the consumers revealed that their attitudes were the same as before the advertising program began.

The second argument in favour of a large scale campaign stems from the proposition that advertising can add a certain positive image to the product. It may be possible through advertising to establish and maintain a favourable image for beef. The most desirable image to the project would be the one which most improves consumer demand for beef.

The case presented in the 1979 study against advertising included five points:

1. The evidence that promotion is likely to be effective is based on sketchy evaluations of advertising programs and is generally unconvincing. Although many marketing boards defend their advertising campaigns as effective means of strengthening consumers' demand for their product, analysis of demand before, during, and after was not done to determine whether or not demand had changed.

2. Consumption is high and demand for beef should remain strong without promotion. Consumption of beef has always been constrained by supply, therefore promotion will not sell any more, regardless of how effective it is.

3. A satisfactory promotion program would require a large investment with a significant risk over an extended period of time. Since producers would be financing the campaign through voluntary checkoff contributions, early indications of advertising effectiveness would be necessary to maintain continued producer support.

4. Even if promotion was successful at stimulating the demand for beef, producer profits may not increase. Any increase in the demand could be met with higher levels of imported beef. If Canada imposed more restrictive barriers towards beef imports, the U.S. most likely would reciprocate with similar barriers towards Canada's beef exports. It is normally in favour of Canadian producers to have unrestrictive trade policies, especially toward the U.S. It is unlikely that the Canadian beef industry would be better off with increased consumer demand created through advertising, but without access to the U.S. market.

5. The retail and the HRI (Hotel, Restaurant, and Institutional) trades make the final sales to the consumer. These industries could realize the benefits of a producer financed promotion campaign simply by increasing their marketing margins on beef.

These arguments against advertising were not perceived as real problems by many in the industry. Some argued that the demand for beef would not remain strong without some promotional push. With respect to the cost of advertising, it was estimated that an advertising campaign of $3 million could be financed by as small an increase in average beef prices as two cents per pound. The likelihood of Canadian advertising strengthening beef demand for foreign suppliers is small. The Beef Industry Council (BIC) is advertising beef nationally in the U.S. If Canadian producers advertise, the consumption and prices in both countries should improve together. Alternately, Canadian advertising may be able to establish and exploit a preference for Canadian beef. When the pros and cons regarding advertising were weighed, the study concluded that the case for advertising narrowly outweighed the case against it. The argument that the industry could control the consumers' image of beef was the deciding factor in favour of advertising.

The results of the initial study convinced members of the CCA that a consumer attitude study was necessary before a promotional strategy could be developed. Cheryl Clark of Actionable Market Research Limited was contracted in November of 1980 to identify exactly how consumers thought and felt about beef. The specific objectives of the study were to determine:

- the current perceptions of beef compared to alternate forms of protein,
- beef usage patterns,
- frequency of in-home and out-of-home beef consumption,
- awareness of, and attitudes towards recipes and information sources,
- how consumers perceive the relationship between beef prices and increases in income.

Women from households in every province were surveyed to arrive at the observations summarized below.

Consumer Perceptions of Beef. Several positive attitudes towards beef were identified. It was rated better than competitive products in terms of taste appeal, versatility, overall convenience, and usefulness on the barbecue. The negatively perceived attribute of beef was its high price relative to other meats. It was ranked third, out of four, in terms of value for money. Perceptions of high calorie and fat content gave beef a low nutritional rating, and some cuts of beef were seen as not convenient to prepare.

Perceptions of beef varied with consumption and with consumers' affluence. As consumption increased, perceived convenience, taste appeal, versatility, value for money, and healthfulness improved. Perceived fat content and expensiveness diminished. Medium users found beef most useful on the barbecue, while light users saw it as having fat content. As consumers' affluence increased, perceived expensiveness increased and perceived value for money and healthfulness decreased. Also, as consumers' affluence increased, their perceptions of beef's usefulness on the barbecue improved.

The overall image of beef was poorer than chicken, equivalent to fish, but somewhat better than pork. Beef use and image were highest in Quebec and the western provinces where the greatest proportions of heavy users resided. In the Maritimes and Ontario, beef has done poorly as a consequence of strong competition from pork and, to a lesser extent, chicken.

Within the beef category, different cuts have different images. Roast beef has by far the best image, while pot roast and stewing beef have far less impressive images. Ground beef, on the other hand, is perceived almost as another product altogether. Heavy users have more positive images of all cuts than medium or light users. They are less inclined to express a desire to eat more of the prime cuts and less of the cheaper cuts. Medium users are more inclined to admit that they would like to eat the prime cuts more frequently and the cheaper cuts less often.

Product Usage. The decline in beef use has been a national phenomenon. Frequency in serving beef as the main course of a meal has slipped more severely than has the size of the portions served. Use of more expensive cuts has fallen far more severely than the use of less expensive cuts. Experimentation in preparation of beef is relatively limited. Common reasons given for the lack of experimentation include fear of wasting money, apathy, and time constraints.

Three categories of beef consumers were identified: heavy, medium, and light users. Heavy and medium users were most likely to choose beef as the highest of the meats in terms of taste appeal, versatility, and convenience. They identified taste appeal as the most important attribute. Light users were more likely to identify chicken or fish as being higher on these attributes. In fact, differentiation between the light and medium user groups was made solely on their respective images of beef relative to other meats. In all other respects such as demographics (income, age, education, etc.), family backgrounds, and beef cuts normally used, both the medium and light user groups were very similar.

Differentiation between medium and heavy users could be made in terms of demographics, psychographics, and cuts of beef purchased. Heavy users were more likely to have an executive as household head, be somewhat more sophisticated in tastes, have a higher income, and purchase more of the expensive cuts. Both medium and heavy users were equally positive on the benefits of beef. What appeared to account for their different levels of consumption was a difference in their abilities to pay for it.

In-Home versus Out-of-Home Consumption. Some form of beef is served in approximately one-half of all meals served at home. Beef is included in about one in three home lunches (consumed mostly by women and children). Forty percent of the lunch market eats at cafeterias or from bagged lunches. Beef is more likely to be eaten in the cafeteria than from a bagged lunch. In fast food restaurants, which account for slightly over one-half of the meals eaten out of the home, beef is featured in almost three out of four meals. It is featured in one out of two meals eaten at family and fancy restaurants. These restaurants account for one in three, and one in six out-of-home meals, respectively.

Information. Most women demonstrated an extensive desire for information on beef. They were interested in learning how to become a better judge of quality, and how to better economize with the product. Pamphlets and brochures were by far the preferred mediums through which women would like to get more information. It was also found that awareness of the BIC was extremely low among surveyed households.

Beef Prices/Income Increases. It was generally believed that beef prices had increased more than incomes over the previous three years. Reasons most commonly cited as responsible for the increase in beef prices include: inflation, rising costs, and excessive profits (taken by packers and the stores).

The Promotion Campaign

On the basis of the advertising effectiveness and the consumer attitude studies, Ms. McDonnell decided to go ahead with the development of a major advertising campaign in 1981. Most of the funding would be raised through the sales check-off of fifty cents per head sold in British Columbia, Alberta, Manitoba, Ontario, and Nova Scotia. In addition, the Alberta government would contribute $900 000 in the first year, and the Saskatchewan government $100 000, on behalf of beef producers in that province.

An advertising consultant was hired to aid and advise the BIC in directing the campaign. The first step was to establish goals. As the primary goal, it was hoped that consumer attitudes towards beef could be improved over the long term through advertising. In the short term, the campaign was expected to stimulate beef demand.

The F.H. Hayhurst Advertising Agency was retained to design the campaign in conjunction with BIC staff. The information obtained from the Actionable Market Research consumer attitude study was used in the campaign development. A target of 18- to 49-year-old women in the medium user category was selected. It was felt that these users could be moved into the heavy user category. Consumers in the light user category had many negative perceptions of beef. As a result, the cost of the message frequency necessary to influence their purchasing habits could be prohibitive. Consumers in the heavy user category already had positive attitudes towards beef which would be reinforced by the advertising.

To promote consumption and improve attitudes towards beef, the campaign was designed to reinforce positive attitudes and downplay the importance of negative attitudes with the hope of altering them. The copy thrust placed emphasis on the positive emotional feelings people have about beef. "Beef Sounds Good" was selected as the campaign theme to be used in all promotion materials.

The F.H. Hayhurst agency developed media materials for use in television, major Canadian magazines, in-store promotions, and direct mailings. The television commercial, "Beef Sounds Good—Any Way You Slice It," was developed. It attempted to sell the steak by selling the sizzle, featuring 31 different images of beef including hamburgers, casseroles, fondue, ribs, prime rib roast, steak Diane, and porterhouse steak— among others. To fix the slogan "Beef Sounds Good" in people's minds, it was sung to a catchy accompanying jingle. The commercial was aired on a network basis for a 22-week period starting September 1982. Meanwhile, other commercials featuring "Beef Sounds Good—On a Barbecue" were in production for airing in the spring and summer of 1983.

Supporting magazine advertisements were carried in *Chatelaine*, *Canadian Living*, and *Homemaker's* (see Exhibit 1). These ads highlighted "Beef Sounds Good—On a Budget" and present information on cutting a cross-rib roast into three meals, recipe messages, and mail-in recipe offers. Presentation of newspaper or radio ads with retail tie-ins were planned for later in the campaign.

The total cost for the first year of the beef advertising campaign was expected to reach $2.8 million by March 1983. Television commercial airing costs were the most significant at $1.8 million. $400 000 was budgeted for magazine advertisements. The remainder would be spent on the development and production of promotion materials, and on evaluation and test market studies.

A detailed tracking study to monitor consumer attitudes was scheduled to be carried out on an ongoing basis by Actionable Market Research. A sample of retailers were requested to report each month the pounds of beef sold on a regular and "special" basis in each of the three categories. In addition, selected test markets were established to receive double exposure of TV commercials, newspaper advertisements, and direct mailings. Ms. Clark of Actionable would be evaluating the effect of these increased exposure rates on consumers' attitudes and purchasing patterns. It was hoped that optimal media mix and frequency rates could be determined for future campaigns.

As she began preparing her report for the upcoming CCA meeting, Carolyn began to wonder about various aspects of the advertising cam-

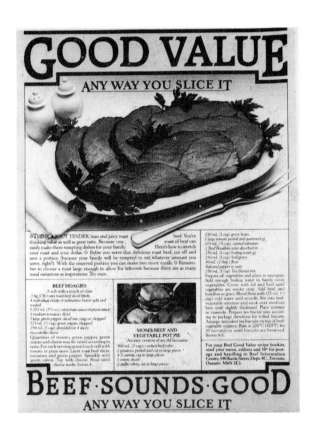

EXHIBIT 1

paign: Had it really addressed the major problems facing the beef industry in Canada? What other courses of action could have been chosen? Was the campaign well-designed? She knew that these were the types of questions she must be prepared to answer.

---

[1]Copyright 1985. This case was prepared by Thomas Funk and Peter Evans, University of Guelph.

---

10. NEW COKE[1]

Situation Summary
On April 23, 1985, Coca-Cola of Canada replaced the 99-year-old classic beverage Coca-Cola with "New Coke." The new soft drink is considerably sweeter than the classic Coca-Cola produced with high-fructose corn syrup in the United States; its sugar content is the same as that of the classic Coca-Cola produced with pure cane sugar in Canada, but the ratio of other ingredients has been changed (Coca-Cola was already sweeter in Canada than its U.S. version.)

In September 1985, Coca-Cola of Canada brings back its original Coca-Cola to compliment the New Coke. Unlike their American counterparts, consumers in Canada seem to prefer the taste of New Coke over its predecessor, now sold under the name Coca-Cola Classic; according to an audit by A.C. Nielsen, New Coke captured 12.8 percent of the total Canadian soft-drink market, compared with 9.4 percent for Coca-Cola Classic during October and November.

Neville Kirchmann has been appointed president of Coca-Cola of Canada. He hopes the new flavour will win converts from other beverages. Whereas soft drinks are the most popular beverage in the United States, in Canada these rank behind coffee and milk, ranking about equal with beer.

Cherry Coke was scheduled to enter test markets in Vancouver and Winnipeg in November 1985, adding to the Coke extension. "Coke is it" was a popular slogan in 1982, but since then the product line has been extended with the introduction of: a) Diet Coke/Coke Light produced according to various ratios of saccharine, aspartame, cyclamates, saccharine-cyclamates and saccharine-fructose; b) Caffeine-Free Coke; c) New Coke;

d) Cherry Coke; as well as e) Coca-Cola Classic. A new campaign is needed.

While Pepsi Cola's advertising expenditures in Canada were $10.9 million in 1984, Coca-Cola of Canada spent $14.3 million. The annual advertising budget will be increased by up to $4.5 million.

Introduction
In 1886, Dr. John Styth Pemberton, pharmacist, developed a sweet-tasting brown syrup which, when mixed with soda fountain water, produced a novel taste. Thinking that it would look good in advertising, Frank M. Robinson suggested the name Coca-Cola and penned it in flowing Spencerian script. On May 8, the new elixir was made available for sale, at Jacob's Pharmacy, for five cents per glass. During that month, the drink was advertised as "Delicious and Refreshing." Pemberton grossed $50 on Coca-Cola that year, having spent $73.96 on advertising; by 1892 advertising expenditures had reached $11 000; by 1920 they reached $2 million. In 1927 Coca-Cola was first advertised on radio, in 1950 on television. In the 1980s, Coca-Cola expanded its product line, and prepared for aggressive advertising for the 1990s and into the twenty-first century.

The Market, the Product, and Positioning
Canadians spend $2.2 billion annually on soft drinks, 50 percent of which are colas. Seven million Cokes are consumed daily in Canada, making it the third highest Coke-consuming country, after the U.S. and Mexico.

In 1983, Coca-Cola of Canada posted profits of $17.1 million (Cdn.) on $432.8 million of sales; it seemed healthy compared to Pepsi Cola's profits of only $4.7 million on $253.2 million of sales. In 1984, profits for Coca-Cola of Canada were down to $11.5 million on $498.7 million of sales. What was even more disturbing for Coca-Cola executives was the steady decline of market share to Pepsi. The response was to create a New Coke, more similar to Pepsi, and to diversify the product line.

Whereas in 1981 there was only one Coke, in 1982 Diet Coke was introduced, positioned "as the *best tasting* drink in a highly developed and competitive low-calorie market." In Western Europe, legal or cultural constraints made it advisable to use the trademark "Coca-Cola Light," positioned slightly differently because of the slow category development of the low-calorie market; thus advertising overseas emphasizes low-calorie attributes rather than taste.

New Coke has four more calories than the old, but two fewer than Pepsi; it is slightly sweeter, yet designed to be less filling. In the U.S., Classic Coke is significantly more popular than New Coke: by a margin of 9 to 1 in Minneapolis, 8 to 1 in New York, 8 to 1 in Dallas, 4 to 1 in Philadelphia, 3 to 1 in Washington, D.C.

Market Share

Coca-Cola was steadily losing market share to its rival Pepsi. Since 1977, Pepsi was outselling Coca-Cola in U.S. food stores; Coca-Cola's supermarket share has been shrinking 1 percent each year since 1981. Unlike in the U.S., Coca-Cola had the lead in supermarket shelf space in Canada.

According to A.C. Nielsen, Coca-Cola had 27.7 percent of all carbonated soft drinks in 1984 and just slightly less in 1985. New Coke was expected to raise Coca-Cola's share of the Canadian soft drink market by 2 percent, boosting sales by $20 million.

Marketing Strategy

Classic Coca-Cola was packaged with the trademarked Spencerian script. For identification and differentiation purposes, New Coke would be advertised in modern script only.

Chairman Robert C. Goizueta announced: "What we are in is the business of creating consumers, not products. Now in these times, more than ever before, marketing must make things happen."

Advertising for New Coke was to induce customers to try the new product and suggest reuse, then increase product usage. However, the public was quite confused. Forty percent of survey respondents were not sure which was new, Coca-Cola Classic or (new) Coke, and 13 percent didn't know, or thought that New Coke was the original and that Coca-Cola was the new product.

Specifically, Neville Kirchmann, president of Coca-Cola of Canada, expected to increase Coca-Cola's share of the soft drink market and widen the gap over Pepsi by an additional two share points. Apart from consumer advertising, separate advertisements were being designed to be shown to franchises, as a campaign to sell to bottlers; the objective was to assure the bottlers that Coca-Cola has a clear vision of its direction, and also to have something new for the fall season.

Target Market

New Coke being sweeter and less bitter than Coca-Cola Classic, its objective was to appeal especially to teenage tastebuds. The cola market in Canada was flat and teenagers were targeted as the only segment of the cola-drinking population having any potential for volume gains. In Canada, the biggest consumers of soft drinks are between the ages of 12 and 19. Given that the degree of acceptance of New Coke tapers off with older consumers, Mr. Kirchmann said that if those consumers are lost in the scramble for the youth market, the company would just have to accept it.

Advertising Strategy and Media Objectives

The goal of Coca-Cola's agency is for advertising to be a pleasurable experience, refreshing to watch, and pleasant to listen to. It should reflect quality by being quality; its aim is to make the audience wish to be drinking Coca-Cola with the people in the advertisement.

Their strategy is to adopt pattern advertising, developed from a prototype concept, created through sharing information among Coca-Cola and advertising agency offices in affluent countries. Then international managers again review the resulting advertisements, determining the specific adaptations to be made in each country.

Coca-Cola wants its advertising to be relevant, lifestyle-oriented, contemporary, fashionable, and up-to-date. The medium of television is used to capture the essence of life today, the same way magazines did for many years.

Product line extensions have laid the groundwork for a megabrand approach. An umbrella approach to New Coke and Coca-Cola Classic seems reasonable.

Creative

When Coca-Cola of Canada first introduced New Coke, the competition printed the following text in the press:

TO ALL BOTTLERS OF PEPSI-COLA AND
PEPSI-COLA COMPANY PERSONNEL:

It gives me great pleasure to offer each of you my heartiest congratulations.

After 51 years of going at it eyeball to eyeball, the other guy just blinked.

Coca-Cola is withdrawing their product from the marketplace, and is reformulating brand Coke. But why? Everyone knows when something is right it doesn't need changing.

Maybe they finally realized what we have known for years . . . Pepsi tastes better than Coke.

There is no question the long-term market success of Pepsi has forced this move.

Well, people in trouble tend to do desperate things . . . and we'll have to keep our eye on them.

But for now, I say victory is sweet, and we have earned a celebration.

Enjoy!

Pepsi Cola's aggressive advertising was targeted at teenagers, with commercials featuring Lionel Ritchie and Michael Jackson. Coca-Cola advertised New Coke with a series of commercials in which Bill Cosby says that he likes New Coke more than its 99-year-old predecessor.

A problem now that Coca-Cola has reintroduced the old brand is that the use of Bill Cosby in an umbrella approach would cause a credibility problem.

One advantage for Coca-Cola of Canada over the Coca-Cola of the U.S. is that much of Coca-Cola's U.S. advertising has been steeped in Americana, creating emotional attachment; the result is resistance against New Coke. Advertising New Coke in Canada may be easier.

Question

You are asked to develop an advertising campaign for New Coke in the Canadian market, focusing specifically on the creative plan.

Appendix
Advertising Themes Used for Coca Cola Since 1886

1886 Drink Coca-Cola
1904 Delicious and Refreshing
1905 Coca-Cola Revives and Sustains
1906 The Great National Temperance Beverage
1917 Three Million a Day
1922 Thirst Knows No Season
1925 Six Million a Day
1927 Around the Corner from Everywhere
1929 The Pause that Refreshes
1932 Ice-Cold Sunshine
1938 The Best Friend Thirst Ever Had
1939 Coca-Cola Goes Along
1939 Wherever You Are, Whatever You Do, Wherever You May Be, When You Think of Refreshment Think of Ice-Cold Coca-Cola
1942 The Only Thing like Coca-Cola Itself. It's the Real Thing
1948 Where There's Coke There's Hospitality
1949 Coca-Cola . . . Along the Highway to Anywhere
1952 What You Want is a Coke
1956 Coca-Cola . . . Makes Good Things Taste Better
1957 Sign of Good Taste
1958 The Cold, Crisp Taste of Coke

1959	Be Really Refreshed	1976	Coke Adds Life
1963	Things Go Better with Coke	1979	Have a Coke and a Smile
1970	It's the Real Thing	1982	Coke Is It!
1971	I'd Like to Buy the World a Coke	1985	It's a Kick; It's a Hit; Coke is it
1975	Look Up America, See What We've Got		

[1]This case was researched and written by Leo-Paul Dana, McGill University and Ecole des Hautes Etudes Commercials.

11. AYLMER FAIR[1]

John White, president of the Aylmer and East Elgin Agricultural Society, was sifting through a marketing report prepared by an external consultant. It was March 1985 and Mr. White was beginning to plan for the August 1985 edition of Aylmer Fair. The consultant indicated that the fair's advertising was not as effective as it could be but Mr. White was unsure as to what specific changes the fair should undertake.

The Fair Industry in Ontario

Almost all the fairs in Ontario were organized by agricultural societies like the one in Aylmer. Each society relied on a large team of volunteers to organize the fair. Each fair had an executive comprised of a past president, president, first and second vice presidents, secretary, and treasurer. Operating under the executive were a series of committees responsible for the activities that form a fair, such as the Cattle Committee, the Reception Committee, the Poultry Committee, the Advertising Committee, etc.

For purposes of scheduling, societies were grouped into 15 districts spanning the province, and within these districts, fairs were given a classification of A, B, or C. In 1984, there were 30 A fairs (including the C.N.E., the Rockton's World Fair, Ancaster Fair, and the Western Fair), 60 B fairs (e.g., Binbrook Fair), and 142 C fairs (such as the Ohsweken Fair and the Burford Fair).

Though as many as 26 fairs could be scheduled at the same time, they would not directly compete with each other because of geographic dispersion. Instead, the major competition to the industry came from other entertainment sources like television, movies, theatre, pageants, festivals, and even Canada's Wonderland.

Aylmer Fair History

First held in 1853, Aylmer Fair had been organized annually by the Aylmer and East Elgin Agricultural Society. Aylmer was a small (Pop: 5500) southwestern Ontario town located ten miles north of Lake Erie between St. Thomas (Pop: 15 000) and Tillsonburg (Pop: 9000) and 25 miles southeast of London (Pop: 300 000). Though originally a one-day spring event, the Aylmer Fair was now five days long, and was scheduled for the third week of August. The Aylmer Fair was classified as a B fair.

The hours of operation for the fair varied from day to day: Wednesday (4 P.M. to 10 P.M.), Thursday to Saturday (10 A.M. to 10 P.M.), and Sunday (12 P.M. to 6 P.M.). The exhibit buildings were open at noon and closed with the fair, while the midway did not start up until 1 P.M. and was operated past midnight.

In addition to the midway, there was lots to see and do at the fair. There were judged exhibits of: work done in high schools (woodwork, metalwork, typing, etc.) and elementary schools (writing, printing, drawing, etc.); baking, preserves, and handicrafts; vegetable, flower, tobacco, 4-H, and grain displays; and a poultry show. While these exhibits did not change on a day-to-day basis, the cattle and horse shows varied over the duration of the fair (e.g., Holstein, Jersey, Guernsey, Ayrshire, and Hereford cattle shows).

Many of the events at the fair were aimed specifically at children. Sunday was Family Day and not only were children under 12 admitted free but also the midway had a special all-day ride passport for sale. Sunday also had a Baby Show where more than 135 babies competed for prizes while accompanied by proud parents and grand-parents. On Wednesday, Children's Day, there were special events for the children to enter ranging from decorated tricycles and bicycles to foot races to bubble gum blowing. Thursday highlighted the Pet Show with classes for cats, dogs, rabbits, gerbils, and in 1984, a minnow-eating duck.

At night, the drawing card was entertainment in front of the grandstand. Wednesday brought the crowning of "Miss Aylmer Fair," the Official Fair Opening by a celebrity (in 1984, Bobby Hull), and a motorcycle thrill show called the "Death Riders" whose highlight was the "Human Bomb." On Thursday rock-and-roll sounds were generated by groups such as "Teenage Head," while Friday, the roar of a Mini-Tractor Pull drew throngs. Saturday night offered the "Chicago Knockers," a troupe of swimsuit-clad female mud wrestlers. On Sunday afternoon the crowd cheered for the Semi-Truck Pull. (Pulls consisted of a vehicle dragging a load which became heavier the father it was pulled; the vehicle which could drag the load the farthest, usually 100 to 200 metres, was declared the winner.) Entertainment highlights of recent years included the "Hell Drivers" (an automobile thrill show), a local Talent Show, and such varied entertainers as Wilf Carter, Sylvia Tyson, and Cheryl and Robbie Rae.

One other feature of the fair was commercial exhibits on view in the arena. These were displays of household wares by local merchants. Some commercial exhibitors included Tates' Home Furnishings, Gulf Farm Service, the London Free Press, the Elgin Co-operative, and Fanshawe College.

Admission charges were levied each day of the fair. Adults paid $3.00 at all times, but children, who usually paid $1.00, were free on Wednesday until 6 P.M. and all day on Sunday. No distinction was made in admission rates for senior citizens and students. Six weeks prior to the fair opening, people had the opportunity to purchase a pass to the fair which offered multiple admissions for $5.00. Passes were valid on any day but could only be used for three admissions in total. At no time was parking, at the rate of $1.00 per car, included with the pass. Should any person need to leave the fair and return at a later time that same day (say to get a sweater), that person was stamped on the back of the hand. The stamp design and colour were changed each day.

The midway also contributed to the fair's revenues. Midway operations were conducted independently of the fair by Conklin's Amusements—the largest supplier of amusements in Canada. Conklin's operated many travelling midways in Ontario to service the fair trade. For Aylmer Fair, the large trucks of equipment usually arrived on the Sunday prior to the fair. The rides and concession stands were set up on Monday and Tuesday and these provided some advance publicity, as they were quite visible to anyone passing through town on Highway 3 (one of the two Ontario Highways that intersected at Aylmer).

Finances and Promotion at the Fair

The fair generated money in four ways: 1) admission charges and parking fees; 2) rentals paid by commercial exhibitors and midway operators; 3) entry fees from exhibitors; and 4) grants and donations. This money was used to pay for: 1) prize money; 2) entertainment; 3) operating expenses; 4) administrative expenses; and 5) advertising. Comparative figures are given in Tables 1 and 2.

In recent years, many directors had been dissatisfied with the performance of the Aylmer Fair. Though the fair built a new cattle barn in 1958, a new secretary's office in 1973 and a new curling club in 1980, financial performance over the past few years had been spotty. The fair had been operating around break-even, showing minimal profits and losses and many wondered how the fair board would be able to pay back the $15 000 bank loan used in the construction of the curling club.

TABLE 1 ATTENDANCE AND ADMISSION CHARGES 1979–84

	1979	1980	1981*	1982	1983	1984
Paid Attendance:						
Adults	13 373	13 185	10 592	12 175	11 903	11 575
Children	2 744	3 213	2 088	2 223	1 681	1 597
Cars Parked	1 855	1 765	1 751	2 004	1 689	1 960
Memberships Sold	1 540	1 348	1 180	1 090	1 026	689
Price: Adults	$2.00	$2.50	$2.50	$2.50	$2.50	$3.00
Children	0.50	1.00	1.00	1.00	1.00	1.00
Parking	1.00	1.00	1.00	1.00	1.00	1.00
Memberships	4.00	5.00	5.00	5.00	5.00	5.00

TABLE 2 SELECTED FINANCIAL DATA 1979–83

	1979	1980	1981*	1982	1983	1984
Revenues:	$62 409	$74 213	$67 513	$77 431	$74 333	$77 481
Admission Charges & Parking	36 132	43 742	36 740	41 377	38 263	42 287
Midway & Commercial Rentals	13 062	15 585	16 596	18 832	20 110	18 094
Exhibitor Entry Fees	3 084	4 152	3 391	3 448	3 870	4 166
Grants and Donations	10 121	10 764	10 846	13 734	12 090	12 934
Expenses:	$65 638	$63 291	$67 996	$70 752	$74 830	$78 815
Prize Money	17 381	17 117	16 825	15 647	17 333	16 682
Entertainment	13 330	13 264	13 728	12 998	10 566	16 288
Operating Expenses	15 216	11 668	12 373	20 045	23 415	23 600
Administration Expenses	16 900	17 192	20 167	16 995	18 020	15 275
Advertising	2 811	4 050	4 911	5 067	5 496	6 970
Profit (Loss) on Operations	$ (3 229)	$10 922	$ (423)	$ 6 679	$ (497)	$ (1 334)

* In 1981, Aylmer Fair experienced 3 days of "off-and-on" rainstorms.

The fair board felt that their position in the people's minds was changing, so Aylmer Fair responded with increased promotion. Two examples are given here. The first was designed to increase the purchase of membership passes. Starting four weeks before the fair, a draw was made on Friday night at the town corners, from all the passes sold to that point in time. Each week, six names were drawn and those lucky people won five dollars. As well, each night of the fair, one ticket was drawn for a $50 cash prize. If that person was at the fair, they would win double the money—$100!

A second facet of the promotional effort was advertising. Ten years ago, the Aylmer fair advertised through three vehicles— the *Aylmer Express*, posters, and word-of-mouth. Some free publicity also was generated by the TV, radio, and newspaper reporters sent to cover the fair as a news item.

In recent years, the attitude toward advertising had changed. Advertising had been directed not only to Aylmer, but to the larger markets of London and St. Thomas through a host of media: BX-93, a country and western FM station in London; CJBK, a pop/rock AM station in London; CFPL-TV, the closest TV station, located in London; CHLO, a middle-of-the-road AM station in St. Thomas; CKOT, a middle-of-the-road AM station in Tillsonburg; the *Elgin County Market*, a free paper distributed to the doorstep of every Elgin county household; and the original three — the *Aylmer Express* (the Wednesday weekly newspaper of Aylmer); posters, and word-of-mouth. In the past five years, advertising expenses have more than doubled.

Radio and television advertising began the week before the fair and continued until the last day of the fair. Ads in the two weekly papers appeared on the Wednesday before the fair and on the opening day. Posters went up two weeks before the fair. There was not enough money in the budget to take advantage of all the media alternatives. Newspapers in Tillsonburg and St. Thomas along with many other London radio stations were not used.

The Consultant's Report

To help the fair improve its performance, an external consultant was hired to review the fair's operations and suggest areas for improvements. Though the report covered all the facets of the fair, two parts of his report related directly to advertising.

During the 1984 Aylmer Fair, the consultant conducted some market research in the form of a self-administered survey. The questionnaire was camouflaged as an opportunity for people to enter a free draw. Everyone who passed through one of the four admission gates was given the survey which was printed on both sides of card stock (about the size and thickness of a post card). None of the seven questions asked were open-ended (other than name and address) and all could be answered with a checkmark or a circle.

The survey was co-sponsored by the St. Thomas AM radio station, CHLO. They had a display in the arena along with the other commercial exhibitors and they provided a drum in which people deposited their cards. A draw was made daily at 10 P.M. from the cards for $25 in cash or a $50 gift certificate from one of the commercial exhibitors. Once the draw was completed, the remaining cards were removed from the drum

so that responses could be compared by day of attendance. The survey card is shown in Exhibit 1.

CHLO & AYLMER FAIR FREE DRAW
$25.00 Cash or $50.00 Purchase Voucher Daily
YOU MUST ANSWER ALL QUESTIONS ON THE
FRONT & BACK TO BE ELIGIBLE TO WIN

•NAME: _____ (Please Print)

•AGE: Under 12☐ 13-21 ☐ 22-35 ☐ 36-45 ☐ 46-55 ☐ 56 & up ☐

•WHICH ADS FOR AYLMER FAIR HAVE YOU SEEN OR HEARD? (☑ ALL That Apply)
   None ☐ CHLO ☐ BX-93 ☐ CJBK ☐ CFPL-TV ☐
   Posters ☐ Aylmer Express ☐ Elgin County Market ☐
•PLEASE CIRCLE ABOVE THE ONE YOU REMEMBER BEST

•DID YOU PAY ADMISSION AT THE GATE?
   Yes ☐ No ☐

•IN THE LAST FIVE YEARS, HOW MANY YEARS HAVE YOU ATTENDED AYLMER FAIR?
   1 year ☐ 2 years ☐ 3 years ☐ 4 years ☐ 5 years ☐

•WHY DID YOU COME TO THE FAIR TODAY? (☑ ALL That Apply)
   Grandstand Show ☐ Midway ☐ Horse Show ☐ Cattle Show ☐
   Agricultural Exhibits ☐ Ladies' Work ☐ Arena Exhibits ☐
   Baby Show ☐ Other ☐

•PLEASE CIRCLE THE ONE ABOVE THAT WAS THE MAIN REASON

•ADDRESS _____ TOWN _____ (Please Print)

•PHONE _____ POSTAL CODE _____

DROP FORM AT CHLO BOOTH IN ARENA
DRAWS AT 9 A.M. DAILY (SUNDAY AT 5)
GOOD LUCK!!

EXHIBIT 1 *The Survey Card (Front and Back)*

Of the approximately 10 000 cards given out, 2915 were returned during the five fair days. The 29 percent response rate was considered to be fairly good for this type of survey. In coding the surveys for analysis on the computer, the sex of the respondent was determined from his or her name, the address indicated the respondent's location and the day of attendance was noted. The results of the survey are presented in Exhibit 2.

The consultant was also able to assign dollars to the media vehicles used for promotion. Table 3 presents a cost breakdown of the advertising dollars spent for the Aylmer Fair.

TABLE 3 **ADVERTISING DOLLAR BREAKDOWN FOR 1984**

Media Used	Cost
Radio: CJBK	$ 384
CHLO	1179
CKOT	780
BX-93	1160
Television: CFPL	1414
Print: *Aylmer Express*	1099
Elgin County Market	653
Posters	301
Total	$6970

The Problem

Given the various pieces of information he had in front of him, John White was uncertain what steps should be taken to improve the advertising for 1985. After all, Mr. White was a volunteer on the Fair Board. The rest of the time, he operated a successful farm operation and raised Jersey Cattle.

Should the advertising budget be increased, decreased, or left at the same level ? Should the distribution of the advertising dollars be changed and, if so, in what manner ? Should any medium be dropped ? Perhaps money was not an issue. Maybe the ads themselves were to blame. Mr. White thought the ads were effective but he had no business experience with advertising.

He needed to know the answers to these questions. The Aylmer Fair Board wanted a profit in 1985 !

EXHIBIT 2 *Summary of Survey Results*

SEX: Male 42.2% Female 57.8%

AGE: 12 & Under 8.9% 13–21 20.3% 22–35 32.3% 36–45 15.0% 46–55 8.4% 56 & Over 15.0%

MOST REMEMBERED AD: CHLO 13.1% BX-93 11.7% CJBK 7.9% CFPL-TV 8.2% Posters 6.8% Aylmer Express 22.1% Elgin County Market 22.2% CKOT 7.1%

ADS SEEN/HEARD: CHLO 35.0% BX-93 32.5% CJBK 23.7% CFPL-TV 26.7% Posters 30.1% *Aylmer Express* 44.9% None 10.0% *Elgin County Market* 51.6% CKOT 23.9% (Percentages do not add to 100% because of multiple responses.)

MOST IMPORTANT ATTRACTION: Grandstand Show 38.0% Midway 23.2% Agricultural Exhibit 5.8% Horse Show 5.1% Cattle Show 4.3% Ladies Work 8.0% Commercial Exhibits 12.2% Baby Show 3.3%

ATTRACTIONS THAT THEY CAME TO SEE: Grandstand Show 58.0% Midway 47.3% Agricultural Exhibit 30.9% Horse Show 16.3% Cattle Show 14.5% Ladies Work 28.0% Commercial Exhibits 44.4% Baby Show 9.6% (Percentages do not add to 100% because of multiple responses.)

RESPONDENTS LOCATION: Urban Aylmer 21.7% Rural Aylmer 18.8% St. Thomas 16.1% Elgin Other 14.5% London 10.1% Middlesex-Oxford 10.3% Other 8.4%

---

12. LULU'S ROADHOUSE[1]

"I don't think that it's a problem yet but it is something we will definitely have to look at in the future." That was Frank Lizzotti's comment about the use of advertising at Lulu's Roadhouse in Kitchener, Ontario. It was June 1987 and as General Manager, Frank had witnessed a plateau and then decline in revenue generated by Canada's largest roadhouse. For the first two years after opening, Lulu's had done no advertising. Two years ago that policy changed but total revenue had not increased since then.

Company Background

Karl Magid had been involved in the commercial and residential real estate market in and around Toronto for many years. In 1977, he was unable to find a buyer for a property in Belleville. He saw this as an opportunity and opened a small restaurant. Having success with this venture he turned to the Kitchener area and opened an 80-seat restaurant. Success led to two more restaurants being opened: one with 120 seats in Kitchener and one with 300 seats in Waterloo.

But Karl Magid was still not satisfied. He had a plan for a restaurant/lounge that could accommodate 3000 people. Working with his bank manager, Mr. Frank Lizzotti, he managed to raise the money needed to bring his idea to life. Besides obtaining a bank loan, he had to sell his other restaurants. In January 1984, following Karl's personal plan, work began on renovating a former K-Mart location which had been vacant for some time. Ninety days later, with workers still putting on the finishing touches, Lulu's Roadhouse was born.

There was approximately 10 000 square metres of space at Lulu's which made it Canada's largest bar room and the fourth largest bar room in the world. As verified by the Guiness Book of World Records, it sported the two longest continuous bars in the world: one measured 100 metres while the other was 80 metres and both were made of oak.

There were several highlights on a tour of the facility: a large stage where the two house bands and featured entertainers would perform; a sunken dance floor with room for 1000; specialty bars which served fuzzy navels, pina coladas, beer, and B-52s; fast food outlets for pizza and finger foods; two restaurant areas serving full meals (see Exhibit 1) with seating for 600; state-of-the-art lighting and sound equipment; and even a lost-and-found/message board near the front. The walls were covered with oak panelling and autographed pictures of the entertainers who had

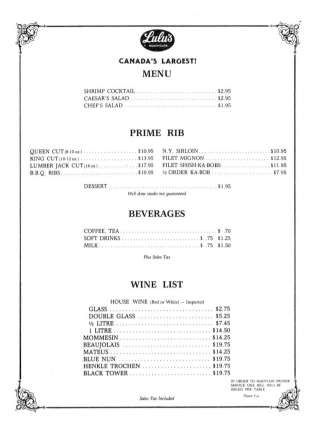

EXHIBIT 1 *Menu from Lulu's Roadhouse*

appeared there. It was difficult to imagine the size of the facility from just a description.

Behind the scenes, there were eight ice machines capable of producing a ton of ice cubes each day. Because of fire regulations, Lulu's had a special inside reservoir containing 550 000 litres of water. The inventory was controlled through computerized cash registers. Inventory turnover was purposely kept high. At the end of a week, there was little liquor or beer remaining and this discouraged pilferage. In an average week, Lulu's would sell 800 cases of beer (24 bottles/case). Lulu's even had a closed-circuit television system that could monitor both patrons and staff.

There was seating for about 2000 patrons while another 1000 could be accommodated at stand-up bars. When Lulu's first opened, the roadhouse operated from Wednesday to Saturday. But

Wednesdays were quickly dropped because the average attendance was only about 350. Instead, when they could be arranged, special concerts were scheduled for Tuesday or Wednesday night (see Exhibit 2). On concert nights as well as on Saturday night, the place operated at capacity. Thursday (Ladies' Night) and Friday nights had an average attendance of about 1250.

EXHIBIT 2 *Schedule of Upcoming Events at Lulu's Roadhouse*

While located in Kitchener, Lulu's drew patrons from cities within an 80 kilometre radius (Exhibit 3). Frank estimated that on a concert or Saturday night 75 percent of the crowd came from out-of-town while on Thursday or Friday night 60 percent of the crowd was out-of-towners. He also noted that Thursday night drew a large number of singles while Saturday was made up predomi-

EXHIBIT 3 *Large Cities Located Near Kitchener*

City	Distance from Kitchener (km)
Brampton	67
Brantford	43
Burlington	56
Cambridge	11
Guelph	24
Hamilton	60
London	82
Mississauga	69
Oakville	64
St. Catharines	105
Stratford	44
Toronto	81
Waterloo	5
Woodstock	43

nantly of married couples. Friday night had an even mix of these two crowds. The roadhouse had been targeted at 30- to 45-year-old people. These people were members of the true "baby boom" generation. Lulu's appeal was its nostalgia theme. While the two house bands played current "Top 40" tunes, the featured performer had produced hits primarily in the 1950s and 1960s. The same theme was evident in the concerts that were scheduled.

Of course, the people who patronized the bar varied from 20 to 70 years in age. People came not only for the music but for the carnival atmosphere as well. Wandering through the bar could be found a man on stilts, who would blow up balloons and twist them into figures, and a "Charlie Chaplin" character, who would perform simple tricks and pantomime. Perhaps one of the most popular features was the large helium-filled message balloons that could be purchased for $1.50. (See Table 1 for the message key.) On an average night 200 balloons were purchased and one occasion one man bought 160 balloons only to give them away to women he met.

When it opened, Lulu's operated with a dining room permit from the Liquor Licensing Board of Ontario. This permit stipulated that no more than

TABLE 1 BALLOON MEANINGS (ACCORDING TO LULU'S ROADHOUSE)

Colour	Meaning
Red	Available woman wanting to dance and party
Blue	Available man wanting to show a lady a fun time
White	Virgin (2 White—Born Again Virgin)
Yellow	Shy coy person
Silver	Those that want to get lucky
Purple	Hot and horny person

60 percent of revenue could come from the sale of liquor with the remainder coming from the sale of food. Lulu's found that it was unable to meet this requirement so that one and a half years later it switched to operating with an entertainment permit. This stipulated that no more than 85 percent of revenue could come from liquor sales. The only problem with the change in permit was that the provincial government imposed an additional 12 percent tax on liquor sold to places operating with an entertainment permit.

Frank's Involvement with Lulu's

Frank Lizzotti had been the Branch Manager at the Royal Bank with which Karl Magid had been dealing. Frank had helped arrange three separate loans for the places that Karl had originally established in Kitchener and then Frank helped Karl secure the financing needed to open Lulu's Roadhouse. Frank had been involved with banking for twelve years when, in late 1985, Karl offered him a job as the General Manager for the roadhouse.

Operations and Advertising at Lulu's

Attendance figures quoted earlier were averages only. Attendance went up somewhat in the spring and fall while the summer and winter attendance dropped. Frank explained that the winter decrease could be attributed to cold weather and hazardous driving conditions while the summer decrease was due to competition from the many outdoor attractions that only operated in the summer. Frank also explained that "out-of-towners" who came to Lulu's were predominantly from Burlington, Hamilton, Oakville, Mississauga, and the west end of Toronto. People from Guelph, Cambridge, Kitchener, Waterloo, and London were not well-represented in the draw of patrons.

Revenue was generated in basically one of three ways: 1) liquor/beer sales; 2) food sales; and 3) cover charges collected at the door. The total revenues for Lulu's is presented in Table 2. Frank was especially concerned about the decline projected for this year.

TABLE 2 REVENUE FIGURES (IN 000's) FOR LULU'S ROADHOUSE

Time Period	Revenues
Apr–Aug 31/84	$2900
Sept/84–Aug 31/85	$5900
Sept/85–Aug 31/86	$6800
Sept/86–Aug 31/87	$6400 (Projected)

When Lulu's first opened it did not advertise. Karl assumed that the publicity surrounding its opening, the size of the bar room and the world-record-length bars would generate all the positive word-of-mouth publicity that he would need. Instead, Karl made certain that people would have a good time at Lulu's and would leave wanting to return. However, two years after opening Karl was willing to consider advertising for the purpose of generating awareness.

For the past two years, the advertising budget had been spent approximately as follows. Radio ads were run on CING-FM (FM 108) in Burlington and on CKKW in Kitchener. About $950 per week was spent on 55 30-second radio spots for the Burlington station. Here a reach plan (where ads would be scattered across the prime and secondary listening times) was used. In Kitchener, $2424 per week was spent on 88 30-second radio spots. These were divided so that 32 were played in the morning while 56 would be played in the evening. As well, Lulu's received some co-operative advertising support equal to $600 per week for the Kitchener ads from sponsors of their concerts (e.g., Hostess Potato Chips).

The only other source of advertising was the *Kitchener-Waterloo Record*. This was the daily paper serving the area. Four or five days a week a 30-line by one-column ad would appear in the entertainment section of the paper. This cost $28.13 per day. About once a week a special 70-line by two-column ad would appear in the entertainment section to promote the special concerts. This ad cost about $70.00. The smaller ad never ran on the same day as the larger ad. (See Exhibit 4 for sample of the large ad.)

Frank had tried a promotion recently but it was too early to tell if it was going to be successful. At the front of the plaza in which Lulu's was located, two Petro-Canada gas stations were situated. Frank arranged with the stations that they

TABLE 3 **POPULATION STATISTICS FOR THE REGION**

City	Population	Number of People 15 & Over Earning More Than $15 000 Per Year
Brantford	74 315	Not Available
Guelph	78 456	38 585
Hamilton (inc. Burlington)	542 095	138 525
Kitchener (inc. Waterloo & Cambridge)	287 801	64 225
London	283 668	67 465
Toronto (inc. Oakville, North York, Mississauga, & Brampton)	2 998 947	804 000

TABLE 4 **ADVERTISING RATES FOR PRINT MEDIA IN THE REGION**

Target Newspaper	Average Paid Circulation	Cost per Line (For 1 Column)	Cost per Line If Order X Lines in Year			
			3350	16 700	33 500	65 000
Guelph Mercury	18 353	$0.84	$0.84	$0.84	$0.84	$0.84
Hamilton Spectator	142 606	$3.32	$3.29	$3.03	$2.92	$2.87
Kit.-Waterloo Record	77 844	$1.77	$1.39	$1.25	$1.22	$1.20
London Free Press	126 971	$3.90	$2.62	$2.49	$2.41	$2.32
Toronto Star	525 669	$12.58	$10.06	$9.49	$9.21	$9.02

Source: Canadian Advertising Rates and Data, 1987.

TABLE 5 **ADVERTISING RATES FOR RADIO MEDIA IN THE REGION**

Target Radio Station	Cost per 30-Second Commercial Using Reach Plan If Number Ordered Per Week Equals . . .			Average Daily Audience
	10	20	30	
Guelph CJOY/CKLA-FM	47.25	44.20	41.65	125 000
Hamilton CING-FM (FM 108)	29.75	25.50	21.25	700 000
Kit.-Waterloo CKKW/CFCA-FM	38.25	34.85	32.30	500 000
London CFPL/CFPL-FM	78.20	71.40	64.60	500 000
Toronto CHUM/CHUM-FM	76.50	72.25	72.25	1 200 000

Source: Local Rates Quoted by Radio Stations, 1987.

would give those of their patrons who purchased 25 litres or more of gas a coupon entitling them to free admission to Lulu's on a Friday night. When the promotion first began, 60 coupons were collected on a Friday night. Most recently 120 coupons were collected.

The Decision for Frank

Two problems were nagging Frank. First, he wondered which was the most effective means of getting more people to come to Lulu's—radio ads, newspaper ads, the coupon promotion or some other means that he hadn't yet considered. Second, he did not feel that the current spending on advertising was generating the proper return but he wasn't certain how to alter the media buy. He had gathered some demographic data and some data on advertising rates for radio and newspapers in the region (see Tables 3, 4, and 5). Some time soon, he would have to sit down and try to sort all of it out.

EXHIBIT 4 *Sample of the Large Ad Run in The Kitchener-Waterloo Record*

[1]Copyright 1987, Marvin Ryder, McMaster University.

13. CLASSY FORMAL WEAR[1]

Stephen Hecht, grandson of Marcus Hecht, the founder of Classy Formal Wear, and now executive vice-president and chief operating officer of the company, was considering how his new line of tuxedos, made in Korea and carrying the Yves Saint Laurent label, should be advertised. It was December 1987. A large quantity of new, black, pure wool tuxedos would be arriving in early 1988 at a cost which would permit a retail price of $295, significantly below that of any comparable tuxedo in the market. The main questions in Stephen's mind were: how large a budget should he allocate for the 1988 advertising campaign, to whom should the advertising be targeted, and what type of research, if any, should be conducted prior to committing Classy to the campaign.

History

Marcus Hecht had founded the firm in 1919 with one of the first formal wear rental stores in Can-ada. At the time, formal wear—tuxedos, full dress black tail coat outfits, and morning suits—was worn almost exclusively by well-to-do men. They wore formal attire to such events as weddings, balls, concerts, and school graduations. Hecht felt that the appeal of this type of dressing could be broadened if quality formal garments were made available at prices which the growing middle class could afford and, hence, he founded Classy as a formal wear rental company. By renting tuxedos, tail coats, and morning suits at a fraction of their retail selling prices, Hecht believed that he could attract substantial numbers of new customers who would otherwise not dress in formal wear.

After a slow start, business in Hecht's single store boomed once Montrealers became aware that they could rent quality formal wear at affordable prices from Classy. Soon Hecht opened a second and a third store. His sons joined the company and even more new stores were opened. Every one of them was a success. This success did not go unnoticed, especially in other Canadian cities. During this period, other enterprising individuals opened formal wear rental stores in Toronto, Hamilton, Winnipeg, Calgary, Edmonton, and Vancouver, as well as in Montreal. By the late 1940s Classy had five stores in Montreal and, in anticipation of competitive expansions, the company began opening stores in new cities. An Ottawa store was opened and in very short order it was successful. In the 1950s the company opened outlets in Toronto and Hamilton and for the first time went head-to-head against other major formal wear specialists. In both of these cities Classy profitably captured a significant share of the market. During the 1960s, Marcus Hecht handed the presidency of the company over to his eldest son, Jack, and he continued Classy's expansion with the successful opening of stores in Vancouver and Quebec City.

Parallel to the growth experienced in the six cities where Classy now had stores, there were two other important developments. First, the company had built an extensive wholesale network to bring Classy's products to cities and towns where there was no Classy store. Through this network, Classy would set up a local men's wear store as an agent to represent and rent the company's line of formal wear. Typically, these stores were given a 30 percent commission for performing these functions. Second, Classy began to offer formal wear for sale on a limited scale through their stores and wholesale agents. A narrow range of formal shirts was made available. A small back-up inventory was held in the company's Montreal distribution centre. The product line was widened further by tuxedos being offered for sale on a made-to-order basis only, with an average delivery time of six weeks.

The Market and Competition
By the 1970s, retail and wholesale sales still accounted for only about 5 percent of total company volume. These sales were basically regarded as an add-on, as opposed to a mainstream con-

tribution to corporate revenues from rentals. Towards the latter part of this decade, two new trends began to make their presence strongly felt.

The first trend was a levelling off in the number of weddings taking place. This is mainly because the baby boom generation born in the late 1940s and early 1950s had by now moved through the early marriage age. Close to 80 percent of formal wear rentals were for weddings, and the stabilization in the number of weddings was not encouraging. The other 20 percent of the market was split about evenly between school graduations and other formal occasions. The second trend was increased competition. In each of the Montreal, Vancouver, and Hamilton markets, Classy had two major competitors while in Toronto there were four.

In 1978 Jack Hecht passed away and left no heirs. His brother Joseph became Classy's president and the trends in the marketplace concerned him as well as his son Stephen, who had been appointed executive vice-president and chief operating officer in the early 1980s. A recent MBA graduate from the University of Western Ontario, Stephen brought a pronounced marketing emphasis to Classy's way of doing business. His research and analysis of the formal wear market showed that the levelling off in the number of weddings was being more than offset by an increasing number of weddings "going formal." In other words, although there was no growth in weddings actually taking place, there were more formal weddings. However, he could not be sure how long this phenomenon would continue.

Classy's Strategy
Stephen decided to establish two fundamental marketing objectives for Classy. The first was to significantly increase the company's share of the formal wear rental market across the country. The second was to substantially increase the level of Classy's retail and wholesale sales.

One of the key strategic tools the company used to help it achieve these objectives was the location and design of Classy stores. First, the company opened stores in new cities, namely, Edmonton, Calgary, Winnipeg, and Kitchener. Also, it developed firm plans to open in other major centres. Second, Classy opened additional stores in Vancouver, Toronto, Ottawa, and Montreal. Third, all the new stores were located in prime retail areas, either in downtown cores or in major regional shopping malls. Finally, all of the company's stores, including the older ones, were fitted with retail merchandising fixtures such as suit racks, shirt display units, and point-of-purchase shelving for formal wear accessories.

Another key strategic action Classy deployed was to increase the availability and inventory levels of its retail merchandise. All stores now carried and displayed a basic line of tuxedos priced from $399 to $599, formal shirts from $39 to $49, and bow tie and cummerbund accessory sets priced from $37. By comparison, very few of Classy's competitors carried any retail stock whatsoever, although they all offered used as well as custom ordered tuxedos for sale.

By late 1987, Classy had 38 retail stores and over 1000 wholesale agents across Canada and was by far the dominant formal wear company in the country (Table 1). Retail sales now accounted for about 10 percent of company revenues. But, in Stephen Hecht's assessment, Classy had barely scratched the surface of the potential retail sales market. Moreover, he felt the company was now well positioned to dramatically increase its sales revenues.

Planning its Sales Revenues

It was with this in mind that Stephen Hecht developed an aggressive plan to make Classy the leading Canadian formal wear retailer. In early 1987, he visited a number of manufacturers of men's suits in Korea. During his three week stay in that country, he discovered that the quality of suits being produced there was equal to and, in many cases, better than those being made in Canada. He also determined that any of the major Korean manufacturers could make quality tuxedos at about 60 percent of the cost of Classy's Canadian suppliers. The same cost structure proved to be the case with the Korean shirt manufacturers. Towards the end of his trip, Stephen Hecht gave an order for 2000 black pure wool tuxedos to one of the suit manufacturers for delivery in early 1988. He also placed a substantial order for formal shirts. On his return to Canada, he actively pursued and secured the exclusive license for the Yves Saint Laurent name and pattern. As a result of this, all of the tuxedos he had ordered from Korea would carry the Yves Saint Laurent label and Classy would be the only formal wear specialist in Canada permitted to sell Yves Saint Laurent tuxedos.

TABLE 1 **LIST OF CLASSY STORES BY CITY AND TYPE OF LOCATION**

City	Downtown Store Locations	Major Regional Mall Locations	Secondary Locations	Total
Vancouver	1	0	5	6
Edmonton	1	2	0	3
Calgary	0	3	0	3
Winnipeg	1*	0	0	1
Kitchener	1	1	0	2
Hamilton	1*	1	0	2
Toronto	3	3	4	10
Ottawa	1	0	2	3
Montreal	1	3	3	7
Quebec City	1*	0	0	1

* These stores are located in downtown regional malls.

The total landed cost to Classy for these Korean produced Yves Saint Laurent tuxedos came to $137.50 including licensing fees. After a thorough analysis of the market, particularly competitive pricing, it was decided to offer the garments at a $295 retail price. There were three basic factors underlying the pricing decision.

First, competition within the retail tuxedo market had become quite active in the previous 18 months as major retailers such as Harry Rosen, Holt Renfrew, Sears, and Moore's, as well as several local retailers began advertising formal wear at prices anywhere between $179 and $1500 as shown in Table 2.

Stephen Hecht and his management team felt that a $295 price for Classy's 100 percent designer label garment would have broad appeal since, in their opinion, it would represent the best value for money in the mid-priced segment of the market.

Second, Classy's management judged that $295 would be the most appropriate price point to begin the process of establishing the company as a major seller of formal wear.

Third, in no previous year had Classy sold more than 500 tuxedos. The company's objective for 1988 was to sell 2000 garments and with no track record of ever having sold this kind of volume, management felt that the $295 price would minimize the risk of falling short of this goal. As well, if demand were to be unexpectedly strong at $295, the price could be quickly increased.

Advertising Decisions

Stephen Hecht, as well as his vice-presidents of marketing and operations, strongly believed that the 100 percent wool fabrication, the Yves Saint Laurent label, and the $295 price represented an inherently attractive package. As they discussed the role of advertising for the new tuxedo line, they agreed that the Classy stores that were located in prime downtown locations and/or in major regional malls would have the greatest sales potential particularly because of their high visibility. Passing traffic would be automatically exposed to these stores' window displays and promotional signage featuring the Yves Saint Laurent tuxedos. However, for the stores which were not so favourably situated, advertising would have to build traffic by getting potential customers to go somewhat

TABLE 2 **ANALYSIS OF CLASSY'S COMPETITION**

Type of Store	Type of Tuxedos Offered	Designer Labels	Retail Prices
Better men's wear stores	Very high quality 100% wool Italian, German & American imports	Giorgio Armani Mario Valentino Gianni Versace Hugo Boss Polo by Ralph Lauren	$749–$1500
Better department stores	High quality 100% wool Italian & British imports & Canadian garments	Mani by Giorgio Armani Emmanuel Ungaro Hardy Aimies	$499–$749
Regular men's wear stores	Good quality polyester/ wool blends from Korea & Canada	Private label	$295–$349
Discount men's wear stores & boutiques	Adequate quality polyester/wool blends from Korea & Eastern Europe	Private label	$179–$299

out of their way to one of Classy's secondary locations.

It was also agreed that advertising would have to start the expansion of Classy's positioning from that of being a leading formal wear renter to being a credible formal wear seller as well. Finally, while it was decided to commence the advertising campaign during the March/April 1988 spring fashion season, advertising support would be heavier in the later summer/early fall to coincide with the start of both the fall fashion and social seasons.

There remained three key decision areas in which Stephen Hecht and his vice-presidents found it difficult to achieve a consensus. After a four and a half hour meeting about these decisions, it was concluded that within the next three days the vice-president of marketing would develop and present a set of proposals regarding:

1. *The advertising budget.* Considering that only 2000 tuxedos would be available for sale, how much should be allocated to advertise the new line throughout 1988? How should this total amount be allocated by month or period?
2. *The target market.* To whom should Classy target the advertising for the Yves Saint Laurent tuxedos? Some people suggested high school graduates, others grooms-to-be and their wedding parties, and another person indicated businessmen and professionals.
3. *Marketing/Advertising research.* Should the company conduct any marketing or advertising research before starting the campaign? If so, what type of research should be performed? If no research is to be proposed, what would be the reasons for not recommending it?

If you were Classy's vice-president of marketing, what would you propose to the group at your up-coming meeting on these topics?

---

[1]This case was written by Harold J. Simpkins, Concordia University.

---

14. THE SHOE TREE[1]

Michael Cassidy was meeting this morning with Joan Hammond, the account executive of the advertising agency that he had hired to develop an advertising campaign for The Shoe Tree. Both were relatively new to the game of advertising. Michael has just been hired as marketing manager, and Joan's agency had recently been established by a former vice-president at the McKim advertising agency's Vancouver office. Both parties were hoping to benefit from this relationship.

The Shoe Tree was a national chain of 105 stores, situated in the 28 major metropolitan areas of Canada. It was founded in 1972 to provide good quality shoes at reasonable prices for every member of the family. It was quite a successful formula, and the chain grew in volume and number of stores to reach 105 in 1990. Total revenues

had reached $60 million for the first time in the history of the company.

The retail chain had never advertised on a national basis, leaving it to the discretion of store managers to advertise special sales or events. However, when Michael took over as marketing manager, he realised that the chain did not have a very clear and consistent image across Canada. Also, individual store advertisements projected different images which contributed to the lack of a strong identity. In the excitement of developing the business, no one has thought of even developing a slogan which would capture the chain's strategy. This is when he approached Joan's agency for some help in developing a national advertising campaign for The Shoe Tree. Michael had known the owner of the new agency for many years, since

TABLE 1 SALES DISTRIBUTION BY PROVINCE AND MONTH

Province	Population %	Sales %	Number of Stores	Month	Sales %
Newfoundland	2.2	3.0	1	January	2
P.E.I.	0.5	0.0	0	February	4
Nova Scotia	3.5	3.6	2	March	5
New Brunswick	2.8	3.1	2	April	4
Quebec	25.8	29.1	36	May	10
Ontario	36.0	38.1	44	June	8
Manitoba	4.2	4.0	4	July	2
Saskatchewan	4.0	3.5	4	August	10
Alberta	9.3	8.1	5	September	19
British Columbia	11.4	7.5	7	October	15
Yukon	0.1	0.0	0	November	11
N.W.T.	0.2	0.0	0	December	10
Total, Canada	*100.0*	*100.0*	*105*		*100*

TABLE 2 DISTRIBUTION OF SALES BY DEMOGRAPHIC GROUPS

Group	Age	Population %	Sales %
Women	13–19	5.3	15
	20–34	13.5	10
	35–54	12.4	8
	55 +	10.1	7
Children	0–6	10.0	22
	7–12	8.4	27
Men	13 +	40.3	11
Total	*all*	*100.0*	*100*

TABLE 3 COSTS GUIDELINES FOR A NATIONAL CAMPAIGN (RETAIL RATES)

Television	$600 per GRP (30-sec. commercial, off-prime)
Radio	$300 per GRP (60-sec. commercial, off-prime)
Newspaper	$80 per Modular Agate Line, black & white
Magazine	$20 000 per page, 4 colours (6 major magazines)
Outdoor/transit	$200 per GRP

Note: A GRP represents 1 percent of the corresponding population (e.g., with TV sets, radio sets, with access to outdoor/transit). A Modular Agate Line (MAL) is 1.8 mm deep by one standard column. A full page is 1800 MALs for a broadsheet and 900 MALs for a tabloid. For fractional sizes use the proportional rule. For more details, consult the appropriate sections in Chapters 5, 6, and 7. For actual rates for vehicles, ask the appropriate vehicle for its retail rate card (or consult the latest CARD catalogue and discount the general rate by 40%).

McKim had handled the advertising business for National Foods, where he had previously worked as a market analyst.

As Michael explained to Joan, his main marketing objective is to continue this growth in sales by 5 percent a year for the next five years. To help achieve this goal, his advertising strategy was to create a strong image for The Shoe Tree, which in turn would generate consistent store traffic over the year, and make the cash register ring more often. Although the initial marketing strategy had been successful, the distribution of sales was uneven across the country, and during the year (see Table 1). Also, the initial target market did not fully materialize; most of the sales were for children and younger woman's shoes (see Table 2).

What Michael wanted was a strong slogan which would project a positive image of The Shoe Tree. He had thought of one slogan: "Shoes fit for a king, at affordable prices." As he saw it, the advertising messages should reflect a number of attributes such as:

- comfort and quality,
- friendliness and good service,
- leadership and authority,
- fashionable yet practical shoes,
- reasonable prices representing good values,
- one-stop shopping for the whole family.

In the past, store managers had mainly used newspaper advertisements, and some had distributed fliers, all announcing a special sale, for example: "Back to school sale." However, Michael felt there was some merit in using radio, television, billboards, mall posters, or even magazines. Table 3 provides some rate benchmarks for a preliminary budget exercise. Of course, Joan would have access to more accurate information on rates by looking at the latest issue of *Canadian Advertising*

Rates and Data. In addition, information on readership could come from NADbank, PMB, and COMB, while information on the broadcast media could come from BBM and Nielsen.

Michael has figured that he could get final approval for a total budget of $1 500 000, with approximately 15 percent of it devoted to producing the ads, and the rest to media expenditures.

The meeting was coming to an end. Joan had agreed to come back in two weeks and present Michael with a preliminary advertising plan, complete with precise advertising objectives, a creative strategy and slogan, some sample advertisements and/or commercials, and a rough media plan.

Questions

1. Prepare a preliminary advertising campaign for The Shoe Tree.
2. Be prepared to justify your recommendations.

---

[1]This case was written by Michel Laroche, Concordia University.

---

15. ASHMAN & BIRI ADVERTISING LIMITED[1]

In late Spring of 1988, Mr. Bill Jorch, newly appointed media director of Ashman & Biri Advertising Limited (A & B), faced a challenging media scheduling assignment. He needed to prepare the 1988–89 media plan for the Corda, a new subcompact which was to be introduced to the Canadian market in September 1988. The car was designed by a leading Canadian automobile manufacturer to compete in the "sporty" subcompact segment of the market.

A & B had obtained the advertising account for the Corda in an intense competition with three other advertising agencies. A & B's creative team had developed a "hot," visually oriented campaign that everyone at the agency and the client's management group was excited about. However, the cost of developing the campaign had exceeded the budgeted level, so Mr. Jorch was under more

pressure than usual to allocate the media budget efficiently. Mr. Jorch's task was to develop a media plan to accomplish the advertising objectives set out by the manufacturer. A total media budget of $1 million had been established and a further $150 000 had been spent preparing television commercials and other advertisements for the campaign.

The Industry

For the past few years, approximately one million cars were sold annually in Canada and sales for 1988–89 were expected to be in that range. While overall car sales had remained flat, in recent years sales of compacts and subcompacts had increased at the expense of larger models. The Corda was designed to compete in the subcompact segment which accounted for 45 percent of total car sales.

In the past two years, total sales of compacts on a regional basis were as follows; Maritimes 8 percent, Quebec 25 percent, Ontario 40 percent, and Western Canada 27 percent. The largest single market for subcompacts was Toronto, which accounted for 26 percent of total national sales.

The comparable regional distribution of the Canadian population was as follows; Maritimes 9 percent, Quebec 26 percent, Ontario 36 percent, and Western Canada 29 percent. Toronto had 13 percent of Canada's population. On a regional basis, total car sales closely approximated population figures.

The leading car models sold in the subcompact market against which the Corda would compete included the Ford Escort EXP, Volkswagen Golf GTI, Honda CRX, Mazda RX-7, Pontiac Fiero, and the Toyota MR2. These models could be described as "sporty" subcompacts. In 1987, the competing manufacturers spent as much as $1 800 000 and as little as $200 000 on advertising these "sporty" compacts. The largest advertisers tended to spend up to 80 percent of their budget on television while the smaller advertisers used magazines almost exclusively.

The Corda

The Corda was positioned as a sporty car with the benefits of exciting styling, superior road handling, and excellent value. The car was designed and priced to provide consumers with an exhilarating, yet affordable driving experience.

During the design and development of the Corda, the automobile manufacturer conducted a number of marketing research studies. The research included market tests of the car with a wide variety of potential customers. Based on this marketing research, the primary market for the Corda was identified as females, aged 18 to 34, in clerical or professional occupations with good income potential. In fact the research had indicated that over 60 percent of Corda sales were likely to be women. With respect to psychographics, these females were outgoing, active, energetic, success-oriented, and in control of their lives. The secondary target was males, aged 18 to

34, in blue collar occupations with average income potential. They regarded themselves as modern, cheerful, and were moderately outgoing.

In a subsequent study of consumers planning to buy a new "sporty" subcompact (Table 1), those who preferred the Corda tended to be single and younger.

TABLE 1

	Preference for Corda %	Preference for Other "Sporty" Subcompacts %
Single	60	35
Under 18	2	2
18 to 24	51	29
25 to 34	41	28
35 to 44	6	37
Over 44	0	4
University degree	35	37

Those who preferred the Corda were interested in sports and social activities. For both target markets, female and male, the major appeal of the Corda was its great styling and that it looked like it was fun to drive. As well, females viewed the car as an extension of their personality while males were impressed by its value for money.

Communication Objectives

Communication objectives were established to promote two consumer benefits. One was to communicate the excitement of driving a fun car and the social satisfaction derived from being seen in it. The Corda should be seen as an extension of the buyer's lifestyle. Second, a factual appeal was required to provide consumers with a reason to purchase on dimensions where the Corda had a competitive advantage. More specifically, the four benefits were value for money, low maintenance, ease of handling, and safety. A research study had been conducted with individuals who rated new cars for various automotive publications. Based on their experience driving prototypes of the Corda, these "experts" had rated the car very favourably on the four benefits.

The Media Budget

After extensive analysis and discussion between A & B personnel and Corda management, the advertising media budget for the 1989 model year—September, 1988 to August 1989—had been set at $1 000 000. This figure was based on an analysis of previous results for other brands in the car maker's product line, competitive analysis, and recognition that building first year sales for the Corda was a major priority of the client. As well, the budget determination included an assessment of how much spending was needed to build awareness of the Corda and to motivate potential consumers to take the first step—going into a Corda dealership.

Mr. Jorch had been actively involved in the budget setting process: "Not all media buyers get to play an active role in budget setting, but at A & B my inputs are significant," he said, "No question about it, this is a budget I can live with."

The Media Objectives

Media objectives were established to guide the media selection process. The main objectives were:

1. Efficiently deliver impressions on a national basis in the hope of targeting all people interested in buying a car.
2. Direct media weight to the most likely targets which were; 1) women, single, 18 to 34, $20 000+ income, and 2) men, single, 18 to 34, $20 000+ income.
3. Match the emotional and rational appeals to the appropriate media.
4. To the extent that the budget allows, extra weight should be applied in markets where subcompact sales are high (in order of priority, Toronto, Montreal, Vancouver).

The Media Planning

Mr. Jorch's task was to select a media mix that accomplished the communication objectives within the guidelines established for the media plan. As Mr. Jorch viewed it, media selection consisted of two important decisions. First, how should the budget be allocated over the various media types (e.g., television, radio, newspapers, magazines, billboards) and second, what specific vehicles (e.g., *Time, Maclean's, Chatelaine*) within media types should be used? A major problem faced by all media buyers was the difficulty in making comparisons across media, since media measures vary across television, magazines, newspapers, and billboards. With these thoughts in mind, Mr. Jorch began reviewing the available information on the major media and their costs and audiences.

He first concentrated on making broad choices among the various media types. While Mr. Jorch knew the main features of the different media types, he needed to use that information to narrow his focus. Because of the visual nature of the ad campaign he had decided that radio was unsuitable for the Corda. Similarly, he felt that given the size of the budget available, TV advertising required strong consideration. Based on his previous experience, he knew that television time should be purchased on a station by station basis, as opposed to purchasing time through a network (e.g., CBC). These station by station purchases, referred to as spot buys because they guaranteed a "spot" within a particular time period (e.g., prime time), cost considerably less than network purchases. Mr. Jorch thought that at least half of the budget should be spent on television advertising and probably much more.

Mr. Jorch was of two minds about newspapers. On the one hand, newspaper ads could be used to target local markets quite precisely and could help support local Corda dealers. On the other hand, he would use only black and white quarter-page ads because the colour reproduction in newspapers was not appropriate to illustrate the Corda. Black and white ads would not have a strong visual appeal. Regardless, if he decided to use newspaper advertising, no more than $100 000 would be spent in this medium.

Billboards were a major imponderable. Seen most by people in cars, they would seem to be a prime advertising vehicle. Their large size and big splash of colour were ideal for conveying the look of a Corda. But little beyond that exciting look could be shown.

Magazines had the advantage of brilliant colour, and the ad copy could be well presented in a magazine ad. Magazines also had a degree of permanency as they remained in the household for a period of time. As well, magazines appeared to be effective at reaching the target market.

Mr. Jorch's assistant had compiled an extensive set of data on the audiences and rates of major Canadian media, as shown in Tables 2 through 6. As well, his assistant had prepared some information on the media habits of Canadians (Tables 7 and 8).

While quantity discounts could be obtained if the Corda bought a large amount of advertising in one media vehicle, Mr. Jorch did not want his planning to reflect those discounts at this time. His past experience had shown that the discounts did not seem to change very much with the media plan for an account such as Corda. This was because the parent company's total advertising was great enough to earn maximum discounts from all major media.

He was not concerned with planning the timing of the campaign. He had no justification for altering the standard pattern in the auto industry of matching advertising levels to buying patterns,

TABLE 2 **SPOT TELEVISION BUY IN SELECTED CITIES WITH POPULATIONS EXCEEDING 100 000 (1987 ESTIMATES)***

| Metropolitan Area | Total Population | Percentage of Total Population That Is | | Cost/GRP** |
		Female 20–34	Male 20–34	
Halifax	309 000	30.6	30.1	$ 25
Quebec City	615 000	29.0	29.7	40
Sherbrooke	124 000	28.7	29.2	19
Montreal (F)	1 899 000	27.2	28.1	105
Montreal (E)	1 016 000	27.8	27.9	95
Ottawa/Hull	809 000	29.0	28.9	65
Sudbury	148 000	23.6	24.2	17
Toronto	3 377 000	28.0	27.5	165
London	286 000	28.4	28.0	30
Kitchener	308 000	27.7	27.7	35
Winnipeg	614 000	27.2	27.8	35
Regina	177 000	29.0	30.0	25
Saskatoon	170 000	31.1	31.5	22
Calgary	664 000	34.3	36.9	55
Edmonton	703 000	32.6	34.3	58
Vancouver	1 392 000	27.6	28.2	83
Total	*12 611 000*	*28.6*	*28.9*	*$874*

* Spot television buys are the purchase of broadcast time on a station by station basis. The costs are based on prime time purchases (6:30 P.M.–11:00 P.M.).

** Cost/GRP is the cost of one gross rating point. It costs $874 to expose 1% of the total population (12 610 000) to one 30-second television ad, of which 28.6% are females, aged 20 to 34 and 28.9% are males aged 20 to 34.

Sources: The Canadian Media Directors' Council Media Digest, 1987/88, Market Research Handbook, Statistics Canada, Catalog 63–224, and *Canadian Advertising Rates and Data*.

with the heaviest spending occurring in the fall (during model introduction) and in the spring.

The Media Decision

Mr. Jorch realized it was now time for him to do what he was best at doing—combining an intuitive feel for the media requirements that a campaign's creative theme demanded with a detailed analysis of masses of data to develop a highly efficient media plan. While there were some in the agency who believed that creative and copy were the dominant areas of advertising effectiveness, Mr. Jorch knew that the only successful campaigns were those that reached their audience.

TABLE 3 **MAGAZINE COVERAGE AND RATES (1987 ESTIMATES)**

	Circulation	Rate Full Page 4 colours	(CPM) Cost per Thousand	Estimated Readership Men 18+	Women 18+
National					
Maclean's	649 281	$19 965	$30.75	585 000	500 000
*Time**	372 239	10 870	29.20	323 000	249 000
Chatelaine (E)	1 109 695	24 580	22.15	456 000	1 262 000
Canadian Living	515 756	14 950	28.99	214 000	590 000
*Marquee***	501 200	8 915	17.79	299 000	236 000
French language					
L'Actualité	265 732	8 650	32.55	224 000	332 000
Châtelaine (F)	304 313	8 420	27.67	130 000	337 000
Toronto					
Toronto Life	97 353	5 778	59.35	82 000	83 000
Starweek (T.V. magazine)	806 193	12 825	15.91	661 000	804 000
Sunday Sun TV	461 260	6 128	13.29	410 000	431 000

* *Time* is a U.S. publication that is not eligible for tax deductible expenses for Canadian advertisers as per Bill C-58. The equivalent cost for a Canadian advertiser requires a 50% surcharge be added to the above cost figures.
** *Marquee* is a free bulk distribution publication and reported numbers have not been verified.

Source: The Canadian Media Directors' Council Media Digest, 1987/88.

TABLE 4 **QUALITATIVE ASSESSMENT OF SELECTED MAGAZINES**

Maclean's	Weekly news publication, estimated 93% duplication of audience with *Time*, 29% with *Marquee*, 90% with *Chatelaine* (English), 19% with *Toronto Life*
Time	Weekly news publication, estimated 28% duplication with *Marquee*, 47% with *Chatelaine* (English) 17% with *Toronto Life*
Chatelaine (E)	Women's monthly English publication
Canadian Living	Average may be somewhat older than target market
Marquee	Entertainment monthly publication, provided free to consumers at movie theatres across Canada
L'Actualité	Weekly French magazine
Châtelaine (F)	Women's monthly French magazine
Toronto Life	Monthly general interest magazine, upscale
Starweek	Television weekly publication in Toronto, small size may not reproduce ads well
Sunday Sun TV (Toronto)	Television weekly publication in Toronto, small size may not reproduce ads well

TABLE 5 **BILLBOARD COVERAGE AND RATES, TOP 20 MARKETS (1987 ESTIMATES)**

	Estimated Population (000)	25 GRPs Daily		50 GRPs Daily		100 GRPs Daily	
		# of Panels	4 Week Rate $	# of Panels	4 Week Rate $	# of Panels	4 Week Rate $
Top Three							
Toronto/Hamilton/Oshawa	4 043.9	59	34 338	118	65 372	237	131 298
Montreal	3 128.5	47	28 435	94	54 050	188	108 100
Vancouver	1 467.9	23	12 581	45	24 435	91	48 685
Total–Top 3	8 640.3	129	75 354	257	143 857	516	288 083
Next Seven							
Edmonton	827.8	14	8 330	27	15 120	54	29 700
Calgary	819.9	14	8 400	28	15 960	55	30 800
Ottawa/Hull	798.7	17	10 965	33	20 592	67	41 808
Winnipeg	657.1	8	4 432	17	8 976	34	17 952
Quebec City	622.5	16	7 200	32	14 080	64	28 160
Kitchener	533.3	15	8 025	30	15 750	—*	—
St. Catharines	457.9	17	9 095	33	17 325	—	—
Total–Top 10	13 357.8	230	131 801	457	251 660	—	—
Next Ten							
London	432.4	11	5 885	22	11 550	44	23 100
Windsor	405.7	9	4 455	18	7 740	35	14 175
Sherbrooke	298.7	7	2 716	15	5 535	30	11 070
Halifax/Dartmouth	289.9	7	3 479	13	6 123	26	12 246
Kingston	264.5	8	3 128	17	6 324	—	—
Regina/Moose Jaw	219.5	5	2 485	9	4 257	19	8 987
Sudbury	213.0	7	2 870	13	5 070	26	9 490
Barrie	204.8	11	5 775	22	10 890	45	20 025
Trois Rivières	193.3	5	1 660	11	3 465	22	6 930
Saskatoon	184.8	4	1 788	8	3 408	16	6 816
Total–Top 20	16 064.4	304	166 042	605	316 022	—	—

* GRP requirements not met

Source: The Canadian Media Directors' Council Media Digest, 1987/88, pp. 57–58.

TABLE 6 **NEWSPAPER COVERAGE AND RATES**

Metropolitan City	Major Newspaper	Circulation*	Rate Black & White Quarter Page	CPM Cost per Thousand
Halifax	*Chronicle-Herald*	80 274	$ 1 278	$15.92
Quebec City	*Le Soleil*	117 235	1 710	14.59
Sherbrooke	*La Tribune*	39 786	846	21.26

TABLE 6   NEWSPAPER COVERAGE AND RATES (continued)

Metropolitan City	Major Newspaper	Circulation*	Rate Black & White Quarter Page	CPM Cost per Thousand
Montreal (F)	*La Presse*	201 875	2 610	12.93
Montreal (E)	*The Gazette*	48 943	2 250	45.97
Ottawa/Hull	*Ottawa Citizen*	188 483	1 994	10.58
Sudbury	*Sudbury Star*	26 803	540	20.15
Toronto	*Toronto Star*	523 458	5 661	10.81
Hamilton	*Hamilton Spectator*	118 522	1 494	12.61
London	*London Free Press*	128 085	1 755	13.70
Kitchener	*Kitchener-Waterloo Record*	77 844	797	10.24
Winnipeg	*Winnipeg Free Press*	172 246	1 841	10.69
Regina	*Leader Post*	73 253	734	10.02
Saskatoon	*Star Phoenix*	59 785	702	11.74
Calgary	*Calgary Herald*	134 553	1 598	11.88
Edmonton	*Edmonton Journal*	170 707	1 827	10.70
Vancouver	*Vancouver Sun*	230 297	4 113	17.86

* Average based on Monday to Friday

Source: Canadian Advertising Rates and Data.

TABLE 7   HOURS VIEWING TELEVISION PER WEEK, PERCENTAGE

Number of Hours	Total Canada	Income Over $20 000
Less than 8	18	24
8–14.9	19	25
15–21.9	19	23
22–32.5	23	16
Over 32.5	21	12
	100	100

MAGAZINES READ PER MONTH, PERCENTAGE

Number Read	Total Canada	Income Over $20 000
One or none	17	5
2 or 3	19	12
4 or 5	20	20
6 or 7	19	26
More than 7	25	37
	100	100

Source: BBM Fall 1986 "BG" Report

TABLE 8   NEWSPAPER AUDIENCE REACH BY DEMOGRAPHICS (30 LARGEST MARKETS)

Group	Percentage Average Reach (Weekday)
Adults (18+)	63
18–24	55
18–34	57
18–49	60
Under $10 000	49
$10–15 000	55
$15–20 000	58
$20–25 000	60
$25–35 000	65
$35 000+	71
Males	68
Females	58

Source: The Canadian Media Directors' Council Media Digest, 1987/88.

[1]This case was prepared by Gordon McDougall, Wilfrid Laurier University and Douglas Snetsinger, University of Toronto.

16. WONDER COLA 1991 CAMPAIGN[1]

Following is a typical media checklist used by Canadian advertising agencies. It is prepared by the account service department and acts as the briefing document from which the agency's media department develops the annual media plan.

Media Plan Checklist

This checklist has been designed to provide a formal collection of the data judged necessary for the development of a media plan. The checklist ensures that no information requirement is overlooked and that a documented data source is available for reference purposes. It is important therefore that information be both accurate and up to date.

The completed checklist will enable the preparation of a media strategy. Upon approval and agreement a full media plan will then be developed. The checklist will be included as an appendix in the final plan.

Client
ACCOUNT: Universal Foods
DIVISION: Soft Drinks
PRODUCT/SERVICE: Wonder Cola

Due Dates
CHECKLIST PREPARED: 27 April 1990
ORIGINAL/REVISED: Original
STRATEGY: 10 May 1990
PLAN—INTERNAL: 24 May 1990
PLAN—CLIENT: 1 June 1990

Timing
FISCAL YEAR: 1 Sept. 90–31 Aug. 91
CAMPAIGN PERIOD: Same

Personnel
ACCOUNT STAFF: L. Martin
MEDIA SUPERVISOR: J. Roy

Budget
WORKING MEDIA: $3 500 000   NET:
PRODUCTION: $250 000   GROSS: X
TOTAL: $3 750 000

SPECIAL DIRECTIVES: Historically, 40 percent of the media budget has been allocated to television time on selected high profile sports programs. Research and sales results have shown the allocation to be effective. However, given the high level of competitive "noise" in the market place, a strategy which would give Wonder Cola more media dominance would be considered by the client.

Regional/Language Requirements
PLAN TO PROVIDE
COVERAGE:
Ethnic Media Coverage.
LIST LANGUAGE
REQUIREMENTS: None
NATIONALLY: X
ENGLISH ONLY:
FRENCH ONLY:

SPECIFIC MARKET LIST: Halifax, Sydney, St. John's, St. John, Charlottetown, Quebec City, Trois Rivières, Chicoutimi/Jonquière, Montreal, Ottawa/Hull, Kingston, Oshawa, Toronto, Hamilton, Sudbury, Timmins, North Bay, London, Kitchener, Windsor, Winnipeg, Regina, Saskatoon, Calgary, Edmonton, Vancouver, Victoria.

Objectives/Strategy
Marketing Objectives

1. To increase market share as follows:
   English Canada—from 3 percent to 4 percent. French Canada—from 2 percent to 2.5 percent.
2. To expand usage of Wonder Cola's 1 litre bottle, from 1 percent of households to 2 percent in English Canada, and from 0.8 percent to 1.5 percent in French Canada.

Marketing Strategy

1. Continue positioning as the lively, better tasting cola that is a real break from ordinary colas. Support positioning with aggressive advertis-

ing and sales promotion throughout the year, with emphasis on summer.

2. Distribution of the 1 litre bottle will be expanded from 40 percent to 50 percent nationally in supermarkets and convenience stores. Trial-inducing price-off deals supported by advertising will be offered in June and December 1990.

3. National distribution will be expanded in sports arenas and sporting events from 75 percent to 90 percent, and the brand will continue to be a sponsor of major sporting events and programs.

4. Regular pricing will be competitive with Coke and Pepsi.

Advertising Objectives

1. Increase unaided brand awareness from 75 percent to 85 percent in English Canada and from 50 percent to 70 percent in French Canada.

2. Increase the past 12-month trial levels as follows: English Canada, from 6 percent to 8 percent; French Canada, from 4 percent to 5.5 percent.

3. Maintain a brand preference rating of 70 percent among triers on a national basis.

4. Encourage adults who are current brand users of the 10 ounce size to purchase the 1 litre size instead of the comparable sizes of competitive brands.

Media History

Brief Details of Previous Media Plan and Budgets: See media plan.

Target Audience

	Percent Population	Percent Prospects	Development Index
Sex			
Male	49.7	55.5	112
Female	50.3	44.5	88

	Percent Population	Percent Prospects	Development Index
Age			
12–17	10.4	20.1	193
18–24	13.4	28.2	210
25–34	17.3	20.3	117
35–49	17.3	14.4	83
50–64	14.0	5.5	39
65 +	9.7	2.6	27
H/Hold Income			
Under $15M	14.5	18.5	128
$15–20M	9.5	23.0	242
$20–25M	8.9	25.7	289
$25–35M	18.9	11.2	59
$35–45M	17.0	12.5	74
$45M +	31.1	9.1	29
Education			
Public or Grade School	21.9	27.5	126
Some High School	23.0	30.7	133
Completed High School	19.4	22.7	117
Community College	19.7	10.3	52
Some University	8.0	4.6	58
Completed University	8.0	4.2	53
Occupation			
Owner/Manager/ Professional	22.9	10.5	46
Clerical	17.6	20.2	115
Sales	10.4	15.5	149
Farmer	6.2	4.2	68
Skilled	25.6	30.1	118
Other Workers	17.3	19.5	113

Other Criteria:
Wonder Cola users tend to be more physically active than the general population. They are above-average participants in and spectators of sporting activities.

Sales Data
By Province

	Percent Population	Percent Category	Percent Sales Brand	Development Market	Indices Brand
Newfoundland	2.2	2.1	2.0	95	91
Prince Edward Island	0.5	0.5	0.4	100	80
Nova Scotia	3.4	3.3	3.2	97	94
New Brunswick	2.7	2.6	2.3	96	85
Quebec	25.5	26.6	19.2	104	75
Ontario	36.8	36.5	41.0	99	111
Manitoba	4.2	4.3	5.4	102	129
Saskatchewan	3.8	3.9	3.9	103	103
Alberta	9.2	8.9	10.5	97	114
British Columbia	11.4	11.1	12.1	97	106
Yukon	0.1	0.1	0.0	100	0
N.W.T.	0.2	0.1	0.0	50	0

By City Size

	Percent Population	Percent Category	Percent Sales Brand	Development Market	Indices Brand
1 000 000 +	29.4	31.0	33.0	105	112
100 000–1 000 000	27.1	27.0	27.0	100	100
Under 100 000	43.5	42.0	40.0	97	92

By Month

	Percent Sales		Monthly Indices	
	Category	Brand	Market	Brand
January	5.5	5.4	66	98
February	5.4	5.2	65	96
March	6.5	6.0	78	92
April	7.1	7.0	85	99
May	9.3	9.2	112	99
June	10.2	11.1	122	109
July	11.4	12.3	137	108
August	11.8	12.0	142	102
September	9.1	8.7	109	96
October	6.9	6.5	83	94
November	6.8	6.5	82	96
December	10.0	10.1	120	101

Market Shares—Competitors
Market and Brand Growth

Percent change past year—market	2.1%
Percent change past year—brand	5.6%

Market Share and Position

| | Share % | Position # | Significant Regional Variations | | | % Change Past Year |
			Region	Share	Position	
Brand	3	5	Maritimes	2.5	6	5.0
Competition	97	—	Quebec	2.0	7	5.2
Coke	24	1	Ontario	3.8	5	6.1
Pepsi	19	2	Prairies	3.0	5	4.8
Seven-Up	8	3	B.C.	3.1	5	4.8

Production Distribution
Describe channels:

Supermarkets and convenience stores	75%
Restaurants and snack bars	15%
Sports arenas and events	10%

Purchase Cycle
1. Single serving sizes—daily, high impulse component
2. One litre size and larger sizes—weekly

Price
Brand: At parity prices except during special price promotions.
Competitors: Same

Competitive Activity
Highly Competitive   X
Moderate Competition
Minimal Competition
No Competition

Competitive Brands	Media Used	Estimated Budgets
Coca-Cola	Television, radio, outdoor, print	$14 000 000
Pepsi Cola	Television, print	$ 9 500 000
Seven-Up	Television	$ 4 750 000

Creative Requirements/Government Regulations
Creative Requirements:
This section provides the Media planner with guidance as to the creative parameters that will be required in the selection of media. It does not necessarily represent any creative executional directives.

	Primary Requirement	Secondary Requirement	Comments/ Rationale
Visual	X		
Demonstration		X	
Package Identification	X		
Sound		X	
Colour		X	
Long Copy		X	
Short Copy	X		
Announcement, News Approach		X	
High Quality Reproduction		X	
Dominance		X	
Mood	X		
Other: sports/active environment	X		

Creative Strategy

Wonder Cola will be presented as the better-tasting alternative to competitive soft drink brands, with particular appeal to teenagers and young adults who are physically active (or who perceive themselves to be so).

Government Regulations

Specify any regulations that could affect media selection/scheduling: Do *not* schedule advertising in time periods whose audience is composed of a majority of children under 13 years of age in Quebec.

Provincial Advertising Taxes

Indicate whether budget includes or excludes allowances for provincial taxes: Budget *excludes* provincial taxes.

Non-Tax-Deductible Advertising

Indicate if U.S. media can be used and how non-deductibility should be accommodated: Double estimated cost of U.S. media for budget purposes.

Spill/Promotional Plans
U.S. Spill-in Advertising

Indicate medium, commercial unit:
Television—30 seconds
Print—Full page, 4 colours

Indicate compatibility in:
Packaging: Same as in Canada
Creative Strategy: Same as in English Canada only

Provide indication of weight levels, markets and seasonality:

June to August   125 GRPs weekly television in all border markets.
April to October: Full page insertion every month in U.S. national issues of *Sports Illustrated, People, Cosmopolitan, Road & Track*.

Special Promotional Plans

Provide dates and content plans:
June 1990—Trial price offer on 1 litre size
December 1990—Trial price offer on 1 litre size

Special Client Directives

Provide details of special client requests that could affect media selection or scheduling:

1. All savings that accrue because of buying effectiveness to be returned to client.
2. When efficient, purchase time on major sporting events, blockbuster movies, and dramatic specials.
3. If using newspapers, ensure placement in sports, food, or entertainment sections.

Attachments: *List of attachments supplied for background:*

1. U.S. media plan with tearsheets of U.S. print advertisements
2. Media plan for previous year
3. Analysis of major competitive promotional activities
4. Samples of competitive print and broadcast media
5. Creative strategy documentation

Assignment

Based on the foregoing information, propose a media plan for Wonder Cola. Include in your proposal a clear statement of media objectives and strategy as well as a blocking chart to illustrate your recommended media schedule by week and by medium.

Assume the following media costs:

Television:	$1000 per GRP (30-second commercial)
Radio:	$650 per GRP (60-second commercial)
Newspapers:	$125 per Modular Agate Line, black & white
Magazines:	$20 000 per page, 4 colours (6 major magazines)
Outdoor:	$400 per GRP

---

[1]This case was written by Harold J. Simpkins, Concordia University.

---

17. SURELOCK HOMES COMPANY[1]

Alan Taylor is the owner of AdVisor, a small advertising agency located in Calgary, Alberta. He has just opened his own agency after working for close to 10 years as a senior account executive with a major advertising agency in Toronto. Being a native of Alberta, he had always wanted to go home and get away from the "rat race" of Toronto, while at the same time using the experience he had acquired. Thus, he was very eager to build his business in Calgary, and establish a good reputation in the business circles.

He has recently been hired by Mr. Watson, the owner of the Surelock Homes Company to develop an advertising campaign to launch a new product. Alan is very excited about the assignment, and he is convinced that if he came up with a very effective campaign for the Surelock Homes Company, this firm had the potential of becoming very successful and his most important account for many years to come.

The Surelock Homes Company

Mr. Watson is the inventor of a revolutionary burglar-proof lock that works without a key. The lock operates with a small device attached to the wrist that, when a button is pressed, emits a special coded sound which opens the lock. The lock itself is connected to the electrical system in the dwelling, with a rechargeable battery operating the movement in case of electrical failure. It could also be connected to an alarm system. In addition to being invisible to potential burglars, this new revolutionary lock has a number of consumer benefits. Among others, with this new lock, a consumer may be able to open a door without dropping packages, searching for the keys, or for the keyhole in the dark. Mr. Watson has named his invention the Surelock, and his firm the Surelock Homes Company.

An electronics firm located in a nearby metropolitan area has agreed to produce the locks, provided that the firm orders at least 5000 units. Initially, Mr. Watson has invested $20 000 of his own money, and a local bank has agreed to give him a loan of up to $50 000. More recently, he has been able to interest some investors and a provincial agency has promised to give him a development grant provided that the manufacturing of the new product is done in the province of Alberta.

Because of his lack of knowledge about marketing, Mr. Watson has not developed any marketing strategy or marketing program beyond the mere branding of his invention. This is a fairly common occurrence among small businesses, especially those founded by an inventor. However, Mr. Watson has indicated to Alan that he thought that $15 to $20 might be a good price for the new lock.

The Market for Locks

Mr. Watson has been able to ascertain the following facts through secondary sources (mainly Statistics Canada), and a small survey conducted in the Calgary metropolitan area using personal interviews:

a. Only owners of private dwellings may be interested in the new lock. When asked, about 40 percent of these owners say they are interested.
b. The vast majority of those interested in the new lock are male heads of households.
c. When *shown* the new lock, 30 percent of those who claim to be interested in the new lock say they intend to purchase on the average two units if the price is between $15 and $20. This proportion drops to 25 percent willing to purchase one unit if the lock is priced between $21 and $30. Above $30, only 10 percent have a positive intention of purchasing the lock.
d. These figures drop dramatically to 10, 5, and 1 percent when the lock is only *described* (i.e., without demonstration).
e. From the 1986 census, the number of owned dwellings in Canada is distributed as in Table 1.
f. Preliminary costing of the new product is indicated in Table 2.

TABLE 1 NUMBER AND DISTRIBUTION OF OWNED DWELLINGS IN CANADA AND THE PROVINCES

	Number (in 000 units)	Distribution %
Newfoundland	127	2.3
P.E.I.	30	0.5
Nova Scotia	212	3.8
New Brunswick	172	3.1
Quebec	1290	23.1
Ontario	2048	36.7
Manitoba	250	4.5
Saskatchewan	251	4.5
Alberta	516	9.2
British Columbia	676	12.1
Yukon and N.W.T.	8	0.1
Canada	*5580*	*100.0*

TABLE 2 AVERAGE COST PER UNIT FOR THE SURELOCK

Volume (in 000s)	Average Cost per Unit
0–5	$ 9.00
5–10	7.00
10–20	5.00
20–100	3.00

Alan's Assignment

Based on the information provided by Mr. Watson, Alan must develop a rough marketing pro-

TABLE 3 NATIONAL COSTS GUIDELINES FOR MEDIA BUYS

Television:	$1000 per GRP (30-sec. commercial)
Radio:	$650 per GRP (60-sec. commercial)
Newspapers:	$125 per Modular Agate Line, black & white
Magazines:	$20 000 per page, 4 colours (6 major magazines)
Outdoor:	$400 per GRP

gram, and a complete advertising plan for the Surelock Homes Company, paying particular attention to the advertising strategy, the campaign objectives, the advertising budget, the media and the creative plans.

Alan knows from experience that one needs at least five repetitions for a television commercial to make the audience learn the message and 12 repetitions for a print advertisement.

National costs guidelines for media buys are indicated in Table 3, and provincial ones could be approximated by using population distribution weights. As for direct mail, he knows from past experience that the cost per mailing would be $1.50 to $2.00, and that the expected response rate would be around 1 percent.

Finally, he knows that a television commercial would cost about $50 000 to produce, while a print advertisement would cost $8 000 in colour and $3 000 in black and white.

[1] This case was written by Michel Laroche, Concordia University.

18. BILL C-51[1]

The Canadian Federal Government has recently introduced Bill C-51 to ban all tobacco advertising and forbid smoking in all federal offices by 1989. The ban will include billboards, magazines, and sponsorship of sports and cultural events. Tobacco advertising, already banned on television and radio, will be forbidden in newspapers on January 1, 1988. Bill C-51 already had passed a first reading early in 1987.

It was in the light of this proposed ban that the big three tobacco companies spent $800 000 to launch a three-advertisement campaign against the Government's proposed ban. The ads appeared in many English and French newspapers and magazines over a several months' period in 1987.

Smoking: Health Effects and Control

Cigarette smoking has been identified as the single most important source of preventable morbidity and premature mortality in each of the reports of the U.S. Surgeon General produced since 1964. The estimated annual excess mortality from cigarette smoking in the United States exceeds 350 000 and in Canada exceeds 35 000. It has been estimated that an average of five and a half minutes of life is lost for each cigarette smoked, on the basis of an average reduction in life expectancy for cigarette smokers of five to eight years. Cigarette smoking is a major cause of deaths from coronary heart disease, cancer, chronic bronchitis, and emphysema.

Exposure to Passive Smoking

Involuntary or passive smoking is defined as the exposure of non-smokers to tobacco-combustion products in the indoor environment. Tobacco smoke in the environment is derived from two sources: "Mainstream" smoke exhaled by the smoker, and "sidestream" smoke arising from the burning end of the cigarette. Sidestream smoke contains a higher concentration of potentially dangerous gas-phase constituents and accounts for about 85 percent of the smoke found in the room occupied by cigarette smokers.

One study found that in smoky environments where carbon monoxide concentrations exceed 30 ppm, the level of carboxyhemoglobin in the blood of passive smokers (extrapolated over an eight-hour period) was equivalent to that in voluntary smokers consuming five cigarettes. Another study, which measured the nicotine concentration in the urine and saliva of non-smokers exposed to the smoke in a typical work environment, found that the amount of nicotine absorbed passively by the non-smokers over a period of four hours produced salivary and urinary concentrations of nicotine similar to those found in light smokers (1 to 10 cigarettes per day).

Among healthy adults, the most common symptoms arising from exposure to passive smoking are eye irritation (69% of those reporting problems), headaches (33%), nasal symptoms (33%), and coughs (33%). Exposure to tobacco smoke precipitates or aggravates (or both) allergic attacks in persons with respiratory allergies, and exacerbates such allergic symptoms as eye irritation, nasal symptoms, headaches, cough, wheezing, sore throat, and hoarseness.

Advertising and Smoking: Some Issues

Douglas Barr, chief executive officer of the Canadian Cancer Society, branded the tobacco industry's $800 000 ad campaign as a pack of lies and an expensive concoction of misleading information and myths about smoking. He estimated that 13 000 Canadian will die next year of lung cancer caused by cigarette smoking. It should also be noted that the dangers of cigarette smoking are manifold. One in four smokers will die of a smoking-related disease. Heart disease remains the number one killer in both men and women and lung cancer has recently overtaken breast cancer as the most common cause of death from cancer in women. Women who smoke and take the pill run about ten times the risk of dying from cardiovascular disease as women who neither smoke nor take the pill. Smokers run the risk of decreased fertility, spontaneous abortion, low birthweight infants, and premature menopause. Absenteeism among smokers is 50 percent higher than among non-smokers.

Though older Canadians are quitting smoking in record numbers, smoking among teenagers has not decreased and more young women are smoking. The number of women aged 20 to 29 who smoke daily increased from 36 percent in 1983 to 45 percent in 1986. Mr. Barr also believed that tobacco/cigarette advertising "glamourizes smoking." Sponsorship of sports is one way that sponsorship provides valuable media time and exposure, leading some industry antagonists to state that by this method the industry gets spurious respectability. In Canada, tobacco companies sponsor Tennis Canada; in America, Virginia

Slims sponsors a major women's tennis tournament; in Britain, Gallaghers Tobacco sponsors Martina Navratilova, and in 1982 at Wimbledon she was dressed in clothing bearing the name and colours of Kim, a cigarette aimed primarily at women. Complaints that year resulted in Martina wearing the colours and not the brand name, Kim.

The Canadian Cancer Society has distributed 50 000 brochures attacking the recent ad campaign and asking all members of the public to write to their members of Parliament in support of Bill C-51, the Tobacco Products Control Act. Mr. Barr said that the society will also mobilize its 350 000 volunteer force to fight the industry.

"It is of great concern that this foreign controlled industry should be spending so much effort to block proposed Canadian legislation," he said. "They want to defeat it, delay it, or water it down."

Tobacco Firms Fight Back: Sales Strategies
In early July 1987, Canada's big three tobacco companies quietly worked out ways to beat the forthcoming ban on their advertising and sponsorship activities. The three firms—Imperial Tobacco Ltd., Montreal, Rothmans Benson and Hedges Inc., and RJR-MacDonald Inc., both of Toronto—planned to change their sales strategies when Bill C-51 becomes law.

Their alternatives include:

• Beefing up sales staff. Retailers will be supplied more frequently, ensuring that fresh product is always on the shelves.
• Paying for better positions on storeshelves or end-of-aisle displays. Competition for visible in-store space will intensify.
• Brightening up cigarette packages to make them more noticeable. This change may backfire if existing brands lose their strong package identification.
• Improved distribution by finding new avenues to sell the product, such as increased numbers and locations of vending machines.

Imperial Tobacco is even broadening its sponsorship program. The company plans to launch a new book prize for fiction which may put Canada in the top ranks of the literary world. The international award, rumoured to be worth $450 000, is expected to achieve the same prestige as Britain's Booker-McConnell prize or France's Prix Goncourt. Imperial Tobacco will probably call the award the duMaurier prize, despite the fact that the proposed Federal legislation allows tobacco companies to use only their corporate names, not brand names, as sponsors.

All three firms agreed that distribution will be the key to survival in an ad-less marketplace.

The tobacco lobby maintained that a ban on Canadian advertising will be ineffective because of the number of cigarette ads carried in U.S. publications sold in Canada. "An ad ban leaves us unable to defend ourselves from U.S. tobacco advertising" said Wilmat Tennyson, president of Imperial Tobacco. However, on the other hand, U.S. cigarettes have less than a 1% share of the Canadian market. That's about 500 million of the total 55.4 billion cigarettes sold annually in Canada.

A total ban would have at least one possible consolation for tobacco companies. Most of the estimated $80 million the tobacco companies spend each year on advertising and promotions should go straight to the bottom line.

Tobacco Firms Fight Back: Advertising Campaign
Before the tobacco companies put their new sales strategies into action, the firms took their case to the Canadian public in an $800 000 advertising campaign. The tobacco firms hoped that public pressure would cause the government to modify its position. The advertisement program was a series of three full-page newspaper and magazine advertisements. The first of the two ads focus on the violation of the Charter of Rights and Freedoms, outright censorship, and the loss of jobs; the second ad states that an advertising ban would not work, that advertising does not make people smoke, and again the question of the loss of jobs. The third ad in the series focuses on the sponsorship issue. The tobacco companies spend a combined $10 million a year supporting a variety of

events ranging from Tennis Canada, Royal Canadian Golf Association, Symphony Nova Scotia, Toronto Symphony, Montreal World Film Festival, Cercle Molière, and Neptune Theatre, for example. The advertisement stressed the fact that under Bill C-51, banned sponsorship of professional sports or cultural activities would become illegal (Exhibit 1).

Every cultural and professional sports group in Canada has the right to accept or reject tobacco brand sponsorship.

The Government wants to take away that right.

EXHIBIT 1

The Backlash Against the Advertisements

There has been ridicule against the three ads placed in newspapers in July, 1987. One ad argues that government bans on tobacco advertisement do not influence behaviour. "If that is so, why do they oppose (the ban) so strongly," one critic said.

The ad also goes on to say that advertising does not encourage people to start smoking or to smoke more, does not encourage young people to smoke, and only encourages them to try different brands. That may be the industry's public stance but not what numerous studies show. In a recent study, most Canadians support the proposed ban, 80 to 90 percent of all smokers would like to kick the habit.

Another ad states that banning tobacco ads just won't work. The ad shows cigarette sales volume in Norway, Singapore, and Finland. The ads show that even with the banning of advertising, the consumption of cigarettes increased after the ban. The critic of the ads, from the Canadian Cancer Society went on to state that the statistics shown in the ad are wrong and misleading. For example, in Singapore from 1976 to 1980 only sales of imported cigarettes increased. Tourist arrivals went up 72 percent in that time and tourists prefer imported cigarettes. So, the argument and the use of statistics needs further analysis, understanding, and discussion.

The third ad attacks the proposed ban on sponsorships that involve the brand names of tobacco products. However, Mr. Barr, executive officer of the Canadian Cancer Society, believed that if tobacco companies are good corporate citizens, they will donate anyway, and if they do not the government may be asked by society to put a surcharge in cigarettes to assist the athletic and cultural organizations. David Allnutt of the Tobacco Manufacturers' Council said cigarette companies are "not in the business of sponsoring charity."

Recently, numerous Canadian luminaries, such as former Ontario Lieutenant-Governor Pauline McGibbon and Arnold Edinborough of the Toronto Musicians Association have supported the tobacco industry's position.

Questions

1. Does the proposed legislation infringe upon the right to freedom of expression for individuals or corporations?

2. What are the rights of the non-smokers, the smokers, and the unborn children?
3. Do you believe that the Federal Government has the right to restrict, or ban, the promotion of products that are not deemed illegal?
4. Does the government have the right to promote good health?

5. Should tobacco companies be sponsoring cultural events mainly "high art"/"high culture"? Why do they do this? Are artists, musicians, concert attendees good "target markets"?

---

19. CANADIAN AMATEUR HOCKEY ASSOCIATION¹

The Canadian National Junior Team had just won the gold medal for first place at the World Championship in Helsinki, Finland. Murray Costello, president of the Canadian Amateur Hockey Association, was returning to Canada elated at the team's success and very proud that the medal had been won through clean, skilful play rather than through the "bullying" that Canadian teams have been known for in the past. He picked up a copy of the *Globe and Mail*, and, on opening it, his heart sank. There on the first page was an announcement that the Minister of Sport was setting up a national commission in order to secure immediate action to curb the violence in Canadian sport, and that he planned to meet in the next few days with various sports leaders. Once again, hockey was singled out in the article as one of the sports most plagued with violence.

"No matter how many positive things we do, our image never changes," he thought. "We're going to have more trouble renewing our insurance, and we may now find ourselves dealing with regulations imposed on us by the government."

The C.A.H.A.
The Canadian Amateur Hockey Association (C.A.H.A.) is the national governing body for amateur hockey in Canada. A non-profit organization, the C.A.H.A., in conjunction with its 12 provincial and regional branches, is engaged in the administration, promotion, and organization of hockey at

the amateur level for the enjoyment and recreation of Canadians from coast to coast. More than a million Canadians participate actively as players, officials, volunteer coaches, managers, and trainers. Exhibit 1 shows a breakdown of this involvement in terms of registrations for the period 1974 to 1984.

The C.A.H.A. also represents its members as the recognized voice for amateur hockey in negotiations with the International Ice Hockey Federation, the federal government, the Sports Federation of Canada, the Canadian Olympic Association, and the professional hockey leagues.

The Board of Directors of the C.A.H.A. consists of eight officers, six council directors and 12 branch presidents. The six councillors play a major role as advisory authorities to the Board by bringing input from the "grass roots" to the formation of policy. Although democratic, this operating style increases the cost of running the association as well as the amount of time spent on communication by the officers and the permanent staff. In co-ordinating the resources and activities of this huge organization, the 20-member permanent staff of the main office must cope with all the typical problems of a volunteer organization:

• the high turnover of volunteers which often results in the breakdown of communication channels and a lack of continuity from year to year;

EXHIBIT 1 **NUMBER OF REGISTERED PLAYERS AS A PERCENTAGE OF POPULATION 9–18 YEARS OLD (1974–1984)**

Year	A Total Number of Registered and Affiliated Players	B Population Ages 9–18	% A of B
1984	463 794	3 632 152	12.77
1983	493 877	3 691 956	13.38
1982	486 002	3 798 653	12.79
1981	466 566	3 920 485	11.90
1980	500 053	4 043 983	12.36
1979	599 480	4 157 653	14.40
1978	545 303	4 263 872	12.79
1977	536 849	4 371 188	12.28
1976	567 521	4 474 480	12.68
1975	584 257	4 569 965	12.78
1974	582 678	4 629 941	12.58

- the casual attitude toward deadlines of people in key positions of responsibility, both volunteer and full-time;
- the high level of internal politics;
- the constant liaison between hockey organizers and corporate sponsors.

The C.A.H.A. national office is divided into three functional departments. Administration coordinates the registration of players, team officials, and referees; records player movements; and coordinates and administers regulations and by-laws; it also provides administrative and accounting services. Development provides liaison with the branches in education programs, prepares coach and referee certification programs, and develops and distributes communication items. Marketing deals with sponsors, who provide over 50 percent of the organization's revenue, and with the media.

The Game of Hockey

In spite of the fact that lacrosse was named Canada's "official" national sport by act of Parliament, most Canadians would identify hockey as the national game. It is, without challenge, the top spectator and participant sport in Canada. The game itself is not a complicated one to watch or play, and it generates much excitement even among crowds to whom it is not well known. Played at its best, it requires a great deal of technical skill and training on the part of the players. It mixes quick and clever play combinations with hard, clean body contact. Because of the speed at which the game is played, players are protected from injury by a helmet and various lightweight padded pieces of equipment.

Amateur hockey competition is well developed in Canada. Some 28 000 teams involving over 500 000 participants, both male and female, play schedules of 40 to 80 games each year. Competition is structured by age groups ranging from five to 20, with rules against body contact for those under 12 years of age in order to allow for the development of skills. While the total number of teams registered and affiliated with the C.A.H.A. has been decreasing every year, it was recently pointed out that when compared to annual population figures—of the number of children between the ages of nine and 18—enrolment in C.A.H.A. programs has not dropped, but has in fact remained quite stable at 12 to 13 percent of the eligible population group.

Evolution to Increasing Violence

It was not so long ago that kids' hockey was primarily a game they organized themselves. They met on ponds, lakes, and rivers, or the part of playground oval for a game of "shinny." A pair of skates, a stick, and newspaper tucked into socks, for shin pads were all the equipment necessary. The best of these played on local teams where the coach had a great deal of authority, and where equipment was usually provided by the local sponsors. Parents turned out to watch the "big" games, but to have one's parents attend practices would have been humiliating.

Today, very little hockey is played on outdoor ice—weather conditions are too unpredictable. As a result hockey is highly structured and organized. For the entire season from September to April, indoor ice arenas have ice time booked long in advance for up to 24 hours a day. In order to learn to play the game, children begin, often as early as five or six years old, with an organized team. Because of the distance to be travelled and the hour at which practices are usually held, children must be driven to and from by parents. Many parents attend practices and games. Those who have played or are still playing the game believe they know how it should be taught and coached. Some parents accost coaches, questioning their game strategies, their use of individual players, and their training techniques. Others frequently become emotionally involved in the competition—shouts of "trip him," "hit him," "who's side are you on, ref," and much worse are often heard.

Coaches have been physically attacked by irate parents whose offspring did not receive, in the parent's view, sufficient ice time, or by parents of the opposing team players as a result of some on-ice incident. Many such disputes have reached the level of the courts. The sport has lost more than a few promising coaches who enjoyed the children but found dealing with the parents "not worth the hassle." Furthermore, some parents have pulled their children out of organized hockey because of the abuses they see at the local level. They complain about the reinforcement of violent behaviour by other parents and coaches and they feel powerless to stop it.

Coaches and referees are drawn from all walks of life. Most have played the game at some time, but this is not a requirement. Some parents volunteer their time because their children are playing, others for the social life or the community status such involvement brings. Still others hope that their abilities may be recognized and they may find a career in the game. A few have authoritarian tendencies. Referees are paid a few dollars per game at the lower amateur levels and up to $5 000 per year at the higher amateur levels. In the N.H.L., a referee earns up to $80 000 per year. Coaches in the amateur ranks volunteer their time, sometimes up to 200 hours per season, although some, particularly at the competitive levels, are "unofficially" paid for their services.

In spite of the fact that only one in 10 000 players reaches the professional ranks, some parents have extraordinarily high expectations for their children. In attempting to vicariously fulfill their own dreams, they do not always consider the youngster's educational and social needs. To the surprise of officials, some parents have gone so far as to move from one district to another in successive seasons in order that their child might find the best career opportunity—and this at a very minor age and skill level. These parents believe that budding talent must be properly managed if a youngster is to have a chance of moving up to the elite levels.

The consensus within the C.A.H.A. is that hockey competition should be confined to the winter season months and that youngsters should be encouraged to participate in a well-rounded schedule of many sports. To do otherwise is to invite the possibility of "burnout" in many young players, or simply a loss of interest through overexposure. Though not as serious, the same "burnout" possibilities exist for volunteers, who give so much of their time during the winter months.

However, the hockey season is getting longer and summer hockey competition and hockey camps have grown in popularity. Summer hockey camps range from a day camp structure given at the local arena to the high-priced residential camps directed by "stars" of the N.H.L. Though C.A.H.A. guidelines provide the basis for many of these programs, the training they offer is ultimately determined by the camp directors alone. At this time the C.A.H.A. does not have the authority to impose quality standards or accreditation requirements on these camps.

A number of entrepreneurs, usually former professional players, offer various products that compete with those of the C.A.H.A.—hockey schools, summer tournaments, training clinics for coaches and referees. Though some members are not pleased to see these products on the market, executives of the C.A.H.A. have always felt that the quality of their own products would allow them to prevail. In the last few years, such competitive products have become more successful. This is partly due to the use of better marketing techniques but also because these programs are somewhat less demanding in terms of their prerequisites and the length of their training sessions.

Professional Hockey

Professional hockey is the best-known form of the sport. The National Hockey League, as the pinnacle of hockey in North America and much of the free world, is associated with fame, wealth, and labour. Individual teams select players from among the amateur players of the world at an annual universal draft. Though the majority of its players are North American, the great heroes and superstars the N.H.L. has produced have been Canadians. The history of inter-city team rivalry has created a great deal of Canadian folklore. To appreciate the fact that Canadians take their hockey very seriously, one need only remember the riots along Ste. Catherine Street in Montreal when in 1955 Clarence Campbell, the president of the N.H.L., suspended the great Maurice Richard for the last five games of the season.

Today, the National Hockey League consists of 21 teams, in seven Canadian and 14 American cities, divided into four divisions. It operates as a business, and a very profitable one for owners of well-located franchises. Players earn salaries in the hundreds of thousands of dollars and are lionized by the press and fans wherever they go. They earn high endorsement fees for selling any number of consumer-oriented products and for speaking at special events. Many players have had careers spanning 15 or 20 years, but presently the average career in the N.H.L. is four years. Most people also consider the junior ranks and above as equivalent to the professional one, since at those levels gate revenues are of primary importance.

The player community has its own culture in which "machismo" and retaliation are very important. Pain and injury are accepted as part of the price of success, and complaining or refusing to play when injured would brand a player as troublesome. There is a code of "on-ice" behaviour providing for instances where physical aggression or retaliation is considered necessary and "legitimate." Sports commentators often refer to certain players as team policemen or "enforcers." The N.H.L. now claims to have eliminated the mass brawls and "goonery" so frequently seen a few years ago, but fighting is still tolerated as a means of "letting off steam." The N.H.L.'s premise is that anger and frustration should be quickly released rather than allowed to build up and eventually explode with the swinging of sticks.

The Media

As Canada's major winter sport, hockey receives a large share of media coverage. The professional ranks receive most of this attention. All too frequently however, coverage of hockey activities is dominated by the sensational or controversial aspects of the game, as is so often true for general news. Ironically, while the sports pages and televised sport reports feature vividly every brawl and fight, individual columnists and commentators raise an outcry about the violence in the sport.

Professional hockey clubs and the various media have an interdependence that is not always helpful in promoting the best aspects of the game. In order to secure media coverage that furthers their financial success, professional clubs employ press officers to provide a continuing stream of statistical data, gossip, and items of note. This material is helpful to sportswriters who have pages of sports news to fill and daily deadlines to meet. For televised games, the play-by-play announcer is assisted by a "colour commentator," usually a former N.H.L. player or coach, who is able to provide "inside" detail on players, coaching methods, trades, contracts, etc. His survival in the position depends, to a large extent, on the approval of team owners and the following he is able to attract, since television stations bid for a season's contract to air games. It is not surprising then that the dominant "macho" attitudes of the player community are provided in positive, even exciting terms, and as the only means to a successful career.

Creating a Safer Game Environment

Over the years, C.A.H.A. officials have frequently found that coaches, officials, and parents pay only lip service to the ideals espoused by the C.A.H.A.—that youngsters learn social and life skills through competition and team effort, and that the game of hockey be a good, recreational activity, fun to play. They have waged a continuous battle against established attitudes, coaching habits and undesirable patterns of behaviour in many areas of the country against those who feel that aggression and rough play are an essential part of the game.

To date, the greatest effort in terms of both time and resources has been directed toward the educational guidance of coaches and officials through the certification programs. These began with "seed" funding from the federal government, and have been ongoing for some 12 years. There are five levels of coaching certification offered, beginning with a four-hour introductory session and leading up to the higher levels, which require as much as a full week of instruction, considerable study with written exams, and on-ice evaluation of coaching style. More and more coaches are becoming certified as many local associations attempt to control the quality of training for their young players by requiring that their coaches obtain minimal certification to coach at various levels.

The higher certification levels are optional, and coaches must be recommended by their branches in order to register for level V. The programs are generally well received, although some coaches have complained that these demands are excessive given the number of hours they volunteer through the winter months.

In an effort to decrease the number of injuries that have occurred in the game at every level in recent years, the C.A.H.A. has adopted changes in recommended equipment and stricter interpretations of the rules. Helmets were made mandatory for all minor hockey players in 1966, and in 1977 the C.A.H.A. made facial protection mandatory. The N.H.L followed with a ruling in 1979 which made helmets obligatory for all rookies entering the league. Three years ago the C.A.H.A. initiated strong penalties for "checking from behind," because there appeared to be a strong connection between this type of "illegal" check and the rise in spinal column injuries. Such checking, though "illegal," is tolerated in the N.H.L. At the 1985 annual meeting of the C.A.H.A., the Board of Directors adopted rigorous "stick work" guidelines which disallowed the use of the hockey stick above waist level. The Quebec branch of the C.A.H.A. has been considering making neck protectors mandatory at every level of minor hockey within its jurisdiction.

Nonetheless, fighting and roughhouse tactics continue to result in injuries. Some observers of the game have commented that the sophistication of the equipment itself, though necessary, has had an unexpected secondary effect. Players are dressed almost like gladiators of old with protective padding from head to toe and helmets with face cages or protective glass, and competition becomes very impersonal as opponents no longer see the human, personalizing features in each other—faces and expressions are covered.

The Model Programs

A few years ago, the C.A.H.A. set out to devise new programs which would allow each participant to play the game at his level or ability and interest. The new Model Programs were labelled Initiation, Recreation, Competition, and Program of Excellence. The Program of Excellence, established in 1981, was the easiest to implement because it was directly conceived and controlled by the national office. An elite program, its purpose was to allow the best players to experience the pressures of international competition at a younger age, so that they might be better prepared to successfully compete in the Olympic Games and the Canada Cup when they reached that level. The fact that the National Junior Team (under age 20) has won three medals in the last four years of competition attests to the success of this approach. The teams have been drawing a great deal of positive media attention because of their successes, and public response has been growing to the extent that some of the players have become widely known even before reaching the professional ranks.

The other three Model Programs were to be introduced by the branches at the local level after a five-year, three-phase development. This was to be followed by evaluation and modification as changes in conditions warranted it.

Phase I— collect the best ideas and test in pilot projects, working with the various local associations

Phase II— develop and produce resource materials such as films, manuals, training programs, and promotional materials to explain and encourage the use of the Model Programs

Phase III—develop Model Program teams which would assist local associations in estab-

lishing the Model Programs in their community, working with and training volunteers.

At the time of writing, the C.A.H.A. had reached Phase III of the plan. The materials had been designed specifically for volunteers to enable them to do their job more easily and in less time.

Later that Monday afternoon, Dennis Mac-Donald, the C.A.H.A.'s Director of Development, was bringing Murray up to date on the progress made with the Model Programs.

"Dennis, do you think we could add a section on the responsibility that coaches bear for the violence in the game? When I meet with the Minister this week, he's going to want to know what further action we can take."

"Indirectly all these programs help us to get our message across, Murray, but you know there's no cure-all. There are so many different influences on the kids."

"I know, but at least think about it, Dennis. See if your people have any ideas. Public opinion is with us and we've got to try to do more to counteract the violence in the game."

Murray sat at his desk for a long time, thinking about the directions in which the C.A.H.A. could move next. Dennis is right, he thought, our job is to change attitudes in many segments: the players, the parents, all the officials—coaches, referees, and our own people—the media, and the N.H.L. Maybe it is impossible!

---

[1]Copyright 1986. This case was written by Denise Costello and Luc Gelineau under the supervision of David S. Litvack, University of Ottawa.

---

20. CANADIAN ADVERTISING FOUNDATION[1]

Pam Frostad, Creative Director at Vickers & Benson Advertising was reviewing the advocacy campaign developed for the Canadian Advertising Foundation (CAF), prior to the presentation to the Annual Meeting of CAF to be held next April 1988.

The objective of the proposed campaign was to enhance the overall economic environment for advertising by raising the level of belief in the *responsibility* of advertising.

Strategy

The selected strategy was to demonstrate that advertising functions in an ethical, responsible, disciplined fashion. The rationale for this strategy was:

The goal of advertising is to communicate to people that advertisers are genuinely interested in and sensitive to the public's opinion of advertising. Advertisers are accessible; "open" to comments and criticism. Advertisers are responsive, committed to creating responsible, ethical, informative, and entertaining advertising.

Support

This was chosen because advertisers want to know what the public thinks of advertising. They spend millions of dollars making sure that they are saying the right things about themselves in a compelling way, so if enough people think their advertising is unacceptable, unethical, or "unlikeable," advertisers want to know about it, without delay, and they want to find out why. Advertisers value and respect the public's opinion.

Positioning

The selected positioning was defined as follows:
Advertising knows it cannot be all things to all people. There will be some people who find some advertising unacceptable. Advertisers owe them an explanation, and welcome the opportunity to talk with them about it. They are inviting the flow of communication to be more than a one-way street. The CAF is an instrument the public can use to respond to advertising. By making this offer the public will perceive advertising as more responsive and receptive and thus more helpful. In turn this should help advertising perform more efficiently.

The creative rationale, as developed by her agency under her direction, is provided in Exhibit 1, and some samples of the proposed print messages are provided in Exhibit 2. As can be seen, the message of the campaign is serious, but the treatment is lighthearted and fun.

Media

Because CAF is a non-profit organization, the messages are run by the media free of charge, but at their discretion. The agency would contact them to ask for their co-operation, provide the media with the proper materials, and monitor the appearance of these messages.

Conclusion

After reviewing the work of her agency, Pam must decide whether to present this campaign as developed, or make some changes before the Annual Meeting, in only three months!

EXHIBIT 1

CAF CAMPAIGN RATIONALE
Prepared by Vickers & Benson Advertising Ltd.

ADVERTISING'S BEST WHEN IT'S TALKED ABOUT

The campaign is based on the relationship between advertisers and the people they talk to because we are dedicated to establishing a better relationship than ever before!

Right now, one might consider this relationship a pretty one-sided affair; in so far as "advertising" has been doing most of the "talking."

Advertising talks to people, day in day out, about everything from RSPs to panty liners. People wake up to us, eat their cereal reading us, drive to work listening to us. We talk to them on buses, in the subway. In fact, some people even spend their working day hearing our points-of-view, and then, they come home, and we're at it again!

They take to the couch and we have a go at them for another couple of hours.

We tell them how to make supper simpler, where to go when you want to know about chicken, Bottom Bottle Openers, No Trouble Gasoline, Light Days, how it feels so good coming down, and just what a swell bunch of guys we are . . .

All of this talking has *impact*.

People react to us. They admit that advertising *does* influence them. It is persuasive stuff. Powerful stuff.

And people have a point-of-view about advertising.

They have opinions as to how we should approach them.
The language we should be using. The attitude we should take.
What we look like and sound like.

However most people don't think that advertisers are genuinely interested in their point-of-view. Or even accessible at all. They believe that they are at the mercy of advertising: that necessary evil.

Our campaign will remind people that the advertising industry does indeed care; in fact, the industry works to codes, guidelines, standards, and they are in place to reflect and respect the public's point-of-view.

The campaign premise is a simple one:

Advertising talks to you.
Did you know that you can talk to the advertiser?

Well, you can, and here's how:
    through the CAF/Box # etc . . .

And guess what?

We'll be glad to hear from you.
To find out what's on your mind.

Our campaign will open up the lines of communication between advertisers and the people who are forced to "consume" it. It will become a genuine reminder that the advertising industry represents a group of people who are ready to respond to your comments, criticism, or queries.

However, this does not mean that we intend to set up the industry as a bunch of wimps ready to kneejerk to every whim or caprice. It's a campaign that says "here we are." Advertising has come forward to say that we don't dodge or ignore issues and concerns. We confront them. Deal with them head on.

And a key part of our campaign is the admission that advertising cannot be all things to all people. There will be advertising that is not unanimously liked, or even acceptable. This is reality.

Although there are industry standards, codes, guidelines, etc., they are discretionary. Open to interpretation. Attitudes, points-of-view will vary with the person you speak to.
Advertising is only human.

"I might find an ad offensive and Tom might love it . . . does that make me right and Tom wrong?"

Who's to say? What's the index?

This is a tough call, but advertisers make it every step of the way.

And make no mistake, while we want people to understand that advertising is a subjective opinion call, we do not intend this as a way to get ourselves off the hook.
The call *can* be made. We simply ask that you respect the subjectivity of it all, recognizing that you cannot please all of the people all of the time . . .

Also, at the heart of our concept is the fact that the industry has a right to believe that advertising, for the most part, does *not* alienate, offend, insult, or stereotype; while at the same time there is a potential for imperfection.
So if you think something's out of line, unclear or misleading, tell us about it, and we'll work it out together.

We respect your right to comment, and believe that you deserve a response.

All of this rhetoric sounds like we're leading up to a pretty heavy duty campaign, but far from it.

This is *advertising* we're representing, so it better be entertaining, interesting. Fun. Right?

The message is straight ahead. But the executive is metaphor.
Part of our objective was to create a great personality for the advertisers, and CAF as their representative.
Something that was warm and intelligent. Approachable.
Take the sterility out the word 'foundation' . . .
We came up with the idea of expressing our concept with the help of animation, a commercial style that pretty well everybody has a hard time casting stones at. In our case, we created two character

metaphors to showcase the difference of opinion that occurs when advertising is the topic. And make no mistake, it *is* a point-of-couch topic lots of times. That's why people will recognize the truth in what we have to say.

Our characters come from different "sides of the couch."

And, they're both right, of course!

Through their banter they set up the classic dilemma, demonstrating the point/counterpoint of any related topic, from the generic topic of advertising to sexism.

The advertising industry, through CAF, enters into the concept as people who celebrate the fact that advertising is being talked about because of course that's when it works best. And the industry is extending this invitation to people to get in touch. We'd like to hear what you've got to say and we can be better communicators when you talk to us.

EXHIBIT 2 *(cont'd)*

EXHIBIT 2 *Proposed Print Messages*

---

[1]This case was written by Michel Laroche from documents provided by Suzanne Keeler, Canadian Advertising Foundation.

APPENDIX 1

BROADCASTING REGULATIONS AND RADIO ADVERTISING

Courtesy Radio Bureau of Canada. See Chapter 7.

The Broadcasting Act directs the CRTC to regulate and supervise all aspects of the Canadian broadcasting system with a view to implementing the broadcasting policy for Canada declared in Section 3 of the Act. The act empowers the CRTC to make regulations applicable to persons holding broadcasting licences respecting the character of advertising and amount of time that may be devoted to advertising.

The Broadcasting Regulations presently require the pre-clearance of commercials promoting beer, wine, cider, food, drugs, cosmetics, and medical devices. In addition, the Commission has placed conditions on the licences of broadcasters requiring adherence to the Broadcast Code for Advertising to Children, which in turn require pre-clearance by the Children's Section of the Advertising Standards Council and le Conseil des Normes de la Publicité, of all broadcast advertising directed to children. The CRTC has a representative in each of these bodies.

The following sections of the CRTC Broadcasting Regulations pertain to advertising on radio:

	Section	
	AM	(FM)
Program logs	4	(5)
Newscasts	5	(9)
Political broadcasts	6	(7)
Commercial messages	7	(8)
Insurance, financial and mining advertising	8	(10)
Liquor, beer, wine, and cider advertising	10	(12)
Food and drug advertising	11	(13)

SECTION 4 (5)
Program logs

Each station shall maintain a program log, and shall cause to be entered therein each day the following the information:

a. the date;
b. the call letters, location, and frequency of the station;
c. the times at which station identification announcements were made;

d. the title and a brief description of each program broadcast, the name of the sponsors, if any, the time at which the program commenced and concluded and the appropriate code word or letter set out in Schedule 1 indicating the language or origin of the program;

e. the time and duration of each commercial announcement broadcast, the total commercial time in each sponsored program and the name of the sponsor of each such announcement and program;

f. the name of the speaker of any talk program and the auspices, if any, under which the talk was given;

g. the name of any candidate for public office speaking on a political broadcast and his political affiliation, if any;

h. the name of every person speaking on a political broadcast on behalf of a political party or candidate together with the name of the party or candidate on whose behalf the talk was given; and

i. in the case of FM stations, the time of the commencement and conclusion of any time segment in which the matter being broadcast is in a foreground format and the code letters set out in Schedule 1 indicating that format.

SECTION 5(9)
Newscasts

AM
No station or network operator shall broadcast any advertising content in the body of a news broadcast and for the purposes of this section, a summary is deemed to be part of the body of the news broadcast.

FM
1. The first 10 minutes of any newscast shall not be interrupted by a commercial message or public service announcement.

2. For the purposes of this section "newscast" includes headlines, reports of news events, and summaries of the news but does not include an announcement that mentions only the place or origin of the news items, the title of the newscasts and the name of the news reader.

SECTION 6(7)
Political broadcasts

Each station or network operator shall allocate time for the broadcasting of programs, advertising, or announcements of a partisan political character on an equitable basis to all parties and rival candidates.

Political programs, advertisements, or announcements shall be broadcast by stations or network operators in accordance with such directions as the Commission may issue from time to time.

SECTION 7(8)
Commercial messages

AM
1. No station shall broadcast commercial messages the total time of which exceeds 250 minutes during the period between six o'clock in the forenoon and twelve o'clock midnight, and the total time of commercial messages in a week shall not exceed 1500 minutes.

2. No station that is by a condition of licence to broadcasting between the hours of sunrise and sunset only shall broadcast commercial messages the total time of which exceeds 200 minutes during the period between sunrise and sunset in any day and the total time of commercial messages in any week shall not exceed 1000 minutes.

FM
1. Between six A.M. and twelve midnight of any day
   a. no station operated by the holder of a joint FM licence shall broadcast commercial messages the aggregate time of which exceed 120 minutes, and

b. no station operated by the holder of an independent FM licence shall broadcast commercial messages the aggregate time of which exceeds 150 minutes.

2. No station operated by the holder of a joint FM licence or an independent FM licence shall, during any clock hour between six A.M. and twelve midnight of any day, broadcast more than 10 minutes of commercial messages.

SECTION 8(10)
Insurance, financial, and mining advertising

1. No station or network operator shall broadcast any program or any flash announcement sponsored by any person for the purpose of promoting:
   a. any act or thing prohibited by the law of Canada or of the province in which the station is located;
   b. any insurance corporation not authorized by law to carry on business in Canada;
   c. the investment in bonds, shares or other securities except:
      i securities of the Government of Canada or any province, municipality or other public authority
      ii certificates issued by any recognized trust company incorporated in Canada as evidence of a term deposit with such trust company, and
      iii debentures of any mortgage loan company incorporated in Canada that are insured or guaranteed by a federal or provincial deposit insurance corporation; or
   d. the sale of mining, oil or natural gas property or any interest in any mining, oil or natural gas property.

2. Subsection (1) does not apply to the broadcasting of a sponsored program of general quotations of market prices presented without comment.

Offensive or objectionable advertising

3. The Commission may, by notice in writing to any station or network operator, require that station or network operator to modify the character of any advertisement broadcast by that station where, in the opinion of a representative of the Commission, the advertisement is of an offensive or objectionable nature.

Good taste

Since broadcast messages are received in the privacy of the home, reaching old and young alike, there are certain subjects which are unsuitable for this intimate medium and others, which, if they are introduced, must be treated with restraint. Personal hygiene is an example of a topic that must be dealt with discreetly.

Only those commercial messages should be broadcast which can freely be introduced into any gathering in the home as a subject of ordinary conversation.

In the past, certain words, phrases or categories of products have been designated as unacceptable. This is no longer the case. This does not imply less concern for good taste but does reflect the view that the decision concerning good taste of a commercial is best made by the broadcast licensee, who is responsible for all material broadcast by his station.

The CRTC relies on the licensee to exercise appropriate care in accepting commercial messages for broadcast, and in deciding the suitable time of day or night for the scheduling of certain commercials.

However, in reviewing scripts, the CRTC may ask for the deletion or substitution of certain words, expressions or may reject complete scripts which it may, in the context, consider not to be in good taste.

SECTION 10(12)
Spirituous liquors, beer, wine, and cider

1. Subject to subsection (2), no station or network operator shall broadcast any com-

mercial message:

   a. advertising, directly or indirectly, any spirituous liquor or any beer, wine or cider; or
   b. sponsored by or on behalf of any person whose principal business is the manufacture or sale of spirituous liquor, beer, wine or cider.

2. Where in any province the advertising of beer, wine, or cider is permitted, a commercial message sponsored by a brewery, winery, or cider-house may be broadcast in the provinces subject to the following conditions:

   a. the advertising shall not be designed to promote the general use of beer, wine, or cider, but this prohibition shall not be construed so as to prevent industry, institutional, public service, or brand preference advertising;
   b. no commercial message shall exceed sixty seconds in duration;
   c. no device and no commercial message, other than a commercial message allowed under this subsection, shall be used to advertise, directly or indirectly, the sponsor or his product; and
   d. no commercial message shall be broadcast unless it is approved by a representative of the Commission prior to broadcast.

3. For the purpose of determining whether a commercial message may be broadcast in a province pursuant to subsection (2), "cider" means that is considered to be an alcoholic beverage by the law of the province relating to the advertising of cider.

Beer, wine, and cider advertising—CRTC procedures

A The main criterion in the approval of scripts is adherence to standards of good taste.

B Advertising shall not
   a. encourage the general consumption of the product, nor should it attempt to influence non-drinkers to drink;
   b. be associated with youth or youth symbols;
   c. attempt to establish a certain product as a status symbol, a necessity for the enjoyment of life, or an escape from life's problems;
   d. show persons engaged in any activity in which the consumption of alcohol is prohibited.

C Six copies of each commercial must be submitted and received by the Continuity Section of the CRTC at least two weeks prior to the meeting. The name of the province where the commercial is to be broadcast must be mentioned.

D Scripts are examined on scheduled dates (usually every second Wednesday). Any modification to a previously approved script must be indicated. The schedule of meetings may be obtained from the CRTC.

E The advertisers or their agents who so desire, may make personal representations concerning their copy when their commercials are examined.

The department of Consumer and Corporate Affairs has deemed that, since beer, wine, and cider are considered "food" under the Food and Drug Act, the regulations pertaining to that act will be enforced as they apply to those products. Accordingly, all radio commercials for these products will be reviewed by a representative of the Department of Consumer and Corporate Affairs. The Commission will review such commercials in accordance with Sections 10 and 11 of its Radio and Television Broadcasting Regulations.

It should be noted that these commercials will now receive a continuity clearance number which will be valid for a period of one year from the date of approval.

A summary of the provincial regulations concerning the advertising of beer, wine, and cider on radio

The advertising of beer, wine, or cider is prohibited on radio in the following provinces:

British Columbia
Saskatchewan
New Brunswick
Prince Edward Island

In all provinces where the advertising of beer and wine is allowed, the advisers must adhere to the CRTC regulations. In addition, each province has specific regulations relating to such advertising.

Guidelines for advertisers are available from the Head Office of the Liquor Boards in each province. The regulations relating to the content of commercial messages as they apply to Radio are essentially the same.

Ontario regulations pertaining to the content of beer, wine, and cider commercial messages

a. Beer, wine, and cider advertising must be within the limits of good taste and propriety, having regard at all times to the need for discouraging abusive drinking patterns and encouraging the legal, moderate, and safe consumption of alcoholic beverages.
b. Beer, wine, and cider advertisers must take into account at all times the likelihood of minors and adult non-users being exposed to their advertising. The probable audience or readership for an advertisement must consist primarily of drinking age adults.

Advertisers are required to prepare at the Board's request an annual report to the Board containing data on the ages of those exposed to their advertising in the previous one year period, based upon independent qualified sources such as the Bureau of Broadcast Measurement and the Print Measurement Bureau.

c. There shall be no endorsement, personally or by implication, either directly or indirectly of beer, wine, or cider products, by any person or group of persons who may be generally known or recognized either by reason of their exposure in the mass media, or by reputation or achievement, and whose

exposure, fame, or prestige is a result of activities, work, or endeavour in an area other than the production of beer, wine, or cider products. Actors or musicians employed in the production of advertising shall not imply that their talent or ability is dependent on the use of the company's product.
d. All such advertisements, commercials, and endorsements shall be directed towards, and emphasize, the nature and quality of the product being advertised, and shall not imply, directly or indirectly, that social acceptance, personal success, business or athletic achievement may be acquired or result from the use of the product being advertised. All such advertisements shall be directed to the merits of the particular brand being advertised so as to promote brand preference and the responsible use of the product and not the merits of consumption or the encouragement of excessive consumption of beer, wine, or cider products.
e. Advertisements must not suggest that the consumption of alcoholic beverages per se, or of a particular category of alcoholic beverage may be a significant factor in the realization of any lifestyle or the enjoyment of any activity.
f. Advertisements must not suggest that participants in work, sports, hobby, recreation, and other similar activities should consume alcoholic beverages per se, or a particular category of alcoholic beverage or a particular brand of alcoholic beverages whilst engaging in their work or other activity. Nor may advertising suggest that consumption of alcohol in any way enhances performance or enjoyment of these activities.
g. Advertisements shall not make any claim, direct or implied, of healthful, nutritive, curative, dietetic, stimulative, or sedative qualities or properties attributable to beer, wine, or cider, or to any product mixed with beer, wine, or cider.

h. No media advertisement shall refer to the price at which the product may be purchased, nor to the brand number, nor that it is available in a particular licensed establishment.

i. Except for advertisements under 2(a) and (b), no corporative name or the name of an organization other than the company displaying the advertisement or on whose behalf the advertisement is displayed shall appear in the advertisement.

j. Advertisements shall not contain scenes in which the product is actually being consumed. Nor shall the face or figure of any person be unduly exploited as the central theme of the advertisement.

k. Advertisements shall not appear to suggest or recommend the consumption of beer, wine, or cider prior to the driving of a motorized vehicle, or participation in any sort of activity in which the participant's safety is dependent upon normal levels of alertness, physical co-ordination, or speed of response, except in authorized messages of moderation. Nor shall any advertisement depict or suggest any activity which is a breach of the Liquor Licence Act or any other Provincial Statute.

l. Advertisements shall not be directed to, or appear to be directed to, consumption by minors. Pictures of minors or persons who could reasonably be mistaken for minors are not permitted.

Source: Directives on Advertising and Sales Promotions for Beer, Wine and Cider Industries, Liquor Licence Board of Ontario.

Provincial regulations limiting the frequency of beer, wine or cider commercial messages on radio

Alberta: No brewery or winery shall be permitted to purchase more than seven announcements per day, each not to exceed 60 seconds in duration.

Manitoba: Permitted only between 10:00 P.M. each evening and 7:00 A.M. the following morning.

Ontario: In any calendar year, no company shall average more than 55 commercial minutes of broadcast per week on any radio station, with a maximum in any calendar week of 75 commercial minutes.

The weekly time limitations may be extended upon application to the LCBO in the case of special cultural or sporting events but in no case shall the maximum weekly average be exceeded in any calendar year.

No company may broadcast commercials during periods when half or more of the audience is, or is likely to be, under the age of majority, as determined by the Bureau of Broadcast Measurement.

Quebec: No specific regulations on frequency.

Nova Scotia: No company shall sponsor more than three hours of radio programming on any radio station in any calendar week, with a maximum of 78 hours in any calendar year. This time limitation may be extended in the case of cultural or sporting events to cover the entire broadcast of such event.

Newfoundland: No Newfoundland regulations. Subject to CRTC regulations.

SECTION 11(13)
Food and Drugs

1. No station or network operator shall broadcast any advertisement or testimonial for an article to which the Proprietary or Patent Medicine Act* applies or for a drug, cosmetic or device to which the Food and Drugs Act applies unless the continuity of the advertisement or testimonial has been approved by the Department of National Health and Welfare and by a representative of the Commission and bears the registra-

---

*The Proprietary or Patent Medicine Act was revoked 1 April 1977, and has been incorporated into the Food and Drug Regulations.

tion number (continuity clearance number) assigned by the Commission.

   a. No station or network operator shall broadcast any advertisement or testimonial for a food to which the Food and Drugs Act applies unless the continuity of the advertisement or testimonial has been approved by the Department of Consumer and Corporate Affairs and by a representative of the commission and bears the registration number assigned by the Commission.

2. No station shall broadcast any recommendation for the prevention, treatment, or cure of a disease or ailment unless the continuity thereof has been approved by the Department of National Health and Welfare and by a representative of the Commission and bears the registration number (continuity clearance number) assigned by the Commission.

The procedure for obtaining approval for broadcast commercials for products or services covered by Section 11

Prior to review by the CRTC, the appropriate government branch of either the Department of National Health and Welfare Canada or the Department of Consumer and Corporate Affairs reviews the commercial.

   Continuities submitted for approval should be forwarded to the commission in triplicate at least two weeks in advance of intended use.

1. All commercials for food products must be reviewed by:

Food Division
Consumer Fraud Protection Branch
Consumer Standards Directorate
Department of Consumer and
Corporate Affairs
Place du Portage, Phase 1
68 Victoria Street
Hull, Quebec K1A OC9

Restaurant commercials

Commercials for food dispensed to consumers from restaurant facilities (including drive-ins) need not be submitted for approval under Regulation 11 if they meet all of the following conditions:

   a. they are local advertisements, specially prepared for a city or metropolitan area;
   b. they are in good taste;
   c. they contain no direct or implied nutritional claims;
   d. they make no negative or derogatory statements;
   e. they make no reference to the safety of the food;
   f. standard foods should be stated by their common name.

Perishable food products

In the case of perishable food products, temporary clearance may be obtained from the Local Inspector of the Department of Consumer and Corporate Affairs when an emergency arises.

   Perishables consist of fresh produce in season, such as fruit, vegetables, fish, and bakery products of a variety that cannot be stored without spoilage. It does not include any manufactured or processed products, either preserved or frozen, which may be stored in a refrigerator.

   To obtain temporary clearance, a total of five(5) copies of the commercial should be prepared, of which two (2) copies should be submitted to the Local Inspector, and three (3) copies mailed to the CRTC and marked to indicate that temporary approval has been obtained.

Stock commercials

The problem of submitting commercials two weeks in advance of broadcast, where the small dealer or local merchant may wish to publicize specials on a particular day, may be met by preparing stock commercials. These may be submitted for approval, then placed on the agency or station file for emergency use.

1. All commercials for drugs or cosmetics must be previewed by:

Drugs & Cosmetics
Product Regulation Division
Bureau of Drug Surveillance
Drug Directorate
Health Protection Branch
Health & Welfare Canada
Place Vanier, Tower B
355 River Road
Vanier, Ontario
K1A 1B8

It is not permitted to advertise prescription or therapeutic vitamin preparations, and drugs for human use which carry a recommended single or daily dosage or a statement of concentration in excess of the limits provided by Section C.01.021 of the Food and Drug Regulations.

The offer of drugs as samples by radio is not allowed.

2. All commercials for "device products" must be reviewed by:

Bureau of Medical Devices
Health Protection Branch
Environmental Health Directorate
Health and Welfare Canada
Tunney's Pasture
Ottawa, Ontario K1A 0L2

Section 19 of the Food and Drugs Act states:

No person shall sell any device that, when used according to directions or under such conditions as are customary or usual, may cause injury to the health of the purchaser of user thereof.

Some examples of device products are:

Health studios or reducing salons, contraceptives, optical supplies (i.e., contact lenses), hearing devices, anti-smoking devices or methods, etc.

CRTC approval

Six scripts are initially submitted to the CRTC at least two weeks in advance of intended use. The CRTC then passes them on to the appropriate department for review. If the proposed commercials are approved by the department concerned and the CRTC, they are assigned continuity clearance numbers which are valid for a period of one year.

The CRTC may make a correction to the commercial while reviewing it. So long as that correction is made in the final script and nothing else is changed, the commercial is considered approved.

Advertisers may appeal modifications, deletions, or rejections of food and drug copy. With supporting evidence for claims made, appeals should be addressed to:

Chairman
Canadian Radio-Television and
Telecommunications Commission
Ottawa, Ontario K1A 0N2

Commercials must be broadcast exactly as cleared. Where any revision in words or visual material, the revised commercial must be forwarded for approval prior to broadcast.

Single phrases or claims cannot be cleared. Commercials must be submitted in their entirety, in the form in which they are to be broadcast.

Since the regulations may change from year to year, yearly approvals are necessary. If circumstances warrant, the copy may be requested for review within that one-year period. Prior to expiration of the one-year period, commercials may be submitted for approval for an additional one-year period.

Although a commercial announcement may be provided with a continuity clearance number, this does not imply any obligation on the part of the broadcaster to broadcast the announcement. Final discretion as to whether an approved commercial shall be broadcast or not rests with the licensee.

APPENDIX 2

ADVERTISING PRODUCTION

This technical appendix provides an overview of the most common tools and techniques used to produce print and broadcast advertisements.

PRINT PRODUCTION

Typography

To someone not familiar with the field of typography, the selection of a type style for a print advertisement may seem like a trivial task. However, there are hundreds of styles to chose from, and these come in myriad sizes and weight.

Different Type Groups

Roman. Roman characters are the most familiar and widely used. They are formed with a succession of broad and thin strokes and contain serifs, which are thin lines on the end of unconnected strokes. Roman faces are easy to read, which explains their popularity and frequent use in the body text of print advertisements. Roman characters are generally classified into two subgroups: Old Style and Modern. Modern roman characters are more formal and precise, have less contrast between thick and thin strokes, and have straight, horizontal serifs. These differences can be observed by comparing a popular Old Style face, such as Garamond, with a commonly used Modern face, such as Bodoni (Figure A1). Some Roman styles, like Baskerville, do not fall clearly into either of the preceding categories, but borrow characteristics from both. Such typefaces are considered to form a transitional group between Old Style and Modern Roman characters.

Sans Serif or Block. After Roman styles, sans serif characters are the most widely used in advertising.

FIGURE A1
Examples of Character Types

Garamond

abcdefghijklmnopqrstuvwxyz
ABCDEFGHIJKLMNOPQRSTUVWXYZ
1234567890 ß &?!£$(.,;:)

Bodoni Bold

abcdefghijklmnopqrstuvwxyz
ABCDEFGHIJKLMNOPQRSTUVWXYZ
1234567890 æøßÆØ &?!£$(.,;:)

Helvetica Medium

abcdefghijklmnopqrstuvwxyz
ABCDEFGHIJKLMNOPQRSTUVWXYZ
1234567890 ß &?!£$(.,;:)

Old English

abcdefghijklmnopqrstuvwxyz
ABCDEFGHIJKLMNOPQRSTUVWXYZ
1234567890 ß &?!£$(.,;:)

Their design is straightforward and contemporary; the letters do not have serifs, and the strokes have a uniform thickness. The typeface Helvetica belongs to this category (Figure A1).

Square Serif or Egyptian. These typefaces represent a mixture of Roman and sans serif, as they take the latter's formality of design and uniformity of strokes, but nevertheless contain thick, square serifs. This type is especially appropriate for display material.

Script and Cursive. This lettering very much resembles handwriting. It is almost never used in the body text of an advertisement but can be used for headlines when a special effect is desired.

Blackletter. This style is rarely used because its ornamented characters are not very legible (Figure A1). However, it conveys antiquity and can be used for products or product lines for which such a connotation would be desirable.

This classification is by no means exhaustive. A multitude of typefaces borrow characteristics from the categories outlined above and are therefore unclassifiable. Some other styles are so original as to form a distinct group. Such styles are frequently used in advertising headlines to capture readers' attention and some are designed exclusively for use in one advertisement.

Type Measurement

A special system of measurement is used in typography. Letter height is measured in points. Each point represents about 0.35 millimetres, so there are about 28.5 points to a centimetre. The most commonly used character sizes are: 6, 7, 8, 9, 10, 12, 14, 18, 24, 30, 36, 42, 48, 60, 72, 84, 96, and 120 points. A height of 12 points is called a *pica*.

The *em* is the unit used to measure both height and width. A character that is ten points high and ten points wide measures ten ems. A 12-point em is generally referred to as a *pica em*.

Principles of Good Typography

Type plays an important role in enhancing an advertisement's effectiveness by making the message more attractive, capturing the reader's attention, and/or conveying extra information about the product or product line. To make the best use of type, a typographer must obey some basic rules, and also use imagination and creativity. In this, one can say that typography is an art as well as a science. Like any art form, it is subject to certain fundamental constraints.

One of the most important standards of good typography is legibility. If an advertisement is difficult to read, the potential consumer in the target audience will not go through the trouble of deciphering it. Among the factors that increase or decrease readability are:

• *Size of letters.* In body text, letter sizes between eight and 12 points should generally be used. Large-sized headings are more likely to attract attention, but spacing should be proportional to the size of type.

• *Spacing.* Words and letters should not be too close together, nor separated by too much blank space because reading becomes more difficult. Readers do not move their eyes in a continuous movement along the page but shift them from one group of words to the next. These shifts are the most time-consuming aspect of reading. To reduce them to a minimum, the distance between words should not be too great. For the same reason, lines should not be too long.

The space between lines—the leading—should ideally be equal to the space between words. There should also be more space between paragraphs than between lines.

• *Length of lines.* It is often necessary to break headings into several lines. Each line should contain a word or group of words that makes sense by itself, so that readers can understand the heading at a glance. Such headings as the following should be avoided:

THE NEW XEROX COPIER: A
BREAKTHROUGH IN OFFICE
AUTOMATION

A more effective heading is:

THE NEW XEROX COPIER:
A BREAKTHROUGH
IN OFFICE AUTOMATION

Uppercase letters are less legible than lower case characters but their appearance is more striking. In the same way, even though italics are useful for emphasizing a word or a group of words, they are less readable and should therefore be avoided for entire body texts.

A good type style should not clash with the mood of the advertisement or the message. For instance, Blackletter characters would be incongruous in a commercial for state-of-the-art IBM microcomputer. A delicate, ornamental script would be appropriate for advertising women's perfume but not after-shave lotion. Type styles carry important connotations for consumers, and advertisers should be careful to avoid using lettering that might weaken the effectiveness of their advertising message.

Typesetting

Once the character style and text format have been selected, the advertisement must be set in type. Many techniques are available for this task.

Metal Typesetting

Until recently, the most widespread techniques of typesetting relied on movable metal characters.

Hand Setting. Hand setting has largely been replaced by more efficient, less expensive methods. It is now mainly used for display material. With hand typesetting, an operator selects the needed characters from a box divided into compartments containing the letters, numbers, punctuation, and various symbols. These are inserted into a composition stick, which is a tray that holds the characters for one line of text. Once a line has been completed, the characters are cast and the resulting mould is placed on a galley tray. The moveable characters are then returned to their respective compartments or job cases in the type font, ready to be used again.

Although this method allows for a greater flexibility than mechanical techniques, it is tedious and expensive, and more practical methods have been perfected.

Machine Setting. Machine setting covers two types of processes: linotype and monotype.

Linotype. A linotype machine somewhat resembles a massive and very complex typewriter. When the operator punches the keyboard, brass characters or matrices are released from the magazine of the machine and form words on the operator's right. Narrow triangular wedges or space bands are inserted between each word. Once a line is completed, the space bands are pushed up, increasing the space between words until the line is just the right length to justify the right- and left-hand margins. After this has been done, the line is cast. The resulting cast (or slug) is deposited onto a galley tray. The matrices are then returned to the magazine, ready to be re-used. Linotype is a very efficient way to set type and is therefore widely used for newspapers. Corrections may be somewhat onerous, since changing an individual character involves resetting the whole line.

Monotype. Monotype avoids the inconvenience of linotype. Letters are cast individually, and individual corrections can thus be made without destroying a whole line. Monotype machines usually comprise two units—a keyboard and a caster. The operator punches words onto the keyboard. The text is then stored in the form of perforations on a paper ribbon. At the end of each line, a calculator integrated with the keyboard indicates the amount of space that must be inserted between words in order to justify the right- and left- hand margins. The operator punches this amount at the end of the line. The ribbon is then fed to the caster, which automatically casts individual letters and places the mouldings on a galley tray. The caster "reads" the ribbon backwards, so that it knows the amount to insert between each word before composing the line. This system is more expensive than linotype and therefore is less commonly used for the body text of advertisements, but it is useful for printing display material.

Phototypography

Printing by using plates composed of moveable metal characters has been almost completely replaced by more efficient methods. The technique of phototypography involves exposing text onto photosensitive paper or film. Phototypography has many advantages, because it allows for more aesthetic lettering, a wider array of letter styles, increased sharpness and quality of detail, and greater versatility.

Photodisplay

This method enables an operator to compose a display manually and then expose it onto photo-sensitive paper or film. This allows for great flexibility, since an artist can compose almost any kind of display or headline without the constraints or costs of metal typography. Semi-automatic photo-display allows the operator to see each character before it is exposed individually, set the right letter size through lenses incorporated into the photo-display machine, and adjust the spacing.

Phototext.

One example of the phototext process is mono-photo, which is based on the same principle as the monotype machine except that the metal matrices are replaced by negatives of letters that are exposed on film. Operators use a keyboard that resembles a monotype keyboard and produces a paper ribbon or magnetic tape onto which the text is coded. The lines are automatically adjusted to the right length, because a calculator incorporated into the machine tells the operator how much extra space must be inserted between words. The paper ribbon or tape is then fed into a photo-processing unit that uses negative film fonts to expose the words on film or photosensitive paper. For advertisements, film is more common.

Other machines are more sophisticated and have electronic features. Such machines are the most widely used in advertising, and include the Alphatype and Linofilm. In an age in which computers are rapidly taking over in all walks of life, typesetting is no exception to this rule. As computers increase in cost-effectiveness and versatility, their use will become even more widespread.

It is possible to print display material with any kind of automatic phototext equipment, but the results are generally inferior to photodisplay equipment.

Phototext equipment for advertising does not develop the film. This must be executed sepa-rately, either by hand or through an automatic film processor. Film allows more flexibility than metal type, and trademarks or logotypes can easily be included. Once the film is obtained, it must be transferred onto a printing plate before the actual printing.

Printing

Generally, in the case of newspaper or magazine advertisements, advertisers have no control over the printing technique which is used, as this depends solely on the newspaper that is carrying the advertisement. With other print advertise-ments, such as catalogues or posters, advertisers must base their choice on such considerations as cost effectiveness and quality of print. The most common techniques for printing advertisements are letterpress, gravure, and offset.

Letterpress. Letterpress has traditionally been the most popular technique and is based on the principle of relief printing. It involves taking a printing plate on which the letters are raised above the non-printing surface, inking the entire sur-face, and then pressing the plate onto the paper. Three kinds of printing presses rely on this pro-cess: the platen or job press, gravure or intaglio, and offset lithography.

With the *platen* or the job press paper is placed on a flat surface and the printing plate is pressed on top of it (Figure A2). This technique is slow and rather impractical for printing large runs. A more convenient method is the *cylinder press*, in which paper is placed on a cylinder that rolls over the printing surface. The most practical and popular method is the *rotary press*, because of its high print-ing speed. Both the printing surface and the print-ing plate are cylindrical, and the paper is fed between the two rolls, either in the form of individ-ual sheets or in the form of a roll. By using several cylinders, it is easy to print in colour or print on both sides of one page simultaneously. Of course, rotary printing involves the additional task of put-ting the printing plate onto a curved surface, either by using stereotypes or electrotypes or flex-ible plastic printing plates.

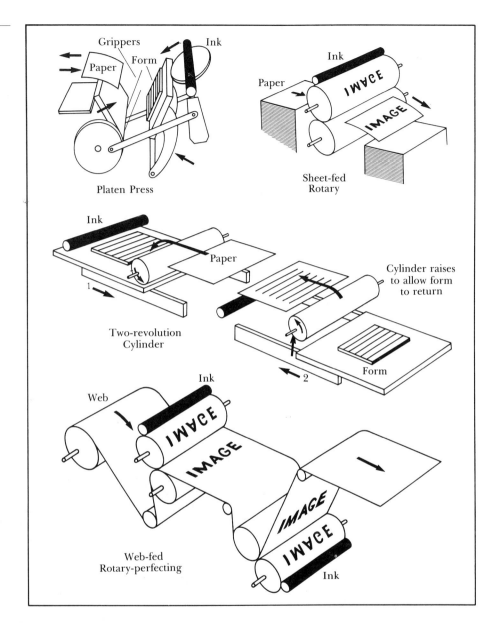

Platen Press

Sheet-fed
Rotary

Two-revolution
Cylinder

Cylinder raises
to allow form
to return

Web-fed
Rotary-perfecting

Gravure or Intaglio. This process involves printing from a depressed surface. It is the reverse of letterpress, since the printing surface is etched into the plate (Figure A3). The ink is deposited on the printing plate by a roller, and then a knife clears the non-printing surface of ink so that ink remains only in the tiny wells etched into the plate. Once this is done, the printing plate is pressed onto a sheet of paper, which absorbs the excess ink.

Offset Lithography. Offset lithography used a smooth surface to print the material (Figure A4). The first phase of offset printing requires the preparation of a special photographic plate made of aluminum or copper. This cylindrical plate is

*The Offset
Lithographic Press*

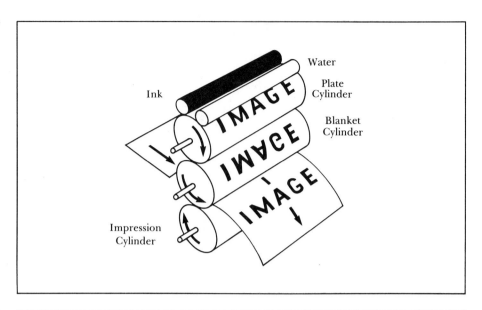

FIGURE A4
A Gravure Press

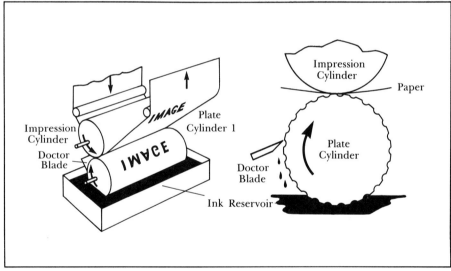

wet, and because of its chemical properties, water remains on the non-printing surface. Next, a greasy ink is applied on the plate. It cannot mix with water, so it adheres only to those parts of the cylinder that are not wet (the printing surface). Next, the printing cylinder is pressed onto a smooth surface or a blanket cylinder. The text is transferred onto the paper by the cylinder, which serves as an intermediary between the actual printing plate and the paper. Offset lithography is relatively inexpensive and easy to carry out.

Photoengraving

Most print advertisements also contain illustrations. Photoengraving is the process of creating special printing plates for reproducing illustrations. There are two main types of photoengraving: line and half-tone.

Line Engraving. Line engravings are generally used for drawings or diagrams that do not contain any shading. First a picture of the drawing is taken in order to obtain a negative. Then light is projected through the negative onto a metallic plate covered with a light-sensitive emulsion. This emulsion hardens on the areas that have been exposed to light. The soft emulsion that coincides with the non-printing surface is then removed. Next, an acid is applied to the plate. The acid eats away at the metal but does not attack the emulsion. Therefore, the surface that is to be printed is raised relative to the non-printing surface. This last phase is etching. Finally, the plate is routed to remove more metal from the non-printing surface and increase the precision and contrast of the drawing.

Half-tone Engraving. The process of reproducing pictures containing different shades of black and white is slightly more complicated than line engraving, although it is similar in principle. The main difference is that the film is exposed through a grid. The light coming from the picture is decomposed into dots that appear on the negative. The size of each dot is proportional to the intensity of the light. A printing plate is created from the negative in much the same way as in line engraving. Although only black and white is used in half-tone, the illusion of different shades of gray can be created by increasing or decreasing the size of the dots. The concentration of black therefore determines an infinity of shades of gray even though only two discrete colours are used.

Colour Photoengraving. The three primary colours—yellow, red, and blue—are mixed with black to obtain a colour photoengraving. Four half-tone plates are produced, one for each of the three primary colours and for black. The plates are obtained by making four distinct negatives, using light filters so that only the desired colour is transferred to each negative. The four half-tones are then reproduced on a sheet of paper. A superimposition of two or more colours can create the illusion of any colour in the spectrum. (See Plate XI).

Duplicating the Advertisement

If an advertisement is to be carried by several newspapers or magazines, an advertising agency must send duplicates of the original printing plates to all the newspaper publishers on its media list. These duplicates can be made by stereotype or electrotype.

Stereotypes. Stereotypes are obtained by pressing the original printing plate onto a mat, which is made of a soft, cardboard-like substance. The mat then takes the shape of the advertisement. It is sent to the newspaper, which can make the stereotype by casting the mats into molten lead. Plastic rather than cardboard can also be used for the mats.

Electrotypes. Electrotypes are more expensive to produce but allow for sharper detail. A mould of the original plate is made with wax or lead. This mould is then plunged into a electrolytic substance, where it is covered with a very thin layer of copper or aluminum. This thin coat is removed from the wax or vinylite, routed, and mounted.

TELECAST PRODUCTION

Choosing the Medium for the Commercial

The two types of media for producing a television commercial are film and videotape. Producers who rely on the former may use 35-mm film or the less expensive, lower quality 16-mm film. If a commercial is intended for extensive national airing, it would be unwise to use anything but the very best quality film. Local advertisers, however, may prefer the cheaper 16-mm film. Taped commercials use one of three standard sizes: 2 inch, 1 inch, and 3/4 inch, although 2-inch tapes are most commonly relied on for good quality pictures.

One of the first decisions a producer must make is whether to use film or videotape. Although film has traditionally enjoyed widespread use, tape is considered by many to be the medium of the future.

In many respects tape is an improvement over film. First and foremost, tape offers the advantage of immediate feedback; editors can see how the commercial will look on TV while it is being taped in the studio. In addition, new computerized techniques have greatly enhanced the speed and effectiveness of editing on tape. All these improvements have reduced the production time from several weeks for a filmed commercial to one or two days. Furthermore, tape is usually less expensive and more durable—a taped commercial can run indefinitely, while film will show signs of wear after about 25 runs. Finally, tape can lend a commercial a more live mood. However, there are drawbacks: tape is considered a cheap medium, whereas film projects a higher quality image. Film also makes for more flexibility than tape and is therefore advised for shooting in remote places. This difference is disappearing rapidly, however, with the advent of less cumbersome portable videotape recorders. Thus there is no clear-cut advantage to using one medium rather than the other. The producer must evaluate each situation individually and decide which means is more appropriate for the mood, circumstances, and technical constraints of the commercial.

After the Commercial is Shot

Once a commercial has been shot, the producer has several yards of film or tape containing numerous versions of each scene. This material, called the *dailies* or *rushes*, is sent to the editor, who selects the best scenes and assembles them into a rough version of the commercial. This work print or rough cut is then submitted to the client for tentative approval. Next, the editor prepares the sound track on separate reel and installs the opticals, which are the special effects intended to provide a smooth transition from one scene to the next. The most commonly used opticals are:

- the *cut*: this is the simplest technique, since one scene simply replaces the next;
- the *matte*: one scene is placed over another so that two or more scenes occupy the screen;
- the *wipe*: the next scene just slides over the previous one, from any direction, or according to some geometric pattern;
- the *dissolve*: as one scene fades out, the next picture gradually appears, so that the two scenes briefly overlap;
- the *zoom*: the camera suddenly focuses on one element of a scene or moves from a closeup to a long shot.

Next, the sound track and the film are synchronized on the same reel, yielding the composite, or optical print. Once this composite print has been approved by the client, it becomes an answer print and is ready for the final stages of production, when the editor puts in the finishing touches, correcting the colour and perfecting the synchronization. From the final print, duplicates (dupes or release prints) are made, and sent to the various stations to be aired.

GLOSSARY

(English/French)

Account *(compte-client).* A term designating a current client of an advertising agency.

Account Executive *(chargé de compte).* A member of the advertising agency's account service group.

Account Service Group *(service de comptes clients).* Group of specialists provided by a full-service advertising agency to ensure a liaison between the client and the agency and to supervise the planning and execution of the client's advertising campaign.

Advertiser *(publicitaire).* A firm or organization that uses advertising with or without the use of an advertising agency.

Advertising *(publicité).* A marketing communication process that directs messages to prospects through the mass media as a means of meeting marketing objectives.

Advertising Agency *(agence de publicité).* An organization providing services to advertisers.

Advertising Appropriation *(allocation publicitaire).* The total sum of money to be spent on advertising within a planning period.

Advertising Budget *(budget de publicité).* A detailed plan specifying how the total amount of money allocated to advertising is to be spent within a planning period.

Advertising Campaign *(campagne de publicité).* A co-ordinated advertising effort conducted over a specified period of time, using messages placed in selected media in order to reach specific objectives.

Advertising Information *(information publicitaire).* The bulk of information that potential buyers receive through the usual advertising media.

Advertising Plan *(plan de publicité).* A plan that describes in some detail the entire advertising program to be followed over a specified period of time.

Advertising Standards Council *(Conseil des normes de la publicité).* A national association of public and business organizations responsible for providing voluntary guidelines to the Canadian advertising industry.

Advertising Strategy *(stratégie de publicité).* An advertising program for the target market segment(s) designed to achieve the campaign's communication objectives within a specified budget and time period.

Advocacy Advertising *(publicité en faveur d'une cause).* Advertising undertaken by an organization to advance a course of action on a controversial public issue.

Affective Attitude Components *(composantes affectives de l'attitude).* Components of the attitude structure that include the feelings and affective reactions provoked by a message.

Affiliate *(membre).* A television or radio station that has a contractual agreement with one network and that must carry specific programs, including commercials.

Agate Line *(ligne d'agate).* A unit of space measurement for newspapers that is one column wide and 1.8 mm (¼ in.) deep.

Agency Charges *(frais d'agence).* Additional costs, chargeable to the client, incurred by the agency in developing the advertising campaign.

Agency Commission *(commission d'agence).* Compensation (usually 15 percent) paid to an advertising agency by the advertising medium for time and space bought by an agency on a client's behalf.

Agency-of-Record *(agence de coordination).* A client that deals with several advertising agencies may select one agency (of record) to assume the co-ordination of media use by the various agencies involved and to qualify for media discounts.

Aided Recall *(rappel assisté).* Percentage of individuals indicating that they know of a brand when presented with that brand name.

A-la-Carte Agency *(agence à-la-carte).* A full service advertising agency that allows clients to choose unbundled services tailored to their needs.

Argumentative Advertisement *(annonce argumentative).* An advertisement that gives potential buyers specific and explicit reasons to buy a product or a particular brand.

Artist *(artiste).* Individual in an agency responsible for developing the visual or audio component of the advertising creative strategy.

Attitude *(attitude).* A hypothetical construct that intervenes between buyers' perception formation process and actual behaviour as they are exposed to stimuli and communications from the marketing environment.

Attitude Structure *(structure des attitudes)*. A system of cognitions, positive or negative evaluations, emotional feelings, and pro or con action tendencies regarding social objects.

Audience *(auditoire)*. An individual or group of individuals for whom a communicator's message is intended.

Audience Duplication *(duplication d'auditoire)*. The number of people or households reached by two media vehicles.

Audience Fragmentation *(fragmentation de l'auditoire)*. A situation of reduced reach and higher costs due to the increasing number of vehicles at any given time.

Audio *(audio)*. Sound portion of a broadcast commercial.

Audit Bureau of Circulation (ABC). An association of advertisers, agencies, and publishers that conducts audits of reported paid circulation of various periodicals.

Availability *(disponibilité)*. Unsold commercial time that is available for purchase by an advertiser.

Background Music *(musique de fond)*. Live or recorded music used in a commercial in order to convey a certain mood or atmosphere.

Backlight *(affiche illuminée de l'arrière)*. An outdoor advertisement printed on reinforced translucent plastic and illuminated from the rear.

Bait (and Switch) Advertising *(publicité appât et substitution)*. Low price offer to induce buyers to come to a store where it is difficult or impossible to buy the product at the advertised price.

Behavioural Segmentation *(segmentation selon les réactions comportementales)*. Segmentation of markets by finding "natural" groupings of consumers with the same consumer needs and problems and similar lifestyles.

Benefit Segmentation *(segmentation selon les bénéfices que les consommateurs retirent des produits)*. Segmentation of markets according to the benefits that users seek from products.

Billing *(facturation)*. A term used by an advertising agency to refer to the total amount an advertiser spends through the agency.

Bleed Advertisement *(annonce à franc bord)*. An advertisement printed to the very edge of a page, thus having no margin.

Blocking Chart *(tableau des périodes)*. A document summarizing the media schedule.

Blow-Up *(agrandissement)*. Enlarged reproduction of print artwork.

Body Copy *(texte descriptif d'une annonce)*. The main copy blocks of an advertisement.

Borrowed Interest *(attention par utilisation d'un intermédiaire)*. A technique that uses someone (e.g., a baby) or something (e.g., a cat or parrot) to attract attention to the advertised product.

Boutique Agency *(agence de création)*. See CREATIVE BOUTIQUE.

Brand *(marque)*. The name, term, symbol, design, or any combination of these elements, that distinguish a firm's products from competing products.

Brand Awareness *(connaissance de la marque)*. Refers to the level of brand knowledge that customers have acquired.

Brand Development Index *(indice de développement du marché)*. An index of per capita sales of a brand in a given market compared to the national figure.

Brand Image *(image de marque)*. The set of attributes that consumers perceive as belonging to a brand.

Brand Image Value *(valeur de l'image de marque)*. A comparison of the brand image against the traits that buyers in the market segment would consider positive or negative for a brand in that product category.

Brand Loyalty *(loyauté à la marque)*. Loyalty of a customer to a particular brand.

Brand Manager *(chef de marque)*. In many large packaged goods companies, this is the individual responsible for planning, executing, and controlling the advertising campaign for one (or a few) brand(s) and for co-ordinating the advertising between the agency and the company.

Brand Name *(nom commercial)*. Name of a product offering or service. It refers to the verbal element of a brand.

Brand Preference *(préférence de marque)*. The degree to which prospects consider a brand acceptable or unacceptable, especially in relation to competitive brands.

Broadsheet *(journal grand format)*. A full-size newspaper approximately 380 mm wide and 560 mm deep (15 in. by 22 in.).

Broadside or Bedsheet *(in-plano)*. A large sheet with full colour illustrations that are folded for direct-mail distribution and used to create high impact.

Brochure *(dépliant publicitaire)*. A high quality booklet used in direct mail advertising.

Bureau of Broadcast Measurement (BBM). A non-profit organization of advertisers, agencies, and broadcasters that provides estimates of radio and television audiences.

Business-to-Business Advertising *(publicité aux gens*

d'affaires). Advertising directed toward a professional audience in any field.

Buy *(achat).* The purchase of time or space.

Buyer *(acheteur).* The individual(s) in the advertising agency responsible for purchasing radio time, and/or television time, and/or space in print media.

Buying Service *(service d'achats média).* See MEDIA BUYING SERVICE.

Campaign Reach *(couverture de la campagne).* See REACH.

Canadian Advertising Rates and Data (CARD). A monthly catalogue of advertising media rates and other related information.

Canadian Advertising Research Foundation (CARF). A non-profit organization supported by advertisers, advertising agencies, and media to improve the effectiveness of advertising through the use of proper research methods.

Canadian Association of Broadcasters (CAB). A national organization of broadcasters that manages a credit rating system of advertising agencies.

Canadian Broadcasting Corporation (CBC) *(Société Radio Canada).* A Crown corporation established in 1936 to provide national broadcasting service. The CBC's Commercial Acceptance Committee must approve all commercials to be aired on its stations.

Canadian Circulation Audit Board (CCAB). An association of advertisers, agencies, and publishers that conducts audits of reported circulations of business publications and some controlled- circulation consumer magazines.

Canadian Community Newspapers Association (CCNA). A national organization of Canadian community newspapers that manages a credit rating system of advertising agencies.

Canadian Daily Newspaper Publishers Association (CDNPA). A national organization founded in 1925 whose membership consists of most major daily newspaper publishers. The association manages a credit rating system of advertising agencies.

Canadian Newspaper Unit *(module standard de publicité).* A unit of space measurement for newspapers that is one standard column wide and 30 MALs deep.

Canadian Radio-Television and Telecommunications Commission (CRTC) *(Conseil de la Radiodiffusion et des Télécommunications Canadiennes).* Commission established by the Broadcasting Act of 1968 to regulate and supervise all aspects of the Canadian broadcasting system.

Caption *(légende).* Text accompanying an illustration.

Car Card Advertising *(publicité dans les voitures de transport en commun).* An advertisement placed inside transit vehicles.

Carry-Over Effect of Advertising *(effet différé de l'action publicitaire).* Advertising expenses for one year may affect subsequent periods but may yield diminishing results as time elapses.

Cents-Off Deal *(offre de réduction promotionnelle).* A sales promotion technique that consists of offering a temporary price reduction to entice consumers to try or repurchase a brand.

Charges *(frais d'agence).* Additional costs the agency incurs in developing the campaign and charged to the client.

Circular *(prospectus).* An advertisement printed on one page and used in direct-mail advertising.

Circulation *(circulation).* The number of copies of a publication that are sold or distributed. Also used for outdoor advertising to refer to the number of people exposed to a poster during a given time period.

Classified Advertising *(annonce classée).* A form of media advertising in which the message may be very short and falls into specific categories grouped together without editorial matter around it.

Closing Date *(date de clôture ou date limite).* The date when advertising material must arrive at a publication to appear in the next issue.

Clucas Method *(méthode Clucas).* A theatre test conducted by J.E. Clucas and Associates.

Clutter *(méli-mélo).* A situation in which an advertisement must compete for attention with many other messages, thus reducing its effectiveness.

Cognitive Attitude Components *(composantes cognitives des attitudes).* Components for the attitude structure that include the knowledge an individual has acquired as well as the evaluation of the importance of information.

Cognitive Dissonance *(dissonance cognitive).* The psychological tension that develops when an individual is exposed to information that contradicts some information already assimilated or that constitutes the personal beliefs of the individual.

Colour Separation *(séparation des couleurs).* Separation of colour copy into primary colours using colour filters.

Commercial *(message publicitaire).* An advertising message in the broadcast media.

Commission *(commission).* See AGENCY COMMISSION.

Communication Channels *(canaux de communication).* The media used to convey a message to an audience.

Communication Task (*tâche de communication*). The intended effect(s) of the advertising campaign on the target audience.

Communicator (*émetteur*). An individual or organization initiating the communication.

Community Antenna Television (CATV). A system for distributing any television signal directly to homes by means of a cable.

Community Newspapers (*hebdos régionaux ou locaux*). Newspapers with a publication frequency of once to three times a week.

Comparative Advertising (*publicité comparative*). A technique for showing how an advertised brand is superior to competitive brands.

Composition (*composition*). Setting of type for printing.

CNU (*MSP*). See CANADIAN NEWSPAPER UNIT.

Conative Attitude Components (*composantes conatives des attitudes*). The components of the attitude structure that refer to an individual's tendency to act toward the attitude object.

Concentrated Marketing (*marketing concentré*). The selection of a small segment of the total market in order to concentrate all a firm's marketing resources to satisfying this single segment.

Conceptual Segmentation Criterion (*critère conceptuel de segmentation*). The defining of various consumer groups on the basis of consumers' needs and desires.

Consumer Advertising (*publicité grand public*). Advertising directed toward the ultimate consumer of products or services.

Consumer Protection Act (Quebec) (*Loi sur la protection du consommateur*). A legislative act passed in April 1980. The Committee for the Application of Articles 248 and 249 decides whether a commercial is directed toward children under 13 years, which is unlawful under this Act.

Contests (*concours*). A sales promotion technique similar to sweepstakes, except that the consumer must demonstrate some skills in answering a question or performing a task.

Continuity of Campaign (*continuité de la campagne*). The overall pattern of advertising exposures over the time horizon of the campaign.

Controlled Circulation Magazines (*revues à circulation contrôlée*). Magazines that are distributed without charge to a specific group of readers.

Co-operative Advertising (*publicité à frais partagés*). Joint advertising between a manufacturer and a retailer whereby the manufacturer covers part of the costs of advertising a brand in the retailer's advertising.

Co-operative Direct Mail (*publipostage co-opératif*). Method for distributing coupons in non-addressed mail.

Copy (*texte de l'annonce*). Original material for a print advertisement, such as text, illustration, or photographs that are put into final form for printing. Also refers to the advertisement's body copy.

Copy Testing (*tests de messages publicitaires*). Verifying whether an advertisement or a commercial has had the intended effect on consumers. May be done before (pretest) or after (posttest) the start of the campaign.

Copywriter (*concepteur-rédacteur*). The individual responsible for developing the verbal or written communication of the advertising creative strategy.

Corporate Advertising (*publicité institutionnelle*). Advertising aimed at enhancing a company's image among selected target groups or the overall population.

Corrective Advertising (*publicité correctrice*). Advertising run (voluntarily or as a result of a court order) to correct a misleading or false advertisement.

Cost per Rating Point (*coût unitaire de couverture brute*). The cost of a schedule divided by the GRPs delivered by that schedule.

Cost per Thousand (*coût par mille*). The cost of reaching one thousand units of the audience of one particular vehicle, calculated as the unit cost of a message in the vehicle divided by its audience size (in thousands).

Coupons (*bons de réduction*). A sales promotion technique consisting of granting price reductions in the form of certificates to encourage consumers to buy or try a certain product.

Coverage (*couverture*). Percent of the members of a target audience who are reached by one print vehicle.

CPM (*CPM*). See COST PER THOUSAND.

CPRP (*CUCB*). See COST PER RATING POINT.

Creative Boutique (*agence de création, studio créateur*). Agency specializing only in creative work for advertisements or commercials.

Creative Plan (*programme créatif*). A plan to address the problem of translating the communication tasks specified in the advertising campaign's objectives into effective advertisements.

Creative Services (*création publicitaire*). Copy, art, and production services offered by an advertising agency.

Cumulative Audience (*auditoire accumulé*). The number of different units reached by successive vehicles.

Dadson Compare Test (*test Dadson de messages publicitaires*). A mall test using a test group and a control group.

Day-After-Recall (*mesure de la mémorisation différée*). A form of copy testing a commercial the day after it was aired.

Dayparts *(intervalles de temps).* Segments of a broadcast day specified by a station as a basis for setting rates.

Demand Elasticity *(élasticité de la demande).* A measure of the percentage change in demand brought about by a 1 percent change in a variable.

Depth Interview *(entrevue en profondeur).* A technique using trained interviewers to probe respondents' reactions to a product, a brand, or message.

Diary Method *(méthode utilisant un journal).* A technique of asking respondents to accurately record in a diary their purchasing of products or the broadcast programs they viewed during a specified period of time.

Direct Mail Advertising *(publicité directe).* Advertising sent by mail to a pre-selected audience.

Direct Personal Information *(information directe).* Buyers receive this information through physical contact with the product.

Direct Response Advertising *(publicité à réponse directe).* Any form of advertising message sent directly to a pre-selected audience through a variety of media and providing the means for a response to the advertiser.

Disaggregative Process *(processus de desagrégation).* The recognition of the existence of an overall market, various demand schedules, or demand functions within this market as various groups of consumers experience different needs and wants.

Distinctive Brand Attributes *(attributs distinctifs de la marque).* The attributes through which a consumer distinguishes among different brands.

Double-Page Spread *(double page).* An advertising space covering two pages facing each other.

Duplication *(duplication).* The number of individuals or homes exposed to two or more vehicles.

Durable (or Hard) Goods *(biens durables).* High-priced products, such as automobiles and appliances, that require a long search process.

Editorial Matter *(texte de fond).* Material other than advertising that is contributed to a publication or a broadcast station.

Electroencephalograph (EEG). An instrument used to measure brain waves.

Evoked Set *(ensemble évoqué).* All the brands that a potential buyer considers as possible purchase alternatives to satisfy the same general need or desire.

Exposure *(exposition).* A contact between one individual (or family) and one vehicle.

Extensive Problem Solving *(résolution longue du problème).* Displayed when a consumer does not know either the product category or the brand.

Fact Book *(classeur regroupant des informations de base sur une marque ou un produit).* Compilation of relevant information concerning a product or brand for advertising purposes.

Fear Appeal Advertising *(publicité véhiculant une peur).* Advertising in which the rationale is to show consumers the negative consequences that may result from non-usage of a product or brand.

Feedback *(retour d'information).* The effect of advertising results on the firm.

Fees *(honoraires).* A type of compensation negotiated between the advertising agency and the advertiser to cover all the services rendered by the agency.

Fixed Position *(position fixe).* In broadcast media, this term refers to contracting the same period for the commercial to be aired.

Flat Rate *(taux uniforme).* Unit rate charged irrespective of volume or frequency of purchase.

Flexform *(annonce de format flexible ou libre).* Any advertising shape that does not conform to the normal rectangular format of print media.

Flight *(vague publicitaire).* The concentrated use of one medium followed by a period of inactivity.

Flighting *(publicité par vague).* A scheduling method of alternating periods of heavy advertising with periods of inactivity.

Focus Group *(groupe d'entretien en profondeur).* A small group of consumers assembled to discuss a given advertising topic by a trained moderator.

Freeform *(annonce de format libre).* See FLEXFORM.

Free-Standing Inserts *(encarts publicitaires).* Four-colour tabloid size inserts that are distributed with a given newspaper issue.

Frequency *(fréquence).* The number of times one member of a target audience is reached by a media vehicle or a media schedule.

Full-Service Agency *(agence à services complets).* An agency that provides clients with a complete range of advertising services.

Gatefold *(encart à volets).* Pages that fold out from a two-page spread advertisement.

General Advertising *(publicité nationale).* Advertising placed by a manufacturer or a wholesaler.

Gross Impressions *(impressions brutes).* The sum of all the audiences of the selected media vehicles, including duplications.

Gross Rating Points *(indice de couverture brute).* The number of messages delivered to the target audience, irrespective of the number of messages received by each individual, expressed as a percentage of the target audience.

GRP *(ICB).* See GROSS RATING POINTS.

Guaranteed Revenue System *(Système de revenu guaranti).* A compensation scheme where the client guarantees a minimum profit target for the agency.

Headline *(gros titre).* The most conspicuous verbal element of a print advertisement.

Hi-Fi Colour *(couleur hi-fi).* The process of pre-printing rolls of high quality colour advertisements that appear in a continuous pattern, bleeding off the top and bottom of the page.

Horizontal Publication *(publication horizontale).* An industrial publication that reaches similar readers across all industries.

Ideal Brand *(marque idéale).* The brand that, if technically and economically feasible, would have all the features and characteristics desired by consumers.

Image Clarity *(clarté de l'image).* The degree to which a brand image is perceived clearly by consumers.

Image Content *(contenu de l'image de marque).* The personality traits characterizing the brand image.

Image Proximity *(proximité de l'image).* How present a brand is in the buyer's mind.

Impact of the Campaign *(impact de la campagne).* All selected physical characteristics (media options) of messages that may increase their effectiveness given a basic creative execution.

Impression *(impression).* A count of every time a message is received by a member of the audience of the media schedule.

Impulse Purchase *(achat par impulsion).* An unplanned consumer purchase.

In-ad Coupon *(coupons insérés dans l'annonce).* Method for distributing coupons when coupons are part of a newspaper advertisement for the brand.

In/On Pack Coupons *(coupons à l'intérieur/sur le paquet).* Method for distributing coupons when coupons are inserted in the package itself or on the package.

In-Store Coupons *(coupons distribués dans le magasin).* Coupons that are distributed in the store itself.

Independent Station *(station indépendante).* A broadcast station not affiliated with any network.

Industrial Advertising *(publicité de produits industriels).* Advertising directed toward a professional audience responsible for evaluating the products an industrial company uses.

In-House Agency *(agence-maison).* Advertising agency owned and operated by an advertiser.

Insert *(encart).* An advertisement printed in advance by an advertiser and bound in or inserted into a newspaper.

Institute of Canadian Advertisers (ICA). A national organization of advertisers.

Institutional Advertising *(publicité institutionnelle).* Advertising aimed at changing the public image of an organization.

Instrumental Relation Hypothesis *(hypothèse de la relation instrumentale).* The hypothesis that an attitude toward any object or situation is related to the end to which the object serves, i.e., to its consequences.

Intended Effect *(effect visé).* The precise objective of a message.

Intensity of Campaign *(intensité de la campagne).* Level of average effort (measured in monthly GRPs) over the time horizon of an advertising campaign.

Interpersonal Information *(information interpersonnelle).* Information following through interpersonal channels as people interact with social groups.

Irregular Purchase Cycle Markets *(marchés à cycle d'achat irrégulier).* Markets characterized by products that are purchased irregularly.

Isopreference Curve *(courbe d'isopréférence).* According to the vector model, all the brand points that are on the same perpendicular to a vector and thus equally liked by the consumer represented by this vector.

Jingle *("jingle" ou refrain publicitaire).* A musical commercial with a short lyric stressing the product.

Layout *(maquette).* A rough draft of a print advertisement.

Lewin's Field Theory *(théorie du champ psychologique de Lewin).* An individual's behaviour is the result of a number of motives and forces in this individual's lifespace.

Limited Problem Solving *(résolution courte du problème).* Displayed when a consumer knows a product category well but not a particular brand.

Line Rate *(taux d'une ligne).* The cost of using one agate line in a publication.

Line *(Ligne).* See AGATE LINE.

Local Advertising *(publicité de détail).* Advertising placed by a retailer at a lower rate than for a national advertiser.

Logotype *(logotype).* A non-verbal symbol used to identify a brand.

Long or Unpredictable Purchase Cycle Markets *(marchés à cycle d'achat long ou imprédictible).* Markets characterized by products for which purchase decisions cannot be predicted.

Loss Leader (*article sacrifié*). Items sold at cost and used to attract attention to a store and/or its advertisements.

Magazine Coupons (*Coupons distribués au moyen des magazines*). Coupons that are distributed through consumer magazines.

MAL (*LAM*). See MODULAR AGATE LINE.

Mall Test (*test dans un lieu public*). A form of copy testing conducted with respondents intercepted in shopping malls and plazas.

Market Aggregation (*aggrégation des marchés*). A strategy that consists of a firm selling its product to as many customers as possible with a single marketing program.

Market Concentration (*concentration du marché*). The share of market enjoyed collectively by the four leading firms in an industry.

Market Development (*développement du marché*). A strategy of adapting existing products to other consumers or other markets.

Market Penetration (*pénétration du marché*). A strategy aimed at increasing the frequency of use of a brand (or product) and its rate of use by a potential market.

Market Segment (*segment de marché*). An identifiable subgroup of purchasers or consumers within a market who share a common characteristic or a special need.

Market Segmentation (*segmentation du marché*). A strategy that accounts for changes in intensity of demand within the same market and thus adjusts the products and their marketing programs accordingly.

Market Share (*part de marché*). One firm's proportion of an industry's total actual volume.

Marketing Macroenvironment (*environnement macro du marketing*). The marketing environment whereby the forces that influence a market are absolutely uncontrollable by the marketing manager (e.g., legal environment).

Marketing Microenvironment (*environnement micro du marketing*). The marketing environment characterized by forces over which marketers have no direct control but which they may attempt to manipulate by means of promotional actions.

Marketing Mix (*marketing mix, ou mix marketing*). The combination of elements of the marketing operation that are within a firm's control. These variables are classified into four groups: product, place, promotion and price.

Marketing Plan (*plan marketing*). A plan that comprises all the elements of the marketing program and is designed to respond to the expectation of the target market(s) over a specified period of time.

Marketing Planning (*planification marketing*). A process for working out a detailed account (most frequently in writing) of a company's self-image, objectives, the market program designed to achieve the objectives, and the methods used to measure the success of the planning effort.

Marketing Program (*programme marketing*). An action program formulated by a firm to respond as much as possible to the needs of a selected target market.

Marketing Strategy (*stratégie marketing*). The general term used to describe the overall program for selecting a particular market segment and then satisfying the customers in that segment through the careful use of the elements of the marketing mix.

Matrices (or Mats) (*flans*). Moulds made of papier mâché used by newspapers to make stereotypes of clients' advertisements.

Media Buying Service (*service d'achat de médias ou service d'achat média*). An agency that specializes in purchasing media time or space for advertisers.

Media Plan (*plan-média*). A planning document that outlines and explains the decisions concerning media objectives, selection, schedule, budget, and research.

Media Schedule (*calendrier d'insertions*). A document listing all the selected media vehicles and describing when and for how long a message is run.

Media Services (*service de médias*). Service provided by a full-service advertising agency. It comprises the development of a media plan and a media strategy, and the purchase of space and time for advertisers.

Media Strategy (*stratégie-média*). A set of decisions concerning the selection of media and the timing of the media replacements.

Media Vehicle (*support publicitaire*). A single advertising medium, like a specific newspaper, magazine, radio or television program, or type of outdoor.

Message (*message*). The set of words, sounds, and images used by a communicator to convey an idea to an audience.

Milline Rate (*coût par mille lignes*). The cost of one thousand lines of newspaper space for each thousand of circulation.

Modular Agate Line (*ligne agate modulaire*). A unit of space measurement for newspapers that is 1.8 mm deep and one standard column wide (52 mm for a broadsheet and 49 mm for a tabloid).

Motivation (*motivation*). The underlying force of any action. This force reduces the state of psychological tension generally aroused by an unsatisfied need or desire, whether physiological or psychological.

Multiplexity (*multiplexité*).   A characteristic of the components of attitude based on the number of elements involved.

Multi-Segment Marketing (*marketing à segments multiples*).   The process of approaching several or all of the defined market segments.

National Advertising (*publicité nationale*).   See GENERAL ADVERTISING.

Negative Motivations (*motivations négatives*).   Motivations that prevent the performance of certain acts through fear, aversion, or inhibition.

Negative Publicity (*publicité négative*).   Editorial matter that reports problems encountered by a product, a service, or a company.

Net Unduplicated Audience (*auditoire sans duplication*).   The number of different individuals reached by several vehicles during a given time period.

Net Unduplicated Reach (*couverture nette sans duplication*).   The number of different individuals or families reached by single issues of several publications.

Network (*réseau*).   A group of broadcast stations that carry the same signal at the same time periods.

Newspaper Marketing Bureau NMB (*bureau de commercialisation des quotidiens*).   An industry organization that promotes newspapers as viable national advertising vehicles.

Nielsen of Canada, A.C.   A privately owned company providing television audience estimates and program ratings. The Nielsen Television Index (NTI) reports on network audiences. The Nielsen Broadcast Index (NBI) reports on local audiences.

Non-Profit Advertising (*publicité sans but lucratif*).   Advertising that seeks to encourage behaviour that benefits society.

Noted (*côte notée*).   The percentage of individuals who have noticed a specific advertisement in a specific publication as measured by Starch ratings.

O & O Station (*station appartenant à un réseau*).   A television or radio station owned and operated by a network.

Objective-and-Task Method (*méthode de détermination des objectifs et des tâches*).   A method of determining an advertising appropriation on the basis of the advertising objectives.

Omnibus Study (*enquête de type omnibus*).   A co-operative survey run by a professional research firm in which several advertisers share the costs of the research.

Out-of-Home Media (*média hors domicile*).   Mainly advertising media that can be viewed only outside the home.

Outdoor Advertising Association of Canada (OAAC).   A national association of outdoor advertising companies that manages a credit rating system of advertising agencies.

Package Inserts (*encarts*).   A sales promotion technique that consists of including in the package a promotional piece about the product, the product line, or a related product manufactured or distributed by a firm.

Packaged Goods (*produits emballés*).   A convenience non-durable item characterized by frequent purchases and extensive distribution.

Pass-Along Circulation (*lecteurs secondaires*).   The number of persons who read a newspaper or a magazine that was not purchased by a member of the household.

Pay-TV (*télévision à péage*).   Television programs transmitted through cable and paid for by subscribers.

People Meter (*audimètre*).   A system of electronic audience measurement for television using a recording device and a panel of families who have ageed to co-operate.

Percentage of Sales Method (*méthode basée sur un percentage des ventes*).   A method of determining the advertising appropriation as a certain percentage of sales.

Perception (*perception*).   A mental configuration that an individual has of a stimulus.

Periodical (*périodique*).   A newspaper, magazine, or other publication that appears at regular intervals.

Periodical Press Association (PPA).   A national organization of publishers of periodicals that manages a credit rating system of advertising agencies.

Personal Selling (*vente personnelle*).   A personal rather than a mass communication (like advertising) directed to a prospect as a means of meeting marketing objectives.

Pica (*pica*).   A unit of measure equal to 4.2 mm ($^1/_6$ in.) and 12 points.

Place (*canaux de distribution*).   One of the four elements of the marketing mix. It refers to the distribution channels through which products flow from producers to consumers.

Plans Board (*réunion spéciale des chefs de service d'une agence, pour la mise au point d'une campagne*).   A board usually composed of the chief executives of a full-service agency, whose responsibility is to approve the advertising strategy developed by the agency before it is submitted to the client.

Pleasant Appeal Advertising (*publicité utilisant un effet agréable*).   Advertising that associates a product or brand with pleasant events, objects, or feelings so that buyers might make the association in the future.

Point *(point).* A unit of measure of the height of type equal to 0.35 mm ($^1/_{72}$ in.).

Point of Purchase Advertising *(publicité au point de vente).* Signs and displays at the point of final sale.

Position *(position).* The place where an advertisement appears or the spot where a commercial is inserted.

Positive Motivations *(motivations positives).* Needs or desires that cause an individual to favour certain acts.

Positive Valence/Negative Valence *(valence positive ou négative).* In terms of Lewin's theory, the forces inducing buyers to purchase or preventing them from making a purchase can be represented by vectors that characterize an individual's motivations.

Poster *(affiche).* An outdoor advertisement printed on paper and placed on a standardized panel.

Pre-emptible Rate *(taux avec possibilité de préemption).* A lower rate given to an advertiser who agrees to give priority to any advertiser paying a higher rate.

Preferred Position *(position préférée).* A specific position requested by an advertiser, who pays a premium for it.

Premium *(prime).* A sales promotion technique that consists of offering consumers, free of charge or sold at or below cost, a product different from the one they purchased.

Price *(prix).* One of the four elements of the marketing mix. It refers to all those aspects of the marketing program relating to the terms of the transaction.

Price Deal *(offre à prix spéciaux).* An offer to sell a product at a lower price (for example, "Buy ten, get one free").

Primary Audience *(auditoire primaire).* The main group(s) targeted by an advertising campaign or primary readers, listeners, or viewers.

Primary Circulation *(lecteurs primaires).* Household members who read a publication through subscription or purchase.

Primary Readership *(lecteurs primaires).* See PRIMARY CIRCULATION.

Prime Time *(heures de pointe).* A period of several consecutive hours in the evening for television or during the morning or afternoon rush hours for radio (also called drive time) when the audience size is the greatest.

Print Measurement Bureau (PMB). A non-profit organization of advertisers, agencies, and magazine publishers that provides readership data on consumer magazines.

Product *(produit).* One of the four elements of the marketing mix. It represents a material offering (tangible) or a service (intangible).

Product Class *(classe de produits).* A group of products or services that share common attributes and compete directly for the same market.

Product Development *(développement du produit).* A strategy of developing a product with new characteristics that is aimed at a present target market.

Product Differentiation *(différentiation des produits).* The degree to which a product has succeeded in establishing an image as unique, especially when this uniqueness is perceived as beneficial.

Product Life-Cycle *(cycle de vie du produit).* The history of a product from its introduction to its demise in terms of sales and profits. It is customarily divided into four stages: introduction, growth, maturity, and decline.

Product Positioning *(positionnement du produit).* Determination of the position of a product relative to the level of its attributes and its life-cycle.

Product Segmentation Strategy *(stratégie de segmentation des produits).* Strategy consisting of designing and marketing products based on the characteristics of the products as perceived by consumers in various market segments.

Product Variety *(variété de la gamme des produits).* A strategy of marketing a variety of products to an entire market, rather than catering to specific market segments.

Production *(production).* Translation of an advertising idea into a print advertisement or a broadcast commercial.

Professional Advertising *(publicité aux professionnels).* A form of business-to-business advertising directed to professionals such as doctors, lawyers, or teachers.

Profile *(profil).* A description of the characteristics of the users of a product or the audience of a medium.

Profile-Matching Strategy *(stratégie d'assortiment des profils).* A media strategy by which the profile of potential users of a product are matched with the audiences of the various print and broadcast media.

Projective Technique *(technique projective).* A research technique whereby respondents are asked to interpret and find meaning in an ambiguous stimulus in order to reveal hidden feelings and opinions.

Promotion *(promotion).* One of the four elements of the marketing mix. It refers to activities initiated by the seller, through communication tools and vehicles, in order to sell a product, service, or idea.

Promotional Mix *(mix promotionnel).* The combination of all the communication means used to affect sales.

Propaganda *(propagande).* A type of mass communication, whose source is not identified and which generally has an exclusively political rather than an economic purpose.

Psychogalvanometer (*psychogalvanomètre*). An instrument that measures the conductivity of the skin, which is affected by perspiration, which in turn is affected by an individual's emotional reactions.

Psychographics (*psychographie*). The characterization of an individual according to various lifestyle dimensions.

Public Relations (*relations publiques*). Communications designed to enhance the image of an individual or an organization.

Publicity (*publicité à titre gracieux*). Promotional activities originated by an advertiser that aim at obtaining free media space or time. Such activities include articles, editorials, and press releases, which are reproduced free of charge by the media.

Pull (*aspiration*). The degree of demand for a product or service from purchasers.

Pull Strategy (*stratégie d'aspiration*). A marketing strategy aimed at building interest in the market for a brand so that consumers recognize it or request it from retailers, thus creating a demand through the distribution channels.

Push Strategy (*stratégie de pression*). A marketing strategy aimed at convincing wholesalers and retailers to purchase a product.

Radio Bureau of Canada (RBC). A non-profit industry organization that promotes the use of radio as an advertising medium.

Rate Card (*carte de tarifs*). A document published by a particular medium that lists prices and other information related to placing messages in a medium.

Rating (*côte*). The percent of TV or (radio) households that are tuned, on the average, to one time period in a particular program.

Reach (*couverture*). The percentage of a target audience reached once by a media vehicle or a media schedule.

Readership (*lecteurs*). The audience of a publication; equal to circulation multiplied by readers per copy.

Read Most (*lu en majeure partie*). The percentage of people who state they have read more than 50 percent of the copy in an advertisement, as measured by Starch.

Rebate (*remboursement*). The additional amount paid by a medium to an advertiser who qualified for a lower rate because of heavier use of the medium than originally contracted.

Recognized Agency (*agence agréée*). An advertising agency entitled to the standard commission based on a credit check by the various media.

Reference Group (*groupe de référence*). A social group to which an individual may belong or aspire to belong.

Refund Offers (*offre de remboursement*). A sales promotion technique by which cash refunds are offered to consumers who buy a given number of items of the same brand.

Regional Edition (*édition régionale*). An edition of a national magazine distributed with some changes in advertising in a specific geographic area.

Reminder Advertising (*publicité de rappel*). An attempt to influence a consumer's memory by reminding of the existence of the product and of the brand.

Retail Advertising (*publicité/détaillants*). See LOCAL ADVERTISING.

Retailer or Seller's Information (*information fournie par le détaillant ou le vendeur*). Product or brand information from retailers or from people in the distribution channels.

ROB (*EOCR*). See RUN-OF-BOOK.

ROP (*EOCI*). See RUN-OF-PRESS.

ROS (*MPCS*). See RUN-OF-SCHEDULE.

Routinized Response Behaviour (*comportement routinier*). Displayed when a consumer is very familiar with a product category and knows the characteristics of competing brands.

Run-of-Book (*emplacement ordinaire, au choix de la revue*). A magazine term indicating that an advertisement will be placed at the discretion of the publisher.

Run-of-Press (*emplacement ordinaire, aux choix du journal*). A newspaper term indicating that an advertisement is to be printed on standard newsprint paper along with editorial matter, at the discretion of the publisher.

Run-of-Schedule (*messages placés au choix de la station*). A broadcast term indicating that the commercial is to be scheduled at the discretion of the station during a given time period.

Sales Promotion (*promotion des ventes*). Promotional activities other than publicity, advertising, and personal selling that are used to promote products and/or services.

Salient Attributes (*attributs importants*). Buyers tend to perceive only those attributes that are important to them.

Sampling (*distribution d'échantillons gratuits*). A sales promotion technique consisting of providing consumers with a sample of a product, at no cost, to induce trial.

Saturation Phase (*phase de saturation*). The part of the maturity stage of a product's life-cycle when all potential buyers have tried the product and sales are only replacement sales.

Selective Attention *(attention sélective).* Individuals filter the stimuli to which they are exposed and perceive only a small proportion of them.

Selective Direct Mail *(publipostage sélectif).* Sending coupons by mail to pre-identified customers.

Selective Distortion *(déformation sélective).* Individuals distort the messages filtered through selective attention so that the meanings are congruent with their need patterns.

Selective Retention *(mémoire sélective).* The propensity of a person to remember informative stimuli that support prior beliefs or feelings and to forget the stimuli that are at odds.

Semantic Differential Scale *(échelle sémantique différentielle).* A type of scale using a pair of opposites, such as dislike/like, or not believable/believable, often with seven points.

Services Advertising *(publicité des services).* Advertising of services such as banking or tourism.

Share-of-Mind Recall *(rappel de la part de la mémoire).* Recall of a brand as a percentage of all brands mentioned unaided.

Short Purchase Cycle Markets *(marché à cycle d'achat court).* Markets characterized by routine purchase decision processes, or by limited problem solving when a new brand is introduced into a market.

Short Rate *(tarif réajusté).* The additional amount paid to a medium by an advertiser who has not met the quantity requirement of the contract. It is the difference between the earned rate and the contracted rate.

Simulcasting *(émission simultanée).* The practice of scheduling the same episode of the same program at the same time as for a U.S. station. Cable companies may be required to substitute the Canadian signal for the U.S. signal.

Sleeper Effect *(effect d'indolence).* Psychological phenomenon which suggests that as time elapses, individuals who are submitted to persuasive communications tend to dissociate the communication content from the source.

Slippage *(Remboursement non-réclamé).* Proportion of customers who are enticed to purchase as a result of a rebate offer, but who fail to request the refund to which they are entitled.

Slogan *(slogan).* A set of words associated with a brand, which embodies an advertising theme. It may last for years.

Soft Goods *(produits "doux" ou articles de consommation intermédiaire).* Shopping non-durable items, moderately priced, featuring a selected distribution. Includes such products as clothing, carpeting, and linens.

Source *(source).* See COMMUNICATOR.

Source Credibility *(crédibilité de l'émetteur).* Before any communication takes place, a source is perceived by an audience as having expertise, trustworthiness, and attractiveness.

Specialty Advertising *(publicité de rappel).* Advertising on a wide variety of commonly used products (e.g., pens, calendars) given free or sold to a related group.

Spectacolour *(spectacouleur).* The process of pre-printing rolls of four-colour advertisements with the dimensions of the newspaper page and cutting and incorporating the advertisements into the newspaper as full pages.

Spectacular *(panneau géant spécial).* An outdoor advertisement designed to be conspicuous.

Speculative Presentation *(présentation spéculative).* An advertising campaign proposal for a product submitted by an agency to a client.

Split-Run *(tirage partagé).* A service offered by some newspapers or magazines whereby the advertiser can run different advertisements in alternate copies of the same publication at the same time.

Sponsor, To *(parrainer un programme).* An advertiser buys all the commercial time available in a given program or segment.

Spot Time *(temps publicitaire).* Commercial time available from local stations and purchased by advertisers on a market-by-market basis.

Storyboard *("storyboard" ou scénario du message publicitaire).* Sequence of drawings designed to portray copy, dialogue, and action for a television commercial.

Subliminal Advertising *(publicité subliminale).* A communication received by a subject at such a high speed that it falls below the subject's perceptual threshold.

Suggestive Advertising *(publicité suggestive).* Advertising that appeals directly to consumers' emotions and feelings and conveys a certain product or brand image.

Superboard *(panneau géant).* Hand-painted or printed designs on structures larger than posters.

Starch Method. A recognition method of testing print advertisements conducted by Daniel Starch (Canada) Ltd.

Sweepstakes *(loterie publicitaire, ou "sweepstakes").* A sales promotion technique that consists of asking consumers to provide their names and addresses to the advertiser who, at a fixed date, selects the winners by random drawing from all entries.

Tabloid *(journal petit format).* A small-size newspaper approximately 254 mm wide and 356 mm deep (10 in. by 14 in.).

Tachistoscope *(tachistoscope).* An instrument that measures the attention levels of various executions by varying the time of exposure to an advertisement.

Target Audience *(cible).* Group(s) of individuals to whom a communication is directed.

Target Market *(marché-cible).* A specific group of consumers selected by the firm and to which it directs one or several of its products (or services).

Telecaster Committee (TC). A committee formed in 1972 that approves all commercials to be aired on a group of CTV affiliated stations plus one independent outlet, using similar criteria.

Telemarketing *(télémarketing).* A form of direct response advertising using the telephone as a means of reaching a selected audience.

Television Bureau of Canada (TVB). A non-profit industry organization that promotes the use of television as an advertising medium.

Testimonial Advertising *(publicité avec témoignage).* Advertising that uses a credible source to testify for the product claims.

Theatre Test *(test d'annonces en salles de cinéma).* A form of copy testing conducted with subjects who preview a program at a theatre.

Theme *(thème).* The basic idea on which an advertising campaign is built.

Top-of-Mind Recall *(test première marque à l'esprit).* The percentage of individuals mentioning a brand as the first one that comes to mind.

Trade Advertising *(publicité destinée au réseau).* A form of business-to-business advertising aimed at wholesalers and/or retailers.

Trade Deals *(promotion/réseau, ou offres spéciales).* Price reduction by a company to an intermediary for a limited period of time to encourage the intermediary to carry the promoted brand.

Trading Stamps *(timbres de réduction).* Technique that consists of offering consumers a set of products in exchange for receipts totalling a given amount or a cumulative number of points.

Traffic Manager *(surveillant de la production).* The individual in an advertising agency who is responsible for co-ordinating and ensuring the timely completion of the work of the various specialists within the agency.

Transit Advertising *(publicité sur les véhicules de transport en commun).* Advertising space on the inside or outside of buses or subway cars or inside the subway stations.

Two-Step Flow of Communication *(communication en deux étapes).* The concept according to which ideas are transmitted through the mass media to opinion leaders and then from these opinion leaders to less active segments of the population.

Ultra-High Frequency Channels (UHF) *(canaux à fréquences ultra-hautes).* Television channels 14 and higher.

Unaided Recall *(souvenir spontané).* The percentage of individuals mentioning a brand when asked to name all brands that come to mind.

Unique Selling Proposition (USP) *(proposition exclusive de vente).* An advertising technique according to which an advertisement should stress an exclusive selling argument.

Valence *(valence).* The intensity of various attitude components.

Vehicle *(support).* See MEDIA VEHICLE.

Vertical Publication *(publication verticale).* A business publication aimed at readers in a specific industry.

Very High Frequency Channels (VHF) *(canaux à très hautes fréquences).* Television channels 2 through 13.

Video *(vidéo).* The visual part of a commercial.

Volume Discount *(réduction de quantités).* A discount to advertisers that is based on the dollar amount spent for advertising.

Wear-Out *(usure).* TV commercials' loss in effectiveness after several viewings

I N D E X E S

Burnkrant, Robert D., 225
Burton, John, 408, 422
Buzzell, Robert D., 442, 472

Cadogan, David, 126
Cady, John F., 472
Calantone, Roger J., 17, 69, 407, 485
Calder, Bobby J., 225, 408, 422, 430–31
Campbell, Donald T., 403
Campbell, Evid M., 230
Cannent, D.W., 252
Caples, John, 336
Carlson, E.R., 233
Cary, Norman D., 353–54
Cash, Harold C., 48
Caves, Richard, 464
Cervin, V.B., 252
Chatel, G., 101, 441
Chebat, Jean Charles, 77, 421, 494
Chéron, Emmanuel J., 49, 232
Chiasson, Gail, 71, 150
Church, John H., 99
Clarke, T.K., 427
Clawson, Joseph, 217
Claxton, John D., 99
Claycamp, Henry J., 31, 373
Clifford, E., 108
Cody, Sherwin, 318
Cohen, A.R., 248, 252
Cohen, Joel B., 476
Colley, Russell H., 278
Comanor, William S., 472
Cook, T., 237
Cossette, Claude, 17, 104–6
Costello, Denise, 585
Courtney, Alice E., 484
Cox, Donald F., 252
Cox, Keith J., 408, 422
Craig, C. Samuel, 326
Crespi, Irwin, 229
Crissy, W.J.E., 48
Cromwell, H., 237
Crowne, D.P., 252
Crutchfield, Richard S., 216
Cunningham, I., 445
Cunningham, W., 445

Dana, Léo-Paul, 513, 535, 548
d'Astous, Alain, 322, 394, 421, 451
Darell, M. Lucas, 18

Darlin, Damon, 449
Darmon, René Y., 37, 107, 224, 342
Davis, Jeff, 207
Day, Georges S., 229, 406
de Bretteville, Irene, 446
de Camprieu, R., 102
De Deo, Joseph E., 475
Dean, Karen, 131
Deneuve, Catherine, 314–15
Desjardins, Louis, 68–9, 287–88, 290–91
Dhalla, N.K., 431
Diamond, Daniel, 347
Dichter, Ernest, 408, 445
Dicksen, Charles J., 482
Dow, Hugh, 135
Drolet, Réjean, 178, 395
Drury, Donald H., 69, 407
Duhaime, Carole, 104
Dunn, S. Watson, 442, 445–46
Dyer, David C., 313
Dyer, Robert F., 494

Ebbesen, Ebbe B., 258
Ebbinghaus, H., 237
Ehrlick, D., 249
Elinder, Erik, 442
Elliott, J.L., 106–7
Engel, James F., 215, 237
Engle, Ralph S., 489
Eskin, Gerald J., 472
Evans, Peter, 545
Ezell, Hazel F., 84

Faria, A.J., 494
Farris, Paul W., 472–73, 492
Fatt, Arthur C., 441
Ferber, Robert, 478
Ferguson, Frank, 154
Ferguson, James M., 472
Festinger, Leon, 234, 248, 350
Field, P.B., 252
Filiatrault, Pierre, 485
Finneran, John, 121, 126
Fishback, S., 235
Foley, William F., 287
Forbes, James D., 34, 99, 107, 277, 286, 288, 367, 431, 485, 494, 497
Frank, Ronald E., 30
Franklin, Benjamin, 114
Fulford, Ethel, 407

Subject Index

on post-usage feelings, 251
on post-purchase feelings, 249–50
on prices, 471–73
on profits, 472
on purchase decision process, 247
on retail prices, 472–73
on stereotypes, 484–85
social effects, 475–88
Electroencephalographs (EEG), 424
Electrotypes, 603
Elevator Advertising, 151
Elliott Research, 407
Em, 598
Emotional Appeals, 14, 234–35, 251–52, 476–78
Environmental Variables, 28–30, 285, 443–49, 452–53
Erratic Pulse Strategy, 392–93
Etching, 601
Ethnic Markets, 104–7
Evoked Set, 215–16, 243, 280, 430
Exaggeration, 477–78
Exclusiveness of Copy Claims, 429
Executional Copy Testing, 421
Experimentation, 403
Express Air Canada Cargo, 532–35
Extensive Problem Solving, 255
External Secondary Sources of Data, 403
Eye-Movement Camera, 424

Facial Action Coding System (FACS), 424
Fact Book, 270–72
Fantasy, 353
Farm Publications, 136
Fairs and Shows, 193, 201
Fear Appeals, 234–35, 251–52
Federal Government Regulations, 489–92
Fees, 67–69
Field of Experience, 13–17
Film, 603–4
Fixed Sum Per Unit Method, 287
Flexform, 119, 129
Flight, 379, 383–84
FM Stations, 165
Focus Groups, 408, 422–23
Foreign Language Publications, 137–38
Forgetting, 237, 260–61
Free Form. *See* Flexform
Free Goods, 202–3
Free Trade, 439
French Canadian Market, 100–106
cultural differences, 101–2
typologies of traits, 102–6

Frequency, 113, 373–75, 385
distribution, 374–75
dominant strategy, 385
Fringe Time, 184
Full-Service Agency, 57–62

Gatefolds, 130, 134
General Rate. *See* National Rate
Gravure, 601
Gross Impressions, 374–75
Gross Rating Point (GRP), 113, 374–81
defined, 113
derived, 375–76
in media planning, 376–81
Guaranteed Positions, 130
Guaranteed Revenue System, 69

Half-Tone Engraving, 603
Hand Setting, 599
Headlines, 331, 333–39
information content, 335–36
selection, 337–39
syntax, 336–37
Hierarchy of Effects Model, 228–29
High-Assay Strategy, 378
History of Advertising, 4–9
Humour in Advertising, 324–26, 357

Idea Advertising, 14
Ideal Point Model, 37–39
Ideal Universe, 404–5
Impact of Campaign, 380–81
Increasing the Consumption Rate, 257
Increasing the Purchase Volume, 258
Independent Stations, 165, 177
In-Depth Interviews, 408, 422
Industrial Advertising, 14–15, 76–77
Industrial Buyer Behaviour, 264–65
Inference Level in a Message, 236
Information Sources
advertising, 218–19
interpersonal information, 219
retailers/sellers, 219
sensorial information, 218–19
Informative Advertising Messages, 233–34
Inherent Brand Attributes, 244–45
In-House Agencies, 62–63
Inserts, 119, 130, 193, 201
Institute of Canadian Advertising, 92–98
Institutional Advertising, 14, 92, 99
Institutional Market Structure, 29

Media Mix Dominance Strategy, 383–84
Media Objectives, 365–72
Media Options, 293, 380–81, 385
Media Plan, 271, 275, 365–97
    decisions about markets, 368–69
    decisions on target audiences, 367–68
    effect of advertising appropriation, 371
    effects of creative factors, 369
    effect of the communication task, 369–71
    executing, 395–97
    media type selection, 381–85
    media vehicle selection, 385–91
    objectives, 365–72
    planning, 372–81
    schedule and budget, 391–95
Media Research, 410–21
Media Schedule, 391–95
Media Scheduling Methods
    high assay method, 378, 394–95
    mathematical programming, 394
    simulation models, 395, 407
Media Services, 59–60, 62
Media Strategy, 372–81
Media Types
    campaign requirements, 384–85
    characteristics, 113–90, 381–82
    competitive analysis, 382–84
    selection, 381–85
Media Vehicle
    availability, 386–87
    characteristics, 385–87
    costs, 387–91
    demographic profile, 385–86
    discount structure, 386
    editorial environment, 386
    psychographic profile, 385–86
    selection, 385–91
Message Creation, 298–99, 308–9
Message Content, 45–46, 302–19
    argumentative, 302–17
    motivation approach, 303–14
    suggestive, 317–19
    target group, 302–3
    USP, 314–17
Message Format, 45–46, 319–26
Metal Typesetting, 599
Micro-Environment, 30
Milline Rate, 388
Misleading Advertising, 486–87, 492–94
Mode of Broadcasting, 164–65
Modular Agate Line, 116–17

Monitoring Services, 409
Monopoly, 29
Monotype, 599
Motivation Approach, 303–14
    advertising theme selection, 308–14
    basic motive selection, 304–8
    Motivations, 216–18
    definition, 216
    influence of advertising on, 216–18, 475–88
    role in buyer behaviour, 216–17
    theories of, 217–18
    valence, 217–18
Motivation Research, 408, 478–79
Multicultural Advertising, 100–108, 438–58
    ethnic markets, 104–7
    French Canadian market, 100–106
    international, 438–58
    regional markets, 107–8
Multi-Segment Marketing, 31–32
Music
    formats in radio, 165–66
    in creating commercials, 354–56, 359–61
Musical Commercials, 361

Naive Methods, 286–88
National Rate, 121–25, 169
Needs. *See* Motivations
Need Creation, 218, 475–77
Network Advertising, 178–79
Network Affiliates, 165
Networks (TV), 177–78
New Brunswick Optical, 508–11
New Coke, 545–48
New Product Development and Advertising, 465–66
Newspapers, 113–27, 138–39
    advantages, 119–20, 138
    advertising rate structure, 121–25
    cost comparisons, 388–89
    disadvantages, 120–21, 138
    evolution, 113–15
    formats, 115–16
    future of, 125–27
    publication frequency, 116–18
Newspaper Audience Databank (NADbank), 120–21, 124, 126
Newspaper Marketing Bureau, 121, 410
Newspaper Research, 410
Nielsen of Canada, A.C., 367, 416–21
Non-Profit Advertising, 14, 99–100
Non-Verbal Elements of a Communication, 322–23
Noted Reader, 425–27

Suspense, 353
Sweepstakes, 200–201
Syndicated Radio, 166

Tabloid, 115–17
Tachistoscope, 424
Target Audience
    decisions about, 278–79, 367–68
    definition, 278
Target Group Approach, 302–3
Target Market, 272–73, 285
Task. *See* Communication Task
Taxicab Advertising, 151
Technological Environment, 29
Telemarketing, 152–53
Telephone Interviews, 406
Television Advertising, 173–88
    advantages, 180–81, 188
    characteristics, 176–80
    cost comparisons, 389–91
    disadvantages, 181–83, 188
    evolution of, 173–74
    future, 186–87
    rate structure, 183–86
    technology, 174–75
Television Bureau of Canada, 416
Television Commercials
    atmosphere elements, 351
    audio elements, 351, 354–56
    creation, 350–59
    evaluation, 356–57
    production, 357–59, 603–4
    visual elements, 350–51
Television Research, 416–21
TELPAK, 374, 391
Testimonial Advertising, 313–14, 353, 357, 361
Theatre, Video Screen Advertising, 152
Theatre Test, 423–24
Time Classification. *See* Daypart
Top-of-Mind Recall, 280, 429
Total Audience Plans (TAP), 184
Total Painted Buses, 148–49
Trade Advertising, 76–77
Trade Deals, 202–3
Trade Promotions, 202–4
Trade Shows, 202–3
Trading Stamps, 193, 201

Traffic Manager, 59, 62
Training Interviewers, 405
Transit Advertising, 148–50
    advantages, 149, 159
    cost comparisons, 391
    creating, 348
    disadvantages, 149–50, 159
    formats, 148–49
    future, 150
    rate structure, 150
Transit Shelters, 145
Trial, 280, 430
Truck Advertising, 152–53
Truth in Advertising, 486–87
Two-Sided Presentation, 236
Two-Step Flow of Communication Theory, 232–33
Type Groups (printing), 597–98
Type Measurement, 598
Typesetting, 599–600
Typography, 597–99

Unique Selling Proposition (USP), 314–17
Ultra High Frequency Stations (UHF), 177
Unaided Recall, 280, 429
Unduplicated Audience, 374
Urgency of the Purchase Situation, 253–54

Verbal Elements, 331, 333–41, 350–54, 360–61
Very High Frequency Stations (VHF), 176–77
Videotape, 603–4
Visual Elements, 330–33, 350–53
    print advertisements, 330–33
    television commercials, 350–53
Voice, 351, 354–55, 360
    announcer's, 354–55
    pitch analysis, 424
    types of, 355
Volume Discounts (Promotion), 202–3

Wearout Factor, 430–31
Wipe, 604
Wonder Cola, 570–74

Yellow Pages, 136–37

Zest, 522–31
Zoom, 604